Assessing and Restoring Natural Resources in Post-Conflict Peacebuilding

Edited by David Jensen and Steve Lonergan

from Routledge

First published 2012
by Earthscan
2 Park Square, Milton Park, Abingdon, Oxon OX14 4RN

Simultaneously published in the USA and Canada
by Earthscan
711 Third Avenue, New York, NY 10017

Earthscan is an imprint of the Taylor & Francis Group, an informa business

Earthscan publishes in association with the International Institute for Environment and Development

© 2012 Environmental Law Institute and United Nations Environment Programme

The right of the editors to be identified as the authors of the editorial material, and of the authors for their individual chapters, has been asserted in accordance with sections 77 and 78 of the Copyright, Designs and Patents Act 1988.

All rights reserved. No part of this book may be reprinted or reproduced or utilised in any form or by any electronic, mechanical, or other means, now known or hereafter invented, including photocopying and recording, or in any information storage or retrieval system, without permission in writing from the copyright holders.

Trademark notice: Product or corporate names may be trademarks or registered trademarks, and are used only for identification and explanation without intent to infringe.

British Library Cataloguing-in-Publication Data
A catalogue record for this book is available from the British Library

Library of Congress Cataloging-in-Publication Data
Assessing and restoring natural resources in post-conflict peacebuilding / edited by David Jensen and Steve Lonergan.
   xviii, 515 pp., 22.86 cm.
   Includes bibliographical references and index.
   ISBN 978-1-84971-234-7 (alk. paper)
   1. Peace-building—Environmental aspects. 2. Peace-building—Environmental aspects—Case studies. 3. Postwar reconstruction—Environmental aspects. 4. Postwar reconstruction—Environmental aspects—Case studies. 5. Natural resources—Management.
6. Natural resources—Management—Case studies. I. Jensen, David. II. Lonergan, Stephen C. (Stephen Colnon), 1950–
   JZ6300.A77 2012
   333.7—dc23
                                                         2012013113

Typeset in Times and Helvetica
by Graphicraft Limited, Hong Kong

Printed and bound by CPI Group (UK) Ltd, Croydon, CR0 4YY

Table of contents

List of figures and tables	vii
Preface	xi
Foreword	xv
Acknowledgments	xvii

Placing environment and natural resource risks, impacts, and opportunities on the post-conflict peacebuilding agenda   1
David Jensen and Steve Lonergan

Part 1: Post-conflict environmental assessments   13

Introduction   15

Evaluating the impact of UNEP's post-conflict environmental assessments   17
David Jensen

Environment and peacebuilding in war-torn societies: Lessons from the UN Environment Programme's experience with post-conflict assessment   63
Ken Conca and Jennifer Wallace

Medical and environmental intelligence in peace and crisis-management operations   85
Birgitta Liljedahl, Annica Waleij, Björn Sandström, and Louise Simonsson

Thinking back-end: Improving post-conflict analysis through consulting, adapting to change, and scenario building   99
Alexander Carius and Achim Maas

Part 2: Remediation of environmental hot spots   107

Introduction   109

Salting the Earth: Environmental health challenges in post-conflict reconstruction   111
Chad Briggs and Inka Weissbecker

Remediation of polluted sites in the Balkans, Iraq, and Sierra Leone   135
Muralee Thummarukudy, Oli Brown, and Hannah Moosa

The risks of depleted uranium contamination in post-conflict countries: Findings and lessons learned from UNEP field assessments   163
Mario Burger

iv   Assessing and restoring natural resources in post-conflict peacebuilding

Linking demining to post-conflict peacebuilding: A case study of
Cambodia 181
Nao Shimoyachi-Yuzawa

Part 3: Restoration of natural resources and ecosystems   199

Introduction   201

Restoration of damaged land in societies recovering from conflict:
The case of Lebanon   203
Aïda Tamer-Chammas

Ecological restoration and peacebuilding: The case of the Iraqi marshes   223
Steve Lonergan

Haiti: Lessons learned and way forward in natural resource
management projects   241
Lucile Gingembre

Peacebuilding and adaptation to climate change   267
Richard Matthew and Anne Hammill

Part 4: Environmental dimensions of infrastructure and reconstruction   283

Introduction   285

Addressing infrastructure needs in post-conflict reconstruction:
An introduction to alternative planning approaches   289
P. B. Anand

Mitigating the environmental impacts of post-conflict assistance:
Assessing USAID's approach   297
Charles Kelly

Challenges and opportunities for mainstreaming environmental
assessment tools in post-conflict settings   311
George Bouma

Environmental assessment as a tool for peacebuilding and development:
Initial lessons from capacity building in Sierra Leone   327
Oli Brown, Morgan Hauptfleisch, Haddijatou Jallow, and Peter Tarr

Natural resources, post-conflict reconstruction, and regional integration:
Lessons from the Marshall Plan and other reconstruction efforts   343
Carl Bruch, Ross Wolfarth, and Vladislav Michalcik

Making best use of domestic energy sources: The Priority Production System for coal mining and steel production in post–World War II Japan 363
Mikiyasu Nakayama

Road infrastructure reconstruction as a peacebuilding priority in Afghanistan: Negative implications for land rights 373
Jon Unruh and Mourad Shalaby

Evaluating post-conflict assistance 389
Suppiramaniam Nanthikesan and Juha I. Uitto

Part 5: Lessons learned **409**

Natural resources and post-conflict assessment, remediation, restoration, and reconstruction: Lessons and emerging issues 411
David Jensen and Steve Lonergan

Appendices

Appendix 1: List of abbreviations 463
Appendix 2: Author biographies 467
Appendix 3: Table of contents for Post-conflict peacebuilding and natural resource management 477

Index 493

List of figures and tables

FIGURES

Medical and environmental intelligence and the life cycle of operations	88
UNEP environmental hot spot cleanup sites in Serbia (Map)	137
Priority assessment sites in Iraq (Map)	149
UNEP cleanup site in Sierra Leone (Map)	154
UN environmental assessment sites in Kosovo, 2000–2001 (Map)	168
UN environmental assessment sites in Serbia and Montenegro, 2001–2002 (Map)	169
UN environmental assessment sites in Bosnia and Herzegovina, 2002–2003 (Map)	170
National assessment sites for depleted uranium in southern Iraq, 2006–2007 (Map)	174
Landmine sites in Cambodia (Map)	184
Cambodian mine action organization chart	187
Land use after landmine removal in Cambodia, 2006	190
Land area cleared by Cambodian Mine Action Center, 1995–2008	192
Landmine clearance methods in Cambodia, 2007	193
Land use after 2007–2008 landmine removal in Tasen Commune, Battambang, Cambodia	194
Location of the southern Iraq marshes, 2008–2009 (Map)	224
Marshes of southern Iraq, 1973 (Map)	225
Marshes of southern Iraq, 2002 (Map)	226
Marshes of southern Iraq, 2006 (Map)	227
Health of southern Iraqi marshes, spring 2009 (Map)	229
Scenario 1: A smaller Iraqi marsh (Map)	232
Scenario 2: Protect the healthy portions of the Iraqi marshes (Map)	233
Scenario 3: Boundaries proposed by the Center for Restoration of the Iraqi Marshlands (Map)	234

Linkages among disaster vulnerability, poverty, and instability 245

Duration of projects covered by the Haiti Regeneration Initiative's 2009 study of lessons learned in managing environmental projects 261

Funding for projects covered by the Haiti Regeneration Initiative's 2009 study of lessons learned in managing environmental projects 262

Climate change adaptation continuum 276

Average per capita official development assistance as a percentage of gross domestic product in years following peace agreement for five selected countries. 312

Concept of the Priority Production System in post–World War II Japan 364

Domestic production and imported coal, Japan, 1930–1965 367

Number of coal mines and workers, Japan, 1950–1970s 368

Monthly coal production and number of miners, Japan, 1944–1946 370

Ring Road and select secondary roads in Afghanistan (Map) 377

TABLES

UNEP 1999–2007 post-conflict assessments: Methodology and policy frameworks evaluated 21

Evaluation of assessment impact indicators for the Federal Republic of Yugoslavia 27

Evaluation of assessment impact indicators for Afghanistan 32

Evaluation of assessment impact indicators for the occupied Palestinian territories 35

Evaluation of assessment impact indicators for Iraq 39

Evaluation of assessment impact indicators for Liberia 44

Evaluation of assessment impact indicators for Lebanon 47

Evaluation of assessment impact indicators for Sudan 52

UNEP's post-conflict assessments: Summary of assessment impacts by case study 53

Summary of assessment impacts by method used for UNEP post-conflict assessments, 1999–2007 54

Activities of UNEP's Post-Conflict and Disaster Management Branch, 1999–2000 66

Spectrum of potential environmental health hazards for deployed personnel as human involvement increases	87
Assessment form and scoring system for environmental vulnerability assessments	89
Hypothetical environmental vulnerability assessment	91
Outcome of the environmental review for Afghanistan's donor assistance database, 2004–2005	317
Outcome of the environmental review for the Iraq Trust Fund, 2004–2005	319
Outcome of the environmental review for the Sudan Work Plan Projects Database, Sudan, 2008	321
Price subsidies and indemnities: Government payments and percent of general account budget, Japan, 1940–1952	365
Inflation rate, Japan, 1944–1955	366
Approaches to post-conflict assessment, remediation, restoration, and reconstruction	450

Preface

Decades of civil wars, international wars, and wars of secession demonstrate the strong relationship between natural resources and armed conflict. Disputes over natural resources and their associated revenues can be among the reasons that people go to war. Diamonds, timber, oil, and even bananas and charcoal can provide sources of financing to sustain conflict. Forests, agricultural crops, and wells are often targeted during conflict. Efforts to negotiate an end to conflict increasingly include natural resources. And conflicts associated with natural resources are both more likely to relapse than non-resource-related conflicts, and to relapse twice as fast.

Immediately after the end of a conflict, a window of opportunity opens for a conflict-affected country and the international community to establish security, rebuild, and consolidate peace—or risk conflict relapse. This window also presents the opportunity to reform the management of natural resources and their revenues in ways that would otherwise be politically difficult to achieve. Capitalizing on this opportunity is particularly critical if natural resources contributed to the onset or financing of conflict—and, if this opportunity is lost, it may never reappear. Moreover, poorly informed policy decisions may become entrenched, locking in a trajectory that serves the interests of a limited few.

Since the end of the Cold War, and particularly since 2000, substantial progress has been made in establishing institutional and policy frameworks to consolidate peacebuilding efforts. In 2005, the United Nations established the Peacebuilding Commission to identify best practices for peacebuilding. The commission is the first body to bring together the UN's humanitarian, security, and development sectors so that they can learn from peacebuilding experiences.

The Peacebuilding Commission has started to recognize the importance of natural resources in post-conflict peacebuilding. In 2009, along with the United Nations Environment Programme, the commission published a pioneering report—*From Conflict to Peacebuilding: The Role of Natural Resources and the Environment*—that framed the basic ways in which natural resources contribute to conflict and can be managed to support peacebuilding. Building on this report, the commission is starting to consider how natural resources can be included within post-conflict planning and programming in Sierra Leone, the Central African Republic, Guinea, and other countries.

Since the establishment of the Peacebuilding Commission, the policies governing post-conflict peacebuilding have evolved rapidly. In his 2009 *Report of the Secretary-General on Peacebuilding in the Immediate Aftermath of Conflict*, UN Secretary-General Ban Ki-moon articulated five priorities for post-conflict peacebuilding, all of which have natural resource dimensions. The following year, in an update to that report, Ban Ki-moon noted the pressing need to improve post-conflict natural resource management to reduce the risk of conflict relapse, and urged "Member States and the United Nations system to make questions of natural resource allocation, ownership and access an integral part of peacebuilding strategies." And a 2011 UN report, *Civilian Capacity in the Aftermath of Conflict*, highlighted approaches for mobilizing civil society to support peacebuilding in many realms, including natural resources.

The World Bank has also begun focusing on natural resources: the Bank's 2011 *World Development Report*, for example, placed the prevention of fragility, conflict, and violence at the core of the Bank's development mandate. Drawing on the Bank's experiences around the world, the report focuses on jobs, justice, and security, and highlights the contribution of natural resources to these goals.

Despite growing recognition of the importance of post-conflict natural resource management, there has been no comprehensive examination of how natural resources can support post-conflict peacebuilding. Nor has there been careful consideration of the risks to long-term peace caused by the failure to effectively address natural resources. Practitioners, researchers, and UN bodies have researched specific resources, conflict dynamics, and countries, but have yet to share their findings with each other at a meaningful scale, and limited connections have been drawn between the various strands of inquiry. As a result, the peacebuilding community does not know what works in what circumstances, what does not, or why.

Given the complexity of peacebuilding, practitioners and researchers alike are struggling to articulate good practice. It is increasingly clear that natural resources must be included as a foundational issue; many questions remain, however, regarding opportunities, options, and trade-offs.

Against this backdrop, the Environmental Law Institute, the UN Environment Programme, the University of Tokyo, and McGill University launched a research program designed to examine experiences in post-conflict peacebuilding and natural resource management; to identify lessons from these experiences; and to raise awareness of those lessons among practitioners and scholars. The program has benefitted from broad support, with the government of Finland—one of the few donor governments to explicitly recognize the role of natural resources in both conflict and peacebuilding efforts—playing a catalytic role by providing core financing.

The research program has been guided by the collective experiences of the four members of the Steering Committee: as the coordinators of the program and the series editors, we have drawn on our work in more than thirty post-conflict countries. Our experiences—which include leading environmental assessments in Afghanistan, developing forest law in Liberia, supporting land reform in Mozambique, and fostering cooperation around water in Iraq—have led to a shared understanding that natural resource issues rarely receive the political attention they merit. Through this research program and partnership, we hope to catalyze a comprehensive global effort to demonstrate that peacebuilding substantially depends on the transformation of natural assets into peacebuilding benefits—a change that must occur without mortgaging the future or creating new conflict.

Since its inception in 2007, the program has grown dramatically in response to strong interest from practitioners, researchers, and policy makers. Participants in an initial scoping meeting suggested a single edited book consisting of twenty case studies and crosscutting analyses. It soon became clear, however, that the undertaking should reflect a much broader range of experiences, perspectives, and dimensions.

The research program yielded more than 150 peer-reviewed case studies and analyses written by more than 225 scholars, practitioners, and decision makers from fifty countries. The case studies and analyses have been assembled into a set of six edited books, each focusing on a specific set of natural resources or an aspect of peacebuilding: high-value natural resources; land; water; resources for livelihoods; assessment and restoration of natural resources; and governance. Examining a broad range of resources, including oil, minerals, land, water, wildlife, livestock, fisheries, forests, and agricultural products, the books document and analyze post-conflict natural resource management successes, failures, and ongoing efforts in sixty conflict-affected countries and territories. In their diversity and number, the books represent the most significant collection to date of experiences, analyses, and lessons in managing natural resources to support post-conflict peacebuilding.

In addition to the six edited books, the partnership has created an overarching book, *Post-Conflict Peacebuilding and Natural Resources: The Promise and the Peril*, which will be published by Cambridge University Press. This book draws on the six edited books to explore the role of natural resources in various peacebuilding activities across the humanitarian, security, and development sectors.

These seven books will be of interest to practitioners, researchers, and policy makers in the security, development, peacebuilding, political, and natural resource communities. They are designed to provide a conceptual framework, assess approaches, distill lessons, and identify specific options and trade-offs for more effectively managing natural resources to support post-conflict peacebuilding.

Natural resources present both opportunities and risks, and postponing their consideration in the peacebuilding process can imperil long-term peace and undermine sustainable development. Experiences from the past sixty years provide many lessons and broad guidance, as well as insight into which approaches are promising and which are problematic.

A number of questions, however, still lack definitive answers. We do not always understand precisely why certain approaches fail or succeed in specific instances, or which of a dozen contextual factors are the most important in determining the success of a peacebuilding effort. Nevertheless, numerous discrete measures related to natural resources can be adopted now to improve the likelihood of long-term peace. By learning from peacebuilding experiences to date, we can avoid repeating the mistakes of the past and break the cycle of conflict that has come to characterize so many countries. We also hope that this undertaking represents a new way to understand and approach peacebuilding.

Carl Bruch
Environmental Law Institute

David Jensen
United Nations Environment Programme

Mikiyasu Nakayama
University of Tokyo

Jon Unruh
McGill University

Foreword

Klaus Töpfer
Former Executive Director
United Nations Environment Programme

In early 1999, one year into my tenure as Executive Director of the United Nations Environment Programme (UNEP), the conflict in Kosovo escalated into an international war. The range of modern weaponry involved and the deliberate targeting of industrial and military facilities made it clear that the Balkans faced not only a humanitarian crisis of tragic proportions, but also potentially serious environmental damage.

In the face of dire predictions of environmental disaster, UN Secretary-General Kofi Annan asked UNEP to conduct an impartial and scientific investigation of the effects of the Kosovo conflict on the environment and human settlements. To conduct the assessment, UNEP and United Nations Human Settlements Programme (UN-HABITAT) established the Joint UNEP/UN-HABITAT Balkans Task Force.

The resulting report, *The Kosovo Conflict: Consequences for the Environment and Human Settlements*, was published in October 1999. In addition to outlining general linkages between armed conflict and environmental damage, the report identified four environmental hot spots—heavily contaminated sites where remediation was essential to protect human health—and recommended, on humanitarian grounds, a series of urgent cleanup measures. On the basis of the report, UNEP raised significant financial resources from the international community to implement remediation efforts, which were undertaken in partnership with local authorities.

This pioneering work raised awareness of the environmental impacts of conflict and paved the way for the development of new expertise within UNEP to address such impacts. The investigation of the environmental consequences of the Kosovo conflict was followed by similar field assessments throughout the Balkans and in conflict-affected regions across the globe, from Afghanistan to Gaza, Iraq, and Sudan. Each assessment was designed to fit the unique geographic, political, and security conditions of the particular situation.

Ultimately, UNEP's work in the Balkans led to the creation of the Post-Conflict and Disaster Management Branch, which is tasked with undertaking assessments that allow war-torn communities to know whether their water is safe to drink, whether their air is safe to breathe, and whether their land can be cultivated without risk. Moreover, such assessments have helped to ensure that environmental and natural resource management issues are included in recovery and reconstruction plans, enabling communities to "build back better"—that is, in ways that bolster sustainable, long-term development and strengthen peace and stability. Today, one of UNEP's six priorities is to assess and address the environmental dimensions of disasters and conflicts; and neutral, objective, post-crisis assessments remain a cornerstone of UNEP's operations.

As global awareness of the complex relationship between natural resources and conflict increases, more national and international organizations are seeking to address the connections. In 2011, for example, the president of the International Committee of the Red Cross identified the protection of the environment during armed conflict as one of four themes that need to be reinforced by humanitarian law. Within the European Union (EU), the policies pertaining to stability and conflict prevention call for the mismanagement of natural resources to be addressed. The UN and the EU have also created a partnership on natural resources and conflict prevention to issue guidance, conduct training, and develop joint programs in fragile states. Within the UN family, the Department of Peacekeeping Operations and the Department of Field Support adopted a new policy, in 2009, to limit the environmental footprint of peacekeeping operations; the UN Peacebuilding Commission has held high-level meetings to examine the ways in which natural resources can support peacebuilding; the Department of Political Affairs has added mediators with expertise on land and water conflicts to its global roster; and Secretary-General Ban Ki-moon, in his July 2010 *Progress Report of the Secretary-General on Peacebuilding in the Immediate Aftermath of Conflict*, formally called on member states and the UN system to "make questions of natural resource allocation, ownership and access an integral part of peacebuilding strategies."

The examples of post-conflict environmental assessments, restoration, remediation, and reconstruction presented in this book make clear that the work of the Balkans Task Force and the Post-Conflict and Disaster Management Branch is only part of the wide range of initiatives being undertaken to manage natural resources to support peacebuilding. The links between natural resources and violent conflict are now generally accepted; the tasks that remain for practitioners, policy makers, and researchers are threefold: first, to help communities address—and ultimately prevent—violent conflict over natural resources, as well as the environmental damage that results from such conflict; second, to transform natural resources so as to maximize opportunities for sustainable livelihoods, employment, economic diversification, and reconciliation without causing new conflict or environmental degradation; and third, to restore the productivity of degraded natural resources and to begin using them on a more sustainable basis. This book, together with the other five edited books in the series, represents an important step toward achieving these goals. I am proud that UNEP's early assessment work in the Balkans helped to catalyze such important follow-up efforts, and I can only hope that the lessons contained in these books improve programming and impact at the field level.

Acknowledgments

This book is the culmination of a four-year research project. It would not have been possible without the efforts and contributions of many individuals and institutions.

The volume editors are grateful to our managing editor, Peter Whitten, and our manuscript editors, Sandy Chizinsky, Meg Cox, and Mary Sebold, for their peerless editorial assistance. We are also thankful for the support of our assistant managing editors Lynsey Gaudioso and Hannah Moosa in overseeing the publication of this book. Nick Bellorini of Earthscan provided guidance; Matt Pritchard, Arthur Green, and Elan Spitzberg created the maps; and Joelle Stallone proofread the manuscript.

Research assistance and publication support was provided by Elliot August, Susan Bokermann, Calin Brown, Kathryn Chelminski, Brandee Cooklin, Mara Goldberg, Katelyn Henmueller, Bradford Hirsch, Brian Judge, Rachel Kenigsberg, Tim Kovach, Mark McCormick-Goodhart, Russell McFall, Phoenix McLaughlin, Vicki Nee, Katarina Petursson, Kate Powers, Sarah Reese, Eva Richardson, Renard Sexton, Elan Spitzberg, and Jessye Waxman.

Peer reviewers were essential to ensuring the rigor of this volume. The authors would like to acknowledge the professionals and scholars who contributed anonymous peer reviews.

A few chapters in this volume have been adapted with permission from earlier published versions. "Environment and Peacebuilding in War-Torn Societies: Lessons from the UN Environment Programme's Experience with Post-Conflict Assessment," by Ken Conca and Jennifer Wallace, is an updated version of an article that appeared in October 2009 in *Global Governance* 15 (4) and has been reprinted with permission. "Medical and Environmental Intelligence in Peace and Crisis-Management Operations," by Birgitta Liljedahl, Annica Waleij, Björn Sandström, and Louise Simonsson, is an elaborated reprint of a 2009 paper by Birgitta Liljedahl, Björn Sandström, Sture Sundström, Claes Nyström, Christina Edlund, and Annica Waleij, "Medical and Environmental Intelligence in Peace Operations and Crisis Management," published in the *Pearson Papers*, and has been reprinted with permission. "Peacebuilding and Adaptation to Climate

Change" by Richard Matthew and Anne Hammill is an adapted version of an article that appeared in *St. Antony's International Review* 5 (2): 89–112. "Natural Resources, Post-Conflict Reconstruction, and Regional Integration: Lessons from the Marshall Plan and Other Reconstruction Efforts," by Carl Bruch, Ross Wolfarth, and Vladislav Michalcik; "Linking Demining to Post-Conflict Peacebuilding: A Case Study of Cambodia," by Nao Shimoyachi-Yuzawa; and "Road Infrastructure Reconstruction as a Peacebuilding Priority in Afghanistan: Negative Implications for Land Rights," by Jon Unruh and Mourad Shalaby, are printed with the permission of the Environmental Law Institute.

Financial support for the project was provided by the United Nations Environment Programme, the government of Finland, the U.S. Agency for International Development, the European Union, the University of Tokyo's Graduate School of Frontier Sciences and Alliance for Global Sustainability, the John D. and Catherine T. MacArthur Foundation, the Canadian Social Science and Humanities Research Council, the Philanthropic Collaborative, the Center for Global Partnership of the Japan Foundation, the Ploughshares Fund, the Compton Foundation, Zonta Club Tokyo I, the International Union for Conservation of Nature's Commission on Environmental Law, the Nelson Talbott Foundation, the Jacob L. and Lillian Holtzmann Foundation, and an anonymous donor. In-kind support for the project was provided by the Earth Institute of Columbia University, the Environmental Change and Security Project of the Woodrow Wilson International Center for Scholars, the Environmental Law Institute, the Global Infrastructure Fund Research Foundation Japan, the Japan Institute of International Affairs, McGill University, the Peace Research Institute Oslo, the United Nations Environment Programme, and the University of Tokyo.

The cover was designed by Nikki Meith. Cover photography is by Per-Anders Pettersson/Getty Images.

Except as otherwise specifically noted, the maps in this publication use public domain data originating from Natural Earth (2009, www.naturalearthdata.com). The designations employed and the presentations do not imply the expressions of any opinion whatsoever on the part of UNEP or contributing organizations concerning the legal status of any country, territory, city or area or its authority, or concerning the delimitation of its frontiers or boundaries.

When available, URLs are provided for sources that can be accessed electronically. URLs contained in this book were current at the time of writing.

Placing environmental and natural resource risks, impacts, and opportunities on the post-conflict peacebuilding agenda

David Jensen and Steve Lonergan

Following conflict, a country's natural resources are the single most important asset available to kick-start economic recovery, employment, and livelihoods, and to sustain basic services. Decisions about the restoration, management, and protection of natural resources have fundamental implications for short-term stability, longer-term sustainable development, and successful peacebuilding. Yet many post-conflict countries lack (1) sound information on the quality or quantity of the natural resource base and (2) an accurate picture of how resources were damaged or destroyed during conflict. Moreover, there is often little understanding of the ways in which natural resources may have provided a lifeline to populations coping with conflict, or of how resources may have become entwined with the conflict economy. An informed understanding of the linkages between natural resources and conflict is essential, however, to capitalize on the peacebuilding potential of resources while avoiding the perils associated with their poor governance.

The immediate post-conflict period provides a window of opportunity to establish security, rebuild institutions, and consolidate peace (see sidebar). This period also offers the chance to rebuild and transform the institutions that are related to the restoration, management, and allocation of natural resources in ways that would otherwise be politically difficult to achieve. Capitalizing on early opportunities is particularly critical if the economy depends primarily on natural resources, if resources contributed to the onset or financing of conflict, or if resources were heavily damaged during conflict.

Too often, there is a misperception that environmental governance, including the sustainable management of natural resources, is distinct from—and sometimes even in conflict with—peacebuilding and development goals. Ensuring that natural

---

David Jensen is the head of the Environmental Cooperation for Peacebuilding Program of the United Nations Environment Programme (UNEP). Steve Lonergan is an emeritus professor in the Department of Geography at the University of Victoria, and the former director of UNEP's Division of Early Warning and Assessment.

2   Assessing and restoring natural resources in post-conflict peacebuilding

> **Post-conflict peacebuilding and natural resources: Key terms and concepts**
>
> Following conflict, peacebuilding actors leverage a country's available assets (including natural resources) to transition from conflict to peace and sustainable development. Peacebuilding actors work at the international, national, and subnational levels, and include national and subnational government bodies; United Nations agencies and other international organizations; international and domestic nongovernmental organizations; the private sector; and the media. Each group of peacebuilding actors deploys its own tools, and there are a growing number of tools to integrate the peacebuilding efforts of different types of actors.
>
> A post-conflict period typically begins after a peace agreement or military victory. Because a post-conflict period is often characterized by intermittent violence and instability, it can be difficult to pinpoint when the post-conflict period ends. For the purposes of this book, the post-conflict period may be said to end when political, security, and economic discourse and actions no longer revolve around armed conflict or the impacts of conflict, but focus instead on standard development objectives. Within the post-conflict period, the first two years are referred to as the *immediate aftermath of conflict* (UNSG 2009), which is followed by a period known as *peace consolidation*.
>
> According to the United Nations, "Peacebuilding involves a range of measures targeted to reduce the risk of lapsing or relapsing into conflict by strengthening national capacities at all levels for conflict management, and to lay the foundations for sustainable peace and development" (UNSG's Policy Committee 2007). In many instances, this means addressing the root causes of the conflict.
>
> There are many challenges to peacebuilding: insecurity, ethnic and political polarization (as well as marginalization), corruption, lack of governmental legitimacy, extensive displacement, and loss of property. To address these and other challenges, peacebuilding actors undertake diverse activities that advance four broad peacebuilding objectives:*
>
> - *Establishing security*, which encompasses basic safety and civilian protection; security sector reform; disarmament, demobilization, and reintegration; and demining.
> - *Delivering basic services*, including water, sanitation, waste management, and energy, as well as health care and primary education.
> - *Restoring the economy and livelihoods*, which includes repairing and constructing infrastructure and public works.
> - *Rebuilding governance and inclusive political processes*, which encompasses dialogue and reconciliation processes, rule of law, dispute resolution, core government functions, transitional justice, and electoral processes.
>
> Although they are sometimes regarded as distinct from peacebuilding, both peacemaking (the negotiation and conclusion of peace agreements) and humanitarian assistance are relevant to peacebuilding, as they can profoundly influence the options for post-conflict programming. Peacemaking and humanitarian assistance are also relevant to this book, in that they often have substantial natural resource dimensions.
>
> Successful peacebuilding is a transformative process in which a fragile country and the international community seek to address grievances and proactively lay the foundation for a lasting peace. As part of this process, peacebuilding actors seek to manage the country's assets—as well as whatever international assistance may be available—to ensure security, provide basic services, rebuild the economy and livelihoods, and restore governance. The assets of a post-conflict country include natural resources; infrastructure; and human, social, and financial capital. Natural resources comprise land, water, and other renewable resources, as well as extractive resources such as oil, gas, and minerals. The rest of the book explores the many ways in which natural resources affect peacebuilding.
>
> ---
>
> * This framework draws substantially from the *Report of the Secretary-General on Peacebuilding in the Immediate Aftermath of Conflict* (UNSG 2009), but the activities described have been regrouped and supplemented by activities articulated in USIP and U.S. Army PKSOI (2009), Sphere Project (2004, 2011), UN (2011), UNSG (2010, 2012), and International Dialogue on Peacebuilding and Statebuilding (2011).

resource restoration and management are placed on the political agenda as immediate post-conflict priorities requires making a strong case regarding both the potential benefits of swift action and the potential risks of inaction.

Since the mid-twentieth century, the international community's responses to the connections between natural resources, conflict, and peacebuilding have been mixed, evolving in fits and starts as various conflicts have revealed the many challenges that need to be addressed. The use of Agent Orange in the Viet Nam War is one of the most visible and acute examples of the environmental impacts of conflict in recent history. It is estimated that between 1962 and 1971, the United States sprayed more than 72 million liters of defoliants, including Agent Orange, over Viet Nam, exposing nearly 17 million people to the risks associated with these chemicals (Briggs and Weissbecker 2012). Apart from the immense human toll, the ecological damage was devastating: some estimates suggest that up to half of South Viet Nam's commercial hardwood forests and mangrove forests were destroyed.

In the aftermath of the war, the international community responded with new legal instruments designed to prevent similar environmental damage in future conflicts:

- The Convention on the Prohibition of Military or Any Other Hostile Use of Environmental Modification Techniques, adopted in 1976 and entered into force in 1978, was intended to prevent states from using tactics or technologies that could alter the weather, and thereby cause catastrophic environmental change.[1]
- Additional Protocol I to the 1949 Geneva Conventions, adopted in 1977, contained two important articles (35 and 55) that were designed to afford the environment some measure of protection during international armed conflict by prohibiting "widespread, long-term and severe" damage to the environment (UNEP 2009b).[2]

These important advances in international law did nothing, however, to prevent the environmental damage that occurred during the 1990–1991 Gulf War, when the retreating Iraqi army destroyed more than 700 oil wells (Briggs and Weissbecker 2012; UNEP 2003); nor did they prevent Saddam Hussein's government, over a period of several years following the 1990–1991 Gulf War, from

---

[1] Convention on the Prohibition of Military or Any Other Hostile Use of Environmental Modification Techniques, December 10, 1976. http://treaties.un.org/doc/Treaties/1978/10/19781005%2000-39%20AM/Ch_XXVI_01p.pdf.

[2] Protocol Additional to the Geneva Conventions of 12 August 1949, and relating to the Protection of Victims of International Armed Conflicts (Protocol I), 8 June 1977, art. 35. The triple cumulative standard called for in Additional Protocol 1, under which all three conditions must be proven for a violation to occur, has been nearly impossible to enforce, particularly given the lack of precise definitions for "widespread," "long-term," and "severe" (UNEP 2009b).

4 Assessing and restoring natural resources in post-conflict peacebuilding

draining 90 percent of the Mesopotamian marshlands in retaliation against an uprising of the Marsh Arabs (Bruch et al. 2009). Nevertheless, the severe environmental damage caused by conflicts in Iraq again prompted a number of important international responses. In 1991, the United Nations Security Council (UNSC) established the United Nations Compensation Commission to provide financial compensation for losses—including environmental damage—resulting from Iraq's illegal invasion of Kuwait (Payne 2013); the inclusion of environmental damage within the scope of compensation constituted an important international precedent.

Also on the normative front, the 1992 Rio Declaration on Environment and Development included principle 24, which recognized that "warfare is inherently destructive of sustainable development. States shall therefore respect international law providing protection for the environment in times of armed conflict and cooperate in its further development, as necessary" (UNGA 1992, prin. 24).[3]

In 2001, the United Nations General Assembly (UNGA), at the urging of the government of Kuwait, established November 6 as the International Day for Preventing the Exploitation of the Environment in War and Armed Conflict—a day for the international community to reflect on the challenge of deliberate war-related environmental damage and take further collective action toward prevention (UNGA 2001). Importantly, UNGA formally recognized that environmental damage during armed conflict impairs ecosystems and natural resources long after conflict has subsided, and often extends beyond the limits of national territories as well as beyond the present generation.

In addition to being subjected to purposeful harm, natural resources play another role in conflict: as financing sources. With the end of the Cold War, in 1989, many countries and armed groups turned to natural resources to fund conflict: since 1990, eighteen internal conflicts have been partially fueled or financed by natural resources (UNEP 2009a). In many cases, natural resources also became the spoils of war: in the wake of conflict, and with little or no regard for transparency, fair terms, or benefit sharing with local communities, resource concession contracts have been handed out by combatants and governments alike.

Where natural resources have been used to finance conflict, the UNSC has in some cases mandated UN peacekeeping missions to address the challenges of natural resource governance (UNEP 2012). So far, five missions have been given direct mandates to help post-conflict countries restore or extend state authority over natural resources (with varying degrees of breadth with respect to the resources addressed and the activities in which the missions engaged): Cambodia, Liberia, Sierra Leone, the Democratic Republic of the Congo, and Abyei, Sudan (UNSC 1992, 2003, 2004, 2008a, 2008b, 2011).[4] To restrict their use in

---

[3] See Bruch et al. (2012) for more information.
[4] In addition, the UN expert group investigating the production and illicit export of diamonds in Côte d'Ivoire had a mandate to cooperate with the UN peacekeeping mission (UNSC 2005).

conflict financing and prevent illegal trade, the UNSC has also imposed a range of sanctions on oil, diamonds, and timber (UNEP 2012). In the early 2000s, two initiatives—the Kimberley Process (KP) and the Extractive Industries Transparency Initiative (EITI)—were established to restrict conflict financing from diamonds and to ensure transparency in oil, gas, and mining revenues, respectively.[5]

The KP and the EITI were also important elements in the expanding set of tools that the international community could use to address the linkages between natural resources, conflict, and peacebuilding. As these linkages became more complex and multifaceted, the UN saw a need to establish new, dedicated capacity to assist member states in addressing them. As a result, in 2005, the United Nations Environment Programme (UNEP) established the Post-Conflict and Disaster Management Branch (PCDMB). PCDMB's mandate is (1) to conduct post-conflict environmental assessments at the request of member states, and (2) to help integrate environmental and natural resource considerations into UN reconstruction, peacebuilding, and humanitarian assistance efforts. In 2008, the task of helping member states to assess and address the environmental dimensions of both conflicts and disasters became one of UNEP's six overarching priorities; and in 2010, the UN Secretary-General called on member states and the UN system to make "natural resource allocation, ownership and access an integral part of peacebuilding strategies" (UNSG 2010).[6]

This book is an initial response to this call. It captures some of the main lessons that have emerged from efforts to integrate post-conflict environmental assessment into peacebuilding. It also illustrates how post-conflict reconstruction efforts can take environmental and natural resource issues into account—and investigates how, as part of the peacebuilding process, environmental hot spots caused by conflict have been remediated, and natural resources damaged by conflict or unsustainable practices have been restored. The aim is to demonstrate why such measures are important; how they can strengthen peacebuilding; and how they can be better integrated into peacebuilding programs, policies, and practices. Finally, the book highlights the necessity, in assessment, remediation, and restoration, of responding to the unique conditions of post-conflict countries.

The twenty case studies included in this book cover twenty-three post-conflict countries and territories (see map on page 6) and were written by thirty-five experts from UN agencies, government ministries, nongovernmental organizations, academia, and the military. The book is organized into four thematic sections: "Post-Conflict Environmental Assessments," "Remediation of Environmental Hot Spots," "Restoration of Natural Resources and Ecosystems," and "Environmental Dimensions of Infrastructure and Reconstruction."

---

[5] See, for example, Grant (2012), Wright (2012), Bone (2012), Mitchell (2012), and Rich and Warner (2012).

[6] Other important policy documents on post-conflict peacebuilding include World Bank (2011), UN (2011), UNSG (2009, 2012), and UNEP (2009a).

6 Assessing and restoring natural resources in post-conflict peacebuilding

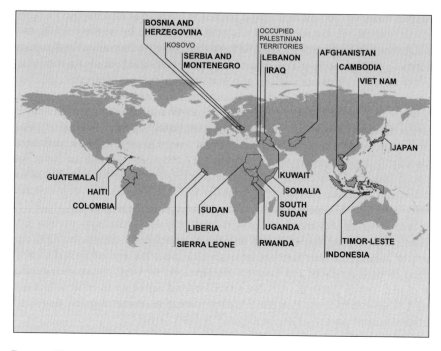

Post-conflict and conflict-affected countries and territories from which lessons have been drawn in this book, either through case studies or broader thematic analyses
Notes: UN member states are set in bold. During the time under consideration in this book, the Palestinian territories were known as the occupied Palestinian territories, and Serbia and Montenegro were one country: first the Federal Republic of Yugoslavia, then Serbia and Montenegro.

POST-CONFLICT ENVIRONMENTAL ASSESSMENTS

The complexity of the potential linkages among natural resources, conflict, and peacebuilding justifies comprehensive assessments at the outset of the peacebuilding process. Such assessments must include three major tasks:

- Identifying the role of natural resources and the environment in contributing to conflict outbreak, financing, perpetuation, and relapse risk.
- Determining the conflict's direct and indirect impacts on natural resources and identifying the associated risks to human health, livelihoods, and security.
- Evaluating opportunities to restore and use natural resources, in order to achieve peacebuilding and sustainable development outcomes while minimizing environmental damage and new grievances.

Environmental assessments in post-conflict countries face a number of challenges: first, many post-conflict countries lack baseline environmental data—

a situation that has often been exacerbated by the conflict itself. Second, key actors with control over natural resources may resist efforts to establish transparency. Third, the "winners" and "losers" in a conflict are typically keen to promote specific agendas—and are therefore not necessarily trustworthy sources of information. Given the lack of reliable data, an objective and verifiable assessment conducted by an impartial actor can be a valuable tool for needs assessments and for the development of priorities.

Individuals, communities, organizations, and nations recovering from conflict also face a number of important decisions about assessment. At what point should an environmental assessment be undertaken? When data are limited, how can sound judgments be made about needs and priorities? How can the assessment address spatial variations in land use, environmental impact, and needs? Can the assessment process itself be used as a platform for community engagement and reconciliation? Who will participate in decision making, and who will set priorities for action? What are the trade-offs associated with different natural resource investments? How can different interventions be sequenced and coordinated? Part 1 of this book provides some initial insight into these challenges, on the basis of case studies from Afghanistan, Albania, Bosnia and Herzegovina, Iraq, Lebanon, Liberia, Macedonia, the occupied Palestinian territories, Serbia and Montenegro, Somalia, and Sudan.[7]

REMEDIATION OF ENVIRONMENTAL HOT SPOTS

Chemical contamination, hazardous waste (including rubble), landmines, and unexploded ordnance are significant threats to human and ecological health in post-conflict settings. The cost of cleanup may be high, but intervention is often crucial to the success of peacebuilding—both as a means of protecting human health, and as a way to demonstrate domestic authorities' capacity for effective response.

When conflict causes environmental hot spots, remediation must address a number of key concerns: What is the minimum level of cleanup needed to avert significant risk? Can remediation projects provide immediate employment for excombatants? Should preexisting levels of contamination and pollution be taken into account in determining the extent of cleanup? Where should hazardous materials be stored or disposed of? When population groups are at odds, can the remediation of hot spots that pose equal threats to all groups be used to build mutual trust, and as an opportunity for cooperation? While there is little question that rapid remediation of hazardous sites is necessary, both domestic and international actors have had difficulty addressing these challenges. The case studies in part 2—which are from Cambodia, Iraq, Lebanon, Serbia and Montenegro, Sierra Leone, Sudan, and Viet Nam—capture some of the key lessons learned to date.

---

[7] Albania and Macedonia are not evaluated as conflict-affected countries but rather are mentioned because each was affected by refugee flows.

8   Assessing and restoring natural resources in post-conflict peacebuilding

RESTORATION OF NATURAL RESOURCES AND ECOSYSTEMS

In addition to having been directly damaged by conflict, natural resources and ecosystems may have been harmed by unsustainable practice before or during conflict. Natural resources are often the very foundation of post-conflict recovery, offering livelihoods and employment (for example, farming, forestry, fishing, and mining); construction materials (such as lumber or reeds); and water for people, agriculture, and livestock. Trying to restore ecosystems and natural resources while simultaneously engineering livelihood recovery may seem like a contradiction. But restoration can be a major source of emergency employment—and, in the longer term, post-conflict livelihoods will depend on the restoration and sustainable management of the natural resource base. Thus, the question is not whether restoration should be undertaken, but how quickly and to what extent.

The key challenges in designing and implementing restoration programs in post-conflict countries include the following: Should restoration efforts be directed by local communities, or by outside organizations that have greater technical expertise? In order to support peacebuilding, can restoration be used both as a source of emergency employment, and as a means of empowering communities? Can the restoration of natural resources and the recovery of human livelihoods proceed simultaneously? What practical steps can be taken if the affected region is no longer ecologically viable? How can restoration be undertaken in the absence of good governance? To what condition should the environment be restored? How should the contributions of nonstate actors be coordinated, and by whom? In part 3, case studies from Haiti, Iraq, and Lebanon highlight key considerations in designing and implementing restoration programs in post-conflict countries. This part of the book also considers the potential implications of climate change for natural resources and peacebuilding.

ENVIRONMENTAL DIMENSIONS OF INFRASTRUCTURE AND RECONSTRUCTION

Reconstruction is always a priority in conflict-affected regions, particularly in relation to water, waste, and energy infrastructure. Any reconstruction efforts must take social, economic, and environmental impacts into account, both from a sectoral perspective (which calls for strategic environmental assessments) and on a project-by-project basis (which calls for environmental impact assessments). Like remediation and restoration, reconstruction faces a number of challenges, including the following: How can competing priorities, particularly for scarce resources such as water, be addressed? How can environmental impact assessments be conducted as rapidly as possible, to avoid delays that could affect peacebuilding? How can investments in natural resource–related infrastructure also support peacebuilding, through job creation, confidence building, and regional cooperation? Part 4 includes case studies from Afghanistan, the Balkans, Iraq, and Sudan, as well as lessons from post–World War II reconstruction efforts. This part of the book also considers the importance, in project evaluations, of assessing a project's potential positive and negative effects on access to natural resources.

FUTURE OUTLOOK

The fragility of post-conflict settings requires immediate attention to natural resources once a conflict has ended—and, in many cases, while it is occurring. Natural resources are essential to most peacebuilding activities, but the design and implementation of post-conflict peacebuilding policies and programs have often failed to effectively analyze, plan for, or address natural resources. This book highlights the important role of environmental assessment, remediation, restoration, and reconstruction in the peacebuilding context, including the implementation challenges that practitioners are likely to face. In addition to stressing the importance of integrating natural resource management and environmental sustainability into peacebuilding, the book offers lessons on how to achieve such integration.

Along with understanding the lessons of the past, it is equally important to assess future risk. For example, the list of fragile states identified in 2011 by the Organisation for Economic Co-operation and Development includes forty-five countries deemed to be at risk (OECD 2011). Of those, about 91 percent contain transboundary waters, globally significant biodiversity hot spots, or both (CI 2005; Wolf, Yoffe, and Giordano 2003); 68 percent contain World Heritage sites (UNESCO 2011); and 80 percent contain extractive resources of strategic global significance (USGS 2010; IEA 2011).

Understanding how to prevent natural resources from contributing to instability and conflict in fragile regions is a critical need, as is the provision of immediate technical and political support in the event of violence. Averting the pillage and plunder of natural resources in fragile states will be one of the key challenges of the next decade. In addition to strengthening post-conflict peacebuilding, this book is intended to provide insights into conducting assessments and designing programs to address the risks and opportunities presented by natural resources in fragile states.

REFERENCES

Bone, A. 2012. The Kimberley Process Certification Scheme: The primary safeguard for the diamond industry. In *High-value natural resources and post-conflict peacebuilding*, ed. P. Lujala and S. A. Rustad. London: Earthscan.

Briggs, C., and I. Weissbecker. 2012. Salting the Earth: Environmental health challenges in post-conflict reconstruction. In *Assessing and restoring natural resources in post-conflict peacebuilding*, ed. D. Jensen and S. Lonergan. London: Earthscan.

Bruch, C., M. Boulicault, S. Talati, and D. Jensen. 2012. International law, natural resources and post-conflict peacebuilding: From Rio to Rio+20 and beyond. *Review of European Community and International Environmental Law* 21 (1): 44–62.

Bruch, C., D. Jensen, M. Nakayama, J. Unruh, R. Gruby, and R. Wolfarth. 2009. Post-conflict peace building and natural resources. *Yearbook of International Environmental Law* 19:58–96.
CI (Conservation International). 2005. *Biodiversity hotspots*. Arlington, VA.
Grant, J. A. 2012. The Kimberley Process at ten: Reflections on a decade of efforts to end the trade in conflict diamonds. In *High-value natural resources and post-conflict peacebuilding*, ed. P. Lujala and S. A. Rustad. London: Earthscan.
IEA (International Energy Agency). 2011. *Key world energy statistics*. Paris.
International Dialogue on Peacebuilding and Statebuilding. 2011. A new deal for engagement in fragile states. www.oecd.org/international%20dialogue/49151944.pdf.
Mitchell, H. 2012. A more formal engagement: A constructive critique of certification as a means of preventing conflict and building peace. In *High-value natural resources and post-conflict peacebuilding*, ed. P. Lujala and S. A. Rustad. London: Earthscan.
OECD (Organisation for Economic Co-operation and Development). 2011. *Ensuring fragile states are not left behind*. Paris.
Payne, C. 2013. Legal liability for environmental damage: The United Nations Compensation Commission and the 1990–1991 Gulf War. In *Governance, natural resources, and post-conflict peacebuilding*, ed. C. Bruch, C. Muffett, and S. S. Nichols. London: Earthscan.
Rich, E., and T. N. Warner. 2012. Addressing the roots of Liberia's conflict through the Extractive Industries Transparency Initiative. In *High-value natural resources and post-conflict peacebuilding*, ed. P. Lujala and S. A. Rustad. London: Earthscan.
Sphere Project. 2004. *Humanitarian charter and minimum standards in disaster response*. Geneva, Switzerland. http://ocw.jhsph.edu/courses/refugeehealthcare/PDFs/SphereProject Handbook.pdf.
———. 2011. *Humanitarian charter and minimum standards in humanitarian response*. Geneva, Switzerland. www.sphereproject.org/resources/download-publications/?search =1&keywords=&language=English&category=22.
UN (United Nations). 2011. *Civilian capacity in the aftermath of conflict: Independent report of the Senior Advisory Group*. New York.
UNEP (United Nations Environment Programme). 2003. *Desk study on the environment in Iraq*. Geneva, Switzerland. http://postconflict.unep.ch/publications/Iraq_DS.pdf.
———. 2009a. *From conflict to peacebuilding: The role of natural resources and the environment*. Nairobi, Kenya. http://postconflict.unep.ch/publications/pcdmb_policy_01.pdf.
———. 2009b. *Protecting the environment during armed conflict: An inventory and analysis of international law*. Nairobi, Kenya. www.un.org/zh/events/environmentconflictday/ pdfs/int_law.pdf.
———. 2012. *Greening the blue helmets: Environment, natural resources and UN peacekeeping operations*. Nairobi, Kenya. http://postconflict.unep.ch/publications/UNEP_greening _blue_helmets.pdf.
UNESCO (United Nations Educational, Scientific and Cultural Organization). 2011. *World Heritage List*. Paris.
UNGA (United Nations General Assembly). 1992. Annex 1: Rio Declaration on Environment and Development. In Report of the United Nations Conference on Environment and Development. A/CONF.151/26 (Vol. I). August 12.
———. 2001. Observance of the International Day for Preventing the Exploitation of the Environment in War and Armed Conflict. A/RES/56/4. November 13. New York.

UNSC (United Nations Security Council). 1992. Resolution 792. S/RES/792 (1992). November 30. New York.
———. 2003. Resolution 1509. S/RES/1509 (2003). September 19. New York.
———. 2004. Resolution 1562. S/RES/1562 (2004). September 17. New York.
———. 2005. Resolution 1643. S/RES/1643 (2005). December 15. New York.
———. 2008a. Resolution 1856. S/RES/1856 (2008). December 22. New York.
———. 2008b. Resolution 1857. S/RES/1857 (2008). December 22. New York.
———. 2011. Resolution 1990. S/RES/1990 (2011). June 27. New York.
UNSG (United Nations Secretary-General). 2009. *Report of the Secretary-General on peacebuilding in the immediate aftermath of conflict*. A/63/881–S/2009/304. June 11. New York. www.unrol.org/files/pbf_090611_sg.pdf.
———. 2010. *Progress report of the Secretary-General on peacebuilding in the immediate aftermath of conflict*. A/64/866–S/2010/386. July 16 (reissued on August 19 for technical reasons). New York. www.un.org/ga/search/view_doc.asp?symbol=A/64/866.
———. 2012. *Report of the Secretary-General on peacebuilding in the aftermath of conflict*. New York.
UNSG's (United Nations Secretary-General's) Policy Committee. 2007. Conceptual basis for peacebuilding for the UN system. May. New York.
USGS (United States Geological Survey). 2010. *Minerals yearbook*. Reston, VA.
USIP (United States Institute of Peace) and U.S. Army PKSOI (United States Army Peacekeeping and Stability Operations Institute). 2009. *Guiding principles for stabilization and reconstruction*. Washington, D.C.: Endowment of the United States Institute of Peace.
Wolf, A. T., S. B. Yoffe, and M. Giordano. 2003. *International waters: Indicators for identifying basins at risk*. Paris: United Nations Educational, Scientific and Cultural Organization.
World Bank. 2011. *World development report 2011*. Washington, D.C.
Wright, J. A. 2012. The Kimberley Process Certification Scheme: A model negotiation? In *High-value natural resources and post-conflict peacebuilding*, ed. P. Lujala and S. A. Rustad. London: Earthscan.

PART 1
Post-conflict environmental assessments

Introduction

In post-conflict environmental assessments, researchers employ investigative technical procedures in a specific geographical area to identify and evaluate the biophysical, social, and other environmental impacts that occurred as the result of a conflict, and to identify needs and the opportunities available to remediate these impacts and restore environmental health. Increasingly, environmental assessments are also investigating how natural resources contributed to the outbreak or perpetuation of conflict, as well as how they can be used to positively transform peacebuilding outcomes without creating new sources of conflict or major environmental impacts. With comprehensive environmental assessments, practitioners are better able to integrate environmental and natural resource considerations into post-conflict planning processes and longer-term decision making.

The post-conflict environmental assessments conducted by the United Nations Environment Programme (UNEP) have evolved and expanded since 1999, when they were first employed. In "Evaluating the Impact of UNEP's Post-Conflict Environmental Assessments," David Jensen reviews the evolution of these assessments and discusses how they are applied in the various policy frameworks they are meant to inform. Environmental assessments can lead to policy change, help to mobilize financing, and attract media coverage. Jensen evaluates the results of seven different post-conflict assessments conducted—in chronological order—in Serbia, Iraq, Afghanistan, the occupied Palestinian territories, Liberia, Lebanon, and Sudan. He quantifies the various impacts and determines the most relevant internal and external explanatory factors for them. Finally, he discusses the strengths and weaknesses of various assessment approaches and highlights the need for national involvement.

Ken Conca and Jennifer Wallace also consider UNEP's post-conflict environmental assessments and review a range of assessments to identify lessons for peacebuilding. Their chapter, "Environment and Peacebuilding in War-Torn Societies: Lessons from the UN Environment Programme's Experience with Post-Conflict Assessment," opens with an overview of the state of knowledge about environmental and natural resource linkages to peace and conflict. The subsequent analysis and discussion highlight four themes: the multiple, often indirect connections between violence and environmental degradation; the political dimensions of environmental assessment as a confidence-building tool; resource and environmental linkages among the formal, informal, illegal, and aid-based economies of war-torn societies; and the environmental dimensions of reconstituting regulations, the state, and the rule of law. Environmental issues create high-stakes choices in post-conflict settings, Conca and Wallace contend, and effective handling of these choices may create a solid foundation for peace and sustainable development; when such choices are handled poorly, however, environmental problems can undercut an already tenuous peace.

16   Assessing and restoring natural resources in post-conflict peacebuilding

The Swedish Armed Forces and the Swedish Defence Research Agency have developed an environmental vulnerability assessment (EVA) framework that has been used to mitigate environmental risks during Swedish peacekeeping operations. In "Medical and Environmental Intelligence in Peace and Crisis-Management Operations," Birgitta Liljedahl, Annica Waleij, Björn Sandström, and Louise Simonsson highlight the need for increased understanding within the peace and security community of the nexus between security, environmental issues, and natural resources. They argue that robust, transparent, and systematically applied tools such as an EVA can aid in the recognition of environmental drivers of conflict and of potential environmental risks to human health. Such tools can also improve the ability to predict and mitigate negative environmental impacts from operations.

Regardless of the specific post-conflict assessment process utilized, three tools can support the consideration of natural resources and enhance the effectiveness of the assessment: consultation, adaptation to change, and the building of scenarios based on the desired end state of the post-conflict transition. In "Thinking Back-End: Improving Post-Conflict Analysis through Consultation, Adapting to Change, and Scenario Building," Alexander Carius and Achim Maas examine these approaches and pose specific questions that can complement crisis analysis and help practitioners to identify and prevent relapses into violence.

The four chapters in part 1 provide a comprehensive overview of the evolution of post-conflict assessments, the main trends in direct and indirect environmental impacts from conflict, the available tools and approaches, and finally the key success factors for integrating environment and natural resource needs into peacebuilding frameworks and recovery plans. One of the key messages is that environmental assessments are critical tools for identifying impacts, risks, and opportunities, as well as for costing and integrating needs within peacebuilding plans. Accordingly, environmental assessments should be conducted on a systematic basis as part of the new UN peacebuilding architecture.

Evaluating the impact of UNEP's post-conflict environmental assessments

David Jensen

In a post-conflict situation, some of the immediate challenges for the international community include defining and prioritizing needs, coordinating responses, and sending the right level and type of support to the right place at the right time. All of this must be accomplished in a way that reflects national priorities and helps stabilize and consolidate the peace process. But efforts often take place in a volatile and complex political environment, where national authorities may lack full legitimacy and public support, have low capacity, or be more interested in their political survival and regime security. Prioritizing the management of natural resources is often difficult, given competing priorities, such as security sector reform; disarmament, demobilization, and reintegration; return of displaced persons; and holding of national elections. Yet natural resources are essential to the peace process because they often underpin other peacebuilding sectors. From water for drinking and agriculture, to forests and rangelands that support livelihoods, to high-value natural resources that can kick-start economic growth and become an engine for recovery, the way natural resources are used can influence the success of peacebuilding endeavors. Furthermore failure to effectively manage natural resources, such as land and water, is often one of the most common sources of local-level conflict.

To ensure that natural resource management and environmental governance needs are reflected in post-conflict relief, recovery, and development plans, the United Nations Environment Programme (UNEP) has built new capacity and technical expertise in conducting post-conflict environmental assessments at the request of national authorities and the United Nations system. UNEP's work, which began in 1999, has been part of an overall process to make UNEP more operational and relevant at the field level. There are three situations in which UNEP can be

---

David Jensen manages the Environmental Cooperation for Peacebuilding Programme of the United Nations Environment Programme (UNEP). He wrote in his personal capacity, so the chapter does not reflect the official view of UNEP. Julien Aguzzoli (University of Grenoble) and Hannah Moosa (University of Toronto) provided research assistance.

18 Assessing and restoring natural resources in post-conflict peacebuilding

requested to conduct a post-conflict environmental assessment—first, when national authorities lack the scientific expertise or operational capacity to conduct a field-based assessment; second, when the conflict causes environmental damage that may involve one or more neighboring countries; and third, when political stakes are high and impartiality is needed to objectively analyze environmental drivers and impacts.

Since 1999, UNEP's post-conflict environmental assessment toolkit has gradually expanded to meet various needs and policy processes. UNEP now offers four distinct types of assessments, each with a different scope, objective, and approach. These include needs assessments, quantitative risk assessments, strategic assessments, and comprehensive assessments. The chapter compares the overall impact of the four methods in seven field operations conducted between 1999 and 2007.

The effects of the assessments are first evaluated according to three indicators: policy influence, financing of environmental needs, and media coverage. For each indicator, the level of impact is categorized on a four-point scale in order to provide a standardized framework for comparison. From the country case studies, successes, failures, and lessons learned are drawn. The chapter then considers a number of questions: Are assessments useful and which methods have worked best? What are the conditions for success? Does more time and funding lead to more impact? How can environmental and natural resource management needs be effectively integrated into peacebuilding plans? How can national ownership be maintained when international actors carry out the assessments?

All of the countries where UNEP conducted post-conflict assessments from 1999 to 2007 are covered.[1] These include the Federal Republic of Yugoslavia (FRY), Afghanistan, the occupied Palestinian territories (oPt), Iraq, Liberia, Lebanon, and Sudan. Assessments conducted by UNEP since 2008 have not been included because their full impact could not yet be evaluated at the time of this writing.

POST-CONFLICT ENVIRONMENTAL ASSESSMENT METHODS

UNEP has developed four types of post-conflict environmental assessments to meet the distinct needs of policy processes. A summary of each method and a list of countries where it was applied are provided below:

- **Needs assessments and desk studies:** During or after a conflict, UNEP can collect preexisting secondary information on environmental trends and natural resource management challenges from international and national sources. The information is compiled into a desk study report that attempts to identify and prioritize environmental needs. Limited field visits of one to two weeks are

---

[1] For another perspective on UNEP's post-conflict assessments, see Ken Conca and Jennifer Wallace, "Environment and Peacebuilding in War-Torn Societies: Lessons from the UN Environment Programme's Experience with Post-Conflict Assessment," in this book.

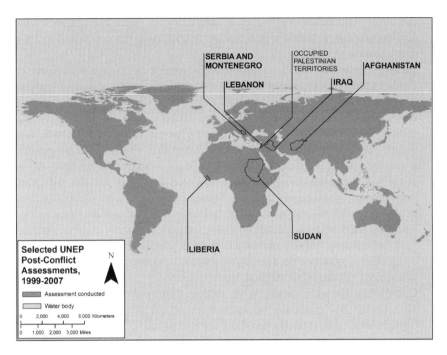

Notes:
1. Post-conflict operations in UN member states are set in bold.
2. At the time of UNEP's respective assessments, the Palestinian territories were known as the occupied Palestinian territories; Serbia and Montenegro comprised the Federal Republic of Yugoslavia; and South Sudan was not yet an independent country.

often conducted to verify data, conduct stakeholder meetings, and validate initial findings. These assessments inform the post-conflict needs assessment (PCNA) process of the UN, World Bank, and European Union (EU). They are also often published as self-standing desk study reports and serve as a basis for further national analysis. The chapter evaluates the impact of UNEP needs assessments and desk studies conducted in the oPt, Iraq, Liberia, and Sudan.

- **Quantitative risk assessments:** These assessments focus on the direct environmental impacts of conflicts caused by bombing and destruction of buildings, industrial sites, and public infrastructure. They were designed to assess environmental damage following short-duration, high-intensity conflicts that often occur in urban environments. Teams of environmental experts conduct rigorous field sampling of possible environmental contamination of water, soil, and air, with a view to identifying serious risks to human health and environmental hot spots. Field missions are conducted in a span of three to four weeks and involve the extensive use of laboratory analysis and satellite imagery. Depending on how soon after a conflict they are conducted, the assessments

can inform humanitarian priorities or early recovery plans. The chapter evaluates the impact of UNEP's quantitative risk assessments conducted in FRY and Lebanon.
- **Strategic assessments:** In addition to the direct environmental effects of conflict addressed by quantitative risk assessments, strategic assessments evaluate the indirect impacts of the survival and coping strategies of local people and the institutional problems caused by the breakdown of governance and capacity. Potential environmental risks to human health, livelihoods, and security, as well as capacity gaps, are then identified. The assessments provide a snapshot of the environmental needs in order to inform larger recovery or peacebuilding strategies. They were designed primarily for use following long-duration, low-intensity conflicts. Strategic assessments are often conducted in two to six months and are based on field missions lasting three to six weeks. They are used when a specific planning or policy process requires updated field information quickly and when there is insufficient time to conduct a comprehensive assessment. The chapter evaluates the impact of a UNEP strategic assessment conducted in Afghanistan.
- **Comprehensive assessments:** When sufficient time and resources exist, UNEP can conduct a comprehensive assessment of the environmental situation. Comprehensive assessments provide a detailed picture of each natural resource sector and the environmental trends, governance challenges, and capacity needs. Based on national consultations with stakeholders, comprehensive assessments attempt to identify priorities and cost the required interventions over the short, medium, and long terms. Comprehensive assessments last from one to two years, depending on the size of the country and area affected by the conflict, the security conditions, and the logistical infrastructure. The assessments contain enough information upon which to build detailed intervention programs. The chapter evaluates the impact of a UNEP comprehensive assessment conducted in Sudan.

The type of assessment used in each case depends on the scope of the request made by the national authority, the conflict, funding, and the time line of the post-conflict policy framework as discussed below. Each assessment is also tailor-made to address the political, security, and logistical conditions in each country. To the extent possible, each assessment methodology involves senior international experts partnered with national experts. UNEP's neutrality and independence are maintained throughout the assessment process, leading to an objective technical evaluation of environmental needs.

POST-CONFLICT POLICY FRAMEWORKS

The findings of post-conflict environmental assessments are used by a number of policy frameworks. This section describes the five post-conflict frameworks used by the UN system and member states where UNEP has taken an active role

Table 1. UNEP 1999–2007 post-conflict assessments: Methodology and policy frameworks evaluated

Case	Assessment methodology	Flash/CAP[a]	PCNA[b]	National recovery plan	PRSP[c]	CCA/UNDAF[d] or equivalent
FRY[e]	Quantitative	X				
Afghanistan	Strategic			X	X	X
oPt[f]	Desk study			X		
Iraq	Desk study	X	X	X		X
Liberia	Desk study		X	X	X	X
Lebanon	Quantitative			X		
Sudan	Desk Study/Comprehensive		X	X		X

a. Flash appeal/consolidated appeal process.
b. Post-conflict needs assessment.
c. Poverty reduction strategy paper.
d. Common country assessment/UN Development Assistance Framework.
e. Federal Republic of Yugoslavia.
f. Occupied Palestinian territories.

in helping national authorities assess environmental issues, identify priorities, and integrate needs. Table 1 summarizes the post-conflict environmental assessment methods and relevant policy frameworks that were used in each of the seven case studies.

- **Flash appeal and consolidated appeal process (CAP):** Following a peace agreement or ceasefire, the UN often issues a flash appeal to respond to urgent humanitarian needs. These usually address food, water, and shelter for refugees and internally displaced persons, as well as other critical services and protection. In some cases, when more planning and analysis are possible, such as during complex emergencies and protracted conflicts, a CAP covers the humanitarian needs for a full year. The flash appeal and CAP are the primary relief instruments used by the international community for identifying needs and coordinating and financing relief efforts. The chapter reviews the impact of environmental assessments on the humanitarian appeals for FRY and Iraq.
- **Post-conflict needs assessment (PCNA):** First used in 2003, PCNAs are undertaken by the UN Development Group, the World Bank, and the EU in collaboration with the national government and donor countries. PCNAs are used for jointly assessing needs, identifying targets, and financing a shared strategy for recovery in post-conflict situations. The PCNA includes the assessment and the national prioritization and costing of needs. Most PCNAs take between two and twelve months to complete and cover two to four years of activities. The chapter reviews the impact of environmental assessments on the PCNA processes for Iraq, Liberia, and Sudan.
- **National recovery plan or development strategy:** In cases when a PCNA was not conducted, or a government chooses to replace the PCNA with a new

strategy, a national recovery plan or development strategy is issued by the transitional or elected national government. The document sets out the costed national priorities and requests assistance from the international community to meet the identified needs. The chapter reviews the impact of environmental assessments on national recovery plans for Afghanistan, oPt, Iraq, Liberia, Lebanon, and Sudan.

- **Poverty reduction strategy paper (PRSP):** Once a post-conflict country has moved from the transition phase to the development phase, interim or full PRSPs are often developed. Designed by the International Monetary Fund (IMF) and the World Bank in 1999, PRSPs are produced in cooperation with governments, stakeholders, and international partners. PRSPs focus on the economic and financial profile of a country and provide a plan for reducing poverty and supporting the economy through various actions. PRSPs are instrumental for a country to obtain financing and debt relief from the IMF and the World Bank. The chapter reviews the impact of environmental assessments within the PRSPs for Afghanistan and Liberia.
- **Common country assessment (CCA) and UN Development Assistance Framework (UNDAF):** In response to a national recovery plan, development strategy, or PRSP, the UN country team conducts a CCA to determine how the UN can meet national priorities. The CCA attempts to focus UN efforts on three or four pillars, or areas of need. Based on the CCA, an UNDAF establishes concrete outcomes and indicators in each area and provides detailed costing. Specific agencies and partners are listed with a time line. In post-conflict countries, CCAs and UNDAFs are typically conducted once the country has moved from the transition phase to the development phase (e.g., three to five years after the conflict). The chapter reviews the impact of environmental assessments within CCAs and UNDAFs for Afghanistan, Iraq, Liberia, and Sudan.

ANALYSIS METHODOLOGY

The seven case studies are presented in chronological order from 1999 to 2007. The impact of each environmental assessment was analyzed according to policy influence, financing of environmental needs, and media coverage. These indicators were selected because objectively verifiable data were available in all seven cases. For each indicator, a standardized four-point scale ranging from none (0), to low (1), medium (2), and high (3) was used to classify the level of impact. Assessments conducted after 2007 were not included because their full impact could not be evaluated at the time of writing.

To analyze the policy impact of an assessment, all relevant post-conflict policy frameworks issued after the release of a UNEP report until January 2010 were collected. The environmental content of each policy framework based on the UNEP assessment report was categorized on the following four-point scale: no impact (0) means that environmental issues were not mentioned in the policy framework; low impact (1) means that a general statement was included on environmental issues, but no specific sectors, targets, indicators, or financial resources were included; medium impact (2) means that environmental needs were included with priorities and sectors, but no targets, indicators, or detailed budget information were included; and high impact (3) means that environmental needs and sectors were included with a detailed budget and targets. To determine the overall policy impact, the individual scores for each policy framework were averaged.

To analyze the financial impact of an assessment, the financial resources that were mobilized by UNEP from donors to address the recommendations of the assessment were calculated. The level of financing raised, compared to the amount requested, was categorized on the following four-point scale: no impact (0) means that UNEP was unable to mobilize any funds for follow-up work; low impact (1) means that UNEP was able to mobilize less than 50 percent of the requested funds for follow-up activities; medium impact (2) means that UNEP was able to mobilize between 50 and 75 percent of the requested funds for follow-up activities; high impact (3) means that UNEP was able to mobilize over 75 percent of the requested funds for follow-up activities. To determine the overall financial impact, the individual scores were averaged. The indicator was restricted to the amount of funding UNEP was able to mobilize for follow-up activities from donors because information on the total amount of funding raised for the environmental sector is not systematically tracked by the UN system or by national governments.

To analyze the media impact of the assessment, four types of media were considered, including print, Web, radio, and television. For each format, the study counted either the presence (yes) or absence (no) of coverage in stream media at the national and international levels. The overall media impact was then categorized on the following four-point scale: no impact (0) means that no coverage was achieved in any media; low impact (1) means that coverage was achieved in only one format; medium impact (2) means that coverage was achieved in two media; high impact (3) means that coverage was achieved in three or four media. To determine the overall media impact, the individual scores were averaged.

Finally, to determine a total impact score, a weighted average calculation was applied to the policy (40 percent), financial (40 percent), and media (20 percent) scores. A weighted process was used because UNEP's objectives relate to the policy and financial impacts, with media coverage a secondary objective. The final impact score was also categorized on the following four-point scale: no impact was 0; low impact was any score less than 2; medium impact ranged from 2 to 2.49; high impact ranged from 2.5 to 3. The scale was arbitrary, rather than robust and quantitative, and was used to compare the cases. Consistent with UNEP's internal categorization, the low category is allocated a wider band than the medium and high categories. A total impact score of 3 means only that the assessment had a high impact within each indicator, rather than a perfect outcome. Following the indicator analysis, each section concludes with a summary of the positive and negative factors that influenced the overall impact of the assessment.

24 Assessing and restoring natural resources in post-conflict peacebuilding

The information presented in this chapter was collected from various public reports and official UN documents, as well as from interviews with UNEP program managers and experts who participated in the assessments.[2] Information on media coverage was collected from UNEP staff and experts who tracked the national and international media coverage of report-launch events and follow-up projects.

The chapter does not attempt to assess subsequent projects developed to address the environmental needs, nor does it analyze the adequacy of the funding allocated or spent in the environmental sector. This kind of analysis would require detailed field-based evaluations and is beyond the chapter's scope. An environmental assessment with a high impact does not automatically translate into a field project with a high impact. Although that may be the case, it is the topic of separate research. Moreover, many of the assessments reviewed occurred before UN reforms were implemented, including the humanitarian cluster system, the UN Peacebuilding Commission, and the environmental toolkit for the PCNA (UN and World Bank 2009). As a result, the possible impact of the reforms on addressing environmental and natural resource needs has not been considered. Not withstanding the limitations, the chapter provides a good opportunity to objectively review and compare the impacts of assessment methods to inform the scope, approach, and substance of future programs.

CASE STUDIES

Case studies that follow are those conducted between 1999 and 2007, and include the Federal Republic of Yugoslavia, Afghanistan, occupied Palestinian territories, Iraq, Liberia, Lebanon, and Sudan.

Federal Republic of Yugoslavia

During the Kosovo conflict in 1999, bombing of industrial sites, military bases, and public infrastructure raised concern about a potential environmental catastrophe from the release of toxic chemicals. The North Atlantic Treaty Organization insisted that sophisticated weapons and targeting minimized collateral damage, yet the government of FRY claimed extensive environmental destruction.[3] Neighboring countries also expressed concerns about possible transboundary water and air pollution.

---

[2] Technical and policy input was provided by Henrik Slotte, Asif Zaidi, Belinda Bowling, Silja Halle, Andrew Morton, Aniket Ghai, Maliza van Eeden, Koen Toonen, and Hassan Partow. Additional research and reviews were conducted by Dennis Hamro-Drotz, Renard Sexton, Fanny Rudén, Divya Sama, and Abigail Sylvester.

[3] On February 4, 2003, the Federal Republic of Yugoslavia changed its name to Serbia and Montenegro. Montenegro became independent on June 3, 2006.

A UN interagency needs assessment mission was deployed May 16–27, 1999, to assess damage and identify humanitarian needs (UN 1999a). The mission, headed by UN Under-Secretary-General Sergio Vieira de Mello, stated that a detailed assessment of the full extent of the environmental impact was urgently required.

To determine the extent of the damage and risks to human health, the UN Secretary-General supported UNEP and the UN Centre for Human Settlements (UNCHS) Programme to undertake an independent, scientific assessment of the effects of the conflict on human settlements and the environment. The scope of the assessment, which started in May 1999, focused on five conflict-related impacts: pollution from bombed industrial sites, damage to the Danube River, harm to protected areas and biodiversity, impacts on human settlements, and the use of depleted uranium weapons (UNEP and UNCHS 2009). A quantitative risk assessment was used to detect contamination and hot spots. The assessment also considered the existing legal and institutional framework for environmental management and national capacity for implementation and enforcement. The joint UNEP/UNCHS environmental assessment report was an input to the UN Consolidated Inter-Agency Appeal for Southeastern Europe Humanitarian Operations in 2000.

Assessment impact

The UNEP/UNCHS assessment report was launched through a series of press conferences in Geneva and Nairobi in October 1999 (UNEP and UNCHS 1999). It consisted of 104 pages detailing the environmental impacts of the conflict and thirty recommendations for addressing risks and building governance capacity. Overall the report concluded that the conflict had not caused an environmental catastrophe. Although some serious pollution and environmental damage had occurred, it was largely limited to four environmental hot spots and did not represent a national or regional threat. Still the hot spots required urgent cleanup on humanitarian grounds in order to prevent health risks and further environmental degradation. The assessment received widespread press coverage at the national and international levels in all media. Local media ran extensive articles about the environmental hot spots, and BBC's *Earth Report* ran a special segment on the environmental consequences of the conflict. A number of television interviews were also conducted by the chairman of the assessment, Pekka Haavisto, former minister for environment and development cooperation in Finland.[4]

The UNEP environmental assessment report was used in the UN Consolidated Inter-Agency Appeal for 2000 (UN 1999b). The UN appeal identified nearly US$200 million of urgent needs in FRY and US$250 million in Kosovo. It

---

[4] Pasi Rinne, UNEP program manager for FRY, personal communication with the author, December 2009.

included US$1.5 million for environmental assessment and further feasibility studies at the four hot spots identified by UNEP. The cleanup of environmental hot spots at bombed industrial sites was seen as an urgent humanitarian priority. This was the first appeal ever to include financing for mitigating environmental risks and set an important precedent for how humanitarian needs were defined. For the first time, human health was directly tied to environmental contamination. Because the UNEP assessment was directly referenced by the appeal, including detailed priorities and budget estimates, the policy impact of the report was considered to be high.

Following further feasibility studies conducted by UNEP and local authorities at the hot spots, US$20 million of cleanup needs were identified. Based on this analysis, an additional US$7 million for hot spot cleanup was included in the 2001 humanitarian appeal and US$5.5 million in the 2002 appeal (UN 2000, 2001). Even though the US$12.5 million raised fell short of the US$20 million of cleanup projects identified, the money did allow the most urgent risks to be addressed. Cleanup financing was provided by a coalition of nine donors, including Denmark, Finland, Germany, Ireland, Luxembourg, the Netherlands, Norway, Sweden, and Switzerland.

UNEP conducted cleanup operations at the four hot spots from August 2000 to December 2003. The primary objective was to reduce the most significant risks to human health and the environment at Novi Sad, Pancevo, Kragujevac, and Bor. It was accomplished through a combination of field-based remediation and rehabilitation projects and complementary capacity-building activities in hazardous waste management, cleaner production practices and technologies, direct foreign investment, sustainable consumption, and multilateral environmental agreements.

In 2003, the UN system decided not to issue an additional humanitarian appeal for Southeastern Europe. The decision reflected a wide consensus that the region was by and large in a phase of increasing stability and was transitioning to development. Moreover donors were shifting their emergency support to other parts of the world. Because the program had cleaned up the environmental hot spots, UNEP closed its field office.

The effect of the assessment was evaluated according to the three indicators in table 2. The weighted average score for all three indicators was 2.8, showing a high overall impact, divided between policy (3.0), financial (2.5), and media (3.0) impacts.

Conclusions and lessons learned

Drawing upon the three indicators selected, the review demonstrated that the post-conflict environmental assessment following the Kosovo conflict had an overall high level of impact. Based on the findings of the UNEP assessment, environmental needs were included within the three humanitarian appeals from 2000 to 2002, and 63 percent of the needs were funded by international donors.

Table 2. Evaluation of assessment impact indicators for the Federal Republic of Yugoslavia

Indicator	Categories	Policy frameworks		
		Humanitarian appeal (2000)	Humanitarian appeal (2001)	Humanitarian appeal (2002)
Policy impact	**No impact (0):** Environmental needs not mentioned **Low (1):** Environmental needs mentioned at a general level, but no detail provided **Medium (2):** Specific environmental needs and sectors mentioned **High (3):** Specific environmental needs and sectors mentioned with budget	3	3	3
Average policy impact:				3.0

Indicator	Categories	Environmental needs	
		Cleanup phase 1 (2001–2002)	Cleanup phase 2 (2003)
Financial impact	**No impact (0):** No financing raised for UNEP follow-up program **Low (1):** Less than 50 percent of UNEP follow-up program financed **Medium (2):** From 50 to 75 percent of UNEP follow-up program financed **High (3):** Over 75 percent of UNEP follow-up program financed	3	2
Average financial impact:			2.5

Indicator	Categories	Media coverage	
		National	International
Media impact	**No impact (0):** No coverage achieved in any media format **Low (1):** Coverage in only one media format **Medium (2):** Coverage in two media formats **High (3):** Coverage in three or four media formats	3	3
Average media impact:			3.0
Weighted total impact:			2.8

Extensive national and international media coverage was also achieved in all types of media. Four factors likely account for the high impact.

First, rather than conducting a broad-based study of all environmental issues, the assessment focused on environmental threats to human health and successfully argued for hot spot cleanup measures on humanitarian grounds. By classifying the cleanup of the environmental hot spots as a humanitarian priority, a high level of visibility was given to the issue with immediate financial support. Timing the findings of the assessment to inform major donor conferences and international assistance frameworks maximized the policy impact.

Second, although the post-conflict environmental assessment was implemented by UNEP in a scientific and impartial manner, a number of national experts and the FRY Ministry of Environment, Mining and Spatial Planning were involved in the process, leading to a high level of national ownership of the findings and interest in follow-up.

Third, UNEP's project office in Belgrade played an important role in disseminating the results of the assessment to decision makers and advocating for cleanup measures to be integrated within the three humanitarian appeals. UNEP also briefed the donor community in Geneva and selected donor capitals to ensure financing was mobilized to meet needs. The briefings included political advocacy by Pekka Haavisto, the chairman of the assessment.

Finally, UNEP's communications strategy was an important factor in the overall impact. By identifying immediate health risks from environmental contamination, the assessment helped to define *environment* in real terms that made sense to people and decision makers alike. The use of photos, maps, and satellite imagery in the final report also helped to maintain reader interest and stimulate media attention.

Afghanistan

Afghanistan has been affected by waves of violence and conflict for decades. When the Bonn Agreement was signed on December 5, 2001, the international community committed to long-term reconstruction support. In terms of assessing and addressing environmental needs, the situation in Afghanistan differed vastly from that in FRY. Before the decades of conflict that began in the 1970s, there was little industrial infrastructure. Therefore few industrial sites could be bombed and become environmental hot spots. Nevertheless the environment was severely damaged by military activities, human displacement, intense exploitation of natural resources, and inadequate institutional capacity for natural resource management. The national government was in disarray and had no capacity to conduct an environmental assessment.

In order to determine the short- and long-term environmental needs of Afghanistan, UNEP developed a new methodology focused on assessing not only the direct environmental impacts of military operations but also the indirect effects of survival and coping strategies and the institutional impacts of the breakdown of governance. Potential environmental risks to human health, livelihoods, and security, as well as capacity gaps were then identified. The new framework was a strategic assessment in that it selected the environmental issues and natural resources that were most relevant to peacebuilding. They included fertile land, rangelands, woodlands, protected areas, water resources, urban environmental infrastructure, waste management, and institutional capacity for environmental governance. The assessment was designed to provide a snapshot of environmental needs that could inform recovery priorities. The national partner in conducting the assessment was the Ministry of Irrigation, Water Resources, and the Environment. The assessment was timed to support the national recovery plan, Securing Afghanistan's Future (SAF) (TISA et al. 2004). But it also provided input into the CCA/UNDAF process and a second national recovery plan, the Afghanistan National Development Strategy (ANDS).

Assessment impact

The assessment report was launched at a press conference in Kabul in January 2003 and the UNEP Governing Council in February 2003 (UNEP 2003a). It consisted of 176 pages of findings with sixty-three sectoral and area-based recommendations. The conclusion was that the environmental degradation of forest, soil, and water resources was so extensive and severe that it threatened to undermine the peace process by contributing to displacement, disease, poverty, and economic instability. The recovery and reconstruction process would need to go hand in hand with sustainable management and restoration of the natural resource base. Although the assessment received widespread press coverage at the international level, national media were still emerging and provided only limited coverage.[5]

The UNEP assessment was primarily designed to identify environmental needs and priorities that could inform a national recovery plan. The SAF presented a broad vision for the reconstruction of Afghanistan, totaling US$27.8 billion for the period 2004–2011 (TISA et al. 2004). A nationally led process with support from international agencies and experts, the plan reflected the findings of the UNEP assessment. In particular, it called for US$1.8 billion of investments in the natural resource sector over the seven-year reconstruction period, approximately 6 percent of the reconstruction budget. The government advocated an integrated approach to natural resource development and management, with efficient and sustainable use of natural resources by communities and the private sector to achieve economic growth and support peacebuilding, security, and equity. Priorities focused on improved management and rehabilitation of fertile land, water, forests, and rangelands; institutional strengthening and capacity building; and development of new supporting policies and laws. The SAF was the first

---

[5] Asif Zaidi, UNEP program manager for Afghanistan, personal communication with the author, December 2009. Information, unless cited otherwise, was obtained from this personal communication and internal project documents.

national reconstruction plan to explicitly link natural resource management and rehabilitation to peacebuilding and security, thus setting an important precedent. An additional US$612 million of investments were included for water supply and sanitation in urban environments. Therefore US$2.4 billion covered natural resource management and related environmental infrastructure, representing 8.6 percent of the entire reconstruction budget.

In addition to the SAF, the UNEP assessment also acted as a critical input to the 2004 CCA and the 2006–2008 UNDAF (UN 2004, 2005a). The CCA emphasized that the contested allocation of natural resources, decades of unsustainable use, and a lack of governance institutions were major risks to peace, security, economic development, and social well-being. Consequently the CCA recommended that the UN focus on three pillars of support to Afghanistan: human rights and peacebuilding; good governance and participatory development; and basic social services and environmental sustainability. It was the first time that environmental sustainability was identified as a critical priority in a post-conflict country.

Based on the analysis contained in the CCA, the 2006–2008 UNDAF recognized the fundamental importance of natural resources to Afghan livelihoods and the economy: roughly 80 percent of Afghans remained dependent on natural resources for income and sustenance. The UNDAF further mentioned that, in order to achieve sustainable development, enhanced natural resource management and environmental governance had to be national objectives. As a result, of the six UNDAF objectives, one addressed environment and natural resources; and a second, sustainable livelihoods. Priorities were developing a legal framework and effective institutions for natural resource management at the national and community levels, and resolving issues related to ownership of and access to land.

Finally the environmental assessment was also used to inform the ANDS (IRA 2007). The ANDS served as Afghanistan's PRSP. Within this strategy, natural resource management needs were divided along two of the eight pillars: infrastructure and natural resources, and agriculture and rural development. Environment was identified as one of six crosscutting issues underpinning the social and development framework of the entire country. For the five-year period of the ANDS, the budget was US$50.1 billion of which 34.1 percent (US$17.1 billion) was dedicated to the infrastructure and natural resources pillar and 8.8 percent (US$4.4 billion) was allocated to agriculture and rural development.

To help respond to the natural resource management and environmental governance needs identified in the SAF, CCA/UNDAF, and ANDS, UNEP designed a multiphase capacity-building program for the Environment Department of the Ministry of Irrigation, Water Resources, and Environment. The proposed program focused on five pillars: institutional development, environmental law and policy, environmental impact assessment and pollution control, environmental education, and community-based natural resource management. Phase 1, covering 2003–2004, was budgeted at US$1 million of which US$936,528 was mobilized (94 percent). Based on this initial work, the Environment Department was eventually transformed into the self-standing National Environmental Protection Agency (NEPA) in 2005.

Therefore Phase 2, covering 2005–2007, focused on extending the capacity-building efforts to NEPA. It was budgeted at US$7 million of which US$6,856,288 was mobilized (98.6 percent). Phase 3, covering 2008–2010, was budgeted at US$7 million of which the full amount was mobilized. The European Commission (EC), government of Finland, and the Global Environment Facility financed the phases. At the time of this writing, a fourth phase for 2011–2014 was being discussed.

The effect of the assessment was evaluated according to the three indicators in table 3. The weighted average score for all three indicators was 2.9, showing a high overall impact, divided between policy (3.0), financial (3.0), and media (2.5) impacts.

Conclusions and lessons learned

The analysis revealed that UNEP's post-conflict environmental assessment of Afghanistan had a high impact based on the three indicators evaluated. The findings of the UNEP assessment were reflected in the SAF, CCA/UNDAF, and ANDS. Within all four documents, the natural resource management and rehabilitation pillar was listed as a major priority for reconstruction and development. To help build national and local capacity for environmental management, UNEP requested US$15 million of which US$14,792,815 was raised (98 percent). Three factors account for the high impact.

First, UNEP's assessment was the first environmental study conducted in the country in over thirty years. In most cases, the environmental degradation was worse than expected, natural resource management capacity was nonexistent, and community management structures had collapsed. The report convinced the national authorities, the UN country team, and donors that long-term peace and security would depend on sustainable management and restoration of natural resources, including land, forests, soils, and water, given that 80 percent of the population was directly dependent on them.

Second, the findings of the UNEP environmental assessment had a direct effect on the priorities and programming of the EC. Within their country strategy papers for 2003–2006 and 2007–2013, the EC recognized the need to establish and support an environmental authority and invest in natural resource management policies and programs (EC 2003, 2007). UNEP was provided seed funding to support the fledgling environmental administration and help navigate it through the national reform process. With this critical support, the NEPA was able to build its internal capacity and effectively advocate elevation of environmental issues and natural resources on the political agenda.

Finally, UNEP's project office in Kabul played a major role in coordinating the environmental sector, strengthening the hand of NEPA, and advocating an environmental agenda. UNEP's approach was inclusive, focused on rebuilding local capacities, empowering communities, and demonstrating the value of sustainable resource management through pilot projects. National ownership and handover were core management principles from the outset.

Table 3. Evaluation of assessment impact indicators for Afghanistan

Indicator	Categories	Policy frameworks		
		SAF[a] (2004–2011)	CCA/UNDAF[b] (2006–2008)	ANDS[c] (2008–2013)
Policy impact	No impact (0): Environmental needs not mentioned Low (1): Environmental needs mentioned at a general level, but no detail provided Medium (2): Specific environmental needs and sectors mentioned High (3): Specific environmental needs and sectors mentioned with budget	3	3	3
Average policy impact:				**3.0**

Indicator	Categories	Environmental needs		
		Follow-up phase 1 (2003–2004)	Follow-up phase 2 (2005–2007)	Follow-up phase 3 (2008–2010)
Financial impact	No impact (0): No financing raised for UNEP follow-up program Low (1): Less than 50 percent of UNEP follow-up program financed Medium (2): From 50 to 75 percent of UNEP follow-up program financed High (3): Over 75 percent of UNEP follow-up program financed	3	3	3
Average financial impact:				**3.0**

Indicator	Categories	Media coverage	
		National	International
Media impact	No impact (0): No coverage achieved in any media format Low (1): Coverage in only one media format Medium (2): Coverage in two media formats High (3): Coverage in three or four media formats	2	3
Average media impact:			**2.5**
Weighted total impact:			**2.9**

a. Securing Afghanistan's Future.
b. Common country assessment/UN Development Assistance Framework.
c. Afghanistan National Development Strategy.

Occupied Palestinian territories

From the outset of the second intifada in 2000, the capacity of the Palestinian Authority to manage and maintain basic infrastructure for water, energy, and waste virtually collapsed. International funding for water and waste management projects evaporated because of donor fatigue and concerns that new infrastructure could not be protected. As public concern over groundwater quality and waste management mounted, there was a need to determine how the environment had been affected and identify risks to human health.

In 2002, UNEP's Governing Council requested that the organization conduct a desk study as a step toward assessing the state of the environment in the oPt. The scope of the assessment was broad, covering water, waste, biodiversity, institutional capacity, and international cooperation. It involved collecting secondary sources of information and traveling on short field missions to hold stakeholder meetings. The assessment was accomplished in close cooperation with the Palestinian Environment Quality Authority and the Israeli Ministry of the Environment. At the time the study was commissioned, it was not designed to inform a specific policy process.

Assessment impact

The UNEP desk study was released at the UNEP Governing Council in Nairobi in February 2003 (UNEP 2003b). It was 188 pages in length and contained 136 recommendations on environmental needs. The conclusion was that institutional collapse from decades of protracted conflict had led to severe declines in environmental quality, especially of water and land. The study flagged the need to increase cooperation on environmental issues between Israelis and Palestinians and to invest in water and waste management infrastructure to protect groundwater resources from contamination. National and international Web, print, and radio media covered the desk study, so the media impact was deemed to be high.

Because the UNEP desk study was mandated by the UNEP Governing Council to provide an overview of the environmental situation, it was not designed to inform a specific policy process. The first opportunity to influence UN recovery policies was the CCA in 2004. Within the draft document, the findings of the desk study were strongly integrated into the needs analysis. Environmental health and water and waste management, which the Palestinian Authority identified as priorities, were addressed in a section of the CCA. But the CCA was never published because of various political events and continued conflict.[6]

---

[6] Aniket Ghai, UNEP program manager for oPt, personal communication with the author, December 2009. Information, unless cited otherwise, was obtained from this personal communication and internal project documents.

The next opportunity for the desk study to influence national planning was the 2005–2007 Medium Term Development Plan (MTDP), within which water and sanitation were identified as the core needs (PNA 2005). The planned budget for water infrastructure, including the installation of desalination facilities and waste management, amounted to US$337 million out of over US$5.6 billion (6 percent of the total). The need for environmental governance was also mentioned. Based on the findings of the desk study and other international reports, emphasis was placed on managing groundwater and land pollution resulting from the unmanaged disposal of wastewater and solid waste and intensive use of hazardous agricultural chemicals. The need for standards, regulations, and monitoring systems for conserving environmental resources, such as water, land, plants, and animals, was also identified. But there was no budget for developing them.

A second MTDP, covering 2006–2008, was also developed, using the desk study. The environment was acknowledged as important for the Palestinians' quality of life (PNA 2006). Of the six national priorities, the last focused on the protection and development of natural resources and recognized the necessity of improving waste and sewage management and neutralizing environmental and health hazards. The required total budget for the three years was estimated to be US$7.2 billion, with US$2.1 billion allocated to "infrastructure support" (including water, energy, and solid waste), and US$40 million to "cultural heritage/ natural resources."

To help build the capacity of the Palestinian Authority to address environmental risks, UNEP initially designed a US$3.5 million capacity-building program for 2004–2006. The proposed program focused on water and waste management, hot spot remediation, and regional cooperation. But given the ongoing conflict, donors were reluctant to invest in capacity building. As a result, UNEP could only mobilize US$157,855, representing only 4.5 percent of program needs. Therefore, although the desk study had a high media and policy impact, it generated little financing.

The effect of the assessment was evaluated according to the three indicators in table 4. The weighted average score for all three indicators was 2.1, showing a medium overall impact, divided between policy (2.7), financial (1.0), and media (3.0) impacts.

Conclusions and lessons learned

Although the CCA and both MTDPs reflected many of the environment and natural resource management issues identified by the UNEP desk study, recurring bursts of violence and insecurity in the area prevented donors from investing in environmental capacity-building programs and remediation efforts. Most funding was channeled into emergency projects and meeting humanitarian needs. The priorities primarily explain the poor financial impact of the assessment. Despite the outcome, identifying the factors that account for the report's relatively high policy impact is important.

Table 4. Evaluation of assessment impact indicators for the occupied Palestinian territories

Indicator	Categories	Policy frameworks		
		CCA[a] (2004)	MTDP[b] (2005–2007)	MTDP (2006–2008)
Policy impact	No impact (0): Environmental needs not mentioned Low (1): Environmental needs mentioned at a general level, but no detail provided Medium (2): Specific environmental needs and sectors mentioned High (3): Specific environmental needs and sectors mentioned with budget	3	2	3
Average policy impact:				**2.7**

Indicator	Categories	Environmental needs
		Capacity-building program
Financial impact	No impact (0): No financing raised for UNEP follow-up program Low (1): Less than 50 percent of UNEP follow-up program financed Medium (2): From 50 to 75 percent of UNEP follow-up program financed High (3): Over 75 percent of UNEP follow-up program financed	1
Average financial impact:		**1.0**

Indicator	Categories	Media coverage	
		National	International
Media impact	No impact (0): No coverage achieved in any media format Low (1): Coverage in only one media format Medium (2): Coverage in two media formats High (3): Coverage in three or four media formats	3	3
Average media impact:			**3.0**
Weight total impact:			**2.1**

a. Common country assessment.
b. Medium term development plan.

First, the fact that the UNEP Governing Council mandated the desk study elevated its political profile and generated interest and momentum in addressing environmental needs. Over 120 countries and ninety ministers participating in the session, including observers from the Palestinian Authority and the Israeli government, unanimously supported the decision for UNEP to conduct a desk study. Klaus Töpfer, executive director of UNEP, held high-level meetings in Ramallah with Yasser Arafat, president of the Palestinian Authority and chairman of the Executive Committee of the Palestine Liberation Organization, and in Jerusalem with Ariel Sharon, prime minister of Israel. Both Middle Eastern leaders backed the assessment process. All parties accepted Pekka Haavisto, former Finnish minister of environment and development cooperation, as chairman of the desk-study team.

Second, the presentation of the desk study at the UNEP Governing Council was an excellent opportunity to attract national and international media coverage. Hundreds of journalists from around the world attended the session to write articles and conduct radio interviews.

Finally, while maintaining strict political neutrality, UNEP conducted the assessments in close coordination with the Palestinian Environment Quality Authority and the Israeli Ministry of the Environment to encourage dialogue and technical cooperation between environmental agencies and ensure transparency. The draft of the desk study was shared with both sides for technical review. The rigor, balance, and transparency of the assessment process led Palestinians and Israelis to support release of the report.

Iraq

Iraq has seen three major conflicts in the last thirty years. Following the U.S.-led military intervention in Iraq in 2003, an environmental-assistance standby group was established by UNEP, at the request of the government of Switzerland, to monitor potential environmental impacts and identify needs. As part of the process, UNEP undertook a desk study of environmental issues. It was released in April 2003, while military operations were ongoing. It included all available information on the environmental impacts of the Iran-Iraq War and the 1990–1991 Gulf War. The study was meant to provide background on environmental needs and isolate priorities that could contribute to an eventual field-level environmental assessment. It was also designed to inform the 2003 humanitarian appeal and the post-conflict needs assessment—the first PCNA ever conducted by the UN system and the World Bank (UN and World Bank 2003).

As part of the desk study, UNEP held three information-sharing sessions in Geneva during the conflict to identify and involve regional experts and organizations that had worked on environmental projects or had collected environmental data in Iraq. The aim of these meetings was to share datasets on environmental quality and identify experts who could participate in a future field assessment. Because of the ongoing conflict, insecurity, and limited lines of communication, authorities in Iraq could not participate.

Assessment impact

The desk study was released at a press conference in Geneva in April 2003 (UNEP 2003c). The ninety-six-page study included twenty recommendations. The most critical issue identified by the study was the need to minimize and mitigate immediate environmental threats to human health from disrupted or contaminated water supplies, oil leaks, and inadequate sanitation and waste systems. Media coverage at the national and international levels was restricted to the Web.[7]

The 2003 Humanitarian Appeal for Iraq directly referenced the UNEP desk study and included a specific section on the need to assess environmental damage, pollution, and risks to human health (UN 2003). A total of US$850,000 was sought to meet the need.

Following the release of the humanitarian appeal, the desk study was used by UNEP to integrate environmental needs into the PCNA process (UN and World Bank 2003). But because Iraq was the first country to utilize the new PCNA methodology, there was no standard approach for addressing environmental issues. Environment was treated as a crosscutting issue, and resource management needs were addressed in the infrastructure sector as well as the agriculture, water resource, and food-security sectors. Of the overall budget of US$35.8 billion, US$6.8 billion was included to address water and sanitation infrastructure, and US$3 billion was included for agriculture and water resource management needs. A number of environmental priorities were also mentioned in the document, including strengthening the Ministry of Environment and environmental governance at all levels, building capacity for environmental impact assessments, cleaning up environmental hot spots, and building public awareness of environmental issues. But addressing these needs was not directly budgeted. Although an estimate of US$3.5 billion by the Coalition Provisional Authority was included for environmental governance and rehabilitation needs, it was not included in the final PCNA budget because there was no agreement on the costing methodology.

The PCNA was the international reconstruction framework for only one year. It was seen as lacking national ownership and not fully reflecting national priorities. It was replaced by the 2005–2007 National Development Strategy (NDS) (MPDC 2005). An approach like that of the PCNA was used to address environment and resource management. Within the budget of US$34.3 billion, US$2.6 billion was included to deal with water and sanitation infrastructure, and US$1.8 billion was included for agriculture and water resource management. Other environmental governance needs were broadly reflected in the NDS but not budgeted. The strategy aimed "to accelerate reconstruction and make [the] citizens [of Iraq] measurably better off, whilst assuring that [the] priceless heritage of natural resources has proper stewardship" (MPDC 2005, viii). A ministry of

---

[7] Koen Toonen, UNEP program manager for Iraq, personal communication with the author, January 2006. Information, unless cited otherwise, was obtained from this personal communication and internal project documents.

environment was called for to ensure environmental quality. But no specific budget was provided.

Based on the NDS, the 2005–2007 UN Assistance Strategy for Iraq (UNAS) fully reflected many of the environmental issues identified in UNEP's assessment (UN 2005b). Agriculture, water resources, and the environment comprised one of the eleven clusters in the strategy, and environmentally sustainable economic growth was mentioned as one of the seven goals. Although it followed most of the NDS recommendations, the UNAS document prioritized the recommendations in a manner that gave more importance to environmental issues. It also included the environmental impacts of the three wars fought since 1980. Precise indicators were incorporated to monitor environmental improvements. Of the budget of US$1.7 billion, US$178 million (10.5 percent) was designated for the agriculture, water resources, and environment cluster with a detailed budget breakdown.

To help build national capacity for addressing environmental needs, UNEP developed an initial US$2 million capacity-building program for 2003–2004. Donors provided US$1.7 million of the program budget, representing 85 percent of the program needs. As follow-up, a second program covering 2005–2006 was developed to address environmental hot spots caused by the looting and abandonment of industrial sites. One hundred percent of the US$4.7 million budget was financed by the government of Japan.

The effect of the desk study was evaluated according to the three indicators in table 5. The weighted average score for all three indicators was 2.4, showing a medium overall impact, divided between policy (2.5), financial (3.0), and media (1.0) impacts.

Conclusions and lessons learned

UNEP's *Desk Study on the Environment in Iraq* was a mixed success, with only a medium overall level of impact. Although the PCNA and NDS mentioned environment and natural resource management as important, they failed to include specific targets, indicators, and budgets. The desk study also failed to generate a high level of national and international media coverage. Nevertheless the desk study did have a high impact on mobilizing financial resources and influencing the content of the humanitarian appeal and the UNAS. The mixed outcome can be explained by three factors.

First, the lack of detailed budget information in the PCNA and NDS on environmental issues stems from the fact that the desk study did not provide detailed budget information. The desk study was structured as an analysis of environmental issues rather than in a manner that could inform reconstruction planning and priorities. Because it was the first PCNA, neither the sector coordinators nor UNEP could include a robust methodology for integrating environmental needs.

Second, the desk study had a low level of involvement of national experts because it was launched and conducted during conflict. Under hostile conditions,

Table 5. Evaluation of assessment impact indicators for Iraq

Indicator	Categories	Policy frameworks			
		Appeal (2003)	PCNA[a] (2004–2007)	NDS[b] (2005–2007)	UNAS[c] (2005–2007)
Policy impact	No impact (0): Environmental needs not mentioned Low (1): Environmental needs mentioned at a general level, but no detail provided Medium (2): Specific environmental needs and sectors mentioned High (3): Specific environmental needs and sectors mentioned with budget	3	2	2	3
Average policy impact:					**2.5**

Indicator	Categories	Environmental needs	
		Follow-up program phase 1 (2003–2004)	Follow-up program phase 2 (2005–2006)
Financial impact	No impact (0): No financing raised for UNEP follow-up program Low (1): Less than 50 percent of UNEP follow-up program financed Medium (2): From 50 to 75 percent of UNEP follow-up program financed High (3): Over 75 percent of UNEP follow-up program financed	3	3
Average financial impact:			**3.0**

Indicator	Categories	Media coverage	
		National	International
Media impact	No impact (0): No coverage achieved in any media format Low (1): Coverage in only one media format Medium (2): Coverage in two media formats High (3): Coverage in three or four media formats	1	1
Average media impact:			**1.0**
Weighted total impact:			**2.4**

a. Post-conflict needs assessment.
b. National Development Strategy.
c. UN Assistance Strategy for Iraq.

achieving effective communication and peer review by national environmental experts and the Ministry of Environment was nearly impossible. Stakeholder consultation was also out of the question. As a result, national ownership of the report's content was low.

Third, the UN agencies that maintained a full-time presence in Baghdad throughout the PCNA and NDS drafting processes had a greater effect on the final content than nonresident agencies such as UNEP. Sending inputs remotely and conducting limited field missions were not adequate substitutes for daily interaction and real-time technical support of national partners. The treatment of environmental issues within reconstruction plans improved once UNEP became a full member of the UN country team (which had been relocated to Amman, Jordan, following the bombing of the Canal Hotel on August 19, 2003). Environmental needs were more effectively integrated within the UNAS, including priorities, indicators, and detailed budgets. Although the hot spot–assessment program was successfully implemented, with two pilot cleanup projects, security conditions continued to decline.[8] Eventually UNEP closed its field-assistance program for Iraq in 2007 and continued providing support on a remote basis only.

Liberia

Two civil wars in Liberia, from 1989–1996 and 1999–2003, resulted in the total collapse of the Liberian state, the displacement of nearly one-third of the population, and destabilization of the entire subregion (UNMIL 2008). Liberia's rich natural resources, particularly timber and diamonds, played a significant role in the conflicts of the region. As part of the reconstruction planning process, the UN was requested to execute a PCNA with the World Bank and the National Transitional Government of Liberia. The PCNA was conducted in November and December 2003 in preparation for a donor conference in February 2004. UNEP was requested to participate in the PCNA as the focal point for the environment and to produce a desk study—to be an input to the PCNA—similar to that conducted on Iraq.

To assess environmental needs, UNEP divided the issues into three areas: human and urban environment, natural resources, and environmental governance and institutions. To conduct the work, all previous environmental studies and information from international organizations, including the United Nations Development Programme (UNDP), the World Health Organization, the United Nations Children's Fund, the Food and Agriculture Organization of the United Nations, and the World Bank, as well as from nongovernmental organizations, such as the International Union for the Conservation of Nature (IUCN), Global Witness, and Fauna and Flora International were collected and analyzed. The national

---

[8] For additional information on the remediation of environmental hot spots, see Muralee Thummarukudy, Oli Brown, and Hannah Moosa, "Remediation of Polluted Sites in the Balkans, Iraq, and Sierra Leone," in this book.

partners were the National Environmental Commission of Liberia (NECOLIB) and the Forestry Development Authority (FDA). Although the Environmental Protection Agency (EPA) of Liberia was legally established in 2002, it was only formally gazetted and created in April 2004, two months after the release of the desk study.

Assessment impact

The UNEP *Desk Study on the Environment in Liberia* was released in New York at an international donors' conference for Liberia in February 2004, in parallel with the PCNA. It was also released in Monrovia (UNEP 2004). At 116 pages, it included sixty recommendations. The conclusion was that the future peace and security of Liberia depended directly on the sustainable management of its natural resources, with transparent concession processes and equitable wealth sharing. Building management capacities for timber and mining and implementing a legal framework for natural resources and environmental governance were priorities. The findings of the desk study were covered by national print media and international Web reporters.[9]

The results of the desk study were used in the PCNA process. The PCNA—known as the Results Focused Transition Framework—was completed in February 2004 and included the priorities for the 2004–2005 transition. It set recovery and reconstruction costs over this period at US$487.7 million (UN and World Bank 2004). In the PCNA document, environmental and natural resource management needs were addressed in two ways. First, environment was listed as one of the crosscutting priorities during the transition period. The document noted that environmental concerns should be properly addressed in the transition period to support the sustainable development of the country's natural resources. Priority needs were related to environmental contamination and human health, environmental danger zones, environmental governance, and conservation. The issues were largely based on the findings of the UNEP desk study. But specific programs to address environmental needs and a dedicated budget were not included. Capacity-building support for the EPA was mentioned as part of forestry reform, but no specific budget was included.

Second, the PCNA recognized that immediate control of Liberia's forests by the government was imperative, given that revenue from timber and other forest resources was misappropriated by combatants and government officials. It noted that "a first priority is that Liberia's forested areas are brought under the effective control of UNMIL [United Nations Mission in Liberia] and the National Transitional Government of Liberia" (UN and World Bank 2004, 25). One of the needs identified by the PCNA was improving stewardship of public finances

---

[9] Grant Wroe-Street, UNEP program coordinator for Liberia, personal communication with the author, December 2003. Information, unless cited otherwise, was obtained from this personal communication.

by relevant government agencies, including proper management of revenues from Liberia's natural resources, such as diamonds and forest products. Policies and practices to address forest management were prioritized, and a budget of US$8.7 million was included (UN and World Bank 2004). One of the needs was to undertake the necessary institutional steps to lift the timber and diamond sanctions. Capacity-building support for the EPA was included, but no detailed budget was provided.

In January 2006, the newly elected president Ellen Johnson Sirleaf was sworn into office. She issued the 150 Day Action Plan, which described how the new government would kick-start the recovery process (ROL 2006). The action plan included a number of important provisions related to natural resources based, in part, on the UNEP desk study—most notably, canceling noncompliant forestry and ports concessions and initiating a process to review the legality of all other concessions and contracts entered into during the tenure of the National Transitional Government of Liberia (ROL 2006). The action plan also committed the country to the Kimberley Process Certification Scheme and to strengthening the capacity of the FDA and the EPA. Increasing access to water and sanitation was also listed as an activity.

As a follow-up to the action plan, a PRSP—Lift Liberia—was released in 2008. It covered 2008–2011 and had a budget of US$1.6 billion (ROL 2008). The PRSP treated the environment as a crosscutting issue and included resource management needs in two sectors: economic revitalization, and infrastructure and basic services. A total of US$38 million was included for food and agriculture needs, and US$143 million was included for water and sanitation. The strategy acknowledged that the sustainable use of natural resources and strong environmental management were crucial for growth, job creation, and poverty reduction. It also committed the government to undertake community-based natural resource management reforms that focus on boosting economic activity through sustainable utilization of timber products, nontimber forest resources, and agroforestry products, while improving environmental management and conservation. Crosscutting issues, including the environment, were allotted US$57.9 million, representing 3.6 percent of the PRSP budget.

In parallel with the PRSP, the UN conducted a CCA in 2006 and finalized a UNDAF in 2007, covering the period from 2008 to 2012 and US$230 million of needs (UN 2006, 2007a). The UNEP desk study was used as an input to both documents. Within the CCA, the environment was treated as one of nine challenges. The CCA acknowledged the importance of natural resources, such as timber, rubber, gold, and diamonds, to the national economy and people's livelihoods. Among other issues, the CCA mentioned a lack of water and waste management, deforestation, loss of biodiversity, and the lack of capacity of environmental agencies. The UNDAF recommended that national capacity for sound natural resource management be developed, transparency in the concession-agreements procedures be enhanced, and environmental impacts of public construction be systematically assessed. Budgetary needs were aligned with those of the PRSP.

To help build national capacity for addressing environmental needs, UNEP developed an initial US$2 million capacity-building program for 2004–2006. Donors provided US$750,000 of the program budget, representing 37.5 percent of the program needs. Because of the shortfall, UNEP's program in Liberia closed at the end of 2007. UNEP was not in a position to assist in the implementation of the UNDAF.

The effect of the desk study was evaluated according to the three indicators in table 6. The weighted average score for all three indicators was 1.6, showing a low overall impact, divided between policy (2.5), financial (1.0), and media (1.0) impacts.

Conclusions and lessons learned

Overall the UNEP desk study had a low impact in Liberia. Although the PCNA mentioned environment and natural resource management as important, it failed to include a detailed budget. The weakness was rectified in the PRSP and CCA/UNDAF, but UNEP was unable to mobilize sufficient financial resources to help rebuild national capacity for resource management and environmental governance. Only 37.5 percent of the program needs were financed, causing UNEP to eventually withdraw from Liberia because of a lack of funds. The low impact of the desk study can be explained by three factors.

First, during the desk study, the EPA did not have the capacity or formal institutional status to be UNEP's national partner. Instead the NECOLIB and the FDA performed this role. When the EPA was formally established two months after the release of the desk study, it did not feel full ownership of the content or the process. The handover process from NECOLIB to the EPA was not smooth, and internal infighting undermined political momentum.

Second, after its establishment, the EPA was starved for funding, was marginalized, and became one of the weakest institutions in the government. It subsequently gained a reputation for a lack of transparency in decision making and financial management, causing donors to hesitate in their support. Instead many preferred to support capacity building of the FDA and the Ministry of Land, Mines, and Energy so that timber and diamond sanctions could be lifted. The two entities attracted the bulk of capacity-building funding, leaving the EPA with few means to engage in and influence policy processes.

Finally, UNEP's desk study for Liberia did not include detailed costing of environmental needs and interventions. As a result, it was difficult to integrate environmental needs and provide detailed budgets in the PCNA. The same weakness was observed in the case of Iraq.

Lebanon

The July 2006 conflict between Israel and Lebanon lasted thirty-four days and resulted in significant civilian causalities and damage to public buildings and

Table 6. Evaluation of assessment impact indicators for Liberia

Indicator	Categories	Policy frameworks			
		PCNA[a] (2004–2005)	150 Day plan (2006)	Lift Liberia (2008–2012)	CCA/ UNDAF[b] (2008–2012)
Policy impact	**No impact (0):** Environmental needs not mentioned **Low (1):** Environmental needs mentioned at a general level, but no detail provided **Medium (2):** Specific environmental needs and sectors mentioned **High (3):** Specific environmental needs and sectors mentioned with budget	2	2	3	3
Average policy impact:					2.5

Indicator	Categories	Environmental needs
		Capacity-building program (2004–2006)
Financial impact	**No impact (0):** No financing raised for UNEP follow-up program **Low (1):** Less than 50 percent of UNEP follow-up program financed **Medium (2):** From 50 to 75 percent of UNEP follow-up program financed **High (3):** Over 75 percent of UNEP follow-up program financed	1
Average financial impact:		1.0

Indicator	Categories	Media coverage	
		National	International
Media impact	**No impact (0):** No coverage is achieved in any media format **Low (1):** Coverage in only one media format **Medium (2):** Coverage in two media formats **High (3):** Coverage in three or four media formats	1	1
Average media impact:			1.0
Weighted total impact:			1.6

a. Post-conflict needs assessment.
b. Common country assessment/UN Development Assistance Framework.

infrastructure in Lebanon. When the Jiyeh power plant was hit, 10,000–15,000 tons of burning oil was released into the sea.

To assess the environmental impact of the conflict in Lebanon, the Lebanese minister of environment requested that UNEP conduct a quantitative environmental assessment. The assessment included five issues: industrial and urban contamination, solid and hazardous waste treatment, polluted water resources, the oil spill, and environmental impacts from the use of weapons (including depleted uranium). Close to 200 samples of soil, sediment, seawater, surface water, and groundwater were taken to evaluate possible environmental contamination. The review was matched with before-and-after satellite images obtained from the UN community, the U.S. Department of Homeland Security, the EU Satellite Centre, and the EU Joint Research Centre. The assessment included various partners, notably the Lebanese Ministry of Environment, UNDP-Lebanon, IUCN, and local counterparts. From the outset, it was designed to inform the national early recovery plan because a PCNA was not requested by the government of Lebanon.

From an environmental assessment perspective, the case of Lebanon is unique because UNDP and the World Bank conducted parallel environmental assessments, each with a different analytical approach. The UNDP assessment—*Lebanon Rapid Environmental Assessment for Greening Recovery, Reconstruction and Reform*—focused more on greening the recovery process than on quantitative data gathering and analysis (UNDP 2007). In contrast, the World Bank report—*Economic Assessment of the Environmental Degradation Due to the July 2006 Hostilities*—evaluated the cost of the environmental degradation caused by the conflict at US$740 million, representing 3.6 percent of Lebanon's gross domestic product (World Bank 2007). It was the first and only time that three separate but complementary post-conflict environmental assessments were issued. Given the three reports, it is difficult to isolate the UNEP report to evaluate its full impact.

Assessment impact

The UNEP post-conflict environmental assessment for Lebanon was released in January 2007 in Berlin (UNEP 2007a). It included 181 pages and twenty-seven institutional and sectoral recommendations. The conclusions of the report were that rubble and waste were environmental risks and that the oil-spill response had been relatively effective in limiting damage. Furthermore no samples contained evidence that depleted uranium had been used during the hostilities. The report received a high level of media coverage at the national level but only medium coverage at the international level.[10]

The governmental recovery and reconstruction plan was issued in September 2006 at the Stockholm Conference for Lebanon's Early Recovery (LER). Entitled *Setting the Stage for Long-Term Reconstruction: The National Early Recovery*

---

[10] Muralee Thummarukudy, UNEP program manager for Lebanon, personal communication with the author, December 2007.

Process, the plan listed eleven types of recovery needs for 2006–2007 (GOL 2006). Environment was one of nine sectors identified within the LER. Issues included the Jiyeh oil spill, rubble from the extensive destruction of buildings, and excess solid waste from reduced ordinary collection and treatment. Two projects were included: an oil-spill cleanup project with an estimated cost of US$52 million and a rubble-cleanup project estimated at US$8 million. Although these needs were reflected in the UNEP assessment, it is difficult to evaluate the precise policy impact of the UNEP report, given the other reports by UNDP and the World Bank. In this case, it is likely that all three had a substantial policy impact on the LER plan because all three were used as inputs.

To assist the Lebanese Ministry of Environment in building its pollution-monitoring capacity, UNEP developed a US$4 million follow-up program on waste management, covering the period 2007–2008. In total, US$1.6 million (40 percent) of the program needs were met by the government of Greece for air-pollution monitoring.

The effect of the desk study was evaluated according to the three indicators in table 7. The weighted average score for all three indicators was 2.1, showing a medium overall impact, divided between policy (3.0), financial (1.0), and media (2.5) impacts.

Conclusions and lessons learned

Overall the UNEP environmental assessment had a medium impact in Lebanon based on the three indicators evaluated. The LER prioritized environmental needs and provided for detailed program budgets. But UNEP was able to mobilize only 40 percent of the funding required to address capacity-building needs for waste management. It is difficult to determine the overall impact of the UNEP report because it cannot be isolated from those of the other two reports. The final score may overrepresent the actual impact of UNEP's assessment.

One notable lesson learned from the three assessments is that the content of the reports differed significantly in their findings on the oil spill. The UNEP report, based on quantitative sampling and technical analysis, concluded that the oil spill did not lead to significant long-term environmental damage. The UNDP and World Bank reports, based on qualitative approaches and expert opinions only, concluded that the environmental impacts were significant. In the end, the government endorsed the UNDP and World Bank reports because they provided stronger support for compensation claims for war-time damage. UNEP's more objective and science-based findings were sidelined. Ideally there should have been better coordination on the three reports and common conclusions.

Sudan

The recent history of Sudan has been marked by turmoil, with several periods of violent conflict and a series of natural disasters leading to massive population

Table 7. Evaluation of assessment impact indicators for Lebanon

Indicator	Categories	Policy framework
		Lebanon early recovery plan (2006–2007)
Policy impact	No impact (0): Environmental needs not mentioned Low (1): Environmental needs mentioned at a general level, but no detail provided Medium (2): Specific environmental needs and sectors mentioned High (3): Specific environmental needs and sectors mentioned with budget	3
Average policy impact:		**3.0**

Indicator	Categories	Environmental needs
		Waste management–capacity building program
Financial impact	No impact (0): No financing raised for UNEP follow-up program Low (1): Less than 50 percent of UNEP follow-up program financed Medium (2): From 50 to 75 percent of UNEP follow-up program financed High (3): Over 75 percent of UNEP follow-up program financed	1
Average financial impact:		**1.0**

Indicator	Categories	Media coverage	
		National	International
Media impact	No impact (0): No coverage is achieved in any media format Low (1): Coverage in only one media format Medium (2): Coverage in two media formats High (3): Coverage in three or four media formats	3	2
Average media impact:			**2.5**
Weighted total impact:			**2.1**

displacement. In addition to the long-standing North-South conflict, low-level conflict ongoing in Darfur for a generation developed into a new regional civil war in 2003. In January 2005, the North-South conflict finally came to an end with the signing of the Comprehensive Peace Agreement (CPA) between the Sudanese government and the Sudan People's Liberation Movement.

In anticipation of the CPA, a PCNA was conducted in 2004 by the UN and World Bank with the government of Sudan and the Sudan People's Liberation Movement for the period 2005–2007. UNEP was requested to be the lead for environmental needs within the PCNA process. But given Sudan's size and the lack of data on the country, UNEP adopted a new approach by splitting the assessment into two major stages. UNEP began with a rapid desk study that provided an initial input to the PCNA. It was followed by an eighteen-month comprehensive assessment in 2005–2006. The comprehensive assessment was designed to inform the National Plan for Environmental Action, the National Strategic Plan (NSP) covering 2007–2011, and the annual UN work plan. To implement the findings and recommendations of the assessment, UNEP established a project office in Khartoum and became a formal member of the UN country team.

Twelve themes were included in the comprehensive assessment: natural disasters and desertification, conflict and peacebuilding, population displacement, urban environment and environmental health, industry, agriculture, forest resources, freshwater resources, wildlife and protected area management, marine environments and resources, environmental governance and awareness, and international aid. Consultation with local and international stakeholders formed a large and continuous part of UNEP's assessment work, with over 1,000 interviewees. Parties consulted included representatives of federal, state, and local governments; nongovernmental organizations; academic and research institutions; international agencies; community leaders; farmers; pastoralists; foresters; and business people. The assessment team was composed of a core UNEP team and a large number of national and international partners who worked collaboratively. UNEP also worked closely with the Government of National Unity (GNU) and the GOSS.

Assessment impact

UNEP's inputs were well reflected in the final document of the PCNA (UN and World Bank 2005a). Environment was addressed not only as a crosscutting sector but also as one of the guiding objectives for eradicating poverty while managing natural resources in an environmentally friendly and sound way. Competition over access to natural resources, including land and water, was also listed as a driving factor in the civil war and a potential threat to peacebuilding. Desertification, land degradation, loss of biological diversity, deforestation, and the pollution of water resources were mentioned as problems. To address environmental needs in a comprehensive way, the PCNA called for a review of the legal framework combined with institutional capacity-building programs and coordination mechanisms at the national and local levels to improve the management and monitoring of natural resources. But only a few specific targets were included in the monitoring framework, and only US$6.5 million was earmarked for specific environmental capacity-building projects (UN and World Bank 2005b).

Following the PCNA, UNEP implemented a comprehensive environmental assessment during 2006–2007. The final report was released in June 2007 at press conferences in Khartoum; Juba; Nairobi; Washington, D.C.; and Geneva (UNEP 2007b). At 354 pages, including eighty-five costed recommendations with designated actors, it was UNEP's largest post-conflict report to date. It concluded that investments in the management and rehabilitation of natural resources were central to conflict resolution and peacebuilding in Sudan. The cost of this report's recommendations was estimated at approximately US$120 million over three to five years. The report was widely covered in all media formats at the national and international levels. UN Secretary-General Ban Ki-moon and Jeffrey Sachs from Columbia University publicly mentioned the report, creating additional press interest.[11]

Due to the detailed nature of the assessment, it was used as a technical input to four major policy processes, including the NSP; the UN work plans of 2007, 2008, and 2009; and the Sudan Country Analysis (SCA) and the UNDAF.

A five-year NSP was prepared for 2007–2011 (NCSP 2006). It was designed to cover North and South Sudan. It built upon the conclusions of the PCNA, setting out new priorities and aiming to improve coordination in the implementation of the CPA in development efforts. UNEP's ongoing comprehensive assessment was used as an input to the NSP. The document lists the abundance of natural resources in Sudan as a strength and development opportunity, and includes deforestation and desertification in parts of the country as threats. Economic priorities were presented, and the need for an optimal use of natural resources and an increase in the contribution of renewable resources to the gross national product were mentioned. Natural resources were linked to security as assets requiring protection from external threats. Environment was also mentioned as one of nine crosscutting issues.

To meet the humanitarian and development needs of Sudan and the goals of the NSP, the UN country team and partner nongovernmental organizations, with government counterparts, developed annual work plans. The comprehensive assessment had a high impact on the work plans that were issued in 2007, 2008, and 2009. Within the 2007 work plan, environmental and natural resource management needs were addressed in two ways (UN 2007b). First, environmental sustainability was listed as one of four crosscutting issues to be addressed by all sectors when relevant. The work plan directly referenced the UNEP post-conflict environmental assessment and included projects for capacity building, dispute resolution, and awareness raising. The plan also addressed natural resource management in the food-security and livelihood-recovery sectors. It noted that tensions

---

[11] Andrew Morton, UNEP program manager for Sudan, personal communication with the author, December 2007.

resulting from competition over natural resources and livestock ownership continued and that conflicts were erupting over access to grazing land and water, especially during the dry season. On the list of development projects, seven natural resource management projects (totaling US$5.4 million) and six humanitarian projects (totaling US$4.5 million) were included. But it was impossible to track all of the projects that either affected or relied on natural resources.

The weakness in tracking environmental-related projects was addressed in the 2008 work plan. For the first time, all projects that either addressed environmental needs directly or mitigated environmental impacts were specifically categorized and mapped as part of a self-standing summary—an important innovation by the UN country team in Sudan that stands as a best practice. A total of 396 projects were listed for US$787 million, nearly 35 percent of the total work plan budget (UN 2008). Within the 2009 work plan, a similar approach was taken. The projects totaled US$552 million (nearly 26 percent of the work plan budget) (UN 2009a). Additionally, the 2009 work plan was the first work plan that included a specific budget line of US$1 million from the Common Humanitarian Fund to promote environmental approaches to humanitarian emergencies. Known as the Green Pot, the fund was to be managed by UNEP to support innovative projects that would kick-start new environmental approaches to humanitarian response. Across the UN system, the Green Pot remains a unique example of a best practice.

The SCA was completed by the UN country team in November 2007 (UN 2007c). It was designed to inform a subsequent UNDAF. The environment and natural resource management sections of SCA were based heavily on the UNEP post-conflict assessment report. Priorities were organized along four pillars: peacebuilding; governance, rule of law, and capacity building; livelihoods and productive sectors; and basic services. Although there were no crosscutting issues identified, environment and natural resource needs were explicitly addressed within all four pillars. The SCA recognized that environmental degradation and mismanagement of natural resources were root causes of insecurity and threats to peace. The analysis also mentioned possible livelihood risks from climate change, environmental degradation, and conflict-induced displacement. It emphasized the need to develop appropriate land use and land tenure practices and to ensure that the potential environmental side effects of the commercial mining and oil industries were contained. The document also highlighted the necessity for sustainable management of water resources, including testing and monitoring groundwater. The SCA is the most comprehensive treatment of environment and natural resources ever achieved in a UN document and stands as a true best practice.

The 2009–2012 UNDAF, also a best practice, integrated environment and natural resource needs (UN 2009b). The UNDAF used the same four-pillar organizational framework as the SCA and incorporated environmental needs within each pillar. Detailed environmental outcomes, budgets, responsible organizations, and partners were included for each pillar. The combined natural resource management projects amounted to US$419 million, about 18 percent of the UNDAF budget of US$2.3 billion. It was the largest allocation made to resource management programs in any UNDAF.

To help the GNU and GOSS build natural resource management and environmental governance capacities, UNEP developed a comprehensive, two-phased capacity-building program covering 2007–2012 for US$30 million, which was financed at a rate of 97 percent. The United Kingdom and the United States provided the majority of the funding (Foster et al. 2010; USAID 2008). The program addresses the environmental drivers of extreme poverty and conflict, recognizing that natural resources provide for the most basic needs of the population. It is coordinated from a central office in Khartoum, with project offices in Darfur and South Sudan. Ongoing activities include integrated water resource management, forestry and energy, waste management, as well as integrating environmental considerations into ongoing humanitarian aid, peacekeeping, and development operations in the country.

The effect of the desk study was evaluated according to the three indicators in table 8. The weighted average score for all three indicators was 3.0, showing a high overall impact, divided between policy (3.0), financial (3.0), and media (3.0) impacts.

Conclusions and lessons learned

UNEP's environmental assessment work has had a higher overall impact on Sudan than on any of the other areas addressed in the chapter. In every policy framework, environment and natural resources were mentioned as priorities, program targets were included, and detailed budgets were provided. In addition, the UN work plans for 2008 and 2009 specifically categorized all projects that either addressed environmental needs or attempted to mitigate environmental impacts. They allowed for transparency in and accountability for tracking environmental investments, stakeholders, and outcomes. The 2009 work plan also included a Green Pot to help kick-start innovations in using environmentally sound approaches to humanitarian response. Nearly US$30 million was mobilized to help build national environmental management capacity. The high level of impact can be explained by four factors.

First, the environmental assessment undertaken by UNEP was conducted in close cooperation with the GNU and GOSS environmental authorities and was well connected to national planning processes. The assessment also underwent six months of consultations with national stakeholders and UN agencies, resulting in a high level of national and international buy-in. These partnerships were crucial to the project's success because they supported the fieldwork, ensured that the study matched local issues and needs, and contributed to national endorsement of the assessment's outcomes. UNEP also worked closely with the GNU and the GOSS on efforts to align UNEP activities with the National Plan for Environmental Management.

52 Assessing and restoring natural resources in post-conflict peacebuilding

Table 8. Evaluation of assessment impact indicators for Sudan

Indicator	Categories	Policy frameworks			
		PCNA[a] (2005–2007)	NSP[b] (2007–2011)	UN Work plans (2007–2009)	SCA/ UNDAF[c] (2009–2012)
Policy impact	**No impact (0):** Environmental needs not mentioned **Low (1):** Environmental needs mentioned at a general level, but no detail provided **Medium (2):** Specific environmental needs and sectors mentioned **High (3):** Specific environmental needs and sectors mentioned with budget	3	3	3	3
Average policy impact:					3.0

Indicator	Categories	Environmental needs	
		Capacity-building program phase 1 (2007–2008)	Capacity-building program phase 2 (2009–2012)
Financial impact	**No impact (0):** No financing raised for UNEP follow-up program **Low (1):** Less than 50 percent of UNEP follow-up program financed **Medium (2):** From 50 to 75 percent of UNEP follow-up program financed **High (3):** Over 75 percent of UNEP follow-up program financed	3	3
Average financial impact:			3.0

Indicator	Categories	Media coverage	
		National	International
Media impact	**No impact (0):** No coverage achieved in any media format **Low (1):** Coverage in only one media format **Medium (2):** Coverage in two media formats **High (3):** Coverage in three or four media formats	3	3
Average media impact:			3.0
Weighted total impact:			3.0

a. Post-conflict needs assessment.
b. National Strategic Plan.
c. Sudan Country Analysis/UN Development Assistance Framework.

Second, the Sudan environmental assessment was the first UNEP report in which recommendations were prioritized and costed over three to five years. The advocacy process for follow-up projects was greatly facilitated by providing concrete project proposals with budgets.

Third, during the implementation of the assessment, the UNEP program manager actively engaged in the UN work-planning process to provide advice on environmental and natural resource issues. Following the release of the assessment, UNEP established a program in Sudan and became the lead on the environment on the UN country team. In this capacity, UNEP was able to fully participate in the annual work-planning process, providing detailed inputs on projects and associated costs. UNEP was also able to ensure that the SCA and UNDAF fully incorporated the results of the environmental assessment.

Finally, a number of donors, including the United Kingdom and the United States, were keen to support environment and natural resource management as a priority. They provided funding to ensure the UN country team could address the issue in a real way and could integrate it throughout the work-planning process.

SUCCESS FACTORS AND LESSONS LEARNED

Across the seven case studies, the post-conflict environmental assessment reports had impacts ranging from low to high (see table 9). Sudan had the highest score (3.0) followed by Afghanistan (2.9) and FRY (2.8). Medium scores were earned by the assessments in Iraq (2.4), oPt (2.1), and Lebanon (2.1). A low score was achieved in Liberia (1.6). On average, desk studies and quantitative assessments have led to a medium impact, strategic and comprehensive assessments have had a high average impact (see table 10). But given the low sample size for strategic and comprehensive assessments, it is difficult to determine if this pattern will continue.

Table 9. UNEP's post-conflict assessments: Summary of assessment impacts by case study

Case	Policy impact	Financial impact	Media impact	Total impact	Impact score	Total value of follow-up (US$)
FRY[a] (1999)	3.0	2.5	3.0	2.8	High	12,500,000
Afghanistan (2003)	3.0	3.0	2.5	2.9	High	14,792,816
oPt[b] (2003)	2.7	1.0	3.0	2.1	Medium	157,855
Iraq (2003)	2.5	3.0	1.0	2.4	Medium	6,392,967
Liberia (2004)	2.5	1.0	1.0	1.6	Low	750,000
Lebanon (2007)	3.0	1.0	2.5	2.1	Medium	1,600,000
Sudan (2007)	3.0	3.0	3.0	3.0	High	29,109,644

Note: To determine the total impact score, a weighted calculation was applied to the policy (40 percent), financial (40 percent), and media (20 percent) scores.
a. Federal Republic of Yugoslavia.
b. Occupied Palestinian territories.

Table 10. Summary of assessment impacts by method used for UNEP post-conflict assessments, 1999–2007

Assessment method	Number of cases	Policy impact	Financial impact	Media impact	Total impact	Impact score
Desk studies	3*	2.56	1.67	1.67	2.03	Medium
Quantitative assessments	2	3.00	1.75	2.75	2.45	Medium
Strategic assessments	1	3.00	3.00	2.50	2.9	High
Comprehensive assessments	1	3.00	3.00	3.00	3.00	High

Notes: To determine the total impact score, a weighted calculation was applied to the policy (40 percent), financial (40 percent), and media (20 percent) scores.
* The Sudan desk study was removed from the total because its impact cannot be isolated from the overall comprehensive assessment that was also conducted.

Success factors

Based on the lessons learned from the assessments, five factors appear to have influenced the overall impact. They include the amount of funding and time available to conduct the assessment, the level of national ownership and involvement, the clear identification of priority needs with a detailed budget, timing an assessment process to coincide with and inform a policy process, and securing early and sustained financial and political support from donors.

Amount of funding and time available to conduct the assessment

In general, the greater the assessment's budget and the time available, the higher its impact was. Although that conclusion may be intuitive, one of the aims of the analysis was to determine if less costly assessments, such as desk studies, had the same impact as more costly and time-consuming comprehensive and strategic assessments. Based on the cases reviewed, there appears to be an increasing impact moving from desk studies to quantitative assessments to strategic assessments to comprehensive assessments. The increase makes sense, given the expanding scope, budget, time, and level of consultation involved in each of the four types.

When time or financial resources are limited, desk studies have provided important inputs to policy processes such as PCNAs. Such inputs have ensured that environmental needs were at least flagged within PCNAs, providing an important justification for follow-up work. Future desk studies should be more tailored to the needs and overall framework of the PCNA, and interventions should be costed. It is encouraging to note that the PCNA process was reviewed and revised in 2007 to take into account more systematically the issue of integrating environmental and natural resource needs (UN and World Bank 2007). A new toolkit for environmental and natural resource needs was included in the revised PCNA framework (UN and World Bank 2009).

To date, the highest overall impact of environmental assessments has been achieved in Sudan, where an initial desk study was conducted for the PCNA, followed by a comprehensive environment assessment. The two-step assessment process may constitute a new best practice.

Overall level of national ownership

Regardless of the precise nature of the assessment, one of the features of a UNEP post-conflict environmental assessment is the institutional neutrality that UNEP maintains throughout the process, combined with independent scientific expertise. On one hand, this ensures that the assessment focuses on the technical state of the environment, rather than political dynamics. On the other hand, the neutrality of the report and the associated process can undermine national ownership and support. Within each assessment, balance must be considered and addressed.

UNEP's experiences in the seven cases highlight the importance of having national experts on the international environmental assessment team. Doing so not only helps to build capacity but also strengthens national ownership of the final product. The success of assessments and their consequent policy impact have also depended in large part on the degree to which UNEP involved stakeholders and conducted awareness-raising efforts to ensure national and local ownership. It may be no coincidence that the Sudan assessment, which invested nearly six months in conducting stakeholder meetings and building national support for the final product, also had the highest policy impact of any report to date.

Clear identification of priority needs with a detailed budget

The review has revealed that the policy and financial impact of an assessment report is significantly influenced by the presence or absence of detailed priorities and costing to address environmental needs. In situations in which environmental needs were not prioritized and budgeted, such as in the PCNA processes for Iraq and Liberia, the resulting policies failed to provide cost estimates for addressing environmental issues in a substantive way. Conversely, in the cases of FRY and Sudan, where all environmental needs were costed in detail, the corresponding policy frameworks and supporting financial budgets included environmental needs.

Timing an assessment process to coincide with and inform a policy process

The cases reviewed suggest that tailoring the assessment time line and output to meet the specific needs of a policy process maximizes the policy impact of an assessment. At the outset of any assessment, the potential policy process should be identified with the engagement windows, focal points, and process requirements. Quantitative risk assessments that target humanitarian appeals or early recovery programs must be issued during the needs-analysis process. Models of such best practices stem from FRY and Lebanon. Similarly more detailed assessments that aim to influence reconstruction and peacebuilding plans should clearly demonstrate how natural resources can support national recovery and peacebuilding priorities. Sudan provides a model of good practice.

Securing early and sustained financial and political support

In most cases, the financial and political support of one or two donors for addressing environment and natural resource issues at an early stage played a role in keeping environment and natural resource management issues on the recovery agenda. In the case of Afghanistan, the EC and the government of Finland provided an initial lifeline to the fledgling NEPA for early capacity-building and institutional-development efforts. Although other ministries tried to downplay the role of sustainable resource management in recovery, NEPA held its ground. After demonstrating the inherent connection between many peacebuilding goals and natural resources, environment eventually became one of six crosscutting national priorities. A similar story can be told about Sudan, where the UK Department for International Development took a strong interest in natural resource management issues and provided early support for integrating them throughout the UN work plan. Japan played a similar role in supporting hot spot assessment and cleanup in Iraq. But it is also important to note that the amount of donor support is also a critical success factor. A program worth at least US$1.5 million per year is needed for UNEP to have any significant impact. Programs that started with less, such as those in Liberia and oPt, failed to have sufficient policy gravity and human resources to have a significant impact.

Lessons learned

Based on analysis of the seven cases, five critical lessons learned can be identified. First, environmental needs that clearly support peacebuilding are often elevated as priorities. Second, field presence is often vital to influence policy and coordinate effectively. Third, national capacity development should be integrated as a crosscutting theme of the assessment process. Fourth, there are multiple approaches to integrating environmental and natural resource management needs within policy frameworks. Finally, the type and scope of the environmental assessment influence the longevity of its policy impact and the extent of media coverage. Each of these lessons is discussed in more detail below.

In addition to the lessons learned, the cases reviewed demonstrate that every post-conflict situation is different and requires an approach custom-made to the geographical and political context and the targeted policy process. Trade-offs must frequently be made between rapid and more detailed assessments, qualitative versus quantitative methods, and the degree of national ownership. In many cases, the scope and duration of an assessment are determined by a number of constraints and boundary conditions. In general, the scope of each assessment should be informed by a conflict's characteristics, including its root causes, duration, intensity, weaponry, and geographic distribution. Matching the assessment content and method to the political needs and processes is always of paramount importance.

Environmental needs that clearly support recovery and peacebuilding are often elevated as priorities

The chapter has demonstrated that environmental and natural resource management needs that clearly support peacebuilding efforts are often elevated as priority issues. The mismanagement of scarce natural resources, such as water and land, contributed to the conflicts in Sudan and Afghanistan. Similarly a lack of water and sanitation infrastructure in the oPt and Iraq worsened instability. Investments in natural resource management and environmental infrastructure were seen as important peace dividends and identified as priorities within the relevant recovery frameworks. Rubble and waste clearing in Lebanon and the cleanup of environmental hot spots in Serbia were also identified as priorities for protecting the health of communities, erasing the visible legacy of war, helping psychological recovery, and protecting critical natural resources such as water.[12] The importance of equitable sharing of high-value natural resources, such as oil in Iraq and Sudan, was also seen as key to peacebuilding and reconciliation.

Field presence is vital to influence policy and coordinate effectively

Simply issuing an assessment report cannot influence policy. The report must be coupled with the development of an action plan and an active field presence in the post-conflict country. Time and significant awareness-raising efforts may be required before environmental issues and other needs are seriously considered within the post-conflict relief, recovery, or development agenda. It is also imperative that the assessment results be structured to precisely fit the needs of the policy framework or programming process. A field presence also helps to ensure that environmental strategies and projects are well coordinated between ministries and other actors. Doing so helps avoid duplication and ensures more coherent programming.

In cases in which different international actors conduct multiple environmental assessments, coordinating the release of the technical findings and ensuring a common communications strategy are important. Multiple assessments with competing or contrasting messages only create confusion and political division that tend to undermine financing of environmental needs. When politically and technically feasible, multiple assessments should be combined into a single report.

---

[12] While the assessment was conducted for the Federal Republic of Yugoslavia, the majority of cleanup operations occurred only in Serbia.

Developing national capacity to address environmental needs should be integrated as a crosscutting theme of the assessment process

At the outset of any assessment, it is critical to take into account existing governance and institutional structures and frameworks already in place in the country. In most post-conflict countries, national capacity for addressing environmental needs remains low. Consequently environmental authorities often have no access to policy and programming processes, and environmental needs are marginalized. Building the capacity of national authorities should be integrated into the design and implementation of the assessment in order to focus not only on technical issues but also on advocating inclusion of the issues in the development of national policy.

There are multiple approaches to integrating environmental and natural resource needs within policy frameworks

There is significant variation in the treatment of environmental and natural resource needs across policy frameworks. Three approaches have emerged. Some frameworks, such as the PCNA for Liberia, the ANDS for Afghanistan, and the 2009 work plan for Sudan, addressed environment in two ways. A natural resource management sector was established, and environment was included as a crosscutting issue within every relevant sector. The success of this approach was mixed. In some cases, although environmental needs were mentioned, targets were rarely set, and activity budgets were not provided. In others, in which UNEP had an active field presence and could supply technical advice, such as in Afghanistan and Sudan, environmental needs were effectively taken into account by the relevant sectors. The outcome demonstrates the importance of an active field presence through which environment can be addressed as a crosscutting issue. The approach seemed to generate the best results in terms of detailed activities and budgets. The Sudan work plan also went a step further by requiring all other projects that use or affect natural resources to be clearly identified. It also provided dedicated funding to kick-start better environmental practices while addressing humanitarian needs. Both of the approaches set important new benchmarks in terms of best practice.

In other cases, such as the UNDAF for Afghanistan and the early recovery plan for Lebanon, environment and natural resources were treated at the highest level as one of the sectors. Although the approach led to targets and detailed budgets for environmental interventions, it also had drawbacks because it isolated environmental projects and prevented the other sectors from considering how they were using or affecting natural resources. Environment became "someone else's problem," rather than a collective challenge and shared responsibility.

In the cases of the CCA for Afghanistan and the SCA and UNDAF for Sudan, a third approach was used. Environmental needs were treated as neither a sector nor a crosscutting issue. Rather problem trees were developed, and root-cause analyses were conducted. In both cases, environmental degradation and natural resource–mismanagement challenges were identified as outcomes of the analyses. The analyses demonstrated that natural resources and environmental quality actually underpinned many other core goals, such as peacebuilding, governance, economic development, and livelihoods. The analyses thus justified why natural resource management should be a national priority and a central part of the UNDAF. The approach not only avoided supply-driven and top-down structures but also demonstrated the inherent connection between many peacebuilding and development interventions and natural resources.

The scope of an environmental assessment influences the duration of policy impact and extent of media coverage

The chapter has shown that quantitative assessments have a shorter-term policy impact—ranging from two to three years—than desk studies, strategic assessments, and comprehensive assessments, which range from four to ten years, primarily due to the more restricted scope of quantitative assessments, which focus on direct environmental impacts and risks to human health. Once critical environmental risks are addressed through cleanup and remediation efforts, their recommendations are less relevant for longer-term development policies.

It is equally important to note that quantitative assessments tend to have a higher media impact (2.75) than desk studies (1.67) and strategic assessments (2.5), most likely because the focus on immediate risks lends itself to a clearer and more striking media message. The media impact of assessments is also enhanced when relevant high-profile figures lead the assessment process and actively engage the media during launch events and follow-up activities. Media coverage can also be increased when assessment reports include dramatic photos, maps, videos, and satellite images depicting environmental damage.

Overall the effective communication of environmental assessment findings and priorities to political leaders, the broader population, and potential funding partners is an important component of impact. Assessments that fail to communicate their content in a manner that captures media attention and public interest often fail to mobilize political support and donor funding for follow-up work. A communications and media strategy must be built into the design of the assessment from the outset.

REFERENCES

EC (European Commission). 2003. Country strategy paper (CSP): Afghanistan, 2003–2006. http://eeas.europa.eu/afghanistan/csp/03_06_en.pdf.

———. 2007. Country strategy paper: Islamic Republic of Afghanistan, 2007–2013. http://eeas.europa.eu/afghanistan/csp/07_13_en.pdf.

Foster, M., J. Bennett, E. Brusset, and J. Kluyskens. 2010. *Country programme evaluation: Sudan.* Department for International Development Evaluation Report EV708. March. Glasgow, Scotland: John McCormick and Company. www.dfid.gov.uk/Documents/publications1/evaluation/country-prog-sudanev708.pdf.

GOL (Government of Lebanon). 2006. *Setting the stage for long-term reconstruction: The national early recovery process.* www.undp.org.lb/early-recovery/docs/Lebanon_Early_Recovery_Framework.pdf.

IRA (Islamic Republic of Afghanistan). 2007. *Afghanistan: National development strategy, 1387–1391* (2008–2013). Kabul. www.embassyofafghanistan.org/sites/default/files/publications/resume_ANDS.pdf.

MPDC (Ministry of Planning and Development Cooperation, Republic of Iraq). 2005. *Iraq national development strategy, 2005–2007.* www.lgp-iraq.org/publications/index.cfm?fuseaction=pubDetail&ID=37.

NCSP (National Council for Strategic Planning). 2006. *The five-year plan (2007–2011).* http://planipolis.iiep.unesco.org/upload/Sudan/Sudan_five_year_plan.pdf.

PNA (Palestinian National Authority). 2005. *Ministry of Planning: Medium term development plan, 2005–2007.*

———. 2006. *Palestinian medium term development plan, 2006–2008.* www.mop-gov.ps/web_files/publishing_file/The%20Medium-Term%20Development%20Plan%202006%202008.pdf.

ROL (Republic of Liberia). 2006. 150 day action plan: A working document for a new Liberia. www.freewebs.com/voiceofliberia/govtofliberiastrategy06.pdf.

———. 2008. *Poverty reduction strategy.* www.imf.org/external/pubs/ft/scr/2008/cr08219.pdf.

TISA (Transitional Islamic State of Afghanistan), Asian Development Bank, UNAMA (United Nations Assistance Mission to Afghanistan), UNEP (United Nations Development Program), and World Bank Group. 2004. *Securing Afghanistan's future: Accomplishments and the strategic path forward.* A government and international agency report. March 17.

UN (United Nations). 1999a. Report of the inter-agency needs assessment mission dispatched by the Secretary-General of the United Nations to the Federal Republic of Yugoslavia. S/1999/662. June 9. www.un.org/peace/kosovo/s99662a.pdf.

———. 1999b. United Nations consolidated inter-agency appeal for Southeastern Europe humanitarian operations. http://reliefweb.int/node/407099.

———. 2000. Consolidated inter-agency appeal for Southeastern Europe. www.reliefweb.int/node/71717.

———. 2001. Consolidated inter-agency appeal for Southeastern Europe. www.reliefweb.int/appeals/2002/files/bal02.pdf.

———. 2003. Humanitarian appeal for Iraq: Revised interagency appeal. www.reliefweb.int/node/128502.

———. 2004. *Common country assessment for the Islamic Republic of Afghanistan.* Kabul. www.undg.org/archive_docs/7403-Afghanistan_CCA.pdf.

———. 2005a. *United Nations Development Assistance Framework (UNDAF) for the Islamic Republic of Afghanistan 2006–2008.* Kabul. www.undp.org.af/Publications/KeyDocuments/UNDAF_2006_2008.pdf.

———. 2005b. *United Nations assistance strategy for Iraq, 2005–2007.* August. www.undg.org/archive_docs/7599-UN_Assistance_Strategy_for_Iraq_2005-2007.doc.

———. 2006. *Country common assessment Liberia: Consolidating peace and national recovery for sustainable development.* Monrovia. www.undg.org/archive_docs/8314-Liberia_CCA_2006.pdf.

———. 2007a. *United Nations Development Assistance Framework for Liberia, 2008–2012*. Monrovia. http://unliberia.org/doc/undaf_doc.pdf.
———. 2007b. *United Nations and partners work plan for Sudan 2007*. http://ochadms.unog.ch/quickplace/cap/main.nsf/h_Index/2007_Sudan_Workplan/$FILE/2007_Sudan_Workplan_VOL1_SCREEN.pdf?OpenElement.
———. 2007c. *Sudan country analysis*. Khartoum. www.undg.org/docs/9996/Sudan-Country-Analysis-2007.pdf.
———. 2008. *Work plan for Sudan, 2008—CCI—environment*.
———. 2009a. *Work plan for Sudan, 2009—CCI—environment*.
———. 2009b. *United Nations Development Assistance Framework (UNDAF) for Sudan, 2009–2012*. Khartoum. www.unops.org/SiteCollectionDocuments/Information-disclosure/UNDAFs/Sudan-UNDAF-2009-2012.pdf.
UN (United Nations) and World Bank. 2003. *Joint Iraq needs assessment report*. http://siteresources.worldbank.org/IRFFI/Resources/Joint+Needs+Assessment.pdf.
———. 2004. *Liberia joint needs assessment*. www.undg.org/archive_docs/3348-Liberia_-_Joint_Needs_Assessment_Synthesis_Report_-_Synthesis_Report.pdf.
———. 2005a. *Framework for sustained peace, development and poverty eradication*. Vol. I of *Sudan Joint Assessment Mission*. www.undg.org/archive_docs/5936-Sudan_JAM_Final_Reports_Volumes_1-3_-_Volume_1__Framework.pdf.
———. 2005b. *Cluster costings and matrices*. Vol. 2 of *Sudan Joint Assessment Mission*. http://reliefweb.int/sites/reliefweb.int/files/resources/DCE6DBAD0504A75349256FFC0021C3AE-jam-sdn-18mar2.pdf.
———. 2007. UN/WB PCNA review: Annex II; Cross-cutting issues. http://ochaonline.un.org/OchaLinkClick.aspx?link=ocha&docId=1118642.
———. 2009. Post-conflict needs assessment and transitional results framework: Note on addressing environmental issues. http://postconflict.unep.ch/humanitarianaction/documents/05_01-07.pdf.
UNDP (United Nations Development Programme). 2007. *Lebanon rapid environmental assessment for greening recovery, reconstruction and reform – 2006*. Beirut. www.undp.org.lb/events/docs/DraftReport.pdf.
UNEP (United Nations Environment Programme). 2003a. *Afghanistan: Post-conflict environmental assessment*. Geneva, Switzerland. http://postconflict.unep.ch/publications/afghanistanpcajanuary2003.pdf.
———. 2003b. *Desk study on the environment in the occupied Palestinian territories*. Nairobi, Kenya. http://postconflict.unep.ch/publications/INF-31-WebOPT.pdf.
———. 2003c. *Desk study on the environment in Iraq*. Geneva, Switzerland. http://postconflict.unep.ch/publications/Iraq_DS.pdf.
———. 2004. *Desk study on the environment in Liberia*. Geneva, Switzerland. http://postconflict.unep.ch/publications/Liberia_DS.pdf.
———. 2007a. *Lebanon: Post-conflict environmental assessment*. Nairobi, Kenya. http://postconflict.unep.ch/publications/UNEP_Lebanon.pdf.
———. 2007b. *Sudan: Post-conflict environmental assessment*. Nairobi, Kenya. http://postconflict.unep.ch/publications/UNEP_Sudan.pdf.
UNEP (United Nations Environment Programme) and UNCHS (United Nations Centre for Human Settlements). 1999. *The Kosovo conflict: Consequences for the environment and human settlements*. Geneva, Switzerland. http://postconflict.unep.ch/publications/finalreport.pdf.
UNMIL (United Nations Mission in Liberia). 2008. History. http://web.archive.org/web/20090122132845/http://unmil.org/1content.asp?ccat=history&zdoc=1.

USAID (United States Agency for International Development). 2008. *Evaluation of the USAID/Sudan "Sudan Transitional Environment Program (STEP)"*. Washington, D.C.: Management Systems International. http://pdf.usaid.gov/pdf_docs/PDACM088.pdf.

World Bank. 2007. *Republic of Lebanon: Economic assessment of environmental degradation due to the July 2006 hostilities; Sector note*. Report No. 39787-LB. http://siteresources.worldbank.org/LEBANONEXTN/Resources/LB_env_Oct2007.pdf?resourceurlname=LB_env_Oct2007.pdf.

Environment and peacebuilding in war-torn societies: Lessons from the UN Environment Programme's experience with post-conflict assessment

Ken Conca and Jennifer Wallace

The environment is not usually viewed as the most important problem in war-torn societies.[1] Humanitarian relief, security, economic reconstruction, and political reconciliation all command attention as urgent priorities. Yet violent conflict does extraordinary damage to the environment on which people depend for their health and livelihoods; human insecurities in such settings have a strong, immediate ecological component as people struggle for clean water, sanitation, food, and fuel in a context of conflict-ravaged infrastructure, lost livelihoods, and disrupted institutions. Over time, more diffuse but equally important environmental challenges emerge: establishing systems of environmental governance, managing pressures on the resource base, creating administrative capacity, dealing with environmental effects of recovery, and finding sustainable trajectories for reconstruction.

The scholarly debate over whether environmental degradation causes violent conflict is ongoing. But as the chapter shows, a growing body of scholarly literature and case documentation indicates that the failure to respond to environmental needs of war-torn societies may greatly complicate the difficult tasks of peacebuilding. At worst, tensions triggered by environmental problems or contested access to natural resources may lead to renewed violent conflict; more generally, failure to meet basic environmental needs undercuts reconciliation, political institutionalization, and economic reconstruction. In the short run, failure to respond to environmental challenges can deepen human suffering and increase vulnerability to natural disasters. In the long run, it may threaten the effective

---

Ken Conca is professor of international relations in the School of International Service at American University, where he directs the Global Environmental Politics program. Jennifer Wallace is a Ph.D. candidate in the Department of Government and Politics at the University of Maryland and an affiliate of the Harrison Program on the Future Global Agenda. This chapter is an updated version of an article that appeared in October 2009 in *Global Governance* 15 (4) and has been reprinted with permission.

[1] The chapter uses the term *war-torn* instead of the more common *post-conflict*, which suggests a neat dichotomy between war and peace that rarely exists in the wake of civil conflict. See de Zeeuw (2001).

functioning of the governmental, economic, and societal institutions necessary for sustained peace.

Along with challenges may come opportunities. An emergent strand of scholarship argues that shared environmental challenges may create peacebuilding opportunities: providing an agenda of shared interests, promoting confidence building, deepening intergroup ties, and fostering the complex task of (re)constructing shared identities. Peace in this context can be thought of as a continuum ranging from the absence of violent conflict to, in its most robust form, the unimagineability of violent conflict (Conca 2002). Peacebuilding, in turn, involves creating the conditions for positive and sustained movement along this continuum.[2] The UN Secretary-General's 2006 progress report on preventing armed conflict stressed both preventive and peacebuilding environmental initiatives. Environmental degradation is flagged as a "risk factor" for violent conflict; environmental protection is identified as a peacebuilding tool "by promoting dialogue around shared resources and enabling opposing groups to focus on common problems" (UNGA 2006, 10). Indeed in the 2010 *Progress Report of the Secretary-General on Peacebuilding in the Immediate Aftermath of Conflict*, Secretary-General Ban Ki-moon calls upon member states and the United Nations system "to make questions of natural resource allocation, ownership and access an integral part of peacebuilding strategies" (UNSG 2010, 12).

Recognizing these connections, the international community's interest in the environmental dimensions of conflict prevention and post-conflict reconstruction has grown. The United Nations Peacebuilding Commission lists building the foundation for sustainable development in its mandate. The need to address the management of natural resources is included within the European Commission's Stability Instrument for conflict-affected countries and fragile states. The United Nations Environment Programme (UNEP) has created a Post-Conflict and Disaster Management Branch (PCDMB), which has conducted assessments in eighteen war-torn countries and regions at the time of this writing.[3] Addressing the environmental dimensions of conflicts and disasters is also one of UNEP's six priorities over the period 2010–2013. Nongovernmental organizations (NGOs) have also engaged the issue; a November 2005 meeting hosted by World Wildlife Fund-U.S. included roughly twenty human rights, conservation, development, and conflict-resolution NGOs (Pendzich 2005).

Yet little is known about the potential role of environmental initiatives in peacebuilding. This chapter seeks to narrow the gap in understanding by drawing lessons from the experiences of UNEP. Through 2010, beginning with Kosovo in 1999, UNEP has conducted assessments in Afghanistan, Albania, Bosnia and Herzegovina, Central African Republic, the Democratic Republic of the Congo, Haiti, Iraq, Georgia, Lebanon, Liberia, the former Yugoslav Republic of Macedonia,

---

[2] On different conceptualizations of peacebuilding, see Haugerudbraaten (1998).
[3] As of May 2012, UNEP has completed a total of twenty assessments.

The UN Environment Programme and post-conflict assessment   65

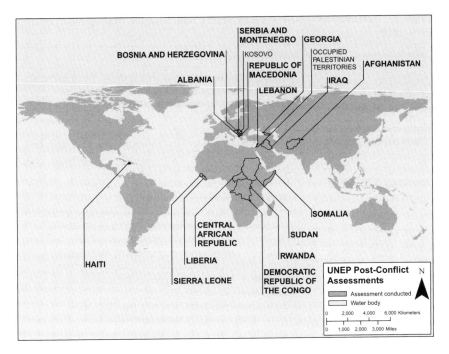

Notes:
1. Post-conflict operations in UN member states are set in bold.
2. At the time of UNEP's respective assessments, Kosovo was part of the Federal Republic of Yugoslavia (FRY); the Palestinian territories were known as the occupied Palestinian territories; Serbia (also formerly part of FRY) was known as the country of Serbia and Montenegro; and South Sudan was not yet an independent country.

Rwanda, Serbia and Montenegro, Sierra Leone, Somalia, Sudan, and the occupied Palestinian territories (see table 1).[4]

UNEP's assessments have been of three main types: rapid appraisals of environmental conditions following conflict, detailed evaluations that approach a national state-of-the-environment report, and issue-specific interventions on targeted questions such as toxic waste, oil spills, human displacement, or depleted uranium weaponry.[5] Although the assessments vary considerably in depth and focus, UNEP's experience offers a unique look at environmental conditions in societies emerging from periods of violent conflict. The goal of the chapter is to use the experience to identify conflict-induced environmental challenges and entry points for environmental initiatives in peacebuilding. In doing so, the chapter

---

[4] UNEP's assessment in Kosovo was undertaken as a joint initiative with the United Nations Centre for Human Settlements (UNCHS). UNCHS was the predecessor of the United Nations Human Settlements Programme, commonly known as UN-HABITAT.

[5] For another perspective on UNEP's post-conflict assessments, see David Jensen, "Evaluating the Impact of UNEP's Post-Conflict Environmental Assessments," in this book.

Table 1. Activities of UNEP's Post-Conflict and Disaster Management Branch, 1999–2010

Country/territory	Principal issues identified
Afghanistan	• Land degradation; water availability; illegal forest harvesting and grazing; urban waste, wastewater and sanitation.
Albania	• Industrial hot spots, environmental impacts of refugees, institutional capacities for environmental management.
Bosnia and Herzegovina	• Depleted uranium weaponry.
Central African Republic	• Role of natural resources in conflict and peacebuilding, land conflicts, illegal mining and deforestation, institutional capacities for environmental management.
Democratic Republic of the Congo	• Mineral concessions, hazardous wastes, deforestation, water availability, sanitation, biodiversity, land degradation, environmental impacts of displaced persons, land tenure, institutional capacity for environmental management.
Former Yugoslav Republic of Macedonia	• Industrial hot spots, environmental impacts of refugees, institutional capacities for environmental management.
Haiti	• Extreme deforestation and disaster vulnerability, waste management, institutional capacities for environmental management.
Georgia	• Industrial hot spots and forest fires from bombing.
Iraq	• Water resources, waste management, oil industry, ecosystem degradation, biodiversity, institutional capacity, depleted uranium weaponry, military ordnance.
Lebanon	• Industrial hot spots, solid and hazardous waste, water resources, coastal and marine environment, military ordnance.
Liberia	• Refugee impacts, energy supplies, water and sanitation, agriculture and food, deforestation, waste management.
Occupied Palestinian territories	• Freshwater, wastewater, hazardous waste, solid waste, conservation and biodiversity.
Rwanda	• Environmental impacts of displaced persons, water availability, biodiversity, land degradation, soil erosion, energy supplies, institutional capacity for environmental management.
Federal Republic of Yugoslavia/Kosovo	• Industrial hot spots, Danube River, protected areas, human settlements, depleted uranium weaponry.
Sierra Leone	• Natural resources and conflict, mineral concessions, land tenure, water management, and waste management.
Somalia	• Resource exploitation (deforestation, land degradation, fisheries depletion), hazardous wastes, human settlements, water and sanitation.
Sudan	• Water resources, refugees and human settlements, industrial and agricultural impacts, deforestation, wildlife and marine resources, resource competition and conflict-related resource exploitation, institutional capacities for environmental management.

Source: Compiled by the authors.
Note: Table excludes assessments focused exclusively on responding to disasters.

notes with caution Roland Paris's observation that peacebuilding "developed into something of a growth industry in the 1990s" (Paris 2004, 3), creating the danger of generically viewing a highly diverse set of conflicts. Clearly, even if war-torn countries had broadly similar ecosystems and natural resource–use patterns (they do not), the heterogeneity of conflicts would make it difficult to develop general formulae about environment-conflict-peace linkages. Much depends on local context.

The chapter draws upon the assessment reports, other documentation, interviews with UNEP's PCDMB staff, and the wider scholarly literature on environment, conflict, and peace.[6] The discussion is organized around four themes: the multiple, often indirect links between violence and environmental degradation; the political dimensions of environmental assessment as a confidence-building tool; resource and environmental linkages among the formal, informal, illegal, and aid-based economies of war-torn societies; and the environmental dimensions of reconstituting the state, regulation, and rule of law. But, first, the chapter provides an overview of the state of knowledge about environmental and natural resource linkages to peace and conflict.

ENVIRONMENTAL CHANGE, NATURAL RESOURCES, VIOLENCE, AND PEACEBUILDING

Early research on environmental change and violent conflict focused on scarcity.[7] The premise was that reduced availability of renewable resources such as forests, soils, croplands, freshwater, and fisheries, or in associated ecosystem services, could trigger intergroup conflict—particularly along preexisting fault lines such as ethnicity, region, or class.

Although many case studies documented links between environmental degradation and violence, skeptics raised important points.[8] First, the many intervening variables—economic factors, state institutions, property rights systems—make it difficult to identify a direct causal link between environmental change and violence. Second, research on civil conflict has found deprivation and grievance, by themselves, to be poor predictors of violent conflict. Third, much of the eco-conflict literature invoked scarcity without paying attention to how social relations create the conditions for resource capture or other forms of social scarcity. Statistical

---

[6] At the time of writing, UNEP's environmental assessments for the Democratic Republic of the Congo (DRC) and Rwanda were still underway. For information pertaining to DRC's assessment, see UNEP's synthesis report, *The Democratic Republic of the Congo: Post-Conflict Environmental Assessment*, available at http://postconflict.unep.ch/publications/UNEP_DRC_PCEA_EN.pdf. For Rwanda's UNEP assessment, *Rwanda: From Post-Conflict to Environmentally Sustainable Development*, see http://postconflict.unep.ch/publications/UNEP_Rwanda.pdf.
[7] See, for example, Homer-Dixon (1994) and Bächler and Spillmann (1996).
[8] For a range of critiques, see Levy (1995); Gleditsch (2001); Peluso and Watts (2001).

tests of association between environmental scarcity and conflict provide some qualified support but remain limited by poor and improperly scaled data.[9]

A separate body of research has asked whether natural resource abundance, rather than environmental scarcity, drives violence, noting the sharp increase in civil conflict in petroleum- and diamond-rich states in particular (Ross 2006). But the precise mechanisms by which resource wealth may induce or sustain violence remain disputed. As Michael L. Ross points out, resource wealth may provide financial sustenance for rebellion, weaken the development of state institutions, increase the likelihood and effects of trade shocks, make capturing the state more attractive, or increase the perceived benefits of separatism (Ross 2006). Again statistical tests have shed some light but not settled the matter, in part due to data limitations and difficulty in using statistical means at a subnational scale.

One important limitation of environment-conflict research has been its failure to examine how social interactions around natural resources and the environment may also create opportunities for cooperation. As Adrian Martin suggests, "environmental scarcity and resource use competition are part of the everyday politics of life. . . . The most usual outcomes are peaceful ones, where broadly accepted rules lead to cooperative outcomes of one kind or another. Thus, theoretically at least, resource use conflict can form part of a virtuous circle, in which cooperative responses contribute to social capital, thus encouraging robust institutions and future cooperation" (Martin 2005, 330). In this view, the key is not abundance or scarcity but whether inherent conflicts are channeled into productive forms of resolution as opposed to violence.

Some scholars have argued that social relations around the environment may create peacebuilding opportunities. Ken Conca and Geoffrey D. Dabelko theorize two pathways for "environmental peacemaking": one emphasizing use of environmental opportunities to improve the "contractual environment" for cooperation among political and economic elites, and another in which environmental interdependencies might strengthen cross-boundary societal linkages (Conca and Dabelko 2002). Richard Matthew and colleagues documented several cases in which "conservation practices may provide a basis for bringing parties who have been or are engaged in conflict together to begin the process of peace building around common environmental concerns" (Matthew, Halle, and Switzer 2002, 5). Although empirical research is in the early stages, there is a growing body of case studies.[10] The picture that emerges is that natural resource management and environmental governance can be a high-stakes point of social interaction and that the characteristics of how resources are governed can be a critical determinant in whether social relations follow a peaceful or violent path. This is particularly true in low-income, resource-dependent economies, under conditions

---

[9] See, for example, Hauge and Ellingsen (1998). For a critique of statistical analysis of environmentally induced conflict, see O'Lear (2006).

[10] See, for example, Martin (2005); Evans (2004); Sundberg (2003); Rogers (1999).

of political instability, or in the context of weak governance institutions—central features of most war-torn societies.

LESSONS FROM UNEP ASSESSMENTS

Four sets of lessons have emerged from the assessments conducted by UNEP: environmental effects resulting from conflict have multiple pathways; militarized environments provide opportunities for confidence building; linkages between the environment and the economy are found in war-torn societies; and environmental governance is dependent upon how state capacity is built and the rule of law is shaped in war-torn societies.

The environmental burden of conflict: Multiple pathways

Many studies have documented conflict's directly harmful ecological effects.[11] Martijn Bijlsma points to the "grave environmental effects of civil conflict" as one reason to incorporate environmental considerations into peacebuilding initiatives, stressing collateral damage, antipersonnel mines, and targeting of the environment as part of military strategy (Bijlsma 2005, 166). The Biodiversity Support Program, a consortium of conservation NGOs funded by the U.S. Agency for International Development, documented extensive effects of armed conflict on biodiversity in sub-Saharan Africa (Shambaugh, Oglethorpe, and Ham 2001).

As table 1 indicates, the principal impacts vary from case to case. In some instances, quick assessments with limited foci—human displacement in Albania and the former Yugoslav Republic of Macedonia, depleted uranium weaponry in Bosnia and Herzegovina and Kosovo—found minimal effects (with the caveat that limitations of time, access, and data left considerable uncertainty). In other instances, protracted conflict has clearly taken a heavy toll, as in Iraq, Afghanistan, and the occupied Palestinian territories. Environmental damage that appears across several of the cases includes the following:

Impacts of human displacement. Difficult human-settlements problems accompany large-scale, rapid displacement of people from their communities due to conflict. UNEP findings are similar to the environmental guidelines of the Office of the United Nations High Commissioner for Refugees, which identify six primary environmental impacts of refugees: natural resource depletion; irreversible impacts on natural resources; social impacts on local populations; and effects on health, social conditions, and the economy (UNHCR 2005). In Darfur, many residents of camps for displaced people make a living by brick making, with the resulting use of fuelwood causing severe localized deforestation (UNEP 2007c). In Sierra Leone, the UNEP assessment found that many unsustainable practices,

---

[11] See, for example, Matthew, Halle, and Switzer (2002).

undertaken out of necessity as survival mechanisms by displaced people, have become institutionalized in the years following the conflict (UNEP 2010).

Toxic hazards from bombardment, oil fires, and conflict in industrial areas. During the 2006 Israeli incursion into Lebanon, the bombing of the Jiyeh power station created a substantial Mediterranean oil spill (UNEP 2007b). North Atlantic Treaty Organization (NATO) air strikes in the Kosovo conflict created localized contamination at a number of industrial facilities (UNEP and UNCHS 1999).

The conflict-deforestation link. This may include any or all of the following: illegal logging, use of timber as a conflict-sustaining financial resource, a legal and administrative vacuum that undercuts sustainable forest management, and pressures on forests from the short-term time horizon of insecure communities. Forests have also been targeted during conflict: in Sudan, evidence was found that trees were felled maliciously, most likely to sever community ties to the land and reduce opportunities for resettlement (UNEP 2007c).

Landmines, unexploded ordnance, and depleted uranium weaponry. Israel's incursion into Lebanon left as many as a million unexploded cluster bombs.[12] In addition to the devastating human toll, landmines and unexploded ordnance can liberate and disseminate toxic materials, displace people onto marginal lands and fragile ecosystems, and disrupt resource management and tourism.[13] UNEP has also weighed in on the ongoing controversy over health effects of depleted uranium weaponry, conducting field tests in Bosnia and Herzegovina, Kosovo, Serbia and Montenegro, and Lebanon.

Water supplies, sanitation, waste disposal, and public health. The challenges of maintaining water and sanitation services and controlling associated problems can be severe. In the conflicts in Lebanon (in 2006) and Gaza (in 2009), solid waste disposal sites became overloaded, contaminating water supplies. In Lebanon, greatly increased streams of hazardous health-care waste were reportedly entering municipal waste sites, promoting disease vectors (UNEP 2007b, 2009a).

These effects may persist long after cessation of violence; in its Sierra Leone assessment, UNEP found that the effects of conflict on water and agriculture infrastructure in rural areas were still observable nearly a decade later (UNEP 2010).

A more important contribution of the UNEP cases is identifying *indirect* pathways by which conflict affects environmental quality, beyond damage from the fighting itself. Among these indirect linkages, three stand out. First, violent conflict imposes an environmental burden on ecosystems that, in nearly all cases, were already straining under severe challenges of pollution, resource degradation, and poor environmental management. Second, violent conflict disrupts state institutions, initiatives, and policy coordination mechanisms. In virtually all cases, conflict yielded poor management, abundant space for illegality, and the collapse

---

[12] See "Report of the Mine Action Coordination Centre, South Lebanon, for the Month of October 2006," cited in UNEP (2007b).
[13] See Torres Nachón (2004).

of positive practices. Third, in the face of violent conflict, desperate people are often forced into choices with unsustainable consequences. Illegality and regulatory lapses cause overharvesting, accelerated extraction, and resource degradation—but so do the pressures of conflict on livelihoods and the resultant changes in people's survival strategies. Each of these indirect linkages deserves a brief elaboration.

First, the direct effects of conflict are compounded by the poor state of the pre-conflict environment, a striking theme in every case. As Pekka Haavisto characterized the occupied Palestinian territories, "There have been direct impacts, caused by military activities; indirect impacts caused by the war-like situation; and an overall environmental degradation due to the lack of administrative management and public awareness" (Haavisto 2003, 2). In Liberia, agriculture, logging, mining, road building, and fuel production had already taken a large toll on forests prior to conflict (UNEP 2004a). In the former Yugoslav Republic of Macedonia, the assessment revealed severe waste management problems: proliferation of illegal dumps, uncontrolled burning, and little or no effective regulation of hazardous wastes (UNEP 2001). Similar problems in Sudan are "directly reflected in the elevated incidence of waterborne diseases, which make up 80 percent of reported diseases in the country" (UNEP 2007c, 13). In Iraq, a combination of poor governance, international sanctions, and minimal regional cooperation created "critical long-term environmental vulnerabilities and risks" related to water quality, ecosystem degradation, waste management, and the oil industry (UNEP 2003d, 28).

A second indirect linkage is the impact of conflict on environmental institutions and governance, which is striking in nearly every case. In Liberia, conflict undercut budgets, staffing, and access for the Forestry Development Authority, leading to failure on several levels: inability to control the explosive growth of logging roads into the forest during the conflict, siphoning of management and reforestation funds accumulated from logging fees, little or no support for community participation, and inability to enforce community rights in forest-concession agreements (UNEP 2004a). In Somalia, the conflict allegedly has enabled some industrialized countries to dump hazardous wastes there, due to political instability, the availability of dumping sites, and low public awareness (UNSC 2011). For the Palestinian Authority, the conflict has imposed a severe burden on waste-processing systems. Some of this is direct, in that facilities have either been targeted or suffered collateral damage, at a time when the general destruction of buildings and infrastructure has greatly increased the waste stream. But there are also second-order effects: It has been difficult to obtain spare parts, and curfews and checkpoint closures disrupt waste collection and transport. Israeli environmental authorities have also been disrupted by violence and are said to have only limited control over the activities of Israeli settlements in the occupied territories (UNEP 2003c). There have been repeated Palestinian allegations that settlements have exploited lax enforcement to attract hazardous industries from Israel (charges denied by Israeli officials) (UNEP 2003c).

Another example of the institutional effects of conflict is Afghanistan, where conflict has disrupted any capacity for effective water management. Deep wells are drilled in uncoordinated fashion; timed releases from storage ponds for drought control or irrigation are done poorly, if at all; and community decision-making structures governing longstanding water systems have largely collapsed (UNEP 2003a). More generally, "local community decision-making structures became unable to deal with the magnitude of the demands being made on the environment, as well as the resulting environmental degradation" (UNEP 2003a, 95).

Third, there are telling anecdotes in the cases about the effects of conflict forcing people to make choices that have unsustainable consequences. In Lebanon, farmers have set bushes ablaze, hoping to set off the unexploded cluster bombs blocking access to farmlands, although this practice can trigger a new round of impoverishment and environmental degradation by worsening soil erosion (UNEP 2007b). Other examples include mangrove-forest harvesting for fuel and charcoal in Liberia; the felling of pistachio woodlands in Afghanistan, due in part to doubts about future access to the resource; and the preemptive release of industrial chemicals in Serbia and Montenegro in anticipation of air strikes (UNEP 2004a, 2003a; UNEP and UNCHS 1999). Positive practices also suffer: UNEP assessments via satellite imagery suggest that the toll of the Israeli incursion into Gaza in 2008–2009 included destruction of or severe damage to an estimated 180 greenhouses (UNEP 2009a).

Confidence-building potential in militarized environments

A second set of lessons relates to environmental confidence building. The emerging literature on environment and peacebuilding posits that creating shared environmental knowledge through cooperative means may be a useful confidence-building tool, particularly when it engages actors beyond the state (Conca 2002; Carius 2006). This raises several questions to which UNEP's experience can speak directly. What are the challenges to environmental monitoring in war-torn societies? Are cooperative-knowledge initiatives even possible in such settings? Which actors have relevant knowledge resources? When uncertainty is extensive, does engagement on environmental issues enhance trust or merely deepen suspicion?

A recurring theme in the cases is that environmental monitoring, data collection, and information sharing are casualties of conflict. Typically, historical data are lacking, monitoring is sporadic, and interagency coordination (when agencies exist and function) is poor to nonexistent. In Afghanistan, "while some ministries reportedly undertake a limited amount of *ad hoc* data collection, it is not consistently collected or routinely shared. The lack of communications between the provinces and central government also hampers data exchange. None of the ministries currently have adequate staff resources to collect environmental information, and in many cases monitoring facilities and equipment have been destroyed during the years of war" (UNEP 2003a, 98).

The cases also underscore the challenging nature of collecting basic environmental information in war-torn societies. In post-conflict Afghanistan and Iraq, ongoing fighting hampered data collection by rendering areas inaccessible to UNEP teams. In Lebanon, unexploded ordnance prohibited access to some sites of interest (UNEP 2007b). The observations reinforce a common theme in peacebuilding literature—that a certain level of public order and security is a prerequisite for sustained peacebuilding activities.[14]

A more hopeful aspect of the cases is the presence of local civil society as a source of grounded knowledge. Although such groups have their own agendas, they can help draw a more comprehensive picture and offer diverse perspectives. UNEP encountered a wide array of environmental and conservation-oriented groups in Liberia, "many of which have played an important role in contributing information and experience to the preparation and review of laws" (UNEP 2004a, 76). Several NGOs supported the UNEP assessment team in Afghanistan, and a few contributed personnel (UNEP 2003a). When ongoing conflict precluded access by the assessment team, a local NGO, Save the Environment Afghanistan, provided data on protected areas in the Ajar Valley (UNEP 2003a). The Environmental Foundation for Africa also played a similar supporting role during UNEP's assessment in Sierra Leone. In Bosnia and Herzegovina, local communities were an important source of information in identifying suspected contamination points from depleted uranium weapons (UNEP 2003b). Exceptions were the Central African Republic, Albania, and Serbia and Montenegro, where the assessments found a weakly articulated civil society and NGOs struggling with membership declines and financial difficulties.[15] In several cases, international NGOs, particularly conservation and forestry organizations, were able to maintain a presence, and in some instances figured prominently as sources of data and expertise.

Even where monitoring capacity exists, cooperative initiatives such as post-conflict cleanup or environmental health projects will depend on access to information, data exchange, and institutional transparency—in settings often dominated by suspicion and exclusion. An example of the barriers to drawing a factual picture came when NATO forces resisted releasing information about their use of depleted uranium weaponry in the Balkans. Several cases also revealed problems of public access to information. In the Palestinian case, UNEP flagged the need for better NGO access to information, including "full transparency on donor-funded environmental projects" (UNEP 2003c, 130). In Afghanistan, the assessment found a lack of transparency, no "clear mechanisms" for public participation, a weak media role, and substantial barriers to women (UNEP 2003a, 103). In Albania, the assessment concluded, "information is often treated as a market good, to be bought and sold for institutional gain, rather than to be shared freely for national benefit" (UNEP 2001, 18).

---

[14] On security governance issues and peacebuilding, see Bryden and Hänggi (2007).
[15] Only ten of forty identified NGOs in Albania were deemed currently active (UNEP 2000).

There are also episodes in which knowledge controversies seem to reproduce and harden mistrust rather than soften it. For example, Palestinian sources repeatedly charged Israel with environmental abuses, including discharge of untreated wastewater, relocation of unregulated hazardous industries from Israeli to Palestinian lands, and excessive use of water in violation of the Oslo II agreements. UNEP was unable to help resolve these controversies, which reflect and deepen mistrust rather than mitigate it. As Pekka Haavisto—the then-chairman of UNEP's Post-Conflict Assessment Unit—put it, "even in the context of a scientific environmental report, some expressions are interpreted in a political rather than a technical way" (UNEP 2003c, 9).[16] A similar dynamic can be seen in the controversies around depleted uranium weaponry.

Given the combination of difficulty gathering information, fragmented and dispersed knowledge resources, and the potential for uncertainty to harden mistrust, a strategic approach is required if generating cooperative environmental knowledge is to serve as a trust-enhancing mechanism. In particular, UNEP's approach has been to trade on its reputation for technical expertise, assume a depoliticized position, and serve as an honest knowledge broker. Klaus Töpfer, UNEP's executive director at the time of the organization's first post-conflict assessment, said on Kosovo, "I am convinced that such a neutral, objective and scientific assessment of the real situation on the ground in a post-conflict situation is essential. This approach provides a much-needed and reliable source of information to the peoples affected" (UNEP and UNCHS 1999, 5).

For an intergovernmental organization, there may be little alternative to this depoliticized approach if UNEP is to work effectively with governments of war-torn societies. Staff consistently named UNEP's reputation for technical expertise and neutrality as its most important resources in dealing with governments; one stressed that how to maintain that position of neutrality while engaging in consultation with governments had been an important part of organizational learning.[17] Some report findings have been controversial, such as those concerning the Jiyeh oil spill in Lebanon, the links between water and conflict in Sudan, toxics issues in the Israeli-occupied Palestinian territories, and depleted uranium weaponry. Staff stressed that although there was a round of consultation with the relevant government when the draft report was ready, the facts of the case would not be changed unless supported by new scientific data.

There are also limits to a depoliticized, predominantly technical approach to environmental knowledge. PCDMB staff described their work as a "bridge-building tool," in which the assessment report served as a starting point, and

---

[16] The Post-Conflict Assessment Unit was the predecessor of Post-Conflict and Disaster Management Branch.
[17] The authors interviewed UNEP PCDMB staff members in September 2007, in Geneva, Switzerland.

stressed the importance of local actors having a sense of ownership. In divided societies ravaged by violent conflict, actors will bring to the table many different ways of knowing and historical reference points; the technical-rational discourse of modern science will be inaccessible to a wide swath of the population; and "facts" will be widely understood to be political things. Under these circumstances, efforts to depoliticize knowledge entail a clear trade-off: they make it more feasible to work under very difficult circumstances but at the risk of reducing the scope of potential ownership in the results. As UNEP embarks on new models of post-conflict environmental assessment—involving a more complex set of partnerships with actors other than simply an environmental ministry—these trade-offs will likely come to the foreground of efforts to cooperate around shared environmental knowledge. For environmental assessments to be not just resource-management guides but also confidence-building tools, the task of widening the audience becomes central.

Reconstruction and economic development: Environment-economy linkages in war-torn societies

Economic development is critical to conflict transformation strategies. As Oliver Richmond suggests, "fieldwork in several different post-conflict environments—from the Democratic Republic of Congo to East Timor and the Balkans—suggests that development is often the major gap in the peace process, despite much effort being redirected toward social justice, economic stabilization, and free market reform" (Richmond 2005, 437). Paris has argued that aggressive structural adjustment and neoliberal reforms, pushed by international actors, have exacerbated tensions or set back progress by undermining the reconstitution of the political system and state capacity (Paris 2004). These reforms, and aid initiatives in general, often target war-torn societies' natural resource sectors, with intensified extraction viewed as a quickly tapped revenue source.

The concept of sustainability provides a link between economic redevelopment and environmental quality.[18] Toward that end, one critical component of peacebuilding is to enhance the security of people's livelihoods while promoting sustainable resource use and better environmental governance.[19] Although not their central focus, several of the UNEP cases identify opportunities to link environmental management and economic development. For example, the Afghanistan assessment proposes a civilian conservation corps to plant trees and promote sustainable forestry, while identifying benefits of a revitalized protected-areas network for tourism (UNEP 2003a). In Liberia, the assessment identifies

---

[18] *Sustainable development* is defined as "meeting the needs of the present without compromising the ability of future generations to meet their own needs" (UNGA 1987, 1).
[19] On the economics of peacebuilding, see Paris (2004); Forman and Patrick (2000).

potential for debt-for-conservation swaps, given the country's heavy indebtedness to multilateral lending agencies (UNEP 2004a).

The UNEP cases also flag many unsustainable practices developed under periods of weak governance, often tied to the pull of export revenues. In Somalia, under weak forest regulation, there has been rampant harvesting of trees for charcoal. Beyond the environmental damage, the practice has led to open conflict between clans, including shoot-outs and laying mines. The same is true of largely unregulated coastal fishing, including overharvesting and destruction of foreign fishing boats by local fishers (UNEP 2005).

Examples of unsustainability include many episodes of inadequate environmental planning in aid and reconstruction. Environmental concerns are often relegated to a secondary level in humanitarian aid, and poorly conceived aid responses can render critical environmental problems worse. The Afghanistan assessment found that international efforts to increase water supplies had in some cases led to digging drinking wells next to septic tanks (UNEP 2003a). In Afghanistan, the UNEP assessment team found "no consistent application of [environmental impact assessment] guidelines used by donors and international organizations" (UNEP 2003a, 97).

The aid economy can also depress the prices of local goods, affecting sectors necessary for sustainable livelihoods. In Somalia, large-scale and sometimes poorly timed delivery of food aid contributed to driving farmers out of agriculture and to the decline in per-capita food production (UNEP 2005). Sudan, on the other hand, highlights the complexity of the matter: "if aid were reduced to encourage a return to agriculture, the result in some areas would be food insecurity and an intensification of land degradation, leading to the high likelihood of failure and secondary displacement" (UNEP 2007c, 16).

In identifying sustainable projects and flagging unsustainable ones, it is critical to keep in mind that "conflict economies" consist of several distinct but intertwined segments: the remains of the formal economy, the international aid economy, the informal economy, and the criminal economy (Kamphuis 2005). The danger is that peacebuilding strategies will overemphasize one strand, fail to recognize the others, or implement initiatives that work at cross-purposes in their effects on the different strands. Debt-for-conservation swaps may make sense for Liberia—but must be assessed not only in terms of debt pressure on the formal economy but also in the context of the consistent failure of state institutions to stop illegal timber extraction (criminal economy) or deliver benefits promised to local communities in forest-concession agreements (subsistence/informal economy). Similarly, rebuilding efforts spurred by international aid must be assessed in terms of their impacts on local livelihoods—as when reconstruction drives demand for timber, which in turn impacts local communities in forested areas.

Another complication seen clearly in some UNEP cases is that conflict is not bad for all forms of business. Conflict economies are embedded in transnational commodity chains, populated by actors who may exploit the situation. The problems of "conflict timber" and "conflict diamonds" in Liberia and their connection to international market demand for the commodities have been well documented.[20] Less well known is the fact that the period 1997–2002 also saw a tripling of Liberian rubber exports, despite declining international prices and escalating violence (UNEP 2004a). UN officials and the new government alleged that unregulated plantations occupied by former combatants and featuring "conditions of slavery" for laborers were able to market their product through transnational buyers, including Firestone (Leighton 2006).

There are some striking examples of production flourishing in conflict zones, including activity that is both illegal and unsustainable. Conflict in Liberia hurt cattle rearing and led to a flourishing illegal trade in bushmeat for local consumption and for export (UNEP 2004a). Some of the principal linkages among the formal, informal, illegal, and aid-based segments of the economy are environmental; effects of activity in one sphere spill over to the others. In particular, actions to rebuild the formal economy via the aid-based economy may spill over in the form of livelihood effects on the informal economy and local communities, and the embeddedness of local economic activities in transnational commodity chains may stimulate unsustainable activities in weakly governed areas.

Reconstituting the state: Environmental governance, state capacity, and the rule of law

A fourth set of lessons involves the reconstitution of environmental governance. How the environment will be managed, and for whom, may be shaped as parties work out political arrangements. Even preliminary peace overtures may have environmental ramifications for human security and social stability, as when lootable resources are used to attract conflicting factions to the peace process. Forest concessions, for example, were used to consolidate power in Cambodia after the 1993 UN-sponsored elections, creating conditions for rampant illegal logging and deepening social conflict (Global Witness 2002).

A common pattern in the UNEP cases is the weakness of administrative systems, regulatory control, and the rule of law for environmental protection and natural resource management. In Afghanistan, environmental management was weak to nonexistent in urban areas, while rural areas suffered from the conflict-induced collapse of traditional community-based systems of resource management. In Iraq, the Environment Protection and Improvement Directorate saw its laboratories looted, critically degrading the country's environmental monitoring capacity (UNEP 2007d). In the Balkans, political and economic turbulence yielded inadequate funding and staffing levels, weak technical capacity, and public skepticism. In all cases, weak implementation, poor interagency coordination, inadequate resources, and gaps in basic information were the norm.

---

[20] See, for example, Global Witness (2005).

But the assessments also provide some examples of institutional development during conflict or in its wake. In Liberia, the conflict years were also a period of rapid development of the legal framework for environmental protection (UNEP 2004a). In Afghanistan, the 2002 *loya jirga* (grand assembly) that came in the wake of the U.S. intervention against the Taliban regime produced the Ministry of Irrigation, Water Resources and Environment—the first ministry in Afghanistan's history with an explicit environmental mandate, later transferred to the independent National Environmental Protection Agency (UNEP 2003a). The Sierra Leone Environment Protection Agency followed a similar path. In the occupied Palestinian territories, the Oslo Peace Accords launched a Palestinian agency with environmental responsibilities.

PCDMB staff point to strengthening capacity of environmental ministries as an important effect of their work. Several assessments contain recommendations that imply a strategic progression from assessment to cleanup and monitoring and then to institution building and development of legal and policy frameworks. In Serbia and Montenegro, a rapid assessment of industrial hot spots led to a feasibility study on cleanup projects, which in turn led to a cleanup program linking UNEP and local authorities.[21] Trade-offs encountered in this work included whether to adhere to the national legal framework or follow international best practices and how to incorporate local human resources. UNEP's choices to emphasize national law and build on local capacity slowed implementation but were also felt to have enhanced local acceptance and the capacity to sustain results (UNEP 2004b).

Liberia, Afghanistan, and Sudan provide test cases in which UNEP assessments have led to more sustained engagement in environmental institution building. The Liberian experience revealed several daunting challenges to effectively institutionalizing sustainable environmental governance. In biodiversity protection, for example, identified institutional constraints include poor infrastructure and administration, understaffing, lack of data, weak enforcement, barriers to institutional cooperation, and weak financial support—all either created or exacerbated by the conflict (UNEP 2007a). Earlier progress in legal development has stalled for want of implementing legislation. Efforts to strengthen community-based natural resource management (CBNRM)—extensively disrupted by conflict and further marginalized in some legal reforms—have developed slowly and unevenly (UNEP 2007a). Although a full assessment of UNEP's post-conflict accomplishments in Liberia is beyond the scope of the chapter, the limits are apparent: UNEP has phased out its in-country program, and one staffer reported that the effort had "influenced the UN but not the government."

The picture in Afghanistan is more complex. A strong international aid presence and a more receptive national government created more operational space. The

---

[21] For more information on the cleanup program in Serbia, see Muralee Thummarukudy, Oli Brown, and Hannah Moosa, "Remediation of Polluted Sites in the Balkans, Iraq, and Sierra Leone," in this book.

preliminary assessment led to a longer-term partnership for "capacity building and institutional development" along five specific dimensions: government institutions, law and policy, impact assessment, environmental education, and CBNRM (UNEP 2006). Early assessments by UNEP and others revealed several barriers to these goals, including the environmental damage from the conflict, the disruption of traditional resource management systems and institutions, and basic challenges of creating communication systems with adequate staff, office equipment, and the like. A 2005 interim progress report described Afghanistan's environmental situation as "an immense challenge that will take decades to achieve" (UNEP 2006, 19).

Progress in Afghanistan has been uneven, with the strongest advances made in agency building, law, and policy (including a national environmental protection agency, national framework legislation, development of human resources, and engagement with several multilateral environmental agreements). Environmental impact assessment was slower because stakeholders struggled before eventually agreeing on a policy framework. Perhaps the least progress has been made in CBNRM, historically the norm in Afghanistan but severely disrupted by conflict. Also, PCDMB staff acknowledge that social-science expertise, which is central to effective support of CBNRM, has been the least-developed link in their work.

UNEP's work in Sudan represents the most ambitious effort to build on its assessment work. The most comprehensive of the UNEP assessments to date, *Sudan: Post-Conflict Environmental Assessment* can be read as a state-of-the-environment report rather than merely a post-conflict snapshot (UNEP 2007c). In the wake of the 2007 assessment, UNEP opened an office in Khartoum. Initiatives have been launched that are intended to yield several specific outputs over the 2009–2012 time frame. One strand of work seeks to enhance the environmental and resource management capacity of the national and state governments, including capacity-building work with Khartoum in the North and Juba in the South. A second strand seeks to promote awareness and action in South Sudan, where a ministry of environment was created. A third strand focuses on Darfur, addressing its environmental situation (with particular attention to water management and reforestation) and raising the profile of environmental concerns in the peace process. Activities are also underway to promote the mainstreaming of environmental awareness and best practices and to address climate vulnerability. The United Kingdom has provided the bulk of financing for the follow-up work combined with contributions from the governments of Italy and the United States.

ENVIRONMENT AND PEACEBUILDING: SUPPORT, CAVEATS, AND STRATEGIC TRADE-OFFS

There are important reasons to promote effective environmental governance and natural resource management in societies emerging from protracted conflict. To be sure, trade-offs with other values abound in such settings. But UNEP's decade of experience underscores several points in the emerging literature on environment and peacebuilding. Systematic failure to manage resources sustainably undercuts social welfare and social justice; social relations around the environment in wartorn societies contain potential pathways to both resurgent conflict and enhanced cooperation; and these facts are only amplified in societies where most livelihoods are tied directly and immediately to the resource base. In other words, environmental issues create high-stakes choices in war-torn societies. Handled effectively, they may create a solid foundation for peace and sustainable development; handled poorly, they risk undercutting an already tenuous peace.

But the UNEP cases also suggest caveats and refinements to how the environmental dimensions of peacebuilding are conceived. First, conflict can do tremendous damage to the environment, yet in these cases, some of the most important pathways are seen in how conflict changes institutions, disrupts livelihoods, and alters social practices. Second, as peacebuilding scholarship posits, cooperative environmental initiatives may have substantial potential to enhance trust and build confidence, but such initiatives are complicated by the challenges of engaging a wide array of societal actors and by the fact that environmental controversies can also harden differences and reinforce conflict identities. Third, aid projects and development initiatives play a crucial role in the prospects for sustainable reconstruction, but they will accomplish little if they do not account for how conflict economies are fragmented into formal, informal, aid-based, and illicit components or for how the fragments are embedded in transnational commodity chains that exploit weak governance to accelerate extraction. Fourth, strengthening environmental law, administration, and management can be an important part of rebuilding the state and reestablishing the rule of law, but such initiatives must reach beyond formal state institutions to engage the societal practices where most resource governance actually occurs.

UNEP's experience also suggests the need for a more strategic, adaptive approach. A depoliticized, technical, honest-broker strategy—in which rapid assessment led to monitoring and cleanup activities, which in turn led to bureaucratic strengthening and legal codification—yielded some useful results in some of the cases. There is also clear evidence of adaptation of this approach through organizational learning. The Sudan assessment involved a wider process of stakeholder engagement, identified local partners for follow-up work, and engaged the separate governing entities in the North and South in bridge-building dialogue. The recommendations, each of which included specific cost estimates and implementing agencies, became part of the UN country team's agenda.[22]

But this approach also runs up against clear political limitations. Disasters and conflicts are now one of UNEP's six strategic priorities, which will strengthen

---

[22] UNEP PCDMB staff, correspondence with author, October 2008.

UNEP's capabilities. But UNEP has neither a conflict-prevention mandate nor the political or logistical resources to conduct extensive on-the-ground operations in war-torn countries. To build on the possibilities, a more strategic, system-wide approach is required: one that coordinates more explicitly with an expanded set of international peacebuilding actors while engaging domestically a wider set of stakeholders.

A key trade-off of the approach is implicit in the first recommendation of UNEP's report on the occupied Palestinian territories: "keep the environment out of the conflict" (UNEP 2003c, 126). UNEP's depoliticized, technically oriented approach is not surprising given the politicization surrounding all aspects of international intervention, no matter how benign and altruistic aid efforts may seem to some in the international community. The position seems to have been vital to achieving the level of cooperation and partnership with host governments seen in several of the cases.

But it is also true that there are inherently political elements to environmental management as a peacebuilding tool. In Liberia, the effects of conflict on traditional dryland agriculture stimulated interest in swamp cultivation to boost critically needed food supplies. Such a shift entails complex environmental and social trade-offs: less pressure on forests but the destruction of mangroves and ill effects of wetlands conversion on biodiversity (UNEP 2004a). Even if this high-stakes choice is made to optimize Liberia's trajectory of sustainable development, it will have the effect of redistributing power, resources, and opportunities among Liberians. War-torn societies and the international community will have made great progress toward peacebuilding when the social conflicts embedded in environmental choices can be managed as well as the technical, legal, and administrative ones.

Finally, UNEP's experience suggests some important steps moving forward. First, as key elements of public health, livelihoods, and recovery, environmental considerations must be present at the earliest stages of the efforts to heal societies and landscapes torn by conflict. Much work lies ahead in mainstreaming effective environmental capacity within the UN's peacebuilding efforts. Second, the role of natural resources in recovery strategies must be fundamentally reevaluated, with an eye toward optimizing an overall trajectory of sustainable development and creating the institutional underpinnings to stay on the trajectory, rather than seeking a quick fix of enhanced commodity exports. Third, perhaps the most important environmental peacebuilding work takes place before conflict even occurs, in the form of proactive, preventive measures. Investment in effective, equitable, and conflict-sensitive strategies for natural resource management may lessen incentives for conflict, reduce the impact on people and the environment when conflict does occur, and enhance the chances for durable peace.[23]

---

[23] These recommendations parallel several made by UNEP (2009b).

REFERENCES

Bächler, G., and K. R. Spillmann, eds. 1996. *Environmental degradation as a cause of war.* Zurich, Switzerland: Rüegger.

Bijlsma, M. 2005. Protecting the environment. In *Postconflict development: Meeting new challenges,* ed. G. Junne and W. Verkoren. Boulder, CO: Lynne Rienner.

Bryden, A., and H. Hänggi. 2007. *Security governance in post-conflict peacebuilding.* Geneva, Switzerland: Geneva Center for the Democratic Control of Armed Force.

Carius, A. 2006. *Environmental cooperation as an instrument of crisis prevention and peacebuilding: Conditions for success and constraints.* Report to the German Federal Ministry for Economic Cooperation and Development. Berlin, Germany: Adelphi Consulting.

Conca, K. 2002. The case for environmental peacemaking. In *Environmental peacemaking,* ed. K. Conca and G. D. Dabelko. Washington, D.C.: Woodrow Wilson Center Press; Baltimore, MD: Johns Hopkins University Press.

Conca, K., and G. D. Dabelko, eds. 2002. *Environmental peacemaking.* Washington, D.C.: Woodrow Wilson International Center for Scholars.

de Zeeuw, J. 2001. *Building peace in war-torn societies: From concept to strategy.* The Hague: Netherlands Institute of International Relations, Conflict Research Unit.

Evans, D. 2004. Using natural resources management as a peacebuilding tool: Observations and lessons from Central Western Mindanao. *Journal of Peacebuilding and Development* 1:140–155.

Forman, S., and S. Patrick. 2000. *Good intentions: Pledges of aid for postconflict recovery.* Boulder, CO: Lynne Rienner.

Gleditsch, N. P. 2001. Armed conflict and the environment. In *Environmental conflict,* ed. P. F. Diehl and N. P. Gleditsch. Boulder, CO: Westview Press.

Global Witness. 2002. *Deforestation without limits: How the Cambodian government failed to tackle the untouchables.* www.globalwitness.org/sites/default/files/library/Deforestation_Without_Limit.pdf.

———. 2005. An architecture of instability: How the critical link between natural resources and conflict remains unbroken. Policy briefing. www.globalwitness.org/sites/default/files/import/An%20Architecture%20of%20Instability.pdf.

Haavisto, P. 2003. Conflict and the environment: Lessons learned. *Environment House News,* no. 8:1–3.

Hauge, W., and T. Ellingsen. 1998. Beyond environmental scarcity: Causal pathways to conflict. *Journal of Peace Research* 35 (3): 299–317.

Haugerudbraaten, H. 1998. Peacebuilding: Six dimensions and two concepts. *African Security Review* 7 (6): 17–26.

Homer-Dixon, T. F. 1994. Environmental scarcities and violent conflict: Evidence from cases. *International Security* 19 (1): 5–40.

Kamphuis, B. 2005. Economic policy for building peace. In *Postconflict development: Meeting new challenges,* ed. G. Junne and W. Verkoren. Boulder, CO: Lynne Rienner.

Leighton, C. 2006. Firestone in Liberia rubber row. BBC News, May 24. http://news.bbc.co.uk/2/hi/business/5013830.stm.

Levy, M. A. 1995. Is the environment a security issue? *International Security* 20 (2): 35–62.

Martin, A. 2005. Environmental conflict between refugee and host communities. *Journal of Peace Research* 42 (3): 329–346.

Matthew, R., M. Halle, and J. Switzer, eds. 2002. *Conserving the peace: Resources, livelihoods and security.* Winnipeg, Canada: International Institute for Sustainable Development.

O'Lear, S. 2006. Resource concerns for territorial conflict. *GeoJournal* 64:297–306.

Paris, R. 2004. *At war's end: Building peace after civil conflict.* Cambridge, UK: Cambridge University Press.

Peluso, N. L., and M. Watts, eds. 2001. *Violent environments.* Ithaca, NY: Cornell University Press.

Pendzich, C. 2005. Remarks at the workshop "Building Partnerships to Reduce Forest Conflict in Asia," United States Agency for International Development, Washington, D.C., December 1–2.

Richmond, O. 2005. Peace and development: Strange bedfellows? *International Studies Review* 7 (3): 437–440.

Rogers, K. 1999. Sowing the seeds of cooperation in environmentally induced conflicts. In *Ecology, politics and violent conflict*, ed. M. Suliman. London: Zed Books.

Ross, M. L. 2006. A closer look at oil, diamonds, and civil war. *Annual Review of Political Science* 9:265–300.

Shambaugh, J., J. Oglethorpe, and R. Ham. 2001. *The trampled grass: Mitigating the impacts of armed conflict on the environment.* Washington, D.C.: Biodiversity Support Program.

Sundberg, J. 2003. Conservation and democratization: Constituting citizenship in the Maya Biosphere Reserve, Guatemala. *Political Geography* 22 (7): 715–740.

Torres Nachón, C. 2004. The environmental impacts of landmines. In *Landmines and human security: International politics and war's hidden legacy*, ed. R. Matthew, B. McDonald, and K. R. Rutherford. New York: SUNY Press.

UNEP (United Nations Environment Programme). 2000. *UNEP Balkans technical report: Institutional capacities for environmental protection in Albania.* Draft. November. http://enrin.grida.no/htmls/albania/reports/tech/docs/tec_inst.pdf.

———. 2001. *Strategic environmental policy assessment—FYR of Macedonia: A review of environmental priorities for international cooperation.* Geneva, Switzerland. http://postconflict.unep.ch/publications/fyromsepa2001.pdf.

———. 2003a. *Afghanistan: Post-conflict environmental assessment.* Geneva, Switzerland. http://postconflict.unep.ch/publications/afghanistanpcajanuary2003.pdf.

———. 2003b. *Depleted uranium in Bosnia and Herzegovina: Post-conflict environmental assessment.* Geneva, Switzerland. http://postconflict.unep.ch/publications/BiH_DU_report.pdf.

———. 2003c. *Desk study on the environment in the occupied Palestinian territories.* Nairobi, Kenya. http://postconflict.unep.ch/publications/INF-31-WebOPT.pdf.

———. 2003d. *Desk study on the environment in Iraq.* Geneva, Switzerland. http://postconflict.unep.ch/publications/Iraq_DS.pdf.

———. 2004a. *Desk study on the environment in Liberia.* Geneva, Switzerland. http://postconflict.unep.ch/publications/Liberia_DS.pdf.

———. 2004b. *From conflict to sustainable development: Assessment and clean-up in Serbia and Montenegro.* Geneva, Switzerland. http://postconflict.unep.ch/publications/sam.pdf.

———. 2005. *The state of the environment in Somalia: A desk study.* Geneva, Switzerland. http://postconflict.unep.ch/publications/dmb_somalia.pdf.

———. 2006. *Progress report on the Capacity Building and Institutional Development Programme for Environmental Management in Afghanistan, 2003–2005.* Nairobi, Kenya. http://postconflict.unep.ch/publications/afg_PR_jan06.pdf.

———. 2007a. *Assessment of the legal, scientific, and institutional frameworks for biodiversity protection in the Republic of Liberia.* Geneva, Switzerland. http://postconflict.unep.ch/publications/liberia_biodiversity.pdf.

———. 2007b. *Lebanon: Post-conflict environmental assessment.* Nairobi, Kenya. http://postconflict.unep.ch/publications/UNEP_Lebanon.pdf.

———. 2007c. *Sudan: Post-conflict environmental assessment.* Nairobi, Kenya. http://postconflict.unep.ch/publications/UNEP_Sudan.pdf.

———. 2007d. *UNEP in Iraq: Post-conflict assessment, clean-up and reconstruction.* Nairobi, Kenya. http://postconflict.unep.ch/publications/Iraq.pdf.

———. 2009a. *Environmental assessment of the Gaza Strip following the escalation of hostilities in December 2008–January 2009.* Nairobi, Kenya. www.unep.org/PDF/dmb/UNEP_Gaza_EA.pdf.

———. 2009b. *From conflict to peacebuilding: The role of natural resources and the environment.* Nairobi, Kenya. www.unep.org/pdf/pcdmb_policy_01.pdf.

———. 2010. *Sierra Leone: Environment, conflict and peacebuilding assessment; Technical report.* Geneva, Switzerland. http://postconflict.unep.ch/publications/Sierra_Leone.pdf.

UNEP (United Nations Environment Programme) and UNCHS (United Nations Centre for Human Settlements). 1999. *The Kosovo conflict: Consequences for the environment and human settlements.* Geneva, Switzerland. http://postconflict.unep.ch/publications/finalreport.pdf.

UNGA (United Nations General Assembly). 1987. Report of the World Commission on Environment and Development. A/RES/42/187. December 11. www.un.org/documents/ga/res/42/ares42-187.htm.

———. 2006. Progress report on the prevention of armed conflict: Report of the Secretary-General. A/60/891. July 18. www.ipu.org/splz-e/unga06/conflict.pdf.

UNHCR (United Nations High Commissioner for Refugees). 2005. *UNHCR environmental guidelines.* Geneva, Switzerland.

UNSC (United Nations Security Council). 2011. Report of the Secretary-General on the protection of Somali natural resources and waters. S/2001/661. October 25. http://unpos.unmissions.org/Portals/UNPOS/Repository%20UNPOS/S-2011-661%20%2825Oct%29.pdf.

UNSG (United Nations Secretary-General). 2010. *Progress report of the Secretary-General on peacebuilding in the immediate aftermath of conflict.* A/64/866–S/2010/386. July 16 (reissued on August 19 for technical reasons). New York. www.un.org/ga/search/view_doc.asp?symbol=A/64/866.

Medical and environmental intelligence in peace and crisis-management operations

Birgitta Liljedahl, Annica Waleij, Björn Sandström, and Louise Simonsson

Deployed personnel in peace and crisis-management operations regularly face an environment that has been negatively affected by the consequences of conflict (Waleij et al. 2005; UNEP 2009). Environmental challenges to such operations have three important aspects: first, potential environmental risks to the health of deployed personnel must be identified and mitigated; second, the overall operation must not cause further damage to the environment; and third, environmental drivers of the conflict or crisis, as well as potential flashpoints that may undermine mission security, must be understood.

Since 2001, the Swedish Armed Forces and the Swedish Defence Research Agency have collaborated on developing tools that facilitate medical and environmental intelligence and, more recently, analyses of environmental vulnerabilities, guided by the notion that environmental considerations and health protection for deployed personnel are two sides of the same coin.[1] This chapter provides a short

---

Birgitta Liljedahl is a senior medical intelligence analyst and project manager at the Swedish Defence Research Agency, specializing in environmental impact assessments and health hazard assessments in conflict and disaster areas. Annica Waleij is a senior medical intelligence analyst and project manager at the Swedish Defence Research Agency, specializing in environmental considerations for military operations. Björn Sandström is a deputy research director at the Swedish Defence Research Agency. Louise Simonsson is an analyst and area manager at the Swedish Defence Research Agency. This chapter is an elaborated reprint of a 2009 paper by Birgitta Liljedahl, Björn Sandström, Sture Sundström, Claes Nyström, Christina Edlund, and Annica Waleij, "Medical and Environmental Intelligence in Peace Operations and Crisis Management," published in the *Pearson Papers*. The authors would like to acknowledge the Swedish Medical Intelligence Network, the Swedish Armed Forces, and the Swedish Ministry for Foreign Affairs for providing research funds for further developing the environmental vulnerability assessment tool.

[1] Some of the geographical areas Sweden has studied include the Aceh Province in Indonesia (Waleij et al. 2005); Afghanistan (Berglind et al. 2002; Edlund, Liljedahl, Waleij, et al. 2004; Liljedahl et al. 2007); Bosnia and Herzegovina (Waleij, Edlund, Eriksson, et al. 2004); Burma, or Myanmar (Swedish Armed Forces Medical Intelligence 2008a); Chad (Swedish Armed Forces Medical Intelligence 2008c); the Democratic Republic of the Congo (Edlund, Follin, et al. 2003); Haiti (Liljedahl 2010); Kosovo (Edlund,

overview of developments within the field of Swedish medical and environmental intelligence and of one of the tools that has been developed, the environmental vulnerability assessment (EVA). The chapter proceeds with a brief discussion of how EVAs have contributed to decision making for Swedish peace and crisis-management operations, and concludes by emphasizing the need for participants in international peace and crisis-management operations to systematically share and coordinate environmental intelligence.

MEDICAL AND ENVIRONMENTAL INTELLIGENCE

Intelligence within the military is a product of a four-phase process: collection, analysis, processing, and dissemination. Intelligence activities are conducted at all levels, from tactical to operational and strategic, and may include a variety of areas of interest.

An overall intelligence assessment can be broken down into a number of components, including medical and environmental intelligence. Developers of each intelligence component conduct their business according to defined structures and functions. In Sweden, environmental intelligence is carried out within the broader framework of the Swedish Armed Forces medical intelligence component.

Deployed personnel may encounter multiple health risks that are not related to combat.[2] These include exposure to toxic substances like mold and asbestos, to chemicals and radiation in damaged civilian industrial facilities, to inadequate sanitary conditions, and to open-pit burning of waste (Waleij et al. 2006; Waleij, Göransson Nyberg, et al. 2011). The mission itself will add to the overall sources of potential hazard exposure, including jet fuel, petrol and diesel fumes, repellents, explosives, and munitions (Wingfors et al. 2007). In addition, personnel may encounter health risks from environmental conditions in the theater of operations, such as endemic diseases, naturally high dust levels, and extreme temperatures (Westholm et al. 2008; see table 1).

When an exposure hazard or health threat to deployed personnel is identified, it must be added to the physiological and psychological stress factors that normally affect a person before, during, and after deployment. All information related to such complex hazards will be of interest for medical intelligence purposes (Stricklin et al. 2007).

The size of a peace or crisis-management operation is likely to have both direct and indirect impacts on the local community. One challenge is to minimize the unintended environmental consequences of the operation, such as depletion

---

Engberg, Fahlander, et al. 2003); Lebanon (Eriksson et al. 2007); Liberia (Edlund, Liljedahl, Lindblad, et al. 2004); Moldova (Edlund, Follin, et al. 2004); Somalia (Edlund, Engberg, Liljedahl, et al. 2003); Sudan (Waleij, Edlund, Holmberg, et al. 2004); and Darfur (Swedish Armed Forces Medical Intelligence 2008b).

[2] Injuries that are not related to combat are sometimes referred to as DNBIs, an initialism for "diseases and nonbattle injuries."

Table 1. Spectrum of potential environmental health hazards for deployed personnel as human involvement increases

	Natural hazards (naturally occurring)	Human-made hazards (incidental)	Attacks with weapons (deliberate)
Chemical	– Fumes from a volcanic eruption – Smoke from forest fires	– Incidental chemical release or pollution due to failure of chemical storage or production facilities – Military or terrorist action that causes incidental release due to collateral damage to chemical storage or production facilities – Improper waste and hazmat management	Chemical weapons attack
Biological	– Endemic disease – Exposure to pathogenic microorganisms	– Antibiotic-resistant disease – Incidental release or pollution due to failure of biotech storage or production facilities – Military or terrorist action that causes incidental release due to collateral damage to biotech storage or production facilities – Improper waste and hazmat management	Biological weapons attack
Radiological and nuclear	– Background radiation – Low-level radiation from naturally occurring materials	– Incidental release or pollution due to failure of radiological or nuclear storage or production facilities – Military or terrorist action that causes incidental release due to collateral damage to radiological or nuclear storage or production facilities – Improper waste and hazmat management	Radiological or nuclear weapons attack

Source: Adapted from Senior Defence Group on Proliferation (2005).

of scarce natural resources, soil erosion, pollution, and chemical spills. Peace and crisis-management operations also generally have a major impact on the host economy by increasing the prices of local housing and accommodations and by placing demands on local producers for staple foods and materials, thereby putting such items financially out of reach for the local community (UNDPKO and UNDFS 2008; Hull et al. 2009).

Efforts to do no harm or build back better, sometimes referred to as a light-footprint or zero-footprint approach, are intended to mitigate these problems. They have resulted in environmental policies (UNDPKO and UNDFS

88 Assessing and restoring natural resources in post-conflict peacebuilding

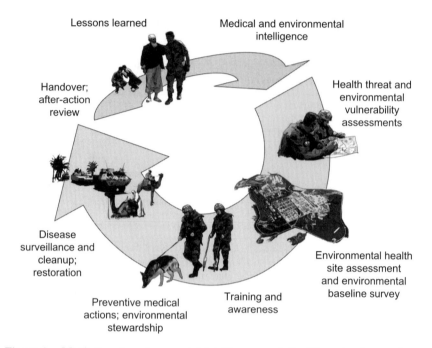

Figure 1.   Medical and environmental intelligence and the life cycle of operations
Source: Adapted from Bosetti et al. (2008).

2009), guidebooks (Bosetti et al. 2008), and concepts (NATO 2010) for military operations and decision making that raise the need for environmental intelligence as early as possible in the planning process and during each phase of the mission life cycle (see figure 1).

To enable evaluation of the full range of environmental issues that might affect or be affected by an operation, an EVA framework has been developed by the Swedish Defence Research Agency. This effort was initially funded by the Swedish Ministry for Foreign Affairs for the purpose of supporting the UN Department of Field Support. It was later implemented as a component of the Swedish Armed Forces medical intelligence framework. With support from the Swedish Armed Forces environmental research and development program, the EVA methodology is being further developed, with the aim of creating a transparent, coherent, and reproducible tool that can inform decision making throughout the life cycle of operations.

ENVIRONMENTAL VULNERABILITY ASSESSMENTS

The Swedish Medical Intelligence Network, which consists of the Swedish Armed Forces and the Swedish Defence Research Agency, has conducted some twenty EVAs so far for areas where Sweden is engaged, or might become engaged in peace or crisis-management operations. Examples include northern Afghanistan, Chad, Darfur, Haiti, and Lebanon. The results have been integrated with Swedish Armed Forces medical intelligence assessments.

The purpose of an EVA is to identify environmental vulnerabilities that should be taken into consideration if a peace or crisis-management operation deploys to a certain region. It is performed in a rapid manner at the outset of the intelligence process and is based on quality-assessed sources of secondary information and on field data when such data are available.

EVAs include an assessment of the causes of differential impacts, together with responses that will prevent, reduce, or offset adverse consequences. The main drivers of vulnerability are identified and then assessed to determine who and what may be exposed to hazards, and when the exposure is likely to occur. The level of sensitivity for each impact is analyzed, together with the capacity to cope with these impacts and other stresses.

The format of an EVA consists of a standard set of questions (see box) combined with an assessment form in a table format (see tables 2 and 3) and supporting maps and geographic information system (GIS) analysis. A color-coded system is used to score the vulnerability estimate for each of the assessment categories. The quality of the underlying data is also scored on a six-point scale.

As a basis for decisions about issues that are context specific and often require in-depth knowledge of critical factors, vulnerability estimates support prioritization and the highlighting of issues that may need immediate and further consideration. Vulnerability assessments should always take into account adaptation options and consider how mitigation could reduce vulnerability. Therefore the assessment should show the present vulnerability level, as well as the level the respective factors would attain after mitigation.

In some cases it is not possible to determine what the mitigation effects will be because of data and information constraints, general uncertainty, or connectivity complexity in time and space. Moreover, sometimes mitigation options are unrealistic or impossible to carry out. For example, in the process of urbanization, the driving forces often cannot be directly affected within the mandate of

Table 2. Assessment form and scoring system for environmental vulnerability assessments

Vulnerability estimate	Reliability of the source		Credibility of the data	
No observable	A	Fully reliable	1	Confirmed by another source
LOW	B	Normally reliable	2	Probably true
ELEVATED	C	Sometimes reliable	3	Possibly true
HIGH	D	Normally not reliable	4	Doubtful
VERY HIGH	E	Not at all reliable	5	Improbable
NA – Not assessed	F	Cannot be assessed	6	Truth cannot be judged

Questions to consider during an environmental vulnerability assessment

I. Environment and conflict relations:
- Is the conflict or crisis linked to environmental factors such as natural resources or environmental degradation? If so, how and to what extent?
- Are the key resources abundant or scarce?
- Is organized crime connected to any natural resources?

II. Institutional capacity and legal framework:
- How are natural resources linked to the war economy?
- Is corruption affecting key environmental issues and natural resource management?
- What environmental legislation, multinational environmental agreements, customary laws, or sending-nation environmental regulations are applicable?
- Does the receiving nation have environmental infrastructure such as water or waste management facilities? If so, are they operational?
- Are large-scale land acquisitions (also known as *land grabbing*) occurring? If so, is it being monitored or addressed?
- Are there transnational environmental concerns or conflicts?

III. Natural resources and environmental changes:
Environmental trends:
- What are the current and predicted future states of the environment and natural resources?
- What are the main relevant ongoing processes of change?

Climate and extreme weather:
- What are the main climatic characteristics of the region?
- What is the type, magnitude, and frequency of extreme weather events?
- What are the main climate change trends, and what are the main predicted concerns regarding future climate changes?

Water:
- What are the hydrological characteristics of the region?
- What are the total natural water withdrawal and recharge rates?

Land and soil:
- Does the region suffer from land and soil degradation?
- What are the current land uses?

Oil and minerals:
- Does commercial mining or oil extraction take place?
- Are there reserves of minerals or oil in the region that have not yet been explored?

Energy:
- What energy production and consumption patterns exist?

Forests:
- How much land is covered by forest?
- What types of forest are there and how are the forests used?
- Does the region suffer from deforestation? If so, to what extent?

Biodiversity and wildlife:
- What is the status of the terrestrial and marine environments?
- Are there protected or endangered species in the region?

IV. Cultural and historical resources and heritage:
- What cultural and historical sites of significance exist (for example, UNESCO* World Heritage sites, graveyards, and spiritual or sacred environments)?
- What key cultural practices exist nationally, regionally, and locally?

V. Socioeconomic and livelihood issues:
- What main livelihoods are permanently or temporarily pursued in the region?
- What are the main socioeconomic trends and their critical characteristics?
- What demography, urbanization, and migration patterns exist?
- What sectors and areas are undergoing rapid expansion?
- What is the situation with respect to gender?
- What is the nutritional status of the population?
- How vulnerable is the area to food insecurity?

---

* UNESCO (United Nations Educational, Scientific and Cultural Organization) administers the World Heritage Convention, which recognizes the world's exceptional demonstrations of natural and cultural diversity. See http://whc.unesco.org.

Table 3. Hypothetical environmental vulnerability assessment

Environmental vulnerability cutoff date June 1, 2011[a]	Vulnerability without mitigation	Expected vulnerability with mitigation	Reliability of the source	Credibility of the data	Comments
Environment and conflict relations					
Competition for natural resources	HIGH	ELEVATED	C	2	Scarce land, food, and water resources.
Illegal trade in natural resources	ELEVATED	LOW	A	1	CITES[b] violations.
Environmental crime	HIGH	LOW	A	1	Illegal off-coast dumping of toxic waste.
Institutional capacity and legal framework					
Legal framework	HIGH	ELEVATED	A	1	Environmental legislation exists but is outdated.
Monitoring and control	HIGH	ELEVATED	A	1	Lack of enforcement and monitoring capabilities; general environmental awareness low.
Illegal trade in natural resources	VERY HIGH	ELEVATED	A	1	Poor waste management infrastructure.
Natural resources and environmental changes					
Climate and extreme weather	HIGH	LOW	C	2	Total annual rainfall extremely low; climate change affects crop production, food security, water resources, human health, population settlement, and biodiversity.
Water resources	VERY HIGH	ELEVATED	B	2	Absence of usable fresh surface water resources; locally extreme arid conditions; saltwater intrusion near the coast.
Land and soil	HIGH	ELEVATED	B	2	Salinization caused by improper irrigation and drainage practices; soil erosion caused by excessive overgrazing and shrub clearing.
Oils and minerals	VERY HIGH	NA	B	2	Majority of commercial mining is for oil; production disturbed by conflict.

[a]The cutoff date is the last day in which information is transferred into intelligence for the purpose of assessing environmental vulnerabilities.
[b]Convention on International Trade in Endangered Species of Wild Fauna and Flora.

Table 3. (continued)

Environmental vulnerability cutoff date June 1, 2011[a]	Vulnerability without mitigation	Expected vulnerability with mitigation	Reliability of the source	Credibility of the data	Comments
Energy	HIGH	LOW	C	3	High energy consumption relative to other countries in the region due to cheap oil.
Forest resources	VERY HIGH	LOW	B	1	Widespread deforestation due to charcoal use.
Biodiversity and wildlife	ELEVATED	LOW	A	2	Sensitive and vulnerable ecosystems by the coast.
Cultural and historical resources and heritage					
Historical or cultural significance	ELEVATED	LOW	A	2	Rock paintings; five UNESCO World Heritage sites.
Religious significance	ELEVATED	LOW	C	3	Ancient graveyards.
Cultural traditions	ELEVATED	LOW	B	2	Local dress codes.
Socioeconomic and livelihood issues					
Urbanization	ELEVATED	NA	C	3	Desertification has accelerated migration to cities; many foreign workers present until recently.
Migration	VERY HIGH	ELEVATED	B	2	Internally displaced persons; induced development possible.
Gender	HIGH	ELEVATED	B	3	Gender-based violence; transit route for human trafficking to Europe and other regions.
Demography	HIGH	NA	B	2	Children are a large proportion of population.
Food security	VERY HIGH	ELEVATED	B	2	Short-term difficulty for food to reach vulnerable groups of people; medium- and long-term disruption to the markets from which farmers secure seeds and fertilizers, which threatens agricultural production and income generation.

the operation. In other cases, the vulnerability level can be reduced from very high to low—for example, if mitigation efforts such as actions to reduce deforestation are carefully planned and implemented.

IMPLEMENTATION OF EVA

Collected experience with and knowledge about environmental considerations in peace and crisis-management operations is considerable, but attention to environmental considerations in the planning and execution of peace and crisis-management operations is often insufficient (Waleij, Östensson, et al. 2011). In a few cases, however, EVAs have informed decision making prior to and during Swedish operations.

In 2007, the Swedish Navy deployed in support of the UN peacekeeping operation in Lebanon. The EVA that was performed in the planning phase of the operation identified areas along the coastline that had sensitive and vulnerable ecosystems, and the Navy then avoided those areas (Eriksson et al. 2007). In 2008 an engineering company was preparing to deploy to Darfur, Sudan, in support of a UN and African Union joint peacekeeping mission (Swedish Armed Forces Medical Intelligence 2008b). Because the EVA pointed out many critical environmental issues, a special predeployment training on environmental awareness was performed for the troops.

Later the same year, an amphibious company deployed to Chad in support of an European Union–led mission. The EVA had identified water scarcity as a major problem in the region, so the company was equipped with dry toilets rather than standard water-flushing toilet units (Swedish Armed Forces Medical Intelligence 2008c). In 2009, an EVA informed an environmental baseline survey in an overseas Swedish deployment and what environmental sampling to perform (Liljedahl et al. 2007). An environmental expert was also embedded in the mission.

SHARING AND COORDINATION OF ENVIRONMENTAL INFORMATION

Although the EVA model is finding its way toward implementation by the Swedish Armed Forces, there is to date no equivalent tool used by other peacekeeping bodies, such as the UN Department of Peacekeeping Operations, and no framework is yet in place for systematically sharing environmental information between international peace operation participants. Efforts are underway to improve assessment and information sharing within the UN–European Union–NATO peace operation community, and the UN Department of Field Support has initiated information sharing between UN peacekeeping missions, as well as between the missions and the department itself.

In multinational and multifunctional operations, general and mission-specific information regarding the environment is usually shared only on an ad hoc basis. Individual nations and military and civilian bodies may regularly conduct environmental assessments or monitor similar environmental risks without coordinating activities or sharing data with one another.

To address this gap, since 2004 Sweden and its partners have undertaken efforts to improve environmental and environmental health information exchange in peace and crisis-management operations. An international military-civilian platform was established in Umeå, Sweden, to address environmental and industrial health hazards (EIHH). It initially operated through biannual workshops, with broad participation from about twenty nations, the UN, and NATO. Within the framework of this collaboration, environmental health concerns in various mission areas were discussed, and the lessons were shared. The network included military and civilian personnel working at strategic, operational, and tactical levels, as well as researchers in a broad variety of disciplines related to environmental health.

Furthermore, in order to test the real-time sharing of environmental information, various pilot projects have been initiated to make medical, environmental, and environmental health information more accessible to key personnel in the field. Examples of such information include locations of industrial sites, data about environmental contaminants, and details about protected areas and cultural heritage sites. Ideally such information is geo-referenced to facilitate GIS integration. However, issues involving operations security and the protection of sensitive information present a key challenge.[3]

The successor to the EIHH network is a new results-oriented project: Effects of Environmental Conditions on Soldiers. The project, consisting of four phases from 2009 through 2012, is funded by NATO's Science for Peace and Security Programme. It was initiated by Canada and Sweden in Stockholm in June 2009, and in 2010 the United States joined the project as an additional partner.

The project calls for a broad-based commitment to the principles of environmental protection, force health protection, and global security, to be reflected in the policies and practices of the science, military, and civilian communities. Participants are from the fields of medicine, engineering, environmental protection, behavioral health, and CBRN (chemical, biological, radiological, and nuclear) research. The aims of the project are to develop a practical, comprehensive approach that combines medical, CBRN, engineering, and environmental doctrines and standards to create tactical best-practices guidelines for NATO operations; to increase interoperability among sending nations and between force health protection and environmental protection; and to reduce the gap between policy and doctrine, on the one hand, and tactical-level performance, on the other. The desired outcomes of the project include the publication of a comprehensive compendium of best practices for environmental health risk assessment, risk communication, and horizon scanning.

---

[3] Operations security is a process that identifies critical information to determine whether friendly actions can be observed by adversaries' intelligence systems and whether information obtained by adversaries could be useful to them, then executes selected measures to eliminate or reduce adversaries' exploitation of critical friendly information.

It is hoped that lessons from the international EIHH network and the NATO project can inform the development of new policies, doctrines, and operational strategies in the areas of force health protection and environmental protection. Ideally, a similar civilian-military network dedicated entirely to environmental considerations in peace and crisis-management operations will be established to mirror and communicate with its predecessors.

CONCLUSIONS

All peace operations and crisis-management deployments are specific regarding objectives, chain-of-command structure, and financial resources. The UN Integrated Mission Planning Process recognizes that each environment is unique, so every operation and mandate must adapt to a different context—form follows function. NATO and other bodies use a comprehensive approach that aims for a high degree of integration, coordination, and cooperation among the many types of participants involved in each mission.

The need is increasing for understanding the nexus between security, on the one hand, and environmental issues and natural resources, on the other. Robust and transparent tools can aid in the recognition of environmental drivers of conflict and potential environmental risks to human health, and they can improve the ability to predict and mitigate negative environmental impacts from operations. Moreover, an early understanding of the environmental drivers of conflict enhances the opportunity to identify and secure monetary and human resources for environmental actions within a mission.

To meet these growing needs, the gathering of environmental intelligence should be carried out as an iterative process throughout the life cycle of the mission. EVAs should be conducted at the outset of strategic planning and should inform the scope of the mission mandate and the budget. During the mission, the environmental situation should be closely monitored, and practitioners should develop EVAs into dynamic tools with a view toward continuously identifying new health risks to personnel, new environmental impacts from mission operations, and new sources of local conflict over natural resources. After the mission, the environmental risks and mitigation approaches should be documented and incorporated into an overall effort to identify lessons learned. Over time, environmental intelligence will produce basic information concerning countries, regions, and other specific fields to improve readiness for new deployments and to enable systematic comparisons among various regions and conditions.

Since the goals of the mission include doing no harm, building back better, and winning hearts and minds, the need for timely EVAs and appropriate environmental protection measures is paramount. Environmental effects may be both immediate and long-term, and operational risk management must balance the significance of these effects with wider operational imperatives.

To prevent overlap and to maximize information sharing and coordination among participants in peace and crisis-management operations, there is an urgent need to agree on the standards for environmental information systems and for data sharing. Assessment tools can improve interoperability in its widest sense: within and between nations, between military and civilian participants in a mission, and between scientists and operators such as planners and people working in the field. The EVA has been operational in the early intelligence phase for a number of deployments and has proved an efficient way to strengthen environmental and natural resource management on strategic, operational, and tactical levels in missions in Sudan, Afghanistan, and elsewhere. It has great potential to support the strategic end goal of the missions themselves and to improve opportunities for sustainable development.

REFERENCES

Berglind, R., C. Edlund, B. Engberg, B. Lagerkrantz, B. Liljedahl, A. Lindblad, L. Melin, B. Sandström, A. Tegnell, A. Waleij, and K. Westerdahl. 2002. *The Afghanistan study: Environmental and health risks.* FOI-R–0426–SE (2002). Umeå, Sweden: Swedish Defence Research Agency.

Bosetti, T., S. Clark-Sestak, C-G. Ebbhagen, S. Kajander, A. Kivipelto, B. Liljedahl, W. Nicholls, S. Olsson, Å. Scott Andersson, T. Schultheis, A. Sovijärvi, H. Uusitalo, and A. Waleij. 2008. *Environmental guidebook for military operations.* FOI-S–2922–SE (2008). Umeå, Sweden: Swedish Defence Research Agency.

Edlund, C., B. Engberg, T. Fahlander, B. Liljedahl, A. Lindblad, L. Melin, K. Persson, B. Sandström, A. Waleij, and K. Westerdahl. 2003. *The Kosovo study: Environmental and health hazards for military and civil deployed personnel.* FOI-R–0790–SE (2003). Umeå, Sweden: Swedish Defence Research Agency.

Edlund, C., B. Engberg, B. Liljedahl, L. Melin, K. Persson, B. Sandström, and A. Waleij. 2003. *The Somalia study: Environmental and health risks for international missions.* FOI-R–0788–SE (2003). Umeå, Sweden: Swedish Defence Research Agency.

Edlund, C., P. Follin, B. Liljedahl, A. Lindblad, B. Sandström, S. Sundström, and A. Waleij. 2003. *Congo DR, 2003: Environmental and health risks for international missions.* FOI-R–0651–SE (2003). Umeå, Sweden: Swedish Defence Research Agency.

Edlund, C., P. Follin, B. Liljedahl, A. Lindblad, A. Tegnell, L. Melin, M. Normark, B. Sandström, A. Waleij, and K. Westerdahl. 2004. *Moldova: Environmental and health risks for personnel to be deployed to Moldova.* FOI-R–1169–SE (2004). Umeå, Sweden: Swedish Defence Research Agency.

Edlund, C., B. Liljedahl, A. Lindblad, L. Melin, M. Normark, U. Qvarfort, B. Sandström, S. Sundström, A. Tegnell, A. Waleij, and K. Westerdahl. 2004. *Liberia: Environmental and health risks for personnel to be deployed to Liberia.* FOI-R–1181–SE (2004). Umeå, Sweden: Swedish Defence Research Agency.

Edlund, C., B. Liljedahl, A. Waleij, A. Lindblad, L. Melin, M. Normark, B. Sandström, S. Sundström, K. Westerdahl, and A. Tegnell. 2004. *Northern Afghanistan: Environmental and health hazards to personnel to be deployed to northern Afghanistan; pre-deployment assessment.* FOI-R–1287–SE (2004). Umeå, Sweden: Swedish Defence Research Agency.

Eriksson, H., B. Liljedahl, J. Sjöström, R. Berglind, M. Normark, B. Sandström, S. Sundström, J. Tegman, and A. Waleij. 2007. *EIHH and CBRN threat assessment of the*

Lebanese coastal area. FOI-R–2270–SE (2007). Umeå, Sweden: Swedish Defence Research Agency.

Hull, C., M. Eriksson, J. MacDermott, F. Rudén, and A. Waleij. 2009. *Managing unintended consequences of peace support operations*. FOI-R–2916–SE. Umeå, Sweden: Swedish Defence Research Agency.

Liljedahl, B. 2010. Environmental and health threat assessment: Haiti. FOI Memo 2988. January 16. Umeå, Sweden: Swedish Defence Research Agency.

Liljedahl B., M. Normark, B. Sandström, S. Sundström, H. Eriksson, and A. Waleij. 2007. *Northern Afghanistan: Environmental and health hazards to personnel to be deployed to northern Afghanistan, Version 3*. FOI-R–2222–SE (2007). Umeå, Sweden: Swedish Defence Research Agency.

NATO (North Atlantic Treaty Organization). 2010. Strategic concept for the defence and security of the members of the North Atlantic Treaty Organisation: Active engagement, modern defence. Adopted by Heads of State and Government in Lisbon. November 19. www.nato.int/lisbon2010/strategic-concept-2010-eng.pdf.

Senior Defence Group on Proliferation. 2005. Draft EAPC (DGP) guidelines on environmental and industrial hazards (EIH). Working paper. NATO/EAPC (DGP)WP(2005)0001-REV1. Working paper. May 30. On file with the authors.

Stricklin, D., B. Sandström, A. Waleij, H. Eriksson, C. Edlund, M. Normark, K. S. Westerdahl, A. Lindblad, R. Berglind, and B. Liljedahl. 2007. *Medical threat assessment models*. FOI-R–2302–SE (2007). Umeå, Sweden: Swedish Defence Research Agency.

Swedish Armed Forces Medical Intelligence. 2008a. Burma (Myanmar): Health threats, industrial hazard objects, environmental vulnerability. May 23. Stockholm: Swedish Armed Forces. On file with the authors.

———. 2008b. Darfur. January 28. Stockholm. On file with the authors.

———. 2008c. Medical hazards and environmental vulnerability for deployments to Chad. January 28. Stockholm. On file with the authors.

UNDPKO (United Nations Department of Peacekeeping Operations) and UNDFS (United Nations Department of Field Support). 2008. *United Nations peacekeeping operations: Principles and guidelines*. New York. http://pbpu.unlb.org/pbps/library/Capstone_Doctrine_ENG.pdf.

———. 2009. *Environmental policy for peacekeeping missions*. New York.

UNEP (United Nations Environment Programme). 2009. *From conflict to peacebuilding: The role of natural resources and the environment*. Nairobi, Kenya. http://postconflict.unep.ch/publications/pcdmb_policy_01.pdf.

Waleij, A., C. Edlund, H. Eriksson, B. Liljedahl, A. Lindblad, B. Sandström, and K. S. Westerdahl. 2004. *Hazards related to NBC or EIHH and PHC within Swedish AOR MNTF (N), Bosnia and Herzegovina*. FOI-R–1352–SE (2004). Umeå, Sweden: Swedish Defence Research Agency.

Waleij, A., C. Edlund, M. Holmberg, B. Lesko, B. Liljedahl, A. Lindblad, L. Melin, M. Normark, B. Sandström, M. Sedig, S. Sundström, and K. Westerdahl. 2004. *Sudan: Environmental and health risks to personnel to be deployed to Sudan, pre-deployment assessment*. FOI-R–1218–SE (2004). Umeå, Sweden: Swedish Defence Research Agency.

Waleij, A., H. Eriksson, C. Edlund, S. Sundström, M. Holmberg, B. Sandström, K. S. Westerdahl, R. Berglind, and B. Liljedahl. 2005. *Aceh Province: Environmental and health hazards for personnel to be deployed to the Aceh Province, Indonesia*. FOI-R–1730–SE (2005). Umeå, Sweden: Swedish Defence Research Agency.

Waleij, A., A. Göransson Nyberg, D. Stricklin, B. Sandström, and A. Hånell Plamboeck. 2011. *Feasibility study for human biomonitoring in peace operations*. FOI-R–3235–SE (2011). Umeå, Sweden: Swedish Defence Research Agency.

Waleij, A., M. Östensson, D. Harriman, and C. Edlund. 2011. *Greening peace operations: Policy and practice*. FOI-R–3112–SE (2011). Umeå, Sweden: Swedish Defence Research Agency.

Waleij, A., Å. Scott Andersson, C. Edlund, I. Svensson, and C. Nilsson. 2006. *Health risks associated with waste management in international operations*. FOI-R–1952–SE (2006). Umeå, Sweden: Swedish Defence Research Agency.

Westholm, L., A. Waleij, B. Liljedahl, and D. Stricklin. 2008. *Exposure to particulate matter to personnel in the Swedish Armed Forces international operations*. FOI-R–2533–SE (2008). Umeå, Sweden: Swedish Defence Research Agency.

Wingfors, H., K. Arnoldsson, D. Stricklin, B. Liljedahl, and A. Waleij. 2007. *Approaches for EIHH air sampling in military operations*. FOI-R–2299–SE (2007). Umeå, Sweden: Swedish Defence Research Agency.

Thinking back-end: Improving post-conflict analysis through consulting, adapting to change, and scenario building

Alexander Carius and Achim Maas

Almost invariably, natural resources are intertwined with violent conflict in multiple ways. They can be the cause of a conflict, they can be damaged during the conflict, or they can be a source of funding for those involved in the violence. In the post-conflict period, natural resources can sustain survivors and contribute to reconstruction. Consequently, natural resources must feature in any long-term strategy to rebuild societies emerging from conflict. Individuals and organizations working in post-conflict societies should consider natural resources in two key ways: first, to ensure that disputes over natural resources do not contribute to a relapse into conflict; and second, to maximize the benefits that natural resource management can have in post-conflict reconstruction. Thus, natural resources need to be included in the analysis and planning conducted in post-conflict situations regardless of whether that planning is undertaken by the peacebuilding, humanitarian, environmental, or business communities.

This daunting challenge requires integrating two complex and crosscutting issues—natural resource management and peacebuilding—at a time dominated by severe and immediate humanitarian needs, high political volatility, pressures to act quickly, and insufficient resources. In addition, reconstruction efforts often last for years or decades; thus, actions taken today may cast a long shadow. Just as post-conflict societies are dynamic in nature, the role of natural resources as a mitigating or contributing factor in violent conflict may change as well. For instance, prices of high-value commodities, which financed reconstruction work in the beginning, may vary significantly over time, thus undermining the reconstruction efforts. Accounting for such changes is another challenge in post-conflict societies.

This chapter argues that successful post-conflict assessment processes and methodologies involving natural resources need to consider three analytical tools: (1) consultation; (2) adapting to change; and (3) building scenarios based

---

Alexander Carius is the cofounder and codirector of Adelphi Research and Adelphi Consult. Achim Maas is a project manager at Adelphi Research. The authors would like to thank Irina Comardicea for many helpful comments and editorial support.

on the desired end state of the post-conflict transition. It concludes with specific questions related to the three analytical tools in an effort to identify and perhaps avoid relapsing into the violence that accompanies a fast-changing world.

ANALYTICAL TOOLS

A multitude of analytical tools are available that either focus on or include natural resources within post-conflict assessment.[1] In addition, several international aid agencies have attempted, with varying success, to develop approaches to link environment and peacebuilding.[2] All of the tools have a set of common features: they focus on identifying the causes and dynamics of conflicts, understanding how natural resources and the environment are related to these dynamics and (to varying degrees) to the broader peacebuilding process, and developing recommendations for peacebuilding interventions.

Consultation

Using analytical tools successfully requires dual ownership: first, by those who apply them; second, by the beneficiaries. The tools are typically applied by governmental agencies, international organizations, donors, or local nongovernmental organizations. In many cases, however, their staff members are burdened with multiple issues and limited resources. Understandably, they may hesitate to integrate yet another issue into their work (Carius, Tänzler, and Feil 2007). The beneficiaries, in turn, may have little awareness of the importance of natural resource management (Maas, Carius, and Wittich, forthcoming). Hence, tools need to include provisions for raising awareness, such as organizing consultative processes to disseminate knowledge, discuss and identify priorities, and widen the horizon of participants. Consultative processes can also give analysts the advantage of gaining a more nuanced understanding of the relevant context and the actors involved, while implementers and beneficiaries may gain innovative ideas from an outside perspective.

Many guidelines and frameworks, however, do not include provisions for conducting consultative activities or integrating results of workshops or surveys in their analysis.[3] If mentioned at all, they often serve as an additional source of information feeding into a larger report (GTZ 2007). It is rarely mentioned that the very participatory nature of workshops, consultation, and deliberation can make consultation an important instrument for improving ownership—and thus acceptance of analytical findings and recommendations.

---

[1] See Tänzler and Altenberg (2010).
[2] For an overview of several agencies plus an exemplary review of the European Commission's activities in this field, see Carius, Tänzler, and Feil (2007).
[3] See, for example, Goor and Verstegen (2000); CPR (2005); GTZ (2007); Hasemann, Hübner-Schmid, and Dargatz (2005); and NZAID (2008).

Identifying the needs of target audiences, how to engage them, and how to present findings should be paramount. Engaging audiences via stakeholder workshops, discussing findings with the participants, and developing comprehensive reports reflecting the key results and priorities may also improve the legitimacy of an analysis, as well as support the development of ownership.

Adapting to change

Analytical tools must also account for the dynamic nature of natural resources and post-conflict situations. Changing circumstances are inevitable, and analysis must be future-oriented. In a post-conflict situation, many forces can have an impact on the resource base: the restart of economic development; return of refugees and internally displaced persons who need shelter; population growth; and resource consumption resulting from reconstruction work. When analyzing the social, political, economic, and ecological contexts, these trends must be addressed so that scenarios can be developed for early identification and avoidance of potentially conflicting or mutually amplifying negative trends.

Analysis of post-conflict situations will be further complicated by climate change, which is likely to alter regional and local environments drastically, as well as redraw political, economic, and social maps. (See Richard Matthew and Anne Hammill, "Peacebuilding and Adaptation to Climate Change," in this book.) Research suggests this process is accelerating beyond what was imaginable only a few years ago, portending significant impacts in just a few decades (Richardson et al. 2009). But after a major conflict at least a generation is necessary for reconciliation to occur and the social contract to be renewed (Lederarch 2005). Thus, analytical tools need to support efforts to visualize the range of ways in which the environment may be significantly altered during a post-conflict transition. For instance, a resource that is abundant at the end of a violent conflict may become critically scarce a decade or two later. If tensions between former warring parties are not resolved, such a change may transform a formerly trivial resource dispute into a trigger for conflict.

This danger is not limited to climate change per se. The goal of limiting global warming to two degrees Celsius above preindustrial levels will require reductions of global greenhouse gas emissions of 80 percent and beyond, implying a radical and massive change from current modes of economic development and management of natural resources, particularly against the background of growing global population and resource demand. Integrating conflict-sensitive adaptation into post-conflict work will be critical in this context (Carius, Tänzler, and Maas 2008; Tänzler, Maas, and Carius 2009).

Building scenarios

Integrating the challenge of a dynamically changing environment will require a scenario-based approach that includes realistic projections of these changes and how they may affect the society in the future. It is imperative to outline, deliberate, and understand the likely shape of the world in which post-conflict reconstruction takes place. Actively integrating stakeholders into such a process is crucial and can improve their ownership and their awareness of environmental concerns. Doing so may support the following activities:

- *Goal setting*: develop an overall framework of goals to be achieved in a post-conflict transition process.
- *Decision making*: provide points of orientation for policy formulation and strategy development for an uncertain future.
- *Communicating*: promote exchange of ideas, disseminate information, and shed light on priorities and trends.[4]

Scenarios are understood here as coherent, structured descriptions of what a desirable future would look like for a post-conflict society. They do not envision an ideal world: the upcoming decades will present a number of interlocking challenges related to environmental change and natural resource management (B. Lee 2009). Thus, a scenario for a desirable future needs to be embedded within the set of anticipated challenges, such as climate change. The boundaries and the timescale of the scenarios need to be clearly defined from the beginning, and the scenario itself should be within a range of plausible developments. For instance, it is necessary to keep in mind those developments that can realistically happen within the proposed time frame. It is also useful to develop a set of alternative scenarios that explore, for example, whether a certain economic sector such as agriculture should remain predominant. When developing such scenarios, caution is necessary, for the post-conflict period is typically politically charged and highly sensitive.

There are a variety of methods to develop scenarios (Kosow and Gaßner 2008). In a post-conflict situation, a creative-narrative approach may be highly suitable: a group or several groups of people jointly develop scenarios in an open, transparent manner, for example via workshops. The result is a narrative with compelling storylines regarding what desirable futures may look like. The people involved should include government officials, experts, business people, and the proverbial "man on the street." Individuals and organizations facilitating such scenario building should provide input on key factors that may influence future developments, such as the potential impacts of climate change. This requires background research, including reviewing available scientific literature. It also involves interviews with experts and local stakeholders regarding how the respective national or subnational contexts have changed over the past years, and how they may likely change in the future.[5]

---

[4] Adapted from Kosow and Gaßner (2008).
[5] For an example of scenario building, see Steve Lonergan, "Ecological Restoration and Peacebuilding: The Case of the Iraqi Marshes," in this book.

Once scenarios are established, backcasting becomes necessary: identifying potential pathways to connect the desirable future with the present situation, including the events that need to happen to realize the scenarios, potential obstacles, and ways to overcome these obstacles.[6] The pathways themselves can be operationalized by defining milestones and indicators for assessing whether a post-conflict society is developing toward a desired future stage. The pathways may serve afterward as blueprints for planning peacebuilding interventions. Both the initial scenario development and the subsequent backcasting can be part of either a prolonged workshop or a series of events. Indeed, in cases of long-running conflicts and deep enmities, a slow process may be necessary, engaging a select number of figures from the parties formerly in conflict. Although scenarios may be disregarded as purely speculative at the beginning, they provide a starting point for discussion.[7]

The farther into the future a scenario looks, the more difficult it is to assess the interaction of different trajectories and trends, thus moving scenarios increasingly into the realm of speculation (J. R. Lee 2009). Despite being hypothetical, however, a well-developed, plausible scenario that offers a pathway for the next fifteen to twenty years may also highlight the need for sustained engagement. For two reasons, periodic reviews (either in the case of approaching milestones or within specific time intervals) will be necessary to assess the validity of the scenarios. First, as has been argued before, the world continues to change rapidly, and new knowledge and information needs to be integrated to assess whether the pathway to the desirable future is still possible. Second, the post-conflict society itself is changing continuously, and a reassessment can determine whether the desirable future itself is still valid.

Scenarios feature in several available guidelines, but in many cases are presented more as an add-on after the main conflict analysis is completed (Hasemann, Hübner-Schmid, and Dargatz 2005; NZAID 2008). The focus is often on potential best- or worst-case scenarios of a situation based on the analytical findings (Hasemann, Hübner-Schmid, and Dargatz 2005). This is exemplified by defining scenarios as "basically answer[ing] the question, 'What happens next?'" (CPR Network 2005, 18). Such an approach is limited in two ways:

- First, it emphasizes the present over the future. Achieving a future of sustainable peace, however, should be the aim of any post-conflict reconstruction process. The future—exemplified by the scenario—should be among the central elements of analytical tools in post-conflict situations. Thus, the

---

[6] For an overview and application of backcasting, see JRC (n.d.) and Future Foundation (2005).
[7] For an example of a slow process including the problem of "speculative problem-solving," see the informal Georgian-Abkhaz dialogue documented in Wolleh (2006).

question should not be, what happens next?, but instead, what should happen next?[8]
- Second, it omits the fact that global change processes and particularly climate change are transforming the context of a post-conflict situation (Maas et al. 2010). An analysis emphasizing the present may overlook the fact that the foundations of the analytical findings will change. The analysis as such becomes devalued.

Conflict analyses play a central part in identifying the key factors that will determine post-conflict transition. As such, they are highly important for developing scenarios by providing the necessary background. Indeed, the future can hardly be conceived without knowing the past (Lederach 2005). However, it is necessary to transcend this stage during a post-conflict transition and refocus the analysis toward the future instead of the present.

Aside from adding another layer of analysis, using a scenario- and future-oriented approach may provide an innovative avenue for environmental peacebuilding. Future threats of climate change are to some extent abstract and thus neutral. They can provide a platform for discussing common future challenges which is less politicized than the present post-conflict situation, including the need for joint action. If mediated by legitimate external actors, this provides a foundation for common action (Feil, Klein, and Westerkamp 2009). However, great sensitivity is needed in discussing this future. Groups which anticipate that the future will result in an adversely changed situation may today take steps to prevent such a future from happening. This may include, for instance, seeking to enhance their vital resources such as water which may today be abundant but may become scarce tomorrow.

CONCLUDING QUESTIONS

Analytical tools focusing on natural resources in a post-conflict situation should take into account the following:

- First, appreciating the nature of post-conflict situations and inherently focusing on the future by taking a scenario-based approach: What should the framework and baselines be for building a new society? What are the necessary building blocks to create such a society? What role do (or could) natural resources play?
- Second, taking into account the different internal trends—such as population growth and economic development—and external trends such as climate change: How resilient will a rebuilt society be to mediate disputes peacefully, internally and externally? What will such a world look like a generation into

---

[8] Several tools do advise developing actions that help a best-case scenario come about (CPR 2005).

the future? Where is there potential for disputes over natural resources, and are there effective endogenous means of resolving these disputes?
- Third, capturing the perspectives and priorities of stakeholders by having strong consultative elements: Is the operational reality of those living and working in a post-conflict situation adequately reflected?

These questions may complement a basic conflict analysis and help to identify not only causes of violence but also reflect on ways to avoid the relapse into violence in a fast-changing world.

REFERENCES

Carius, A., D. Tänzler, and M. Feil. 2007. *Addressing the interlinkages between natural resource management and conflict in the European Commission's external relations.* Report commissioned by the European Commission's Directorate-General for External Relations (DG RELEX). Rotterdam, Netherlands: Ecorys Evaluation Consortium.

Carius, A., D. Tänzler, and A. Maas. 2008. *Climate change and security—Challenges for German development cooperation.* Eschborn, Germany: Deutsche Gesellschaft für Technische Zusammenarbeit GmbH.

CPR (World Bank Conflict Prevention and Reconstruction Team). 2005. *Conflict analysis framework (CAF): Draft report.* http://siteresources.worldbank.org/INTCPR/214574-1112883508044/20657757/CAFApril2005.pdf.

CPR Network (Conflict Prevention and Post-Conflict Reconstruction Network). 2005. *Peace and conflict impact assessment (PCIA) handbook.* http://reliefweb.int/sites/reliefweb.int/files/resources/8D6B8844543EE82F8525711F00607481-PCIA%20Handbook.pdf.

Feil, M., D. Klein, and M. Westerkamp. 2009. *Synthesis report: Regional cooperation on environment, economy, and natural resource management. How can it contribute to peacebuilding?* Brussels, Belgium: Initiative for Peacebuilding.

Future Foundation. 2005. Rural futures project: Scenario creation and backcasting. www.ncl.ac.uk/cre/publish/otherpublications/ruralfuturesprojectfinaldec05.pdf.

GTZ (Deutsche Gesellschaft für Technische Zusammenarbeit GmbH). 2007. *Peace and conflict assessment: A methodological guidance note for tailoring development cooperation to issues of peace and conflict* [Ein methodischer Rahmen zur friedens– und konfliktbezogenen Ausrichtung von EZ-Maßnahmen]. Eschborn, Germany.

Hasemann, A., K. Hübner-Schmid, and A. Dargatz. 2005. Using conflict analysis for developing recommendations on socio-political cooperation programmes [Konfliktanalyse zur Entwicklung von Handlungsoptionen für gesellschaftspolitische Kooperationsprogramme]. www.frient.de/publikationen-service/dokumente/library/konfliktanalyse-zur-entwicklung-von-handlungsoptionen-fuer-gesellschaftspolitische-kooperationsprogr.html.

JRC (Joint Research Centre). n.d. Backcasting. http://forlearn.jrc.ec.europa.eu/guide/3_scoping/meth_backcasting.htm.

Kosow, H., and R. Gaßner. 2008. *Methods of future analysis. Overview, assessment, and selection criteria.* Bonn: German Development Institute.

Lederach, J. P. 2005. *The moral imagination. The art and soul of peacebuilding.* New York: Oxford University Press.

Lee, B. 2009. Managing the interlocking climate and resource challenges. *International Affairs* 85 (June): 1101–1116.

Lee, J. R. 2009. *Climate change and armed conflict: Hot and cold wars*. London: Routledge.

Maas, A., C. Briggs, V. Cheterian, K. Fritzsche. 2010. *Shifting bases, shifting perils. A scoping study on security implications of climate change in the OSCE region*. Berlin, Germany: Adelphi Research / Chatham House / Cimera.

Maas, A., A. Carius, and A. Wittich. Forthcoming. From conflict to cooperation? Environmental cooperation as a tool for peacebuilding. In *Environmental security: Frameworks for analysis*, ed. R. Matthew and R. Floyd. Cambridge, UK: Cambridge University Press.

NZAID (New Zealand Agency for International Development). 2008. Conflict-risk assessment guideline. http://nzaidtools.nzaid.govt.nz/sites/default/files/conflist-risk-assessment-1306615_0.pdf.

Richardson, K., W. Steffen, H. J. Schellnhuber, J. Alcamo, T. Barker, D. Kammen, R. Leemans, D. Liverman, M. Munasinghe, B. Osman-Elasha, N. Stern, and O. Wæver. 2009. *Synthesis report for climate change: Global risks, challenges, and decisions*. Copenhagen, Denmark: University of Copenhagen. http://climatecongress.ku.dk/pdf/synthesisreport/.

Tänzler, D. and J. Altenberg. 2010. *EC-UN partnership—Strengthening capacities for the consensual and sustainable management of land and natural resources. A capacity inventory*. Berlin, Germany: Adelphi Research. www.undp.org/cpr/documents/conflict/United%20Nations%20Capacity%20Inventory.pdf.

Tänzler, D., A. Maas, and A. Carius. 2009. Adaptation of climate change in the character of conflicts and crises. *Die Friedens-Warte: Journal of International Peace and Organization* 84 (February): 73–92.

van de Goor, L, and S. Verstegen. 2000. Conflict prognosis: A conflict and policy assessment framework; Part two. The Hague, Netherlands: Clingendael Institute. www.clingendael.nl/publications/2000/20000602_cru_paper_vandegoor.pdf.

Wolleh, O. 2006. A difficult encounter—The informal Georgian-Abkhazian dialogue process. Berghof Report No. 12. Berlin, Germany: Berghof Research Center for Constructive Conflict Management.

PART 2

Remediation of environmental hot spots

Introduction

Environmental hot spots are sites whose conditions pose a serious risk to the health and safety of local communities. These conditions can be caused by the release of toxic chemicals during the bombing of infrastructure and industrial sites, by the presence of depleted uranium weaponry and landmines, or by the creation of vast quantities of rubble and waste during conflicts. Remediation of conditions at these sites can build confidence between communities, reinforce government legitimacy, and provide short-term employment for excombatants. These potentially important peacebuilding benefits deserve more focused attention. At the same time, it is important to recognize that hot spot remediation is especially challenging in post-conflict situations where laws and governance are weak, social relations are divisive, and capacity to handle hazardous waste is poor.

Severe environmental damage caused by conflict can have major implications for human health. In the first chapter of part 2, "Salting the Earth: Environmental Health Challenges in Post-Conflict Reconstruction," Chad Briggs and Inka Weissbecker argue that although the health impacts of wartime environmental destruction are commonly not obvious, the effects—as measured by morbidity and mortality rates—can persist for decades. The authors also discuss the cascading effects of environmental damage on social and political stability. The specific experiences they cover include the long-term effects of Agent Orange and other defoliants in Viet Nam; the environmental health impacts of landmines and cluster munitions in Iraq and Lebanon; and the linkages between water, sanitation, and health in refugee camps in Darfur.

Taking an in-depth look at United Nations Environment Programme (UNEP) remediation projects at environmental hot spots in the Balkans, Iraq, and Sierra Leone, Muralee Thummarukudy, Oli Brown, and Hannah Moosa draw lessons that will be useful for remediation efforts in other countries. In "Remediation of Polluted Sites in the Balkans, Iraq, and Sierra Leone," they focus on many of the considerations that environmental experts must take into account when conducting cleanup operations in post-conflict countries, including cleanup thresholds to be used, the involvement of local communities, disposal and transport of waste, and the building of new capacity for pollution control and cleaner production.

Depleted uranium, which is toxic to humans, is a component of conventional weapons in the arsenals of some countries and—when deployed—may present health and environmental risks following conflict. Mario Burger led field assessment teams to study depleted uranium in the Balkans and Iraq. In "The Risks of Depleted Uranium Contamination in Post-Conflict Countries: Findings and Lessons Learned from UNEP Field Assessments," he presents findings from that fieldwork. His chapter highlights the ways that depleted uranium behaves in the environment and discusses the main exposure pathways and risks. Burger concludes with detailed recommendations for post-conflict mitigation of risks resulting from the use of depleted uranium munitions.

Cambodia is one of the countries most heavily affected by the presence of landmines. Mine clearance operations there have had significant implications not only for safety but also for land distribution and peacebuilding. In the concluding chapter of part 2, "Linking Demining to Post-Conflict Peacebuilding: A Case Study of Cambodia," Nao Shimoyachi-Yuzawa examines the demining strategy and operations of Cambodia and draws lessons for connecting mine clearance to peacebuilding. In particular, she explains that Cambodia has developed a decentralized mechanism to set priorities and prepare land use plans for minefields. She demonstrates that participatory, bottom-up approaches to mine clearance and subsequent land use planning can be effective mechanisms for community reconciliation and local-level peacebuilding. If mine-cleared land is mismanaged, however, it can be grabbed by the elite and become a source of tension and grievance, thereby undermining peace at the local level. Therefore, Shimoyachi-Yuzawa recommends that mine clearance go hand in hand with land registration, titling, and land use planning.

Together, these four chapters highlight many of the key considerations and unique field conditions that must be taken into account when practitioners are identifying health risks and implementing hot spot remediation projects in post-conflict countries. The critical need to combine the technical aspects of remediation with the political aspects and with the needs of peacebuilding is one of the main messages from part 2.

Salting the Earth: Environmental health challenges in post-conflict reconstruction

Chad Briggs and Inka Weissbecker

Without a comprehensive understanding of the environmental and health challenges faced by post-conflict countries and regions, aid may be misapplied and vulnerable populations may be neglected. While economic and political benchmarks are often used to gauge the success of peacebuilding and reconstruction policies, the status of environmental and public health is often a secondary issue.

Environmental conditions and their links to public health remain understudied and inadequately addressed in post-conflict reconstruction (Feldbaum et al. 2006; Brown 2004). Armed conflicts destroy large tracts of land and consume enormous resources, which are often deliberately targeted to undercut the ability of combatants to fight or communities to rebuild. Displaced populations place new pressures on available resources, directly and indirectly causing risks to health.

This chapter reviews the often complex interconnections between environment and health in post-conflict countries. Following a summary of the general health effects of armed conflict and challenges to data collection, examples of environmental health risks in Viet Nam, Iraq and Kuwait, Lebanon, and Sudan are presented. The chapter concludes with suggestions for post-conflict needs assessments and linking public health efforts to peacebuilding.

CONFLICT, ENVIRONMENT, AND PUBLIC HEALTH LINKAGES

There has been much discussion over the past two decades of the connection between the environment and conflict. Tales of a great flood in the Old Testament and the Epic of Gilgamesh may have been based on abrupt climate shifts that changed the course of the Euphrates River around 3200 BC, prompting a series of internecine wars between the Akkadian and Sumerian cities of the region. Following the Third Punic War in Carthage (149–146 BC), Roman troops

---

Chad Briggs holds the Minerva Chair of Energy and Environmental Security in the U.S. Air Force. Inka Weissbecker is the global mental health and psychosocial advisor at the International Medical Corps.

destroyed their enemies' agricultural land by salting it (Ridley 1986). Warring parties barracked troops in the winter and timed conflicts to precede monsoon seasons and severe weather (Essberger 1995). The acclimation difficulties and tropical diseases suffered by European crusaders in the medieval Middle East prompted colonial powers to establish institutes to address tropical medicine (Crosby 2004). Recognition of militaries' impacts on the environment and environmental health resulted in the 1976 Convention on the Prohibition of Military or Any Other Hostile Use of Environmental Modification Techniques.[1] In 1999, the United Nations Environment Programme (UNEP) also established dedicated capacity to conduct post-conflict environmental assessments to identify risks to human health, livelihoods, and security.[2]

The direct casualties of conflict often overshadow the health effects of wartime environmental destruction. Yet measured in terms of excess morbidity and mortality, health impacts can persist for decades (Murray et al. 2002). The environment, natural or built, underlies public health risks, which interact with economic and social factors to create vulnerabilities in a community. Understanding the real health effects and perceived notions of injustice that perpetuate conflict is crucial to reconstruction (Briggs, Walji, and Anderson 2009; McDonnell 2004; Renner and Chafe 2007).

Direct effects of conflict on health understandably dominate second-order, or indirect, impacts. Armed conflict profoundly affects the physical and mental health of both combatants and civilians (Levy and Sidel 1997). Whereas 14 percent of all deaths were civilian in World War II, the proportion reached 90 percent in several wars during the 1990s (Garfield and Neugut 2000), partly because of the increased number of intrastate conflicts (World Bank 2008). Moreover, beginning with World War I, technology has played a greater role, in combat preparation and operations, affecting the environment and health—through toxicological and radiological impacts and direct destruction—far more than in the past. The total-war model has since been used to justify direct and indirect violence against civilians and destruction of civilian infrastructure.

The indirect health effects of conflict on civilian populations may take years to manifest and may be missed in post-conflict needs assessments (Harris 1999). The indirect impacts can result from destruction of essential infrastructure, including health care facilities and water supplies, transportation, and waste-management systems (Levy and Sidel 1997). Furthermore, widespread violence can affect the environment and natural resources by contaminating soil, food, and water. It can also disrupt livelihoods and leave behind unexploded ordnance (UXO). The destruction and contamination of natural resources can lead to food insecurity and water scarcity, as well as to malnutrition and food- or waterborne illnesses (Levy and Sidel 1997, 2009; Toole and Waldman 1997). Displacement

---

[1] See www.un-documents.net/enmod.htm.
[2] For more information, see www.unep.org/conflictsanddisasters/.

of people creates new settlement patterns and overwhelms built environments that are generally unable to cope with increased demands for food, hygiene, and sanitation.

For every combatant killed, it is estimated that one civilian is killed directly and eight more die from lack of food, clean water, shelter, and health care (Murray and Lopez 1996). Although the ratio of indirect to direct conflict-related deaths has frequently been estimated to be nine to one (Levy and Sidel 1997), an empirical basis for the approximation has not been established (Murray et al. 2002).

Even higher numbers of individuals suffer the nonfatal, long-term consequences of conflict, including injuries, physical and mental illnesses, and disabilities (Murray et al. 2002; Levy and Sidel 2009; Pedersen 2002). Christopher J. L. Murray and Alan D. Lopez estimated that nonfatal outcomes of conflict have resulted in 4.8 million disability-adjusted life years (DALYs) lost worldwide, about the same number of years lost due to fires and more than half those lost due to road-traffic injuries (Murray and Lopez 1996).[3] By 2020, conflict is expected to be one of the top ten causes of DALYs lost (Murray and Lopez 1996).

CASE STUDIES OF THE ENVIRONMENTAL AND HEALTH IMPACTS OF CONFLICT

Understanding public health risks from environmental degradation caused by conflict requires pre-conflict, or baseline, and post-conflict data in order to identify trends and major risk factors (Liljedahl et al. 2010). Case studies of the direct and indirect environmental and health risks identified in Viet Nam, Iraq and Kuwait, Lebanon, and Sudan, as well as responses and associated challenges, illustrate the importance of gathering and evaluating reliable data.

Viet Nam

Conflict began with the Japanese occupation of French Indochina in 1940. Clashes with French colonial forces erupted in the 1950s, and more intense fighting against U.S. military forces followed from the early1960s until the U.S. withdrawal in 1973. Hostilities between North and South Viet Nam lasted until 1975 and between reunified Viet Nam and Cambodia until 1979. The direct health impacts of the wars are well documented, but the long-term effects have been difficult to analyze. Total military and civilian casualties numbered in the millions, and millions of Vietnamese were internally displaced or made refugees (Allukian and Atwood 2000). Reconstruction has taken many years, and the environmental health legacy of the conflict, from chemical defoliants used by the U.S. military to UXO, has not been fully addressed.

---

[3] DALY is a measure of overall disease burden, expressed as the number of years lost due to ill health, disability, or early death.

114 Assessing and restoring natural resources in post-conflict peacebuilding

Chemical defoliants

American military leaders approved use of defoliants by the U.S. Air Force because North Vietnamese insurgents used the thick, tropical forest to lie in ambush against U.S. and Army of the Republic of (South) Viet Nam forces. The chemicals thinned the forest cover, reducing surprise attacks; opened up fire zones in communist-allied areas of the rural South, especially in the Mekong Delta; and destroyed food supplies of insurgent forces and their sympathizers. Over 72 million liters of chemicals were sprayed over Viet Nam between 1962 and 1971, exposing approximately 17 million people in South Viet Nam, as part of Operation Ranch Hand. The defoliants, and particularly Agent Orange (named for the identifying stripe on the barrel in which it was delivered), belonged to a larger family of chemicals that often contained the active ingredient 2,4,5-T, a teratogen (an agent that causes developmental abnormalities). Many of the mixes also had 2,3,7,8-TCDD (dioxin) as a by-product, a more controversial chemical that the U.S. Environmental Protection Agency did not list as a probable carcinogen until 1992 (U.S. EPA 2001; Nguyen 2009).

The ecological damage to Viet Nam was acute: up to half of South Viet Nam's commercial hardwood forests and mangrove forests were destroyed (Zierler 2011). Ecosystems were severely affected, and food production was sharply curtailed. The public health impacts were less well documented, but attention to the chemicals' adverse effects finally resulted from political pressure exerted by American veterans concerned about their exposure during their tours of duty. After long and contentious debate in the United States, they won compensation under the Agent Orange Act of 1991 (Palmer 2005). But Vietnamese not living on U.S. territory have received no direct compensation from the U.S. government. In 2000, the Vietnamese government established the Agent Orange Central Payments Programme, which provided monthly payments between US$3.40 and US$7.14 to adults and children suffering from spina bifida and related ailments. However, program funds are insufficient for the approximately over 1 million Vietnamese affected, and the health impacts of Agent Orange continue to drain the economy and family incomes (Nguyen 2009; Palmer 2005). Food production and ecosystem health have not recovered fully because foliage remains damaged and UXO prevents farming in some areas.

Unexploded ordnance

Viet Nam is extensively contaminated by UXO, primarily artillery shells, aerial bombs, and landmines. Although not traditionally considered an environmental risk, UXO fits the definition of a contaminant and is considered a key environmental health issue by the U.S. military (U.S. AEC 1999). Between 1975 and 2009, approximately 42,000 Vietnamese were killed by landmines, and many times more suffered severe injuries. Some 6.5 million hectares—nearly 20 percent of the total land area—remain contaminated with UXO (VVAF and BOMICEN 2009). Although over 4 million landmines and bombs have been cleared since 1975, 600,000 tons of UXO, including landmines, remain. As of 2010, the UN Children's Fund (UNICEF) and the Vietnam Veteran's Association of America have each donated US$10 million to mine clearance, and the U.S. government has contributed US$42 million. Because removal of a single mine can cost up to US$1,000, large-scale clearance is cost prohibitive. Thirty years after the conflict, Vietnamese are still exposed to UXO, and agricultural land remains fallow (VVAF and BOMICEN 2009).

Responses

By the end of the 1970s, UXO and chemical contamination posed enormous difficulties for environmental and health management in Viet Nam. In 1975, many

Western nations, led by the United States, imposed sanctions on Viet Nam, largely cutting the country off from the rest of the world for two decades. Soon after, Viet Nam lost Chinese patronage following disputes over Cambodia. International scientists had little access for many years, and Vietnamese scientists and physicians were not privy to peer-reviewed literature on dioxin or environmental management techniques. Agent Orange remained unstudied in Viet Nam, although anecdotal reports from Vietnamese led to common understanding of the developmental health risks. Likewise, the Vietnamese government, lacking means to remove landmines, left either large areas of the country off-limits or allowed residents to face continued risk of death and injury.

Both concerns were compounded by actions of the Vietnamese government and demographic shifts. Many Vietnamese fled from North Viet Nam after the 1954 peace talks; many more fled from rural areas to avoid fighting, which included B-52 bomber strikes that left large rural areas uninhabited (Allen 2001). After 1975, the Vietnamese government forced millions to relocate in a deliberate attempt to break up communities and encourage them to adopt communist teachings. Millions more left Viet Nam in the 1970s. In total, some 5 million Vietnamese (although the number may count people multiple times) became refugees or internally displaced persons (IDPs). Once population shifts occurred, land use patterns shifted drastically. Traditional land management ceased because of relocation and loss of property rights.

It is impossible to determine exactly how environmental issues affected health, especially in a country where monitoring of both issues was quite weak. Yet the conflict left Viet Nam and its people more vulnerable to conflict-specific and environmental health risks.

In June 2011, the United States and Viet Nam announced a limited joint environmental cleanup program. The US$32 million project will remove dioxin from twenty-nine hectares of land at the Da Nang air base, where chemical levels are 300 to 400 times higher than international guidelines. Two other former U.S. air bases in the southern locations of Bien Hoa and Phu Cat (located near Qui Nhon) have also been identified for cleanup of soil and groundwater contamination (AP 2011). The United States and Viet Nam hope that the measures will be the first phase of a larger effort to reduce the risks to public health left by the conflict.

Iraq and Kuwait

The cumulative environmental impacts and health risks caused by the war between Iran and Iraq in the 1980s, the 1990–1991 Gulf War (Desert Storm), subsequent UN sanctions, the U.S.-led invasion of Iraq in 2003, and the ensuing insurgency are complicated and extremely difficult to unravel. Fully assessing the environmental conditions in Iraq has been overshadowed by political events and continued violence. In 2005, UNEP reported that destroyed or abandoned industrial sites in Iraq had become environmental hot spots (areas of severe contamination);

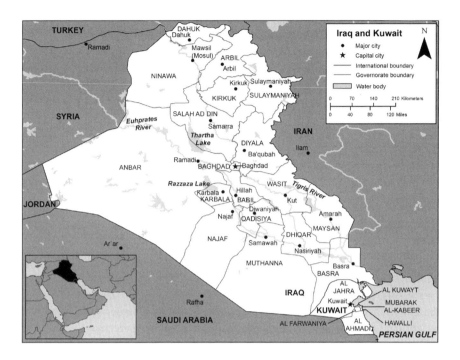

however, due to lack of access, UNEP could not assess other long-term structural and indirect environmental impacts.

Oil spills and fires

Deliberate actions during Desert Storm created human and ecological health risks. As they retreated from Kuwait, Iraqi forces deliberately opened oil pipelines into the Gulf, destroyed drill heads in advance of allied forces, and sank oil freighters in the harbor of Kuwait City. Off Kuwait's coast, two oil slicks merged to cover 2,000 square kilometers (km^2) (Readman et al. 1996), the largest-ever marine oil spill. The oil damaged ecologically sensitive regions off the coasts of Kuwait and Bahrain and mangrove forests in Saudi Arabia; however, the long-term effects of the spill to the region remain unclear. Earthworks to deter movement of invading allied vehicles and destruction of Kuwait's main sewage treatment plant further damaged the environment (UNEP 1993).

The oil fires started when Iraqi military forces detonated explosives on the oil heads of some 700 oil wells (igniting more than 600) across Kuwait and southern Iraq to provide cover, destroy infrastructure, and deny Kuwait and its allies access to oil (UNEP 2003). Dark smoke and soot affected human health in Kuwait and other Gulf states and weather as far away as India. Daily, the smoke carried approximately 50,000 tons of sulfur and 100,000 tons of carbon, significantly increasing the risk of respiratory illness (Campbell, MacKinnon, and Stevens 2010).

Depleted uranium

The 1990–1991 Gulf War was one of the first known conflicts that employed widespread use of depleted uranium (DU) ammunition. Since that time, DU's military merits have been seriously debated, but its long-term health effects have remained largely unstudied. DU was used in antitank rounds, particularly in the 30-millimeter cannon shells fired by U.S. Air Force A-10 attack bombers, whose cannons were capable of firing high-explosive incendiary rounds at 3,900 rounds per minute. It was also used extensively in U.S. Army M1A1 tank armor.

During the 1990–1991 Gulf War, allied (mostly U.S.) forces used over 350 tons of DU, primarily in army and air force antitank shells (U.S. DOD 2000). During the 2003 invasion, an estimated 1,000 tons of DU munitions were fired, usually on cities (U.S. DOD 2000). DU tends to disintegrate on impact, creating oxidized particles that can be absorbed over time.[4] The amount of these particles, or aerosols, that are released depends largely on the type of surface with which the munitions make impact. If the round connects with a harder surface, such as an armored vehicle or a building, a significantly higher percentage of the DU will be released as aerosols than if the round misses its target or strikes a softer surface (Hindin, Brugge, and Panikkar 2005). Medical reports and epidemiological evidence from Iraq and Kuwait suggest a strong connection between contaminated areas and developmental abnormalities in children, although, like Agent Orange in Viet Nam, strong causality is difficult to substantiate (Hindin, Brugge, and Panikkar 2005).

The U.S. Department of Defense claims that DU use in Iraq and Kuwait has not significantly threatened human health. Consequently, it does not feel legally obligated to fund cleanup or compensate those who claim DU has affected their health. Unlike landmines, the geographic range and the unclear exposure-risk relationship can make costs of cleanup high and responsibility for assistance to those harmed uncertain (Arfsten et al. 2006; Graham-Rowe 2003; Marshall 2008). Although operating in a conflict zone, like Iraq, and gathering reliable data on the DU discharged into the environment can be challenging, conducting assessments of potential contamination sites is possible if the parties involved in the conflict provide data on the amount and geographic distribution of the DU ammunition discharged. While the United States has not been forthcoming in

---

[4] According to a study by Rita Hindin, Doug Brugge, and Bindu Panikkar, "normally 10–35% and up to 70% of the DU is estimated to be aerosolized on impact or when DU catches fire. Most of the dust particles are reported to be smaller than 5 μm in size, i.e., of a size to be inhaled or ingested by humans. They usually remain windborne for an extended time. There is empirical documentation that DU aerosols can travel up to 26 miles and theoretical documentation that they can travel further" (Hindin, Brugge, and Panikkar 2005, 2).

providing this data for Iraq, UNEP has undertaken such surveys in southern Iraq (based upon information provided by the United Kingdom) as well as in other post-conflict situations.[5]

Unexploded ordnance

UXO from landmines and other explosive devices poses an environmental and health hazard throughout Iraq. Since conflicts in the early 1960s, artillery shells and cluster munitions have contaminated 1,718 km² in Iraq. Another 6,370 km² are largely off-limits due to approximately 25 million landmines and 8 million unexploded remnants of cluster bombs (Dolan and Hussein 2009; IMMAP 2006). In 2008, responsibility for cleanup was turned over to the Iraqi Ministry of Environment. In 2009, it described the UXO problem as the country's single biggest environmental problem, one it lacked the resources to handle.

The Mines Advisory Group reported 932 deaths and 1,512 injuries from landmines and UXO in 1991 (Carstairs 2001). Risk of injury or death has continued since, especially in the northern, Kurdish parts of the country and along the Iran-Iraq border. Regions near Basra and on the southern borders are heavily contaminated, often with cluster munitions, which may account for over 20 percent of injuries among children. Injuries to livestock are thought to be much higher and impose significant costs on farmers, although reliable records do not exist (Schreuder 2009). Insurgent or terrorist groups routinely incorporate UXO in improvised explosive devices, which they use against international forces and civilians.

Complete removal of UXO from Iraq will require resources beyond the limited funding and expertise of the UN, United States, Iraq, or nongovernmental organizations. By 2005, removal programs decreased sharply because of inadequate funding and security concerns. The Iraqi government acceded to the UN Convention on the Prohibition of the Use, Stockpiling, Production and Transfer of Anti-Personnel Mines and on Their Destruction (the Ottawa Convention) in August 2007.[6] Yet at the present rate of removal, Iraq will be unable to meet its legal obligation to be mine free by 2018. With current manpower and funding, landmines could remain an issue for the next seventy years. Many areas of the country remain uninhabitable, and reconstruction projects (such as a water treatment plant in Basra) have been postponed because of UXO. Up to 15 percent of the residents have been injured or killed as a result of landmines or cluster munitions (IWPR 2009).

Water and infrastructure

Water was scarce prior to the conflicts between Iraq and Iran, and irrigation already limited the availability of freshwater. The salinity of irrigation water now

---

[5] For a more detailed discussion, see Mario Burger, "The Risks of Depleted Uranium Contamination in Post-Conflict Countries: Findings and Lessons Learned from UNEP Field Assessments," in this book.
[6] For the convention, see www.apminebanconvention.org/overview-and-convention-text/.

approaches 2,000 parts per million by the time it reaches the Gulf (Ryan 2009). Other factors, such as climate variability and drought, increased food demand, changing land use patterns, and increased upstream use of water, have resulted in chronic water shortages that adversely affect ecosystems (especially riparian areas), food security, and water quality (U.S. DIA 1991). Food production has dropped dramatically; once a substantial exporter of wheat, Iraq is now one of the world's largest importers (Al-Ansary 2012). Malnutrition and vaccine shortages have contributed to outbreaks of measles and mumps. There were over 8,000 cases of mumps reported in the first half of 2004, a twenty-fold increase over 2003 (Peplow 2004).

Damage to environmental infrastructure, notably waste treatment facilities and water treatment plants, has compounded the lack of drinking water. Most sewage in urban areas is released untreated into rivers, and other areas have little access to working sewers or clean drinking water. Cholera outbreaks are routine because of inadequate access to drinking water and little investment in infrastructure (Ryan 2009). Of four major sewage treatment plants that operated in Baghdad before the 2003 invasion, not one remained operational by 2009. Displaced populations, in particular, have poor access to potable water and adequate sewage facilities. Most physicians have fled abroad, and curfews have hampered access to existing medical care. And notably, the insurgency was strongest in areas under severe environmental health pressure (Hill and Fittipaldi 2007).

Responses

Political, international development, and especially public health responses to the wars in Iraq have been largely uncoordinated. Allocation of authority to regional governments and earlier attempts by the Coalition Provisional Authority (CPA) to privatize many services left the federal government fragmented, unable to handle environmental management and health services effectively (Wilson et al. 2009). After 2003, Baghdad had little ability or jurisdiction to address health holistically; the Iraqi constitution did not empower the federal government to address cross-border threats to health. Many international organizations, including the UN, were unable to operate effectively during reconstruction, and insurgent attacks on infrastructure prevented delivery of environmental and health services to significant areas of the country.

The CPA's approach to governance relied heavily on free-market theories of response.[7] As a result, administration, enforcement of regulations, and prioritization of environmental and health needs suffered (Chandrasekaran 2007; Phillips 2005).

---

[7] Free-market theories of response hold that the reconstruction of Iraq can be achieved by simple and rapid privatization of state-run industries. Naomi Klein, with her so-called "shock doctrine," and Rajiv Chandrasekaran each have criticized the free-market approach in Iraq (Klein 2007; Chandrasekaran 2007).

Environmental health challenges in post-conflict reconstruction 121

Effective health policies require monitoring of environmental conditions and action in advance of emerging risks. There should be structures that disseminate information about risks, such as the location of UXO and ways to reduce risks; strategies for adaptation; and processes for redressing harm caused by hazardous environmental conditions. In post-2003 Iraq, most of the responsibility was left to individuals and communities, assisted by international organizations that often could not operate safely or lacked resources.

Lebanon

Lebanon endured sixteen years of civil war and violent conflict from 1975 to 1991, which damaged the economy and the public health infrastructure (Sibai and Sen 2006). Hostilities between Israel and the Lebanese Shiite militia Hezbollah

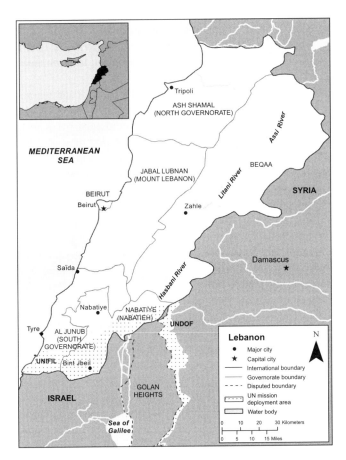

Note: United Nations Interim Force in Lebanon (UNIFIL) and United Nations Disengagement Observer Force (UNDOF) are UN peacekeeping missions.

continue on Lebanon's border with Israel, with clashes erupting in the summer of 2006 after Hezbollah forces kidnapped two Israeli soldiers. The conflict, which continued for thirty-three days until the UN brokered a ceasefire, caused over US$7 billion of damage to the economy and infrastructure of southern Lebanon (Mooney 2007; Darwish, Farajalla, and Masri 2009). More than 1,200 people were killed, and over 5,000 were wounded, mostly civilians (Sibai and Sen 2006).

Unexploded ordnance

Remaining cluster munitions and other UXO from past conflicts pose an ongoing threat, especially in southern Lebanon. Cluster munitions are designed to scatter and explode upon landing but often fail to detonate immediately, making them de facto landmines. Since 1975, mines and UXO have affected an estimated 150 million square meters (m^2) of land in Lebanon (E-MINE 2009). Approximately 4 million cluster munitions were dropped on southern Lebanon during the last days of the 2006 conflict, contaminating an estimated 48 million m^2, and approximately 1 million unexploded munitions remain (WHO 2009). By the end of August 2008, an estimated 30 percent of contaminated land remained uncleared (E-MINE 2009).

Two-thirds of the land contaminated by UXO is used for agriculture (Landmine and Cluster Munition Monitor 2009), which is the main source of income for 30 to 40 percent of Lebanese. Approximately 545 cultivated fields were damaged or made inaccessible by UXO. Farmers face death and disability but have few alternatives for making a living (Landmine and Cluster Munition Monitor 2009). Attention has focused, at the expense of agriculture, on the impact of the conflict on infrastructure, industry, and tourism (Darwish, Farajalla, and Masri 2009). Current and projected losses of agricultural production lie between US$22.6 and US$26.8 million (Crowther 2008).

Most of those killed or injured by cluster munitions are civilians, who engage in farming, herding, and collecting wood, as well as children, who find the brightly colored casings attractive. Cluster munitions are particularly dangerous because, unlike landmines, they tend to inflict damage on the eyes and brain (WHO 2009). They not only cause physical but also psychological disability and distress that require years of rehabilitation and support (WHO 2009). As of 2007, there were approximately 2,704 survivors of cluster bombs and landmine explosions living in Lebanon (Landmine and Cluster Munition Monitor 2009).

Responses

Since the 2006 conflict, most of the U.S. funding for post-conflict stabilization and reconstruction has been allocated to military, security, and humanitarian relief programs. Although there has been some U.S. support for demining efforts and water, sanitation, and health projects, fewer resources have been directed toward strengthening economic and social programs (Mooney 2007). In May 2007, the Lebanese government issued the National Mine Action Policy, which laid out principles and basic provisions for mine clearance, risk education, and, through the Lebanon Mine Action Center, mine victims' assistance. The policy aimed at ensuring medical, psychological, and economic support for victims of landmines and explosive remnants of conflict. It also supported activities to help victims regain full legal rights and reintegrate into society (LMAC 2007). Advocacy against cluster bombs and landmines has increased, resulting in the Convention on Cluster Munitions,[8] which was signed by ninety-four countries in December 2008. The convention, which has received strong support from Lebanon, bans cluster munitions and requires countries to destroy stockpiles within eight years of signing and to clear land contaminated with cluster munitions within ten years. Party states are also obliged to provide financial, medical, and psychological support to those affected by cluster munitions (WHO 2009).

After the June 2009 parliamentary elections, the U.S.-backed, predominantly Sunni, Christian, and Druze alliance retained control of the Lebanese parliament, and the United States sent aid to the Lebanese military for the first time in almost thirty years. With support from the United States and other countries, the World Health Organization, UNICEF, the International Committee of the Red Cross, the Lebanese army, and the UN Interim Force in Lebanon have continued to clear UXO, but more financial support is needed to complete clearance and give economic support and rehabilitation to those affected by UXO (E-MINE 2009).

Sudan

Sudan has been riddled with destabilizing violence and intertribal and ethno-religious conflict for all but ten years since its independence in 1956. Indeed, within its geographical boundaries, several conflicts have persisted simultaneously (Maitre 2009; Omeje 2010). They have been driven by many factors, including competition for political power; cultural identity; religious, ethnic, and tribal divisions; economic marginalization; and historical feuds (UNEP 2007). While not the sole triggers of conflict, the environment and natural resources, particularly oil and gas reserves, Nile waters, rangeland and rain-fed agricultural land, have been inextricably linked to all levels of feuding between the warring factions. Many of Sudan's conflicts have resulted from tension over the use of natural resources, and persistent conflict has, in turn, harshly affected resources. In all, an estimated 60 percent of the country has been directly harmed by protracted conflict (UNEP 2007).

North-South civil war

Sudan's North-South conflict, which started shortly after independence, came to an official end in January 2005 with the signing of the Comprehensive Peace Agreement between the northern-based National Congress Party and the southern-based Sudan People's Liberation Movement (SPLM).

---

[8] See http://treaties.un.org/Pages/ViewDetails.aspx?src=TREATY&mtdsg_no=XXVI-6&chapter=26&lang=en.

124 Assessing and restoring natural resources in post-conflict peacebuilding

Notes:
A – The Hala'ib Triangle is claimed by Sudan and de facto administered by Egypt.
B – The Abyei region's status is not yet determined (UNDFS 2011).
C – The Ilemi Triangle has been claimed by Ethiopia, Sudan, and Kenya and de facto controlled by Kenya.

While the North-South conflict started long before oil was discovered in central Sudan, competition for ownership of and wealth from the country's vast oil and gas reserves has been widely recognized as further fuelling and prolonging the civil war. Oil has fostered grievances in the South and has been used as a rallying cry by the SPLM, which charged the Sudanese government with exploiting the resources without benefiting local populations (Haysom and Kane 2009).[9]

---

[9] Most current oil production occurs in the disputed border areas between the North and the South, thus enhancing the strategic significance of these areas and severely complicating efforts to demarcate borders. Additionally, roughly 75 percent of Sudan's proven reserves of 6.3 billion barrels of oil lie in the South, but the only export pipeline that carries the oil to export terminals and refineries runs through the North.

During the civil war, the Sudanese government reportedly engaged in indiscriminate attacks on civilians to depopulate oil-rich areas and further develop infrastructure in partnership with foreign oil companies (Helly 2009). Chinese, Malaysian, and Indian oil investors faced mounting pressure from human rights groups and the wider international community, which were alarmed by the systematic mass killings and lootings by the Sudanese army and its counterinsurgency allies (ICG 2003; Richter et al. 2007).

Competition for benefits accruing from the use of surface water through the Jonglei Canal Project contributed to the 1983 resumption of the North-South conflict (UNEP 2007). Launched in 1980, the plan was to bypass the Sudd wetlands in Southern Sudan to more quickly capture water for downstream users in North Sudan and Egypt. Ultimately, however, the project lacked local support and acceptance and, as a result, sparked violent conflict between the government of Khartoum and the pastoralists, fishermen, and local communities. Tension over attempts to restart the project continues to run high (UNEP 2007).

Conflict in Darfur

For decades, rivalry between sedentary African farmers and nomadic Arab herders over grazing and agricultural lands and water has driven most local confrontations in Darfur. Deforestation, climate change, desertification, and declining agricultural productivity, as well as the rapid spread of deserts southward, have further devastated the dwindling natural resource base (UNEP 2007).

Until 2003, fighting was primarily confined to tribal and local conflicts. But in early 2003, hostilities escalated into a full-scale military confrontation across the three states of Darfur. The conflict, characterized by a scorched-earth campaign by government-sponsored Janjaweed militias, has resulted in mass killings, forced displacement of millions, and looting and burning of villages (Richter et al. 2007; Jaspars and O'Callaghan 2008).

Livelihood and environmental health impacts

While natural resources have significantly contributed to local tension, the protracted civil wars, in turn, have devastated the environment, resource base, and livelihoods of the people (Young et al. 2009).

The conflict has resulted in severe depletion of natural assets through looting or destruction, unsustainable coping strategies, loss of access, displacement, and restricted mobility. Conventional weaponry, such as bombs, artillery shells, and mortars, has led to cratering and has damaged or destroyed buildings, trees, and industrial facilities. Militias, particularly those in Darfur, have deliberately targeted vital natural resource–related infrastructure, such as rural water pumps, and have burned crops and pastures. Minefields, which have been abandoned without marking, continue to cause human casualties and impede access to large areas of land. Dumping waste on UXO, coupled with the impacts of deforestation and soil erosion, has rendered further tracts of land unusable for agriculture and grazing (UNEP 2007). Obtaining firewood increases security risks, and competition over firewood has led to further conflict between pastoralists and IDPs (Jaspars and O'Callaghan 2008). Lack of pasture and water and a shortage of vaccines have increased disease in livestock (Young et al. 2005). As in other cases, forced displacement has destroyed traditional natural resource management practices and cooperative agreements, as well as the social capital necessary for proper public health efforts.

Approximately 2 to 3 million people have died in the conflicts in Sudan—half a million in the Darfur conflict alone. Over 4 million people are internally displaced as a result of the decades-long conflicts, and an estimated 9 million continue to receive humanitarian assistance (UN OCHA 2010).

The health situation has remained grave, with high rates of preventable diseases such as tuberculosis, malaria, and diarrhea, as well as outbreaks of meningitis, measles, and cholera (Wakabi 2008). South Sudan has the highest maternal mortality rate in the world; skilled staff attend only 5 percent of births (Moszynski 2008). Food insecurity, lack of access to drinking water or sewage systems, and a severe shortage of qualified health care providers contribute to poor population health. Humanitarian relief agencies, which provide most of the health care, have difficulty accessing vulnerable populations because of the absence of infrastructure and persistent insecurity (Moszynski 2008). Inaccessibility of natural resources and food insecurity have also contributed to high rates of malnutrition and infant mortality; 31 percent of children in Sudan are underweight (UNICEF 2006). Continued displacement further jeopardizes health. Large numbers of people, increased violence and riots, risk of disease outbreaks, and high rates of mental disorders such as depression characterize IDP camps (Jaspars and O'Callaghan 2008; Kim, Torbay, and Lawry 2007). Oil extraction has also taken a toll on population health, not only by contributing to violence and conflict but also by reportedly contaminating soil and drinking water with saline water to maintain the pressure of oil reservoirs and dumping industrial waste without safeguards (Calain 2008).

Responses

Because of the humanitarian crisis, most donors have funded emergency aid rather than development (Moszynski 2008). However, addressing natural resource and livelihood issues is vital to finding lasting solutions to the conflict (Young et al. 2009). The 2005 Comprehensive Peace Agreement mandated that a joint technical committee of representatives from the national government and Southern Sudan evaluate contracts with social and environmental problems in mind. The committee was to plan for the consultation and participation of communities in the management of natural resources, specifically oil, as well as for equitable sharing of wealth (ICG 2006).

In July 2009, an international tribunal in The Hague redefined the borders of the disputed area of Abyei, and the government of Sudan and the SPLM accepted the tribunal award.[10] The new borders placed two major oil fields outside the newly defined Abyei area, and as such those oil fields reverted to Northern Sudan. The residents of the Abyei area, as defined by the tribunal, were supposed to exercise the right of self determination in a referendum, to be undertaken simultaneously with the referendum of Southern Sudan, to decide whether the Abyei area would be part of North or South Sudan. However, because of the failure of the government of Sudan and the SPLM to agree on who are the residents of Abyei area, the referendum did not take place on January 9, 2011, as planned. Consequently, violence erupted again in the run-up to South Sudan's formal independence on July 9, 2011. In May 2011, the government of Sudan accused the SPLM of masterminding the death of a number of Northern soldiers inside Abyei, and few days later the government took over the whole of Abyei.

Significant challenges remain in rebuilding public health infrastructure and aiding the return of IDPs and refugees across the country. Recommendations for recovery and reconstruction in Sudan include the development of alternative livelihoods and restoration of natural resources through reforestation, improved agricultural techniques, better water management, alternative fuels, and upgrading local capacity for natural resource management (Jaspars and O'Callaghan 2008; Hassan, Hertzler, and Benhin 2009). It has also been suggested that interventions around common goals, such as animal health, could provide opportunities for local-level conflict resolution by reestablishing relationships and rebuilding trust between conflicting parties (Almond 1990; Minear 2001). Furthermore, through better natural resource management, sources of the conflict, livelihoods, and food security can be addressed to improve human health.

CONCLUSIONS, CHALLENGES, AND SOLUTIONS

Environmental impacts and associated health risks are difficult to prevent during conflict and may affect survivors well into post-conflict reconstruction and development. Immediate post-conflict hot spots are often the focus of UNEP efforts and humanitarian response. However, the long-term risks, from persistent contaminants, destroyed infrastructure, and degraded natural resources, are equally important to address during peacebuilding. Therefore, peacebuilding practitioners must understand that health and environment are related, based not only on exposure to contaminants but also on how effectively livelihoods and resources are managed in order to reduce disease, increase food security, and mitigate exposure to disasters.

Reliable data are one of the greatest challenges to successfully addressing environmental impacts and public health risks. During and after armed conflict, gathering data on mortality and morbidity is difficult because of the breakdown of infrastructure and health systems and political motivations in obscuring data

---

[10] For more information, see Salman (2012).

or preventing access to the field. Direct conflict-related deaths are difficult to measure from household surveys, census data, government reports, and press coverage, and indirect deaths and nonfatal consequences of conflict are even more difficult to quantify (Murray et al. 2002). Baseline data on environmental conditions are frequently unavailable or unreliable.

New approaches to gathering data are emerging, including surveying family health when gathering household data on mortality (Murray et al. 2002) and rapid environmental assessments (Liljedahl et al. 2010). But more research and monitoring are needed to document the effects of conflict on public health (Utzinger and Weiss 2007), including indirect effects through environmental factors. Madelyn H. Hicks and Michael Spagat suggest calculating a "dirty war index" using data on prohibited and unacceptable combat outcomes, including civilian deaths, torture, disappearances, and use of prohibited or indiscriminate weapons such as antipersonnel landmines (Hicks and Spagat 2008). The index would also account for the destruction of hospitals, as well as food and water infrastructure and resources. Because assessing the consequences of conflict falls within several fields, political scientists, environmental managers, and public health researchers must collaborate more closely (Murray et al. 2002).

Another challenge is finding ways to connect protecting public health to peacebuilding. Fortunately, the links have been increasingly recognized. In 1980, the Pan American Health Organization coined the phrase "health as a bridge to peace," which the 51st World Health Assembly formally accepted in 1998 as a feature of its Health for All in the 21st Century strategy (PAHO 1988; Loretti, Leus, and Van Holsteijn 2001). Furthermore, "peace through health" has been proposed as a new way to investigate "the downward spiral of war and disease and the positive symbiosis of peace and health" (MacQueen et al. 2001, 1460). "Health-peace initiatives" intend to "improve the health of a population and to simultaneously heighten [a] population's level of peace and security" (MacQueen and Santa-Barbara 2000, 293).

Health-peace initiatives can promote dialogue by identifying population health as a superordinate goal upon which conflicting parties and stakeholders can agree (Santa-Barbara and MacQueen 2004). Peace through health has had some success in countries such as El Salvador, the Democratic Republic of the Congo, and Afghanistan, where UNICEF and others have negotiated ceasefires during "days of tranquility" to vaccinate children (Weekes and Teagle 1991; Tangermann et al. 2000; MacQueen et al. 2001). Health personnel from conflicting sides can also be engaged in joint health training, programming, and service-delivery initiatives, such as a project involving Israeli and Palestinian health professionals (Skinner et al. 2005).

Collaboration among formerly conflicting parties on environmental cleanup efforts may also build trust and counteract dehumanization of the other side (Winter and Cava 2006; Conca and Dabelko 2002). Environmental grants could be made conditional on contending parties' working together on a project (MacQueen and Santa-Barbara 2000). Peace-through-health initiatives show some promise but need to be subjected to more careful empirical analysis and investigation (MacQueen and Santa-Barbara 2000; Santa-Barbara and MacQueen 2004; MacMahon and Arya 2004). Several authors have begun to develop frameworks to aid development and evaluation of initiatives (Bush 2003; Schmelzle 2005).

Natural resource management and restoration can similarly contribute to the socioeconomics of peacebuilding by recreating opportunities for sustainable livelihoods. Public health systems, when coupled with proper environmental management and participation, can help stabilize communities where conflict has left behind long-term risks and chronic health concerns. Addressing environmental health risks (including perceived risks) can help mitigate feelings of injustice and resentment toward national and subnational groups and can have greater political dividends than disability payments long after a conflict has ended.

Environmental and social factors that influence post-conflict public health often remain unaddressed, either through a lack of proper post-conflict assessments or failure of reconstruction policies. At the expense of environmental health, reconstruction efforts often focus on economic and political metrics, not on decreasing the number of vulnerable people, addressing environmental risks, or restoring public health.

Humanitarian response in post-conflict regions may temporarily address acute environmental health risks, but measures remain largely disconnected from longer-term development policies. Post-conflict environmental management could improve health conditions significantly, but it must be acknowledged and prioritized. Early efforts to monitor and assess environmental health needs and vulnerabilities are also required.

REFERENCES

Al-Ansary, K. 2012. Iraq to raise wheat output by 74% by 2015, state company says. Bloomberg, January 17.

Allen, G. W. 2001. *None so blind.* New York: Ivan R. Dee.

Almond, M. 1990. *Pastoral development and OXFAM in Sudan.* Khartoum: Oxfam.

Allukian, M., and P. L. Atwood. 2000. Public health and the Vietnam War. In *War and public health*, ed. B. S. Levy and V. W. Sidel. Washington, D.C.: American Public Health Association.

AP (Associated Press). 2011. Vietnam and US in joint venture to clean up Agent Orange damage. June 17. www.guardian.co.uk/world/2011/jun/17/vietnam-us-agent-orange-damage.

Arfsten, D. P., D. J. Schaeffer, E. W. Johnson, J. R. Cunningham, K. R. Still, and E. R. Wilfong. 2006. Evaluation of the effect of implanted depleted uranium on male reproductive success, sperm concentration, and sperm velocity. *Environmental Research* 100 (2): 205–215.

Briggs, C., M. Walji, and L. Anderson. 2009. Environmental health risks and vulnerability in post-conflict regions. *Medicine, Conflict and Survival* 25 (2): 122–133.

Brown, V. 2004. Battle scars: Global conflicts and public health. *Environmental Health Perspectives* 112 (17): A994–A1003.

Bush, K. 2003. *Hands-on PCIA: A handbook for peace and conflict impact assessment.* Under the auspices of the Federation of Canadian Municipalities and the

Canada-Philippines Local Government Support Programme. www.mendeley.com/research/handson-pcia/.
Calain, P. 2008. Oil for health in sub-Saharan Africa: Health systems in a "resource cursed" environment. *Globalization and Health* 4 (10). www.globalizationandhealth.com/content/4/1/10.
Campbell, P. J., A. MacKinnon, and C. R. Stevens. 2010. *An introduction to global studies.* West Sussex, UK: John Wily and Sons.
Carstairs, T. 2001. Humanitarian mine action in Northern Iraq. *Journal of Mine Action* 5 (3).
Chandrasekaran, R. 2007. *Imperial life in the Emerald City: Inside Iraq's Green Zone.* New York: Vintage.
Conca, K., and G. D. Dabelko. 2002. The problems and possibilities of environmental peacemaking. In *Environmental peacemaking*, ed. K. Conca and G. D. Dabelko. Washington, D.C.: Woodrow Wilson International Center for Scholars.
Crosby, A. 2004. *Ecological imperialism.* New York: Cambridge University Press.
Crowther, G. 2008. Counting the cost: The economic impact of cluster munition contamination in Lebanon. London: Landmine Action. www.clusterconvention.org/files/2011/01/Counting_the_cost.pdf.
Darwish, R., N. Farajalla, and R. Masri. 2009. The 2006 war and its inter-temporal economic impact on agriculture in Lebanon. *Disasters* 33 (4): 629–644.
Dolan, J., and J. Hussein. 2009. Iraq halts clearing landmines even as huge toll keeps rising. *McClatchy*, June 2. www.mcclatchydc.com/homepage/story/69310.html.
E-MINE (Electronic Mine Information Network). 2009. Lebanon. www.mineaction.org/country.asp?c=16.
Essberger, R. 1995. Military surprise and the environment. *GeoJournal* 37 (2): 215–224.
Feldbaum, H., P. Patel, E. Sondorp, and K. Lee. 2006. Global health and national security: The need for critical engagement. *Medicine Conflict and Survival* 22 (3): 192–198.
Garfield, R. M., and A. I. Neugut. 2000. The human consequences of war. In *War and public health*, ed. B. S. Levy and V. W. Sidel. Washington, D.C.: American Public Health Association.
Graham-Rowe, D. 2003. Depleted uranium casts shadow over peace in Iraq. *NewScientist*, April 15. www.newscientist.com/article/dn3627-depleted-uranium-casts-shadow-over-peace-in-iraq.html.
Harris, G. 1999. *Recovery from armed conflict in developing countries.* London: Routledge.
Hassan, R., G. Hertzler, and J. Benhin. 2009. Depletion of forest resources in Sudan: Intervention options for optimal control. *Energy Policy* 37 (4): 1195–1203.
Haysom, N., and S. Kane. 2009. Negotiating natural resources for peace: Ownership, control and wealth-sharing. HD Centre Briefing Paper. Geneva, Switzerland: Henry Dunant Centre for Humanitarian Dialogue. http://siteresources.worldbank.org/EXTOGMC/Resources/336929-1266445624608/negotiating_peace_haysom_kane.pdf.
Helly, D., ed. 2009. *Post-2011 scenarios in Sudan: What role for the EU?* ISS Report No. 6. November. www.iss.europa.eu/uploads/media/Post-2011_scenarios_in_Sudan.pdf.
Hicks, M. H., and M. Spagat. 2008. The dirty war index: A public health and human rights tool for examining and monitoring armed conflict outcomes. *PLoS Medicine* 5 (12): e243.
Hill, T. E., and J. Fittipaldi. 2008. *Reducing an Insurgency's Foothold: Using Army sustainability concepts as a tool of security cooperation for AFRICOM.* Arlington, VA: Army Environmental Policy Institute.

Hindin, R., D. Brugge, and B. Panikkar. 2005. Teratogenicity of depleted uranium aerosols: A review from an epidemiological perspective. *Environmental Health* 4 (17). www.ncbi.nlm.nih.gov/pmc/articles/PMC1242351.
IMMAP (Information Management and Mine Action Programs). 2006. *Landmine impact survey: The Republic of Iraq; 2005–2006.* www.uniraq.org/documents/Iraq_Landmine _Impact_Survey_Final_Report,_iMMAP,_09_07.pdf.
ICG (International Crisis Group). 2003. Sudan's oilfields burn again: Brinkmanship endangers the peace process. Africa Briefing. February 10. www.crisisgroup.org/~/media/ Files/africa/horn-of-africa/sudan/B013%20Sudans%20Oilfields%20Burn%20Again%20 Brinkmanship%20Endangers%20The%20Peace%20Process.ashx.
―――. 2006. Sudan's comprehensive peace agreement: The long road ahead. Africa Report No. 106. www.crisisgroup.org/~/media/Files/africa/horn-of-africa/sudan/Sudans %20Comprehensive%20Peace%20Agreement%20The%20Long%20Road%20Ahead .pdf.
IWPR (Institute for War and Peace Reporting). 2009. Basra plagued by mine menace. July 3. http://iwpr.net/report-news/basra-plagued-mine-menace.
Jaspars, S., and S. O'Callaghan. 2008. Challenging choices: Protection and livelihoods in Darfur. Humanitarian Policy Group Working Paper. www.odi.org.uk/resources/download/2616.pdf.
Kim, G., R. Torbay, and L. Lawry. 2007. Basic health, women's health, and mental health among internally displaced people in Nyala Province, South Darfur, Sudan. *American Journal of Public Health* 97 (2): 353–361.
Klein, N. 2007. *The shock doctrine: The rise of disaster capitalism.* London: Allen Lane.
Landmine and Cluster Munition Monitor. 2009. Lebanon. In *Landmine Monitor Report 2009.* www.the-monitor.org/index.php/publications/display?url=lm/2009/countries/lebanon.html.
Levy, B. S., and V. W. Sidel, eds. 1997. *War and public health.* New York: Oxford University Press.
―――. 2009. Health effects of combat: A life-course perspective. *Annual Review of Public Health* 30:123–136.
Liljedahl, B., A. Waleij, A. S. Andersson, R. Doran, M. Bhatta, and S. Olsson. 2010. Environmental impact assessment in peacekeeping operations. https://community.apan.org/ apcn/m/apcnmedia/23321.aspx.
LMAC (Lebanon Mine Action Center). 2007. National mine action policy 2007. www.lebmac.org/files/publications/National_Policy__March_2007.pdf.
Loretti, A., X. Leus, and B. Van Holsteijn. 2001. Relevant in times of turmoil: WHO and public health in unstable situations. *Prehospital and Disaster Medicine* 16 (4): 184–191.
MacMahon, M., and N. Arya. 2004. Editorial: Peace through health. *Student BMJ* 12:438.
MacQueen, G., R. Horton, V. Neufeld, J. Santa-Barbara, and S. Yusuf. 2001. Health and peace: Time for a new discipline. *Lancet* 357 (9267): 1460–1461.
MacQueen, G., and J. Santa-Barbara. 2000. Peace building through health initiatives. *BMJ* 321 (7256): 293–296.
Maitre, B. R. 2009. What sustains "internal wars"? The dynamics of violent conflict and state weakness in Sudan. *Third World Quarterly* 30 (1): 53–68.
Marshall, A. C. 2008. Gulf War depleted uranium risks. *Journal of Exposure Science and Environmental Epidemiology* 18 (1): 95–108.
McDonnell, S. M. 2004. The role of the applied epidemiologist in armed conflict. *Emerging Themes in Epidemiology* 1 (4): 1–9.

Minear, L. 2001. Pastoralist community harmonization in the Karamoja Cluster: Taking it to the next level. Feinstein International Famine Center Working Paper Series. Medford, MA: Tufts University.

Mooney, W. K., Jr. 2007. Stabilizing Lebanon: Peacekeeping or nation-building. *Parameters* Autumn:28–41.

Moszynski, P. 2008. Health in southern Sudan is still critical despite truce. *BMJ* 336:1093.

Murray, C. J. L., G. King, A. D. Lopez, N. Tomijima, and E. G. Krug. 2002. Armed conflict as a public health problem. *BMJ* 324 (7333): 346–349. http://gking.harvard.edu/files/armedph.pdf.

Murray, C. J. L., and A. D. Lopez. 1996. *The global burden of disease: A comprehensive assessment of mortality and disability from diseases, injuries, and risk factors in 1990 and project to 2020.* Cambridge, MA: Harvard University Press.

Nguyen, T. 2009. Environmental consequences of dioxin from the war in Vietnam: What has been done and what else could be done? *International Journal of Environmental Studies* 66 (1): 9–26.

Omeje, K. 2010. Markets or oligopolies of violence? The case of Sudan. *African Security* 3 (3): 168–189.

PAHO (Pan American Health Organization). 1988. *Health as a bridge for peace: Priority health needs in Central America and Panama.* Washington, D.C.

Palmer, M. G. 2005. The legacy of Agent Orange: Empirical evidence from central Vietnam. *Social Science and Medicine* 60:1061–1070.

Pedersen, D. 2002. Political violence, ethnic conflict, and contemporary wars: Broad implications for health and social well-being. *Social Science and Medicine* 55:175–190.

Peplow, M. 2004. Iraq faces growing health crisis. *Nature*, October 13.

Phillips, D. L. 2005. *Losing Iraq: Inside the postwar reconstruction fiasco.* New York: Basic Books.

Readman, J. W., J. Bartocci, I. Tolosa, S. W. Fowler, B. Oregioni, and M. Y. Abdulraheem. 1996. Recovery of the coastal marine environment in the Gulf following the 1991 war-related oil spills. *Marine Pollution Bulletin* 32 (6): 493–498.

Renner, M., and Z. Chafe. 2007. *Beyond disasters: Creating opportunities for peace.* Washington D.C.: Worldwatch.

Richter, E. D., R. Blum, T. Herman, and G. H. Stanton. 2007. Malthusian pressures, genocide, and ecocide. *International Journal of Occupational and Environmental Health* 13 (3): 331–341.

Ridley, R. T. 1986. To be taken with a pinch of salt: The destruction of Carthage. *Classical Philology* 81 (2): 140–146. www.jstor.org/stable/269786.

Ryan, M. 2009. Drought takes toll on Iraq revival efforts. Reuters, July 23. www.reuters.com/article/2009/07/24/us-iraq-water-idUSTRE56N01Q20090724.

Salman, S. M. A. 2012. The Abyei territorial dispute between North and South Sudan: Why has its resolution proven difficult? In *Land and post-conflict peacebuilding*, ed. J. Unruh and R. C. Williams. London: Earthscan.

Santa-Barbara, J., and G. MacQueen. 2004. Peace through health: Key concepts. *Lancet* 364 (9431): 384–386.

Schmelzle, B. 2005. *New trends in peace and conflict impact assessment (PCIA).* Berghof Research Center for Constructive Conflict Management. www.berghof-handbook.net/documents/publications/dialogue4_pcianew_complete.pdf.

Schreuder, S. 2009. Iraq: Facing the legacy of landmines and explosive remnants of war. *Journal of Mine Action.* http://maic.jmu.edu/JOURNAL/11.2/focus/Schreuder/Schreuder.htm.

Sibai, A., and K. Sen. 2006. Can Lebanon conjure a public health phoenix from the ashes? *BMJ* 333:837–838.
Skinner, H., Z. Abdeen, H. Abdeen, P. Abner, M. Al-Masri, J. Attias, and K. Avraham et al. 2005. Promoting Arab and Israeli cooperation: Peacebuilding through health initiatives. *Lancet* 365 (9466): 1274–1277.
Tangermann, R., H. F. Hull, H. Jafari, B. Nkowane, H. Everts, and R. B. Aylward. 2000. Eradication of poliomyelitis in countries affected by conflict. *Bulletin of the World Health Organization* 78 (3): 330–338.
Toole, M. J., and R. J. Waldman. 1997. The public health aspects of complex emergencies and refugee situations. *Annual Review of Public Health* 18:283–312.
Tuyet, L. T. N., and A. Johansson. 2001. Impact of chemical warfare with Agent Orange on women's reproductive lives in Vietnam. *Reproductive Health Matters* 9 (18): 156–164.
UNDFS (United Nations Department of Field Support). 2011. Sudan. Map No. 4458. October. www.un.org/Depts/Cartographic/map/profile/sudan.pdf.
UNEP (United Nations Environment Programme). 1993. *Updated scientific report on the environmental effects of the conflict between Iraq and Kuwait.* UNEP/GC.17/lnf.9. March 8. www.unep.org/Documents.Multilingual/Default.asp?DocumentID=307&ArticleID=3894&l=en.
———. 2003. *Desk study on the environment in Iraq.* Geneva, Switzerland. http://postconflict.unep.ch/publications/Iraq_DS.pdf.
———. 2007. *Sudan: Post-conflict environmental assessment.* Nairobi, Kenya. http://postconflict.unep.ch/publications/UNEP_Sudan.pdf.
UNICEF (United Nations Children's Fund). 2006. *Progress for children: A report card on nutrition.* New York. www.childinfo.org/files/PFC4_EN_8X11.pdf.
UN OCHA (United Nations Office for the Coordination of Humanitarian Affairs). 2010. Where we work: Sudan. www.unocha.org/where-we-work/sudan.
U.S. AEC (United States Army Environmental Command). 1999. US Army UXO environmental remediation and active range clearance technology strategic plan. Report No. SFIM-AEC-PC-CR-2002028. http://aec.army.mil/usaec/technology/stratplan.pdf.
U.S. DIA (United States Defense Intelligence Agency). 1991. Iraq water treatment vulnerabilities. www.gulflink.osd.mil/declassdocs/dia/19950901/950901_511rept_91.html.
U.S. DOD (United States Department of Defense). 2000. Environmental exposure report: Depleted uranium in the Gulf (II). www.gulflink.osd.mil/du_ii/.
U.S. EPA (United States Environmental Protection Agency). 2001. Dioxin reassessment: An SAB review of the Office of Research and Development's reassessment of dioxin. May. http://yosemite.epa.gov/sab/sabproduct.nsf/C3B2E34A9CD7E9388525718D005FD3D2/$File/ec01006.pdf.
Utzinger, J., and M. G. Weiss. 2007. Editorial: Armed conflict, war and public health. *Tropical Medicine and International Health* 12 (8): 903–906.
VVAF (Vietnam Veterans of America Foundation) and BOMICEN (Technology Center for Bomb and Mine Disposal). 2009. *Report on Vietnam unexploded ordnance and landmine impact assessment and rapid technical response.* Hanoi, Viet Nam. www.ngocentre.org.vn/node/16730#attachments.
Wakabi, W. 2008. Health situation remains grave in southern Sudan. *Lancet* 372 (9633): 101–102.
Weekes, R., and P. Teagle. 1991. *Humanitarian ceasefires: Peacebuilding for children; Report of a conference to promote the implementation of paragraph 25 of the World Summit for Children plan of action.* Ottawa, Canada: Centre for Days of Peace.

Wilson, K., D. P. Fidler, C. W. McDougall, and H. Lazar. 2009. Establishing public health security in a postwar Iraq: Constitutional obstacles and lessons for other federalizing states. *Journal of Health Politics, Policy and Law* 34 (3): 381–399.

Winter, D., and M. Cava. 2006. The psycho-ecology of armed conflict. *Journal of Social Issues* 62 (1): 19–40.

WHO (World Health Organization). 2009. Banning cluster munitions. *Bulletin of the World Health Organization* 87: 8–9.

World Bank. 2008. *Mini-atlas of human security*. Washington, D.C.

Young, H., A. M. Osman, A. M. Abusin, M. Asher, and O. Egemi. 2009. *Livelihoods, power and choice: The vulnerability of the northern Rizaygat, Darfur, Sudan*. Medford, MA: Feinstein International Center, Tufts University.

Young, H., A. M. Osman, Y. Aklilu, R. Dale, B. Badri, and A. J. A. Fuddle. 2005. *Darfur: Livelihoods under siege*. Medford, MA: Feinstein International Center, Tufts University.

Zierler, D. 2011. *The invention of ecocide: Agent Orange, Vietnam, and the scientists who changed the way we think about the environment*. Athens, Georgia: University of Georgia.

Remediation of polluted sites in the Balkans, Iraq, and Sierra Leone

Muralee Thummarukudy, Oli Brown, and Hannah Moosa

Countries emerging from conflict face myriad complex challenges, including restoring peace and security, rebuilding infrastructure and the economy, and providing for the basic needs of their people. The natural environment is often harshly affected during conflicts, and restoring and rehabilitating ecosystems to ensure long-term sustainability is an additional challenge that post-conflict societies must address. In many instances, contamination of soil and groundwater by chemicals and other substances; dispersion of hazardous waste from fires, looting, bombings, and oil spills; and accumulation of municipal waste and hazardous health-care waste pose significant risks to human health and the environment and urgently require remediation.

This chapter takes an in-depth look at cleanup activities the United Nations Environment Programme (UNEP) has undertaken in the Balkans (2000–2004), Iraq (2004–2006), and Sierra Leone (2009–2011). It provides an overview of the findings and recommendations from the environmental site assessments UNEP conducted following the cessation of hostilities, and it details the objectives and achievements of cleanup projects that were implemented. Drawing on the successes and failures of the cleanup activities in these three situations, the chapter concludes with some general lessons for remediation of polluted sites in post-conflict situations.

THE BALKANS, 2000–2004

Following the suspension of NATO air strikes in June 1999, UNEP and the United Nations Centre for Human Settlements (UNCHS)[1] initiated a neutral, independent,

---

Muralee Thummarukudy is chief of disaster risk reduction at the United Nations Environment Programme (UNEP). Oli Brown is an environmental affairs officer for the United Nations Integrated Peacebuilding Office in Sierra Leone and a program coordinator for UNEP. Hannah Moosa is a Ph.D. student at the Munk School of Global Affairs and the Department of Political Science at the University of Toronto.

[1] UNCHS is currently known as the United Nations Human Settlements Programme, or UN-HABITAT.

scientific assessment of the environmental effects of the conflict in what was then the Federal Republic of Yugoslavia (UNEP 2004a).

In order to conduct the assessment and field missions, UNEP and UNCHS established the Balkans Task Force, which comprised more than sixty international experts from six UN agencies, nineteen countries, and twenty-six scientific institutions and nongovernmental organizations (NGOs). The task force also included ten national experts who served as local advisors for the team.

UNEP's post-conflict environmental assessment

Between July and October 1999, UNEP and UNCHS conducted four expert missions in the region, visiting a range of sites, including Pancevo, Novi Sad, Kragujevac, Bor, Pristina, Nis, Novi Beograd (a municipality of Belgrade), Kraljevo, the Iron Gate Reservoir on the Danube River (near the Romanian border), Lepenica River (which runs through Kragujevac), and Morava River (UNEP 2004a).

Following extensive fieldwork in the conflict-affected areas, in October 1999 UNEP and UNCHS published a report titled *The Kosovo Conflict: Consequences for the Environment and Human Settlements*, which concluded that the Kosovo conflict had not caused an environmental catastrophe affecting either the Balkans region as a whole or the territory of the Federal Republic of Yugoslavia (UNEP and UNCHS 1999). However, the report did find that the conflict had more localized effects on the environment, which in some cases were linked to the region's long-term legacy of poor environmental management. Furthermore, in its report UNEP identified four hot spots—in Pancevo, Novi Sad, Kragujevac and Bor—that presented serious risks to the environment and human health, and thus required urgent cleanup action (see figure 1).

Following the publication of the post-conflict assessment, UNEP conducted a feasibility study to define in more detail the scientific and financial requirements of the hot spot cleanup measures. Finalized in April 2000, the feasibility study identified twenty-seven cleanup projects for the four sites, with an estimated combined cost of US$20 million (UNEP 2004a). Donors from ten different countries contributed a total of US$12.5 million for the most critical cleanup projects. These countries were Denmark, Finland, France, Germany, Ireland, Luxembourg, the Netherlands, Norway, Sweden, and Switzerland.

UNEP's cleanup program

In November 2000, UNEP partnered with the United Nations Office for Project Services to begin implementation of the cleanup program (UNEP 2004b). Partnerships with local and national stakeholders, as well as corresponding coordination mechanisms, were also developed and maintained throughout the program in order to ensure local ownership and cost-effective implementation of cleanup objectives.

Remediation of polluted sites in the Balkans, Iraq, and Sierra Leone 137

Figure 1. UNEP environmental hot spot cleanup sites in Serbia
Source: UNEP (2004).

Pancevo petrochemical plant (HIP Petrohemija)

UNEP's post-conflict assessment and subsequent feasibility report demonstrated that Pancevo, with fourteen priority projects, had the greatest remediation needs of the four hot spots; therefore, a larger portion of program resources were allocated to Pancevo, and specifically to its industrial complex, than to efforts elsewhere. Cleanup efforts were first undertaken at Pancevo's petro-chemical plant (HIP Petrohemija) and focused primarily on remediation of soil and groundwater contamination and rehabilitation of wastewater treatment facilities (UNEP 2004b).

Ethylene dichloride contamination. The NATO bombings of April 1999 damaged tanks holding ethylene dichloride (EDC), resulting in roughly 2,100 metric tons of EDC being released, an estimated 50 percent of which is believed to have infiltrated the soil. The International Agency for Research on Cancer has classified EDC as a possible human carcinogen (U.S. EPA 2006). Site investigations conducted in May 2000 indicated the presence of an EDC free-phase pool in the backfilled sand at the top of the clay layer where the damaged EDC storage tanks were located.[2] EDC concentrations detected in groundwater samples collected from the shallow aquifer were an estimated 5.6 grams per liter (g/L) (UNEP 2004b). In comparison, Dutch environmental-quality objectives for groundwater require remediation if EDC concentrations are above 400 milligrams per liter (mg/L).

The aim of UNEP's project at the Pancevo petrochemical plant was to reduce the level of EDC contamination in groundwater and the soil in order to decrease the health risks for factory workers and to protect groundwater resources and the Danube River (UNEP 2004b). Following detailed site investigations and a preliminary human health and environmental risk assessment, it was determined that the remedial target for the EDC cleanup should be the removal of the free-phase EDC and a reduction of the dissolved phase to 1.0 g/L.[3]

Working in close collaboration with HIP Petrohemija and Czech partners, UNEP launched the EDC remediation project in June 2001. Between January and July 2002, comprehensive subsurface characterization works and pilot tests (pump-and-treat remediation and steam-enhanced extraction tests) were performed so workers could select the best available technology for soil and groundwater remediation at the vinyl chloride monomer (VCM) plant. The tests indicated that the VCM plant's treatment facilities could treat fluids containing chlorinated hydrocarbons that resulted from groundwater remediation. The cleanup project upgraded the capacity of these facilities from 3.5 cubic meters per hour (m^3/h) to 5.5 m^3/h by August 2002, and to 8.0 m^3/h by late November 2003 (UNEP 2004b).

Following project investigations and data evaluation, a general design for the cleanup of the upper aquifer was prepared. By January 2004, the interim remedial system, which focused on the shallow aquifer, had recovered over 400 metric tons of EDC, including approximately 93 metric tons of free-phase EDC and 316 metric tons of pure EDC recovered through the treatment of contaminated groundwater.

In order to ensure continued risk reduction, an upgraded full-scale system was commissioned and transferred from the cleanup program to the site owner in April 2004.

Wastewater treatment facility. Although the wastewater treatment facility at Pancevo's petrochemical plant was not directly targeted during the 1999 NATO bombing, damage to the oil refinery and the VCM and chloro-alkali plants led to the discharge of roughly 170,000 m^3 of raw materials, petrochemical products, and firefighting water (UNEP 2004b). This flow overloaded the wastewater treatment

---

[2] The term *free-phase pool* refers to a collection of a liquid toxin that is freestanding, that is, not dissolved in another medium.
[3] The term *dissolved phase* refers to a toxin that is dissolved in an aqueous medium, usually groundwater.

facility's capacity, clogged the units with contaminated sludge, damaged the processing equipment, and cracked or otherwise damaged concrete retaining structures.

The aim of UNEP's cleanup efforts at the wastewater treatment facility was to rehabilitate the treatment plant in order to protect the Danube River system and downstream water supplies. The project began in 2001 in collaboration with HIP Petrohemija. By June 2004, the process equipment had been replaced, the trickling filter and pH regulating facilities repaired, and the activated sludge rehabilitated (UNEP 2004b). The facility's hydraulic and treatment capacity were restored and significantly improved in comparison to pre-conflict levels, and the pollutant-loading into the Danube River and its associated risks to downstream water supplies were reduced.

In April 2004, the project was handed over to the site owner, who was required to provide regular reports to national authorities and provincial environmental authorities on the operation of the rehabilitated facilities.

Pancevo oil refinery (NIS-RNP)

Between April and June 1999, the Pancevo oil refinery (NIS-RNP) was the site of heavy NATO aerial strikes. As a result, an estimated 80,000 metric tons of oil products and crude oil burned, and an additional 5,000 metric tons of oil and oil products leaked into the soil and sewer system, releasing sulphur dioxide and other noxious gases (UNEP 2004b). The bombings further damaged the refinery's sewer system and wastewater pretreatment unit.

Construction of a concrete basin for oil sludge. In addition to destroying some of the refinery's production and storage facilities, the bombings caused large quantities of oil to spill into the ground, the sewer network, and the refinery's wastewater pretreatment facilities, and finally to flow into the Danube River. Because storage facilities were not sufficient, the spilled oil and oil products could not be removed and disposed of safely.

UNEP's cleanup project aimed to provide safe temporary storage for oily wastes that were removed during rehabilitation of the sewer pipeline and the pretreatment unit, as well as to provide temporary storage for other oil wastes from the refinery. By April 2003, working in close collaboration with NIS-RNP, UNEP completed the cleanup works (UNEP 2004b). The project successfully provided 1,700 m^3 of temporary storage capacity for the cleanup operations at the refinery, thereby making possible remediation in the pretreatment facilities and sewage system.

Cleaning and repair of sewer pipelines and oil separators. Throughout the conflict, large amounts of oil, debris, and other materials clogged and partly damaged the sewer pipes, oil separators, and discharge pipelines. Following the conflict, the refinery's wastewater was being discharged directly into a wastewater canal and the Danube River without final treatment at the HIP Petrohemija's integrated wastewater treatment plant.

Overall, this UNEP cleanup activity aimed to protect the Danube River system (UNEP 2004b). More specifically, it would reestablish the NIS-RNP wastewater pretreatment facilities, ensure that wastewater from the refinery met the input specifications for final wastewater treatment at HIP Petrohemija's wastewater treatment plant, enable transport of pretreated wastewater from NIS-RNP to that plant, assess the refinery's sewer networks, and outline a strategy for rehabilitation and priority repairs.

Working with the NIS-RNP, UNEP began its rehabilitation activities in December 2001. The wastewater pretreatment facilities were successfully repaired and upgraded, including repairs to the oil separators' structures. By April 2004, the wastewater pipeline between the refinery and the petrochemical plant had been repaired, so pretreated wastewater could be transported from the refinery to the wastewater treatment plant before it was discharged into the wastewater canal (UNEP 2004b).

As part of its efforts to assist the refinery in defining its rehabilitation strategy and prioritizing its work, UNEP partially cleaned the refinery's sewer network, performed a geodetic survey, and completed design preparation. When it handed the project over to the site owner in April 2004, it delivered a study on technical solutions for rehabilitation of the refinery's sewage system and for the proper management of wastewater.

Pancevo fertilizer factory (HIP Azotara)

During the 1999 Kosovo conflict, the Pancevo fertilizer factory (HIP Azotara) was struck by a NATO aerial attack. The nitrogen-phosphorus-potassium plant and the fuel-oil tanks were destroyed, and the ammonia plant was damaged. As a result, significant quantities of hazardous substances flowed into the wastewater canal and poured into the Danube River. In an effort to avoid potential health risks for the workers and the surrounding population, the site managers released approximately 250 metric tons of ammonia into the wastewater canal and the Danube.

Investigations conducted by UNEP in 1999 and 2000 confirmed that high concentrations of pollution originating from industrial wastewaters had contaminated the canal. Specifically, EDC concentrations in the sediment's top layer varied from 130 milligrams per kilogram (mg/kg) to 300,000 mg/kg, indicating the presence of free-phase EDC in some of the canal's bottom layers (UNEP 2004b). Additionally, significant concentrations of mercury (from 1.4 to 40 mg/kg) and petroleum hydrocarbons (from 5,000 mg/kg to 32,000 mg/kg) were found in the canal sediment. High concentrations of these pollutants were also discovered in deeper layers of the sediment, indicating chronic pollution of the canal. Finally, a considerable amount of polyvinylchloride dust was later identified in the canal sediment. It was determined that there was an urgent need to protect downstream drinking-water resources and prevent the discharge of dissolved and sediment-associated pollutants into the Danube River system.

Phase one of the project involved preparing technical documentation and designing an environmentally acceptable remediation strategy. Working in close collaboration with Serbian environmental authorities and local stakeholders, UNEP completed the predesign investigation work in 2001 (UNEP 2004b). Findings from the investigations confirmed that the canal contained 41,000 m^3 of sediment that had significant concentrations of mercury and mineral oils. Further investigations in 2002 and 2003 revealed that EDC concentrations in the sediment had been reduced to almost negligible values, while roughly 550 metric tons of mineral oils and 260 kg of mercury were estimated to still be present in the canal.

In 2003, preliminary environmental impact assessments and general designs were developed for two remedial options: dredging the sediment and depositing it in a new landfill, and dredging and dewatering the sediment and treating it with thermal desorption (UNEP 2004b). By April 2004, a review of the preliminary environmental impact assessment and a general design for the thermal desorption option were completed. National environmental authorities and relevant stakeholders in Pancevo expressed their commitment to technical preconditions for sustainable remediation measures, and a potential donor was identified for remediation of the pollution in the canal.

Overall, UNEP's cleanup program allowed for seven out of the fourteen feasibility study projects for the Pancevo industrial complex to move forward. Although UNEP's remediation efforts in Pancevo led to a considerable reduction in the extent and magnitude of conflict-related environmental problems, chronic environmental problems such as industrial air pollution and improper waste management remain. They require continued investment and improvements to management practices.

Novi Sad oil refinery (NIS-RNS)

During the 1999 Kosovo conflict, the Novi Sad oil refinery (NIS-RNS), which was constructed on backfilled sand, was the target of several aerial strikes. As a result, several storage tanks and pipelines at the refinery were damaged, and over 70,000 metric tons of crude oil and oil products burned or leaked into the wastewater collection system and the ground, causing severe contamination of the soil and groundwater (UNEP 2004b). Visual inspection and analysis of groundwater samples indicated the presence of free-phase oil in the groundwater table. UNEP's post-conflict environmental assessment identified the potential risk to drinking-water wells downstream from the refinery as a key environmental concern. The site has also been a source of long-term and ongoing pollution, which has exacerbated the risks posed to human health and the environment.

Taking into account UNEP's feasibility study, as well as budget constraints, the Novi Sad cleanup program concentrated on protecting the Ratno Ostrvo drinking-water wells in the area between the Novi Sad oil refinery and the Danube

River, comprehensively monitoring the area's groundwater resources, and initiating efforts to address the contamination source zone within the oil refinery.

Remediation of free-phase oil in groundwater. Working in close collaboration with the Novi Sad oil refinery, UNEP delineated areas within the refinery compound where free-phase oil was present in the groundwater table. After reviewing various remediation alternatives, UNEP conducted pilot studies of techniques in order to select the most appropriate one for risk remediation. By January 2004, roughly 4.5 metric tons of free-phase oil had been recovered (UNEP 2004b). By February 2004, the mobile abstraction and separation unit was handed over to NIS-RNS, which was then responsible for the continued operation of the unit and for submitting regular progress reports to various national and provincial environmental authorities.

Although the remediation project achieved its objectives, it provided only a limited solution to the refinery's historic and more recent pollution problems.

Construction of a hydraulic barrier at the eastern refinery border. Not only had the conflict caused oil spillage, the Novi Sad oil refinery had historically been an ongoing source of pollution, so the entire refinery area was considered a potential source from which contamination could migrate. Since the Ratno Ostrvo drinking-water wells were located near the refinery, immediate measures for protecting the wells from groundwater contamination were considered the highest priority during remediation.

UNEP, together with Novi Sad Waterworks, began the construction of a hydraulic barrier between the refinery and the drinking-water wells in summer 2001 (UNEP 2004b). By April 2002, the project was handed over to the Novi Sad authorities. Although the project achieved its preventive objectives, additional measures were identified for addressing contamination sources at the refinery in the long term.

Groundwater monitoring. Close monitoring of the groundwater sources, both inside and outside the refinery area, was required in order to provide early warning of contaminant migration in the region. Starting in November 2000, UNEP worked in close collaboration with Novi Sad Waterworks, the Novi Sad oil refinery, the Novi Sad Institute of Chemistry, and the Swiss Agency for Development and Cooperation to monitor groundwater quality in the area and has determined the extent of groundwater pollution from spills at the oil refinery. This program modeled the velocity and preferential pathways of contaminant migration from the source zone, and the results confirmed the long-term risk to the drinking-water wells. The data made possible early warning of pollutant migration from the refinery and provided the basis for determining when to start up the hydraulic barrier operation. The monitoring program did not identify any immediate threat to the quality of groundwater abstracted from the water-supply wells in Ratno Ostrvo (UNEP 2004b).

In February 2004 the program was handed over to NIS-RNS and the Novi Sad Waterworks. Following this handover, the oil refinery site owner and the Novi Sad Waterworks were responsible for reporting monitoring results to the national and provincial environmental authorities.

Repair of the sewage collector outside the refinery. An approximately two-kilometer-long buried concrete collector conveys wastewater from NIS-RNS across the Ratno Ostrvo water-well area to the Danube. The collector and the wells are operated and maintained by Novi Sad Waterworks. The 1999 NATO bombing may have further damaged the collector, which was reportedly in bad condition prior to the conflict. Severe leakage from the damaged collector has been polluting groundwater and threatening nearby drinking-water wells.

UNEP's objective was to assess and repair the wastewater collector in order to prevent wastewater from leaking into the groundwater and polluting nearby drinking-water wells. Working in close collaboration with the Novi Sad Waterworks, UNEP completed the project in September 2003. Workers sealed the collector's cracked and leaking parts, preventing further pollution. The project was handed over to Novi Sad Waterworks and the municipality of Novi Sad in February 2004 (UNEP 2004b).

Overall, UNEP's remediation efforts in Novi Sad enabled three of the seven priority projects identified in the feasibility study to be fully addressed. Throughout the process, UNEP encouraged national and international stakeholders to provide additional inputs to risk-reduction efforts.

Kragujevac industrial complex

In April 1999 Kragujevac's Zastava industrial complex—including a power station, car assembly line, paint shop, computer center, and truck line—was heavily damaged by NATO bombings, and some areas of the facility were completely destroyed. The most significant risk identified at this site was the high concentrations of polychlorinated biphenyls (PCBs) and dioxins detected on the Zastava Automobili paint-hall floor and in nearby wastewater pits, PCBs within the Zastava Energetika power plant's transformer station, and sediments in the Lepenica River. The assessment further revealed that an estimated 2,150 kg of PCB-containing oil had leaked from damaged transformers.

UNEP's feasibility study identified five priority projects for the Zastava industrial complex. Cleanup efforts concentrated on remediation of PCB contamination of the concrete floor at the paint hall, cleaning of the wastewater pits and decontamination of wastewater in the paint hall, remediation of PCB contamination at the transformer station, and transportation and treatment abroad of hazardous waste generated by the Kragujevac remediation projects (UNEP 2004b).

Remediation of PCB contamination of paint-hall floor. Due to the bombings, an estimated 2,150 kg of PCB-containing oil leaked out of two paint-hall transformers and flowed onto the concrete floor and toward nearby wastewater pits. Analyses of samples taken during UNEP's assessment missions in 1999 and 2000 revealed high levels of PCBs, dioxins, and furans in the debris on the floor. Further analysis by UNEP in 2001 confirmed that PCBs had penetrated approximately 150 square meters (m^2) of the paint hall's concrete floor to a depth of roughly 25 centimeters, thereby contaminating the soil below the floor in some places. An estimated 30,000 mg/kg of PCBs were found in the top layers of concrete near the former transformers, while elsewhere in the paint hall the concentrations were less than 50 mg/kg (UNEP 2004b). Roughly 400 m^2 of less contaminated concrete were identified in the remainder of the paint hall and in the area toward the new basic paint pit. Very low concentrations of dioxins and furans were found in the concrete, so PCBs were the primary concern for the cleanup project.

The main risk from the PCB contamination was exposure of the paint-hall workers. As a result, UNEP's cleanup project aimed to reduce health risks for factory workers, to prevent any further cross-contamination, and to pack and store waste properly to allow for future transportation.

Working in close collaboration with the Zastava car factory and the University of Kragujevac's Institute of Chemistry, UNEP started implementation of the project in December 2001. Contaminated layers of concrete and soil were removed and packaged, and decontamination of these layers was verified. When the project reached its target of reducing PCB concentrations in the remaining soil to less than 50 mg/kg, the soil was covered with concrete, and antistatic epoxy resin was placed over the concrete. The cleanup efforts also included removing damaged transformers and debris created by the conflict. In all, an estimated 135 metric tons of hazardous waste resulting from remedial activities were characterized, properly packed, labeled, temporarily stored, and later transported and incinerated abroad (UNEP 2004b). The cleanup activities were completed in August 2002, allowing for the reuse of the affected part of the paint hall.

Cleaning of wastewater pits and decontamination of wastewater. PCBs leaking from the two transformers damaged by the bombing reached the open wastewater pits in the Zastava paint hall and mixed with water, paint sludge, and debris. Since oils containing PCBs are denser than water and not very soluble, they were mainly confined to the sediment at the bottom of the pits. In all, an estimated 6,000 m^3 of PCB-contaminated wastewater was found to be in the pits (UNEP 2004b).

The cleanup project aimed to reduce health risks to factory workers; prevent further cross-contamination; protect water resources from further contamination, particularly through uncontrolled sewage discharges into the Zdraljica River and Lepenica River; and properly pack the cleanup waste to allow for transportation at a later date.

Working in close collaboration with the Zastava car factory and the University of Kragujevac's Institute of Chemistry, UNEP began implementation of the project in August 2001. An estimated 6,000 m^3 of PCB-contaminated wastewater, with a maximum concentration of 0.7 mg/L, was removed from the pits and treated using a remediation method elaborated by national experts and reviewed by international experts.

Once the wastewater was purified, its PCB content was less than 0.0005 mg/L. In all, 120 metric tons of contaminated debris and bottom sediment were removed. An additional ten metric tons of equipment from the pits were dismantled, decontaminated, and disposed of. The resulting hazardous waste was characterized, properly packed, labeled, and later transported and incinerated abroad. Following verification of the decontamination work, the cleanup project was completed in April 2002 (UNEP 2004b). The project not only ensured that workers were protected by an improved environment, it also allowed for reuse of the wastewater pits.

Remediation of PCB contamination at transformer station. The 1999 NATO bombings damaged a transformer at the substation near Zastava Energetika headquarters, causing PCB-containing oil to leak. UNEP assessment missions in 1999 and 2000 revealed high concentrations of PCBs, dioxins, and furans in the concrete and a nearby rainwater gully. The contaminated concrete area was estimated to be 150 to 200 m^2.

UNEP's cleanup project aimed to reduce the health risks to factory workers by removing the damaged transformer and cleaning up the site, as well as allowing for reuse of the transformer station, which supplies the factory and provides heating to the municipality.

Working together with Zastava Energetika and the University of Kragujevac's Institute of Chemistry, UNEP began remedial activities in September 2002 (UNEP 2004b). The transformer was removed and temporarily stored at an access-restricted site designated specifically for used PCB equipment. Once the contaminated concrete and soil layers from the transformer pit and adjacent concrete surface were removed and replaced, the old transformer was replaced by one that does not use oil containing PCBs. In total, an estimated 50 metric tons of hazardous waste was characterized, properly packed, labeled, and later transported and incinerated abroad.

The remedial project not only protected workers and improved the environment, it also allowed for reuse of the transformer station.

Transportation and treatment of hazardous wastes from remediation projects. The primary objective of this activity was to treat and finally dispose of roughly 150 metric tons of hazardous waste resulting from all UNEP cleanup projects in Kragujevac, in accordance with environmentally sound management requirements, thereby eliminating risks arising from the waste's storage on factory premises.

By October 2003, UNEP, working in collaboration with Zastava factory officials and national authorities, and in accordance with the Basel Convention on the Control of Transboundary Movements of Hazardous Wastes and Their Disposal, had successfully transported and treated the hazardous waste resulting from its cleanup efforts in Kragujevac (UNEP 2004b).

Overall, UNEP's remediation efforts in the Zastava complex enabled the completion of four of the five priority projects identified in the feasibility study. National environmental authorities implemented the fifth project, regarding the monitoring of the Lepenica River. Local and national stakeholders played a critical role in ensuring the successful implementation of all activities.

Due to the successful implementation of all priority projects, a joint final-assessment mission conducted by UNEP and national authorities concluded that the designation "environmental hot spot" no longer applied to Kragujevac (UNEP 2004a).

Bor

NATO bombings in May 1999 struck the RTB Bor mining and smelting complex, damaging the transformer station that provided the site with electricity. UNEP's subsequent assessment of the complex revealed localized PCB contamination at the destroyed transformer station. Furthermore, the assessment raised concerns regarding severe and chronic air pollution that resulted from the plant's long-term operations.

Bearing in mind both the wider environmental problems in the Bor region and the post-conflict environmental assessment, cleanup activities at Bor focused on assessing and reducing remaining PCB-related risks at the transformer station and the dump site, and strengthening the overall environmental management capacity of local stakeholders (UNEP 2004b).

UNEP assessment missions in 1999 and 2000 obtained soil and sand samples at the transformer station that revealed PCB values ranging from 3.35 to 682 mg/kg of soil as based on dry matter. During that same period, local stakeholders took the initiative to move PCB-contaminated debris and material, including approximately 120 capacitors, from the destroyed transformer station to the RTB Bor dump site. UNEP's remedial activities aimed to identify and reduce the potential health risks to workers from PCB contamination, and to enable redevelopment of the transformer station area. A UNEP risk assessment conducted in September 2001 concluded that no further remedial activities were needed at the transformer station site. In 2002–2003, a new transformer station was erected at the same site with Norwegian funding.

UNEP's risk assessment of the RTB Bor dump site, which was finalized in February 2003, revealed that there were no immediate risks to groundwater resources from PCB contamination, but recommended that measures be taken to protect workers' health and to reduce risks at the site (UNEP 2004b). In December 2003, approximately 150 PCB-containing capacitors, which had been removed from the damaged transformer station and stored near the RTB Bor dump site, were removed, packed, and transported abroad for final treatment.

UNEP's remediation activities provided support for enhancing local capacity in the fields of environmental planning and monitoring, particularly the monitoring of air pollution. UNEP further assisted in enhancing local environmental planning capabilities by supporting the formulation of the first Local Environmental Action Plan for Bor.

IRAQ, 2004–2006

UNEP has been actively working in Iraq since the end of the 1990–1991 Gulf War. Following the end of those hostilities, UNEP undertook field assessments in Iraq, Kuwait, and Saudi Arabia to identify the environmental consequences of the conflict, including the effects of the intentional destruction of over 700 oil wells (UNEP 2003). Although major risks to human health and livelihoods were identified by the UNEP reports, the political situation prevented sustained cleanup efforts.

In 2001 UNEP extended its work in Iraq by monitoring and assessing the degradation and demise of the Mesopotamian Marshlands. This study found that the geographical area of the marshlands had declined by 90 percent due to a combination of dams, intentional diversion, and mismanagement of water resources.[4]

In February 2003, as coalition forces planned their second invasion of Iraq, UNEP initiated a desk-based environmental surveillance program to monitor the conflict as it occurred. UNEP's work resulted in the publication of the *Desk Study on the Environment in Iraq* in April 2003 (UNEP 2003). Two key needs were identified in the desk study and subsequent progress report: first, the need for an environmental assessment of selected contaminated sites; and second, the need to build and strengthen the environmental governance capacity of the Iraqi administration and provide specific training to experts from the Ministry of Environment in several key areas (UNEP 2003, 2005).

Following completion of the desk study and a subsequent post-conflict needs assessment conducted between June and October 2003, UNEP, in consultation with the Iraqi Ministry of Environment, helped develop a project titled Strengthening Environmental Governance in Iraq through Environmental Assessment and Capacity Building (UNEP 2005). The program included a comprehensive package of activities for building the Ministry of Environment's capacity to conduct assessments of contaminated sites, develop sound environmental policies, and monitor environmental quality. It was divided into five components: assessment of contaminated sites; capacity building in technical and policy areas; institutional capacity assessment; improvement of infrastructure and equipment; and monitoring of the Mesopotamian marshlands. Funded by the government of Japan, the project activities were carried out from July 2004 to December 2005, with training activities conducted in Jordan, Switzerland, and the United Kingdom.

---

[4] For a more detailed discussion, see Steve Lonergan, "Ecological Restoration and Peacebuilding: The Case of the Iraqi Marshes," in this book.

148   Assessing and restoring natural resources in post-conflict peacebuilding

Although capacity building and institutional capacity assessment were crucial components of the program, this chapter focuses primarily on the assessment and cleanup of contaminated sites.

Environmental site assessments

Regarding the assessment and cleanup of contaminated sites, the UNEP program had two key objectives. In the short term, it would identify and remediate the environmental hot spots that posed the most immediate risks to human health and the environment. In the long term, it would build institutional capacity, knowledge, and expertise within the Ministry of Environment for the establishment of a national site assessment program, remediation activities, and improvements in hazardous waste management (UNEP 2005).

Traditionally, UNEP's methodology for conducting hot spot assessments has been to assemble a team of international experts who partner with local institutions and government scientists to conduct field sampling. UNEP then divides the samples into a number of batches, which UNEP analyzes independently, using internationally accredited laboratories, while national counterparts conduct the analyses in parallel. This approach maximizes transparency and ensures that the findings are informed by sound science. It also facilitates capacity building at the local level and local ownership of issues arising from assessments.

However, such an approach was not feasible in the context of a deteriorating security situation in Iraq, particularly following the bombing of the Canal Hotel in Baghdad in August 2003 and the subsequent withdrawal of UN staff members. As a result, UNEP adopted an alternative approach that focused on building a team of national experts to conduct environmental site assessments (ESAs) at each hot spot according to UNEP standards and on the basis of UNEP training and quality-control procedures.[5] UNEP independently analyzed the resulting field samples at internationally accredited laboratories. The national team was primarily from the Ministry of Environment and was provided with UNEP training in neighboring countries, including Bahrain, Egypt, Jordan, and Syria (UNEP 2005).

Site selection for priority assessment was led by the Ministry of Environment, with UNEP acting in an advisory role. UNEP's previous environmental assessments had provided information on a number of sites, and this was complemented by secondary data. UNEP compiled an initial list of over fifty sites, mainly in industrialized regions surrounding Baghdad, all of which were damaged or in environmentally poor condition due to fires, looting, armed conflict, or poor operating practices. This list was presented to the Ministry of Environment for review and discussion, and the source-pathway-receptor model was used to identify the sites with the most acute risks. The top five sites, selected on the basis of security and access considerations, were Qadissiya, Suwaira, Khan Dhari,

---

[5] UNEP has developed environmental site assessment as an approach for post-conflict countries, based on international best practices in environmental assessment.

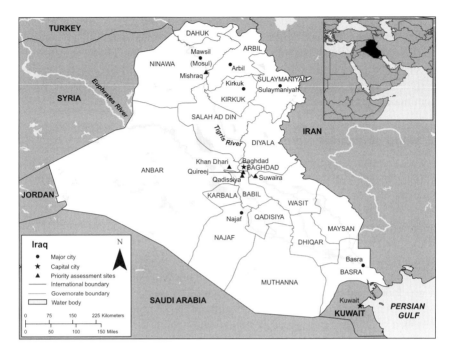

Figure 2. Priority assessment sites in Iraq
Source: UNEP (2005).

Mishraq, and Quireej (UNEP 2005; see figure 2). Cleanup operations would be conducted on a pilot basis for training purposes at the sites with the greatest immediate environmental risks to human health.

Qadissiya metal-plating facility

Constructed in the 1980s and located on the urban fringes approximately thirty kilometers south of Baghdad, the Qadissiya military industrial site operated continuously until March 2003. During the conflict in 2003, it suffered damage from ground conflict as well as air strikes. The unsecured site had previously contained a complex of metal-plating and machining units, all of which were partially or completely demolished. Particularly, the site contained pure sodium cyanide, a toxin with a lethal dose of less than one gram by ingestion (UNEP 2007). Following the conflict, the site was repeatedly looted, and piles of cyanide were deposited on open ground. Photographic and laboratory evidence revealed a significant volume of highly hazardous waste dispersed across the site. Chemical analysis of the waste piles indicated that the principal contaminants were heavy metals—specifically lead, nickel, copper, and antimony.

UNEP's ESA found that the Qadissiya facility represented a severe danger to human health, the principal risk arising from direct contact with hazardous waste by site trespassers, particularly children. Dispersed piles of sodium cyanide pellets were found to pose the greatest hazard. Uncontrolled demolition potentially increased the volume of hazardous waste, much of which could have been covered by or mixed in with demolition rubble (UNEP 2007). The ESA noted that if no corrective action was taken, high levels of hazard from chemical waste would continue for up to a decade.

Suwaira pesticides warehouse complex

Located approximately fifty kilometers southeast of Baghdad, less than two kilometers north of the Tigris River, and three kilometers north of the town of Suwaira, the Suwaira warehouse facility was used to store, mix, and dispatch a range of pesticides over a thirty-year operating period (UNEP 2007). Empty imported pesticide containers were washed and reused for the local sale of pesticides, and some damaged drums were dumped on site. The warehouse complex held a large quantity of obsolete and highly toxic methyl mercury pesticide.

The Suwaira warehouse facility operated normally until March 2003, when it was looted and the majority of the pesticides, as well as containers at the site, were stolen. The buildings on the site suffered only limited damage, but looters smashed containers and spread pesticides throughout the building and in parts of the compound in the process of stealing material. As of July 2005, the facility was secure but idle, and no cleanup had been carried out. The warehouses contained roughly 100 m^3 of waste pesticides, and at least three of the warehouses were considered unsafe to use or even enter until they could be decontaminated. Still, UNEP's ESA found that the site represented only a low priority to human health because security conditions prevented access to the contaminated warehouses.

Khan Dhari petrochemicals warehouse site

Located thirty-five kilometers west of Baghdad near the town of Abu Ghraib, the Khan Dhari petrochemicals warehouse site was administered by the Midland (Al-Doura) Refinery Company. The site contained a complex of eighteen warehouses and two support buildings (UNEP 2005).

The Khan Dhari warehouse operated normally until March 2003. Immediately following the 2003 conflict, the site was looted for machinery, empty drums, fittings, and chemicals, and looters poured the contents of containers full of chemicals onto the ground. According to site staff, 6,000 empty barrels contaminated with chemicals were stolen from the warehouse complex. Looters also started a fire that destroyed four warehouses, as well as the chemicals stored indoors and in the adjacent yard. Photographic and laboratory evidence revealed a significant volume of hazardous waste, mostly from fire-damaged drums, spilled heavy liquids, and burnt residues that were dispersed across the site.

UNEP's ESA found that the Khan Dhari site represented only a low risk to human health, primarily because of the site controls that were in place. In the absence of remedial action, however, large parts of the site represented a moderate risk to the health of site workers and were therefore deemed unfit for normal use. The principal threat arose from direct contact with and inhalation of lead dust and oxidized organic chemicals.

Mishraq sulphur mining complex

Located fifty kilometers south of Mosul, the Mishraq sulphur mining and processing complex was in operation from 1972 to early 2003. In March 2003, production ceased, and between April and July 2003 the site was comprehensively looted (UNEP 2005).

In June 2003, a fire set by looters burned continuously for almost a month. Reports indicate that the volume of sulphur burned ranged between 300,000 and 400,000 metric tons. Twenty-five villages and three towns were affected, with at least two deaths and many hospital reports of respiratory problems. A large part of the local population evacuated their villages at the time of the fires. There were also reports of extensive damage to wheat crops in the surrounding areas, most likely due to acute acid burns to the exposed plants, which resulted in stunted growth and plant death. As of July 2005, the entire site was shut down and secured, and it was lying idle and semiderelict.

UNEP's ESA found that the Mishraq site represented a low risk to human health and the environment, and that the primary risk was related to acidic surface-water ponds. Maintenance of site security could minimize this hazard, but failure to engage in corrective action would result in high levels of hazard from chemical waste for decades. Following the June 2003 sulphur fire, initial investigations indicated that the short-term damage to vegetation was severe close to the plant, but damage to the environment as a result of the fire was not widespread or long-term. Rainwater ponds, drainage ponds, and gullies close to the sulphur-processing and acid plants were found to contain hazardous levels of acid. Runoff from these areas could affect local river quality.

Quireej military scrapyard site

Located roughly fifteen kilometers south of Baghdad, the Quireej military scrapyard was primarily vacant land prior to 2003 (UNEP 2005). Between 2003 and 2004, it was used as a storage site and active scrap-recovery facility for damaged and redundant Iraqi military and civilian vehicles and equipment. Uncontrolled dumping and scrapping of vehicles resulted in localized contamination. Today the site is idle.

UNEP's ESA found that the Quireej military scrapyard site represented a moderate risk to human health, primarily to site workers but also to site residents. The primary toxicity risk was found to be to workers who came into direct contact with and inhaled chemicals in the process of transporting, cutting, sorting, and burning the scrap. The mixing of civilian and military scrapping activities was found to be exacerbating the problem.

UNEP's cleanup activities

Following completion of the ESA, which identified the key sites posing acute risks to human health and the environment, UNEP developed a cleanup project for the two sites with the greatest immediate risks. At the Suwaira warehouses the cleanup focused on the collection and containment of toxic pesticide residue, including chlorophenyl mercury and calcium cyanide. The cleanup also involved the design and creation of on-site, secure storage for the hazardous waste that was collected. At the derelict Qadissiya metal-plating facility, cleanup focused on the collection and containment of sodium cyanide, hexavalent chromium salt, and sodium hydroxide. By focusing cleanup efforts on the two sites that posed the most immediate threats to human life, the project further aimed to build the capacity of the Ministry of Environment, of other ministries, and of contractors so these entities could manage hazardous wastes, coordinate and implement cleanup works, and solve similar problems throughout Iraq in the future (UNEP 2007).

Suwaira site

At the Suwaira site, residue from the warehouse was collected in plastic bags and sealed in storage drums that were clearly labeled in Arabic and English to indicate that the contents were "toxic, environmentally hazardous, not to be touched, and flammable" (UNEP 2007, 38). The drums were numbered serially, and samples taken from each drum were cross-referenced with the same serial number. In total, 149 drums were filled. Ninety contained hazardous waste such as soil, dust, and bird guano mixed with chlorophenyl mercury; twenty-seven contained chlorophenyl mercury; thirty-one contained calcium cyanide; and one contained seeds. The drums were stored at the end of the warehouse and enclosed with warning tape (UNEP 2007).

Once the pesticide residue was collected, the Suwaira warehouse was extensively cleaned. The walls, windows, and doors were repaired, and holes were filled. The ceiling and walls were thoroughly scrubbed and washed with water jets. The floor-cleaning process was then repeated for a second time. Thereafter, a special concrete-polishing machine was used to remove stains and discoloration from the surface of the concrete floor. Following this cleaning process, the warehouse was washed with a warm soap solution and a hypochlorite solution, and then cleaned and washed a second time to reach a satisfactory state (UNEP 2007). Manholes in the floor were cleaned, and new covers were installed. Finally, the outside of the warehouse was cleaned and washed.

Qadissiya site

At Qadissiya, UNEP successfully collected, labeled, and stored all identified chemicals in steel barrels. In total, 150 drums of sodium cyanide, 228 drums of hexavalent chromium salt, and 68 drums of sodium hydroxide were collected

(UNEP 2007). Contaminated liquids found inside the plating basins were pumped out, placed into jerrycans, and stored inside the Qadissiya storage facility. A total of 220 jerrycans were filled with a mixture of hexavalent chromium salt and cyanide salt. One hundred bags of asbestos were collected and packed into larger plastic bags, which were then placed inside a third layer of plastic bags. The bags were sewn tight with a special sewing machine and stored. Samples were also taken of all drums, and the bags containing the samples were clearly labeled.

A hangar was constructed to store the contaminated soil and concrete that the chemicals had been lying on, as well as all related equipment, which included empty storage containers, drums, chemical wash tanks, and a cyanide salt annealing vessel with solidified chemicals. The hangar, which covered an area of 360 m^2, was constructed with concrete floors, closed walls, and a sealed roof (UNEP 2007).

SIERRA LEONE, 2009–2011

When peace was declared in 2002 after more than a decade of conflict, the small West African nation of Sierra Leone was left to tackle a number of serious environmental problems from the conflict. These included direct impacts, such as the destruction of infrastructure and large-scale displacement of skilled workers; indirect impacts on people's coping strategies; and institutional consequences of the almost entire collapse of governance during the conflict, including basic natural resource management (UNEP 2010).

Recognizing the critical value of the environment and natural resources, the government of Sierra Leone included them as key peace and development priorities, most notably in its *An Agenda for Change: Second Poverty Reduction Strategy* (ROSL 2008). In 2009 it requested that UNEP contribute to the *UN Joint Vision for Sierra Leone*, which outlines UN support for the *Agenda for Change* (UNIPO 2008).

When UNEP began an in-country capacity-building program to improve the governance of natural resources in July 2010, one immediate issue was the cleanup of a cache of toxic chemicals that had been left at an old oil refinery site in Kissy, a densely populated area in the eastern part of the country's capital, Freetown (see figure 3). The chemical in question was tetraethyl lead (TEL), which before 2000 was used around the world as an additive to gasoline to boost its octane rating and prevent engine damage.

TEL can be unstable; it is flammable, explosive, and highly toxic. Lead is a neurotoxin that is volatile in its organic form and is easily absorbed into the body through inhalation, absorption, or ingestion. Once organic lead is converted into inorganic lead, the risk of absorption into the body is reduced considerably (Innospec 2011).

In the mid-1990s operations at Kissy Refinery wound down, and the site was abandoned by its owners as a result of the civil war. The site was left without adequate supervision by trained personnel and was seriously affected during the attacks on Freetown by the Revolutionary United Front (RUF) in the latter part

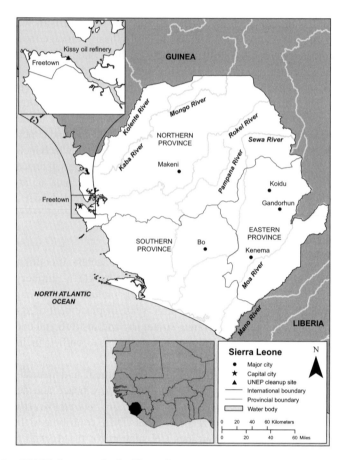

Figure 3. UNEP cleanup site in Sierra Leone
Source: UNEP (2011).

of the 1990s. During this time a number of empty and partially filled drums were buried in unlined "grave sites" in a manner contrary to accepted standards for the disposal of TEL compound drums (Innospec 2011).

There are also unverified reports that RUF rebels may have tried to empty the TEL drums into the local water source, only to be discouraged by the approximately 300-kilogram weight of the drums. If this did happen, it would constitute a serious attempted war crime.

Site investigations at Kissy Refinery, Freetown

Preliminary investigations by a team of researchers from Sierra Leone's Environment Protection Agency (EPA-SL) and Fourah Bay College triggered an official request to UNEP's regional office for Africa for assistance in the analysis and disposal of the toxic stockpile at Kissy Refinery (UNEP 2009). UNEP's regional office launched a field mission to Freetown in July 2009 to conduct a quantitative assessment of the situation, to advise on proper measures to minimize the risks, to train managers on safety issues, and to draft a comprehensive remediation plan that would address final cleanup of the site.

The assessors found a total of forty-two metal drums of TEL stacked in an open shed on the premises of the refinery. At least two of these drums were showing signs of serious corrosion. Two large mounds of earth purported to be the burial site for another twenty-one drums were also identified. Once the cleanup was initiated, it turned out that there were fifty-one buried drums in varying states of corrosion in four separate burial sites. In total, ninety-three barrels of toxic waste would need to be decontaminated.

Sizable parts of the forty-two-acre refinery comprise a community market garden, where local residents grow fruit, vegetables, and staple crops, most of which are sold to nearby markets. The research team noted that absorption and bioaccumulation of toxic components of liquid fuel and gas by these crops were highly likely, but this required further investigation. The preliminary investigation further highlighted other breaches of environmental standards; for example, caretaking personnel were not being properly protected from the effects of the refinery's chemical fumes (UNEP 2009). UNEP's assessment determined that the significant quantities of TEL at Kissy Refinery posed a severe risk to the health, livelihoods, environment, and security of nearby communities.

Cleanup efforts

Following UNEP's technical assessment, Innospec, a UK-based private contractor and the world's only producer of TEL, submitted a commercial proposal for the final decommissioning and decontamination of TEL drums at Kissy Refinery (Innospec 2011). UNEP provided technical assistance and cofunding for the remediation operation, which was driven and managed by EPA-SL.

The cleanup project began in May 2011 and was originally scheduled to last for twenty-seven days. However, because more buried barrels were discovered after cleanup operations commenced—many of them heavily corroded—the project was extended to fifty-three days.

Innospec imported much of the special equipment required for the project, including a storage and transport vehicle, pumping equipment, and safety gear for the workers. The Innospec project managers hired and trained ten local workers, who began a supervised process of tapping and siphoning the drums to move the liquid into a transport container. The liquid TEL recovered from the site was transported to the United Kingdom for further treatment (Innospec 2011).

The empty drums were then cut open and flame-washed (blasted with an oxy-acetylene torch) to decontaminate any remaining liquid. Some of the oxidized sludge was mixed with cement to create stable concrete blocks that safely lock in the lead content. The burial sites were lined with a membrane layer and backfilled to minimize any further contamination.

There were several challenges involved in carrying out such an operation in a country like Sierra Leone. First, given the low level of development in the country and the lack of an existing chemicals industry, there was very low technical capacity related to chemicals management. Obtaining in-country support in terms of trained personnel and appropriate equipment was very challenging. Second, the safety and security conditions at the refinery were not ideal: hot and humid temperatures posed a risk to the TEL itself and were difficult for workers to withstand while wearing hazmat suits. The operation also needed to be completed before the rainy reason, meaning operations had to be conducted nearly continuously during daylight hours. It was also difficult to secure the site in order to protect the public from potential risks and to prevent equipment theft. Third, Sierra Leone is not a party to the Basel Convention on the transport of hazardous waste. This meant that although it was possible to transport liquid TEL outside of the country because it is considered a chemical product, it was not possible to export any TEL sludge for reprocessing outside of the country because the sludge is considered hazardous waste. This necessitated employment of a domestic solution: in situ containment in concrete.

By the end of June 2011, ninety-three TEL drums had been successfully decontaminated with no incidents, accidents, or contamination to the local workforce, population, or environment. This amounted to almost 12,000 liters, or nineteen metric tons, of TEL (Innospec 2011). Soil samples were taken from the area to provide a preliminary assessment of the extent of any ground contamination. Depending on the results of the soil analysis, further investigation may be required to determine whether a second phase of ground remediation work should be conducted.

LESSONS LEARNED

UNEP's experiences in the cleanup of contaminated sites in the Balkans, Iraq, and Sierra Leone yield several key lessons.

Timing

In order to be effective, post-conflict environmental assessment and cleanup efforts should start as rapidly as possible following the cessation of hostilities. Where potentially severe environmental damage may arise from a conflict, an independent, objective assessment must take place as soon as the security situation allows.

The sooner action is taken, the more effective the outcomes are likely to be in terms of protecting the environment and human health from further risks and effects. Early action is also justified by the fact that cleanup costs often increase with time, especially in the case of contaminants that can migrate through the soil and affect groundwater. It is crucial that sufficient financial resources for a comprehensive cleanup effort are secured as early as possible in order to facilitate a fast start to the program and ensure a sustainable and effective remediation project.

Scope of remediation

It is important for designers of remediation programs to identify the multiple ways in which a specific site has been contaminated. In addition to direct or indirect impacts from the conflict, some level of environmental contamination often predates the conflict. This was the case, for example, at the Pancevo fertilizer factory (HIP Azotara) in Serbia.

When project leaders are setting the scope of a remediation program, they must address three major questions: What causes of contamination, both preexisting and conflict-related, should be addressed during remediation? What overall degree of remediation and restoration should the project achieve (for example, a return to natural conditions or only pre-conflict conditions)? What existing or new sources of pollution may recontaminate the site?

Ideally, cleanup efforts should not focus solely on reversing the conflict's negative effects on the environment, but should kick-start long-term environmental restoration and lay the foundation for environmentally sound site management. Furthermore, cleanup operations should be conducted only where sustainability can be demonstrated. This entails both stopping all other forms of contamination related to the site and preventing new contamination. Sometimes cleanup operations at industrial sites need to go hand in hand with technology upgrades and training in cleaner production methods. In many instances, the availability of funding, the time frame for remediation activities, and the prevailing security situation will influence the overall scope of remediation.

Flexibility in remediation design and contingency planning

A thorough understanding of the local security, political, and socioeconomic context is critical for the design of remediation programs for post-conflict situations. Although it is necessary to draw on existing methods for post-conflict environmental assessment and remediation, strategies must be flexible and adaptable to the particular post-conflict situation and the evolving security situation on the ground. A one-size-fits-all approach or strict adherence to a project framework should be avoided. UNEP's cleanup work in Iraq clearly demonstrated the need for a flexible and adaptive approach when experts had to modify their projects amid a deteriorating security situation and maintain an appropriate balance between security considerations and the quality and cost of remediation.

When designing remediation programs, project leaders should also anticipate that cleanup sites involving abandoned industrial areas may have significant subsurface dump sites. Contingency planning should take this risk into account.

Cleanup operations in Sierra Leone demonstrated the need to adapt to changing conditions when additional drums of TEL were discovered in subsurface dump sites.

Furthermore, project leaders should anticipate additional challenges and costs when conducting remedial work in a context that lacks a strong industrial sector. In Sierra Leone the absence of a well-established industrial sector posed unexpected difficulties in implementation of the remediation project, both in terms of costs and the lack of skilled workers with the requisite background in handling hazardous chemicals.

Although effective cleanup programs should be tailored to fit the specific country context, practitioners should also attempt to achieve remediation that meets the best international standards—rather than local standards—so the country can establish a higher benchmark for future remediation and learn about best practices. In exceptional cases, however, a risk-based analysis may indicate that a lower standard can be used.

Prioritization of sites

In a post-conflict situtation, the number of contaminated sites may outweigh the amount of financing available for cleanup and remediation. It may be necessary to prioritize certain sites and to justify pursuing remediation at those sites rather than at alternative locations. This was the challenge facing UNEP in both Iraq and Serbia.

In situations where cleanup demand exceeds available financing, a transparent decision-making framework should be developed that allows stakeholders to rank and prioritize sites. This process should be informed by technical assessments that use the source-pathway-receptor approach to identify which sites pose the greatest immediate risks. UNEP's assessment in Iraq demonstrated the value of this approach. Although five sites were determined to be potential hot spots, only two of the sites represented immediate risks to human health on the basis of the source-pathway-receptor analysis.

Ideally, the first sites to undergo cleanup should be used as pilot cases to help build the capacity of stakeholders and raise public awareness of potential risks. Early and successful efforts can help build political momentum and public support for additional cleanup operations.

Life cycle approach to hazardous waste

When remediation works are conducted, the complete life cycle of hazardous waste must be taken into account from the outset of project design through collection, storage, transport, treatment, and final disposal. As was the case in Sierra Leone and Iraq, sites containing valuable scrap metal, equipment, or chemicals that can be sold on local markets will need to be secured to discourage theft and looting.

Because many post-conflict countries lack sufficient capacity and expertise to treat and dispose of hazardous waste, the best solutions are often regional.

Neighboring countries with internationally accredited treatment and disposal facilities should be used to the extent possible. Where regional solutions cannot be found, facilities farther away should be sought. When local contractors transport hazardous wastes to local treatment and disposal sites, chain-of-custody systems with appropriate levels of monitoring and enforcement should be used to prevent illegal dumping.

When the transport of hazardous waste crosses international borders, compliance with the Basel Convention on the Control of Transboundary Movements of Hazardous Wastes and Their Disposal is essential. Special efforts may be needed to train port and customs authorities regarding remediation equipment that needs to be imported and exported. Customs delays were experienced in all three cases, in particular during the importation of specialized cleanup equipment.

Public awareness and communication

From the outset, planning should incorporate media strategies and public awareness and consultation measures. This is especially critical when sites represent an immediate health risk and access cannot be easily restricted, as with the sites in Sierra Leone and Iraq.

Awareness campaigns should include basic information on the risks posed by specific contaminated sites and hazardous materials, and on ways to limit public exposure. When key resources such as drinking water have been contaminated, the public must be provided with clear guidance regarding treatment options and alternative sources. All forms of media, including TV, radio, Internet, and print, should be used to disseminate information to the public, and awareness workshops or door-to-door visits should be conducted in communities in the immediate vicinity. However, the timing of media campaigns needs to be carefully planned to avoid creating public panic before safeguards, risk-exposure guidance, or alternative measures are in place.

Proper photographic records of contaminated sites and remediation efforts should be created to help communicate problems and to highlight progress in cleanup efforts. Furthermore, follow-up monitoring should be instituted to track the presence of hazardous materials and ensure that the remediation work has been sufficiently carried out. Ideally this should be taken on as a core responsibility of the host government.

Partnerships

To be successful, any remediation program must include an effective framework for sustained engagement, coordination, and collaboration among site owners, local and national stakeholders and authorities, and international actors, including UN agencies, NGOs, and donors. Such an approach yields four major benefits.

First, it allows for the establishment of more sustainable projects and of solutions that are specific to the local context, thereby increasing acceptance of remediation activities among local residents and site owners. Second, it prevents overlap between projects and helps to identify synergies between related projects. Third, consistent and concerted engagement with local and national counterparts ensures a smoother handover to site owners and local authorities once the remediation project has come to an end. Finally, partnerships and collaboration create the space and interest for long-term, sustained investment in follow-up remediation efforts and environmental restoration projects.

Cleanup as an opportunity for capacity building and local employment

UNEP's work in the Balkans, Iraq, and Sierra Leone demonstrate that remediation programs go beyond physical cleanup activities and risk reduction; these projects play an important role in building local capacity, technical competence, and political visibility, as well as in generating local employment. For example, UNEP's remediation efforts in the Balkans were complemented by a range of training courses, seminars, and workshops that covered issues such as hazardous waste management, local environmental action plans, cleaner production, sustainable consumption, foreign direct investment, and multilateral environmental agreements.

In Iraq training topics included environmental emergency response, environmental inspection and control, environmental impact assessment, multilateral environmental agreements, environmental law, biodiversity and natural resource management, and office management. A detailed training program on assessing depleted uranium contamination was delivered to the Radiation Protection Center of the Iraqi Ministry of Environment (see Mario Burger, "The Risks of Depleted Uranium Contamination in Post-Conflict Countries: Findings and Lessons Learned from UNEP Field Assessments," in this book). In addition to training, UNEP provided lab and field equipment, established an environmental information center containing 1,500 publications, and facilitated participation in regional and international meetings.

In all cleanup efforts, the role of UNEP, the UN, and the wider international community should be to assist and advise national authorities and stakeholders while offering objective scientific and technical expertise. National authorities and stakeholders should manage cleanup efforts and take overall responsibility for operations. In the case of Sierra Leone, the EPA-SL's ownership of the project was critical to its success, particularly the EPA-SL's support in negotiating local services, hiring a local workforce, and clearing the necessary equipment through customs.

When possible, remediation and cleanup efforts should be designed to serve as a platform for building national and local environmental management capacity, initiating reform of local and national environmental governance institutions, and contributing to the resumption and strengthening of regional and international environmental cooperation.

Cleanup operations should also be designed to generate employment and procurement contracts that prioritize local companies. During UNEP's cleanup operation in Serbia, 80 percent of the staff were national experts, and 75 percent of contracts were awarded to local companies or institutions that employed local experts and used local technologies. When the UNEP program closed down, many of the staff employed by the program went on to open their own highly successful engineering companies.

CONCLUSIONS

Remediation of contaminated sites is often only one small step in the much longer and larger process of environmental restoration and governance required in post-conflict countries. In many cases, cleanup of environmental hot spots can be used as a starting point for raising environmental awareness and building greater public support for projects that safeguard the environment. When possible, cleanup operations should be used to catalyze greater political interest in tackling broader environmental challenges facing the country. In both Iraq and Serbia, the environmental risks posed by contaminated sites helped to bring environmental issues and governance needs to the political agenda and into national reconstruction plans.

REFERENCES

Innospec. 2011. Report for the tetraethyl lead (TEL) drum remediation project at Kissy Refinery, Sierra Leone, 27th July 2011. Ellesmere Port, UK.

ROSL (Republic of Sierra Leone). 2008. *An agenda for change: Second poverty reduction strategy (PRSP II) 2008–2012*. Freetown. http://unipsil.unmissions.org/portals/unipsil/media/publications/agenda_for_change.pdf.

UNEP (United Nations Environment Programme). 2003. *Desk study on the environment in Iraq*. Geneva, Switzerland. http://postconflict.unep.ch/publications/Iraq_DS.pdf.

———. 2004a. *From conflict to sustainable development: Assessment and clean-up in Serbia and Montenegro*. Geneva, Switzerland. http://postconflict.unep.ch/publications/sam.pdf.

———. 2004b. *From conflict to sustainable development: Assessment of environmental hot spots; Serbia and Montenegro*. Geneva, Switzerland. http://postconflict.unep.ch/publications/assessment.pdf.

———. 2005. *Assessment of environmental "hot spots" in Iraq*. Geneva, Switzerland. http://postconflict.unep.ch/publications/Iraq_ESA.pdf.

———. 2007. *UNEP in Iraq: Post-conflict assessment, clean-up and reconstruction*. Nairobi, Kenya. http://postconflict.unep.ch/publications/Iraq.pdf.

———. 2009. Field mission report: Kissy Refinery. Geneva, Switzerland.

———. 2010. *Sierra Leone: Environment, conflict and peacebuilding assessment; Technical report*. Geneva, Switzerland. http://postconflict.unep.ch/publications/Sierra_Leone.pdf.

———. 2011. UNEP supports clean-up of toxic waster dump in Sierra Leone. UNEP News Centre, June 30. www.unep.org/newscentre/default.aspx?DocumentID=2645&ArticleID=8796.

UNEP (United Nations Environment Programme) and UNCHS (United Nations Centre for Human Settlements). 1999. *The Kosovo conflict: Consequences for the environment and human settlements.* Geneva, Switzerland. http://postconflict.unep.ch/publications/finalreport.pdf.

UNIPO (United Nations Integrated Peacebuilding Office). 2008. *Joint vision for Sierra Leone of the United Nations family.* Freetown.

U.S. EPA (United States Environmental Protection Agency). 2006. Toxicology. In *Lead scavengers compendium: Overview of properties, occurrences, and remedial technologies.* www.epa.gov/oust/cat/Section_5-Toxicology.pdf.

The risks of depleted uranium contamination in post-conflict countries: Findings and lessons learned from UNEP field assessments

Mario Burger

Many of the world's armies possess, or are thought to possess, depleted uranium (DU) munitions—conventional weapons that have been used in warfare on several occasions (Harley et al. 1999). DU is a dense metal used in munitions for its penetrating ability and on armored vehicles as a protective material. In warfare production, DU is an alternative for tungsten, which is more expensive and has fewer offensive capabilities. Munitions containing DU were used in Iraq during the 1990–1991 and 2003 Gulf wars, in Bosnia and Herzegovina in 1994–1995, and in the Kosovo conflict in 1999, including southern Serbia and Montenegro.

DU is the main by-product of enriching natural uranium ore for use as fuel in nuclear reactors and nuclear weapons. It is mildly radioactive, with approximately 60 percent of the radioactivity of natural uranium from which it is distinguished by its concentrations of uranium isotopes. Natural uranium has a uranium-235 (U-235 or 235U) content of 0.7 percent, whereas DU has a U-235 content of 0.2–0.3 percent. Like naturally occurring uranium, DU is an unstable, chemically toxic, radioactive heavy metal that emits ionizing radiation of three types: alpha, beta, and gamma. The scientific community is investigating the extent to which DU can filter through soil and contaminate groundwater as well as how wind or human activity can resuspend DU as dust.

DU ammunition forms a dust cloud on impact. Because the metal is pyrophoric (i.e., the reaction of the metal to oxygen in the air causes it to ignite spontaneously), the dust cloud burns and forms an aerosol of fine uranium oxide particles. The amount of DU transformed into dust depends on the type of munitions, the nature of the impact, and the target. Normally, 10–35 percent (up to 70 percent) of the penetrator becomes an aerosol upon impact with a hard target, such as a tank or an armored personnel carrier. Ignition of the DU-dust cloud can therefore cause total destruction of an impacted vehicle because

---

Mario Burger is head of the Radioactivity Group at the Swiss government's Spiez Laboratory and a regular consultant to the United Nations Environment Programme (UNEP) as a senior scientific advisor. The views expressed in this chapter do not necessarily reflect those of the laboratory or UNEP.

of the secondary explosion of carried ammunitions (tanks carry a number of battle ammunitions that can explode). After an attack with DU munitions, DU is deposited on the ground and other surfaces as pieces of DU metal, fine fragments, and dust. If the DU catches fire, it is deposited as uranium oxide dust. Most of the DU dust lands within one hundred meters of a target (Nellis AFB 1997). When DU hits soft surfaces such as nonarmored vehicles and soft ground, it does not produce as much dust as it does when it encounters hard surfaces such as battle tanks and concrete surfaces.

DU AND HUMAN HEALTH

A variety of international studies examining the behavior of DU in the natural environment and medical aspects and risks have been published by international, regional, and national institutions, including the World Health Organization (WHO), the Scientific and Technological Options Assessment of the European Union, the National Research Center for Environment and Health in Germany, the Italian Ministry of Defense, the British Royal Society, and the Swedish Defence Research Agency (WHO 2001; EC 2001; Roth et al. 2003; MOD 2004; Royal Society 2001, 2002; and Waleij et al. 2004).

The effects of DU on human health depend on the types and magnitudes of exposure, as well as on characteristics such as particle size, chemical form, and solubility. Where DU munitions have been used, the penetrators, penetrator fragments, and jackets (or casings) can be found on the ground or buried at varying depths, where they have the potential to contaminate air, soil, water, and vegetation.

Human exposure to radiation from DU can be external (through contact with the skin) or internal (through inhalation or ingestion of DU particles). Radiation may increase the risk of cancer, with the degree of risk depending on the part of the body exposed and the dose rate (EC 2001). The estimated annual radiation doses that can arise from exposure to DU residues are low, estimated to be less than 0.1 mSv[1] (IAEA 2010). This radiation dose is less than those received on an annual average by individuals from natural sources of radiation in the environment (2.4 mSv). It is also below the internationally recommended annual dose limit for members of the public (1 mSv) and below the annual action level of 10 mSv established by the International Commission on Radiological Protection (ICRP) (ICRP 1999; IAEA 2010). While people who handle objects hit by DU or DU remnants will not likely receive doses that exceed the annual

---

[1] The sievert (Sv) is the International System of Units–derived unit of dose equivalent radiation (the biological effect of ionizing radiation) equal to an effective dose of a joule of energy per kilogram of recipient mass. One millisievert (mSv) is one thousandth of a sievert. The unit is named after Rolf Maximilian Sievert, a Swedish medical physicist, renowned for work on radiation-dosage measurement and research into the biological effects of radiation.

action level, a person present during an attack may receive a higher dose by inhaling air with a high concentration of DU dust (IAEA 2003; ICRP 1999).

Like naturally occurring uranium and other heavy metals, DU is chemically toxic when ingested or inhaled. If certain uranium compounds accumulate in the kidney tubules and kidneys, severe poisoning can result within hours or days. DU's chemical toxicity is usually considered the dominant risk factor, relative to its radioactivity.

But comparison of the chemical and radiological hazards of uranium is complex given the following:

- *The insufficiency of chemical toxicity data for long-term ingestion of uranium.* Currently, literature only covers intermediate-term adverse effects on animals.
- *Noncomparable standards for radiation doses and chemical toxicity.* For radiation and cancer-inducing effects of toxic substances, a linear dose-to-effect relationship is assumed at low doses and low-dose rates; the occurring probability of an adverse effect is therefore not reduced by the selection of a standard.[2] At low doses, the absence of linearity in the dose-effect curve for noncancerous effects of toxic substances allows identification and selection of nonadverse-effect levels.

The absence of comparability can be illustrated by the ingestion of uranium. The U.S. Agency for Toxic Substances and Disease Registry (ATSDR) estimated a tolerable daily intake (TDI) of pure uranium in its natural-isotope composition for use in calculating the annual limit on intake (ALI) of the element.[3] The value obtained (for a 70 kilogram (kg) body weight) is equal to 51.2 milligram (mg) (ATSDR 1999; WISE n.d.). But according to the WHO, the ALI is 15.3 mg (WHO 1998: WISE n.d.).

The ICRP, whose methodologies are based on radiological hazard studies, uses an annual dose-rate threshold of 1 mSv to define the ALI for the public.[4] This methodology gives ALI values for natural uranium (with progeny) of 31.5 mg, for uranium with natural isotope composition (without progeny) of 813 mg, for enriched (3.5 percent U-235) uranium of 251 mg, and for depleted (0.2 percent U-235) uranium of 1,410 mg (WISE n.d.). The variability of ALI for uranium composed of natural isotopes (without progeny) calculated with the chemical toxicity methods (51.2 mg, according to ATSDR, and 15.3 mg, according to WHO) and the ALI calculated with radiation methods (813 mg) is therefore relatively significant.

---

[2] Doses and dose rates include the toxicological and radiological dimensions (milligram/kilogram (mg/kg), Sv, mg/kg/time, Sv/time).
[3] The TDI relates to the chemical toxicity of a substance.
[4] The field of radiation protection distinguishes between members of the public and radiation workers. For the public, the annual radiation-exposure limit is 1 mSv; for radiation workers, it is 20 mSv.

Taking into account the radioactivity of uranium, a member of the public weighing 70 kg would be allowed to ingest fifteen times more naturally composed uranium than the ATSDR chemical toxicity of the uranium would allow. But in both cases, there would be a very low probability of harm.

For uranium inhalation, under the toxicological approach, the minimal risk level (MRL) sets the daily human exposure to a hazardous substance at or below the level at which the substance is unlikely to pose a measurable risk of adverse and cancerous effects. MRLs are calculated for specific pathways (inhalation and oral) over a specified time period (acute, intermediate, or chronic). In the case of highly soluble uranium salts, the ATSDR value for intermediate-period inhalation is 0.0004 milligram per cubic meter (mg/m^3), and the value for chronic inhalation is 0.0003 mg/m^3. The MRL for intermediate inhalation of insoluble uranium–compounds is 0.008 mg/m^3 (WISE n.d.).

Using the radiological risks posed by the inhalation of uranium radioisotopes, it is possible to calculate derived-air concentrations (DACs) based on the annual 1 mSv value for the public, with a breathing rate of 0.9 m^3/hour on a continuous exposure (WISE n.d.). The DACs and the associated values are more or less comparable to the MRLs. The values are generally in the low microgram-per-cubic-meter range.

For the DU assessments conducted in the Balkans (see below), the approach was to estimate the hazard posed by the DU contamination at a selected location, using the ICRP methodology. In the cases of intermediate and chronic inhalation, the results were comparable to the radiological and chemical risks. In the case of ingestion, chemical toxicity is the dominant factor. The consequences of radiation were considered insignificant for doses less than 1 mSv/year and significant for doses higher than 1 mSv/year.

ASSESSMENTS OF DU

For the safety of local populations and international workers in post-conflict situations, accurate information must be available in order to evaluate the risks to human health from the environmental consequences of the conflict and to take appropriate measures for mitigation. Where DU munitions have been used during conflict, environmental assessments should be undertaken to determine potential risks.

The United Nations Environment Programme (UNEP) has conducted three comprehensive environmental assessments of DU in the Balkans. The first was carried out in Kosovo in 2000–2001. It was followed by assessments in Serbia and Montenegro in 2001–2002 and in Bosnia and Herzegovina in 2002–2003. Because security constraints prevented international experts from traveling to Iraq during 2003–2007, UNEP focused on delivering capacity building and training to national staff to enable them to conduct DU-assessment fieldwork in the country during 2006–2007. In 2010, the International Atomic Energy Agency (IAEA) published the outcomes of the national assessments in Iraq.

In conducting the various DU assessments, which included a combination of fieldwork and laboratory analysis, UNEP worked with the IAEA and WHO.

UNEP managed the assessment process, including the field sampling and laboratory analysis. IAEA made all calculations necessary to determine radiological conditions in areas contaminated with DU residue and discussed the results with partner organizations. WHO calculated the toxicity of DU, developed scenarios, and published health-related materials on the basis of UNEP's findings.

Kosovo, 1999–2001

UNEP first conducted a fact-finding mission to Kosovo in August 1999. The mission determined that DU contamination was likely not widespread because no traces of DU were detected. Although site-specific contamination could not be ruled out, the mission was unable to identify the locations where DU had been used because it lacked essential information from the North Atlantic Treaty Organization (NATO) on firing locations and targets. Even though the preliminary findings helped quell public fears about widespread contamination, there was still an urgent need to conduct more detailed site-specific analysis.

In 2000, NATO provided UNEP with vital information on the use of DU during the Kosovo conflict, including maps, number of rounds fired, and coordinates of targets. The data enabled UNEP to carry out the first international environmental assessment of DU in a conflict situation.

Because more than a year had elapsed since the conflict, the overall aim of the UNEP mission of autumn 2000 was to examine risks posed by remaining DU contamination of soil, water, and plants, as well as by intact and fragmented DU penetrators still in the environment. The mission faced the following key questions: What were the levels of DU contamination in Kosovo? What were the corresponding radiological and chemical risks, then and for the future? Was there any need for remedial measures or restrictions? If so, which measures were reasonable and realistic?

Eleven out of a total of 112 known sites were selected for analysis by UNEP (see figure 1). A total of 361 samples were collected from the eleven sites, including 249 soil, 13 smear,[5] 46 water, 37 botanical, 3 milk, 7 penetrators, and 6 jackets. UNEP independently chose sites that were most heavily targeted, as well as sites that were in or closest to inhabited areas. In selecting the sites, diversity was also sought in the surrounding natural environment, soil types, and vegetation. Sampling in some areas was limited by the fact that the sites had not been cleared of mines and unexploded ordnance. In *Depleted Uranium in Kosovo: Post-Conflict Environmental Assessment* (UNEP 2001), UNEP reported that low levels of radiation had been detected in the immediate vicinity of the points of DU impact and that mild contamination from DU dust had been measured near the targets. However, the report concluded that there was no significant risk related to the

---

[5] Smear sampling of undisturbed surfaces is one of the most precise methods for detecting DU. UNEP has detected the impact of as little as two 30-millimeter DU penetrators of 300 grams each and has confirmed the presence of DU within 300 meters of a target.

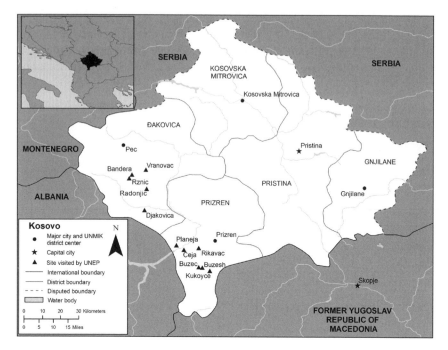

Figure 1. UN environmental assessment sites in Kosovo, 2000–2001
Source: UNEP (2001).
Note: As with UN peace operations in other countries, UNMIK (United Nations Interim Administration Mission in Kosovo) defines its own districts. Each district has a district center and a responsible international commander. In a district, UN-mandated troops are present.

points in terms of possible contamination of air, water, or plants. Analyses of the samples collected also showed only low levels of radioactivity. Furthermore, there was no detectable, widespread contamination of the ground surface by DU. The results suggested that there was no immediate cause for concern regarding toxicity.

But major scientific uncertainties persisted about DU's long-term environmental behavior and potential adverse impacts. The assessment concluded that many DU munitions on the ground surface or hidden in the ground constituted a risk of future DU contamination of groundwater and drinking water. Therefore, UNEP called for precaution and recommended cleaning up polluted sites, raising the awareness of the local population, and monitoring environmental quality.

Serbia and Montenegro, 2001–2002

During the Kosovo conflict, a few sites in Serbia and Montenegro were also targeted with ordnance containing DU. Thus a second phase of scientific work started in September 2001 and was concluded in March 2002 with the publication of *Depleted Uranium in Serbia and Montenegro: Post-Conflict Environmental Assessment in the Federal Republic of Yugoslavia* (UNEP 2002). Eight sites were

Figure 2. UN environmental assessment sites in Serbia and Montenegro, 2001–2002
Source: UNEP (2002).
Notes:
1. At the time of UNEP's assessment, Serbia and Montenegro was one country, called the Federal Republic of Yugoslavia.
2. This figure shows the general location of assessment sites. A few sites are too close in proximity to reflect all eight visited.

selected for analysis based on their accessibility and the high number of rounds fired (see figure 2). A total of 129 samples were collected, including 54 soil, 4 smear, 11 water, 30 botanical, 17 air, 9 penetrators, and 4 fragments of jackets or penetrators.

The report confirmed the findings of the Kosovo assessment, provided additional information, and revealed important discoveries about the environmental behavior of DU. More than two years after the conflict, DU dust could be detected in soil samples and sensitive bio-indicators like lichens. However, because levels were extremely low, only state-of-the-art laboratory analyses could detect them. Based on the findings, UNEP confirmed that targeted sites were

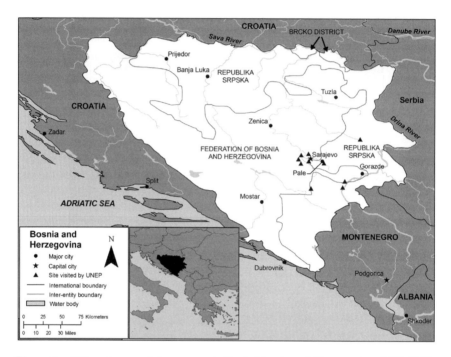

Figure 3. UN environmental assessment sites in Bosnia and Herzegovina, 2002–2003
Source: UNEP (2003).
Note: This figure shows general location of assessment sites. Some sites are too close in proximity to reflect all fifteen visited.

contaminated, though experts measured no significant levels of radioactivity. One or two meters from the impact holes, the amount of DU dust detected fell below the natural presence of uranium in the soil.

The UNEP team also used air-sampling techniques to detect airborne DU particles at two sites. Although all levels detected were below international safety limits, valuable information on DU's behavior was obtained. Discussions began on decontamination and construction standards for DU-contaminated sites.

As in the Kosovo report, UNEP called for precautionary measures such as monitoring groundwater in populated areas and raising awareness of the local population. The report included detailed recommendations for cleanup and decontamination, which started during the assessment.

Bosnia and Herzegovina, 2002–2003

DU was also used in Bosnia and Herzegovina during the conflict of the mid-1990s, and UNEP undertook an assessment of its effects in September 2002. Fifteen sites with reportedly high use of DU ammunition and evidence of environmental consequences were selected for analysis (see figure 3). Five of the sites were areas where NATO had reported using DU munitions. The local population and authorities were concerned that DU had been used in the other ten. A total of 132 samples were collected, including 4 penetrators, 46 surface soil, 3 soil profiles of 60 cm each, 5 smear, 2 scratch, 19 water, 24 air, and 29 vegetation.[6] The final report, *Depleted Uranium in Bosnia and Herzegovina: Post-Conflict Environmental Assessment*, was released in March 2003 (UNEP 2003a).

In addition to confirming the results of the earlier DU assessments, the report presented four new findings. First, detailed laboratory analyses of surface-soil samples revealed low levels of localized ground contamination. Although local ground contamination could be detected up to 200 meters from the impact zone, it was typically found within a 100-meter radius.

Second, penetrators buried near the surface had decreased in mass by approximately 25 percent over seven years. The correlation between these findings and the results of previous UNEP studies proved the relatively short time in which DU decomposed. Within twenty-five to thirty years, DU penetrators can completely degrade into uranium oxides and carbonates as a result of pitting corrosion.[7] Degradation products with different chemical and toxicological properties remain, and radioactivity does not change.

Third, DU-contaminated drinking water was found for the first time at one of the surveyed sites. The concentrations were very low, and the corresponding radiation doses were insignificant to human health. Nevertheless, because the mechanism that governs the contamination of water in a given environment is not well understood, UNEP recommended that water sampling and measurements continue for several years and that an alternative water source be used when DU was found in the drinking water. In Hadjici (west of Sarajevo), the local authorities shut down the contaminated well used by local workers, and added the site to a water-quality survey.

Fourth, DU contamination was found in the air in and around two buildings that had been hit by DU. Resuspension of DU particles by wind or human activity was the most likely cause. The concentrations in the air were very low, and calculated radiation doses from inhaling the dust were insignificant. However, precautionary decontamination and cleanup steps were recommended for the buildings, which the military and civilians used.

Overall, the findings of the study were consistent with those of UNEP's earlier assessments in the region: the levels of DU contamination were not a cause for alarm, but there was potential for groundwater contamination from penetrator-corrosion products or bioaccumulation of uranium salts from degraded DU dust.

---

[6] A scratch sample is a solid sample of material scraped off of a supposedly contaminated medium or structure.
[7] When a DU penetrator makes contact with an object, the penetrator's surface cracks deeply. When the metallic uranium reacts with the environment, cavities, pores, and corrosion pits result.

Iraq, 2004–2007

The 1990–1991 Gulf War was the first conflict in which DU munitions were used extensively. In total, some 300 metric tons of DU-containing munitions were fired by the United Kingdom and the United States in the course of the war, and DU remained in the environment as dust or small fragments. To date, no independent scientific assessment of the impacts of the 1990–1991 conflict has been conducted in Iraq.

The 2003 Gulf War, which the United States named Operation Iraqi Freedom, began on March 19, 2003. Approximately 120,000 troops from the United States, 45,000 from the United Kingdom, and smaller forces from other nations (collectively called the Coalition Forces) were deployed to Iraq.

The war itself was preceded by air attacks, which continued during the land invasion. Several air attacks were conducted by A-10 Thunderbolt II aircraft, which fired DU munitions. UK and U.S. tanks also launched DU munitions in several land battles, mainly against Iraqi tanks. The UK Ministry of Defence reported that its troops fired approximately 1.9 metric tons of DU munitions during the conflict, and in June 2003 it provided UNEP with the coordinates of DU-firing points of the UK Challenger 2 tanks. The United States has not made available information concerning the quantity of DU munitions it used and the corresponding coordinates of firing points.

Rumors about health effects from a high concentration of DU residue on the battlefield concerned Iraqis and the international community. In July 2004, UNEP was requested to strengthen environmental governance in Iraq and was provided funding through the Iraq Trust Fund from the government of Japan. In addition, the United Kingdom funded an assessment of the environmental consequences of the conflict and helped build the capacity of Iraqi authorities to assess the potential risks caused by the use of DU munitions during the 2003 war.

In April 2005, UNEP convened a meeting in Geneva with the IAEA and WHO to discuss, coordinate, and plan work on the environmental and health effects of DU residue in Iraq. The three organizations agreed to collaborate on DU-related matters with the Iraqi Radiation Protection Center (RPC) of the Iraqi Ministry of Environment.

Because security constraints prevented international experts from traveling to Iraq, UNEP's DU capacity-building project had five main objectives: first, to train Iraqi experts to undertake a field-based assessment of DU using internationally accepted methodologies and modern equipment; second, to provide those trained with precise information on sites to assess and the type of samples to collect; third, to supervise the assessment remotely and retrieve samples for detailed analysis in the Swiss Spiez Laboratory on ISO/IEC 17025 accredited procedures;[8] fourth, to evaluate the field observations, monitoring

---

[8] ISO/IEC 17025 specifies the general requirements for competence to carry out tests and calibrations, including sampling. It covers testing and calibration performed using standard, nonstandard, and laboratory-developed methods.

results, and samples to draw conclusions on the effectiveness of the capacity-building activities; and, fifth, to review the results and provide recommendations for follow-up to the Ministry of Environment. The outcomes of the capacity-building project were detailed in a report published in August 2007 (UNEP 2007).

UNEP trained Iraqi experts from the RPC in three workshops designed to cover all aspects of conducting DU assessments. The first workshop, which was held at the Spiez Laboratory in May 2004, focused broadly on environmental inspections and laboratory analyses. UNEP and Spiez Laboratory experts trained participants on the basics of environmental inspections, as well as on soil, air, and water pollution; hazardous chemicals; and waste management.

The second workshop—on DU site–investigation techniques—took place in June 2005 in Amman, Jordan. The objective of the workshop was to provide training, equipment, and technical assistance to staff from the Ministry of Environment's RPC and from the Ministry of Health. Participants were trained to use portable field instruments and laboratory equipment, which were then handed over to the head of the delegation from the Ministry of Environment.

A third workshop held in Geneva in August 2005 concentrated on site-investigation techniques in urban areas. The practical training session of the workshop had a comprehensive agenda covering nearly all the measurement techniques useful in urban areas. It also comprised detailed training on sampling methods, cleanup, and small-scale decontamination measures. The practical fieldwork focused on realistically simulating the conditions of a site targeted by DU weapons. Measurement and cleanup techniques were demonstrated by the UNEP team and tried by each participant. Sampling strategies and techniques were also developed.

Based on the training and documentation received from UNEP and Spiez Laboratory (UNEP 2005, 2006), Iraqi staff collected environmental samples at selected sites in southern Iraq during sampling campaigns conducted in 2006–2007. Four areas in southern Iraq were selected for analysis, namely, Samawah, Nasiriyah, Basra, and Zubayr (see figure 4). The basis for site selection included battle reports, mainly collected through extensive Internet research; high-resolution satellite images, taken as close as possible to the end of the war; and UK coordinates of DU firing sites. The Iraqi team collected 520 soil, water, vegetation, and smear samples.

In order to ensure scientific reliability, samples were shipped to UNEP in Geneva for analysis by Spiez Laboratory. Analysts measured the content of uranium isotopes (U-238, U-236, U-235, and U-234), using high-resolution inductively coupled plasma mass spectrometry.

The radioanalytical results were shared with UNEP and the IAEA to estimate the radiation doses and corresponding exposure risk to Iraqis living at the four locations investigated. On the basis of the measurements and the committed doses calculated, analysts concluded that DU residues in the environment did not pose a

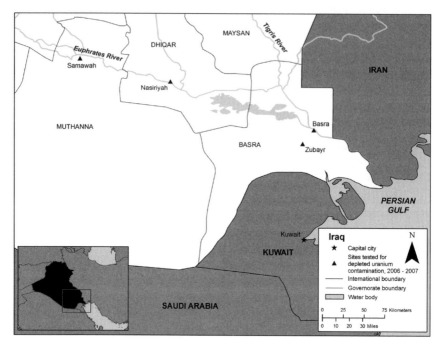

Figure 4. National assessment sites for depleted uranium in southern Iraq, 2006–2007
Sources: UNEP (2005, 2006).

radiological hazard to the population of the four studied locations, as long as people took minimum safety measures. The precautions included not entering vehicles hit by DU munitions, not undertaking long activities around objects hit by DU, not collecting penetrators or shrapnel that could contain DU residues, and not recycling or processing objects hit by DU. If these steps were taken, the estimated annual radiation doses that could arise from exposure to DU would be low (less than 0.1 mSv)—below the annual doses received by Iraqis from natural sources of radiation and therefore of little concern. The doses were also far below the annual action level of 10 mSv suggested by the ICRP as a criterion for determining whether remedial action is necessary.

Analysts concluded that a person would receive a significant dose of radiation only if he or she handled DU penetrators and penetrator fragments for a considerable period of time. A higher radiological risk was found where people entered vehicles hit by DU ammunition. Of particular concern were scrapyards where destroyed military equipment was stored and scrapping operations were conducted. But the doses received by workers involved in remelting DU-contaminated scrap metal were difficult to measure. Despite the lack of relevant data, not mixing DU-contaminated scrap metal with other scrap metal would be prudent. Using protective equipment, authorized personnel should dispose of scrap in accordance with international recommendations.

From a scientific point of view, the conclusions cannot be extrapolated to other locations in Iraq where DU ammunition was used because they depend on the amount of DU munitions fired, geographical and meteorological conditions, land use practices, and the population's habits. Without knowing the exact coordinates and firing data, it is difficult to predict potential contamination levels at other sites with any certainty. However, places exhibiting characteristics like those of the sites sampled would likely show similar contamination levels.

In 2010, the IAEA published the findings in *Radiological Conditions in Selected Areas of Southern Iraq with Residues of Depleted Uranium: Report by an International Group of Experts*, as part of the Radiological Assessment Reports Series (IAEA 2010).

LESSONS LEARNED AND RECOMMENDATIONS

The assessments resulted in a number of lessons learned and detailed recommendations to address and mitigate risks from the use of DU munitions. The recommendations are valid for any location potentially contaminated by DU.

Lessons learned

The main lessons learned from the post-conflict assessments of DU contamination are the following:

General

- Obtaining precise information on the location of DU-targeted sites, as well as secure site access, is an essential prerequisite for conducting effective measurements of DU contamination. Parties to conflicts should release the target coordinates and the number of rounds of DU fired in advance of any DU assessment.
- Localized surface contamination (i.e., a couple of grams of DU) can occur through four main pathways: dispersion and deposition (aerosolization) of fine DU particles immediately following an attack; weatherization of metallic DU pieces into corrosion products; dispersal of penetrators, smaller fragments, and dust on the soil surface, mainly through dilution by rainwater; or further redistribution by wind or flowing water, as in the case of smaller fragments and DU dust.
- The inner and outer surfaces of armored vehicles destroyed by DU ammunition will often be heavily contaminated by DU dust.

- Lichens appear to be reliable indicators of airborne DU contamination but only if they are within 200 meters of the zone attacked.
- Environmental effects of DU can be long-term, with resuspension of particles and groundwater contamination.

Soil

- Detailed laboratory analyses of surface-soil samples in areas where DU munitions had been used revealed low levels of localized ground contamination up to 200 meters from a weapon's impact.
- None of the sites showed contamination over large surfaces 200 meters from the target.
- Ground-surface DU contamination detectable by portable beta- and gamma-radiation detectors was typically limited to areas within one to two meters of penetrators and localized points of contamination caused by a penetrator's impact.

Corrosion of penetrators

- Penetrators buried near the surface of the ground and recovered had decreased in mass by approximately 25 percent over seven years. This finding, combined with UNEP's earlier studies of penetrators, shows that a DU penetrator can be fully oxidized into corrosion products (e.g., uranium oxides and carbonates) twenty-five to thirty-five years after impact.
- Penetrators lying on the ground showed significantly lower corrosion rates than those buried near the surface.

Drinking water

- In all the assessments conducted, DU was clearly identified in only one drinking-water sample. A second drinking-water sample from a well also showed traces of DU, but it was detectable only through use of mass spectrometric measurements.
- Contamination of the well may have occurred because of its position in the line of air attack.
- The concentrations found in the drinking-water samples were very low, and the corresponding radiation doses were insignificant to human health. This is also true considering the chemical toxicity of uranium as a heavy metal.

Air

- DU has been measured in air samples at a few sites, including buildings and vehicles hit by DU ammunition.

Depleted uranium contamination in post-conflict countries 177

- The most likely cause of DU in the air is resuspension of DU particles by wind and human activity from contamination points, corroded penetrators, or fragments on surfaces.
- The concentrations of DU in air samples were very low, and resulting radiation doses were minor and insignificant. Inhalation and ingestion can have different exposure limits.
- If many penetrators hit hard surfaces and are aerosolized on impact, people nearby may inhale airborne DU dust.

Recommendations

In post-conflict countries where DU munitions have been used, governments should do the following:

General

- As a precaution, raise awareness of DU. Programs should cover DU in general, the risks incurred from inhaling and touching DU, the hazards posed by handling and storing remnants of DU weapons, and contact information of relevant authorities. The leaflet *Depleted Uranium Awareness* provides information on the DU ammunition problem (UNEP 2003b).
- Launch a campaign to train people, particularly children, not to pick up, play with, or chew DU penetrators, fragments, or casings.
- Publicize locations where DU ammunition has been used.
- Take steps to prevent people from entering military vehicles hit by DU munitions.
- Apply precautionary measures after a conflict, giving high priority to reducing risks associated with DU. Move military equipment hit by DU to zones inaccessible to the public, and clean surfaces contaminated by DU penetrators, DU fragments, and DU-related ammunition parts.

Handling of DU-contaminated material

- Avoid scrapping and remelting DU-contaminated military equipment.
- Identify secure areas for storing DU-contaminated equipment.
- Assess all conflict-related equipment for DU and, when positively identified, move it to secure locations.
- Restrict access to secure locations and scrapyards where DU-contaminated equipment is stored.
- Avoid trying to decontaminate DU-contaminated equipment in order to prevent radiation and toxicological hazards and management problems associated with the radioactive and toxic waste generated.
- Task authorized personnel with removal of DU residue (DU penetrators, penetrator fragments, and corrosion products) from surfaces in targeted zones, using international best-storage practices.

Groundwater

- Have local authorities monitor drinking-water quality on a regular basis at sites attacked by DU ammunition and in surrounding zones. Because there is uncertainty about the mobility of DU and DU-corrosion products from the ground to groundwater, further research is justified to better understand the dispersion of DU in conflict zones and the efficacy of removing DU penetrators and remnants.
- Use an alternative water source if DU is found in drinking water.

Buildings

- Remove penetrators and fragments from buildings and conduct precautionary surface decontaminations of rooms in which there could be DU remnants.

The findings and lessons learned should help the international community form a better understanding of DU risks in real conflict situations. The knowledge gathered from the assessments and capacity-building activities conducted since 1999 can help post-conflict countries to measure potential risks from contamination of air, soil, water, and vegetation as well as design cleanup operations and longer-term environmental monitoring.

REFERENCES

ATSDR (United States Agency for Toxic Substances and Disease Registry). 1999. *Toxicological profile for uranium.* Atlanta, GA: United States Department of Health and Human Services.
EC (European Commission). 2001. *Opinion of the group of experts established according to article 31 of the Euratom treaty: Depleted uranium.* http://ec.europa.eu/energy/nuclear/radiation_protection/doc/art31/2001_03_opinion_en.pdf.
Harley, N. H., E. C. Foulkes, L. H. Hilborne, A. Hudson, and C. R. Anthony. 1999. *Depleted uranium.* Vol. 7 of *Gulf War illnesses.* Santa Monica, CA: Rand Corporation. www.rand.org/pubs/monograph_reports/2005/MR1018.7.pdf.
IAEA (International Atomic Energy Agency). 2003. *IAEA safety standards series: Remediation of areas contaminated by past activities and accidents.* Vienna, Austria. www-pub.iaea.org/MTCD/publications/PDF/Pub1176_web.pdf.
———. 2010. *Radiological conditions in selected areas of southern Iraq with residues of depleted uranium: Report by an international group of experts.* Radiological Assessment Reports Series. Vienna, Austria. www-pub.iaea.org/MTCD/publications/PDF/Pub1434_web.pdf.
ICRP (International Commission on Radiological Protection). 1999. *Protection of the public in situations of prolonged radiation exposure.* Publication No. 82. Oxford, UK: Pergamon Press.
MOD (Italian Ministry of Defense). 2004. Parliament, commission IV: Defense commission stenographic hearing. No. 15. June 29. www.camera.it/_dati/leg14/lavori/stencomm/04/audiz2/2004/0629/pdfel.htm.

Nellis AFB (Nellis Air Force Base, United States Air Force). 1997. Resumption of use of depleted uranium rounds at Nellis Air Force Range: Target 63-10. Nellis AFB, NV: United States Army Corps of Engineers.

Roth, P., V. Höllriegl, E. Werner, and P. Schramel. 2003. Assessment of exposure to depleted uranium. *Radiation Protection Dosimetry* 105 (1–4): 157–161.

Royal Society. 2001. *The health hazards of depleted uranium munitions: Part I.* http://royalsociety.org/The-health-hazards-of-depleted-uranium-munitions-Part-1-Full-Report/.

———. 2002. *The health hazards of depleted uranium munitions: Part II.* http://royalsociety.org/The-health-hazards-of-depleted-uranium-part-II/.

UNEP (United Nations Environment Programme). 2001. *Depleted uranium in Kosovo: Post-conflict environmental assessment.* Geneva, Switzerland. http://postconflict.unep.ch/publications/uranium.pdf.

———. 2002. *Depleted uranium in Serbia and Montenegro: Post-conflict environmental assessment in the Federal Republic of Yugoslavia.* Geneva, Switzerland. http://postconflict.unep.ch/publications/duserbiamont.pdf.

———. 2003a. *Depleted uranium in Bosnia and Herzegovina: Post-conflict environmental assessment.* Geneva, Switzerland. http://postconflict.unep.ch/publications/BiH_DU_report.pdf.

———. 2003b. *Depleted uranium awareness.* Flyer. Geneva, Switzerland. http://postconflict.unep.ch/publications/DUflyer.pdf.

———. 2005. *Local expert DU site assessment package I: As Samawah and Az Zubayr.* Geneva, Switzerland.

———. 2006. *Local expert site assessment package II: Al Basrah and An Nasiriyah.* Geneva, Switzerland.

———. 2007. *Technical report on capacity-building for the assessment of depleted uranium in Iraq.* Geneva, Switzerland. http://postconflict.unep.ch/publications/Iraq_DU.pdf.

Waleij, A., C. Edlund, H. Eriksson, B. Liljedahl, A. Lindblad, B. Sandström, and K. S. Westerdahl. 2004. *Hazards related to NBC or EIHH and PHC within Swedish AOR MNTF (N), Bosnia and Herzegovina.* FOI-R–1352–SE (2004). Umeå, Sweden: Swedish Defence Research Agency.

WHO (World Health Organization). 1998. Guidelines for drinking-water quality. 2nd ed. Addendum to vol. 2, *Health criteria and other supporting information.* WHO/EOS/98.1. Geneva, Switzerland. www.who.int/water_sanitation_health/dwq/2edaddvol2a.pdf.

———. 2001. *Depleted uranium: Sources, exposure and health effects.* Geneva, Switzerland. www.who.int/ionizing_radiation/pub_meet/Depluraniumintro.pdf.

WISE (World Information Service on Energy). n.d. Uranium toxicity. WISE Uranium Project. www.wise-uranium.org/utox.html.

Linking demining to post-conflict peacebuilding: A case study of Cambodia

Nao Shimoyachi-Yuzawa

Landmines are one of the most significant obstacles to post-conflict peacebuilding and development. Long after a battle has ended and peace agreements are signed, landmines remain underground, where they explode to kill and maim people above. Mines delay the return and resettlement of refugees and internally displaced persons (IDPs) and block access to vital resources and social services, including farmland, water, roads, schools, and health clinics. Furthermore the costs of mine removal and victim assistance weigh heavily on countries struggling to recover from conflict and rebuild their societies.

Mine clearance progresses slowly. Although more efficient demining tools, such as mine detection dogs and machines, are used widely, manual metal detectors remain the primary technique for attaining humanitarian mine clearance, or ridding an area of all mines. The Mine Ban Treaty,[1] which was signed in 1997 and entered into force in 1999 as a result of a unique partnership between nongovernmental organizations (NGOs) and states, obliges states' parties to clear all antipersonnel mines in their territories within ten years of becoming party to the treaty and to prohibit the use, stockpiling, production, and transfer of anti-personnel mines. Approximately two-thirds of the sixteen states failed to meet their 2009 deadlines and requested extensions (ICBL 2009). As of August 2009, the International Campaign to Ban Landmines (ICBL), a coalition of more than one thousand NGOs around the world, believed that more than seventy countries were still affected by mines and that the total mined area was less than 3,000 square kilometers (km^2). The ICBL also stated that at least 1,100 km^2 of mined areas were cleared from 1999 to 2008, including 158 km^2 in 2008 (ICBL 2009). At the current rate, the world would be free of mines in twenty years.

Nao Shimoyachi-Yuzawa is a research fellow at the Japan Institute of International Affairs. This chapter was developed with support from the Center for Global Partnership of the Japan Foundation.

[1] The treaty's official name is the Convention on the Prohibition of the Use, Stockpiling, Production and Transfer of Anti-Personnel Mines and on their Destruction. For more information, see www.un.org/Depts/mine/UNDocs/ban_trty.htm.

182 Assessing and restoring natural resources in post-conflict peacebuilding

Landmines must be removed to protect populations and put mine-affected countries on the path to recovery and development with post-clearance land use plans. Scholars and policy makers in international organizations have advocated linking demining to peacebuilding and development, but only a handful of countries has actually succeeded in doing so (Harpviken and Skåra 2003; Harpviken and Isaksen 2004; GICHD 2009).

This chapter examines the demining strategy and operations of Cambodia, one of the most heavily mine-affected countries in the world, and attempts to draw lessons for connecting mine clearance to peacebuilding. Although the United Nations initiated improvement of demining operations after the Mine Ban Treaty, ensuring effective use of mine-cleared land—a qualitative aspect of demining— remains a challenge for many countries. While absorbing many new trends in international mine action,[2] Cambodia is developing a decentralized mechanism to set priorities and prepare land use plans for minefields. The chapter first provides an overview of Cambodia's landmine problem and then examines its demining strategy and operations with regard to land management and peacebuilding. A focus is placed on a bottom-up approach that engages local communities affected by mines. The chapter then explores international assistance, especially that of Japan, one of the largest donors in the field, and concludes by presenting lessons from the case of Cambodia.

THE LANDMINE PROBLEM IN CAMBODIA

Cambodia's landmine problem resulted from a nearly three-decade-long civil war that started in 1970 during the Cold War. Internal factions, backed by the United States, the Soviet Union, China, and Viet Nam, competed for power and left the country contaminated by landmines and explosive remnants of war. Landmines were used as a key weapon in the 1980s in the battle between the socialist government, which was supported by Viet Nam and the Soviet Union, and the communist, China-backed Khmer Rouge, whose reign (1975–1979) left an estimated 1.7 million people dead from overwork, malnutrition, and execution.[3] As the government army pushed the Khmer Rouge guerrillas toward the border with Thailand, the northwestern provinces, notably Battambang and Banteay Meanchey, became the most densely mined areas in Cambodia (see figure 1). Reflecting the nature of the conflict, some thirty different varieties of antipersonnel mines, manufactured mostly in the Soviet Union, China, and Viet Nam, were planted in Cambodia (CMAC and JICA 2007). The peace process began in October 1991 with the

---

[2] *Mine action* means more than removing landmines from the ground. According to the UN Mine Action Service (UNMAS), the five pillars of mine action are clearance of mines and explosive remnants of war, mine risk education, victim assistance, advocacy of a mine-free world, and destruction of mine stockpiles. See E-MINE (2010).

[3] The exact death toll is debated. The Yale Cambodian Genocide Program at Yale University gives an estimate of 1.7 million, and political scientist R. J. Rummel offers the figure of 2 million (Yale University 2010; Rummel 1994). See also ICRC (1996).

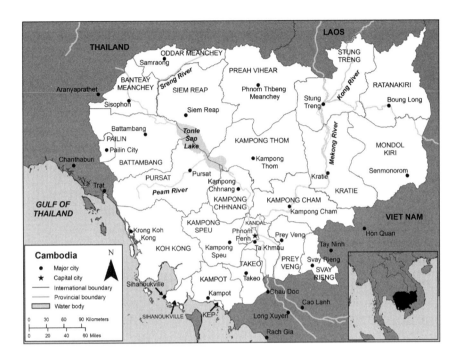

Paris Peace Accord, which brought together four factions to form the Supreme National Council. The Khmer Rouge soon withdrew from the agreement to continue waging guerrilla war in the northwestern mountains. The conflict did not truly end until 1998 when Pol Pot, the Khmer Rouge leader, died.

The first national survey of minefields in Cambodia (the Level 1 Survey), completed in 2002 with the support of the Canadian government, ascertained that the number of villages affected by mines was 6,422, or 46 percent of the total number of villages, and stated that the contamination put more than 5 million people, or about 45 percent of the population, at risk (CIDA and CMAC 2002). Because both the government army and Khmer Rouge militias used mines heavily as offensive weapons, antipersonnel and antitank mines were mixed randomly, and more than one layer of mines was created. The Khmer Rouge laid landmines not only in battlegrounds but also in civilian communities to terrorize and extend social and economic control over the population (Davies and Dunlop 1994). Few records were kept about the location of the mines, making mine removal extremely difficult (ICRC 1996).[4] Under the Mine Ban Treaty, which the Cambodian government signed in December 1997 and to which it became a state party in January 2000, Cambodia was required to clear all antipersonnel

---

[4] Protocol II to the 1980 Convention on Certain Conventional Weapons requires that records be kept of the locations of pre-planned minefields. Parties to a conflict should also endeavor to keep records of the locations of other minefields laid during hostilities.

184 Assessing and restoring natural resources in post-conflict peacebuilding

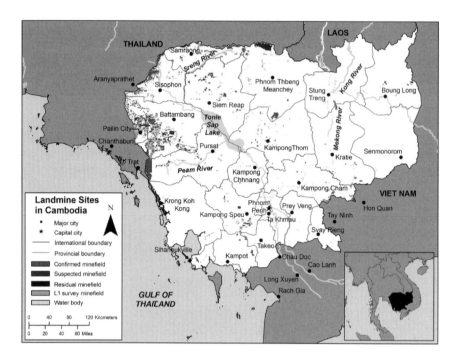

Figure 1. Landmine sites in Cambodia
Source: CMAC (2008).

mines no later than January 1, 2010. But in 2009, the country estimated that 649 km² still required demining and applied for a ten-year extension at a projected cost of US$330 million (ICBL 2009).[5]

According to Cambodia Mine/UXO Victim Information System, there were 7,300 reported casualties from landmines and unexploded ordnance (UXO)—approximately 92 percent of them civilian—between the end of hostilities in 1998 and May 2009 (ICBL 2009).[6] Casualties occurred primarily when villagers were farming or tampering with mines or pieces of UXO (RGOC 2005). Agriculture, which is the major means of making a living in Cambodia, accounts for 34 percent of gross domestic product and employs 70 percent of the population (NIS 2008a, 2008b). The overwhelming majority of minefields are located in the once-prosperous northwestern agricultural provinces of Battambang and Banteay Meanchey. When the peace agreement was signed in 1991, the Cambodian government announced plans for the return of refugees and IDPs, but some

---

[5] According to ICBL, Cambodia demined 373.53 km² of land in the previous decade (ICBL 2009). The country's efficiency increased year by year; 63.36 km² of land was cleared in 2008.
[6] People involved in demining activities in Cambodia say there are, by far, more unreported than reported casualties.

heavily mine-affected districts of these provinces had to call off the plans owing to high casualty rates. Even people who forced their way back found that up to 80 percent of the arable land had been lost to landmines (Davies and Dunlop 1994). Recognizing the extent of the problem, Cambodia listed mine clearance in its 2006–2010 National Strategic Development Plan (NSDP) as one of the key strategies for enhancing the agricultural sector (RGOC 2006).

NATIONAL DEMINING STRATEGY

Cambodia is one of a few countries that has incorporated demining programs into their national poverty-reduction and development strategies. A study by the International Peace Research Institute, Oslo and the United Nations Development Programme, *Reclaiming the Fields of War*, surveyed eleven mine-affected countries and found that only two countries—Cambodia and Laos—had clearly linked mine action to their poverty reduction strategy papers (PRSPs). The study stated that "Cambodia's PRSP is the one that comes closest to having mainstreamed mine action" (Harpviken and Isaksen 2004, 65).

International mine action has become increasingly systematic and professional since the Mine Ban Treaty. Driven by the UN Mine Action Service (UNMAS), international mine-action policy has promoted the use of modern technologies to map and measure the extent of the global landmine crisis (Mather 2002). Mine-affected countries are encouraged to conduct national surveys, known as level one surveys, to measure the extent of their landmine problems. The results are stored in a standardized data management system (the Information Management System for Mine Action), which was developed by the Geneva International Centre for Humanitarian Demining (GICHD). To ensure safety and improve efficiency in mine action, GICHD has also developed demining guidelines, which have been updated periodically. Although landmines have long been considered an issue of safety and security, the UN has begun emphasizing integration of mine clearance in broader national programs for reconstruction and development (UNGA 2004; Harpviken and Isaksen 2004; GICHD 2009). Still in most mine-affected countries, mine clearance is largely conducted apart from peacebuilding and development because it is considered a highly technical sector, whose practitioners often have military backgrounds (Kjellman et al. 2003; Harpviken and Isaksen 2004).[7]

Cambodia completed a nationwide survey of minefields in 2002 and appended a demining objective to the eight Millennium Development Goals (MDGs) shared by all developing nations. In 2005, the country incorporated the MDGs into its new NSDP. According to the NSDP, "de-mining operations are not only humanitarian

---

[7] The ICBL also stated, "efforts continue to mainstream mine action into development. Yet, despite references to demining in many development plans or poverty reduction strategy papers and the existence of an online network for practitioners, the extent of mainstreaming on the ground still appears limited" (ICBL 2008, 28).

and security related but have significant social and economic implications, particularly on land distribution and the security of poor farming households in remote areas. They open up avenues for rural development" (RGOC 2006, 60).

Cambodia's primary demining agencies are the Cambodian Mine Action Center (CMAC), the national operator, and the Cambodian Mine Action and Victim Assistance Authority (CMAA), the national regulatory body. CMAC was originally established in June 1992 as part of the UN Transitional Authority in Cambodia (UNTAC), which ran from 1992–1993 and was tasked with implementing the peace accord. Although mine clearing assistance was included in its mandate, UNTAC busied itself with ensuring a successful election and helping to write a new constitution, which it regarded as its primary missions. Driven by necessity, the UN undertook demining indirectly through training, but the organization and its member states were reluctant to allow their mine specialists stationed at UNTAC's Mine Clearance Training Unit to work in dangerous minefields and, instead, decided to train Cambodian deminers. As UNTAC force commander Lt. General John Sanderson put it, demining was dismissed as "a Cambodian problem" (Davies and Dunlop 1994). The international community considered CMAC a Cambodian institution for tackling the mine problem over the long term. Ironically CMAC became one of the most effective government institutions (Davies and Dunlop 1994).

In July 1993, just after the first election, CMAC became a Cambodian national institution by absorbing UNTAC's Mine Clearance Training Unit. Under the direct control of the prime minister, CMAC is responsible for mine/UXO clearance, training, minefield surveys, and risk education. With a staff of 2,300, it has an annual budget of approximately US$10 million, of which more than 90 percent comes from foreign donors (CMAC 2008; Sang Onn 2009). The other demining agencies include international NGOs, such as the Mine Advisory Group and the Halo Trust, and the Royal Cambodian Armed Forces (see figure 2).

In 2000, the CMAA was set up to regulate and coordinate all demining activities, a responsibility previously assigned to CMAC. Often described mockingly as "a father born from his children," CMAA has had difficulty overseeing all the demining operations because of a lack of capacity and funding (Rotha 2009).

MINES AND LAND MANAGEMENT

Coordination between mine clearance and land registration is indispensable to ensure fair distribution of land. In Cambodia, where large-scale land acquisitions (often referred to as land grabbing) by people with power and authority is rampant, there are reports of poor people who laid mines to protect their land or built their houses deliberately on minefields to prevent arbitrary confiscation (JCBL 2003). The problem is exacerbated by the fact that Cambodia's land tenure remains unclear largely because private ownership of all property, including land, was abolished during the Khmer Rouge regime (1975–1979). Just prior to the

Demining and peacebuilding in Cambodia 187

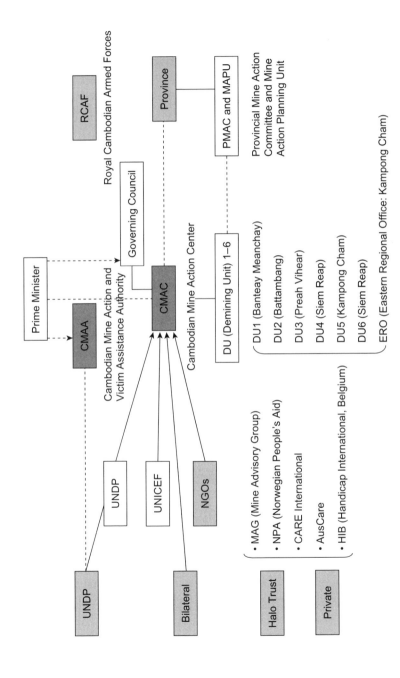

Figure 2. Cambodian mine action organization chart
Source: Yaginuma (2009).

Vietnamese withdrawal in 1989, the Cambodian government introduced laws that allowed farmers to pass land titles to their children and permitted householders to buy and sell real estate (Chandler 2008). Nevertheless vast tracts remain classified as state land. All provinces have conducted land registration activities, but only some have carried out systematic registration. Most landowners still do not hold legal title to their property (Vanna 2007).

Determining land ownership

A year after the Level 1 Survey was completed in 2002, the Cambodian government conducted a pilot project to address land ownership in mine-affected areas. With the support of the government and private sector of Canada, the Land Administration in Mine Affected Areas (LAMAA) project designed a program for distribution of mine-cleared land in the Svay Chek District of Banteay Meanchey Province.

The first step was to provide the local population with information on topics such as the obligations of landowners, so they could successfully claim land titles. This was accomplished during meetings at easily accessible places, such as pagodas. The second step—the demarcation of parcels and adjudication—was based on the Level 1 Survey but involved more extensive field investigations and interviews with landowners and their neighbors concerning the history of the land and its owners, information on mines, household occupations and incomes, and the village's development priorities. It also utilized high-resolution satellite data. The information collected was put into a database. The third step was a thirty-day public exhibit of the results of the investigations for the landowners and other concerned people. Again held at an accessible location, the public display was the last chance for local people to lay and modify claims to land. LAMAA officials were available to explain and answer questions. The final step was the issuance of land titles, which were given out by the General Department of Cadastre and Geography in Phnom Penh and the provincial director or local manager, and were presented to locals at a public ceremony (Vibol 2009).

The project eventually awarded 3,578 titles in January 2004 in four villages in Svay Chek Commune and one village in Treas Commune in Svay Chek District. Along the way, there were nineteen disputes: six cases concerned boundary clarification at the time of demarcation; three involved misunderstandings over family inheritances or gifts; two related to compensation for improvements made by nonowner occupants; two were caused by a misinterpretation of land law; two occurred on borrowed land, which the borrower mistakenly thought he owned or was at least entitled to compensation for improvements; one arose over the lack of a fence on a property boundary; one dealt with an excombatant who claimed land on returning from service; one concerned the construction of a village road; and one had to do with the alleged abandonment of land by a poor farmer. LAMAA personnel resolved all but one dispute with assistance from the village chief, family members, and the participants (Vibol 2009).

Bottom-up priority setting

The Cambodian government also considered establishing an institutional process to prioritize minefields and guarantee effective use of mine-cleared land. In 1998, CMAC organized a workshop in Battambang that resulted in placing the province at the center of the process. In the following year, CMAC established a land use planning unit (LUPU) under the Provincial Rural Development Committee of Battambang Province. LUPUs were later introduced in four other provinces (AVI and CMAA 2008).[8] But CMAC failed to consult land authorities and the regulatory agency of mine action (CMAA) and left unclear the responsibilities of the Ministry of Land Management, Urban Planning, and Construction and the CMAA. The project also lacked sustainable funding; three LUPUs eventually lost support in November 2003.[9]

Learning from their failure, CMAA drafted in August 2003 a sub-decree designed to establish a bottom-up land use–planning process that involved all concerned agencies, including provincial authorities, demining operators, relevant ministries, and international donors. Sub-decree 70, Socioeconomic Management of Mine Clearance Operations, was adopted in September 2004.

The key agencies in this process were the Provincial Mine Action Committee (PMAC) and the Mine Action Planning Unit (MAPU). PMAC is an impermanent committee chaired by a vice governor and is composed of provincial representatives, officials from relevant ministries, demining operators, and donors. The committee approves the annual Provincial Mine Clearance Work Plan, which prioritizes minefields for clearance in the next year in line with national and provincial development plans. MAPU is a permanent technical unit of PMAC, tasked with coordinating mine-affected communities and demining and development agencies (Sang Onn 2009).

Planning for mine clearance runs on an annual cycle. It begins in January or February with a commune meeting where village chiefs and commune council members discuss and propose priority areas for demining, based on information ascertained through the Level 1 Survey that included village sketches, aerial photos, and village and minefield profile data. Proposals must be backed by good reasons, such as the frequency of mine accidents; a lack of schools, roads, health centers, and other infrastructure; and poor access to resources, such as agricultural land and water. The areas are ranked, and by March, the commune council finalizes the demining plan for the next year. The plan is then sent to the district where the District Working Group (DWG)—consisting of representatives of the district, NGOs, MAPU, and CMAC—selects minefields to clear in light of villagers' needs and donors' plans. The DWG meeting is usually held by August. In September and October, MAPU and CMAC conduct field investigations to verify

---

[8] The four provinces were Banteay Meanchey, Oddar Meanchey, Pailin, and Preah Vihear.
[9] Information was obtained from the CMAA during research for this chapter, and is on file with the author.

that areas selected for demining comply with criteria for intended land use, beneficiary selection, land ownership, and so on. Usually by the end of November, the PMAC determines priority minefields in line with the national mine-action plan, which reflects the needs of national and local development and poverty-reduction programs. National priority is currently given to residential land, agricultural land, infrastructure development, and safety. The final plan is submitted to CMAA (Sang Onn 2009; Vibol 2009; Vanna 2007).

Mine clearance is conducted according to the plan, and mine-cleared land is then distributed to local people, following the procedure set out by the pilot project for managing mine-affected land. The process was first introduced in the five provinces of Banteay Meanchey, Battambang, Oddar Meanchey, Pailin, and Preah Vihear with the support of Australian Volunteers International and Canada's GeoSpatial International Inc. and was later expanded to include three additional provinces—Siem Reap, Kampong Thom, and Pursat. Thus eight out of Cambodia's twenty-three provinces now have in place the community-based, bottom-up mechanism to clear landmines.

Senior CMAC and CMAA officials in Phnom Penh suggested that the annual planning process was working fairly well, but CMAA admitted that funding did not yet allow sufficient monitoring for full analysis.[10] According to CMAA, of the land cleared in 2006 (35.4 km^2), roughly 60 percent was allocated for agriculture and resettlement (including dual-purpose land) followed by roads and other infrastructure (see figure 3) (MOFA 2008). Overall the result was consistent with the priorities set nationally. Battambang Province reported that rice fields increased by 8,000 hectares between 2005 and 2006 because of mine clearance and cultivation of abandoned land. With the average rice yield estimated to be 2.2 tons per hectare, mine clearance led to production of up to 17,600 tons of additional rice (BDA n.d.).

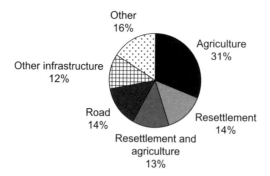

Figure 3. Land use after landmine removal in Cambodia, 2006
Source: MOFA (2008).

---

[10] The author interviewed senior officials, including Oum Sang Onn, the director of planning and operations at CMAC, and Chan Rotha, the deputy secretary-general of CMAA, on February 25, 2009, in Phnom Penh, Cambodia.

INTERNATIONAL ASSISTANCE

Despite its initial dismissal by the international community as a "Cambodian problem," the removal of landmines from Cambodia attracts international, bilateral, and nongovernmental donors, thanks largely to awareness raised by the international campaign that led to the Mine Ban Treaty. But the nature of the international assistance points to challenges that Cambodia faces in promoting ownership of mine action and linking mine clearance to peacebuilding.

Heavy dependence on foreign aid

In 2007, thirteen countries and the European Commission reportedly provided US$30.8 million to mine action in Cambodia, and Cambodia's national government supplied US$1.15 million. According to the Five-Year Mine Action Plan for 2005–2009, approximately US$170 million was needed for the full term—or US$34 million per year—to address all aspects of mine action. As noted by the UNMAS, insufficient funding is a primary factor impeding mine action in Cambodia (ICBL 2008).

CMAC receives the largest part of the international assistance. In 2007, the Cambodian national demining agency collected US$9.4 million in aid, which accounts for some 30 percent of the money donated to Cambodia's mine action and 95 percent of the annual budget of CMAC. But most of the assistance is provided through one-year contracts, making the agency's financial foundations weak (Yaginuma 2009).

CMAA regularly calls coordination committee meetings, which are attended by international donors and development partners. Heavy dependence on foreign aid means that donors tend to drive the actual demining, depriving CMAA of oversight and coordination. Furthermore the involvement of many donors, without coordination, leads to inefficiency at CMAC and CMAA because they have to prepare different versions of reports for each donor—one of the structural problems of international aid administration.

Official development assistance (ODA)

In 2007, Japan was the largest donor to mine action in Cambodia; it provided US$5.9 million (697 million yen).[11] Japan regards Cambodia as one of its most important recipients of foreign aid; the Japanese government sent its first peacekeeping forces to the country in 1992 and began providing development assistance. Japan's assistance to Cambodian mine action began in 1999 as part of the Zero Victim Campaign that the Japanese government announced on its signing of the Mine Ban Treaty in 1997. The campaign provided US$8.5 million (10 billion

---

[11] In 2008, Japan was overtaken by Australia in the amount of financial assistance provided to Cambodia's mine action efforts. See ICBL (2009).

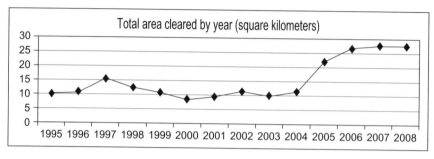

Figure 4. Land area cleared by Cambodian Mine Action Center, 1995–2008
Source: CMAC (2009).

yen) in aid to more than thirty countries between 1998 and 2002. In 2003, the government listed demining assistance as a peacebuilding priority in its revised Official Development Aid (ODA) Charter. The government regards CMAC as its ODA partner in Cambodia and, in 2007, provided US$5.9 million (697 million yen) to assist the country's mine action.

Characteristic of Japan's ODA for Cambodia's mine action is its heavy focus on efficiency. Of the assistance provided in 2007, about US$4 million (480 million yen), or 69 percent, went to research and development of demining machines. Brush cutters are key; they are used to remove vegetation before clearing mines. In tropical Cambodia, fast-growing trees and ground cover pose significant obstacles to demining, especially during the rainy season. Put into full operation in 2005, the machines are credited with almost doubling mine clearance: the land cleared in 2005 was more than twice that in 2004 (see figure 4). Of the twenty-seven operational brush cutters in 2007, all but one was supplied by Japan.

However, demining machines have shortcomings. First, not only do they miss mines but they also can only be used where there are no antitank mines because antitank mines can destroy the machines when exploded. Because many of Cambodia's minefields contain a mixture of antipersonnel and antitank mines, most mine clearance (63 percent) is still conducted manually using metal detectors (see figure 5) (CMAC 2008). Second, researchers have argued that, by removing all vegetation, the machines can severely undermine soil structure and texture. Such damage, whether caused by inherent flaws in equipment design, improper use, or lack of skill, can often be irreversible (Morin 2008). These limitations and concerns suggest the need for taking into account local needs and situations, in addition to seeking efficiency in mine clearance.

NGO assistance

Because demining tasks are dangerous, they are usually left to specialists. But in poor, rural areas of Cambodia, untrained villagers have demined their land because there is no economic alternative to farming minefields. The high casualty

Demining and peacebuilding in Cambodia 193

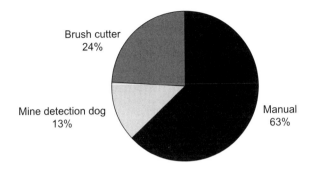

Figure 5. Landmine clearance methods in Cambodia, 2007
Source: CMAC (2008).

rate in rural Cambodia is often attributed to the practice. Community-based demining (CBD), introduced by CMAC, is designed to pay villagers to learn proper mine clearance in order to prevent accidents.[12] As of 2007, five CBD platoons, each consisting of thirty-three people, had been positioned in Battambang, Banteay Meanchey, and Preah Vihear provinces. Of the five platoons, three have been deployed since 2006 in Battambang, where Japan Mine Action Service (JMAS), a Japanese NGO, has assisted them in cooperation with CMAC. They receive annual financial support of US$0.6 million (75 million yen) from the Japanese government.

The CBD site in Tasen Commune in Kamrieng District of Battambang Province, sits on the border with Thailand, where fierce battles were fought between the government army and Pol Pot's forces in the 1980s. Most of the residents of the commune, which consists of six villages, are former Pol Pot guerrillas, who returned from Thailand to make their living by clearing jungles. The average annual household income is somewhere between US$700 and US$800. Ninety-nine percent of the villagers are peasants, and many of them have no other means of livelihood than cultivating mined land. Thus of the fifty-eight mine accidents that occurred between 1998 and 2007, some 60 percent injured or killed farmers (Takayama 2009).

In recruiting deminers, the Japanese NGO gives priority—in order of importance—to mine victims from poor families, widows or widowers from poor families, and members of landless poor families (CMAC 2008). As a result, in July 2008, forty-five of the ninety-nine deminers in Tasen Commune were women (JMAS 2008). Recruited villagers are sent to a training center run by CMAC in Kampong Chhnang for a six-week technical training program before undertaking demining tasks. The monthly salary is US$105 (Takayama 2009).[13]

---

[12] Mine-action practitioners debate whether villagers should be trained in demining techniques. See, for example, Bottomley (2003).
[13] The net monthly salary is US$72, of which CMAC deducts US$30 for retirement and US$3 for mutual aid money (Takayama 2009).

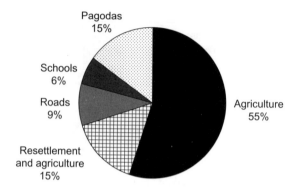

Figure 6. Land use after 2007–2008 landmine removal in Tasen Commune, Battambang, Cambodia
Source: JMAS (2008).

Priority setting for minefields and planning for community building follows the PMAC/MAPU process. Between June 2007 and June 2008, the three CBD platoons deployed in Tasen Commune cleared a total of 0.625 km^2, of which more than half was subsequently used for farmland (see figure 6).

When compared with the 2006 national statistics in figure 3—although the periods covered are not exactly the same—the findings suggest that CBD reflects the needs of local people. Though resettlement figured highly in national statistics, more priority was given to agriculture in Tasen, where people returned to the land before the mines were cleared and nearly all the residents were engaged in farming, virtually the sole source of income. By giving local people priority-setting and decision-making authority, the community-based approach enhanced their sense of ownership in the rehabilitation and development of the community. Because opportunities for education were limited in Tasen, the villagers decided to build two primary schools and one junior high school on the mine-cleared land, as well as a two-kilometer-long road leading to the junior high school. They also installed fifty-nine tubewells to improve the community's sanitary and health conditions (Takayama 2009).[14] The CBD project assisted by JMAS is much smaller in scale than the Japanese ODA in terms of budget and areas covered. Nevertheless the case suggests that coping with landmines in post-conflict situations means more than just removing mines: cleared land must benefit vulnerable people.

CONCLUSION

Given the limited resources and time-consuming nature of demining, minefields must be prioritized and efficiency in clearing them must be improved. Furthermore,

---

[14] Previously villagers used pond water, which often led to malaria and other infectious diseases (Takayama 2009).

prioritization should be consistent with broader post-conflict reconstruction and development plans. In this sense, mine-action programs must be integrated into national poverty-reduction and development strategies, as advocated by the UN in recent years.

Cambodia's experience indicates that land management is key to linking mine clearance to peacebuilding. Land is closely associated with rebuilding life after conflict, which includes the return and resettlement of refugees and IDPs and access to vital resources and social services, such as farmland, water, health care, and education. Yet if mismanaged, mine-cleared land can be grabbed by the elite and become a source of tension and grievance, thereby undermining peace at the local level. Therefore mine clearance must go hand in hand with land registration and titling.

This case study also suggests the efficacy of a decentralized, bottom-up approach. Involving local communities in prioritizing areas for demining and developing land use plans ensures that mine-free land benefits vulnerable people and contributes to community development. In designing a community-based mechanism, Cambodia's history shows that demining agencies must coordinate with other ministries and donors, including authorities in charge of land management and rural development.

Enhancing mine clearance productivity and efficiency, the chief objective of the UNMAS and GICHD, is still critical. Efforts must continue given the still-slow pace of demining. Demining programs and the international community need to pay more attention to local needs and situations in order to link mine clearance to post-conflict reconstruction and peacebuilding.

REFERENCES

AVI (Australian Volunteers International) and CMAA (Cambodian Mine Action and Victim Assistance Authority). 2008. Mine action planning units and the mine action planning process. Phnom Penh, Cambodia. CD-ROM.

BDA (Battambang District Administration, Royal Government of Cambodia). n.d. Economy. www.battambang-town.gov.kh/city_info/anzeige/redaktionssystem/main/show .cfm?region_id=27&lang_id=3&id=252&modul_id=5.

Bottomley, R. 2003. Balancing risk: Village demining in Cambodia. *Third World Quarterly* 24 (5): 823–837.

Chandler, D. 2008. *A history of Cambodia*. 4th ed. Boulder, CO: Westview Press.

CIDA (Canadian International Development Agency) and CMAC (Cambodia Mine Action Centre). 2002. Cambodia National Level 1 Survey: Executive summary. www.sac-na.org/pdf_text/cambodia/executive%20summary.htm.

CMAC (Cambodian Mine Action Center). 2008. *Annual report 2007*. Phnom Penh. http://cmac.gov.kh/userfiles/file/ar2007.pdf.

———. 2009. *Annual report 2008*. Phnom Penh. www.cmac.gov.kh/userfiles/file/annual2008 .pdf

CMAC (Cambodian Mine Action Center) and JICA (Japan International Cooperation Agency). 2007. *What is Cambodian Mine Action Centre?* Phnom Penh. www.jica.go.jp/project/cambodia/0701732/pdf/cmac.pdf.

Davies, P., and N. Dunlop. 1994. *War of the mines: Cambodia, landmines and the impoverishment of a nation*. London: Pluto Press.

E-MINE (Electronic Mine Action Information Network). 2010. What is mine action? www.mineaction.org/section.asp?s=what_is_mine_action.

GICHD (Geneva International Centre for Humanitarian Demining). 2009. *Linking mine action and development: Guidelines for policy and programme development*. Geneva, Switzerland. www.gichd.org/publications/linking-mine-action-and-development-guidelines-for-policy-and-programme-development-en.

Harpviken, K. B., and J. Isaksen. 2004. *Reclaiming the field of war: Mainstreaming mine action in development*. Oslo, Norway: International Peace Research Institute, Oslo / United Nations Development Programme. www.prio.no/sptrans/-446551233/Harpviken%20Isaksen%20(2004)%20Reclaiming%20the%20Fields%20of%20War.pdf.

Harpviken, K. B., and B. A. Skåra. 2003. Humanitarian mine action and peace building: Exploring the relationship. *Third World Quarterly* 24 (5): 809–822.

ICBL (International Campaign to Ban Landmines). 2008. *Landmine monitor report 2008: Toward a mine-free world*. Ottawa: Mines Action Canada. www.the-monitor.org/lm/2008/translations/LMES_2008_07_withMaps.pdf.

———. 2009. *Landmine monitor report 2009: Toward a mine-free world*. Ottawa: Mines Action Canada. www.the-monitor.org/lm/2009/res/Landmines_Report_2009.pdf.

ICRC (International Committee of the Red Cross). 1996. *Anti-personnel landmines: Friend or foe?; A study of the military use and effectiveness of anti-personnel mines*. Geneva, Switzerland. www.icrc.org/eng/assets/files/other/icrc_002_0654.pdf.

JCBL (Japan Campaign to Ban Landmines). 2003. Landmines and human beings [Jirai to Ningen]. Tokyo: Iwanami.

JMAS (Japan Mine Action Service). 2008. *Community-based demining annual report: 26 June 2007–25 June 2008*. http://jmas-ngo.jp/ja/english/CBDCompletionReport2008-6/CBDRep2008-1p.htm.

Kjellman, K. E., K. B. Harpviken, A. S. Millard, and A. Strand. 2003. Acting as one? Co-ordinating responses to the landmine problem. *Third World Quarterly* 24 (5): 855–871.

Mather, C. 2002. Maps, measurements, and landmines: The global landmines crisis and the politics of development. *Environment and Planning* 34:239–250.

MOFA (Ministry of Foreign Affairs of Japan). 2008. Project assessment report of grand aid project in Cambodia [Mushoshikin Kyoryoku ni Okeru Project Level Jigo Hyoka Chosa Cambodia].

Morin, A. 2008. Demining and the environment: A primer. *Journal of Mine Action* 11 (2). http://maic.jmu.edu/journal/11.2/feature/morin/morin.htm.

NIS (National Institute of Statistics, Royal Government of Cambodia). 2008a. Gross domestic product (GDP): Economic activity 2003–2007. www.nis.gov.kh/nis/NA/Summary.pdf.

———. 2008b. 2008 General population census of Cambodia. http://celade.cepal.org/khmnis/census/khm2008.

RGOC (Royal Government of Cambodia). 2005. Cambodian strategy and 2005–2009 plan to implement article 5 of the Ottawa Convention. Paper presented to Nairobi Summit on Mine Free World First Review Conference. www.mineaction.org/downloads/Cambodia%20Plan%20.doc.

———. 2006. National strategic development plan 2006–2010. Phnom Penh. www.cdc-crdb.gov.kh/cdc/aid_management/nsdp.pdf.

Rotha, C. 2009. Interview by author of the deputy secretary-general of Cambodian Mine Action and Victim Assistance Authority. February 25. Phnom Penh.
Rummel, R. J. 1994. *Death by government*. New Brunswick, NJ: Transaction Publishers.
Sang Onn, O. 2009. Interview by author of the director of planning and operations at Cambodian Mine Action Center. February 25. Phnom Penh.
Takayama, R. 2009. Interview by author of chief technical advisor of Japan Mine Action Service. February 26–28. Tasen Commune, Battambang, Cambodia.
UNGA (United Nations General Assembly). 2004. Resolution 58/127. A/RES/58/127 (2004). February 17.
Vanna, M. 2007. Detail presentation on risk management/land release workshop on 20–21 June 2007, GICHD, Geneva, Switzerland. www.gichd.org/fileadmin/pdf/risk_management/workshop-june2007/DetailPresentation-LR-RM-Workshop-June2007.pdf.
Vibol, K. 2009. Interview by author of Land Management and Administration Project representative. February 24. Phnom Penh, Cambodia.
Yaginuma, R. 2009. Interview by author of Japan International Cooperation Agency expert and Cambodian Mine Action Center consultant. February 24. Phnom Penh, Cambodia.
Yale University. 2010. Cambodian Genocide Program. www.yale.edu/cgp.

PART 3

Restoration of natural resources and ecosystems

Introduction

Ecological restoration seeks to return a specific natural resource or ecosystem to its previous state of health and functionality. Usually restoration of natural resources and related ecosystems achieves not a full return to a previous state, but a compromise that reflects various socioeconomic and political constraints. In the case of post-conflict countries, additional challenges to and constraints on restoration activities must be taken into account. Part 3 highlights three cases in which conflicts and related survival strategies have significantly degraded natural resources and related ecosystems, and examines attempts to restore them. It also considers the potential implications of climate change on natural resources and the risks it poses for peacebuilding.

Land in South Lebanon was damaged during the 2006 armed conflict between Israel and Lebanon. In "Restoration of Damaged Land in Societies Recovering from Conflict: The Case of Lebanon," Aïda Tamer-Chammas notes that to be successful restoration must address not only the technical side of ecosystem restoration, but also political, socioeconomic, and structural issues. In post-conflict countries such as Lebanon, for example, it is necessary to reinstate access to land that is essential to livelihoods, resolve land disputes in the absence of clear land tenure laws, and eliminate security risks from cluster bombs. Tamer-Chammas observes that restoration activities can provide strategic support for reconciliation and peacebuilding by creating an opportunity for cooperation and confidence building between divided communities.

Ecosystem resilience has limits. In some cases, political decisions need to be made on how to adapt a damaged ecosystem—as well as the social systems and livelihoods dependent on it—to a new functional state. This has been the case in the Iraqi marshlands, a unique ecological area that Saddam Hussein targeted during internal conflicts with the Marsh Arabs following the 1990–1991 Gulf War. In "Ecological Restoration and Peacebuilding: The Case of the Iraqi Marshes," Steve Lonergan focuses on the importance of transboundary management in the marshlands and the need to engage neighboring countries in restoration plans involving shared waters. He concludes that despite all of the restoration activities to date, the long-term outlook for the marshlands appears to be dim, given all of the development pressures, capacity constraints, and expected future risks from climate change.

In Haiti, a long history of internal conflicts and crushing poverty has severely degraded the environment and has increased the country's vulnerability to natural disasters. In the chapter "Haiti: Lessons Learned and Way Forward in Natural

Resource Management Projects," Lucile Gingembre outlines the Haiti Regeneration Initiative and reviews lessons learned from various restoration projects in the country. Her conclusion reinforces that of other case study findings: community participation and empowerment are essential components of restoration. In addition, integrated resource management, continuous monitoring, and institutional capacity building are high priorities.

Climate change is becoming an increasingly important consideration in peacebuilding in terms of how it may affect the distribution and availability of natural resources and thereby affect livelihoods. In "Peacebuilding and Adaptation to Climate Change," Richard Matthew and Anne Hammill examine the various pillars of peacebuilding activities and discuss how the pillars depend on natural resources and ecosystems and how they might be affected by climate change. Drawing on examples from Rwanda, Sierra Leone, and the Democratic Republic of the Congo, they illustrate how failure to introduce climate change adaptation into peacebuilding activities can leave countries ill equipped to manage climate risk. On the other hand, as Matthew and Hammill discuss, there are ways in which adaptation to climate change can be a positive influence on peacebuilding.

The case studies presented in this part reveal that successful restoration of damaged or degraded natural resources in a post-conflict situation can be critically important for restoring livelihoods and providing a visible peacebuilding dividend. However, this can occur only when restoration is led and owned by the affected communities and supported by local authorities. Restoration projects are complex and long-term endeavors requiring flexibility, innovation, and adaptive management. Furthermore, it is essential to consider the potential risks from climate change in designing restoration programs because future environmental conditions may not resemble those of the present. When practitioners are considering how natural resources can support livelihood recovery, it is essential that they understand the potential implications of a changing and more variable climate—and that they ensure that suitable climate-proofing measures are undertaken as part of peacebuilding.

Restoration of damaged land in societies recovering from conflict: The case of Lebanon

Aïda Tamer-Chammas

Societies emerging from armed conflict face multiple social, political, and economic challenges. Natural resource management has been hailed as a tool for post-conflict peacebuilding because it can support economic recovery, development of sustainable livelihoods, dialogue, cooperation, and confidence building (UNEP 2009).

This chapter covers the process of restoration of natural resources, essentially the land and its products, and infrastructure services, such as water, wastewater, and energy, which were damaged in southern Lebanon during the conflict between Hezbollah and Israel in the summer of 2006. It assesses the impact on peacebuilding of measures taken following the conflict until 2009 by the United Nations (UN) and the government of Lebanon (GOL) and draws lessons for other areas of the world that are emerging from conflict.

Fieldwork took place in the South between August 2008 and August 2009.[1] Localities were selected based on their differences in size and location to lend some diversity to the analysis. All had high levels of poverty prior to the conflict and were severely damaged by it. Included were Bint Jbeil, a small village of four thousand inhabitants on the border with Israel, which was flattened during the conflict, and the relatively large towns of Tyre and Nabatiye, situated farther from the border.[2] Public officials and inhabitants were interviewed through semi-structured interviews rather than focus groups. The Mine Action Coordination Center South Lebanon (MACC SL) in Tyre was visited, and a demonstration of demining was attended.[3] The Lebanon Mine Action Center (LMAC); the

---

Aïda Tamer-Chammas is a researcher in international environmental and international humanitarian law at the School of Oriental and African Studies, University of London.

[1] Lebanon is divided into six governorates, including North Lebanon, South Lebanon, Beqaa, Beirut, Nabatiye, and Mount Lebanon. In this chapter, "the South" includes the governorates of South Lebanon and Nabatiye.

[2] The towns of Nabatiye and Bint Jbeil are in the Nabatiye Governorate. Tyre is in the South Lebanon Governorate. Bint Jbeil, Tyre, and Nabatiye are among the poorest places in the South (CRI 2007).

[3] At the time of the first visit in August 2008, MACC SL was still the UN Mine Action Coordination Center, South Lebanon.

ministries of agriculture, environment, energy, and water; United Nations Development Programme (UNDP) officers in Beirut; and academics at the American University of Beirut were consulted.

The chapter is based on the meetings and pertinent literature but does not intend to provide a complete picture of the problems in the South or of post-conflict remediation of all environmental destruction from the conflict. Environmental damage included a fifteen-thousand-ton oil spill, which was caused by Israel bombing two fuel tanks of a power station located on the Mediterranean Sea coast, near Beirut. Air was polluted by demolition waste; roads and bridges were destroyed or damaged; cultural property, including Byblos, a site on the World Heritage List, was harmed; and the Palm Islands Nature Reserve, a protected area, was damaged.

The chapter first presents the background of the conflict and discusses relevant concepts. It then evaluates restoration projects by describing the pre-conflict state of the resource or infrastructure concerned, the impact of the conflict, and the measures taken. It also attempts to link the initiatives discussed to peacebuilding. Attention finally turns to the constraints that may undermine peacebuilding operations and to lessons on the potential effect of natural resource management on peace.

BACKGROUND OF THE CONFLICT

The conflict between Israel and Hezbollah during the summer of 2006 lasted thirty-four days and wrought extensive devastation and suffering on the land and people of Lebanon.[4] Although explanations for the conflict differ (Harel 2006; Külbel 2006), it primarily resulted from the state of enmity between Israel and Lebanon since the 1948 Arab-Israeli war in which Lebanon participated.[5] The March 23, 1949, General Armistice Agreement between Israel and Lebanon was never implemented, and subsequent peace processes failed.[6] The 1969 Cairo Agreement between Lebanon and the Palestine Liberation Organization (PLO) gave PLO fighters in Lebanon the right to bear arms, which they used to attack

---

[4] This background section focuses on the conflict between Israel and Lebanon, including the role of Hezbollah. It does not cover the civil war or Syria's full role in Lebanon.

[5] The 2006 conflict is generally assumed to have started when Israel crossed into Lebanon in pursuit of Hezbollah who had abducted two Israeli soldiers (Harel 2006). Others consider the kidnapping the pretext for a conflict in planning (Külbel 2006). The 1948 and 1967 wars brought with them an influx of Palestinian refugees into Lebanon. Approximately 400,000 Palestinians have voluntarily registered as refugees with the United Nations Relief and Works Agency in Lebanon (UN 2007c).

[6] The 1989 Taif Agreement, which was signed by Lebanese factions gathered in Saudi Arabia after a period of instability and a war against Syria waged by Lebanese Army General Michel Aoun, mentioned the need to revive the 1949 General Armistice Agreement with Israel.

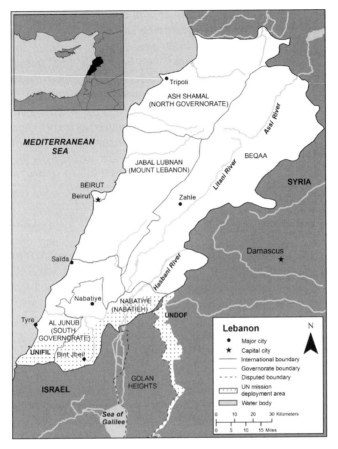

Note: United Nations Interim Force in Lebanon (UNIFIL) and United Nations Disengagement Observer Force (UNDOF) are UN peacekeeping missions.

Israel from Lebanese soil (Lacouture, Tueni, and Khoury 2002).[7] Thus Lebanon found itself embroiled in the intractable Israeli-Palestinian conflict.

Israel breached Lebanon's territorial sovereignty with frequent aerial raids and repeatedly attacked the country in retaliation for attacks on its territory, culminating in a full-scale Israeli invasion that reached Beirut in 1982. Arduous peace negotiations between Israel and Lebanon led nowhere, and in 1984 Lebanon

---

[7] The agreement was signed on November 3, 1969, by Yasser Arafat, head of the newly formed PLO, and Lebanese Army General Emile Boustani. The agreement was repudiated by a unanimous vote of the Lebanese Parliament in 1978, after adoption the same year of United Nations Security Council Resolution 425 (UNSC 1978a). Resolution 425 called for Israeli withdrawal from all Lebanese territories and was the only resolution on the subject to draw a unanimous vote.

repudiated the treaty signed a year earlier with Israel.[8] Beginning in 1978, Israel occupied the South for twenty-two years with an "iron fist" policy (Petran 1987), and from 1976 to April 2005, Syrian armed forces remained in Lebanon.[9] Hezbollah, a Shiite movement created with help from Iran and with Syria's blessing (Harik 2005), launched an armed resistance to the occupation in the South.[10] Under Syrian domination, the Lebanese government did not send its army to the South.[11] Israeli operations continued unabated, notably in two destructive military campaigns—Operation Accountability in 1993 and Operation Grapes of Wrath in 1996—that reinforced local support for Hezbollah (Harik 2005). In 2000, Israel finally withdrew from the South, except from Shebaa Farms and the village of Ghajar. United Nations Security Council (UNSC) Resolution 1559 called for "disbanding and disarmament of all Lebanese and non-Lebanese militias," but Hezbollah decided to keep its arsenal (UNSC 2004, 1).

By 2006, Lebanon was in political chaos. The 2005 assassination of Prime Minister Rafik Hariri in a car explosion in Beirut prompted huge manifestations of popular outrage and precipitated the withdrawal of Syrian troops from Lebanon. A two-year period of instability followed, and there was a wave of politically motivated murders of prominent personalities who had campaigned against Syria's role in Lebanon. Political institutions and processes proved ineffective in the face of strong internal divisions. Despite many rounds of negotiations among Lebanese politicians, there was no agreement over Lebanon's defense strategy, the issue of Hezbollah's arms, or the Special Tribunal for Lebanon (STL) (UNDP 2007c).[12]

In this context, Hezbollah kidnapped two Israeli soldiers in 2006, igniting the conflict of July 2006. UNSC Resolution 1701, adopted on August 11, 2006,

---

[8] After Israel's invasion of Lebanon in 1982, a U.S.-brokered peace agreement was signed on May 17, 1983. It was rescinded by Lebanon in March 1984.

[9] In early April 1986, Israeli prime minister Yitzak Rabin declared in the Knesset—the Israeli legislature—that he would pursue a scorched-earth policy of all-out retaliation if the attacks continued (Petran 1987). Assessments of Syria's role in Lebanon differ: "In 1976 the Syrian Army invaded Lebanon, a move later construed as an Arab peacekeeping force, the Arab Deterrent Force (ADF), but in reality the beginning of a Syrian occupation" (Knudsen 2005, 2).

[10] Hezbollah transformed itself into a political party with a military wing before it participated in Lebanese parliamentary elections in 1992. The United States and Israel consider Hezbollah a terrorist organization. Others consider it a resistance movement.

[11] Under Syrian suzerainty, the "Syrian intelligence grew to become a dominant force in Lebanon with power to veto all important political decisions" (Knudsen 2005, 11). Syria established rules that were to govern relations between the GOL and Hezbollah and the role of the resistance in the South (Harik 2005).

[12] The creation of an international criminal tribunal to investigate Hariri's death was, and is still, extremely divisive and led in November 2006 to the resignation of pro-Syrian, especially Hezbollah, ministers from the government one day before it approved the tribunal's statutes after eight months of UN-Lebanon negotiations. The political coalition opposed to the government organized a sit-in in central Beirut that lasted almost two years, destroying economic life in the heart of the city. Furthermore, the parliament was incapacitated because its speaker, a member of the antigovernment coalition, refused to open a session.

called for full cessation of hostilities on August 14; authorized an increase in UN Interim Force in Lebanon (UNIFIL) troops; extended their mandate until August 31, 2007; and expanded their duties, which were first outlined in 1978 in UNSC resolutions 425 and 426 (UNSC 1978a, 1978b, 2006).[13] There is nothing in Resolution 1701 concerning restoration of natural resources, and there remains no peace agreement between the two countries.

Post-conflict

Post-conflict means that "one form of high-profile political violence comes to a virtual end through negotiated settlement among the main protagonists or through military defeat" (Call 2008, 175). It is misleading, however, when a formal peace agreement is signed and violence continues or when there is a military defeat because a regime fell (Call 2008).

Even though Lebanon is recovering from armed conflict, it is not in a post-conflict situation. There was no negotiated settlement between the belligerents, and no side admitted military defeat. The country is in diplomatic limbo, neither at war nor at peace, which has implications for peacebuilding operations.

An uneasy quiet prevails in the South.[14] Israel and Hezbollah exchange threats of new conflict, and both sides have violated Resolution 1701. Israel regularly flies over Lebanon. In July 2009, a hidden arms depot, assumed to belong to Hezbollah, exploded, and allegations of arms transfers from Syria to Hezbollah have surfaced (Galey and Mroueh 2010).

Peacebuilding

There are many definitions of *peacebuilding*, reflecting the different mandates and interests of the participants (Chetail 2009). The "polymorphous concept" offers a framework for the measures needed to rebuild a country, its divided society, and national institutions following intrastate conflicts. A peacebuilding strategy is multipurpose but should essentially aim for transformation of governance structures and relationships to prevent further conflicts (UNEP 2009).

The UNDP Peace Building Strategy for Lebanon, designed to run from March 2006 to January 2008, was implemented between January 2007 and December 2010. It defined peacebuilding as "a process that facilitates the establishment of a durable peace and prevents the recurrence of violence by addressing the root causes and effects of conflict" (UNDP 2007a, 8). Natural resource management was not considered an element in peacebuilding but was part of socioeconomic programs. A crisis prevention and recovery program has operated in parallel since 2009.[15]

---

[13] UNIFIL's mandate has been regularly renewed since then.
[14] UNIFIL intervened to build a fence when tensions increased at the border when an Israeli cow crossed it (*Daily Star* 2009).
[15] Tajia Kontinen-Sharp, UNDP Lebanon program officer, Crisis Prevention and Recovery, personal communication with the author, August 2009.

Although the 2006 conflict was not a civil war, Lebanon needs conflict prevention because it remains extremely divided over whether or not to be at the forefront of armed combat with Israel (Ghoraieb 2009), reflecting the conflicting goals of the government and Hezbollah (Harik 2005). The South would benefit most from recovery measures because, except for the southern suburbs of Beirut, it was hardest hit. It is also the most economically deprived region and Hezbollah's base.

Peacemaking

Peacemaking involves negotiations through diplomatic channels of an agreement to end a conflict (Peacebuilding Initiative 2008). *Environmental peacemaking* refers broadly to natural resource management measures taken in the wake of an interstate conflict (Conca and Dabelko 2002), but it is irrelevant to Lebanon because of the extremely tense situation with Israel. It will not be explored in the chapter.

THE CASE OF SOUTHERN LEBANON

The South is essentially a rural agricultural area of small villages and towns. Agriculture is the only source of income for half of the working population and provides approximately 70 percent of total household income (FAO 2006). The region is the poorest in Lebanon (CRI 2007) and suffers from high rates of extreme poverty that reach 11 percent (Lebanese Republic 2007).[16]

During the conflict of 2006, Lebanon withstood tremendous casualties, disruptions, and displacement of nearly 1 million people, one-quarter of its population.[17] Its environment, economy, social and physical infrastructure, agriculture, and food security were damaged.

Direct expenditures for early recovery and reconstruction were estimated to be US$2.8 billion, of which the GOL was to cover US$1.75 billion. The indirect costs of the conflict were approximately US$2.2 billion, and private sector losses—mainly in agriculture and tourism—were to be alleviated by up to US$950 million in government financial assistance (Lebanese Republic 2007). As of 2010, approximately US$909 million had been committed, of which US$674 million had been disbursed. Grants amounting to US$2.1 billion had been pledged, of which US$1.6 billion had been formally committed (Lebanese Republic 2010).

International organizations surveyed conflict-related environmental impacts through studies. For example, the United Nations Environment Programme (UNEP) as well as UNDP and Earth Link and Advanced Resources Development performed environmental assessments (UNEP 2007; UNDP 2007); the Food and Agriculture Organization of the United Nations (FAO) assessed

---

[16] Rates of extreme poverty in Beirut and some regions of Mount Lebanon do not exceed 1 percent (Lebanese Republic 2007).
[17] In 2006, Lebanon's population was approximately 3.9 million (Lebanon Info Center n.d.).

recovery needs of agriculture, fisheries, and forestry sectors (FAO 2006); the European Commission and European Union Satellite Center conducted a preliminary damage assessment on public infrastructure (EC and EUSC 2006); and the World Bank reported on the costs of the environmental damage (World Bank 2007). The Association for Forests, Development and Conservation, a local non-governmental organization (NGO), examined the South's forests and olive groves (AFDC 2007), and the Consultation and Research Institute conducted the *Post-Conflict Social and Livelihoods Assessment in Lebanon* to document the social and economic conditions of the most vulnerable (CRI 2007). The oil spill received additional attention through an international independent study (Steiner 2006) and a research project at the American University of Beirut (Sabra 2007). Human Rights Watch and Amnesty International filed their own reports (HRW 2008; Amnesty International 2006).

A difficulty common to all of the assessments was the lack of reliable baseline data on the environment, infrastructure services, and social conditions before the conflict. The UNDP and UNEP assessments were thorough, broad in their coverage, and complete with proposals for green recovery and reconstruction. Both were circulated to donors and government ministries in Lebanon.

Since the 1960s, the UN has been active in Lebanon through its many agencies and three regional offices, and it has cooperated with various government ministries since 1991.[18] UNDP started planning for post-conflict recovery on August 2, 2006, by appointing a UN resident coordinator and coordinating projects with the Lebanese government through its policy advisory units and with the Council for Development and Reconstruction, the key Lebanese agency in charge of infrastructure and service projects, as well as relevant ministries and local municipalities. But the efficiency of donor communication and program coordination is hard to ascertain. The infrastructure rehabilitation project, funded by the European Commission Humanitarian Aid Department (ECHO) and implemented by UNDP, showed cooperation among peacebuilding participants (ECHO and UNDP n.d.a).[19]

Recovery activities were divided into projects to be launched immediately after the end of the conflict and during early and sustained recovery phases.[20]

---

[18] Following the 1989 Taif Agreement, Lebanon recovered some political stability under Syrian tutelage, enough to encourage UNDP and the GOL to launch an innovative strategic partnership in 1991.

[19] The implementation of the ECHO and UNDP Rapid Rehabilitation of Key Municipal Infrastructure for Local Service Delivery project started in October 2006 and ended in January 2007.

[20] There were five Quick Starting and High Impact Early Recovery priorities, including (1) support to municipalities for removal of rubble and debris; (2) reactivation of public administration services; (3) support for national coordination of recovery efforts with the establishment of (a) a reconstruction and recovery cell in the office of the prime minister, (b) a development assistance database, and (c) a multi-donor trust fund, the Lebanon Recovery Fund; (4) initial oil spill cleanup (from surface water); and (5) restoring fishermen's livelihoods. (UNDP 2007d).

The link between the livelihood recovery projects and the peacebuilding strategy is difficult to evaluate, although some findings from the assessments were used in the planning (Klap and Yassin 2008).

Recovery priorities

Assessments identified immediate needs and directed recovery priorities, which included removal of demolition waste, clearance of cluster bombs, and livelihood projects in the agricultural sector.

Rubble removal

After the conflict, removal of demolition waste scattered in villages that were reduced to rubble and along roads was prioritized (Fisk 2009). Waste estimates ranged from 2.5 to 3 million cubic meters (m^3) (UNDP 2007), although the actual volume of waste removed reached 5.75 million m^3, including 3.32 million m^3 from the South (World Bank 2007).[21]

UNDP financed approximately US$800,000 of rubble removal in 101 villages and towns in the South, each of which received up to US$25,000 (ECHO and UNDP n.d.b).[22] The implementation was left to municipalities that sometimes contracted private sector haulers with disastrous results. In Beirut, demolition waste was dumped in four sites.[23] In the South, municipalities with relatively little waste used it to fill depressions in roads or in construction. Where the amount of rubble was extensive, it was dumped, after removing most hazardous domestic material, on nearby land and in ecologically sensitive valleys, ponds, and riparian areas (World Bank 2007). Scattered all over the South were hundreds of piles of heterogeneous material, which were observed in 2007 and 2009 (UNDP 2007).

As an alternative to dumping, UNDP proposed recycling waste using fixed or mobile equipment (UNDP 2007), but only a limited rubble-recycling project was implemented in Kawnine and Shaqra, where approximately 65,000 tons of rubble were crushed (UNDP 2006). Mobile equipment was rented from a private company, and a service provider, monitored by the Bint Jbeil municipality, was hired to operate it (Seoud 2009). The experience was scaled up in Nahr El Bared Camp, where all the demolition material was recycled using

---

[21] In 2006, approximately 130,000 housing units were destroyed or damaged in Lebanon. Ninety-three thousand were in the South Lebanon Governorate and the Baalbeck Hermel region in Beqaa, and 4,500 were in Beirut (World Bank 2007).
[22] The southern suburbs of Beirut received US$200,000 for rubble removal.
[23] Of the four sites, two were "in low-lying areas located by the sea and one on the other side of the road within the Choueifat cadastral area, and a temporary dumpsite along the airport road" (World Bank 2007, 45).

fixed recycling equipment.[24] Although the use of green-building equipment has expanded over the past two years, the Lebanese government has issued no laws enforcing green building–reconstruction standards.

Cluster-bomb clearance

The 2006 conflict left behind approximately 1 million unexploded submunitions from the 4 million cluster bombs launched over the South in the last seventy-two hours of the conflict (UNDP 2007d).

Clearance activities started immediately after the conflict and were prioritized by realities on the ground. First, roads were cleared for public safety, followed by clearance of paths to houses and schools. Activities then turned to clearance of agricultural fields, because "access to natural resources is key as it underlies all livelihoods" (Halle, Matthew, and Switzer 2002, 16). Farmers desperate to recover their land have attempted to explode bombs, burned fields after demarcating bombs, and paid US$6.50 per bomblet disposed using artisanal methods (FAO 2006). Despite many awareness campaigns, injuries and fatal accidents still occur.

Clearance operations, projected to end in 2007 (UNDP 2007), will now end in 2012, according to UNDP (UNDP 2008b). Reassessments revealed that previous estimates of unexploded ordnance (UXO) were too low. Israel refused to turn over the maps of their strikes to the UN or the Lebanese until 2009. As of September 2009, approximately 21.1 million of 36.7 million UXO-contaminated square meters (m^2) had been cleared (Fehmi 2008).[25] Still unclear are the extent of agricultural land involved and the method used to calculate the area of cultivated land contaminated by UXO.[26] Environmental damage may have been aggravated by technical choices, such as the refusal by some factions to use remote-sensing drones to establish the density of cluster bombs prior to clearance operations.[27]

A national institution, the Lebanon Mine Action Center (LMAC), was created, and a national mine-action policy and an end-state strategy for mine action were developed. Although international technical advisors still work with the LMAC, it has offered to train members of the Lebanese Armed Forces. The UN has provided institutional and capacity-building support to the National

---

[24] Nahr El Bared, a Palestinian camp, was destroyed during a battle with the Lebanese army in 2007.

[25] Estimates of the total area contaminated in 2006 vary. According to UNDP, approximately 38 million m^2 were contaminated by UXO in 2006 (UNDP 2008b). In December 2008, the UN Mine Action Coordination Centre, South Lebanon, reported that the total area contaminated was forty-eight square kilometers (km^2), but in May 2009, the LMAC lowered the figure to 35.36 km^2 (E-MINE 2009a, 2009b).

[26] The FAO estimates that 26 percent of agricultural land is contaminated. (FAO 2006).

[27] One interviewee claimed that the techniques could reveal hidden caches of armaments and were, therefore, opposed by one party on the ground. The claim could not be verified.

Demining Office (Klap and Yassin 2008). The success of the project may be due to the involvement of the UN over a long period of time.[28]

Forests, olive groves, and agriculture recovery

Thirteen and a half percent of Lebanon's forests lie in the South, and 42 percent of the land in the South is used for agriculture. People graze animals; collect pine nuts and wood; produce charcoal and honey; and cultivate olives, citrus, other fruit, and medicinal and aromatic plants. Olive groves are essential to the economy of the South and account for approximately 39 percent of Lebanese olive groves (AFDC 2007). Forty-nine percent of crops are under irrigation, except in the Nabatiye Governorate where there is little irrigation infrastructure.[29]

During the conflict, raging fires caused most of the damage to land and forests. Civil defense personnel, including firefighters, were already stretched by helping a fleeing population (AFDC 2007). Farmers were unable to access their fields to harvest crops at their peak and, after the conflict, could not prepare their land for the following season because of cluster bombs (CRI 2007). The irrigation infrastructure was destroyed, and the loss of animals, crops, fisheries, and forests amounted to approximately US$280 million (FAO 2006).

Concern was raised about the "unknown effects of bomb-induced soil contamination on crop production and human health" (FAO 2006, 7). The declining fertility of the soil and trees—confirmed during fieldwork—might be attributed to the intensity of the bombardments, the size or type of bombs, and the extreme heat; it has not been factored into the recovery plan. The local population has noticed the disappearance or reduced production of fruit and vegetables. Since 2006, olive crops have decreased below the usual minimum yield in Tebnine, a village east of Tyre, and olive trees have not borne any fruit in Sarba, a village east of Saida (Farran 2009).[30]

UNDP recommended remediation measures for forested areas damaged by fire (UNDP 2007), but there was no follow-up. Small projects, such as installation of a laurel press and funding of beekeeping and agricultural cooperatives, were included in the ECHO and UNDP early-recovery initiatives (ECHO and UNDP n.d.b). In August 2007, the FAO launched a US$3.3 million program to help restart agriculture in the South. It provided fertilizer, seeds, animal

---

[28] The UN has been involved in peacekeeping in the South since 1978, in capacity development and mine clearance since 1998, and in mine action–capacity building since 2001. In January 2002, the UN Mine Action Coordination Centre, South Lebanon, was established to coordinate mine action within the UNIFIL mission area south of the Litani River. It transferred primary responsibility on January 1, 2009, to the LMAC. Lebanon could be in full control by the end of 2012 (E-MINE 2009a). UNDP lends its support to the National Demining Office (renamed LMAC in 2007) through a policy advisory unit at the Ministry of Defense.

[29] See footnote 1 on the governorates. In Nabatiye, only 5 percent of crops are irrigated.

[30] The minimum yield (or alternate or biennial bearing) is the tendency of fruit trees to produce a heavy crop one year and a light crop the following year.

stock, and assistance in renovating greenhouses. To mitigate the impact of cluster bombs on people's livelihoods, two other projects, totaling US$421,934, aided cultivation of medicinal and aromatic plants (MAP projects) (UNDP 2007b, 2008a). To participate, communities had to have access to irrigation water, fertile soil, and a willingness to irrigate and bear the costs of irrigation. UNDP rented suitable land, provided seeds and plants, and helped install irrigation systems.

A three-pillared approach of assessment, monitoring, and evaluation could be used for natural resource management. In the South, there has been little evaluation, and it has concentrated on easily met objectives. Although the different initiatives of early recovery support by UNDP were judged exemplary (Klap and Yassin 2008), focus groups complained about the total lack of irrigation and facilities to process crops such as tobacco (CRI 2007). Data to evaluate the effect of FAO projects on livelihoods were insufficient, but a Ministry of Agriculture official suggested it was small (Nasrallah 2009). MAP projects were limited in their economic impact and had no effect on dialogue or confidence building because their beneficiaries belonged to a single community group.

Proposals for the agricultural sector made by UNDP (UNDP 2007) were not applied. Nothing was done to promote sustainable cropping patterns, possibly due to a lack of human and financial resources at the Ministry of Agriculture and conflicting political priorities resulting in a preference given to other projects such as those involving MAP. Through the poverty-reduction program, some assistance was provided to trout farmers to help revitalize freshwater aquaculture in the Assi River.

Natural resource issues require both a short- and a long-term approach (Whittemore 2008). But the extent to which a strategy for transition to sustainable recovery guides UNDP and its partners has been questioned (Klap and Yassin 2008). FAO recommended further studies before planning medium- to long-term recovery projects (FAO 2006).

Infrastructure services and recovery

Priority was also placed on the restoration and development of Lebanon's infrastructure services, including its water and wastewater sectors and energy sector, which were in poor condition due to neglect prior to the conflict.

Water and wastewater sectors

Lebanon has forty streams and rivers and 2,000 springs. It has one of the highest per capita water ratios in the Middle East (UNEP 2007). Freshwater is probably Lebanon's single most important resource. Unfortunately it is wasted.

While water services reached 90 percent of the population in 2008, one-quarter of the population did not have regular access to safe water at the household level (UN-HABITAT 2008). Untreated domestic sewage, agricultural runoff, industrial pollution, open dumping, and overpumping of underground water in coastal regions have long compromised the quality of surface and groundwater (UNEP 2007).

214 Assessing and restoring natural resources in post-conflict peacebuilding

According to post-conflict assessments, the water and sanitation infrastructure were in a derelict state, and there was an acute deficiency in wastewater treatment capacity (UNEP 2007). In rural areas, such as in the South, only 20 percent of households were connected to the wastewater infrastructure (UN-HABITAT 2008). Most houses used cesspools and septic tanks, which can pollute underground water, and sewage sludge was typically disposed of on land or dumped in empty boreholes (UNEP 2007).

Water and sanitation infrastructure were affected considerably by the conflict; rivers were polluted by industrial facilities and with waste from bridge demolition. Water transmission lines, water tanks, pumping stations, artesian wells, and water treatment systems were heavily damaged or destroyed. Water and sanitation services were disrupted and effectively came to a halt.

Priority was given to restoration of infrastructure services (Chehab 2009).[31] UNDP implemented a US$2 million project to fund initiatives targeting quick repair of water and wastewater networks, cleanup and rehabilitation of the sewage system, and reinstalling street lights in 143 communities in the South.[32] Instead of scaling up existing infrastructure, UNDP favored including nearly all municipalities (including those not covered previously) to foster equity and prevent conflict (Klap and Yassin 2008).

Energy sector

The energy sector has long been in deep crisis and is heavily subsidized, draining public finances. Insufficient supply leads to daily power shortages, and consumers pay a heavy price for private backup electricity (World Bank 2008).

After the 2006 conflict, which negatively affected the electricity network, ECHO, UNDP, and foreign donors financed improvements at the municipal level.[33] A renewable energy initiative (CEDRO)[34] was launched in 2007 as an early recovery project—with a budget of approximately US$2.7 million (phase 1)—to introduce new technology, such as solar water heaters (SWHs), to public institutions such as schools and hospitals, in south Beqaa and Akkar (in the North Lebanon Governorate) (M. Khoury 2009; Seoud 2009). It grew into a successful national project: it was extended until 2012, and its budget was increased to US$9.7 million.

Three hundred interested municipalities submitted applications for sixty projects in CEDRO's first phase. While important in many municipalities, CEDRO's national impact will be negligible because it will only directly cover approximately

---

[31] By September 2007, 1,465 units of water and wastewater networks, which were destroyed by the conflict, were repaired (Rebuild Lebanon 2007).
[32] The project was implemented by UNDP and funded by ECHO.
[33] For example, in Bint Jbeil Qada (a *qada* is a geographical division in Lebanon), Iran offered money for one or two generators per village, depending on the cost of repair of the electrical grid and fuel, among other things.
[34] CEDRO stands for Community Energy Efficiency and Renewable Energy Demonstration Project for the Recovery of Lebanon.

3 to 4 percent of the general energy needs of the South and, indirectly, approximately 10 percent. Still, it is in line with the government's policy and complements other SWH projects funded by Sweden and Greece (P. Khoury 2009).

The benefits of CEDRO will continue once donor support ends. The participating public institution and ultimately the relevant ministry own the SWHs.[35] UNDP provided training to the recipients of the appliance and to those responsible for its installation and maintenance. The contractor that installed the heaters also conducted initial monitoring, and UNDP will ensure monitoring of CEDRO until the Lebanese Centre for Energy Conservation takes over.

Factors affecting outcomes

A number of limiting factors and constraints may undermine the effectiveness of peacebuilding measures in Lebanon.

Land tenure

Land tenure in rural Lebanon is affected by the monopoly of landlords and corrupt administrative practices, unclear or overlapping land rights due to legal ambiguity and de facto practices, land encroachment and illegal settlers, and zoning difficulties caused by land left unsurveyed (UN-HABITAT 2008).

Infrastructure prior to the 2006 conflict

Considering their poor state before 2006—the result of decades of neglect by the government—infrastructure services in the South require major development, not simply restoration, which could lead to only marginally sustainable economic recovery and growth.

Important projects include comprehensive reform of the energy sector (Lebanese Republic 2007), construction of seventeen dams to remedy the problem of groundwater quality deterioration due to extraction from wells built haphazardly in areas where water is unavailable (UN-HABITAT 2008), and better management of water resources under a national institution.[36] But implementation will take time, and needs in the South are immediate.

Environmental awareness

Although most Lebanese were shocked by the 2006 oil spill, they remain generally unaware of the importance of protecting natural resources. Their main concerns

---

[35] The public sector in Lebanon is centralized. Every ministry supervises public institutions under its scope and ultimately owns the buildings used by the institutions. For example, the Ministry of Education owns public school buildings.

[36] An agreement was signed on May 14, 2010, between the GOL, UNDP, and Italy. A grant of €1.8 million was provided to conduct a hydrological study and launch the Lebanese Centre for Water Management and Preservation (*Daily Star* 2010).

are security and the economy, as in most post-conflict societies. "Security is a priority whereas conservation of natural spaces is perceived as a luxury" (Halle, Matthew, and Switzer 2002, 23). Natural resources are valued in the South because they contribute to livelihoods and among foreign interventionists for preservation (Makhzoumi 2009).

Limited Enforcement of environmental regulations

The Ministry of Environment lacks human resources, technical capacity, and financial means.[37] Political divisions, infighting between it and other ministries, and corruption can hamper application and enforcement of environmental laws (Malek 2009).

Communities' interests

Every project in Lebanon must handle sectarian and regional interests equitably. To balance an FAO project of US$3.3 million in the South, US$2.5 million, originally designated for agricultural development in the South, was dedicated to relieving poverty in the North Lebanon Governorate.

Disarmament, demobilization, and reintegration

Because Hezbollah remained armed, livelihood and economic development projects could not address disarmament, demobilization, and reintegration of combatants.

Private sector engagement

The private sector, which substantially helped refugees during the conflict, has not participated significantly in financing reconstruction or natural resource restoration.[38] Lebanese civil society organizations tend to focus on the needs of different categories of people (such as orphans, people disabled by the war, children in need of school scholarships, and so forth), as opposed to the environment itself. "Involvement of the private sector in Lebanon takes place on an ad hoc basis, and their capacity to influence decision-making is somewhat hampered by a lack of structure, limited resources, sectarianism and political differences" (ETF 2010, 2). Recognizing its lack of involvement, UNDP is strengthening its

---

[37] The Ministry of Environment was created in 1993—quite recently compared with other ministries. It has only approximately fifty employees. Monitoring the twenty-five officially authorized quarries rests on the shoulders of only two agents, each of whom earns approximately US$800 a month.

[38] The private sector is changing: in 2010, a Lebanese bank, the Banque du Liban et d'Outre-Mer, launched a credit card arrangement under which the commissions due the bank on every transaction would be donated to a fund for the Lebanese armed forces involved in mine clearance in the South.

cooperation with the business community at the local level and in the Lebanese diaspora (UNDP and UNPF 2009).

Scope of peacebuilding

The UNDP Peacebuilding Strategy has focused on internal political reconciliation (UNDP 2007c) because sectarianism has historically been among the root causes of conflict in Lebanon (UNDP 2006). But there is danger in ignoring the international aspect of a conflict (Beydoun 2009; CPHS and CERI 2006) and "addressing past problems rather than those that shape the immediate post-conflict condition" (Peacebuilding Initiative 2008). Current internal divisions revolve around the defense strategy of Lebanon and the Special Tribunal for Lebanon (STL), are closely intertwined with opposing regional influences (UNDP 2007c).

Role of international actors

In some specific cases, reconstruction should be implemented by impartial international institutions rather than by specific belligerent groups (Gheciu and Welsh 2009). For example, mistrust of central authority by inhabitants of southern Lebanon was reinforced in the aftermath of the conflict. The population often feels more indebted to Hezbollah than to the government because, with Iran's financial backing, Hezbollah has built new roads and provided electricity generators. Furthermore, to build a sustainable peace, the complex politics of post-conflict reconstruction requires that combatants be engaged in dialogue (Gheciu and Welsh 2009). As of June 2011, the two main political coalitions have not resolved their differences, and UN agencies—neutral politically—may not intervene in internal political discussions.[39]

Visibility of UNDP

Few Lebanese outside the UNDP circle know the extent of UNDP involvement in peacebuilding (Klap and Yassin 2008). Unbeknownst to most citizens, the small amounts of money UNDP donated to municipalities were helpful in making urgent repairs of the infrastructure and removing rubble. Publicizing more widely these facts would demonstrate that the GOL was both determined to respond to the needs of its citizens in the South and able to mobilize the support of the international community in an efficient manner, countering Hezbollah's status as provider of resources for citizens in the South.

---

[39] A new government was formed on June 13, 2011, dominated by the Hezbollah coalition despite its minority status in parliament, after its resignation from the government in January 2011 over the STL's procedure. On June 30, 2011, the STL handed to Lebanon's state prosecutor its indictment, naming four Hezbollah members as suspects, a decision dismissed by Hezbollah leaders.

CONCLUSION AND LESSONS LEARNED

The first step toward recovery from conflict is evaluation of the damage and its impact on the population. Assessments were made relatively quickly and provided a clear picture of the needs on the ground. Coordination among the different programs seems to have succeeded to a certain extent.

Most important, from the perspective of natural resource management, is reinstating access to land essential to livelihoods and eliminating the security risk from cluster bombs. Several companies have participated in mine-clearance operations under the umbrella of the Lebanese Mine Action Centre (previously the UNMAC). Demining progresses steadily but will not be complete for at least another two years. Foreign funds have dried up, yet the project is absolutely imperative to full recovery of the South.

Removal of demolition waste was an enormous project. Dumping rubble in ecologically sensitive sites may have damaged the environment. Although infrastructure services were restored only to their dismal pre-conflict levels, their return did give daily life the semblance of normalcy. A renewable energy initiative has been introduced successfully, even though its impact has been small. The task is far from over, and construction of new infrastructure services is essential. The agricultural sector was seriously affected by the conflict, though limited recovery and livelihood projects (such as MAP projects) provided a small amount of income to a few communities, which also benefited from the FAO projects.

It would be premature to conclude that natural resource management has had a substantial impact on economic recovery and sustainability of livelihoods in the South. Dialogue, cooperation, and confidence building have not been positively influenced. The divisions between factions have not diminished since the end of the conflict, and relations with Israel are still tense. But sound, inclusive natural resource management remains essential to rebuilding Lebanon, restoring the environment, reconstituting the social fabric of the country, and supporting economic growth. Consequently, it may still play a role in promoting peace and preventing conflict in Lebanon.

The following six lessons learned from Lebanon highlight the role natural resource management may have on peace:

1. *Natural resource management may have only a minor effect on political divisions.* According to Robert Ricigliano, three types of post-conflict initiatives are necessary for successful peacebuilding: the political (focused on reaching agreement among the parties), the social (transformation of underlying relations and perceptions), and the structural (institutions, good governance, rule of law, development, and economic justice) (Ricigliano 2003). Ideally, natural resource management should underpin the three dimensions. In Lebanon, it can affect social and structural issues, with little influence on entrenched political divisions.
2. *Programs must engage opposing communities.* For management of natural resources to play a successful role in confidence building and dialogue at the national level, there must be a project that requires involvement of all citizens.

In Lebanon, opposing communities have not participated together to a conflict-prevention measure. There could be a national campaign to raise money from Lebanese to fund clearance of UXO as part of a land restoration project.
3. *Peacebuilding strategies must be regional.* Natural resource management, on its own, will not prevent a relapse of conflict. When a society emerging from conflict is mired in internal fragmentation that is worsened by regional politics and substate tensions, diplomacy on a regional level must accompany natural resource management as part of a peacebuilding strategy (Gheciu and Welsh 2009).
4. *Recovery cannot wait for full peace.* Although most Lebanese agree on the necessity of regional diplomacy for sustainable peace, internal recovery cannot wait for this distant goal.
5. *Projects should address the needs of those most affected by conflict.* Lebanon is due to enter a phase of sustained recovery. Projects should be adapted to the real needs and aspirations of the population. Construction of new infrastructure services, neglected for decades in the South, is essential for development, poverty reduction, and economic growth. It may also help build confidence in the central authority and reinforce a feeling of national belonging—if not identity.

The agricultural sector would benefit from modernization of irrigation, a reassessment of production yields, and restoration of soil fertility. Large-scale initiatives must be envisaged, and attention must be given to sustainable medium- to long-term recovery projects.
6. *Environmental assessments or capacities are often ignored.* There should be monitoring of implementation of recommendations. In Lebanon, interventions proposed for mitigating the environmental impacts of the conflict (such as sustainable management of demolition waste) and green recovery (such as promotion of sustainable cropping patterns) were ignored (UNDP 2007). Although the agricultural sector is essential to the economy, declining soil fertility has not been factored into recovery plans.

REFERENCES

AFDC (Association for Forests, Development and Conservation). 2007. *War impact on forest resources and olive groves in South Lebanon.* Final report. May. www.afdc.org.lb/admin/pictures/AFDC_-_War_Impact_on_Forests_and_Olive_Groves_Assessment_in_South_Lebanon.pdf.

Amnesty International. 2006. Israel/Lebanon: Deliberate destruction or "collateral damage"? Israeli attacks on civilian infrastructure. MDE 18/007/2006. August. www.amnesty.org/en/library/asset/MDE18/007/2006/en/4a9b367a-d3ff-11dd-8743-d305bea2b2c7/mde180072006en.pdf.

Beydoun, A. 2009. *La dégénérescence du Liban ou la réforme orpheline.* Arles, France: Sindbad-Actes Sud.

Call, C. T. 2008. Knowing peace when you see it: Setting standards for peacebuilding success. *Civil Wars* 10 (2): 173–194.

Chehab, E. 2009. Interview by the author of project manager for United Nations Development Programme. April. Beirut, Lebanon.

Chetail, V., ed. 2009. *Post-conflict peacebuilding: A lexicon.* New York: Oxford University Press.
Conca, K., and G. D. Dabelko, eds. 2002. *Environmental peacemaking.* Washington D.C.: Woodrow Wilson International Center for Scholars.
CPHS (Center for Peace and Human Security) and CERI (Centre d'Etudes et de Recherches Internationales). 2006. *Integrated approaches to peace building: A round-table discussion.* Conference report. June 2.
CRI (Consultation and Research Institute). 2007. *The post-conflict social and livelihoods assessment in Lebanon.* http://lebanon-support.org/Uploads/2009-05/News1737.pdf.
Daily Star. 2009. Staff report. August 14.
———. 2010. Italy donates 1.8 million euros to Lebanon for water study. May 15.
EC (European Commission) and EUSC (European Union Satellite Center). 2006. *Rapid preliminary damage assessment—Beirut and S Lebanon.* Brussels, Belgium. http://reliefweb.int/sites/reliefweb.int/files/resources/8090711DCC7E7187C12571DC0035466F-eu-lbn-31aug.pdf.
ECHO (European Commission Humanitarian Aid Department) and UNDP (UN Development Programme). n.d.a. *Rapid rehabilitation of key municipal infrastructure for local service delivery.* Beirut. www.undp.org.lb/communication/publications/downloads/Rapid_Rehab_English.pdf.
———. n.d.b. *Restoration and preservation of lives and livelihoods.* Beirut. www.undp.org.lb/communication/publications/downloads/Echo_EngBrochure.pdf.
E-MINE (Electronic Mine Information Network). 2009a. Lebanon. www.mineaction.org/country.asp?c=16.
———. 2009b. *Lebanon: Landmine monitor report 2009.* www.the-monitor.org/lm/2009/countries/pdf/lebanon.pdf.
ETF (European Training Foundation). 2010. Lebanon: EFT Country information note. www.etf.europa.eu/pubmgmt.nsf/(getAttachment)/9A159D86BC44EDEDC12577060032804F/$File/NOTE84JCSR.pdf.
FAO (Food and Agriculture Organization of the United Nations). 2006. *Lebanon: Damage and early recovery needs: Assessment of agriculture, fisheries and forestry.* TCP/LEB/3101. Rome. www.fao.org/newsroom/common/ecg/1000445/en/LebanonDNAMFinalReportTCP.pdf.
Farran, M. 2009. Interview by the author of professor from the American University of Beirut and advisor to the Ministry of Agriculture (during the post-conflict phase). August. Beirut, Lebanon.
Fehmi, M. 2008. Interview by the author of brigadier general director of the Lebanon Mine Action Center. August. Beirut.
Fisk, R. 2009. "Lebanon's Madoff" bankrupted after bouncing US$200,000 cheque to Hizbollah. *The Independent*, September 8.
Galey, P., and W. Mroueh. 2010. Israel: Attackers will be sent years "backwards." *Daily Star*, May 28.
Gheciu, A., and J. Welsh. 2009. The imperative to rebuild: Assessing the normative case for postconflict reconstruction. *Ethics & International Affairs* 23 (2): 121–146.
Ghoraieb, I. 2009. L'identité retrouvée. *L'Orient-Le Jour*, June 9.
Halle, M., R. Matthew, and J. Switzer. 2002. *Conserving the peace: Resources, livelihoods and security.* Winnipeg, Canada: International Institute for Sustainable Development. www.iisd.org/pdf/2002/envsec_conserving_peace.pdf.
Harel, A. 2006. Hezbollah kills 8 soldiers, kidnaps 2 in offensive on northern border. *Haaretz*, July 13.

Harik, J. P. 2005. *Hezbollah: The changing face of terrorism*. London: I. B. Tauris.
HRW (Human Rights Watch). 2008. *Flooding South Lebanon: Israel's use of cluster munitions in Lebanon, in July and August 2006*. www.hrw.org/sites/default/files/reports/lebanon0208webwcover.pdf.
Khoury, M. 2009. Interview by the author of project manager for United Nations Development Programme's Community Energy Efficiency and Renewable Energy Demonstration Project for the Recovery of Lebanon. April. Beirut.
Khoury, P. 2009. Interview by the author of official from the Lebanese Center for Energy Conservation in the Ministry of Energy and Water. September 4. Beirut.
Klap, A., and N. Yassin. 2008. *Outcome evaluation: Conflict prevention and peace building*. www.undp.org.lb/WhatWeDo/Docs/UNDP_LEB_CPR_Outcome_Evaluation.pdf.
Knudsen, A. 2005. Precarious peacebuilding: Post-war Lebanon, 1990–2005. CMI Working Paper. Bergen, Norway: Chr. Michelsen Institute. http://bora.cmi.no/dspace/bitstream/10202/103/1/Working%20paper%20WP%202005-12.pdf.
Külbel, J. C. 2007. La longue route d'Israël vers la guerre de Juillet 2006. *Voltaire Édition Internationale*, January 3. www.voltairenet.org/article143782.html.
Lacouture, J., G. Tueni, and G. D. Khoury. 2002. *Un siècle pour rien: Le Moyen-Orient Arabe de l'Empire Ottoman à l'Empire Americain*. Paris: Éditions Albin Michel.
Lebanese Republic. 2007. *Lebanese republic: Recovery, reconstruction and reform*. "International Conference for Support to Lebanon," Paris, January 25. www.rebuildlebanon.gov.lb/images_Gallery/Paris%20III%20document_Final_Eng%20Version.pdf.
Lebanon Info Center. n.d. Lebanon statistics. www.lebanoninfocenter.eu.org/encyclopedia/lebanon/en/lebanon-statistics.html.
Makhzoumi, J. M. 2009. Unfolding landscape in a Lebanese village: Rural heritage in a globalising world. *International Journal of Heritage Studies* 15 (4): 317–337.
Malek, S. 2009. Interview by the author of head of International Legal Affairs, Ministry of Environment. August. Beirut, Lebanon.
Nasrallah, H. 2009. Interview by the author of member of the research department in the Ministry of Agriculture. August. Beirut, Lebanon.
Peacebuilding Initiative. 2008. Debates. www.peacebuildinginitiative.org/index.cfm?fuseaction=page.viewpage&pageid=1766.
Petran, T. 1987. *The struggle over Lebanon*. New York: Monthly Review Press.
Rebuild Lebanon. 2007. Projects in progress. Water sector: Water and wastewater rehabilitation progress report. www.rebuildlebanon.gov.lb/english/f/default.asp.
Ricigliano, R. 2003. Networks of effective action: Implementing an integrated approach to peace building. *Security Dialogue* 34 (4): 445–462.
———. 2010. Lebanon country profile 2010. www.finance.gov.lb/en-US/finance/ReportsPublications/DocumentsAndReportsIssuedByMOF/Documents/Sovereign%20and%20Invensment%20Reports/Country%20Profile/2010%20Lebanon%20Country%20Profile.pdf.
Sabra, A. H. 2007. Oil spill contaminants in selected vertebrates and invertebrates of the eastern Mediterranean Sea. Master's thesis, American University of Beirut.
Seoud, J. 2009. Interview by the author of project manager for United Nations Development Programme. August. Beirut, Lebanon.
Steiner, R. 2006. *Lebanon oil spill rapid assessment and response mission: Final report*. www.greenline.org.lb/new/pdf_files/document_2_lebanon_oil_spill_rapid_assessment_and_response_mission.pdf.

UNDP (United Nations Development Programme). 2006. Projects database: An integrated waste management plan for mixed demolition waste in South Lebanon. www.undp.org.lb/ProjectFactSheet/projectDetail.cfm?projectId=52.
———. 2007a. Projects database/Peace building: A strategy for conflict prevention in Lebanon. www.undp.org.lb/ProjectFactSheet/projectDetail.cfm?projectId=45.
———. 2007b. Projects database/Promoting cultivation of medicinal and aromatic plants for livelihood recovery in South Lebanon. www.undp.org.lb/ProjectFactSheet/projectDetail.cfm?projectId=68.
———. 2007c. *United Nations common country assessment: Lebanon.* Beirut. www.un.org.lb/Library/Files/CCA/UNDAF/CCA%20Report%20Dec07%20English.pdf.
———. 2007d. *UNDP's participation in Lebanon's recovery in the aftermath of the July 2006 war.* www.undp.org.lb/PROFORMA.pdf.
———. 2008a. Projects database/Small scale MAPs cultivation to reduce the risks associated with cluster bombs in South Lebanon. www.undp.org.lb/ProjectFactSheet/projectDetail.cfm?projectId=132.
———. 2008b. Support to the National Demining Office. www.undp.org.lb/ProjectFactSheet/projectDetail.cfm?projectId=28.
UNDP (United Nations Development Programme). 2007. *Lebanon rapid environmental assessment for greening recovery, reconstruction and reform.* Beirut. www.undp.org.lb/events/docs/DraftReport.pdf.
UNDP (United Nations Development Programme) and UNPF (United Nations Population Fund). 2009. Draft country programme document for Lebanon (2010–2014). DP/DCP/LBN/1. May 29. www.undp.org.lb/WhatWeDo/Docs/CPD_Lebanon_2014.pdf.
UNEP (United Nations Environment Programme). 2007. *Lebanon: Post-conflict environmental assessment.* Nairobi, Kenya. http://postconflict.unep.ch/publications/UNEP_Lebanon.pdf.
———. 2009. *From conflict to peacebuilding: The role of natural resources and the environment.* Nairobi, Kenya. http://postconflict.unep.ch/publications/pcdmb_policy_01.pdf.
UN-HABITAT (United Nations Human Settlements Programme). 2008. *Country programme document 2008–2009: Lebanon.* Nairobi, Kenya. www.unhabitat.org/pmss/listItemDetails.aspx?publicationID=2706.
UNSC (United Nations Security Council). 1978a. Resolution 425. S/RES/425 (1978). March 19. http://unispal.un.org/unispal.nsf/d744b47860e5c97e85256c40005d01d6/e25dae8e3ce54fb5852560e50079c708?OpenDocument.
———. 1978b. Resolution 426. S/RES/426 (1978). March 19. http://unispal.un.org/unispal.nsf/d744b47860e5c97e85256c40005d01d6/db9fd6b989bc0381852560e50079a532?OpenDocument.
———. 2004. Resolution 1559. S/RES/1559 (2004). September 2. http://unispal.un.org/UNISPAL.NSF/0/764DC777BFC4307E85256F08005098BF.
———. 2006. Resolution 1701. S/RES/1701 (2006). August 11. http://unispal.un.org/UNISPAL.NSF/0/3E1D31CCD699DF0C852571CB0052D40B.
Whittemore, L. 2008. Intervention and post-conflict natural resource governance: Lessons from Liberia. *Minnesota Journal of International Law* 17 (2): 387–433.
World Bank. 2007. *Republic of Lebanon: Economic assessment of environmental degradation due to the July 2006 hostilities; Sector note.* Report No. 39787-LB. http://siteresources.worldbank.org/LEBANONEXTN/Resources/LB_env_Oct2007.pdf?resourceurlname=LB_env_Oct2007.pdf.
———. 2008. *Republic of Lebanon: Electricity sector public expenditure review.* Report No. 41421-LB. www.wec-lebanon.org/attachments/WB-Electricty_Sector_Overview_2008.pdf.

Ecological restoration and peacebuilding: The case of the Iraqi marshes

Steve Lonergan

The marshes of southern Iraq—often called the Iraqi marshlands or the Mesopotamian marshlands—were once among the largest wetlands in the world, covering more than 10,000 km^2 (roughly the size of Lebanon) and supporting diverse flora and fauna and a human population of approximately 500,000 (Coast 2003). Fresh water for the marshes came almost entirely from the two major rivers of the region—the Tigris and Euphrates—and their tributaries. Both rivers have their source in southeast Anatolia in Turkey and eventually flow into Iraq, coming together in the marshes to form the Shatt al-Arab River. The Shatt al-Arab then flows through the city of Basra into the Persian Gulf (see figure 1).

Eighty-eight percent of the runoff that contributes to the flow of the Euphrates comes from Turkey; the rest, from Syria. Turkey supplies 42 percent of the flow of the Tigris; Iraq, 32 percent; Iran, 26 percent; and Syria, less than 1 percent (Altinbilek 2004). Iraq, including the marshes, is almost completely dependent on the two river systems for its water. The ecology of the marshes requires periodic flushing from floodwaters to remove pollutants and sustain the wetlands.

Historically three marshes merged during times of high water: the Central Marshes (between the two rivers), Hawizeh Marsh to the northeast, and the Hammar Marsh to the southwest (see figure 2). The marsh dwellers depended on a healthy marsh ecosystem for fishing, agriculture (including livestock), building materials, drinking water, and transportation—all intricately linked to fresh water. The marshes were also home to a variety of wild plants, birds, and animals, including endangered migratory birds and many fish that provided sustenance for marsh dwellers and the broader Iraqi population. Prior to 1990, 60 percent of the fish consumed in Iraq came from the marshes (Ochsenschlager 2004; Tkachenko 2003).

Steve Lonergan is a professor emeritus in the Department of Geography at the University of Victoria in Canada. He led a project funded by the Canadian International Development Agency that focused on the restoration of the Iraqi marshlands. From 2003 to 2005, Lonergan served as director of the Division of Early Warning and Assessment of United Nations Environment Programme.

224   Assessing and restoring natural resources in post-conflict peacebuilding

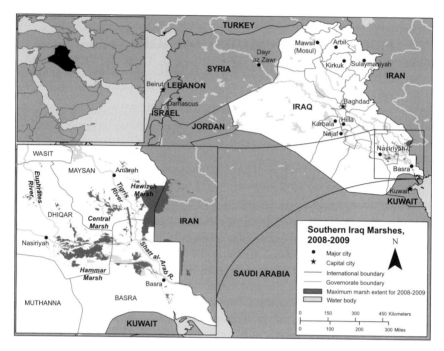

Figure 1.   Location of the southern Iraq marshes, 2008–2009
Source: CIMI (2010).

   The importance of the marshes and the surrounding area goes far beyond the borders of Iraq. Many consider the marshes the cradle of civilization and the site of the biblical Garden of Eden. They are close to cultural and religious centers, such as Sumer, Babylon, and Najaf, and their historical, cultural, and ecological importance is unquestioned. Nevertheless because of security issues and the difficulty of traveling to or within the marshes, few outsiders have spent time in the region in the past thirty years.[1]
   In addition to their historical and ecological significance, the marshes have been of strategic interest to the government of Iraq, particularly since 1980. During the 1980s, much of the fighting in the Iran-Iraq War was in the marshes, and subsequent invasions by the United States and its allies in 1991 and 2003 went through them. Basra, Iraq's second largest city, located just south of the marshes, was the center of protests against the government of Saddam Hussein and pro-Iranian sympathy in the early 1990s. Although the security situation in

---

[1]   For historical readings on the marshes, see Maxwell (1957); Sluglett (2003a); Thesiger (1964); and Young and Wheeler (1977).

Peacebuilding and ecological restoration of the Iraqi marshes 225

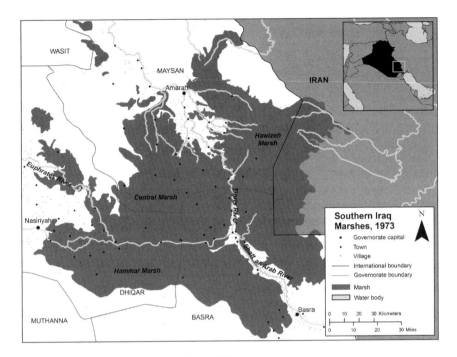

Figure 2. Marshes of southern Iraq, 1973
Source: CIMI (2010).

the marshes is relatively stable, there are independent militia operating in and around them, and conflict may erupt at any time.[2]

This chapter identifies factors that have imperiled the Iraqi marshlands, from Saddam Hussein's systematic draining of the marshes in the 1990s to a severe drought in 2009 to infrastructure projects and changes in land use in the Tigris and the Euphrates basins. The chapter reviews the varying extent of Iraqi marshlands from 2002 to 2009, as compared to the boundaries of the marshes in 1973, and provides three scenarios for the future of the marshes, based upon ten recommendations put forth by the Canada-Iraq Marshlands Initiative. The chapter examines international restoration efforts and regional cooperation attempts among Iraq, Iran, Syria, and Turkey—the neighboring riparian states. It concludes with lessons learned and discusses the connection between ecological restoration and peacebuilding.

---

[2] Information on activities in the marshes came from Iraqi participants in the Canada-Iraq Marshlands Initiative, a three-year project to restore the marshes. Meetings were held twice a year with local sheikhs, university researchers, governorate officials, and national ministry representatives. For more information, see www.iraqimarshlands.com or CIMI (2010).

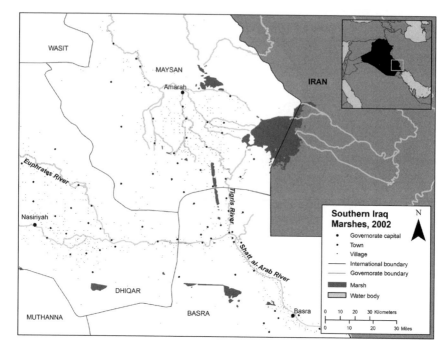

Figure 3. Marshes of southern Iraq, 2002
Source: CIMI (2010).

DRAINING THE MARSHES

In 1951, the British developed a plan to drain the marshes to reclaim land for agriculture. When Turkey, Syria, and Iraq began a series of irrigation and hydroelectric projects in the 1980s, human activities started to have a negative impact on the region. Despite the potential for decreased water flow in the Euphrates (less so in the Tigris), the primary concern of the Iraqi government in the 1980s was the Iran-Iraq War (Sluglett 2003b). The marshes remained relatively healthy and were allocated ample water to make entry of Iranian troops difficult.

Following the 1990–1991 Gulf War, the situation changed dramatically. The government of Saddam Hussein began a systematic effort to destroy the marshes and the people living there, initially through aerial bombing and burning villages. When the United Nations resisted, the government brought forth a plan to drain the marshes and displace the population, ostensibly to reclaim them for agriculture. With the construction of major drainage canals linked to the Euphrates and Tigris, by 2003, the marshes were reduced to less than 10 percent of their pre-1990 size (see figure 3), and the population declined to fewer than 80,000 (France 2006). Satellite photos showed the extent of the destruction, and reports from refugees documented the hardships endured by local residents. The UN and the World Bank identified the draining as a major environmental and humanitarian disaster (Partow 2001).

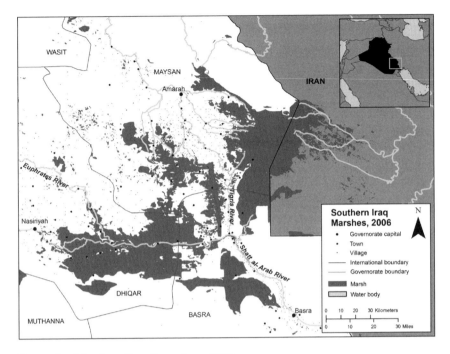

Figure 4. Marshes of southern Iraq, 2006
Source: CIMI (2010).

MARSH RESTORATION

The fall of Saddam Hussein's regime in 2003 allowed assessment of damage to the marshes and restoration efforts. The United States, Japan, Italy, and Canada, along with the United Nations Environment Programme (UNEP), and subsequently the United Nations Development Programme, promoted ecological restoration, funded new development programs, and provided basic services. In all cases, the focus was on building a sustainable peace through marsh rehabilitation. Efforts included facilitating multi-stakeholder processes, engaging the international community through environmental agreements, and inviting other riparian states, particularly Turkey and Iran, to discussions. Initial assessments showed that the reduced size of the marshes, poor water quality, saline soils, and pollution from industries and leftover military ordnance would make full restoration difficult, if not impossible. The conversion of marsh to agricultural land, oil under the marshes, and significant growth in upstream impoundments in Turkey, Syria, and Iraq worsened matters. Nevertheless ad hoc efforts by local residents, who destroyed some of the earthen dams, and ample rain and snowfall in the mountains of Turkey and northeastern Iraq markedly improved the extent of the marshes and water volume by 2006 (see figure 4). Many migratory birds returned, and there was some cause for optimism that ecological restoration would be successful (Richardson and Hussain 2006). But four troubling issues remained.

First, very few former residents had returned to the marshes. Although the evidence is anecdotal and drawn largely from discussions with sheikhs and local government officials, the ongoing security problems in the region and the lack of economic opportunities had made return unattractive. In addition, there were few basic amenities, including drinking water. Many former residents had re-established their families in urban centers such as Basra or Nasiriyah. The number of returnees may be no more than 40,000—less than 10 percent of those originally displaced (CIMI 2010).

Second, the three marshes had been reduced to two; the Central Marshes had completely disappeared, and there was no connection between the remaining wetlands, even during times of high water. (The government hopes to reintroduce water to the Central Marshes but has not.) In addition, the health of the remaining marshes was very poor in certain places, particularly in the Hammar Marsh, southeast of Nasiriyah. Soil salts had reached the surface through capillary action, and farther downstream, tidal flow had polluted a large part of the area.

Third, agricultural land now occupied a significant part of the former wetlands, so reflooding them would have lowered economic output from a region that was already poor.

Fourth, and most important, upstream infrastructure projects and increased demand for water for nonagricultural uses had severely reduced the flow of water to the marshes. With more dams in Turkey and new dams and dikes under construction in Iran, some stakeholders had turned their attention from ecological restoration to modifying local and regional expectations for the marshes.

Current conditions

Draining by Saddam Hussein's regime had a catastrophic impact on the marshes' ecology, hydrology, and people. Despite this destruction, hopes were raised that at least a partial restoration would be possible when the marshlands expanded from 9 to 10 percent to roughly 35 percent of their 1973 size between 2003 and 2006. However, these expectations were soon lowered due to the effects of infrastructure projects in the Tigris and the Euphrates basins and severe drought conditions in 2008–2009. By the fall of 2009, with a severe drought affecting the entire country, the marshes' size had approached that of 2002.

Perhaps more importantly, information on infrastructure development in Iran came to light. Since 2006, Iran has dammed many of the small rivers that provided water to the Hawizeh Marsh. Even more devastating was Iran's construction along its border with Iraq of a six-meter-high dike, which effectively divided the Hawizeh Marsh into two, when it was completed in the spring of 2009. The dike in Hawizeh restricted water flow into the Iraqi part of the marsh. Security—against the drug trade—was Iran's primary justification for construction of the dike, although drilling for oil and the desire to reduce water flow into Iraq may have played a role. Iran held no discussions with Iraq prior to building the dike and even installed guard towers.

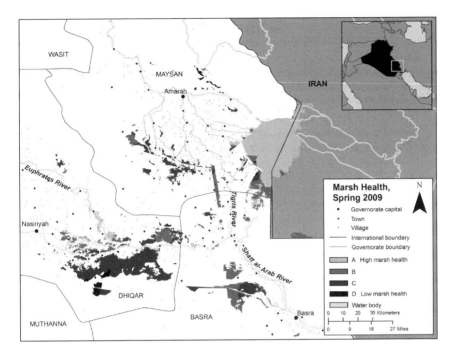

Figure 5. Health of southern Iraqi marshes, spring 2009
Source: CIMI (2010).

The marshes now suffer from three conditions: First, the low, 2002 level of the marshes is no longer strictly the result of political factors; infrastructure development, changes in land use, and climate change are also responsible. Second, the marshes have become very fragmented. Ecological fragmentation threatens the survival of many species, the health of the marshes, and the people, whose livelihoods depend on the environment. Third, the Hawizeh Marsh, which is now a Ramsar site,[3] has been badly affected and will only suffer more from the Iranian dike along the border.

The health of the ecosystem is related to the marshes' size. Detailed water sampling and analysis conducted since 2005 demonstrate that only a portion of the remaining marshes is healthy enough to support flora and fauna and provide drinking water for humans and animals. Lack of periodic flushing, continued encroachment of salt from tidal flow, and agricultural runoff have adversely affected the ecosystem of much of the region (see figure 5). The marshes could recover but not without return to the flow regime that existed prior to 1990.

---

[3] In early 2008, Iraq became a party to the Convention on Wetlands of International Importance, commonly known as the Ramsar Convention. The Hawizeh Marsh is listed as a site of international importance under this convention. For the complete text of the convention, see www.ramsar.org/cda/en/ramsar-documents-texts-convention-on/main/ramsar/1-31-38%5E20671_4000_0__.

The Iraqi government continues to talk about the importance of restoring the marshes for ecological and humanitarian reasons. It allocated US$300 million to the new Ministry of State for the Marshlands to improve infrastructure and support basic services for marsh residents. But the government is paying little attention to the ecology of the marshes and the resources they provide. Acknowledging that there may never be enough water to restore the wetlands, the Ministry of Water Resources proposes adhering to the 1973 boundaries of the marshes, disallowing existing and future agricultural and oil development, and labeling the remaining land and wetlands the "marshes" (CRIM 2009). Division within the national government, lack of intergovernmental coordination, and emphasis on economic development and growth have made the marshes a low priority in the future of Iraq.

Future of the marshes

Internal and international discussions now refer to the marshes' survival as much as to their restoration. Like many ecological and social systems, the marshes have been remarkably resilient to external stresses, climate or security related. But deliberate draining and reduced water flow from upstream have overcome their natural resiliency. In the absence of significant management interventions, the marshes will only exist during years of high rainfall. In dry years, the marshlands will diminish, continuing only as a small, brackish water marsh in the southern part of the original marshes. The following ten recommendations put forth by the Canada-Iraq Marshlands Initiative in its 2010 report "Managing for Change: The Present and Future State of the Iraqi Marshlands" (CIMI 2010) will be required to protect even the healthiest and most permanent areas of the marshes.

1. **Reaching agreement with Turkey and Syria regarding upstream withdrawal and ensuring that a minimum flow of water enters Iraq.**
   Although Syria and Iraq signed a treaty (consisting of joint minutes of a meeting) in 1979, Turkey has been recalcitrant to discussing water allocations—from either the Tigris or Euphrates rivers. Discussions on economic cooperation between Iraq and Turkey did not cover water, and the Iraqi parliament has resisted signing any agreement unless water is explicitly addressed. There is little question that the large irrigation and hydroelectric projects in Turkey have affected, and will increasingly affect, the flow of the two rivers.
2. **Reaching agreement with Iran regarding dams and, in particular, the dike in Hawizeh to ensure survival of the Hawizeh Marsh.**
   In recent years, Iran has dammed some of the streams and rivers that flow into the Hawizeh Marsh. To make up for the dams, in fall 2009, Iran began trucking water to Basra to help Iraq deal with drought. Discussions between the two countries about Iran's dike in the Hawizeh Marsh have been unproductive.

3. **Rationalizing the upstream withdrawals and storage of water within Iraq to ensure that a minimum flow of water reaches the marshes.**
   Dam construction within Iraq has also reduced the flow of water to the marshes. The demand for electricity and irrigation in the northern and central regions of the country continues to affect the amount of water reaching the marshes.
4. **Reducing tidal flow to the southern areas of the marshes.**
   The health of the marshes is dependent on periodic flushing by floodwater from the north. The flushing keeps tidal water from the Persian Gulf from moving into the southern marshes, which are, for the most part, below sea level. The desiccation of the marshes has allowed tidal flow to move farther north, resulting in higher salinity levels in the southernmost sections of the marshes.
5. **Reducing the flow of untreated wastewater and pollution into the marshes.**
   The lack of strong regulations on wastewater treatment and discharge and the relaxed enforcement of existing regulations further threaten the quality of water in the marshes. As the Iraqi economy expands, more attention must be focused on controlling the movement of wastes into the marshes.
6. **Addressing competition for water.**
   Agriculture, industry, and domestic users compete for water from the marshes. As the sectors grow, so will their water demands, leaving little in the marshes.
7. **Reducing the negative impact of drought.**
   Because many residents of the marshes lack basic services, long-term climate change is understandably not a high priority. But the severe drought of 2009 revealed the need for a drought-management strategy that addresses the magnitude and frequency of drought and other extreme weather events, which are expected to increase according to all projections of global warming. Long wet and dry periods will affect all aspects of marsh ecology and society.
8. **Promoting better community stewardship of water resources within and adjacent to the marshes.**
   In the past, periodic flushing and the overall size of the marshes made the wetlands resistant to most human activities, such as fishing with poisons and waste disposal. Best management practices need to be introduced and implemented by villagers and the general population.
9. **Ensuring that economic development in the region does not negatively affect the marshes.**
   The main economic driver in Iraq is oil, and much of the country's reserves lie in the marshes. The sensitive ecology of the region will likely not be a factor in decisions to drill for oil. Accordingly steps must be taken to ensure that the effects of drilling and transportation—and other economic activities—are minimal. Environmental impact assessments are now required for all projects in the marshlands, although how seriously resulting recommendations will be taken remains unclear.

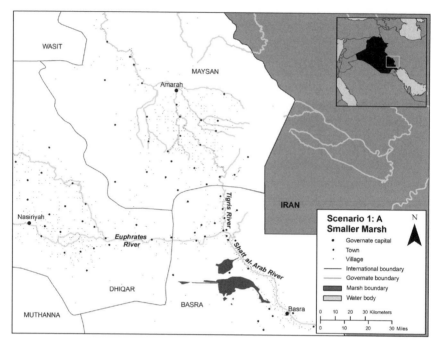

Figure 6. Scenario 1: A smaller Iraqi marsh
Source: CIMI (2010).

10. **Developing a land use strategy to ensure the sustainability of the marshes.** Land use activities may greatly affect the sensitive wetlands ecosystem. For its survival, a land use strategy must be developed to minimize negative impacts. Despite the designation of the marshes as a Ramsar site, and its status as a proposed World Heritage site and protected area, activities within and adjacent to the marshes may still destroy them.

The Canada-Iraq Marshlands Initiative used the ten recommendations to develop scenarios for the future of the marshes (CIMI 2010). Without a managerial intervention and some progress on the first, second, and third issues, the marshes will probably not survive, except as brackish wetlands north of Basra, fed by backflow from the Shatt al-Arab (see figure 6). When the scenario was presented to marsh residents and representatives from local and national governments, there was general acceptance that the near-complete drying of the marshes was a real possibility.

A second, and more optimistic, solution includes protecting the healthiest sections of the marshes (for example, Hawizeh) and addressing most of the factors above to ensure the survival of smaller marshes that might expand over

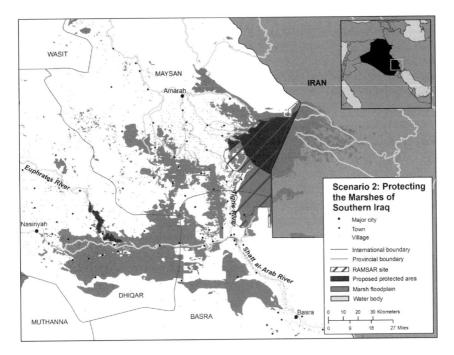

Figure 7. Scenario 2: Protect the healthy portions of the Iraqi marshes
Source: CIMI (2010).
Note: This scenario would lead to the survival of approximately 20 percent of the original marshes.

time to support many flora and fauna. Roughly 20 percent of the original marshes would remain (see figure 7).

A third scenario (see figure 8), which the Iraqi government promotes, is quite remote, particularly given the existing and future land uses and the amount of water available to the marshes (CIMI 2010). The government hopes that engineering solutions—constructing more dams and canals—will lead to the survival of up to 70 percent of the original marshes.

Despite the optimistic assessment of the Iraqi government and the efforts of donor agencies and countries to restore the marshes, the future of the wetlands and the society and culture that are based on them is dire. Water is a necessary—but not necessarily sufficient—condition for the survival of the marshes. The ten recommendations listed above pose tremendous challenges to the future of the marshes. Despite some reflooding after 2003 and an increase in native and exotic plant and animal species, the wetlands remain extremely vulnerable to further disruptions in water flow, chemical pollution, and saltwater intrusion. Reflooding of the marshes does not necessarily mean restoration of the wetlands environment. In some cases, reflooding has released toxins from chemical pollution and military ordnance in the soil. Water quality and ecosystem health have declined.

234 Assessing and restoring natural resources in post-conflict peacebuilding

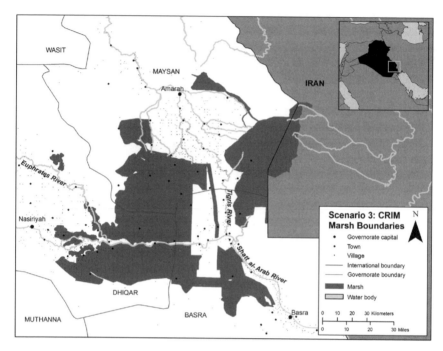

Figure 8. Scenario 3: Boundaries proposed by the Center for Restoration of the Iraqi Marshlands
Source: CIMI (2010).
Note: This scenario would lead to the survival of up to 70 percent of the original marshes.

Ongoing restoration efforts

A few countries and UN agencies remain committed to the restoration of the marshes. As early as 2001, UNEP began monitoring changes using satellite data and established the Iraq Marshlands Observation System to provide information to the international community (UNEP 2006). Subsequent efforts by UNEP, funded mostly by Japan, focused on improving water supply to marsh residents using environmentally sustainable technology. They also conducted studies of a drainage canal, which was constructed by Saddam Hussein's regime, to determine whether the water was suitable to redirect to the marshes (Aoki, Kugaprasatham, and Al-Lami 2013). Work is underway to help treat the canal water before it enters the marshes.

The Italian government has spent considerable funds on hydrological modeling to determine the amount of water necessary to sustain a marsh of reduced size. Its analysis has been incorporated into plans of the Ministry of Water Resources, but insufficient water and little consideration of social and economic factors weaken the hydrological and engineering modeling (Iraqi Ministries 2006).

The U.S. and Canadian governments have focused on training Iraqi students and professors in water-quality monitoring and analysis and geographic information systems to improve wetlands science and basic understanding of the marshes. Although educational programs have been successful, insufficient access and government and academic capacity have hampered full implementation of water resource management of the marshes. Restoration is further hindered by the absence of a coordinated approach.

Regional cooperation

By almost any measure, most countries in the Middle East are water scarce. Wealthy countries, such as Saudi Arabia, can afford expensive desalination, but managing water demand and investing in regional solutions are required to protect the Nile River Basin, the Jordan River, and the Tigris and Euphrates rivers. International and regional conflicts often have devastating planned and accidental impacts on water and sanitation infrastructure and water quality. But despite the rhetoric, there has been little evidence—since the 1950s—that the region will engage in conflict over water.

After the fall of Saddam Hussein's regime in 2003, there was some optimism that international furor over loss of the wetlands would set the stage for regional cooperation between Turkey, Syria, Iraq, and Iran, resulting in peace initiatives. In 2004, UNEP opened dialogue between Iraq and Iran, which share the marshes. (See Muralee Thummarukudy, Oli Brown, and Hannah Moosa "Remediation of Polluted Sites in the Balkans, Iraq, and Sierra Leone," in this book.) The catalyst was a UNEP study that demonstrated that over 90 percent of the marshlands had dried into salt pans, which had grown quickly because of construction of extensive drainage works (UNEP 2006). Iran and Iraq requested that UNEP facilitate dialogue between them.

The process began at a seminar on integrated water resource management at a neutral venue in Geneva, where parties studied best practices in transboundary water management. The meeting was exclusively technical, and the outcome was left completely open. The agenda moved from basic concepts of water management to best practices from around the world and the case of the marshlands. By progressing from the broad to the specific, the meeting encouraged dialogue between the parties before sensitive issues were discussed. Prior to hearing formal presentations from both sides, UNEP presented technical details from its assessments of water consumption in the area and focused on rapid changes, including degradation, reflooding problems, and emerging threats. UNEP experts noted challenges and possibilities for restoration on both sides of the border. The independent analysis placed indisputable facts on the table that could become the basis for joint problem solving.

Only after the technical priming were the delegates asked to express their countries' water-related concerns. The Iraqi side emphasized restoration and the need for a regional approach. In contrast, the Iranians advanced a nationalist view, including plans to build a dam and dike across the transboundary marsh. The diverging visions revealed the urgency of continuing the dialogue and improving technical cooperation on both sides of the border. Although additional meetings were planned, dialogue was eventually placed on hold following the deterioration of the security situation in Iraq and diplomatic challenges following the Iranian presidential elections in 2005. Even though talks over a shared environmental problem can initiate cooperation, sustainability can be a major challenge when larger political or security issues are at play.

Despite the lack of cooperation during the UNEP discussions, Iraq moved forward and in early 2008 became a party to the Convention on Wetlands of International Importance (Ramsar Convention) (Rubec 2008). International cooperation, one of the three pillars of the convention, obligates countries to consult each other when wetlands extend across international borders, as in the case of Iran and Iraq, and to "endeavour to co-ordinate and support present and future policies and regulations concerning the conservation of wetlands."[4] Although the convention cannot force parties to cooperate, it can be used to apply "moral pressure" when conflicts arise (Dudley 2008, 73). But, on the marshes, the response from Iran has been minimal.

Iraq has also been working with the United Nations Educational, Scientific and Cultural Organization and UNEP to have portions of the marshes designated a World Heritage site—a natural and a cultural treasure—and has become a party to the Convention on Biological Diversity.[5] Still discussions with Iran on cooperative management of the marshes have been unsuccessful.

The situation between Iraq and its neighbors, Turkey and Syria, regarding the flow of the Euphrates and Tigris into Iraq is more promising because it only indirectly involves the marshes. A 1990 Iraqi protocol ratified the minutes of a meeting with Syria on the provisional division of Euphrates waters and provided Iraq with 58 percent of the Euphrates water entering Syria from Turkey (Wolf 2010). The UN Convention on the Law of Non-Navigational Uses of International Watercourses—the only global freshwater convention—was adopted by the UN General Assembly in 1997 and obligates parties to "cooperate on the basis of sovereign equality, territorial integrity, mutual benefit and good faith in order to attain optimal utilization and adequate protection of an international watercourse."[6] Although Syria and Iraq have ratified the convention, Turkey and Iran have not. Only sixteen of the thirty-five countries needed for the convention to enter into force have become parties. Economic diplomacy between Iraq and Turkey has not touched on water flow from the Tigris or the Euphrates. Iraqi parliamentarians have insisted that water allocations be a component of any agreement (CIMI 2010).

Despite the need for a continuous flow of water to sustain the marshes and the hopes of many that discussions over the future of the marshes might stimulate further cooperation and peacebuilding between riparian states, there has been

---

[4] Art. 5, para. 2.
[5] For the complete text of the convention, see www.cbd.int/convention/text/.
[6] A/RES/51/229, art. 8, para. 1. For the convention, see http://untreaty.un.org/ilc/texts/instruments/english/conventions/8_3_1997.pdf.

little productive discussion, let alone action, by basin states. Indeed there is more dam construction, and water flow into the marshes continues to decrease.

LESSONS LEARNED

The Iraqi marshes have changed drastically since 1991, first because of politics and later because of infrastructure developments upstream. The Iraqi government has converted many of the wetlands into agricultural land, and there are plans to develop oil resources under some of the existing and former marshes. The government has identified the areas leftover as marshlands, whether they contain water or not. But it has not explained the strategy to the local population. The tribes and local residents—at least those who remain in the marshes—still expect their lives to return to the way they were prior to the 1990–1991 Gulf War.

Four lessons have emerged from the case of the Iraqi marshes:

1. Restoration efforts must consider environmental changes caused by conflict and involve local communities. Restoration to the marshes' original condition and peacebuilding may be incompatible. Raising expectations for the marshes that existed for thousands of years may inhibit peacebuilding.

2. Ecosystem resilience has a limit. Even if all the water were available and there were no other activities on land, the marshes' resiliency might be exhausted. There is some indication that small sections of the marshes, which were reflooded after 2003, are recovering naturally. Pollutants were flushed from the system; native reeds returned; and biodiversity increased. The natural resiliency of the wetlands was very much intact. Yet other areas changed into a brackish water marsh. Nonnative species that thrive under stress (such as catfish) are outcompeting native species for food, and the natural flushing of the marshes' floodwaters has been permanently disrupted.

3. Although environmental agreements, such as the Ramsar Convention, endorse multilateral discussions, they cannot force parties to meet, even when environmental damage might affect all parties. When countries want to cooperate, the conventions provide a useful institutional structure. But when they do not want to cooperate, environmental conventions are little incentive for discussion.

4. Many governments in post-conflict situations have limited capacity to implement broad change, particularly when it requires collaboration. The Iraqi national government remains fragmented, and corruption is rife. There is little cooperation between levels of government despite assurances that decision making will be more decentralized in the future. In the case of the marshlands, the US$300 million initially allocated to the governorates for restoration were withdrawn and given to the new Ministry of State for the Marshlands, ostensibly because the governorates were using the funds to support urban activities outside the marshes.

CONCLUSIONS AND STEPS FORWARD

The winter rains of late 2009 and early 2010 increased water flow into the marshes, which cover roughly 20 percent of the area they did in 1973—far less than in 2006. The government has redirected the flow of the Main Outflow Drain, south of Nasiriyah, into the Hammar Marsh, even though it is still studying the effect on marsh health. The Ministry of Water Resources is considering the construction of more impoundments and regulators to facilitate the flow of water into the marshes.

Despite the efforts, the long-term outlook for the marshes appears dim. First, further controlling the flow of water upstream eliminates the annual pulse of water that cleansed the marshes of salts and other pollutants. Second, the reduced flow of water from Iran poses increasing problems to the extent and health of the Hawizeh Marsh. The long-term effects of the Iranian dike and other dams are uncertain, but there are already signs of a reduction in the extent and volume of the marsh. Third, there is a strong likelihood that climate change will cause longer and more severe droughts in the region, further shocking an already-vulnerable ecosystem. Fourth, agricultural development and oil drilling are higher priorities for the Iraqi government than ecosystem restoration. Although economic development and marsh restoration are not incompatible, the present course makes it unlikely that the marshes will be able to provide the renewable resources they once did.

Partly due to the lack of interest of neighboring states, problems will probably remain unaddressed. There can only be ecological reconciliation, a coming to terms with new wetlands. The Iraqi government should designate Hawizeh (and possibly other areas) as a protected area and restrict development to at least establish a front against further deterioration of the wetlands. Still some agreement with Iran is essential to ensure a healthy flow of water into Hawizeh.

REFERENCES

Altinbilek, D. 2004. Development and management of the Euphrates-Tigris Basin. *International Journal of Water Resources Development* 20 (1): 15–33.

Aoki, C., S. Kugaprasatham, and A. Al-Lami. 2013. Environmental management of the Iraqi marshlands in the post-conflict period. In *Water and post-conflict peacebuilding*, ed. E. Weinthal, J. Troell, and M. Nakayama. London: Earthscan.

CIMI (Canada-Iraq Marshlands Initiative). 2010. *Managing for change: The present and future state of the Iraqi marshlands*. University of Victoria, Canada. www.lonergansleanings.com/storage/Marshlands%20Book.pdf.

Coast, E. 2003. Demography of the Marsh Arabs. In *The Iraqi marshlands: A human and environmental study*, ed. E. Nicholson and P. Clark. 2nd ed. London: Politico's Publishing.

CRIM (Center for Restoration of the Iraqi Marshlands). 2009. A land-use plan for the Iraqi marshlands. Presentation at the CIMI-Beirut Meeting. Beirut, Lebanon.

Dudley, N., ed. 2008. *Guidelines for applying protected area management categories*. Gland, Switzerland: International Union for Conservation of Nature.

France, R., ed. 2006. *Sustainable redevelopment of the Iraqi marshlands*. Oxford, UK: Routledge.

Iraqi Ministries (Iraqi Ministry of Environment, Ministry of Water Resources, and Ministry of Municipalities and Public Works). 2006. *New Eden master plan for integrated water resources management in the marshlands area*. http://citeseerx.ist.psu.edu/viewdoc/download?doi=10.1.1.98.2941&rep=rep1&type=pdf.

Maxwell, G. 1957. *A reed shaken by the wind*. London: Longmans, Green.

Ochsenschlager, E. L. 2004. *Iraq's Marsh Arabs in the Garden of Eden*. Philadelphia: University of Pennsylvania Museum of Archeology and Anthropology.

Partow, H. 2001. *The Mesopotamian marshlands: Demise of an ecosystem*. Nairobi, Kenya: United Nations Environment Programme.

Richardson, C. J., and N. A. Hussain. 2006. Restoring the Garden of Eden: An ecological assessment of the marshes of Iraq. *BioScience* 56 (6): 477–489.

Rubec, C. D. A., ed. 2008. *Draft management plan for the Hawizeh Marsh Ramsar site of Iraq*. Vols. 1 and 2. Sulaymaniyah, Iraq: Nature Iraq.

Sluglett, P. 2003a. The international context of Iraq from 1980 to the present. In *The Iraqi marshlands: A human and environmental study*, ed. E. Nicholson and P. Clark. 2nd ed. London: Politico's Publishing.

———. 2003b. The marsh dwellers in the history of modern Iraq. In *The Iraqi marshlands: A human and environmental study*, ed. E. Nicholson and P. Clark. 2nd ed. London: Politico's Publishing.

Thesiger, W. 1964. *The Marsh Arabs*. London: Longman, Green.

Tkachenko, A. 2003. The economy of the Iraq marshes in the 1990s. In *The Iraqi marshlands: A human and environmental study*, ed. E. Nicholson and P. Clark. 2nd ed. London: Politico's Publishing.

UNEP (United Nations Environment Programme). 2006. *Iraqi Marshlands Observation System: UNEP technical report*. Nairobi, Kenya. http://postconflict.unep.ch/publications/UNEP_IMOS.pdf.

Wolf, A. 2010. International freshwater treaty database. www.transboundarywaters.orst.edu/database/interfreshtreatdata.html.

Young, G., and N. Wheeler. 1977. *Return to the marshes: Life with the Marsh Arabs of Iraq*. London: Collins.

Haiti: Lessons learned and way forward in natural resource management projects

Lucile Gingembre

Haiti is the ultimate example of a country where the environment, poverty, and instability are intrinsically interconnected. Rehabilitation of the largely degraded environment is essential to the development of the country and the well-being of its population.

Over the past few decades, many rehabilitation projects have been conducted, and substantial investments have been made in environmental improvement. However, results have been meager. A number of technically sound one-off interventions in the environmental sector have been successful, but these were implemented on a small scale, there was little follow-through after the projects were completed, and the projects were neither replicated nor systematized. Consequently, environmental degradation worsens, environmental governance remains ineffective, and the vicious cycle of poverty, instability, and vulnerability to natural disasters continues.

Given this situation, the United Nations Environment Programme (UNEP), in collaboration with the government of Haiti and a consortium of UN agencies, nongovernmental organizations (NGOs), and technical institutes, is now developing an integrated, long-term effort called the Haiti Regeneration Initiative. This program aims to reverse environmental degradation and thus reduce poverty and vulnerability to natural hazards. To assist in the design and implementation of the initiative, UNEP conducted an analysis of the experiences, lessons, needs, and challenges from past environmental projects in the country. The study examined forty-three projects and programs pertaining to natural resource management and the environment in Haiti, twenty-seven of which were still in progress at the time of the study. This chapter outlines the linkages between environmental degradation, poverty, conflict, and instability in Haiti and presents the main findings of the lessons-learned study.

Lucile Gingembre is associate program officer for the Post-Conflict and Disaster Management Branch of the United Nations Environment Programme (UNEP). She participated in the design, planning, and implementation of UNEP's Haiti country program.

ENVIRONMENTAL CHALLENGES

Haiti is the poorest, least stable, and most environmentally degraded country in the Caribbean, and its situation reflects how poverty, instability, disaster vulnerability, and environmental problems are tightly intertwined.

Deforestation and erosion

Uncontrolled deforestation, which began in colonial times, and associated erosion are severe in Haiti. Forests cover less than 3 percent of Haitian territory; by contrast, they cover approximately 28 percent of territory in the neighboring Dominican Republic. Twenty-five of Haiti's thirty major river basins are severely eroded. Each year, 42 million cubic meters of soil are swept away (UNEP, Ministry of the Environment, and University of Quiskeya 2010). Haiti's land area, measuring 27,700 square kilometers, is primarily mountainous. According to the Food and Agriculture Organization of the United Nations (FAO), 63 percent of Haiti's land has a slope of over 20 percent, and over 40 percent of the country is above 400 meters in elevation (FAO 2001).

In spite of these challenges, approximately 58 percent of the area of Haiti is used for some form of agriculture. On the steep slopes, farmers make a living by practicing rudimentary and unsustainable agriculture. They cut down trees to access new farmland, acquire firewood to meet their household needs, and make charcoal to sell. Wood fuel (firewood and charcoal) supplies 70 percent of Haiti's energy, further jeopardizing remaining forests (Energy Sector Management Assistance Program 2007). By 1995, Haitian peasants were felling some 30 million trees each year to produce approximately 3.5 million tons of firewood. By 2003, annual consumption of wood was more than 4 million tons, 33 percent of which was transformed into charcoal. The volume of firewood gathered annually exceeds the trees' ability to regenerate naturally. Since the 7.0-magnitude earthquake on January 12, 2010, the already dire environmental conditions have deteriorated further. In particular, deforestation has accelerated, partly because of the increased demand for construction material.

Deforestation and unsustainable agricultural practices cause erosion, loss of soil fertility, landslides, and reduction in water retention. On the slopes, crop yields decrease and become less reliable, and extensive damage to soil occurs. In downstream river areas, effects include unwanted sediment deposition and increased flood surges, which lead to loss of fertile land in the upper floodplains and catastrophic flooding in the vulnerable townships of the lower floodplains.

In marine and coastal zones, mangrove swamps, seagrass beds, and coral reefs are badly degraded. Sedimentation caused by the erosion of upper watersheds, overexploitation of resources for fuel and fishing, land-based pollution, and habitat encroachment threaten ecosystems. As a consequence, fish catches are plummeting and mariculture is declining. Because low-tech fishing gear and

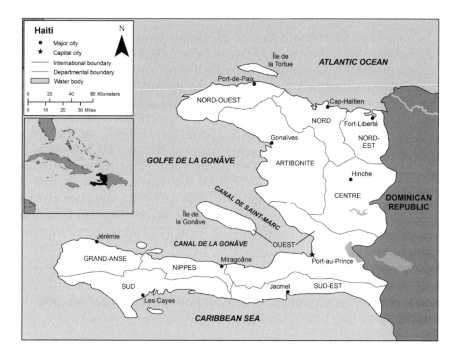

inappropriate fishing techniques prevent Haitian fishers from accessing new fishing grounds farther offshore, near-shore fisheries are overexploited. Although the status of Haitian deepwater fisheries is unknown, it is acknowledged that foreign fishing fleets exploit them illegally (Wiener 2009). Between 1980 and 2005, mangrove forests decreased in area from 17,800 to 13,000 hectares (UNEP, Ministry of the Environment, and University of Quiskeya 2010). Severely degraded mangrove forests and coral reefs cannot function as buffers against hurricanes and other storms, and their diminishment limits the development of international coastal-resort tourism, an important source of income for Caribbean islands.

Vulnerability to disasters

Haiti is the most disaster prone of all the small-island developing countries (UNDP 2004). This can be explained partly by its mountainous topography and its location on two major fault lines and in an active hurricane region. Water-catchment degradation exacerbates Haiti's vulnerability to flooding and other natural disasters, which especially affect the inhabitants of lower watersheds.

Between 1900 and 2004, Haiti recorded the fifty greatest disasters in its history; it suffered seventeen hurricanes, twenty-six major floods, and seven droughts in that period (UNEP, Ministry of the Environment, and University of Quiskeya 2010). The years from 2004 to 2008 were marked by several hurricanes that left hundreds of thousands of victims and massive infrastructure loss in their wake. In 2004, Hurricane Jeanne killed an estimated 3,000 people and adversely affected another 300,000 (4 percent of the population) (UNEP, Ministry of the Environment, and University of Quiskeya 2010; GORH 2010). The economic cost was estimated to be equivalent to 7 percent of Haiti's gross domestic product (GDP) (GORH 2010). In August and September 2008 alone, four hurricanes hit the country, affecting 826,000 people and costing the equivalent of approximately 14.6 percent of Haiti's GDP, or over US$897 million (GORH 2008).

The 2010 earthquake was a tipping point. It caused not only social and economic upheaval but also massive environmental damage, further diminishing the country's capacity to recover from chronic crisis. According to the Haitian government, 222,570 people died, over 300,000 were injured, and some 2.3 million were displaced (OCHA 2010; IASC 2010). The earthquake cost Haiti US$4.3 billion in physical damage and US$3.5 billion in economic losses, or more than 120 percent of the country's 2009 GDP. It is the first time in thirty-five years that the cost of a disaster was so high relative to the size of a country's economy (GORH 2010).

Links between environmental degradation, poverty, conflict, and instability

Poverty—combined with natural hazards, vulnerability, poor governance, weak institutions, uncontrolled population growth, insufficient economic opportunities, urban overpopulation, and economic and social inequities—produces resentment and fuels instability and political turmoil (see figure 1).

Haiti's population is expected to increase from 9.92 million in May 2009 to 11.74 million by 2020 (IHSI 2009, 2007). Fifty-six percent of the population lives below the extreme poverty line of US$1 per day; 78 percent live on under US$2 per day. Haiti's largely destroyed rural environment cannot fully feed its population or support adequate livelihoods. Around 50 percent of food is imported; 60 percent of the population suffers from food insecurity. Approximately 1 million families practice subsistence farming in precarious circumstances (ICG 2009). Because about 70 percent of Haiti's energy needs are met with firewood and charcoal, harvesting forests for revenue or fuel is a key coping mechanism that the impoverished population often relies on for survival, furthering environmental deterioration and eroding Haiti's ability to escape the negative spiral in which it finds itself.

Dwindling agricultural production, poor basic services, and a lack of employment opportunities in rural areas have spurred massive flight from the land, primarily to large cities such as Port-au-Prince, Cap-Haïtien, Les Cayes, and Gonaïves. According to an International Crisis Group study, 75,000 migrate yearly to the capital in search of work, taking up residence in overcrowded slums. Before the earthquake, Port-au-Prince was home to 2.5 million people, more than one-quarter of Haiti's total population (ICG 2009). Average population growth is 3.63 percent per year in urban areas (5 percent in the capital), but just 0.92 percent in the countryside.

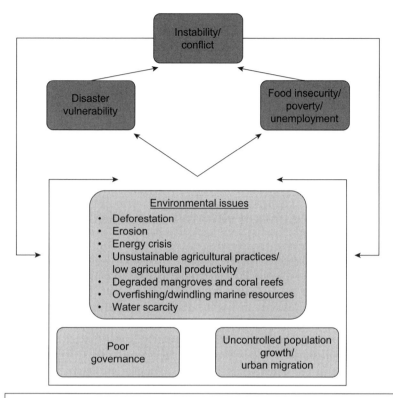

Figure 1. Linkages among disaster vulnerability, poverty, and instability

Continued overcrowding of urban slums by poor rural migrants with no remaining links to the countryside makes for an explosive social mix. Many children, now shantytown residents, have become *zenglendons* (common criminals, in Creole) because their parents are unable to pay for their schooling (ICG 2009). After the uprising of 2004, armed gangs of zenglendons took over many slums by systematically looting, kidnapping, and killing.

Since the earthquake, there have been massive and chaotic shifts in population from the directly affected Ouest and Sud-Est departments to less affected departments. The difficult living conditions and lack of food, water, sanitation, and energy in quake-affected areas and new urban settlements also jeopardize the country's stability and security. The 1.5 million migrants who have fled the earthquake zone compete with rural families for natural resources to fill their reconstruction and energy needs.

Haiti is now locked in a deepening social, economic, and environmental crisis that causes untold hardship for the great majority of the population and threatens the country's stability. Reversing the trend of environmental destruction would enable Haiti's development and enhance security and peacebuilding. Along with family planning, education, health care, access to basic services and employment, and urban planning, sound natural resource management could improve conditions in the country. Over the past few decades, there have been many projects and substantial investment in rehabilitating Haiti's environment, but with the exception of a number of small, technically sound, one-off interventions, results have been meager. Moreover, ineffective environmental governance further perpetuates the vicious cycle of poverty, vulnerability, and instability.

THE HAITI REGENERATION INITIATIVE AND LESSONS-LEARNED STUDY

Following a request from the Haitian government and the United Nations, UNEP established a country office in Port-au-Prince in 2008 to play a catalytic role in developing the Haiti Regeneration Initiative, a large-scale, long-term program that aims at reducing poverty and vulnerability to natural hazards by restoring ecosystems and establishing sustainable natural resource management. The initiative is anticipated to last around twenty years and to have a budget of over US$1 billion, with approximately 20 percent coming from foreign aid. Over fifty partners will participate in the initiative at the local, national, and international levels. UN agencies, government entities, NGOs, and technical institutes are consulting on the initiative's development.

To guide the design phase, from June to December 2009 UNEP conducted a study of lessons learned in environmental management and restoration projects in Haiti (Haiti Regeneration Initiative 2010). The study found substantial evidence that many international assistance programs had not been successful and that with smaller, beneficial projects there had been no follow-up. The lack of systematization and failure to disseminate lessons drawn from the past is a major obstacle to improving natural resource management in the country.

To record recent trends, extract key lessons, and identify best practices, evaluators analyzed forty-three projects, twenty-seven of which were still in progress at the time of the study. They conducted approximately forty follow-up interviews with project personnel, visited and inspected several sites, and identified potential improvements.

The projects involved international organizations, government institutions, NGOs, bilateral donors, and rural organizations, and they varied in duration, financing, and geographic coverage. They were chosen for the study according to several criteria, including their location in areas where the Haiti Regeneration Initiative would be implemented; their use of techniques, models, or frameworks relevant to the initiative; their duration, which needed to be sufficient to yield lessons; and the availability of information from current and former program officers.

The study found that to reverse the negative cycle in Haiti, future projects should take five key findings into account. These involve taking an integrated and comprehensive approach to natural resource management and environmental rehabilitation, involving and empowering the local community, linking income generation to natural resource management projects, recognizing the necessity of national ownership and institutional capacity building, and remaining in place for the long term. Each of these findings is described in more detail in the following sections. Though the study took place in 2009 and therefore does not reflect strategic changes that were adopted in response to the 2010 earthquake, many of the observations are still valid in the aftermath of the disaster.

Natural resource management and environmental rehabilitation: The need for a comprehensive approach

For sustainable management of microwatersheds or whole watersheds, projects need to concurrently tackle issues such as governance, economic and social development, disaster risk reduction, agricultural productivity and food security, energy and water access and management, and conflict resolution.

Past trends in natural resource management projects

In the past, sectoral approaches prevailed in the implementation of environmental projects. A United States Agency for International Development (USAID) report lists the different natural resource management models applied in Haiti. From the 1950s to the 1970s, the commonly adopted approach was the landscape engineering strategy: "Soil conservation was considered to be a strictly technical problem to be solved by engineers installing mechanical structures, mainly rock walls and contour ditches, using paid labor. Neither land tenure nor the interest of peasant landowners were taken into account" (USAID 2007, 19). Most of the programs proved unsustainable and ended in failure; the abandoned structures can still be seen throughout the country.

In the 1980s, NGOs and peasant organizations started to promote agricultural extension and natural resource conservation programs using biological conservation structures, reforestation, and agroforestry techniques. Even though the projects succeeded in rehabilitating small areas of ecosystems and watersheds, they tended to target scattered plots of land and failed to restore whole watersheds or reduce their vulnerability to flooding, erosion, or deforestation. Moreover, coordination between development organizations was poor. Donors had no clear geographic focus or institutionalized system for sharing information. Duplication of efforts, overlapping of activities, and squandering of financial resources resulted.

The new watershed-based approach

A trend toward geographic coherence and greater coordination started to emerge in the late 1990s. Donors and organizations are now concentrating their efforts and investments on vulnerable zones, partly because of the rapid expansion of integrated watershed-management and development programs.

Large donors, such as the Inter-American Development Bank (IDB), USAID, Canadian International Development Agency (CIDA), and the United Nations Development Programme (UNDP), are rehabilitating larger, more vulnerable geographic areas on a ridge-to-reef basis, upstream to downstream in whole water catchment areas. Most of them have planned their interventions on the basis of rankings by USAID and Haiti's Ministry of Agriculture, Natural Resources, and Rural Development.[1]

For example, CIDA works on the middle and upper parts of the Artibonite watershed, UNDP on the lower section. The IDB works across the Ennery-Quinte (Artibonite); Grande-Rivière-du-Nord (Nord); and Ravine du Sud, Les Cayes, and Cavaillon (Sud) watersheds.[2] USAID has opted to concentrate its efforts on the Montrouis (Ouest) and Limbé (Nord) watersheds under the Economic Development for a Sustainable Environment (DEED) project, and on the Cul-de-Sac (Sud-Est) and Gonaïves (Artibonite) watersheds through the Watershed Initiative for National Natural Environmental Resources (WINNER) project. Spain's Ministry of Foreign Affairs and Cooperation (Ministerio de Asuntos Exteriores y de Cooperación, or AECID) focuses on the Sud-Est Department with its Araucaria and Pedernales programs.

The largest donors not only have improved the geographic distribution of their interventions throughout the country, but also have aimed to reduce duplication and overlap. Interinstitutional mechanisms include the newly created Inter-Ministerial Committee for Land Use Planning (Comité Interministériel pour l'Aménagement du Territoire), which coordinates land use planning interventions, and the Sectoral Group on Watersheds, which includes the main donors and international cooperation agencies like the IDB, World Bank, USAID, European Union, AECID, UNDP, and UNEP.

Small-budget projects have started to work on contiguous plots and at the microwatershed level. Project officers of the NGO Floresta, the FAO-CIDA Local Development Project for Integrated Natural Resource Management, the

---

[1] The Ministry of Agriculture, Natural Resources, and Rural Development prioritized the watersheds but did not use clearly defined criteria. USAID adopted a systematic approach to ranking watersheds by level of vulnerability (USAID 2007).

[2] The IDB is giving greater attention to upper watersheds than before; emphasis had previously been on agricultural intensification in the lower parts of the watersheds. The IDB has now decided to allot the major part of its funding to upper watersheds in order to reduce vulnerability downstream. Two-thirds of its investments are devoted to upstream management, and one-third to downstream management—the opposite of the previous allocation (Damais 2009).

Environmental Protection and Sustainable Development in Marmelade project (the Marmelade Project), and the CIDA–Oxfam Quebec Support for Local Development and Agroforestry project in Nippes (PADELAN) have been trying to intervene on adjacent plots at the microwatershed level. The Lambi Fund, which finances projects submitted by community organizations, concentrates on the Artibonite, Sud, and Ouest departments. Evaluators of over one hundred projects funded by Lambi over the past ten years recommended creation of "project concentration pockets" to reduce projects' geographic spread; promote an integrated, regional approach; and enable sharing of economic and social services (Lambi Fund of Haiti n.d.).

Cross-sectoral and integrated interventions

In areas targeted for environmental projects, organizations have shifted to a more holistic and cross-sectoral approach that aims to improve concurrently the natural, economic, social, and political environment. But few projects focus on coastal and marine issues, and when they do, they address immediate local threats and not activities upland. Likewise, climate change adaptation strategies are still systematically ignored.

The move toward implementation of comprehensive cross-sectoral strategies at the microwatershed or watershed level requires larger-scale interventions and, therefore, improved coordination and partnership building, particularly among small programs that must pool efforts in order to scale up their activities. Successful and sustainable programs have brought together donors; stakeholders; and local, national, and international levels of government. For over ten years, the Marmelade Project has tackled local governance, watershed rehabilitation, disaster management, and job creation through the work of a bamboo-products factory; supported education by providing locally produced milk to pupils; and addressed energy issues by installing solar streetlights and planting sustainably managed forests for firewood and timber production. It has linked community leaders, local authorities, international donors (such as Dutch, Canadian, and Japanese development assistance agencies), the European Union, the FAO, and a Taiwanese company.

Of the forty-three projects studied, only six involved the Dominican Republic, despite the interdependence of the two countries' ecosystems, their shared vulnerability to natural disasters, and their need to improve relations with each other. The few cross-border projects had difficulties with design and implementation. Such projects typically require much more time and effort in terms of coordination and negotiation, as compared to national projects. Cross-border projects also call for strong commitment from the two governments and the implementing agencies.

Lessons learned

A review of past natural resource management and environmental rehabilitation projects in Haiti yields three key lessons. First, it is important to integrate natural resource management interventions into comprehensive cross-sectoral strategies that take land use planning into consideration. Similarly, promoting cooperation among partners to scale up efforts and tackle issues at the microwatershed and watershed levels is necessary for the success and sustainability of natural resource management projects. Finally, increasing donor coordination and improving information-sharing mechanisms are crucial for ensuring efficient use of funds and for preventing duplication and overlap of efforts.

Local empowerment and community participation

Organizations involved in natural resource management projects in Haiti all acknowledge that community participation is critical to success. Yet project beneficiaries and civil servants often say that projects are inadequate for local needs, communities often feel little ownership, and interventions are often unsustainable.

Ensuring community participation involves more than informing or even consulting the population. Communities must help identify the challenges they face, find solutions, choose methodologies, and organize project activities. They must be involved at all stages of the project, including needs assessment, project design, implementation, monitoring, and evaluation. Participation is effective when stakeholders have sufficient and equal input and can openly express aspirations and concerns during the decision-making process. It involves accountability and clear definition of the roles and responsibilities of community members. Financial and material contributions from the population need to be agreed upon beforehand through establishment of partnership agreements.

Haitian community organizers can provide appropriate technical support to facilitate participatory planning and project implementation and can ensure effective communication and transparency in decision making. Information can be provided to the communities to help them understand the challenges, define a strategy, and solve problems. The Economic and Social Assistance Fund (Fonds d'Assistance Economique et Sociale, or FAES) and the German Society for International Cooperation (GTZ at the time) cite the importance of entrusting facilitation of community participation to Haitians who understand the issues, power structure, and local sensibilities (Adam and Odnel 2009; Hiriel 2009).

In some cases, participatory projects initially satisfy communities less than short-term, quick-impact programs do, but eventually, as in the case of the Marmelade Project, they usually result in a higher level of community engagement and ownership. Participation in establishing protected areas also encourages compliance and reduces the need for and cost of extensive systems of enforcement.

The NGO Floresta noted the positive aspects of ensuring community participation. In one case, farmers communicated their need for a water tank, and with the Floresta's support, they contributed to financing and building it by producing and selling seedlings (Paraison 2009). Under the WINNER project, sanitation and irrigation associations are supported for three years while they develop their capacity for self-management. The associations agreed by contract to collect fees and maintain irrigation canals after the project ends. Through its high-altitude biodiversity preservation and development program, the NGO Helvetas trained 600 farmers in sustainable agriculture and paid for seedlings and organic fertilizer. In return, the farmers helped replant forest clearings with trees native to Haiti and were required to train others—an approach that greatly increased the project's impact in a short period of time.

Permanent participatory structures

Rather than launch a new participatory process for every project, a few programs (notably PADELAN, DEED, the Marmelade Project, and the UN Capital Development Fund Local Development and Governance Programme in Haiti's Nord-Est Department) established permanent structures for participation and dialogue, such as local development councils and watershed-management committees. They involve local authorities, the private sector, civil society, cooperatives, farmers, workers, women, schools, tradespeople, fisherfolk, and members of the opposition. Local institutions and elected officials are tasked with coordinating these participatory structures; this confers democratic legitimacy on the committees.[3] Project officers, including those from PADELAN and the Marmelade Project, say that the structures need to be in existence for ten years before they can function sufficiently on their own (Vial 2009; Brutus 2009).

By enabling sustained and extensive consultation among stakeholders, permanent participatory structures offer several advantages. They reinforce the capacities of local people, especially local authorities, in democratic governance and in planning, implementing, and monitoring development projects. For example, when a local committee is responsible for monitoring a program, the whole community can easily access firsthand information on the intervention's environmental impact. Moreover, project monitoring is more efficient and economically attractive than creating a system of controls.

Permanent participatory structures also facilitate elaboration of coherent, sustainable development strategies, including consensus-based, local development frameworks and watershed-management plans that can include environment and natural resource management interventions. These plans also make possible additional mobilization of resources. Donors are more willing to finance projects that are part of a comprehensive action plan for a locality.

These structures are also resilient in cases of political change. For example, after external involvement in the Marmelade Project ends and elections bring new officials to power, the development committee, which is empowered by decentralized civil servants, should continue to operate autonomously.

---

[3] These local institutions include—at the communal-section level, for example—the local government council, or CASEC (Conseil d'Administration de la Section Communale), and the local assembly, or ASEC (Assemblée de la Section Communale).

By promoting constant dialogue among community members, permanent participatory structures reduce conflict, enhance social cohesion and peace, decrease political polarization, and support the involvement of women and vulnerable people in the development process. They also promote partnerships and synergy, and they favor involvement of the private sector through private-public partnerships. For example, Taiwanese experts supported the Marmelade Project by starting a bamboo nursery to encourage reforestation, soil conservation, and furniture making.

Project coordination structures at the local level

Having a project office on-site facilitates the participatory process, maximizes capacity building, and enables effective monitoring. Many interviewees confirmed that these are positive aspects of local project coordination structures. The coordinating body may be a governmental entity; an implementing partner like Development Alternatives International on the DEED project or Oxfam Quebec on PADELAN; or the donor's field representatives. Or, preferably, it can be a mixed steering committee that, as in Marmelade and Gonaïves, can bring together local authorities and field representatives of the organization managing the project. Such a steering committee builds ownership and develops institutional capacity.

Coordinators in an on-site support office can earn the trust of local communities and authorities because they are accessible. They can make quick decisions to advance the project, respond quickly to challenges that arise, and reorient the project if necessary. Local staff provide knowledge of local customs and needs, allowing the project to be more adapted to the specific context. Their daily presence also simplifies community participation and facilitates ongoing training and capacity building. Community responsiveness to awareness-raising campaigns and other communications about the project increases as a result. Finally, local structures reduce transaction costs and allow greater financial focus on a program's activities.

One of the Marmelade Project evaluations mentioned a high level of initial mistrust on the part of the population (FAO 2005)—which is fairly typical in rural Haitian communities, particularly during the long diagnostic phase prior to implementation. Yet on-site organizers, immersed in the community, gradually established trust and proved their commitment.

Building on existing organizations and knowledge

Although the increasingly common practice of forming local coordinating structures supports positive outcomes, building on relevant existing structures is no less critical to a project's success. However, external projects often bring about new structures or initiatives where similar local ones exist. Haitian peasants have a long history of labor organization and shared work, especially in agriculture. Several peasant organizations are engaged in soil conservation and restoration work, and cooperate in microwatershed management. Others have created simple cooperatives. The widespread tradition of *konbit* (grouping people for a common goal, in Creole) reflects the long-standing culture of cooperation, particularly among peasants in rural Haiti, and lies at the core of Haitian society. Strengthening existing local structures rather than creating new, ad hoc ones results in more community acceptance and sustainability. Existing associations are the primary channels for diffusion and adoption of technical innovations and awareness-raising messages.

Understanding land tenure through community participation

Understanding and addressing land tenure are important for developing successful environmental projects. Indeed, land tenure problems cause many community-level disputes. Illegal exploitation of land threatens investment in natural resource management and environmental protection.

Much of Haitian land officially belongs to the state, but there is no functioning national cadastral system. Many peasants therefore cultivate state lands or harvest wood from them illegally. In rural Haiti, informal arrangements regarding land tenure are more important than formal titles, which are more expensive and less flexible. Land tenure ranges from direct access by virtue of ownership to indirect access through tenancy or usufruct. According to a USAID study, investment decisions are based on the duration of access to a plot regardless of formal tenure, and duration of access depends on a farmer's social capital and position (Smucker et al. 2005). The authors reported that "FAO-funded research by the Haitian Institute of Agrarian Reform (INARA) drew the following remarkable conclusion: *the judicial system is incapable of guaranteeing land tenure security even for those able to take full advantage of it*" (Smucker et al. 2005, 26; italics in the original). Tenure insecurity reduces incentives for people to make long-term environmental investments in plots of land because they always face risk of dispossession.

Tenure insecurity is not an insurmountable barrier to developing natural resource management projects and technologies (Smucker et al. 2005). The participatory approach helps in diagnosing land tenure and population trends and should precede any natural resource management project. By consulting the population, development practitioners have been able to understand informal land tenure systems and support the development of well-designed natural resource management projects. Conversely, projects that have skipped participatory analysis of land tenure have often stalled when tenure problems crop up. Frequently, for example, after restoration has been undertaken on a plot of land, someone will profess ownership and attempt to claim the land. Researchers from USAID and other organizations have concluded that "the primary challenge is to harness farmer incentives to cooperate across garden boundary lines by building collective social capital, motivated by the prospect of increased revenues or decreased risk" (Smucker et al. 2005, v).

Lessons learned

One of the main lessons about community participation and empowerment that were learned from past natural resource management projects in Haiti—one that is consistent with experience elsewhere—is the need to involve communities in all stages of the project cycle. Entrusting the facilitation process to Haitians who are familiar with the local context and experienced in running participatory processes is an effective way to ensure community participation. Drawing up partnership agreements with community members prior to the start of activities to clarify their roles in and responsibilities for project implementation and follow-up can promote the long-term sustainability of these efforts. It is also important to integrate the environment and natural resources into participatory local development frameworks and watershed-management plans. Finally, setting up and reinforcing local permanent participatory structures with capacity to lead in the planning, implementation, and monitoring of sustainable local development projects is an especially effective way to encourage long-term community involvement. In particular, capitalizing on and reinforcing the work of existing organizations prevents overlap of efforts and can contribute significantly to long-term success.

Natural resource management and income generation

Most of the projects analyzed in the 2009 Haiti Regeneration Initiative study link natural resource management and income generation, a widespread trend that reflects learning from earlier experiences. In a country like Haiti, which faces severe poverty and instability, any action aiming to restore the environment needs to improve beneficiaries' socioeconomic condition and provide economic alternatives. In the 1980s, USAID, FAO, and the Ministry of Agriculture, Natural Resources, and Rural Development led widespread traditional hardwood-reforestation projects, but these projects proved unsustainable. Most of the trees were cut down, were eaten by cattle, or died because peasants had no interest in caring for them. Natural parks–management projects have to create economic alternatives for communities that need to be resettled because mere prohibitive and regulatory approaches have not proved to be effective in preserving trees. Although environmental protection is not the primary consideration for most peasants invested in natural resource management, people might build up and conserve soils, and they might plant and preserve trees if they can benefit economically in a short time.

Sustainable forestry and agroforestry projects

In the 1990s international development experts began seeking to link natural resource management projects with increases in communities' incomes and to create economic alternatives through farmers' cooperatives. The market-opportunity approach holds that stimulating the market can positively affect natural resource management. For example, approximately half of the projects analyzed included an agroforestry component. These projects have mostly encouraged the planting of trees yielding high-value fruit, such as mangoes, avocados, citrus fruits, and breadfruit, and they have supported the development of community-based nurseries or have trained local farmers in planting and grafting. Distribution of free or subsidized seedlings has proved successful and has led to a high return on investment.

To conserve soil, projects have also encouraged the planting of living fences (hedgerows) of perennials, such as pineapple, plantain, and sugar cane, as well as annuals, such as yams and sweet potatoes. In addition to stabilizing soils and reducing erosion, the living fences yield wood, nourish the soil, and function as windbreaks, especially on the plains. In the past three decades, peasants have maintained the fences with no external support, and farmers elsewhere have copied the practice.

In the Marmelade Project, the FAO is supporting establishment of a sustainable management system for a community forest that will satisfy demand for wood products, respond to energy needs, and create revenue from timber and charcoal. The initiative plans exploitation modalities for the long term (more than twenty years) and is part of a broader strategy for community development, increasing the chance of sustainability after the project comes to an end. Studies predict high profitability and return on investment in ten years. The pilot project demonstrates an alternative to bans on charcoal production and consumption. Seventy thousand tons of charcoal could be produced in projects like it, but this is still less than one-quarter of current overall consumption (Energy Sector Management Assistance Program 2007).

Jatropha, a large perennial shrub that can grow on arid and eroded land, produces an oil that can be used as a biofuel. As a result, many people in Haiti advocate cultivating it as a solution to the country's energy shortage and as erosion protection. However, many are concerned that Haiti's food insecurity might be aggravated if small producers replace food crops with jatropha.

In many reforestation projects, trees have been chosen because they grow rapidly and yield revenue quickly, even if they are nonnative, invasive species that can disrupt ecosystems and impair ecosystem reconstruction. This is the case for casuarina, bamboo, eucalyptus, and neem, for example, whereas native species could be planted instead. Fewer trees are felled when communities can choose to plant culturally acceptable and common species that are well adapted to the ecosystem and profitable to grow. Therefore, technical assistance in forestry should be provided to enable communities and project managers to select species wisely, taking all of these factors into account.

Natural resource value chains

Local economic development can "build up the economic capacity of a local area to improve its economic future and the quality of life for all. It is a process by which public, business and non-governmental sector partners work collectively to create better conditions for economic growth and employment generation" (World Bank n.d.). Such development requires implementing market-driven strategies and improving marketing links. Past experience has shown that projects aiming to protect natural resources should pay close attention to market conditions and value chains. In the development of a value chain, all the products and processes essential to the production of a good or service need to be taken into account. For example, in the case of fruit tree yields, all key elements such as planting, financing, processing, storage, packaging, and distribution need to be considered in project design and implementation.

The Organization for the Rehabilitation of the Environment (L'Organisation pour la Réhabilitation de l'Environnement, or ORE), an NGO that has worked for more than twenty years in southern Haiti to improve environmental, agricultural, and economic conditions in rural areas, developed fruit tree value chains for mangoes, avocados, and citrus. ORE has taught farmers how to graft mango trees to produce commercial-quality fruit, has strengthened regional mango cooperatives, has built a factory to process and package dried mangoes, and has negotiated with exporters. These activities add value and create revenue in the region (Finnigan 2009).

Practitioners should carefully study every aspect of the supply chain to identify bottlenecks and to remove them with targeted investments. For example, ORE mango producers close to Camp-Perrin (in Sud Department) claimed that they could sell only one-tenth of their crop to exporters because poor roads made it difficult to transport their product to market. The state of the infrastructure, including roads and transportation, needs to be taken into account in the project-planning process. Likewise, the credit situation of the area needs to be considered. Project beneficiaries may need financing to participate in the project, for example, to buy inputs or extra fuel. In rural areas, access to credit is often limited, so a project could seek to reinforce existing local credit institutions, guarantee beneficiaries' loans to facilitate access to credit, or set up a local fund to be managed by the community.

The food- or cash-for-work approach and conditions for success

Temporarily paying local labor to protect or restore the environment combines revenue generation with environmental rehabilitation and balances immediate socioeconomic needs and environmental sustainability. Workers may repair rural railroad tracks, improve sanitation, or construct gabions to regulate rivers and terraces to fight erosion.

Interventions that respond immediately to urgent food-security and financial needs are popular in vulnerable communities. For example, through a World Food Programme–UNDP–International Labour Organization project to prevent natural disasters and rehabilitate the environment through revenue-generating activities in Gonaïves, laborers were paid half in kind (one World Food Programme ration per workday) and half in cash.[4] Another example is the market-opportunity approach taken by the Foundation for the Protection of Marine Biodiversity in its environmental rehabilitation project for coastal communities of the Arcadins (northwest of Port-au-Prince). For that project, people were hired to guard the mangroves and care for the tree nursery. With a relatively small investment, the mangroves were protected, awareness of proper resource management was raised, and substantial profits were made.

Following the January 12, 2010, earthquake, the UN and various NGOs widely promoted cash-for-work schemes, particularly for clearing rubble from roads and removing waste. While earning small wages to cover critical needs, workers helped preserve stability and provided vital reconstruction services.

If the benefits supported by cash-for-work arrangements are to be sustainable, community engagement and ownership need to be addressed from the beginning. Community members who are remunerated for construction projects often expect to be paid for maintenance and repair work as well. From its inception, the USAID WINNER project included maintenance in initial contracts with community organizations. For three years, management committees received technical assistance until communities could take over the maintenance of installations themselves.

The staff coordinating and implementing cash-for-work projects must consider environmental guidelines and be trained in fields such as engineering, agronomy, pedology, and hydrology to ensure quality and sustainability. Careful selection of the target population, on the basis of objective criteria, is also crucial to a project's positive outcome. Even though cash-for-work programs are responses to emergency situations, they need to include planning for the long term and ideally be integrated into a comprehensive development strategy for the area.

Lessons learned

Offering people cost-effective solutions that provide an incentive for preserving natural resources is crucial to the success and sustainability of any natural resource management project. This can be achieved through a variety of different mechanisms, depending on the circumstances. One way to create incentives for preserving natural resources is to encourage farmers to develop high-value products from sustainable forestry and agroforestry. Similarly, promotion of soil-conservation structures that not only prevent erosion but replenish the soil's nutrients and provide rural families with food and wood have proved successful. Carrying out cash-for-work projects related to natural resource management is another option. Local communities will be able to maintain these projects if they are integrated into longer-term, comprehensive development interventions. Likewise, for reforestation

---

[4] The daily rations the World Food Programme provides can vary greatly, depending upon location, circumstance, and population being served. One ration generally provides 2,100 kilocalories of energy to the recipient. See www.wfp.org/nutrition/WFP-foodbasket.

initiatives, it is important to provide communities with technical assistance in forestry and with information about appropriate plant species. Finally, prior to the implementation of any natural resource management project, it is crucial to identify and analyze local competitive natural resource–related value chains, taking into consideration possible bottlenecks, key actors, and potential partnerships.

National ownership and institutional capacity building

A lack of national ownership of and commitment to natural resource management projects seriously undermines their sustainability. Too often the Haitian government is hardly consulted or involved and has little control over project programming, monitoring, or financing. At times, projects are directly implemented by NGOs with no interaction whatsoever with the government.

Government involvement

Overlapping mandates and competencies, competition, and the occasional disinterest of Haitian government institutions are significant obstacles to government involvement in environmental projects. Because the environment is a crosscutting issue, responsibilities for its protection and rehabilitation are divided among several government ministries, mainly the Ministry of the Environment; the Ministry of Agriculture, Natural Resources, and Rural Development; and the Ministry of Planning and External Cooperation. In practice, the Ministry of Agriculture, Natural Resources, and Rural Development has the biggest mandate and the largest budget for environmental activities.

The success of several projects was hampered by the complexity of governmental management. For example, the World Bank's Forest and Parks Protection Technical Assistance Project involved the Ministry of the Environment and the Ministry of Agriculture, Natural Resources, and Rural Development (through the Forest Resources Service, the National Parks Service, and the Center for Research and Agricultural Development, Directorate of Training and Continuing Education); an independent body, FAES; and numerous NGOs and firms, including the organization CARE, the Centre d'Etude et de Cooperation Internationale, and the local NGO ASSODLO (Toussaint 2008). Several technical experts from the Ministry of the Environment said that institutional complexity hindered the project. The new Inter-Ministerial Committee for Land Use Planning (Comité Interministériel pour l'Aménagement du Territoire), which was started in 2009, may facilitate coordination and enable governmental entities to steer projects more effectively.

Institutional capacity

Haitian institutions have very limited resources and few skilled workers who can participate in decision making and day-to-day monitoring. The Ministry of the Environment is particularly weak in human and financial resources and lacks political influence. According to a 2010 report on the state of Haiti's environment, "the operations of the MOE [Ministry of the Environment] were mainly confined to the implementation of projects based on external funding, such as the management of protected areas or focused on local development, and on the production and follow up of basic environmental information" (UNEP, Ministry of the Environment, and University of Quiskeya 2010, 14).

The last decree on environmental affairs, which was passed on January 20, 2006, was intended to encompass all national policies and make government management and citizen use of the environment compatible with sustainable development goals.[5] But a lack of political and financial support has hindered the Ministry of the Environment's leadership and enforcement of the decree; in practice the measures are hardly implemented.

More recently, the 2010 earthquake killed a number of Ministry of the Environment staff and considerably damaged equipment and buildings, such as the National Geographic Information Systems Center, resulting in substantial loss of technical capacity and institutional memory.

Stability

Chronic instability in the country has led to frequent governmental reorganization and political unrest. It has also contributed to frequent changes in strategy and interruptions in project implementation and follow-up. Even though the government has been increasingly willing to reverse environmental degradation, its involvement often remains too limited.

Still, achieving political support and government ownership is key to a project's success and sustainability. The government deployed full-time staff to participate in project formulation and execution with the Marmelade Project and with World Food Programme–UNDP–International Labour Organization disaster-rehabilitation projects in Gonaïves. In other cases, the government has decided to dedicate significant financial resources. These positive signs of engagement demonstrate political will for specific project support.

Few of the projects studied focused on institutional capacity building and policy development at the national level. Yet according to an International Crisis Group study:

> The catastrophic state of the environment is closely related to the country's deep-seated institutional, political and governance problems. Coherent national socioeconomic development policies have been mostly absent, due to management and political limitations and the narrow interests of those holding economic power, thus contributing to the problem. The extreme environmental vulnerability also stems from the state's institutional weakness and poor governance, especially at the local level (ICG 2009, 5).

---

[5] Decree Concerning the Environmental Management and Regulation of the Conduct of Citizens for Sustainable Development.

Natural resource management in Haiti calls for a strong legislative framework and reinforcement of knowledge-management capacities, project monitoring, management tools, and material means. Buildings, vehicles, computers, and hardware may be required. Development of financial and report-writing skills may encourage more meaningful involvement of staff in project management.

The Ministry of Environment's Environmental Management Support Program (Programme d'Appui à la Gestion de l'Environnement), which is financed and supported by UNDP, is the most important of the few programs that directly target national institutional capacity building for environmental governance and management. The program played a central role in the creation of the National Environment and Vulnerability Observatory (Observatoire National de l'Environnement et de la Vulnérabilité). The observatory's role is to disseminate information; produce and monitor environmental data; and offer technical and monitoring services to all organizations that address the environment and vulnerability. It has great potential to increase knowledge management on environmental issues and to improve governance and management of institutions. However, the observatory is still at an early stage; it continues to lack leadership, it struggles to gain donors' confidence, and progress has been slow.

Although efforts to reinforce capacity at the national level are still limited, many donors and international organizations have sought to strengthen decentralized and devolved authorities so they can effectively manage natural resources in rural areas. Many interventions support mayors, local administrative councils, and devolved authorities of the Ministry of Agriculture, Natural Resources, and Rural Development with material support, such as computer equipment, and with technical training in natural resource management, local governance, program management, finance, and agronomy. Empowered local structures that have been involved from the outset have assumed responsibility for management of projects and have ensured their continuity.

Lessons learned

The experiences of past natural resource management projects in Haiti yield several lessons regarding the promotion of national ownership of and government commitment to such projects. First, prior to project implementation, it is important to realistically assess the capacity of governmental structures. This assessment should be followed by efforts to reinforce both national and local capacity, which involves supporting the government in developing and updating enabling legal and policy frameworks for natural resource management and environmental protection, including frameworks for energy, protected areas, and waste management. Encouraging cooperative relationships between government agencies with clearly defined roles and responsibilities for project management is also important. This can be accomplished with the establishment of clear partnership agreements prior to implementation. Finally, in order to ensure sustainability, it is important to establish project-monitoring or steering committees to build ownership and improve follow-up.

Long-term intervention and follow-up

Protecting Haiti's environment must go hand in hand with improving socioeconomic conditions, raising general environmental awareness, strengthening institutional capacity and empowering communities. Reinforcing capacity and developing a sense of ownership are lengthy processes that call for long-term commitment and a high level of financial investment, whether from large donors or from smaller agencies that build solid partnerships to ensure the impact of their interventions. However, environmental interventions are often short-term, small-scale, and ill-adapted to the resolution of longstanding, complex issues. Prevailing short-term approaches and isolated small investments have not succeeded, and will not succeed, in solving long-term natural resource management issues and reversing environmental degradation.

Project duration and financing

Extremely short project cycles of less than one year prevent the establishment of plans for follow-up and in nearly every case lead to unsustainability. Most projects are still short- to medium-term programs of two to five years, though there is a tendency to extend them. Fortunately, compared to past decades, more projects—particularly those involving local development and watershed management and rehabilitation—are designed to last longer (see figure 2).

Of the forty-three projects covered in the Haiti Regeneration Initiative's 2009 study of lessons learned in managing environmental projects, twenty-six were small- or medium-scale (below US$5 million). Just three projects received between US$5 million to US$10 million, and ten received more than US$10 million. The largest donors included the IDB, USAID, and the World Bank (see figure 3).

International aid for Haiti is extremely unstable. The massive influx of international aid under President Aristide in 1990–1991 was followed by an embargo during the military regime in 1992–1994 (World Bank 2006). Total official development assistance dropped from just under US$200 million in 1991 to US$112 million in 1992–1993. Between 1995 and 2000, official development

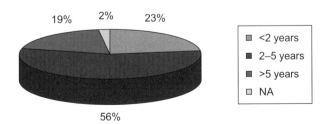

Figure 2. Duration of projects covered by the Haiti Regeneration Initiative's 2009 study of lessons learned in managing environmental projects

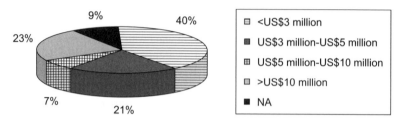

Figure 3. Funding for projects covered by the Haiti Regeneration Initiative's 2009 study of lessons learned in managing environmental projects

assistance resumed, reaching an annual average of US$383 million. After the disputed elections in 2000, aid declined to US$195 million, or 6 percent of GDP, from 2000 to 2004. These fluctuations have repercussions on project financing: project funding is frequently suspended, and short-term projects are often not renewed.

Four factors contribute to lack of continuity and follow-through in funding: changes in donor strategies, chronic instability, failure of projects, and political changes.

First, donors often redefine their strategies and cut off funds suddenly. For example, the entire environmental component of the USAID Hillside Agriculture Program was removed during implementation. The Marmelade Project came close to joining the long list of abandoned programs after the Netherlands terminated its funding. Programs such as the Substitution of Energy for Protection of the Environment project, implemented by CARE/Haiti and funded by USAID, carried through to the end of their terms but were not renewed, even though studies and promising results called for a next phase.

Smaller organizations suffer most from donor inconstancy. These organizations have relatively low financial capacity and are therefore obliged to develop their budgets and plan their activities for short periods of one to three years. The smallest organizations remain dependent on annual budgeting, although they are aware that results can only be achieved in the medium term of six to seven years.

Second, in periods of crisis, many donors withdraw from Haiti. During the military regime in 1992–1994 and the political unrest of 2000–2004, some donors stopped all of their interventions and suspended programs that were underway. USAID and the World Bank interrupted several projects as a consequence of the unrest in 2000–2004, only to reinvest in Haiti a couple of years later with new projects that were in tune with new strategies.

Third, some projects are suspended or not renewed because midterm or final evaluations conclude they have not met their objectives. Their failure may be due to unrealistic schedules, inability to adapt to local needs, or lack of local ownership.

Finally, Haitian electoral cycles disrupt policy development and program funding. New governments often make clean sweeps of projects supported by their predecessors. For example, a European Union cross-border environmental program suffered from, among other things, the different visions of two successive governments. Thus some activities had to be completely abandoned during the second phase of the project.

Building a long-term presence

For assimilation of new techniques, concepts, and practices to happen, communities need continuous support. Training must be spread over time, targeting ever-larger groups or new beneficiaries as trust in a project and its staff gradually builds.

Long-term presence is critical to projects that deal with chronic and structural issues and require a change in attitudes. CIDA's involvement in Nippes (first through an agroforestry project and then through PADELAN) and FAO's participation in Marmelade illustrate the importance of a continuing presence. Even though the communities were at first discouraged by slow progress, they later acknowledged that the extensive time spent to build their capacity in local governance and to shape local development committees was crucial to the creation of public-private partnerships and the achievement of results. After close to ten years of engagement, the community members, supported by decentralized authorities, can plan and manage sustainable local development. Cooperating organizations can now withdraw gradually, passing on information, coordination responsibilities, and management with no major risk of diminished activity.

Once a sense of ownership has been developed, transferring the costs of project management to the government, the community, and the private sector is easier. The UNDP Carrefour Feuilles solid waste management project strove for public-private partnership and for financing by institutional, private, and community agents. It was scheduled to last three years (2006–2009), and its goal was to reduce armed violence, social unrest, and poverty by instituting sustainable solid waste management and revenue-generating activities, including the manufacture and sale of artificial charcoal briquettes made of solid waste. This pilot project, which employed 385 people, would not have lasted without continued financial support from UNDP. With stronger management capacity and several years' additional financial backing, the project may be able to achieve full autonomy (Nicolini 2009).

Finally, many high-quality technical studies have examined Haiti's environment, but systematic management of environmental information is lacking. Longer projects allow time to do an inventory and compile existing and new information as well as build on lessons learned from past interventions.

Lessons learned

Past natural resource management projects in Haiti yield some lessons for project duration and financing. First, interventions need to follow appropriate timelines. Long-term projects that build ownership and capacity are often necessary, and they should be designed to address deeply rooted problems. It is essential to allocate sufficient time to conduct a preliminary analysis of existing information and studies on relevant themes and geographic areas. Finally, achieving long-term financial stability through strong managerial partnerships is crucial to the development and implementation of successful and effective natural resource management projects.

CONCLUSION

Despite the large number of natural resource management projects conducted in Haiti and the considerable investments made in the past few decades, widespread vulnerability, poverty, and instability remain. Recently, however, there have been gradual improvements in the effectiveness and sustainability of international assistance, and institutional leaders have been able to adopt, better coordinate, and scale up integrated projects, particularly for water catchment management and sustainable local development.

To be effective in the long term, natural resource management programs must be characterized by an extended duration of five years or more; local ownership, with community participation in all phases of the project cycle; and integration of environmental concerns into rural livelihood frameworks. They must build institutional capacity and support the development of enabling policies and legal frameworks; roles and responsibilities of participating institutions must be clearly agreed upon; and information must be gathered, analyzed, and shared so practitioners can learn from past experiences and improve the sustainability of future interventions.

With external support for natural resource management augmenting its own significant human resources and resilient grassroots social structure, Haiti has the capacity and opportunity to address its environmental challenges.

REFERENCES

Adam, A., and D. Odnel. 2009. Interview by author of environment program director and deputy general director, respectively, of the Economic and Social Assistance Fund. July. Port-au-Prince, Haiti.

Brutus, P. M. 2009. Interview by author of national director for the Environmental Protection and Sustainable Development in Marmelade project. May. Marmelade, Haiti.

Damais, G. 2009. Interview by author of natural resource and environment specialist for the Inter-American Development Bank. March 11.

Energy Sector Management Assistance Program. 2007. *Haiti: Strategy to alleviate the pressure of fuel demand on national woodfuel resources.* Washington, D.C. www.esmap.org/esmap/sites/esmap.org/files/TR_11207_Haiti%20Strategy%20to%20Alleviate%20the%20Pressure%20of%20Fuel%20Demand%20on%20National%20Woodfuel%20Resources_112-07.pdf.

FAO (Food and Agriculture Organization of the United Nations). 2001. Land resources information systems in the Caribbean. World Soil Resources Report No. 95. Rome. www.fao.org/DOCREP/004/Y1717E/y1717e13.htm.

———. 2005. *Rapport d'évaluation du Projet Marmelade: Développement local et aménagement des terres pour un programme national de sécurité alimentaire et de gestion des ressources naturelles.* On file with author.

Finnigan, D. M. 2009. Interview by author of general director of L'Organisation pour la Réhabilitation de l'Environnement. November. Camp-Perrin, Haiti.

GORH (Government of the Republic of Haiti). 2008. *Rapport d'évaluation des besoins après désastres, cyclones Fay, Gustave, Hanna et Ike.* November. www.ht.undp.org/_assets/fichier/publication/pubdoc35.pdf?PHPSESSID=a2aeb8fd103700a3b3db61373bc72c3c.

———. 2010. *Haiti earthquake PDNA: Assessment of damage, losses, general and sectoral needs.* March. http://siteresources.worldbank.org/INTLAC/Resources/PDNA_Haiti-2010_Working_Document_EN.pdf.

Haiti Regeneration Initiative. 2010. *Study of lessons learned in managing environmental projects in Haiti.* http://oneresponse.info/Disasters/Haiti/Environment/publicdocuments/Lessons%20learned%20in%20managing%20environmental%20projects%20in%20Haiti.pdf.

Hiriel, J. 2009. Interview by author of project manager for German Society for International Cooperation (GTZ). May. Port-au-Prince, Haiti.

IASC (Inter-Agency Standing Committee). 2010. *Response to the humanitarian crisis in Haiti following the 12 January 2010 earthquake: Achievements, challenges, and lessons to be learned.* www.humanitarianinfo.org/iasc/downloaddoc.aspx?docID=5366.

ICG (International Crisis Group). 2009. Haiti: Saving the environment, preventing instability and conflict. Latin America and Caribbean Policy Briefing No. 20. www.crisisgroup.org/~/media/Files/latin-america/haiti/aiti___saving_the_environment__preventing_instability_and_conflict.ashx.

IHSI (Institut Haïtien de Statistique et d'Informatique). 2007. *Estimation et projection de la population totale urbaine et rurale et économiquement active.* www.ihsi.ht/pdf/projection/ProjectionsPopulation_Haiti_2007.pdf.

———. 2009. *Population totale, population de 18 ans et plus—ménages et densités estimés en 2009.* March. www.ihsi.ht/pdf/projection/POPTOTAL&MENAGDENS_ESTIM2009.pdf.

Lambi Fund of Haiti. n.d. Executive summary of the evaluation of the first ten years of the Lambi Fund of Haiti. www.lambifund.org/content/10_yr_evaluation.pdf.

Nicolini, E. Interview by author of project chief for United Nations Development Programme's cash-for-work program. May. Port-au-Prince, Haiti.

OCHA (United Nations Office for the Coordination of Humanitarian Affairs). 2010. Haiti earthquake. OCHA Situation Report No. 25. March 1. http://haiti.humanitarianresponse.info/Portals/0/Information%20Management/Sitrep%202010/OCHA_Haiti_Sitrep%2025_Earthquake_01_03_10.pdf.

Paraison, G. 2009. Interview by author of Floresta program director for Haiti. May. Port-au-Prince.

Smucker, G. R., G. Fleurantin, M. McGahuey, and B. Swartley. 2005. *Agriculture in a fragile environment: Market incentives for natural resource management in Haiti.* Port-au-Prince: United States Agency for International Development. http://pdf.usaid.gov/pdf_docs/PDACN884.pdf.

Toussaint, J. R. 2008. *Révision et synthèse des leçons apprises des interventions dans la zone d'intervention du Parc National Macaya.* Barahona, Dominican Republic: Fundación Taiguey. www.google.com/url?sa=t&rct=j&q=&esrc=s&source=web&cd=2&cts=1331072229938&ved=0CDMQFjAB&url=http%3A%2F%2Ftaiguey.org%2Fforum-ap

-haiti%2Ffiles%2Flecons_Macaya_2.doc&ei=3YxWT6ybH-Lw0gG3lbGmCg&usg=A
FQjCNEq9Vz1dECyYH95uYE4G1UU0DGcCg&sig2=idMSpBdudcPs6yANinMmOg.
UNDP (United Nations Development Programme). 2004. *Reducing disaster risk: A challenge for development.* New York. www.undp.org/cpr/whats_new/rdr_english.pdf.
UNEP (United Nations Environment Programme), Ministry of the Environment, and University of Quiskeya. 2010. *GEO Haiti: State of the environment report.* Port-au-Prince. www.pnuma.org/deat1/pdf/GEO_Haiti2010_IN(web).pdf.
USAID (United States Agency for International Development). 2007. *Environmental vulnerability in Haiti: Findings and recommendations.* http://pdf.usaid.gov/pdf_docs/PNADN816.pdf.
Vial, F. 2009. Interview by author of PADELAN project officer. May. Port-au-Prince, Haiti.
Wiener, J. 2009. Interview by author of director of the Foundation for the Protection of Marine Biodiversity. March 12. Port-au-Prince, Haiti.
World Bank. 2006. Interim strategy note for the Republic of Haiti for the period FY07–FY08. http://siteresources.worldbank.org/INTHAITI/Resources/HaitiInterimStrategyNotein English.pdf.
―――. n.d. What is local economic development (LED)? http://go.worldbank.org/EA784ZB3F0.

Peacebuilding and adaptation to climate change

Richard Matthew and Anne Hammill

Since the early 1990s, peacebuilding has matured into a complex capacity-building process through which conditions amenable to sustainable development are created or recreated in post-conflict societies. Contemporary peacebuilding entails the design, sequencing, and implementation of diverse capacity-building strategies that provide basic security and encourage socioeconomic recovery and growth, and that also address the conditions, attitudes, and actions associated with past violent conflict in order to prevent its recurrence (UNEP 2009). Various United Nations agencies play a critical role in this process, as do nongovernmental and civil society organizations, aid agencies and development banks, private businesses, and national governments. While coordination is a daunting challenge and there is no single recipe for success, empirically grounded guidance notes and best practices are now available to focus and guide efforts, and there are many examples of operations widely regarded as successful, such as Liberia, Namibia, Rwanda, and South Africa (Jeong 2005).

Since the release of the *Fourth Assessment Report* of the Intergovernmental Panel on Climate Change, in 2007, climate change has come to be regarded as both an immediate and long-term threat to sustainable development and an amplifier of violent conflict.[1] Changes in precipitation patterns, rising sea levels, and increases in the frequency and intensity of extreme weather events are already undermining livelihoods, reducing the productivity of key economic sectors, disrupting human health, and affecting settlement and migration patterns (IPCC

Richard Matthew is a professor of international and environmental politics at the School of Social Ecology and the School of Social Science at the University of California, Irvine, and founding director of the Center for Unconventional Security Affairs. Anne Hammill is a senior researcher for both the climate change and energy and the environment and security programs of the International Institute for Sustainable Development. This chapter was adapted, with permission, from Anne Hammill and Richard Matthew, "Peacebuilding and Climate Change Adaptation," *St. Antony's International Review* 5 (2): 89–112. Copyright 2010 *St. Antony's International Review*.

[1] See Brown and Hammill (2007); Campbell (2008); CNA (2007); German Advisory Council on Global Change (2008); and Stern (2006).

2007). Little research has been carried out on climate impacts in fragile post-conflict situations. However, there is reason to believe that such impacts add considerable stress to the governance structures and other institutions that provide basic services and protect people from injury and loss, thereby weakening people's confidence in the social order. Additional challenges posed by climate impacts include increased displacement, reduced agricultural outputs, and a heightened risk of conflict recurrence (Smith and Vivekananda 2009). Concerns that climate change has and will continue to (1) contribute to violent conflict and (2) obstruct sustainable development have important implications for peacebuilding.

Climate change could affect peacebuilding in at least two ways. First, climate impacts could undermine existing peacebuilding operations by making the transition to sustainable development more difficult and costly. For example, climate change may damage the natural resource base upon which many post-conflict societies rely for economic recovery and sustainable livelihoods (UNEP 2009). This is especially true in agricultural economies, which are typical in peacebuilding countries. In Sierra Leone, for example, over 70 percent of employment is in the natural resource sector, mainly in agriculture (UNEP 2010). Shifting cultivation is practiced throughout Sierra Leone, and crops are rain fed. Although data are limited, significant anecdotal evidence collected during five field missions between 2008 and 2010 suggests a typical pattern of climate effects, including higher-than-normal variability in rainfall and atypical flooding and drought, all of which add stress to the country's most important source of livelihoods (Ogundeji 2010).

Dwindling resources may also increase competition and tensions in volatile settings. Again, in Sierra Leone, where the population obtains some 75 percent of its protein from fish, the country's extensive coastal fisheries will be affected as climate change modifies water temperature and currents (FAO n.d.). And changing climate conditions (in particular, more frequent and intense extreme weather events) are overwhelming institutional capacities even as they are being built up, increasing demands for disaster response and diverting scarce capital away from other priorities, such as rebuilding infrastructure. To the extent that climate change intensifies processes that have the potential to undermine peace—by, for example, increasing population displacement or causing further setbacks in development, it risks fostering conflict relapse. Even if one is skeptical about the contribution of climate change to conflict recurrence, it clearly has the potential to undermine capacity building and slow or halt the transition to sustainable development.

The second way that climate change may affect peacebuilding is by requiring a shift in peacebuilding approaches and priorities, to enable fragile societies to better cope with the additional stress of climate impacts. At a minimum, this would mean the more systematic use of climate data to inform early peacebuilding decisions (e.g., regarding land use planning, resource prospecting, and investment) that commit post-conflict countries to certain longer-term development pathways. It would also mean greater emphasis on early warning or on tools and strategies to reduce disaster risk.[2] The authors believe, however, that a more comprehensive integration of climate change adaptation into the pillars of peacebuilding is desirable, and may be essential for a transition to sustainable development. To this end, the chapter examines the challenge of integrating peacebuilding and climate change adaptation into a unified approach to support the transformation of post-conflict states.

The chapter is divided into five major sections: (1) a general discussion of peacebuilding; (2) a consideration of the relationship between peacebuilding and climate change; (3) a discussion of climate change adaptation; (4) a description of potential strategies for integrating peacebuilding and climate change adaptation; and (5) a brief conclusion. Throughout, examples from field research in post-conflict countries in Africa (the Democratic Republic of the Congo, Rwanda, and Sierra Leone, in particular) are used to illustrate the discussion.

PEACEBUILDING

The end of the Cold War provided an opportunity to revive elements of the UN's mission that had been severely compromised by decades of ideological and military rivalry between the United States and the Soviet Union, countries that had veto power in the United Nations Security Council (Brahimi 2007; Paris 2004). In 1992, in response to this opportunity, UN Secretary-General Boutros Boutros-Ghali published *An Agenda for Peace* (UNSG 1992), a report that stimulated interest in peacemaking, peacekeeping, and peacebuilding on the part of academics, policy makers, and practitioners around the world. This interest was remarkably productive: in 2003, for example, Jacob Kreilkamp argued that in a single decade, the "U.N. peacekeeping work has undergone a richly documented transformation" (Kreilkamp 2003, 619).

Although there is no single definition of peacebuilding that is used consistently within the UN, let alone beyond it, peacebuilding is often defined as an element in a broader process.[3] The first step in this process, peacemaking, generally refers to a diplomatic effort that may involve UN, governmental, and nongovernmental actors, and is designed to bring together the various parties that are engaged in violent conflict so that they can explore—and, ultimately, agree to implement—a peace agreement that will end hostilities. This agreement, in turn, creates the setting for peacekeeping, which is typically a multilateral process that involves dispatching military forces to a conflict zone: (1) to monitor, and

---

[2] Similarly, the presence of conflict risks in an area vulnerable to the impacts of climate change may call upon societies to confront climate impacts in a different way, so as to reduce the likelihood of conflict.

[3] Editors' note: The conceptual framework for the post-conflict peacebuilding process presented in this chapter is similar to, but distinct from, the framework articulated earlier in this book. More details can be found in the introductory chapter, in the box titled "What Is Peacebuilding?", and in the introduction to Bruch et al. (2012).

perhaps assist with, the implementation of the peace agreement; (2) to deter hostile parties from resorting to violence; and (3) to provide safe spaces for nonmilitary activities to begin.

Peacebuilding, the third phase of the process, overlaps with peacekeeping. The 2004 Utstein study of peacebuilding, whose findings are reflected in the conceptualization of peacebuilding published by the Development Assistance Committee of the Organisation for Economic Co-operation and Development (OECD) in 2008, provides a useful overview of the main elements of peacebuilding (OECD/DAC 2008).[4] The Utstein study—carried out by the International Peace Research Institute, Oslo—examined 336 peacebuilding projects implemented over a ten-year period by the four Utstein governments: Germany, the Netherlands, Norway, and the United Kingdom (Smith 2004). In both the OECD and the Utstein reports, peacebuilding is structured into four mutually reinforcing pillars of activity.[5]

Pillar 1, the social, economic, and environmental dimension, focuses on the socioeconomic drivers of conflict, such as wealth disparities, marginalization of particular social groups or geographic areas, environmental degradation, and competition over natural resources. Activities under this pillar include repatriating and reintegrating refugees and internally displaced persons (IDPs), and generating employment through investments in the productive sectors of the economy. Attention is also given to constructing and repairing infrastructure; restoring and reforming key government functions, such as water supply and sanitation; and developing and providing basic public services, such as education and health care. To further strengthen this pillar, government agencies and other institutions seek international assistance to build technical and financial capacity.

Pillar 2, the governance and political dimension, is concerned with consolidating the legitimacy, capacity, and effectiveness of key institutions. Activities under this category include state building (that is, taking measures to reconstruct and strengthen political authority and administrative capacity) and capacity building for civil society. Various democratizing initiatives—such as organizing elections, developing power-sharing structures, and instituting participatory processes—are undertaken. Programs fostering transparency, accountability, and anticorruption programs are also implemented.

Pillar 3, the security dimension, focuses on the protection and provision of state and personal security. Security is typically achieved through programs that support disarmament, demobilization, and the reintegration of former combatants

---

[4] As defined on the web site of the U4 Anti-Corruption Resource Centre, the Utstein Group "is a group of Ministers responsible for Development Co-operation, working in a concerted way to drive the development agenda forward, focusing on implementing the international consensus.... The 'core group' consists of the respective Ministers of Germany, the Netherlands, Norway and the United Kingdom" (U4 Anti-Corruption Resource Centre 2002).

[5] The description of the four pillars is based on OECD/DAC (2008) and Smith (2004).

into local communities; programs may also be developed to clear mines and other unexploded ordnance, and to control access to small arms. Security sector reform, another key component of this pillar, involves rebuilding and improving the security and justice apparatus, including a country's military, police, judiciary, and penal services.

Pillar 4, the truth and reconciliation dimension, is designed to encourage dialogue, peaceful resolution of disputes, healing, and justice. Often, an important element of this pillar is to make available precise details of what happened. Exhibitions, memorials, documentaries, and other public displays may be created, archives may be opened to the public, and opportunities may be created for individuals to confess their roles and seek the forgiveness of their communities.

These pillars of peacebuilding are not monolithic. Within each pillar, the priorities and needs vary throughout a society, and it is essential to carefully consider and manage both differences and continuities within and across national and subnational levels of political, economic, and social organization. Post-conflict Sierra Leone, for example, has given considerable emphasis to the reform of the mining and minerals sector, partly because of the attention focused on conflict diamonds during the 1991–2002 conflict.[6] To address the connection between mining and conflict, the national government has worked to reform the governance of the mining sector (pillar 2), negotiating new concession agreements with foreign investors and making the mining sector a prototype for vastly improved accountability, transparency, and participation. Outside Freetown, Sierra Leone's capital, the focus is more on the sector's socioeconomic value (pillar 1). Communities that are adjacent to mining operations typically have a list of specific concerns and priorities, such as employment opportunities, compensation, environmental impacts, displacement, and the provision of community services (UNIPSIL 2009).

Part of the peacebuilding effort has focused on managing unrealistic expectations about the benefits that would flow from this sector after the conflict, and on building support for the strengthening of other sectors of the economy.[7] Many communities believe that they have not received real benefits from the mining sector since the end of the conflict, and are therefore suspicious about the real intentions of the government's reform efforts. In a contentious sector like mining and minerals, it is perhaps inevitable that some communities will assume that reform initiatives unfolding in the capital are providing cover for new modes of

---

[6] As defined by the United Nations, "conflict diamonds are diamonds that originate from areas controlled by forces or factions opposed to legitimate and internationally recognized governments, and are used to fund military action in opposition to those governments, or in contravention of the decisions of the Security Council." (UN n.d.)

[7] The statements in this paragraph are based on information gathered by Richard Matthew—who, as a member of the United Nations Environment Programme's Expert Group on Conflict and Peacebuilding, participated in two UN peacebuilding missions to Sierra Leone.

corruption. Moreover, regardless of its intentions, a national government that is in need of capacity building will never be able to satisfy all of the urgent post-conflict needs of its people.

Given the tension between the desire to channel limited resources toward capacity building and the desire to respond to immediate needs, much of the success of peacebuilding depends on negotiations among various stakeholders about the following issues:[8]

- What are the country's priorities within each pillar and at each level of government (including local, regional, and national).
- How these priorities can be welded into a viable peacebuilding plan that can guide action for three to five years.
- How to mobilize external funding for elements of the plan.

These negotiations must occur within in a complicated context:

- The post-conflict society may be fearful, suspicious, and deeply divided.
- Stakeholders may have to work with a government that is corrupt.
- Negotiators may face pressure from peace spoilers who have found ways to benefit from conflict and lawlessness.
- Negotiations may be complicated by insufficient data, which can introduce uncertainty into planning and decision making.
- Negotiations may be undermined by destabilizing regional dynamics, especially where there are urgent humanitarian needs.

These conditions have rendered peacebuilding in Sierra Leone extraordinarily difficult; as a consequence, the five-year plan that was in place at the time of writing was the product of seven years of observation, discussion, projects, and experiments in peacebuilding.

PEACEBUILDING AND CLIMATE CHANGE

As understanding of peacebuilding has evolved since 1992, so has the grasp of the dynamic and interactive variables that contribute to insecurity and conflict. An important part of the post–Cold War rethinking of peace and security has been the increasingly sophisticated analysis of environmental change as a cause (and symptom) of insecurity.[9] A growing body of literature now explores the many pathways through which environmental degradation and resource depletion

---

[8] Stakeholders include the government, civil society groups and nongovernmental organizations, UN agencies, donors, and private investors.
[9] See Barnett (2001); Matthew, Halle, and Switzer (2002); Conca and Dabelko (2002); and Hammill et al. (2009).

threaten human well-being—and even survival—as much as, or even more than, the threat of military aggression.[10] This threat is especially worrisome for developing countries, where the link between the availability of, or access to, ecosystem services and human well-being is generally more direct,[11] governance is weak, and the capacity to deal with stresses is limited. Indeed, for these societies—and especially for the more marginalized and disadvantaged groups within them—environmental degradation and scarcity mean a greater chance of becoming further impoverished and being made more vulnerable to shocks and disruptions such as disease, famine, extreme weather, and market collapse. In some instances, protracted vulnerability and insecurity can become grounds for insecurity in the more traditional sense: open violent conflict.

The latest iteration of efforts to examine the link between human security and environmental change involves examining the effects of climate change on security.[12] Expressing a view that is in keeping with much of the literature on this topic, *World in Transition: Climate Change as a Security Risk*, a report published by the German Advisory Council on Global Change, states that "climate change will overstretch many societies' adaptive capacities within the coming decades" (German Advisory Council on Global Change 2008, 1). Similarly, CNA's 2007 report, *National Security and the Threat of Climate Change*, envisions a future in which "climate change acts as a threat multiplier for instability in some of the most volatile regions of the world" and fosters "tensions even in stable regions" (CNA 2007, 6–7). The findings of these and many other assessments were carefully synthesized in a 2009 report prepared by Achim Maas and Dennis Tänzler, who conclude that "climate change is first and foremost a challenge for development and individual or human security, which could halt or reverse developmental achievements and threaten livelihoods" (Maas and Tänzler 2009, 3). Maas and Tänzler also note the "potential impacts of climate change on the existing (armed) conflicts and unstable regions or the potential for emerging conflicts and zones of turmoil" (Maas and Tänzler 2009, 3).

In a 2007 report, Dan Smith and Janani Vivekananda argue that there are "46 countries—home to 2.7 billion people—in which the effects of climate change interacting with economic, social and political problems will create a high risk of violent conflict" (Smith and Vivekananda 2007, 3). It is not certain, of course, that climate change will make conflict more intractable or introduce new conflicts

---

[10] See Homer-Dixon (1999); Deudney and Matthew (1999); Bannon and Collier (2003); Collier (2000a, 2000b); Conca and Dabelko (2002); and German Advisory Council on Global Change (2008).
[11] The term *ecosystem services* refers to the transformation of natural assets into things that humans value. An example is the fact that fungi, worms, and bacteria transform sunlight, carbon, and nitrogen into fertile soil. See Ecosystem Services Project (n.d.).
[12] See Brown and Crawford (2009); Brown and Hammill (2007); Campbell (2008); CNA (2007); German Advisory Council on Global Change (2008); Rogers (2010); and Stern (2006).

into states that are fragile, at war, or in a post-conflict phase. Climate change impacts may be largely invisible in areas where misery and violence are already acute. Furthermore, it is at least conceivable that climate change could create enormous pressure to cooperate and take action, which could generate resources for fragile and post-conflict states and impart a sense of shared fate in vulnerable and fractious areas such as South Asia. It is also likely that in some cases, climate change will introduce new opportunities for settlement and new livelihoods, although current wisdom suggests that this is more likely in places like Canada and Siberia than in the arc stretching from West Africa through the Middle East and into South Asia, where the majority of contemporary violent conflict is located. Thus, insofar as climate change is expected to threaten development efforts and to amplify or create conflict risks, peacebuilding needs to incorporate climate change adaptation.

CLIMATE CHANGE ADAPTATION

Adaptation is a socioecological process of adjustment to new or modified circumstances.[13] Within the context of climate change, adaptation is understood as actions that people take in response to, or in anticipation of, changing climate conditions, in order to reduce adverse impacts or to take advantage of opportunities (Tompkins and Adger 2003). The need for, type, and scale of adaptation depend on the kind of change taking place and on the vulnerability of people and natural systems to this change. Vulnerability in this context refers to both a system's exposure to disruptive shocks and trends and to its ability to prepare for, cope with, and recover from the impacts of such shocks and trends. Thus, adaptation has a temporal aspect: human systems can be adjusted in anticipation of change or as a reaction to its consequences.

The research highlights two general approaches to decision making about anticipatory adaptation: a top-down approach uses information about future climate conditions to identify and quantify impacts on different ecosystems and economic sectors, which is then used as a basis for devising adaptation options. A bottom-up approach looks at historical and current climate variability and existing strategies for coping with this variability, and determines how existing strategies might be modified to take account of climate change. The bottom-up approach has the advantage of not relying on elaborate climate projections, which are fraught with uncertainty and limited in their depiction of social interactions and capacities—both of which are important determinants of vulnerability. But the bottom-up approach also carries the risk of incorrect extrapolations based on current or historical conditions, which could lead to maladaptation. The ideal approach draws from both options, allowing decision makers to develop strategies that address current vulnerabilities and development priorities, while trying

---

[13] This section of the chapter is informed by McGray, Hammill, and Bradley (2007).

to ensure the long-term sustainability of such strategies through a basic understanding of future projections. This hybrid approach to adaptation, which draws from multiple data sources (historical records, current observations, and future projections) and tries to reconcile different timelines, is often referred to as the climate risk management approach (UNDP 2002).

Adaptation can involve a wide range of policies, decisions, and activities implemented at different scales, from a farmer's decision to shift crop varieties, to a village-level malaria awareness campaign, to a municipal plan to expand a storm drainage system, to a national policy to strengthen and expand community-based response to forest fires. These examples are within the purview of traditional development programming, however. The question is, what exactly distinguishes adaptation from traditional development?

The adaptation continuum proposed by Heather McGray and colleagues provides a useful framework for describing the range of possible climate change adaptation activities and how they relate to traditional development (see figure 1) (McGray, Hammill, and Bradley 2007). The continuum features four sequential but overlapping areas of focus for adaptation efforts. At the far left are the more familiar development activities that reduce vulnerability to an array of development stressors, and at the far right are activities designed specifically to reduce vulnerability to the known or anticipated impacts of climate change.

The purpose of this continuum is to demonstrate that climate change adaptation includes a wide range of decisions and activities. Even those development activities that fall on the left side of the spectrum are forms of adaptation: although they appear to have little relation to the specifics of climate change, they build resilience and capacity to manage stress in general, including climate-related stress. Thus, an assessment of current and future climate-related vulnerabilities, and of the range of options for reducing them, may still lead to the adoption of familiar development policies and activities. However, adopting familiar development activities without considering climate issues risks fostering maladaptation—that is, leaving people more vulnerable to climate-related hazards, especially over the longer term, and thereby undermining or reversing development gains.

For example, in post-conflict Rwanda, in the years immediately after the conflict, the pressure of settling millions of IDPs and returning refugees shortened the government's time horizon for planning. As a result, people were settled in protected forest areas and allowed to cultivate steep hillsides: no attempt was made to integrate climate risk management into peacebuilding.[14] On the basis of numerous discussions with officials, it appears that the risks associated with these new settlements may have been underestimated.[15] The government is now

---

[14] In some cases, moreover, people settled wherever they could find space, leaving the government to cope with a fait accompli.
[15] Personal communication, Rwandan officials, Kigali, August 2007.

Figure 1. Climate change adaptation continuum

1	2	3	4
Addressing the drivers of vulnerability	Building response capacity	Managing climate risk	Confronting climate change
Reducing poverty, addressing conditions that make people susceptible to harm from all types of stressors, not just climate related.	Laying the foundation, setting up systems for problem solving and more targeted action.	Using climate information in decision making to reduce negative impacts, maximize positive impacts.	Almost exclusively addressing impacts of climate change; targeting climate risks outside of historic climate variability; benefits are realized only with climate change.
For example, literacy, women's rights, HIV/AIDs.	For example, planning and monitoring processes, communications structures, natural resource management practices.	For example, cropping practices, climate proofing infrastructure.	For example, relocation of communities due to address rise in sea level; management of glacial lake outburst floods.[a]

⬅ Vulnerability focus　　　　　　　　　　　　　　　　　　　Impacts focus ➡

Source: Adapted from McGray, Hammill, and Bradley (2007).
a. Glacial lake outburst floods are caused by the release of water that had been held back by a glacier or a moraine.

attempting to move some people from fragile environments into new villages, but the process has not been easy.

Today, Rwanda is frequently subject to torrential rains—which the Stockholm Environment Institute describes as a possible example of climate change—displacing communities, creating costly humanitarian demands, washing away vast quantities of topsoil, and threatening the long-term productivity of the agricultural sector (Downing, Watkiss, and Dyszynski 2010). There is little climate resilience at any level of Rwandese society, and no obvious way to reduce the risk of more frequent and severe climate-related disasters in the years ahead.[16] The lesson being learned in Rwanda and elsewhere is that information on climate impacts should inform peacebuilding, even if the activities in question appear to be familiar; what is new and additional is the assessment of risk that goes into robust designs that will enhance sustainability and have an overall development impact.

---

[16] See UNEP (2011).

INTEGRATING PEACEBUILDING AND CLIMATE CHANGE ADAPTATION

Peacebuilding is a fairly complex and evolving process that has not always delivered on its goals. Would integrating climate change adaptation with peacebuilding strengthen the process? Would such integration be straightforward? Finally, when climate change adaptation has faced significant obstacles even in stable countries, one might ask whether it would simply add another layer of complexity—and more trade-offs to negotiate—to post-conflict situations, where so many factors work against against cooperation. As a first step toward answering these questions, this section considers the opportunities and challenges associated with integrating climate change adaptation into the four pillars of peacebuilding discussed earlier.

Measures within the security pillar focus on bringing stability to post-conflict societies and reducing the risk of conflict relapse. The reconciliation pillar addresses community healing, justice, peaceful means of dispute resolution, and reparations. Opportunities to integrate climate change adaptation into either of these domains are limited. There may be some possibilities in the area of reintegration, however, which typically falls under the security pillar and involves settling soldiers and providing them with new livelihoods. For example, after the conflict in Sierra Leone ended in 2002, over 70,000 rebels were effectively disarmed and demobilized (Kaldor and Vincent 2006). The reintegration has proven challenging, however—and as of this writing, unemployment and underemployment were serious problems, especially among youth. As evidence mounts that Sierra Leone's agricultural sector, which is based on shifting, rain-fed cultivation, is unsustainable and inadequate for its growing population, and that the country is vulnerable to climate change impacts, it is becoming clear that job creation programs are essential to managing the security risks associated with large numbers of unemployed youth (UNEP 2010).

With respect to the governance pillar, one way to integrate climate change adaptation into peacebuilding is to assist the new government to enhance its capacity for managing climate risk. For example, functioning meteorological services could support the collection and analysis of climate data—which could, in turn, help to establish early-warning systems to prepare for, and minimize, the impact of events such as storms, floods, disease outbreaks, and famine.[17] Measures that encourage governments to create adaptation-related ministerial and departmental posts, establish interdepartmental coordination units, take a long-term perspective, and are flexible in planning and policy development can further develop adaptive capacity and encourage wider participation. Such activities would likely fall within category 2 ("building response capacity") on the adaptation continuum.

---

[17] One reason that Rwanda, for example, is poorly positioned to manage climate risk is that the collection of weather data virtually came to a halt during the 1994 genocide and has never been fully restored. Consequently, the country lacks the necessary data to set priorities and optimize preparedness in this area.

The socioeconomic development pillar offers the greatest opportunities to integrate climate change adaptation into peacebuilding. In Rwanda, for example, where refugees and IDPs numbered over 2 million in 1994, many families were resettled in marshes and steep hillsides, increasing their exposure to climate-related hazards such as flooding and landslides (Cutts 2000). Although there is typically enormous pressure to accommodate refugees and IDPs as quickly as possible, it is in the country's long-term interest to ensure that even the most urgent actions reflect current understanding of climate change: allowing settlements on steep terrain, in floodplains, or on coastlines, for example, can create costly problems that will persist far into the future.

Another immediate need is for infrastructure. Inevitably, post-conflict societies want functional transportation, communication, and water and energy systems to be the focus of government policy and donor support. Climate proofing this critical infrastructure (for example, by constructing higher bridges and wider drainage systems to deal with changing water levels and precipitation patterns, respectively) and introducing new infrastructure (such as sea walls to deal with sea-level rise and storm surges) would be important for protecting early investments and managing climate risks longer term. Yet it can be challenging to apply this climate lens when designing and constructing infrastructure in a post-conflict setting. These projects are typically framed as urgent and "quick wins," which do not lend themselves to additional climate analysis, and the capacity needed to undertake such an analysis is often limited. Climate risk management and adaptation benefits are more likely to be additional (often unintended) consequences of more efficient and environmentally friendly infrastructure design. An example of this is in Sierra Leone, where efficient water infrastructure has been introduced on a small scale.

With respect to health care, it may be tremendously valuable to determine whether climate change is causing shifts in disease patterns (e.g., the expansion of malaria and other water- and vector-borne diseases) and to ask what measures can be taken to address this issue. Education can be key to increasing adaptive capacity at all levels of social organization. In particular, training in disaster risk reduction and climate risk management can be incorporated into the curricula at all educational levels.

Finally, it may be very important to think carefully about changes to supply chains that may result from climate change and to avoid encouraging investment in climate-vulnerable sectors, unless adequate insurance is part of the investment package. Thus, during the peacebuilding phase, it may be desirable for donors to climate screen their own investments (that is, to make model investments), especially since one of the typical goals of donor investment is to identify and create conditions that will be attractive to external investors beyond the donor community. In the case of Sierra Leone, for example, foreign investment in mining operations and in plantation agriculture for biofuels has proceeded without any attention to possible climate effects, an oversight that may one day prove costly.

In general, the authors believe that the integration of climate change adaptation into peacebuilding is highly desirable, and that some of the problems being experienced by places like Rwanda could have been mitigated, had climate change adaptation been integrated into peacebuilding in the past. Specifically, resettlement patterns immediately after the genocide led to a dramatic reduction in forest cover, an increase in the cultivation of very steep hillsides, and settlement in swamps, all of which intensified vulnerability to the heavy rains and intense droughts predicted by climate change science.

There are many grounds for being encouraged about the viability of integrating considerations of climate change adaptation into peacebuilding because the two processes are similar in important ways: both focus on building capacity and resilience, and both promote the adoption of a longer-term perspective, while requiring enough flexibility to react to changing circumstances. Moreover, because both processes are context dependent, interventions need to be informed by context-specific conflict analysis, capacity assessments, vulnerability assessments, and scenario planning. The stakes are high in both cases, as failure or ineffectiveness can translate into heightened vulnerability, loss of lives, and development setbacks. Finally, the development aspects of peacebuilding are often valuable to supporting the wider recognition of underdevelopment as a root cause of conflict. The development community has not always found the right balance between short-term, externally driven results and the less glamorous medium- to long-term capacity building. Peacebuilding provides an opportunity to rethink development, and integrating adaptation into peacebuilding can make both more sustainable.

On the other hand, there are important differences between the two processes. In particular, what is good for peacebuilding may not always be good for climate change adaptation, and vice versa. For example, settling people in and around Virunga National Park was critical to jump-starting livelihoods and stabilizing communities in the Democratic Republic of the Congo, as it permitted access to forest resources for construction, fuel, food, and medicinal needs (Crawford and Bernstein 2008). The resulting degradation of ecosystem services, however, may have undermined the longer-term adaptive capacity of the system. Similarly, putting money into climate forecasting may seem extravagant when people are struggling to meet daily needs. In sum, climate change adaptation (like development in general) involves trade-offs, some of which may directly conflict with peacebuilding initiatives. Further complicating matters, even if one wished to integrate climate change adaptation into peacebuilding, assessments of climate risk may be difficult or impossible to obtain in the time frame available, and it is always hard to plan and act under conditions of great uncertainty.

CONCLUSION

Smith and Vivekananda contend that "the double-headed problem of climate change and violent conflict thus has a unified solution—peacebuilding and adaptation are effectively the same kind of activity" (Smith and Vivekananda 2007, 4). At a high level of abstraction, these authors may be correct in arguing that "peacebuilding and adaptation are effectively the same kind of activity, involving the same kinds of methods of dialogue and social engagement, requiring from governments the same values of inclusivity and transparency" (Smith and Vivekananda 2007, 4). The authors of this chapter agree that the integration of climate change adaptation into peacebuilding is attractive in many ways and might even be critical to helping build the needed capacity to transform post-conflict environments into settings of enduring peace and sustainable development. In their own work in the Democratic Republic of the Congo, Rwanda, and Sierra Leone, the authors observed many examples demonstrating that the failure to introduce climate change adaptation into peacebuilding meant that decisions with long-term consequences were not considered from a climate perspective; as a result, these countries are now ill equipped to manage climate risk.

REFERENCES

Bannon, I., and P. Collier, eds. 2003. *Natural resources and violent conflict: Options and actions.* Washington, D.C.: World Bank. www-wds.worldbank.org/servlet/WDSContentServer/WDSP/IB/2004/05/24/000012009_20040524154222/Rendered/PDF/282450Natural0resources0violent0conflict.pdf.

Barnett, J. 2001. *The meaning of environmental security: Ecological politics and policy in the new security era.* London: Zed Books.

Brahimi, L. 2007. State-building in crisis and post-conflict countries. Paper presented at the 7th Global Forum on Reinventing Government, Building Trust in Government. Vienna, Austria. June 26–29. http://unpan1.un.org/intradoc/groups/public/documents/UN/UNPAN026305.pdf.

Brown, O., and A. Crawford. 2009. *Rising temperatures, rising tensions: Climate change and the risk of violent conflict in the Middle East.* Winnipeg, Canada: International Institute for Sustainable Development. www.iisd.org/pdf/2009/rising_temps_middle_east.pdf.

Brown, O., and A. Hammill. 2007. Climate change as the "new" security threat: Implications for Africa. *International Affairs* 83 (6): 1141–1154.

Bruch, C., D. Jensen, M. Nakayama, and J. Unruh. 2012. *Post-conflict peacebuilding and natural resources: The promise and the peril.* New York: Cambridge University Press.

Campbell, K. M., ed. 2008. *Climatic cataclysm: The foreign policy and national security implications of climate change.* Washington, D.C.: Brookings Institution.

CNA. 2007. *National security and the threat of climate change.* Alexandria, VA. http://securityandclimate.cna.org.

Collier, P. 2000a. Economic causes of civil conflict and their implications for policy. World Bank. http://reliefweb.int/sites/reliefweb.int/files/resources/B7598814338CA6DEC1256C1E0042BE82-civilconflict.pdf.

———. 2000b. Doing well out of war: An economic perspective. In *Greed and grievance: Economic agendas in civil wars,* ed. M. Berdal and D. Malone. Boulder, CO: Lynne Rienner.

Conca, K., and G. D. Dabelko, eds. 2002. *Environmental peacemaking.* Washington, D.C.: Woodrow Wilson International Center for Scholars.

Crawford, A., and J. Bernstein. 2008. *MEAs, conservation and conflict: A case study of Virunga National Park, DRC*. Winnipeg, Canada: International Institute for Sustainable Development. www.iisd.org/pdf/2008/meas_cons_conf_virunga.pdf.

Cutts, M. 2000. The Rwandan genocide and its aftermath. In *The state of the world's refugees 2000: Fifty years of humanitarian action*. New York: Oxford University Press.

Deudney, D., and R. Matthew. 1999. *Contested grounds: Security and conflict in the new environmental politics*. Albany, NY: State University of New York Press.

Downing, T., P. Watkiss, and J. Dyszynski. 2010. *Economics of climate change in Rwanda*. Stockholm Environment Institute. http://sei-international.org/publications?pid=1579.

Ecosystem Services Project. n.d. What are ecosystem services? www.ecosystemservicesproject.org/html/overview/index.htm.

FAO (Food and Agriculture Organization of the United Nations). n.d. National aquaculture sector overview: Sierra Leone. www.fao.org/fishery/countrysector/naso_sierraleone/en.

German Advisory Council on Global Change. 2008. *World in transition: Climate change as a security risk*. London: Earthscan.

Hammill, A., A. Crawford, R. Craig, R. Malpas, and R. Matthew. 2009. *Conflict-sensitive conservation: Practitioners' manual*. Winnipeg, Canada: International Institute for Sustainable Development.

Homer-Dixon, T. 1999. *Environment, scarcity and violence*. Princeton, NJ: Princeton University Press.

IPCC (Intergovernmental Panel on Climate Change). 2007. *Climate change 2007: Impacts, adaptation, and vulnerability*. Contribution of Working Group II to the Fourth Assessment Report of the IPCC. New York: Cambridge University Press. www.ipcc.ch/ipccreports/ar4-wg2.htm.

Jeong, H. 2005. *Peacebuilding in postconflict societies: Strategy and process*. Boulder, CO: Lynne Rienner.

Kaldor, M., and J. Vincent. 2006. *Human security: Evaluation of UNDP assistance to conflict-affected countries; Sierra Leone*. New York: United Nations Development Programme. http://web.undp.org/evaluation/documents/thematic/conflict/SierraLeone.pdf.

Kreilkamp, J. 2003. U.N. postconflict reconstruction. *International Law and Politics* 35:619–670.

Maas, A., and D. Tänzler. 2009. *Regional security implications of climate change: A synopsis*. Berlin, Germany: Adelphi Consult.

Matthew, R., M. Halle, and J. Switzer, eds. 2002. *Conserving the peace: Resources, livelihoods and security*. Winnipeg, Canada: International Institute for Sustainable Development.

McGray, H., A. Hammill, and R. Bradley. 2007. *Weathering the storm: Options for framing adaptation and development*. With contributions by E. L. Schipper and J.-E. Parry. Washington, D.C.: World Resources Institute. http://pdf.wri.org/weathering_the_storm.pdf.

OECD/DAC (Organisation for Economic Co-operation and Development, Development Assistance Committee). 2008. Evaluating conflict prevention and peacebuilding activities: Factsheet 2008. www.oecd.org/dataoecd/36/20/39289596.pdf.

Ogundeji, O. 2010. Climate change threatens food security in Sierra Leone. *In Profile Daily*, September 6. www.inprofiledaily.com/index.php?option=com_content&view=article&id=2315:climate-change-threatens-food-security-in-sierra-leone&catid=1:headlines&Itemid=56.

Paris, R. 2004. *At war's end: Building peace after civil conflict*. New York: Cambridge University Press.

Rogers, P. 2010. Climate change and security. International Security Monthly Briefing. Oxford Research Group. September. www.oxfordresearchgroup.org.uk/sites/default/files/Sept10En.pdf.

Smith, D. 2004. *Towards a strategic framework for peacebuilding: Getting their act together; Overview report of the Joint Utstein Study of Peacebuilding*. Brattvaag, Norway: Royal Norwegian Ministry of Foreign Affairs. http://reliefweb.int/sites/reliefweb.int/files/resources/16A12BCAEAD0E411852573AE007570A3-International%20Alert_Climate%20of%20Conflict_07.pdf.

Smith, D., and J. Vivekananda. 2007. *A climate of conflict: The links between climate change, peace, and war*. London: International Alert. www.international-alert.org/sites/default/files/publications/A_climate_of_conflict.pdf.

———. 2009. *Climate change, conflict and fragility: Understanding the linkages, shaping effective responses*. London: International Alert. www.international-alert.org/press/Climate_change_conflict_and_fragility_Nov09.pdf.

Stern, N. 2006. *The economics of climate change: The Stern review*. Cambridge, UK: Cambridge University Press.

Tompkins, E. L., and W. N. Adger. 2003. Building resilience to climate change through adaptive management of natural resources. Tyndall Working Paper 27. Norwich, UK: Tyndall Centre for Climate Change Research. www.tyndall.ac.uk/sites/default/files/wp27.pdf.

U4 Anti-Corruption Resource Centre. 2002. The Utstein Group principles. http://web.archive.org/web/20071212220026/http://www.u4.no/projects/utstein/utsteinprinciples.cfm.

UN (United Nations). n.d. Conflict diamonds: Sanctions and war. www.un.org/peace/africa/Diamond.html.

UNDP (United Nations Development Programme). 2002. A climate risk management approach to disaster reduction and climate change adaptation. UNDP expert group meeting: Integrating Disaster Reduction with Adaptation to Climate Change. Havana, Cuba. June 19–21. www.undp.org/cpr/disred/documents/wedo/icrm/riskadaptationintegrated.pdf.

UNEP (United Nations Environment Programme). 2009. *From conflict to peacebuilding: The role of natural resources and the environment*. Nairobi, Kenya. http://postconflict.unep.ch/publications/pcdmb_policy_01.pdf.

———. 2010. *Sierra Leone: Environment, conflict and peacebuilding assessment; Technical report*. Geneva, Switzerland. http://postconflict.unep.ch/publications/Sierra_Leone.pdf.

———. 2011. *Rwanda: From post-conflict to environmentally sustainable development*. Nairobi, Kenya. http://postconflict.unep.ch/publications/UNEP_Rwanda.pdf.

UNIPSIL (United Nations Integrated Peacebuilding Office in Sierra Leone). 2009. *Joint vision for Sierra Leone of the United Nations' family*. www.sl.undp.org/1_doc/joint_un_vsion_sl_final.pdf.

UNSG (United Nations Secretary-General). 1992. *An agenda for peace: Preventive diplomacy, peacemaking and peace-keeping*. Report of the Secretary-General pursuant to the statement adopted by the Summit Meeting of the Security Council on January 31, 1992. A/47/277–S/241111. June 17. www.un.org/Docs/SG/agpeace.html.

PART 4

Environmental dimensions of infrastructure and reconstruction

Introduction

Provision of basic services and reconstruction of infrastructure are crucial to post-conflict recovery, but it is also necessary to ensure that the environment is not unduly affected by these activities and that specific natural resources are used sustainably and are distributed in a fair and equitable manner. Decisions on natural resource consumption, access, and distribution can easily become locked in, leading to degradation of resources, inequity in access, and potentially new sources of conflict. Part 4 begins with a focus on the use of environmental impact assessments, strategic environmental assessments, and other tools to identify and mitigate potential social and environmental effects from infrastructure and reconstruction projects in post-conflict settings. It then moves into lessons about how countries with a history of violence can use a regional plan for reconstruction and a cooperative approach to natural resource management as a means for building better and more integrated post-conflict futures, and ultimately a more durable peace. This part ends with a focus on the challenges of monitoring and evaluating projects that affect or use natural resources in post-conflict countries.

A number of challenges can affect infrastructure reconstruction in post-conflict settings. In "Addressing Infrastructure Needs in Post-Conflict Reconstruction: An Introduction to Alternative Planning Approaches," P. B. Anand describes five challenges: lack of financial transparency and mechanisms for cost recovery, inequitable distribution of benefits, weak governance capacity, poor legal systems and rule of law, and short-term spikes in insecurity. He then outlines ways to adapt general planning models to address post-conflict infrastructure reconstruction, and he discusses the problems inherent in choosing particular approaches. Anand observes that environmental and social impact assessments undertaken in post-conflict countries are often constrained by a lack of access to baseline environmental data, by poor community-level participation, by inconsistent monitoring, and by noncompliance with mitigation plans. He also emphasizes that to achieve legitimacy with and ownership by local residents, any approach should include in-depth stakeholder consultation.

The U.S. Agency for International Development (USAID) attempts to systematically assess and mitigate the potential environmental impacts of post-conflict humanitarian and development projects. Charles Kelly outlines USAID's strategy in "Mitigating the Environmental Impacts of Post-Conflict Assistance: Assessing USAID's Approach." Kelly confronts the perception held by some policy makers that environmental reviews of peacebuilding projects slow recovery and hinder clear demonstration of peace dividends to conflict victims and, particularly, to former combatants. Sometimes political interests and demands for quick recovery lead policy makers to bypass or ignore environmental reviews; Kelly discusses how this can result in more damage to the environment and increased hardship for victims, which can sow seeds for future conflict. Focusing on four environmental-review documents that cover post-conflict assistance in Afghanistan, Indonesia, Uganda, and the West Bank and the Gaza Strip, Kelly explains how USAID balances the imperative for timely post-conflict assistance with the need to assess the environmental impacts of that assistance.

An alternative to project-level environmental impact assessments (EIAs) are strategic environmental assessments (SEAs) conducted at the sector level. In "Challenges and Opportunities for Mainstreaming Environmental Assessment Tools in Post-Conflict Settings," George Bouma considers whether practitioners can tailor SEAs to specific post-conflict situations by using donor assistance databases as an entry point to discover key environmental risks at the sector level and to identify a range of environmental safeguards that should be applied. Drawing on his experiences of conducting environmental reviews of donor assistance databases in Afghanistan, Iraq, and Sudan, Bouma concludes that SEAs may be a useful tool for understanding the environmental implications of reconstruction plans and for prioritizing mitigation measures at the sector level when there is limited national capacity to conduct EIAs.

In Sierra Leone, the minerals sector has played an important role in the conflict history and is likely to shape the nation's economic future. The country is likely to become a significant producer of iron ore, gold, and oil, as well as diamonds. In order to maximize the benefits from these resources the government needs to manage large-scale investment, attract responsible investors, ensure a fair financial return to the nation, and promote and protect the well-being of the environment and its citizens. To meet these objectives, the government is building new capacity to conduct EIAs of the extractives sector in order to identify and mitigate potential impacts, as well as to build confidence with local communities. The head of the Sierra Leone Environment Protection Agency, Haddijatou Jallow, together with Oli Brown, Morgan Hauptfleisch, and Peter Tarr, evaluates the utility and feasibility of using EIAs in the chapter "Environmental Assessment as a Tool for Peacebuilding and Development: Initial Lessons from Capacity Building in Sierra Leone." The authors begin by outlining post-conflict peacebuilding efforts and the challenges for governance and peace consolidation in Sierra Leone, particularly with respect to natural resource management. They explain that natural resources are vital to Sierra Leone's economy and that there are high expectations that development in the natural resource sectors be a stabilizing political force. At the same time, they recognize that environmental impacts associated with the mining sector could be a source of conflict if the impacts undermine local livelihoods. EIAs have been a catalytic intervention for environmental governance that has long-lived implications for the sustainability of extractive industries. The authors contend that focused and sustained capacity building for environmental authorities is also essential.

Regional integration and cooperative management of resources is another way to promote post-conflict peacebuilding. In "Natural Resources, Post-Conflict Reconstruction, and Regional Integration: Lessons from the Marshall Plan and Other Reconstruction Efforts," Carl Bruch, Ross Wolfarth, and Vladislav Michalcik review resource-related experiences from the Marshall Plan and compare them with other (often less successful) regional experiences in Central America, the Balkans, and elsewhere. In particular, they focus on how the Marshall Plan enabled Europe's recovery by providing external support for regional cooperation and for integration based on natural resources—particularly coal and steel. The plan helped form the basis for international institutions that still persist, including the predecessors of the Organisation for Economic Co-operation and Development and the European Union.

Mikiyasu Nakayama continues with the post–World War II years in his review of lessons from Japan's Priority Production System, used from 1945 to 1951 to successfully to rehabilitate the coal mining and steel industries, as well as to provide jobs for excombatants, displaced people, and unemployed workers. In "Making the Best Use of Domestic Energy Sources: The Priority Production System for Coal Mining and Steel Production in Post–World War II Japan," Nakayama shows that the success of the Priority Production System relied on strict national control of key natural resources (coal and steel), combined with cheap and abundant labor. However, important trade-offs need to be considered in decisions about using such a system, including the risk of inflation and of rising unemployment once coal resources are exhausted or are no longer economically competitive.

Competing priorities often stymie planners of reconstruction efforts. In "Road Infrastructure Reconstruction as a Peacebuilding Priority in Afghanistan: Negative Implications for Land Rights," Jon Unruh and Mourad Shalaby identify the problematic interaction between the reconstruction of roads and the government's attempts to stabilize the land rights situation in the country. The chapter provides an example of the potentially negative interaction between two peacebuilding activities that are both extremely important and of high priority.

Evaluation of projects can play a key role in identifying lessons and shaping more effective interventions in post-conflict and post-crisis settings. In "Evaluating Post-Conflict Assistance," Suppiramaniam Nanthikesan and Juha I. Uitto argue that where people's livelihoods are at stake and situations remain fluid, there is an urgency to ensure not only that emergency responses and development interventions are on track but that those actions do not further exacerbate problems. The authors highlight the risk that external interventions in post-conflict situations may worsen inequalities that could have contributed to the original causes of the crisis, or may weaken the unifying ties among conflicting communities. Therefore, evaluations should look at the unintended consequences of projects, including effects on natural resource access. The authors also emphasize the importance of integrating natural resource considerations into peacebuilding policies and into long-term strategies beyond individual projects, in order to achieve sustainable benefits for conflict-affected populations.

Collectively, these cases highlight some of the key considerations in minimizing the environmental and social impacts of the reconstruction process, while also maximizing opportunities for job creation and regional cooperation based on natural resources. For these goals to be achieved, institutional capacity building must be prioritized from the outset of the peacebuilding process. International partners must also systematically apply best international practices and resist the temptation to use the post-conflict institutional vacuum as an excuse to neglect social and environmental safeguards.

Addressing infrastructure needs in post-conflict reconstruction: An introduction to alternative planning approaches

P. B. Anand

The term *infrastructure* refers to both hard and soft entities: it encompasses institutions and human capabilities, as well as material and physical processes and structures. Economic infrastructure often includes transportation, energy, communications, and financial services. Social infrastructure includes water and sanitation services, schools, hospitals, and health care. And institutional infrastructure includes the facilities, equipment, and personnel required for governance at the local and national levels.

Infrastructure is often heavily damaged and destroyed during conflict. Because institutions of governance are often fragile in post-conflict situations and because some infrastructure requires a sizable investment over a long period, securing investments and achieving necessary partnerships between the public and private sectors can be difficult (FRIDE 2009). This chapter identifies post-conflict challenges pertaining to infrastructure restoration and then introduces and compares the various approaches to planning infrastructure investment in post-conflict countries.

INFRASTRUCTURE CHALLENGES IN POST-CONFLICT COUNTRIES

In most post-conflict countries, access to infrastructure suffers: electricity consumption per capita decreases while electricity transmission and distribution losses increase, fewer people have access to telephones and communication services, and access to sanitation services and improved sources of water declines (*Foreign Policy* and Fund for Peace 2010; World Bank Group 2010). As a result, restoration of infrastructure can be a major dividend of peace and a key factor in the success of post-conflict recovery. As Merriam Mashatt, Major-General Daniel Long, and James Crum note: "In conflict-sensitive environments, the condition of infrastructure is often a barometer of whether a society will slip further into violence or make a peaceful transition out of the conflict cycle. The rapid restoration of essential services, such as water, sanitation, and electricity,

---

P. B. Anand is a reader in environmental economics and public policy at the Bradford Centre for International Development, University of Bradford. His work focuses on human development, institutions, and governance issues related to public services including water and sanitation.

assists in the perception of a return to normalcy and contributes to the peace process" (Mashatt, Long, and Crum 2008, 1).

Post-conflict investment patterns analyzed by the World Bank reveal that telecommunications investments, particularly in mobile networks, materialize soon after the end of a conflict. Electricity generation and distribution projects are often completed about three years after the conflict and increase in frequency after year five. Private investments in transport and water tend to come much later. Within the transport sector, seaports receive the majority of private investment (Schwartz, Hahn, and Bannon 2004).

Restoration of infrastructure in post-conflict countries must address five main challenges. First, major infrastructure projects often require significant financial investments and cost-recovery measures. However, because some infrastructure exhibits properties of public goods—it is impossible or too costly to restrict access to the good, so it is not feasible to charge a fee for it—it is difficult to recover costs and therefore to attract foreign investors. For example, Jordan Schwartz, Shelly Hahn, and Ian Bannon find that the private sector rarely invests in large-scale power generation and distribution infrastructure in the years immediately after a crisis. They do note, however, that small-scale providers are quick to mobilize resources to take advantage of the demand for services and the relative lack of regulation (Schwartz, Hahn, and Bannon 2004).

Second, the distribution of the costs and benefits of infrastructure projects can be skewed, creating winners and losers. In such cases, though an infrastructure project may result in a net benefit to society at large, a group of persons may end up as losers. This can be a serious source of local conflict, adding to post-conflict instability.

Third, weak governance capacity often translates into corruption, dysfunctional regulatory oversight, and poor management and maintenance of public infrastructure. Post-conflict governments also find it extremely difficult to coordinate myriad infrastructure projects and the many people involved.

Fourth, post-conflict legal systems often provide inadequate protection for large private sector infrastructure investments. This can be a major disincentive to foreign investment and support.

Finally, infrastructure projects must be planned in a way that addresses the possibility of spikes in insecurity as well as short-term shifts in political support. For example, in Afghanistan deteriorating security is a primary cause for delays in completing U.S.-funded projects in the energy sector (SIGAR 2010).

Restoration of infrastructure also involves trade-offs in relation to natural resources. The dilemma is whether to focus on infrastructure that will aid in the rapid extraction and exportation of natural resources so the country can earn much-needed foreign exchange to pay for recovery or, alternatively, to focus on services that have a more significant impact on nonincome dimensions of human development. When state institutions are controlled by nonstate entities whose goal is to extract income from natural resources, infrastructure investments may be distorted and misused in an effort to facilitate resource extraction and sale (Verstegen 2001; Bardhan 2004; Addison and Bruck 2009).

Another challenge involves ownership of and access to land and related natural resources that may be needed for, or may be negatively affected by, a major infrastructure project. Resolution of land use disputes and compensation for damage or lost access are often key prerequisites to infrastructure development (Brookings Institution and University of Bern 2007; Solomon et al. 2009). Environmental and social impact assessments are often needed to identify and help mitigate potential effects. However, such assessments are often constrained by a lack of access to baseline environmental data, poor community-level participation, inconsistent monitoring, and noncompliance with mitigation plans.

ALTERNATIVE PLANNING APPROACHES

Overcoming the challenges to infrastructure reconstruction and connecting infrastructure investments to the peacebuilding process are overarching objectives of post-conflict recovery. Planning approaches that have been adopted to address infrastructure reconstruction needs include incrementalism; imposed strategic planning; stakeholder consultations and bottom-up planning; demand-based approaches; and human freedoms, rights, and security approaches.

Incrementalism

A common approach in post-conflict countries is to base infrastructure investments on initial work conducted during humanitarian operations. In other words, rather than conducting detailed needs assessments and systematic mapping of infrastructure damage, the incremental approach focuses on what has already been provided and simply scales up services from the starting point of these early successes.

The advantage of incrementalism is that risks are minimal as new infrastructure investment is made in services that are already operating to some degree. The disadvantage is that although certain services are crucial for immediate humanitarian relief, they may not be the most appropriate starting points for long-term reconstruction. Also, path dependence in terms of what already exists may mean that other important options are not considered or fully evaluated. Scaling up from relief also means that those who are involved in relief may influence the direction and nature of reconstruction, even if what they recommend are not the most appropriate solutions for the given context. The distribution of benefits and potential social impacts are also often neglected.

For example, in Afghanistan an incremental approach has largely been used in the energy sector. Although this approach has increased Afghanistan's electricity production, the Special Inspector General for Afghanistan Reconstruction has raised concerns (SIGAR 2010). In particular, his 2010 report to the U.S. Congress noted that many energy projects are being implemented across the country in an ad hoc manner, rather than as part of an integrated strategy. Ways in which specific energy projects can support broader strategic goals and overall peacebuilding are rarely considered. The report further notes that the government faces serious challenges in coordinating projects and sustaining existing facilities; for instance, it lacks the capacity to collect revenue from end users and to maintain power plants and transmission lines. The report calls for an updated energy master plan to establish priorities and time frames, taking into consideration the current security context and broader strategic goals.

Imposed strategic planning

Imposed strategic planning occurs within the context of a top-down reconstruction plan or development strategy that is largely based on a needs assessment by international actors or national authorities. This needs-based approach is often undertaken by international and national experts with only a minimal degree of stakeholder consultation. It is used primarily when a post-conflict government lacks either the capacity or the legitimacy to carry out a national consultation process.

The advantage of imposed strategic planning is that an integrated plan can be developed and financed at an early post-conflict stage. The plan can also provide an effective framework for coordination and for monitoring progress against milestones. However, although such top-down plans may provide effective solutions to meet post-conflict infrastructure needs, the lack of local ownership can be a major weakness. Local people may accept the plan as long as donor resources are available; however, acceptance can rapidly switch to disownment if problems arise, or when the responsibilities for the services created are transferred to the local communities.

For example, the initial post-conflict needs assessment in Iraq was conducted by the World Bank, the UN system, and the Coalition Provisional Authority with only minimal local-level consultation. The needs assessment identified US$35.8 billion worth of reconstruction needs over a four-year period (UN and World Bank 2003). However, the needs assessment was the main international reconstruction framework for only one year. It lacked local ownership and did not fully reflect national priorities. It was replaced by the 2005–2007 National Development Strategy, which the newly established interim Iraqi government developed, using a more extensive consultation process.

By way of contrast, in Aceh, after the devastation caused by the December 2004 tsunami, a locally owned reconstruction plan was developed by the state planning agency BAPPENAS (Badan Perencanaan dan Pembangunan Nasional) in 2005. An Asian Development Bank study noted that 94 percent of key performance indicators set in the master plan (and revised in 2008) had been achieved (Asian Development Bank 2009).

Stakeholder consultations and bottom-up planning

A third approach to infrastructure planning is to rely on detailed stakeholder consultations and to conduct bottom-up planning. Focus groups, small sample surveys, and, where the context permits, full-scale representative sample surveys may be used to determine specific needs and priorities on a local level (Anand 2011).

The advantage of this approach is that a cross section of stakeholders is consulted and needs that are specific to a geographic region can be identified. The disadvantages are that wide-ranging consultations require a considerable amount of time and that a policy vacuum exists while consultations are taking place. If shortcuts are taken in the consultation process, the whole exercise may be considered to lack legitimacy, especially by those who do not sufficiently benefit from the plans. Another downside is that sometimes stakeholders cannot reach consensus on infrastructure priorities, in which case technical experts make final decisions.

Demand-based approach

A fourth approach is to use more detailed analysis not just of needs but also of the demand for various infrastructure and design strategies. The advantage of a demand-based approach is that services can be targeted and tailored according to what is likely to generate the most benefits. Involving the private sector and developing public-private partnerships is easier using this approach. The disadvantage is that a demand-based approach may not be suitable for many services with the properties of pure public goods. Demand-based planning can result in a bias toward services for which willingness to pay exists. Thus services that the poorest and most vulnerable households need the most could be the ones most neglected or given least priority; in this case existing vertical inequalities would be reinforced.

A World Bank–International Labour Organization study of demand-driven approaches to post-war reconstruction concludes, "We are still very much in the 'learning phase' regarding the benefits, applications and optimal methodologies for demand-driven approaches" (Goovaerts, Gasser, and Inbal 2005, 12). The study further notes: "The potential benefits and pitfalls associated with demand-driven approaches suggest that there is need to carefully design such approaches, to ensure that they are applied in the most beneficial way possible" (Goovaerts, Gasser, and Inbal 2005, 14).

Human freedoms, rights, and security approaches

A fifth approach focuses on enhancing substantive freedoms, human rights, and human security. This approach places citizens at the center of decision making. Instead of alternative proposals being evaluated against technical criteria, demand, or net present value, proposals are considered according to the extent to which they have been chosen by citizens themselves and to which the proposals will contribute to enhancing citizens' freedoms, rights, or human security. When this approach is being used, infrastructure interventions that empower individuals and increase their freedom and security will be given greater priority over other projects (Anand and Gasper 2007).

In a people-centered approach, infrastructure planning has to address both freedom from want and freedom from fear. Individuals from many different social groups—women, children, the elderly, the disabled, the unemployed, and the impoverished—are seen as active agents of change rather than passive recipients waiting to receive services or aid from elsewhere. At the same time, freedoms come with responsibilities: no person or group of persons should interpret freedom as a license to inflict violence on others.

Normally this approach has the advantage that it is focused on the individuals affected by the conflict and on enhancing their freedoms. However, at the field level, there are two major challenges in its practical application. First, infrastructure planners may lack the expertise to understand the potential impacts of infrastructure on human freedoms, rights, and security. They could argue that the question of trade-offs between the winners and losers of infrastructure projects is a political one that should be left to local or national authorities. Planners can become excessively focused on the well-being of the individuals concerned rather than accepting that citizens may place more importance on having a voice and that they may sacrifice well-being in order to achieve higher-level freedoms. These tensions can enlarge the divide between conflict resolution and the promotion and protection of human rights—as Albert Gomes-Mugumya notes in the case of Northern Uganda (Gomes-Mugumya 2010).

Second, in post-conflict countries where the rule of law and basic government capacity are lacking, human rights approaches that emphasize the need for identifying both rights holders and duty bearers can be difficult to apply in practice. Planners need to consider the limits of their efforts and must ask how trade-offs can be made and whether the freedoms and rights of insurgent groups should also be considered.

CONCLUSIONS

It is challenging to pursue justice and fairness when peace is fragile and relies temporarily on windows of reprieve from unresolved historical injustices or group inequalities. In the immediate aftermath of a conflict, planners may take initial steps using incrementalism, but such an approach cannot be sustained for long-term recovery. A coherent and coordinated reconstruction framework will require strategic planning, and such planning requires in-depth stakeholder consultation to achieve legitimacy with and ownership by local citizens. Stakeholder consultations can pave the way for some degree of shared vision and buy-in. However, consultation is not the same as ownership, and stakeholders may perceive the process as being top-down window dressing that limits their role to that of passive recipients rather than creating a real opportunity to actively participate.

Demand-led approaches can be useful in attracting much-needed investment but may not be appropriate for infrastructure projects that involve significant public good dimensions or externalities. On the other hand, an approach that emphasizes human freedoms, rights, and security offers a new way to understand the potential benefits and impacts of infrastructure.

To be in a position to choose an approach is often a luxury in post-conflict reconstruction. Where institutional conditions and the local reality do present such a choice, it may be necessary to use a combination of these approaches to maximize peacebuilding dividends of infrastructure investments. Cutting across all approaches is the need to anticipate, identify, and mitigate the potential environmental and social impact of infrastructure investments and to see such investments as part of a wider effort to promote freedoms and justice.

REFERENCES

Addison, T., and T. Bruck, eds. 2009. *Making peace work: The challenge of social and economic reconstruction.* London: Palgrave Macmillan.

Anand, P. B. 2011. Right to information and local governance: An assessment. *Journal of Human Development and Capabilities* 12 (1): 135–152.

Anand, P. B., and D. Gasper. 2007. Human security, well-being and sustainability: Guest editorial and introduction. *Journal of International Development* 19 (4): 449–456.

Asian Development Bank. 2009. Indonesia: Aceh-Nias rehabilitation and reconstruction. Progress report. Manila, Philippines.

Bardhan, P. 2004. *Scarcity, conflict and co-operation.* Cambridge, MA: MIT Press.

Brookings Institution and University of Bern. 2007. *Addressing internal displacement in peace processes, peace agreements and peace-building.* Washington, DC: Brookings–Bern Project on Internal Displacement.

FRIDE (Fundación para las Relaciones Internacionales y el Diálogo Exterior). 2009. *Public aid policies and private sector participation in post-war reconstruction processes and promoting development.* A Development in Context Report. Madrid.

Foreign Policy and Fund for Peace. 2010. Failed states index 2010. Washington, D.C.

Gomes-Mugumya, A. 2010. Reflections on rights and conflict from Uganda. Berghof Handbook Dialogue No. 9. Berlin, Germany: Berghof Conflict Research.

Goovaerts, P., M. Gasser, and A. Inbal. 2005. Demand driven approaches to livelihood support in post-war contexts: A joint ILO–World Bank study. Social Development Paper No. 29. Washington, D.C.: World Bank. http://siteresources.worldbank.org/INTCDD/214574-1107382173398/20877452/WP29_Web.pdf.

Mashatt, M., D. Long, and J. Crum. 2008. Conflict-sensitive approach to infrastructure development. Special Report. Washington, D.C.: United States Institute of Peace. www.usip.org/files/resources/sr197.pdf.

Schwartz, J., S. Hahn, and I. Bannon. 2004. The private sector's role in the provision of infrastructure in post-conflict countries: Patterns and policy options. Social Development Paper No. 16. Washington, D.C.: World Bank.

SIGAR (Special Inspector General for Afghanistan Reconstruction). 2010. Afghanistan energy supply has increased but an updated master plan is needed and delays and sustainability concerns remain. SIGAR Audits, 10-4. Arlington, VA.

Solomon, A., Y. Bouka, J. O'Neil, G. Pouliot, and S. Al-Sarraf. 2009. Forced displacement and housing, land, and property ownership challenges in post-conflict and reconstruction. INPROL Consolidated Response (09-003). Washington, D.C.: International Network to Promote the Rule of Law.

UN (United Nations) and World Bank. 2003. *United Nations/World Bank joint Iraq needs assessment.* New York. http://siteresources.worldbank.org/IRFFI/Resources/Joint+Needs+Assessment.pdf.

Verstegen, S. 2001. Poverty and conflict: An entitlement perspective. CPN Briefing Paper. Brussels, Belgium: Conflict Prevention Network.

World Bank Group. 2010. World Development Indicators database. Washington, D.C.

Mitigating the environmental impacts of post-conflict assistance: Assessing USAID's approach

Charles Kelly

Donors frequently provide post-conflict assistance with the assumption that helping people in immediate need outweighs possible negative environmental consequences. Moreover, because of higher per capita levels of international assistance, the post-conflict period is usually characterized by more intense development than at times of peace. As development accelerates, the potential for adverse environmental impacts intensifies.

Providers of assistance and policy makers alike often believe that environmental reviews of assistance projects slow recovery and hinder clear demonstration of the peace dividends to conflict victims and, particularly, former combatants. Why wait six months for an environmental review when conflict-affected people need homes, jobs, and all the features of a peaceful society? Political interests and demand for quick recovery can lead to bypassing or ignoring environmental reviews, resulting in more damage to the environment, increased hardship for victims, and sowing seeds for future conflict.

Post-conflict assistance is one of several mechanisms used to build peace and often includes physical aid, such as rebuilding schools and infrastructure, together with capacity building, such as training and institutional development. The manner in which post-conflict assistance and, specifically, the management of natural resources are conducted is critical to successful peacebuilding. For example, if one group of former combatants believes another group benefits more from allocation of land for resettlement, conflict might arise.

This chapter describes attempts by one organization, the U.S. Agency for International Development (USAID), to balance the imperative for timely post-conflict assistance with the need to assess the environmental impacts of assistance.

Charles Kelly has over thirty years of experience in humanitarian assistance and has been involved in strengthening the incorporation of environmental issues into humanitarian response for the last fifteen years. He is a member of the ProAct Network and has worked in over forty-five countries on humanitarian activities. All views expressed in the chapter are those of the author, not those of any organization or entity. An earlier draft was reviewed by U.S. Agency for International Development staff.

The chapter focuses on four environmental-review documents that cover post-conflict assistance in Afghanistan, Indonesia, Uganda, and the West Bank and the Gaza Strip (West Bank/Gaza) (USAID 2006).[1] Each case is summarized, and issues arising from the four regions are discussed. The chapter concludes by identifying the strengths and challenges of the USAID environmental-review process.

USAID was selected because it follows clearly defined environmental-review policies and procedures after a conflict. The procedures have been used for decades and are well known within the organization and by most implementing partners. USAID requires that senior staff in Washington, D.C., concur with impact assessment results. The process somewhat tempers field-level pressure to overlook environmental issues in order to provide post-conflict assistance quickly.

USAID'S ENVIRONMENTAL REVIEWS

USAID's environmental-review procedures are set out in the Code of Federal Regulations at 22 CFR 216, commonly referred to as Regulation 216 (USAID 1976). After the Environmental Defense Fund sued USAID in 1975, the agency developed environmental-review procedures that reflected the U.S. National Environmental Policy Act (USAID 2004).

Regulation 216 includes two key exemptions—international disaster or emergency assistance and foreign-policy sensitivities (USAID 1976). The first exemption is commonly applied in initial stages following a conflict, when there are significant humanitarian needs. But the justification for the exemption diminishes with time; 180 days after a conflict should be sufficient time to plan longer-term assistance and implement review procedures.

In summary, USAID's environmental impact–review process involves the following:[2]

- An initial environmental examination (IEE) to determine whether there is need for further review of environmental issues. An IEE normally generates one of three outcomes: (1) a categorical exclusion, (2) a negative determination, or (3) a positive determination (USAID 1976). A *categorical exclusion* indicates that the proposed action has been determined in advance not to result in negative environmental impacts, and no further environmental review is needed.[3] A *negative determination* is given when no significant environmental

---

[1] The bureau environmental officer for USAID's Democracy, Conflict and Humanitarian Assistance Bureau provided the reviews for Afghanistan, Uganda, and West Bank/Gaza.
[2] The full set of USAID's environmental-review procedures can be found at www.usaid.gov/our_work/environment/compliance/regulations.html.
[3] Note that exclusions are at the review stage, whereas exemptions related to emergencies arise from policy and negate the need for environmental impact assessments. Where an exemption is used, there is an implicit reliance on minimal international technical standards for humanitarian assistance to address environmental issues or impacts.

impact is expected. A negative determination can be classed as "with conditions," indicating that the proposed action could have harmful effects on the environment. Measures to address these harmful effects can be incorporated into the project design without a more extensive environmental review. A negative determination with conditions is usually given when both the expected negative impacts and mitigation measures are understood. When an IEE indicates that no significant environmental issues exist, no further review is needed. A *positive determination* indicates that one or more significant negative impacts may occur. A positive determination triggers a scoping statement and full environmental review.

- A scoping statement to define issues that require further evaluation in the case of a positive determination at the IEE level.
- An environmental assessment, when an in-depth review of the proposed actions is needed based on a scoping statement. An environmental assessment identifies alternatives to proposed actions that may have significant negative impacts on the environment and defines a plan for mitigation and monitoring.

USAID environmental officers manage the review process. At the mission (field) level, there is at least one mission environmental officer (MEO). The MEO is backed by a regional environmental advisor (REA) and, at the Washington level, a bureau environmental officer (BEO).[4]

Many USAID officials—including technical staff and mission directors, overseas and office directors, and BEOs in Washington—need to approve environmental reviews. Employees are liable for negative audits and evaluations, and experienced staff realize that conducting environmental reviews prevents harm to intended beneficiaries and decreases problems with American taxpayers.

USAID has made considerable effort to formalize the review process and train agency staff and implementing partners. As a result, the agency has a clear step-by-step review process and a cadre of individuals, from USAID, partner organizations, and the private sector, who can undertake, manage, and complete processes for final evaluation and decisions by BEOs.

Afghanistan Stabilization Initiative

The U.S. government considers Afghanistan a "rebuilding country." The Afghanistan Stabilization Initiative, a US$35 million project, is intended to provide options for "advancing the writ of GIRoA" (USAID 2009b, 6).[5] USAID's activities, supported by the Office of Transition Initiatives (OTI), were to:

---

[4] For more information, see www.usaid.gov/our_work/environment/compliance/22cfr216.htm#216.3.
[5] The abbreviation *GIRoA* in quoted material refers to the government of the Islamic Republic of Afghanistan.

facilitate collaborative decision making processes related to small in-kind grant activities.

Other initial planned activities could include:

- Supporting local media organizations to assist them in providing accurate information to communities;
- Training GIRoA employees on stabilization programming best practices (USAID 2009b, 6).

These activities were to take place within two larger programmatic objectives to "create conditions that build confidence between communities and GIRoA through the improvement of the economic and social environment in the region; and, to increase public access to information about GIRoA's social, economic, and political activities and policies in Afghanistan" (USAID 2009b, 5).

The environmental impact–review process focused on the types of activities to be undertaken, such as repairing schools, rather than on specific activities, such as fixing particular schools based on damage reports. This lack of precision is common during transitions from conflict to recovery.

The documents considered by the environmental impact–review process included a program rationale; a summary of environmental conditions in Afghanistan; an evaluation of potential environmental impacts; recommendations on IEE determination and mitigation, monitoring, and evaluation; environmental-review procedures; guidance on staffing to support environmental issues; a section on environmentally sound design and management; Afghan environmental laws and regulations; USAID rules for pesticide use; and an environmental screening form and management plan. OTI contractors, who implemented the program, were to follow the guidance provided in the environmental-review document.

The IEE process led to two determinations:

- "A **Categorical Exclusion** from environmental examination [for] . . . short-term technical assistance, training for strategic planning, strategic communications, surveying/polling, financial management, commodity procurement, information dissemination, provision of equipment, dialogue support, media programming and transmission, communications support to government and NGOs, and creating public forums for communities" (USAID 2009b, 9).
- "A **Negative Determination with Conditions** . . . for projects involving activities such as repair and rehabilitation of public facilities (schools, clinics, government buildings, market places, parks, sidewalks, roads, flood controls, irrigation channels, small-scale water/sanitation projects), tree planting, small animal husbandry" (USAID 2009b, 9).

For the negative determination with conditions, guidance was provided on how to address or limit possible negative environmental impacts. For example, for road rehabilitation, reference was made to the chapter "Rural Roads," in *Environmental Guidelines for Small Scale Activities in Africa* (USAID 2009a), and *Low-Volume Roads Engineering: Best Management Practices Field Guide* (Keller and Sherar 2003).

The outcome of the IEE process also included an environmental screening form and an environmental management plan for use in assessing possible adverse environmental impacts and the risk of their occurring during the assistance effort. The results of the screening were to be used in identifying environmental risks that needed to be mitigated or avoided during implementation of project activities (USAID 2009b).

The environmental review was finalized in mid-May 2009, and the program was projected to start in June 2009. The review was conducted by the OTI Afghanistan program manager and was cleared by the USAID Afghanistan MEO, USAID Afghanistan mission director, Democracy, Conflict, and Humanitarian Assistance (DCHA)/OTI/Asia and Middle East (AME) team leader, DCHA/OTI director, and DCHA BEO, and was endorsed by the AME BEO and the USAID Asia REA.[6]

Indonesia: Immediate Support to Conflict-Affected Communities within the Framework of the Peace Agreement Implementation in Indonesia

Following the peace agreement between the government of Indonesia (GOI) and the Free Aceh Movement, the GOI requested assistance to aid conflict-affected communities in reintegrating former combatants into civil life (USAID 2006). The US$2 million project focused on supporting peace and sustainable reconstruction through quick-impact, community-focused development activities. USAID/Jakarta conducted the environmental impact–review process, and a grantee implemented the project.

The time frame and focus of assistance covered both the immediate and medium term at the individual and community levels. The project included a transitional reintegration package, information campaigns, counseling and referral services, infrastructure repair and reconstruction, training, support for cooperatives, social and cultural events, commodities requested by communities, and material support to restart livelihoods.

The environmental-review document included a summary of findings, recommended environmental actions, descriptions of activities, and discussion of environmental impacts.

It determined that livelihood assistance, training, meetings, information-related activities, materials provision, and technical assistance met the criteria for a categorical exclusion. Activities related to reconstruction, rehabilitation, agriculture, and similar efforts met the criteria for a negative determination with conditions. The conditions included submission of a pesticide evaluation report and safe-user plan (PERSUAP) and measures to limit environmental effects, including controlling erosion, legally sourcing building materials, managing wastewater, and providing fishing boats and equipment only to people who lost

---

[5] This level of consensus, which is standard for issuing a USAID review, was required for the other USAID review documents included in the chapter.

them because of the conflict. The conditions were presented in the review document as instructions to the grantee that implemented the project.

The review was prepared by USAID employees in early March 2006 and was approved within a week by USAID officials.

Uganda: Healthy Practices, Strong Communities Program (HPSC)

HPSC is intended to assist war-affected populations in the health and agricultural sectors in Northern Uganda. The goal of the US$19.8 million, five-year (2008–2013) program is to "support the return and economic recovery of selected communities in Northern Uganda that have been displaced for years by internal strife" (Mercy Corps 2009, 2).

The project involves activities in the following areas:

- *Agriculture.* Improving access to food by planting women's gardens and demonstration plots, working through existing peace structures, strengthening high-value agricultural value chains, increasing funding for producers, facilitating the provision of inputs (such as seeds and tools), improving animal health care, supporting extension agents, linking private and public institutions, using food-for-work programs to improve feeder roads, and adopting environmentally sound agricultural practices.
- *Health.* Bettering delivery of health care and nutrition by increasing access to mother-child health and nutrition services, training health-care staff, providing vitamin A supplements, improving health-seeking behavior, promoting optimal dietary practices, and promoting home gardens.
- *Water.* Increasing availability of safe water and sanitation facilities by assessing existing water points;[7] rehabilitating, constructing, and maintaining wells; promoting proper water storage; encouraging adoption of improved sanitation and hygiene practices; rehabilitating, constructing, and maintaining sanitary facilities; and promoting personal hygiene.

The environmental-review document included a summary of findings, a background and activity description, country and environmental information, recommended actions, an environmental management form, and a table setting out proposed activities and their environmental-impact determinations.

Most HPSC activities were covered by categorical exclusions. Activities related to small-scale gardening and rehabilitation, construction, and maintenance of sanitation facilities were given negative determinations.

Activities linked to increasing funds for producer groups and those involved in raising the value of products; providing inputs (e.g., non-pesticide-treated seeds and tools); improving feeder roads, agricultural demonstration plots, and diet diversification; and the rehabilitation and construction of water points received

---

[6] Water points are places from which people access water, such as wells, and water sources are places from which water originates, such as streams.

USAID's approach to mitigating impacts of post-conflict assistance 303

negative determinations with conditions. It is not clear why the rehabilitation, construction, and maintenance of sanitation facilities was given a negative determination, while rehabilitation and construction of water points was given a negative determination with conditions because both involve construction and possible indirect negative impacts on the environment (e.g., increased production of wastewater).

Actions to mitigate the negative environmental effects of activities with a negative determination with conditions were listed in the review document. The review also made considerable reference to USAID and other documents that offer guidance on how to mitigate or avoid negative environmental impacts.[8] The review document also referred to other USAID environmental reviews, such as a PERSUAP for pesticide and livestock treatment, which could be used to steer program activities.

The review document was first prepared in December 2007 and was revised in September 2009, in both cases by Mercy Corps staff. The revised review document was approved by USAID on November 24, 2009.

West Bank/Gaza Transition Initiative

The West Bank/Gaza Transition Initiative was intended to "respond to political openings following Palestinian leadership changes and Israel's disengagement from Gaza and parts of the northern West Bank" and had "two broad objectives to support emerging, moderate Palestinian leaders and strengthen civil society organizations, citizen groups, and other constituencies for peace to generate grassroots demand for change" (USAID 2007b, 4). The US$25 million project began in 2005, and the review document covered an extension from mid-2007 to mid-2009. The document was prepared by USAID and detailed how a contractor would conduct program activities.[9]

As in Afghanistan, the nature and location of program activities could not be determined at the time of review. Planned activities were divided into two groups:

- Social services and training, with a focus on local groups and civic education, information dissemination, and sports and livelihoods support.
- Repair, reconstruction, or construction of infrastructure, including repairs to public buildings; small-scale public works such as parks; and small-scale water supply, wastewater management, and transportation infrastructure.

The environmental-review document included a summary of findings, background and description of activities, information on the targeted region and

---

[7] See, for example, USAID (2007a).
[8] The USAID mechanism used to fund the project, Support Which Implements Fast Transitions (SWIFT), was also used in Afghanistan. SWIFT is an administrative arrangement under which USAID can contract vetted suppliers to implement services quickly.

environmental conditions, evaluation of environmental impacts, recommended mitigation activities, and impact-review instructions and forms.

The first set of program activities was given a categorical exclusion and the second, a negative determination with conditions. The review included procedures for minimizing or mitigating negative impacts discussed and referred to *Environmental Guidelines for Small Scale Activity in Asia Near East* (USAID n.d.), *Humanitarian Charter and Minimum Standards in Disaster Response* (Sphere Project 2004), and *Low-Volume Roads Engineering: Best Management Practices Field Guide* (Keller and Sherar 2003).

The review document said that the project had failed to follow USAID requirements for the use of pesticides by not earlier completing a PERSUAP. As a result, any pesticide use or training about pesticide use in the first set of activities was given a deferral, that is, a further review of activities was needed before any program activity could involve pesticides in any way.

The review document, which USAID staff drafted, was submitted for approval in mid-June and was approved by USAID on July 11, 2007.

DISCUSSION

The four environmental-review documents had similar structures, as expected in a standardized process, and likely drew on more detailed program descriptions. At the same time, the level of detail in the review documents varied; some documents, such as that on Uganda, were specific, and others, such as those on Afghanistan and West Bank/Gaza, were fairly general.

Use of categorical exclusions

The reviews made considerable use of the categorical exclusion option. For some programs, most of the planned activities were given categorical exclusions.

But the potential for cumulative and indirect impacts suggests a possible flaw in applying categorical exclusions. For example, former soldiers can be taught, under an activity covered by a categorical exclusion, how to make furniture to improve their livelihoods and fill a market need. The wood they use can come from local forests, which survive a conflict relatively undisturbed only to be overexploited because of increased demand for furniture and capacity to produce furniture created by the training program. The Indonesia review attempted to address indirect effects by providing boats only to previous boat owners. Similar consideration of indirect or cumulative impacts was not obvious in the other reviews.

Avoiding a positive determination

That none of the reviews resulted in a positive determination probably reflects three characteristics of the projects. First, they all involved routine activities such as repairing buildings or training. None of the projects involved building a large dam, opening virgin lands, or digging a mine, all efforts that would likely trigger a positive determination and require funding by international financial institutions or the private sector.[10]

Second, all the reviews incorporated mitigation measures for potential negative impacts or, in the case of West Bank/Gaza, because of a negative determination with conditions. Including mitigation measures accomplished the following:

- Lessened the likelihood of a positive determination.
- Reduced the likelihood of a negative determination with conditions, which is, in effect, a positive determination that can be resolved without a full environmental review.

The identification and resolution of environmental problems at the design stage is good practice. More importantly for the post-conflict situation, preemptive action on environmental issues can reduce the time needed for an environmental review and reduce delays in project implementation.

Third, the work and time burden that a positive determination can impose probably dissuaded project designers from selecting activities that could prompt a full assessment. Whether the threat of a positive determination prevented the selection of more effective activities than those actually chosen is unclear.

Flexibility through the use of standard references and guidance

The reviews indicated the extent to which USAID uses standard references and formats to guide the post-review process. As is common in USAID environmental reviews of projects in more peaceful parts of the world, several of the documents mentioned use of a PERSUAP to manage selection and application of pesticides.

Reference was also frequently made to standardized guidance, for instance the *Environmental Guidelines for Small-Scale Activities in Africa* (USAID 2007a) and the online resource *Environmental Guidelines for Small Scale Activity in Asia Near East* (USAID n.d.). Incorporation of these resources into the review document (as well as project documents) avoids the need for each program to develop guidance and procedures and saves time and effort in design and implementation.

The use of standard references and guidance also allows flexibility, which is useful after a conflict when projects must be implemented rapidly. Applying standard guidance to Afghanistan and the West Bank/Gaza, where specific activities were not identified in advance, led to identification of potential negative impacts and mitigation measures to be used in program implementation.

---

[9] None of the projects involved demining, which can open previously closed areas to exploitation and necessitate an extensive environmental review.

Structures for monitoring and evaluation

The USAID process also emphasizes regular monitoring, evaluation, and reporting. Although the monitoring varied in the four cases studied, it usually required completing the following:

- A separate environmental-review document for each activity before it began (for example, before rehabilitation of a road).
- An environmental review of every subproject, particularly when activities were not detailed in the initial review (for example, West Bank/Gaza).
- Regular reporting on a set of impact indicators, continuing the environmental review and monitoring during program implementation.

A progressive review also makes decisions on negative determinations with conditions easier because follow-up monitoring catches problems that might arise during a project.

Continual monitoring also allows program implementers more flexibility in designing activities and leads to a regular review of environmental impacts, as in Afghanistan and West Bank/Gaza. Flexibility is useful in post-conflict situations where there may be no time to generate the detailed program designs that are common in development assistance in situations not affected by conflict.

Post-conflict, peacebuilding, and environmental reviews

Uganda and Indonesia are clearly in the post-conflict period, while Afghanistan and West Bank/Gaza face ongoing conflict. Although the projects in all four areas aim to support peacebuilding, the Ugandan and Indonesian programs focus on building peace after a conflict, whereas those in Afghanistan and West Bank/Gaza concentrate on creating conditions for peace during conflict.

The Afghanistan, Indonesia, and West Bank/Gaza reviews tend to emphasize types of intervention, not locations and methodologies, and the need for quick approval and implementation. Clearly, urgent mid-conflict or immediate post-conflict environmental reviews have less information to work with and rely more on monitoring during a project to ensure that project activities comply with the review and good environmental practice. The case cited in the West Bank/Gaza review, in which a previous instruction to conduct a review of pesticide use was not followed, indicates that ongoing monitoring may not always be effective.

Compliance with local environmental-review procedures

Although national and local environmental governance structures in post-conflict countries may be weak, international assistance organizations—specifically, non-governmental organizations and contractors—are generally obliged to follow the laws of countries where they work. However, not all of the reviews presented in this chapter considered local environmental conditions and environmental regulations.

Complying with host country laws should be an integral element of the USAID review process, if only to speed implementation. Furthermore, as USAID uses the post-conflict period to bolster national and local capacities to manage environmental issues, the apparent failure to follow host-country laws is notable.

Beyond the natural environment

The four reviews focused primarily on the effects of recommended activities on the natural environment. None discussed links between the proposed actions and the potential social, economic, security, and political aspects associated with environmental impacts in the target locations. For example, the Afghanistan review did not cover the impact of repairing roads on illicit activities such as increased timber harvesting. The links may be covered in other USAID documents, but their absence made the reviews less thorough.

CONCLUSION

The four USAID environmental reviews covered in this chapter demonstrate that international assistance organizations can establish standard processes to conduct rapid environmental reviews, which do not delay project implementation. Four strengths of the USAID environmental-review process include a clearly defined process with well-trained staff and compliance; flexibility regarding the amount of information needed for a review; continual monitoring and review of environmental issues during project implementation; and the use of standard references and forms to guide the review process and help in implementing activities in an environmentally sound manner.

The USAID approach, nonetheless, faces several challenges. First, the extensive use of categorical exclusions may result in overlooking indirect and cumulative impacts. Although harmful environmental impacts may be identified and mitigated during the USAID monitoring process, identification of the impacts in advance might prevent them in the first place.

Second, the USAID process is labor intensive. Only individuals with specific skills and training can conduct the reviews, and they are not always available when needed. Finding individuals willing to work in demanding, often dangerous post-conflict situations is many times difficult. Moreover, USAID requires both project implementers and USAID staff to monitor programs regularly while working in difficult post-conflict environments.

Third, the assessment process seems generally limited to the physical impact of planned activities and does not consider social, economic, security, and political linkages, even though they should be examined during an environmental review, particularly when weighing indirect and cumulative impacts and cost-benefit trade-offs. Expanding the USAID process to consider these linkages would reduce unanticipated and unintended negative outcomes of international assistance.

Finally, as shown by the four case studies, USAID does not seem to systematically collaborate with local structures or necessarily observe local regulatory requirements when conducting rapid environmental reviews for development projects in conflict-affected situations. Opportunities to strengthen conflict-affected governments through peacebuilding are therefore lost.

The degree to which target populations were consulted during the reviews or on the environmental trade-offs incorporated into the final review decisions was not clear. Consultations with intended beneficiaries are a core principle of development assistance and should be part of the environmental-review process, even in conflict-affected countries.

Overall, USAID's environmental-review process appears well adapted for use in post-conflict situations. It does not impose long delays on implementation or demands for information not normally available from program-design documents. The process can be adopted or adapted by other organizations to help avoid negative impacts on post-conflict environments.

Indeed, if there were a uniform cross-donor process based on that of USAID, there would be a more consistent approach to identifying and addressing the potential adverse environmental impacts of post-conflict assistance. There could also be a single consolidated environmental review of similar activities funded by different donors.[11] A common process could also lead to more effective use of staff to serve several projects and organizations at the same time and more opportunities to involve national and local government and nonprofit sectors in reviewing and monitoring post-conflict and peacebuilding assistance. Combining environmental-review processes could facilitate and speed assistance, reduce negative environmental impacts, and certainly benefit conflict survivors. The key challenges would be coordination, consistent application, and compliance monitoring.

REFERENCES

Keller, G., and J. Sherar. 2003. *Low-volume roads engineering: Best management practices field guide*. Final report prepared for the United States Agency for International Development, in cooperation with the United States Forest Service and Virginia Polytechnic Institute and State University. www4.worldbank.org/afr/ssatp/Resources/HTML/LVSR/English/Added-2007/2003-LVR-Engineering-FieldGuide-USA-by-GKeller.pdf.

Mercy Corps. 2009. Uganda/Mercy Corps and IMC FY08-FY12 multi-year assistance program—Healthy Practices, Strong Communities program (HPSC). Kampala, Uganda.

---

[10] A USAID programmatic environmental assessment (PEA) covers a set of the same or similar activities in more than one location. For an example of a PEA, see www.ehproject.org/PDF/ehkm/ivm-env_assessment.pdf.

Sphere Project. 2004. *Humanitarian charter and minimum standards in disaster response.* Geneva, Switzerland. http://ocw.jhsph.edu/courses/refugeehealthcare/PDFs/SphereProject Handbook.pdf.

USAID (United States Agency for International Development). 1976. Environmental procedures. www.usaid.gov/our_work/environment/compliance/22cfr216.htm.

———. 2004. Legal and policy requirements related to environmental review of all USAID activities: Legal provisions affecting certain types of environmental activities. www.encapafrica.org/meo_resources/GenCounsel_re_Env_Rvw_Considerations_4-04.doc.

———. 2006. Environmental threshold decision. File No. ANE 06-60 Indonesia ETD immediate support. (On file with author.)

———. 2007a. *Environmental guidelines for small-scale activities in Africa: Environmentally sound design for planning and implementing development activities.* Washington, D.C. www.encapafrica.org/egssaa.htm#cover.

———. 2007b. USAID DCHA initial environmental examination and factsheet: West Bank/Gaza Transition Initiative. Washington, D.C.

———. 2009a. Rural roads. In *Environmental guidelines for small scale activities in Africa: Environmentally sound design for planning and implementing development activities.* Washington, D.C. www.encapafrica.org/EGSSAA/roads.pdf.

———. 2009b. USAID DCHA initial environmental examination (IEE) and factsheet: Afghanistan Stabilization Initiative. Washington, D.C.

———. n.d. *Environmental guidelines for small scale activity in Asia Near East.* www.usaid.gov/our_work/environment/compliance/ane/ane_guidelines.htm.

Challenges and opportunities for mainstreaming environmental assessment tools in post-conflict settings

George Bouma

The foundation of official development assistance (ODA) in post-conflict settings reflects the desire to build peace and stability, improve social dividends for the vulnerable and poor, and create self-sustaining governance and policy that encompass sustainable growth. Progress in this direction is supported by the program and project procedures of bilateral agencies and multilateral aid organizations. However, aid assistance in post-conflict situations is often geared more toward structural and macroeconomic governance than toward social and environmental dividends (Collier and Hoeffler 2004).

The rapid disbursement of financial resources on a large scale to alleviate urgent humanitarian needs and support post-conflict recovery and reconstruction often generates environmental risks. Periods of post-conflict rehabilitation are often characterized by hyperdevelopment, which may result in severe environmental impacts. For example, the need for an increased supply of timber for reconstruction can cause widespread deforestation.

This chapter examines issues surrounding the environmental sustainability of reconstruction investments in these settings—specifically the relevance and application of environmental impact assessment (EIA) and strategic environmental assessment (SEA).[1]

The chapter begins by discussing the integration of environmental issues within post-conflict ODA and then compares environmental assessment methodologies—including for EIA, SEA, and their streamlined variants—as applied in post-conflict

---

George Bouma is a policy advisor for the Environment and Energy Group in the Bureau for Development Policy at the United Nations Development Programme in New York. Between 2004 and 2009, he worked as a staff member and consultant to post-conflict and post-disaster projects for the United Nations Environment Programme in Afghanistan, China, Indonesia, Mongolia, Rwanda, Sudan, and Ukraine.

[1] SEA can apply either to proposed or existing plans, policies, or programs. They may be stand-alone procedures or integrated into the formulation of the plan, policy, or program.

312 Assessing and restoring natural resources in post-conflict peacebuilding

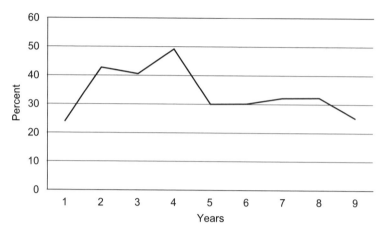

Figure 1. Average per capita official development assistance as a percentage of gross domestic product in years following peace agreement for five selected countries
Source: Compiled by author with data from the World Bank (2011).
Note: The selected countries are Afghanistan, the Democratic Republic of the Congo, Ethiopia, Rwanda, and Timor-Leste.

situations. Environmental assessment tools, if they are to be applied consistently, must seek an entry point through the ODA process. The chapter identifies three such points: donor assistance databases, UN multi-donor trust funds, and the annual work plans of the UN and its partners. The chapter proceeds with an examination of these three tools in pilot studies in Afghanistan, Iraq, and Darfur, respectively. It concludes with a discussion of lessons learned, lessons that suggest that streamlined SEA and other tailored environmental assessment methodologies may be more effective than traditional EIA procedures for understanding the environmental implications of reconstruction plans in a post-conflict situation and for prioritizing mitigation measures.

INTEGRATING ENVIRONMENTAL ISSUES WITHIN POST-CONFLICT OFFICIAL DEVELOPMENT ASSISTANCE

ODA tends to peak in the years immediately following a peace agreement and to gradually decline thereafter (see figure 1). External private investment does occur in post-conflict situations, but because of the risks in such environments, it is usually in the form of small- and medium-sized enterprises seeking marginal gains from small investments. ODA constitutes the majority of capital flow after conflict, so it is the primary avenue for bringing peace and stability (Schwartz and Halkyard 2006).

In 2008, funding to fragile states represented 31 percent (US$34.6 billion) of all ODA to developing countries, with 51 percent of that assistance benefiting just six out of forty-three fragile states and territories (OECD 2009).[2] The capacity for disbursement of ODA is dependent on governance and on policy development with a broad range of stakeholders (Collier and Hoeffler 2004). Where governance is weak and policy development around environmental issues is poorly framed, sustainability is unlikely to figure prominently in the post-conflict period (Verheem et al. 2005). A failure to integrate environmental sustainability into development policy is common in developing countries (Hugé and Hens 2007), and this situation is exacerbated in post-conflict countries, where national development and poverty-reduction strategies take years to evolve.

Yet aid to post-conflict countries needs to be more effective if the Millennium Development Goals are to be achieved by 2015 (McGillvray and Feeney 2008).[3] This includes goal 7, the achievement of environmental sustainability, which has as much relevance in fragile states as anywhere else because a society that projects itself onto a sustainable development pathway may have less chance of relapsing into conflict (International Development Association 2004; UNEP 2009). At the same time, conflicts can have a wide array of environmental effects, including direct effects, such as degradation of land and water by pollution, destruction, and waste; indirect effects, such as overuse of natural resources caused by displacement and dislocation of local communities; and institutional effects, such as destruction of infrastructure and institutional capacity, which can slow development. Post-conflict migration can place increasing demands on services and infrastructure, making environmental health issues a larger problem and further exacerbating poverty brought on by the conflict. These issues need to be taken into account in the allocation of ODA to post-conflict countries and in the design, approval, and implementation of reconstruction projects. Both EIA and SEA have been proposed as tools to meet this objective.

COMPARING EIA AND SEA IN POST-CONFLICT SITUATIONS

EIA is a robust methodology that can aid decision makers in understanding both the positive and negative impacts of a development project on natural resources and the environment. It integrates both social and environmental sustainability in the assessment process (Cashmore, Bond, and Sadler 2009; Elling 2009; Sadler 1996, 2004; Weaver et al. 2008; Westman 1985; Wood 2003). In the developed world, the effectiveness and limitations of a project-based EIA are well understood.

---

[2] In a fragile state, the government lacks capacity and willingness to perform key state functions for the benefit of all. The effects of fragility stretch beyond poor services to include conflict, state collapse, loss of territorial control, extreme political instability, clientelist policies, and repression of or denial of resources to subgroups of the population. Post-conflict countries form a specific subset of fragile states. The six fragile states and territories that benefitted the most from ODA in 2008 were Iraq, Afghanistan, Ethiopia, the West Bank and the Gaza Strip, Sudan, and Uganda.

[3] For more information on the Millennium Development Goals, see www.unmillenniumproject.org/goals/index.htm.

However, in the developing world, policy, governance, and technical challenges reduce its effectiveness (Ali 2007; Kolhoff, Runhaar, and Driessen 2009; Rajaram and Das 2008; Rossouw and Wiseman 2004; Wood 2003). Major challenges for developing countries include incomplete regulatory frameworks, weak governance capacities, limited technical skills, and a lack of government administration and private sector engagement.

These challenges are exacerbated in post-conflict situations where transitional governments often perform the functions of a state until democratic elections occur. Until laws can be passed and implemented by legitimate government authorities, EIA processes are generally applied by development agencies in concert with their own policies and practices. Often EIA obligations are relaxed if the situation calls for emergency assistance.[4] In many cases, EIAs are seen as an additional administrative burden to reconstruction processes and provoke calls for fast-track mechanisms.

EIAs are not easily performed in post-conflict countries where there is weak governance, poor or confusing legal frameworks, insufficient technical skills, and limited baseline data. For example, in Afghanistan from 2004 to 2006, only six environmental impact statement documents were provided to the National Environmental Protection Agency. These were submitted only for information and comment and not for approval as required under law.[5] In Ethiopia, the EIA system has developed more as a result of donors' demands than as a response to the desires of politicians and decision makers (Ruffeis et al. 2010). As a result, it has been a top-down process that often lacks national ownership and consistent application.

Addressing environmental and social safeguards in bilateral reconstruction projects through EIAs is not prominent in post-conflict situations. Post-conflict governments are often overwhelmed with coordinating aid and understanding institutional responsibilities. Adding environmental criteria into this process is not a priority. Furthermore, it can take ten or more years to develop a functional project-based EIA system that is fully integrated into the fabric of governance and applied as a decision-making tool. Given these constraints, alternative approaches are needed in post-conflict countries.

SEAs may provide an alternative tool kit. If EIAs focus on positive and negative environmental impacts at the project level, SEAs move one level up by focusing on policies, programs, and plans. The 2005 Paris Declaration on Aid Effectiveness, which addresses increasing donor effectiveness and national ownership, calls for donors and partners to "develop and apply common approaches for 'strategic environmental assessment' at the sector and national levels" (OECD 2005, 7).

---

[4] See, for example, Charles Kelly, "Mitigating the Environmental Impacts of Post-Conflict Assistance: Assessing USAID's Approach," in this book.
[5] Personal experience of author as international focal point for EIA capacity building in Afghanistan.

A comprehensive description of the SEA process is contained within the Organisation for Economic Co-operation and Development (OECD) guidelines, *Applying Strategic Environmental Assessment: Good Practice Guidance for Development Co-operation* (OECD 2006). Two characteristics of the SEA process should be highlighted. First, SEA is a family of approaches that uses a variety of tools; it is not a single, fixed, prescriptive approach. Second, a good SEA is tailor-made for the context in which it is applied. This means that an SEA process can be designed with the existing post-conflict institutional capacity and legal framework taken into consideration, and with the option for elaboration as capacities increase or laws change.

With the growing acceptance of SEA, there are emerging views about its application in post-conflict situations (OECD 2006, 2008; Verheem et al. 2005). To date, there is limited evidence of its successful use in the development of post-conflict policies, programs, and plans. A common theme in the literature is recognition of various phases in post-conflict processes and the need to find suitable entry points for each phase (Verheem et al. 2005; OECD 2008). Rob Verheem and colleagues identify three broad areas in which SEA has a role to play in post-conflict situations: when environmental issues or natural resources are a source of conflict; when badly planned reconstruction actions may seriously damage the environment; and when environmental programming could open opportunities to strengthen cooperation, democratization, or other peacebuilding activities (Verheem et al. 2005). Given these criteria, there are few if any post-conflict situations in which SEAs would not apply.

The OECD SEA guidance suggests that a full SEA will be effective only where an institution (usually a state institution) exists in a country that has a mandate, the capacity, and the willingness to follow up on the key results of the actions agreed to in the SEA (OECD 2006). Another critical precondition for undertaking an SEA is that stakeholders are both willing and able to participate without risk. As these conditions do not often exist in a post-conflict country, the OECD has also issued a specific guidance, *Strategic Environmental Assessment (SEA) and Post-Conflict Development* (OECD 2008). This guidance describes how a streamlined SEA process can be designed to take into account the unique conditions of a post-conflict country.[6] The guidance specifically identifies potential entry points that could be used as the starting point for an SEA process. These include donor assistance databases, UN multi-donor trust funds, and UN work plans. The main aim of using these instruments is to identify the sectors that may cause the largest potential environmental impact so practitioners can focus on a broad set of mitigation measures or safeguards.

---

[6] A streamlined SEA typically is conducted more rapidly, with less consultation, and may focus on fewer issues (that is, the issues of greatest significance). It also needs to make use of existing baseline data through the use of quick appraisal techniques, with less time to collect new data, let alone generate new data.

THREE CASE STUDIES

The following sections summarize experiences and lessons learned in using donor assistance databases, UN multi-donor trust funds, and UN work plans in Afghanistan, Iraq, and Darfur, respectively. The objective of the analysis is to examine these three instruments to determine whether they provide suitable platforms and entry points for streamlined SEA or other environmental assessment processes.

Afghanistan's donor assistance database, 2004–2005

Afghanistan's 1383–1384 (2004–2005) national development budget was coordinated through its Ministry of Finance with assistance from the World Bank.[7] With a total value of US$4.2 billion, the budget received most of its funding from ODA. In order to centralize, track, and coordinate donor projects, a donor assistance database (DAD) was established. In 2004–2005, the DAD included 432 projects that either had been funded or were in the process of being funded.[8] Within the database, an information sheet for each project was included, containing information on the budget, start and end dates, proponents, and implementation status, as well as a summary of the major outputs. Projects involved UN agencies, nongovernmental organizations (NGOs), and government ministries and bodies.

In order to understand the scope and magnitude of potential environmental impacts of the various projects, the National Environmental Protection Agency, with the support of UNEP, developed a system of environmental markers within the DAD. Each project information sheet required project proponents to categorize potential environmental impacts according to three main grades: a grade of A meant that there was potential for significant environmental impacts; a B indicated that there was potential for moderate impacts; and a C signified potential for small or insignificant impacts.

However, problems eventually arose with the consistency of the categorization process. As a result, the Ministry of Finance modified the approach and thereafter required proponents only to flag any project that may have an impact on the environment (a binary yes/no marker). In 2004–2005, a total of 188 projects out of a total of 432 (44 percent) were identified as likely to have some impact on the environment (a breakdown by sector is shown in table 1). This analysis was an important first step toward understanding the potential magnitude of environmental impacts from donor projects, as well as the distribution of those impacts among sectors. It was an essential step toward identifying the sectors most at risk and in need of further attention and analysis. However, the main limitation of the approach was that the database lacked any information on the magnitude or geographic location of each project, so it was difficult to understand which specific resources could be affected and what the cumulative impacts could

---

[7] Afghanistan, as a Muslim country, operates on a lunar calendar.
[8] The author assessed the database while working for UNEP in Afghanistan.

Table 1. Outcome of the environmental review for Afghanistan's donor assistance database, 2004–2005

Sector and subsector	Number of projects	
Energy, mining, and telecommunications	50	
Energy generation and supply		26
Mineral resources, mining, and energy		24
Transport	41	
Road infrastructure		36
Other		5
Natural resource management	75	
Irrigation (including emergency projects)		31
Livelihoods (food and livestock)		14
Forest, rangeland, and resource management		23
Governance and policy development		7
Urban development and management	22	
Land use planning		3
Infrastructure (roads)		3
Water and sanitation		16
TOTAL	188	

be. It therefore fell short of a full SEA, but it did generate important lessons. Furthermore, the political will to actually implement environmental safeguards for projects with potential impacts eventually weakened.

Iraq Trust Fund, 2004–2005

Sustainable development was one of the guiding principles in the Iraq reconstruction program. The UN strategy for Iraq recognized the need to mainstream environmental and natural resources management within all operations and policies, reflecting the recent drive toward the achievement of the Millennium Development Goals (GOI and UN 2008). Building on experiences from Afghanistan, a new approach was pilot tested in Iraq. All UN projects submitted to the Iraq Multi-Donor Trust Fund (also called the Iraq Trust Fund) would undergo an environmental screening and categorization process to determine their potential impacts prior to approval. However, rather than UN agencies being asked to grade the environmental impact of their projects, proposals were evaluated by an environmental expert from UNEP, who sorted the projects into three categories: A for projects with potential for significant impacts; B for projects with potential for moderate impacts; and C for projects with potential for small or insignificant impacts. For each project, UNEP provided an analysis of the potential environmental impacts, coupled with mitigation recommendations at the project and sector levels. This approach focused on only UN agencies since these agencies would be more likely to adhere to an overall policy directive through the UN country team and that they would therefore comply with mitigation recommendations.

In the 2004–2005 period, the total value of the Iraq Trust Fund was estimated at US$1.5 billion. Within this figure, a total of forty-seven UN projects representing nearly US$350 million (23 percent of the Iraq Trust Fund budget) were assessed for environmental impacts (UNEP 2006). The forty-seven projects were divided among four main clusters: agriculture, food security, environment, and natural resource management (cluster A); education and culture (cluster B); health and nutrition (cluster D); and infrastructure and rehabilitation (cluster E). Projects in the other clusters—governance and human development (cluster C), internally displaced persons and durable solutions (cluster F), and support to the electoral process (cluster G)—either were considered to be of an urgent humanitarian nature or did not involve physical infrastructure and were therefore not assessed for environmental impacts.

The results of the assessment are listed in table 2. In total, eleven out of the forty-seven projects (23 percent) were classified as category A, while fourteen out of the forty-seven projects were category B (30 percent). According to the findings from the screening process, the three most common potential environmental impacts in the reviewed projects (over 50 percent) involved the protection of surface-water quality and quantity; the safe disposal of solid wastes; and the sustainable use of biological resources, including plants, trees, wildlife, and fisheries. Potential impacts in the areas of air quality and groundwater quality were also identified in more than 30 percent of the projects.

Although the original intention of the screening process was to help UN agencies identify and mitigate potential environmental impacts across projects and development sectors, not a single project was amended and no safeguards were adopted. The administrator of the Iraq Trust Fund eventually determined that the outcome of the environmental screening was only "for consideration" by project proponents. There was no requirement to demonstrate that potential project impacts had been mitigated, nor was the question of mitigation considered during the final project approval process. Furthermore, no efforts were conducted to address the potential environmental impacts across the main sectors, nor the cumulative effects. The UN system backed down from adhering to the Millennium Development Goals because this was not a priority of the Iraqi administration.

There are a number of additional reasons why projects were not amended to mitigate environmental impacts. First, the majority of projects were reviewed only during the approval stage and not during project design. Donors and agency headquarters had already signed off on the projects, and additional revisions would have led to significant delays—an outcome that was not desirable given the urgent needs and the pressure to meet those needs. A second reason is that the Iraq Trust Fund did not allocate funds for mitigation. Eighty percent of the Iraq Trust Fund was already earmarked, so it was difficult to increase project costs in order to address potential environmental concerns. Third, many agencies lacked the technical expertise to redesign the projects in order to mitigate environmental impacts. Finally, although some agencies noted that they would attempt to minimize

Table 2. Outcome of the environmental review for the Iraq Trust Fund, 2004–2005

Cluster	Number of projects	
Cluster A: Agriculture, food security, environment, and natural resource management	17	
Category A		2
Category B		5
Category C		10
Cluster B: Education and culture	6	
Category A		0
Category B		1
Category C		5
Cluster C: Governance and human development	N/A	
Cluster D: Health and nutrition	7	
Category A		1
Category B		2
Category C		4
Cluster E: Infrastructure and rehabilitation	17	
Category A		8
Category B		6
Category C		3
Cluster F: Internally displaced persons and durable solutions	N/A	
Cluster G: Support to the electoral process	N/A	
TOTALS	47	
Category A		11
Category B		14
Category C		22

Notes: Category A: Projects with potential for significant environmental impacts. Category B: Projects with potential for moderate environmental impacts. Category C: Projects with potential for small or insignificant environmental impacts. Clusters C, F, and G were not assessed because they were considered to be of an urgent humanitarian nature or did not involve infrastructure.

impacts during the implementation process, there was no mechanism to verify this claim, so the level of compliance with this commitment is unknown.

The experience in screening UN projects supported by the Iraq Trust Fund illustrates both the potential and limitations of SEA—even streamlined SEA—in post-conflict settings. Aggregating the environmental screening results for many projects provides insights into the types of projects that are most likely to have potential environmental impacts, as well as the types of impacts that are of greatest concern. However, there was no evidence of analysis of cumulative environmental impacts—one of the central aspects of SEA. Moreover, the screening sought to inform specific projects, perhaps because most of the funding had already been allocated, so a programmatic approach would not have had as much impact as one that focused on the existing proposed projects. As such, the environmental-review process provided a vision of how a streamlined SEA might be pursued, even if it was not effective in this particular context.

UN and Partners Work Plan for Sudan, 2008

Given the high level of resource scarcity and environmental degradation in Darfur, a strategy for mainstreaming environmental assessments was also pilot tested for the UN and Partners Work Plan for Sudan in 2008, covering UN and NGO humanitarian and recovery projects. UNEP environmental experts screened the projects, using the 2008 Work Plan Projects Database, and categorized the projects by sector into impact categories.[9] The overall objective of the screening was to identify projects that either addressed environmental needs or had the potential for environmental impacts. The intended outcome was to promote sustainable resource management across all projects and major sectors of the work plan. Feedback was provided to project proponents in each sector on the level of impact and options for environmental management, including sustainable forestry and energy management, alternative construction technologies, and integrated water resource management.

The initial review was concerned with the assessment of projects recorded in the Work Plan Projects Database and occurring in the Darfur region only. Of 197 such projects, valued at US$935 million, 109 (55 percent), valued at US$230 million, were identified as likely to have some environmental impact (a breakdown by sector is shown in table 3). Eventually the review process was expanded to cover the entire Sudan work plan. A total of 396 projects were identified, valued at US$787 million (nearly 35 percent of the total work plan budget).

Aggregating the results of the environmental reviews of the various projects identified some of the most common environmental impacts. The most common potential impacts centered around the unsustainable use of groundwater, fuelwood, and construction materials, in particular near camps for internally displaced persons. The need to address the sustainable management of natural resources in support of livelihood recovery programs was also a common issue, as was waste management. Another interesting observation was that UN agencies were responsible for the larger-scale and more complex projects, while NGOs were responsible for many smaller projects. This finding had important implications for the targeting of mitigation measures.

The screening process had two major benefits. First, the UN country team and partners began to understand the potential environmental impacts of each sector and started to more systematically include environmental issues from the outset of project design. Second, groundwater monitoring finally became a common practice for all water and sanitation projects across Darfur and a key sectoral safeguard.

---

[9] The author assessed the database while working for UNEP in Sudan.

Table 3. Outcome of the environmental review for the Sudan Work Plan Projects Database, 2008

Sector and project description	Number of projects	
Building construction	25	
Schools, clinics, and similar building construction		25
Humanitarian	15	
Food aid supply/agricultural substitution		2
Camp operation		1
Provision of shelter materials		12
Health	27	
Health clinic operation and mobile immunization programs		27
Infrastructure	5	
Rehabilitation or maintenance of highways or rural roads		3
Irrigation and drainage—small scale		2
Livelihoods	7	
Livestocking/veterinary programs—large scale		7
Mine action	2	
Mine action—large scale		2
Water and sanitation	28	
Rural water supply and sanitation		26
Humanitarian water supply and wastewater collection and treatment—medium to large		2
TOTAL	**109**	

The screening approach was replicated in the 2009 work plan. In addition, a specific budget line of US$1 million from the Common Humanitarian Fund, known as the Green Pot, was available to kick-start new ways of mitigating the environmental impacts of humanitarian response.

The heightened environmental awareness that resulted from the screening process had a major influence on the approach taken during the drafting of the UN Development Assistance Framework (UNDAF) for 2009–2012.[10] Development priorities were organized according to four main pillars: peacebuilding; governance, rule of law, and capacity building; livelihoods and productive sectors; and basic services. Detailed environmental outcomes were included for each pillar, together with budgets and lists of responsible organizations and partners. The total combined natural resource management projects amounted to US$419 million, approximately 18 percent of the total UNDAF budget (US$2.3 billion).

---

[10] UNDAF is an understanding between the UN country team and a host-country government regarding activities deemed to be the most effective in achieving national development goals.

LESSONS LEARNED

All three cases demonstrate that these instruments—donor assistance databases, UN multi-donor trust funds, and UN work plans—can be an initial starting point for conducting environmental assessments in post-conflict situations. This includes both screening for project-specific impacts and aggregating those reviews into broader sectoral assessments—a process that may lead to an SEA or a de facto streamlined SEA. At the very least, the proportion of projects that may have an environmental impact can be identified, together with the key sectors and actors. However, transforming this information into a full SEA leading to changes in plans, policies, and programs has been more challenging.

One of the main challenges relates to information accuracy and consistency of impact grading. The accuracy of each grade depends on the quality of the data supplied by a range of stakeholders, as well as a common understanding of what constitutes an environmental impact. In Afghanistan, project information sheets contained wide variation in the amount of project information that was provided. Although practitioners were required to flag projects that would have some impact on the environment, there was often inadequate guidance about what constituted an impact. Also, practitioners who believed that a high grade could lead to project delays may have had an incentive to misclassify their projects. The many project managers from various agencies and NGOs also varied in their technical competence and attitudes toward environmental mainstreaming; this also led to a great deal of variation in the tendency to flag projects for potential environmental impacts.

Where UNEP undertook the classification of projects, as it did in Sudan and Iraq, a consistent categorization approach was developed. However, in many cases, project information sheets and associated project documents did not contain sufficient information to make an accurate classification. In particular, the precise geographic locations, scale of the projects, and environmental baseline conditions were not included.

The downside of using an external entity to conduct a screening process for environmental impacts was also revealed when the number of projects exceeded a certain threshold. Screening forty-seven projects in the Iraq Trust Fund was manageable for a single expert, but screening all 396 projects in the Sudan work plan was not. Furthermore, many of the projects require screening in parallel, rather than sequentially, and thus require a significant increase in screening capacity. Third-party screening can also shift responsibility away from project proponents. If proponents are not involved in the classification process and do not take some level of ownership at the outset, it is possible that they will not undertake environmental mitigation measures during project implementation.

Another challenge relates to the selection of projects to include in the screening process. In both Afghanistan and Iraq, all projects of a humanitarian nature were excluded from the screening process, even if they had potential implications for environmental factors such as water quality. Because humanitarian projects were considered life-saving in nature, potential approval delays caused by the need to mitigate environmental impacts were not seen as justifiable. This mind-set eventually changed with the Sudan work plan, when all projects, both humanitarian and recovery, were included in the screening process. One of the main lessons learned from Darfur is that humanitarian operations associated with camps for internally displaced persons have significant environmental impacts caused by unsustainable use of groundwater, fuelwood, and construction materials. The mitigation of those impacts in subsequent years demonstrated the utility of the screening process—and shaped programmatic development and delivery.

Finally, this analysis revealed that basic environmental management requirements are poorly integrated into donor and UN projects, despite higher-level policy directives and commitments to sustainability. Myriad recovery projects have been implemented in which the majority of proponents had little or no exposure to environmental training or the sustainable management of natural resources. Furthermore, even when potential environmental impacts of projects and sectors were identified by third parties and technical assistance was offered to mitigate impacts, few proponents changed their project design. In the case of Iraq, UN agencies were not required to adopt mitigation plans prior to project approval, despite a high-level commitment to sustainability within the overall work plan. Furthermore, no monitoring or compliance mechanisms were in place for project proponents who did make specific mitigation commitments.

If these screening instruments are to be used as the entry points for conducting post-conflict environmental assessments in the future, several conditions need to be met. First, a consistent way to categorize environmental impacts needs to be established at the outset, together with a clear allocation of responsibility. Ideally, project proponents should be required to undertake the classification and to consider environmental issues at the outset of project design. Only when an insufficient number of proponents have the capacity to conduct the classification should third parties take responsibility.

Second, all projects—humanitarian as well as recovery and development—should undergo environmental screening. This screening is important both for reducing the environmental side effects of the projects and for guiding sectoral approaches. Systematic screening of all projects and aggregation of the screening results will help to identify the projects and sectors that are most in need of environmental mitigation.

Third, additional information should be incorporated into project information sheets, in particular simple geographic coding. This would allow a more fine-scale review of geographic areas where projects are to be concentrated and a better analysis of potential impacts and cumulative effects.

Finally, national stakeholders need support to identify and mitigate the environmental risks inherent in relevant sectors and to develop capacity for compliance monitoring. Environmental screening and SEA can be initial starting points for mitigating environmental impacts at the sector level, but a broader policy of project-specific EIA should eventually be adopted. Capacity-building programs should keep longer-term EIA needs in mind as SEA approaches are developed.

CONCLUSIONS

When ODA to a post-conflict country reflects national policy priorities, a basis can be created for an effective reconstruction strategy that is supported by a well-coordinated aid-management architecture (Schiavo-Campo 2003). However, the rapid disbursement of financial resources on a large scale to alleviate urgent humanitarian needs and to support post-conflict recovery and reconstruction often generates environmental risks. This chapter has reviewed alternative approaches to assessing and mitigating environmental risks, together with potential entry points.

In most post-conflict countries, establishing a traditional project-based EIA system is not feasible or is inhibited by weak legal, policy, and technical capacity. Nascent environmental protection agencies that lack political authority and financing often struggle with cumbersome EIA processes. Baseline data on the environment have often been lost or destroyed or are not current, and there is often little political will to establish environmental safeguards. Members of the private sector often fail to understand the benefits of EIA processes. Finally, public participation is often lacking, and people tend to be unaware of their rights concerning natural resources. It can take ten years, or more, to establish a functional EIA system that is integrated into the fabric of governance and applied as a decision-making tool.

Unless significant additional technical resources are provided, traditional EIA approaches will not be prepared to grapple with the large inflows of ODA that occur in post-conflict periods. The application of tailor-made environmental assessment approaches is an alternative model.

This chapter has reviewed lessons learned from using donor assistance databases, UN multi-donor trust funds, and UN work plans as entry points to screen for major environmental impacts across project sectors. These sectors can be identified on the basis of the number, location, and type of projects being undertaken. The process enables practitioners to recognize the main environmental risks associated with each sector so they can establish a range of environmental safeguards. Streamlined SEA processes can also help to identify substantial cumulative effects of plans, programs, and policies—especially in a particular sector—that might be missed in a process that only considers potential impacts of individual projects. Such approaches could aid in the integration of sustainability efforts into post-conflict development and could be an important step toward the achievement of 2005 Paris Declaration aims and the Millennium Development Goals. In implementing a streamlined SEA, however, it is essential that the assessment be undertaken sufficiently early in the process that it can inform the development and implementation of the plan, program, or policy.

Use of the instruments assessed in this chapter is one approach for identifying priority sectors and issues. There is definitely scope for developing other approaches with broader social and environmental aims. Whatever methods are employed, they need to be flexible and must be undertaken within relatively rapid time frames, given the dynamic pace of post-conflict development.

ODA tends to operate according to neoliberal principles of development, prioritizing the establishment of a market-oriented economy in fledgling democracies recovering from conflict. Where natural resources are abundant, there is often a reliance on commercial exploitation of these resources to drive growth and stability in an insecure environment, and social and environmental considerations can often be overlooked, with negative consequences for communities and livelihoods. If there is to be a shift in the development paradigm in post-conflict situations toward sustainability, there is a pressing need for environmental assessments (including SEAs) to be applied to ODA. Reviews of donor assistance databases, UN multi-donor trust funds, and work plans can help to identify risks and inform sector-wide mitigation approaches. This strategy should be further developed, with commitments from donor countries, aid agencies, NGOs, the UN system, and recipient governments.

REFERENCES

Ali, O. M. M. 2007. Policy and institutional reforms for an effective EIA system in Sudan. *Journal of Environmental Assessment, Policy, and Management* 9:67–82.

Cashmore, M., A. Bond, and B. Sadler. 2009. Introduction: The effectiveness of impact assessment instruments. *Impact Assessment and Project Appraisal* 27 (2): 91–93.

Collier, P., and A. Hoeffler. 2004. *Aid, policy and growth in post-conflict societies.* World Bank Policy Research Working Paper No. 2902. Washington, D.C.: World Bank.

Elling, B. 2009. Rationality and effectiveness: Does EIA/SEA treat them as synonyms? *Impact Assessment and Project Appraisal* 27 (2): 121–132.

GOI (Government of Iraq) and UN (United Nations). 2008. *United Nations Iraq assistance strategy 2008–2010.* http://planipolis.iiep.unesco.org/upload/Iraq/Iraq-UN_Assistance-Strategy-2008-2010.pdf.

Hugé, J., and L. Hens. 2007. Sustainability assessment of poverty reduction strategy papers. *Impact Assessment and Project Appraisal* 25 (4): 247–258.

International Development Association. 2004. *Aid delivery in conflict-affected IDA countries: The role of the World Bank.* Washington, D.C. http://siteresources.worldbank.org/IDA/Resources/AidDeliveryConflictAffectedIDAcountries.pdf.

Kolhoff, A. J., H. A. C. Runhaar, and P. J. Driessen. 2009. The contribution of capacities and context to EIA system performance and effectiveness in developing countries: Towards better understanding. *Impact Assessment and Project Appraisal* 27 (4): 271–282.

McGillvray, M., and S. Feeney. 2008. *Aid and growth in fragile states.* Research Paper No. 2008/03. Helsinki, Finland: United Nations University / World Institute for Development Economics Research.

OECD (Organisation for Economic Co-operation and Development). 2005. Paris declaration on aid effectiveness. Paris. www.unrol.org/files/34428351.pdf.

———. 2006. *Applying strategic environmental assessment: Good practice guidance for development co-operation*. DAC Guidelines and Reference Series. Paris.

———. 2008. *Strategic environmental assessment (SEA) and post-conflict development*. Paris. www.oecd.org/dataoecd/51/58/42628169.pdf.

———. 2009. *Ensuring fragile states are not left behind*. Paris. www.oecd.org/dataoecd/50/30/42463929.pdf.

Rajaram, T., and A. Das. 2008. A methodology for integrated assessment of rural linkages in a developing nation. *Impact Assessment and Project Appraisal* 26 (2): 99–113.

Rossouw, N., and K. Wiseman. 2004. Learning from the implementation of environmental public policy instruments after the first ten years of democracy in South Africa. *Impact Assessment and Project Appraisal* 22 (2): 131–140.

Ruffeis, D., W. Loiskandl, S. B. Awulachew, and E. Boelee. 2010. Evaluation of the environmental policy and impact assessment process in Ethiopia. *Impact Assessment and Project Appraisal* 28 (1): 29–40.

Sadler, B. 1996. *Environmental assessment in a changing world: Evaluating practice to improve performance*. Ottawa: Canadian Environmental Assessment Agency.

———. 2004. On evaluating the success of EIA and SEA. In *Assessing impact: Handbook of EIA and SEA follow-up*, ed. A. Morrison-Saunders and J. Arts. London: Earthscan.

Schiavo-Campo, S. 2003. Financing and aid management arrangements in post-conflict situations. Conflict Prevention and Reconstruction Working Papers No. 6. Washington, D.C.: Environmentally and Socially Sustainable Development Network.

Schwartz, J., and P. Halkyard. 2006. *Post-conflict infrastructure: Trends in aid and investment flows*. Washington, D.C.: World Bank. http://rru.worldbank.org/documents/publicpolicyjournal/305Schwartz_Halkyard.pdf.

UNEP (United Nations Environment Programme). 2006. Lessons learned: Environmental review of the Iraq Multi-Donor Trust Fund. Unpublished report. Geneva, Switzerland.

———. 2009. *From conflict to peacebuilding: The role of natural resources and the environment*. Nairobi, Kenya. http://postconflict.unep.ch/publications/pcdmb_policy_01.pdf.

Verheem, R., R. Post, J. Switzer, and B. Klem. 2005. *Strategic environmental assessments: Capacity-building in conflict-affected countries*. Social Development Paper. Washington D.C.: World Bank.

Weaver, A., J. Pope, A. Morrison-Saunders, and P. Lochner. 2008. Contributing to sustainability as an environmental impact assessment practitioner. *Impact Assessment and Project Appraisal* 26 (2): 91–98.

Westman, P. 1985. *Ecology, impact assessment, and environmental planning*. Hoboken, NJ: Wiley and Sons.

Wood, C. 2003. *Environmental impact assessment: A comparative review*. Harlow, UK: Pearson Education.

World Bank. 2011. World Development Indicators (WDI) and Global Development Finance (GDF) database. http://databank.worldbank.org.

Environmental assessment as a tool for peacebuilding and development: Initial lessons from capacity building in Sierra Leone

Oli Brown, Morgan Hauptfleisch, Haddijatou Jallow, and Peter Tarr

A decade after the end of Sierra Leone's civil war, the country's rich mineral and agricultural potential is generating considerable interest from foreign investors. The general public in Sierra Leone holds high expectations of an investment-accelerated peace dividend that will provide jobs and economic growth on the basis of rich natural resources. But the legacy of governmental collapse during the conflict, together with the historical tendency of extractive companies to underdeliver on promises of social benefits and environmental protection, present risks for the peacebuilding process, as well as for efforts to promote inclusive socioeconomic development.

The challenge for the government of Sierra Leone and, in particular, its Environment Protection Agency (EPA-SL), is to put in place systems, regulations, and mechanisms to select investments that will benefit the country; to monitor investors' activities; and to ensure that investors live up to their promises. With more than one hundred mining companies operating in Sierra Leone, 82 percent of its land area already allocated to exploration or exploitation licenses, and nearly 10 percent of its arable land under negotiation for use by agribusiness, mining and industrial agriculture will undoubtedly shape the future of the country—for better or worse.

Since July 2010 the United Nations Environment Programme (UNEP) has had a program in Sierra Leone working with the EPA-SL on a variety of natural resource–related projects. One focus has been to build the EPA-SL's capacity to enforce the effective use of environmental impact assessments (EIAs) and strategic environmental assessments (SEAs) through a "South-South" collaboration with

---

Oli Brown is an environmental affairs officer for the United Nations Integrated Peacebuilding Office in Sierra Leone and a program coordinator for the United Nations Environment Programme, Sierra Leone. Morgan Hauptfleisch is a principal scientist for the Southern African Institute for Environmental Assessment. Haddijatou Jallow is the executive chair of the Environment Protection Agency–Sierra Leone. Peter Tarr is the executive director of the Southern African Institute for Environmental Assessment.

the Southern African Institute for Environmental Assessment (SAIEA), based in Windhoek, Namibia.[1]

This chapter argues that investing in environmental assessment is a focused and cost-effective intervention in post-conflict states because EIAs are a catalytic intervention for environmental governance that has long-lived implications for the sustainability of extractive industries. The timing and sequencing will vary depending on the specific case, but such an intervention should move in step with increased investment activity in a post-conflict country. This chapter outlines some of the challenges to that process in Sierra Leone and describes the ways in which these challenges have been addressed.

ENVIRONMENTAL HISTORY OF SIERRA LEONE

The small, West African nation of Sierra Leone ranks low in the Human Development Index (158th out of 169 countries) but is rich in natural resources and beautiful landscapes (UNDP 2010).

Though diamonds are its best-known mineral—the third largest diamond in the world, the 969 carat "Star of Sierra Leone," was found here in 1972—the country also holds valuable reserves of iron ore, gold, bauxite (for aluminum), and rutile (from which titanium oxide is produced). As with other West African nations, oil may one day become a valuable export: in late 2010 the U.S. exploration firm Anadarko announced the discovery of commercially recoverable quantities of offshore oil and gas near the Liberian border (AP 2010).

Meanwhile, the country's year-round warm temperatures, fertile soil, plentiful fresh water, and proximity to European markets make it an attractive prospect for agribusiness: the government has identified as priority crops sugarcane for ethanol and palm oil for the food industry. Sierra Leone's coastline, fed by the rich Guinean maritime current, provides the fish that make up 80 percent of the animal protein consumed by its people (FAO n.d.). Finally, the country's beautiful beaches fostered a small but valuable tourism industry until civil war spilled over from neighboring Liberia in 1991.

---

[1] An EIA is an analytical process that systematically examines the possible environmental consequences of the implementation of a project, program, or policy (UN 1997). In the case of Sierra Leone, proponents of a project are required to complete a scoping document that lays out the scope and scale of their proposed project. On the basis of that scoping document, the EPA-SL determines whether to direct them to commission an independent consultant or company to produce an EIA of appropriate detail. This EIA is reviewed by the EPA-SL and has to be available for public disclosure and comment in at least three places. If the EIA and the resulting environmental management plan are to the EPA-SL's satisfaction, an environmental license is awarded. Acquisition of an environmental license is a precondition to applying for a mining license. SEAs comprise a range of "analytical and participatory approaches that aim to integrate environmental considerations into policies, plans and programmes and evaluate the inter linkages with economic and social considerations" (OECD 2006, 24).

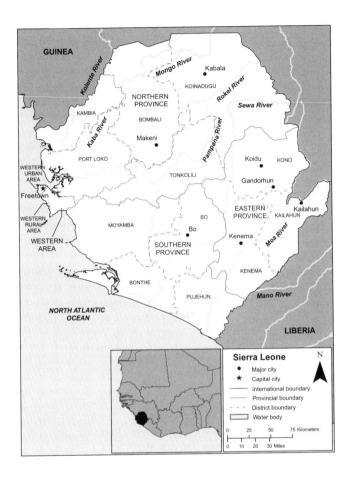

The civil war—which ravaged the country for eleven years, killing tens of thousands and displacing an estimated 2 million people—was triggered by widespread resentment over uneven division of the benefits from the country's natural resources, which were mostly captured by the Freetown-based elite while large portions of the rural population languished in destitution and unemployment. Natural resources financed and perpetuated the conflict: diamonds and other minerals were used to fund combatants and became the spoils of war. Capturing valuable diamond areas became a strategic objective of the Revolutionary United Front (RUF) and other warring parties (UNEP 2010). A report by the United Nations Panel of Experts on Sierra Leone estimated that beginning in 1998 the RUF and their allies funded their operations with smuggled diamonds that had an estimated value of between US$25 and US$125 million each year (UNSC 2000).

In addition to the direct human cost, the conflict had a devastating impact on the environment and economy of Sierra Leone. Transport and service infrastructure was destroyed across the country, industrial mining stopped, and even basic government functions, including environmental management, almost entirely ceased.

PEACEBUILDING EFFORTS

Successive negotiations attempting to draw the conflict to a close finally resulted in the Lomé Peace Accord between the government and the RUF, which was signed in the Togolese capital in 1999. The accord was supported by the United Nations Mission in Sierra Leone (UNAMSIL), one of the largest UN peacekeeping missions ever relative to the size of the population: 17,000 UNAMSIL soldiers in a country with a population of 5.2 million. However, continuing guerrilla fighting meant that the end of hostilities was not declared until January 2002. By that time the process of disarmament, demobilization, and reintegration had disarmed over 72,000 combatants (UNEP 2010).

Starting in 2002, UNAMSIL began to draw down its soldiers and, in line with its mandate, fully withdrew at the end of 2006 (UNEP 2010). In June 2006 Sierra Leone became an agenda country of the newly formed UN Peacebuilding Commission, and the Sierra Leone Peacebuilding Cooperation Framework was adopted in December 2007. By late 2008 the United Nations Integrated Peacebuilding Office in Sierra Leone (UNIPSIL) was created to coordinate the UN's work to consolidate peace and ease the transition to long-term development.

Today, Sierra Leone is at a unique juncture in the process of peace consolidation. In many post-conflict situations fragile governments face the daunting challenge of managing belligerent groups. Sierra Leone is different. The RUF has completely disbanded and has not dissolved into a system of warlords or criminal gangs; most discussions about the group are debates on its history rather than its possible resurgence. As long as the 2012 elections occur without major incident, UNIPSIL aims to be the first peacebuilding mission to complete a planned withdrawal.

But many challenges remain. The major one is sustaining Sierra Leone's economic recovery. In the absence of a significant manufacturing or service sector and with widespread unemployment, future economic growth must come from the exploitation of Sierra Leone's natural resources, at least in the short to medium term.

A 2010 assessment by UNEP found that the civil war significantly damaged the basic environmental resources of the country, namely water and agricultural land, and seriously undermined institutional capacity (UNEP 2010). The assessment also found that although the conflict ended some years ago, its environmental effects and continued unsustainable natural resource exploitation present challenges to development and peace consolidation. These include unmet expectations from natural resources, low levels of transparency and accountability, poor sharing of benefits, and perceptions that low-level violence over natural resources has increased. In addition, many of the coping strategies from the large-scale population displacement resulted in unsustainable forestry, agricultural, and mining practices that became entrenched and persist to this day. The assessment warned that many of the risk factors for conflict that existed in the 1980s and 1990s have not yet been adequately addressed (UNEP 2010).

On a more positive note, the report concluded that if managed effectively, the country's natural resources and environment could play an important peacebuilding and developmental role, constructing the foundation for sustainable jobs and economic growth. In particular, the report recommended making sustainable livelihoods a development priority, improving participation and consultation, building environmental governance capacity at the national and local levels, and establishing joint management of water and agricultural resources. Supporting this process is the underlying rationale for a UNEP program of assistance to Sierra Leone that began in July 2010 as part of the 2009–2012 UN Joint Vision for Sierra Leone (UNIPO 2008).

NATURAL RESOURCE MANAGEMENT

Restarting a viable economy after a civil war remains one of the most difficult challenges of peacebuilding (UNEP 2009). Sierra Leone's natural resources could play a major role in the country's regeneration. Its high-value resources hold the prospect of economic growth, macroeconomic stability, increased employment, and government revenue for desperately needed basic services in a country that has some of the highest rates of adult illiteracy and child and maternal mortality in the world.

In a September 2010 briefing to the United Nations Security Council, the Secretary-General's Executive Representative for UNIPSIL, Michael von der Schulenburg, underlined the importance of natural resources to peacebuilding in Sierra Leone. He noted that the exploitation of Sierra Leone's mineral resources could give the country the impetus it needs to pursue its development goals and could help break its dependency on outside donors, which is essential to offset the country's severe trade imbalance and to supplement government revenue (EconomyWatch 2011). Sierra Leone, he argued, "may be at the verge of turning from [a] major recipient of foreign assistance to becoming a major exporter of primary mineral and hydrocarbon products" (von der Schulenburg 2010).

However, he warned that experience in other parts of the world showed that countries dependent on the export of raw materials often suffered social dislocations, huge income disparities, rampant corruption, and environmental degradation. He noted that the sheer scale of mining agreements could be a "game-changer" for Sierra Leone. There is concern about the agreements' compliance with Sierra Leone's 2009 mining law, the transparency of contract negotiations, and the degree of economic power being conferred on a small number of investors (von der Schulenburg 2010).

Challenges for governance and peace consolidation

The growing influence and rising economic power of the country's natural resource sector create challenges for governance and peace consolidation in Sierra Leone in at least five ways. First, the government's management of its natural resource sector is a proxy for its overall effectiveness. Any democratic system emerging from a period of conflict is under pressure to provide jobs, create revenue, and generate a tangible peace dividend. In the absence of a manufacturing or service economy, most post-conflict countries rely on their natural resources to kick-start economic growth, a situation that is especially true in Sierra Leone. Effective management of Sierra Leone's natural resources from an early stage can help to build confidence in the wider political process of peace consolidation. On the other hand, if large extractive operations begin to dominate local service provision (for example, by being the sole providers of health care and education) the legitimacy of public authorities as providers of services might suffer.

Second, the influx of significant foreign investment in Sierra Leone is generating high expectations of rapid job and economic growth among the general public. Local communities may have unrealistic expectations of what external investors are able and willing to provide. For example, people may expect that jobs will be available regardless of the applicants' skills or literacy. And investing companies have exaggerated the benefits they intend to provide, promising schools, hospitals, and other amenities. Whatever the cause, a gulf can emerge between the popular conception of a project and its reality. Unmet expectations can quickly spread into a wider sense of disappointment with the government and anger at the company.

Third, the way that natural resources are allocated can fundamentally change the balance of political power. In Sierra Leone, natural resources provide one of the few routes for wealth creation and livelihood support, so the way resources are allocated can alter power politics. On the one hand, equitable sharing of benefits may alleviate poverty. On the other, elites often capture the benefits of natural resources and use them to reinforce their position and privilege, breeding resentment among the general population.

Fourth, some of the large investments promise to increase the government's revenue significantly. Such investments would outweigh the country's thin tax base and could widen a democratic deficit if the government becomes more responsive to its major investors than to the general population. Already there are indications that large investors have excessive influence over political processes in the country, particularly given the often favorable treatment they receive in the local media.

Fifth, the operations of extractive companies may undermine efforts to increase transparency and build accountability. The majority of resource-intensive operations in the country are carried out by "juniors," small extractive companies that often have low standards for corporate responsibility. When these low standards meet low pay rates, a bureaucracy with numerous hurdles for business, and a culture that can be permissive of corruption, an increase in the importance and prominence of natural resources in the country's economy can put accountability and transparency at risk.

The mining sector

Mining is often seen as a barometer of Sierra Leone's well-being. The country's considerable reserves of diamonds, rutile, bauxite, gold, and iron ore were first tapped in the 1930s. Run down by successive kleptocracies before the civil war, many of the mining areas were extensively damaged during the fighting. By the end of the conflict, the mining sector was providing just 1 percent of government revenues and 4 percent of GDP, down from 8 percent of government revenues and 20 percent of GDP in 1995 (Ministry of Mineral Resources 2010; Statistics Sierra Leone 2006).

However, mining has played an important role in Sierra Leone's post-conflict economic recovery. Between 2001 and 2006 the rate of growth in the mining sector exceeded the average of 8 percent per annum growth that the rest of the economy experienced for four out of five years (Adam Smith Institute 2007).

Meanwhile, rising commodity prices are generating renewed interest in Sierra Leone's mineral resources: worldwide exploration budgets quadrupled from US$1.9 billion in 2002 to an estimated US$7.5 billion in 2006, and much of the spending was for exploration in Africa (Ministry of Mineral Resources 2010). Anadarko recently discovered commercially recoverable quantities of offshore oil near the Liberian border (AP 2010). Many Sierra Leoneans look to the resurgent mining sector as their path away from reliance on donors and toward financial independence (UNEP 2010).

Large-scale mining has accelerated since the end of the civil war. By 2009 more than 150 prospecting and exploration licenses had been granted to more than one hundred companies; the licenses cover approximately 60,000 square kilometers (82 percent of the country's surface area) (National Advocacy Coalition on Extractives 2009). Three large-scale mechanized mines have been reactivated. The Adam Smith Institute, which has worked extensively on the issue of mining in Sierra Leone, estimated in 2007 that mining reform could raise official mining revenues from US$174 million in 2006 to US$1.2 billion by 2020. The World Bank estimates that between 200,000 and 400,000 people (between 4 percent and 8 percent of the population) depend on artisanal mining for the greater part of their livelihood (Adam Smith Institute 2007).

Although mining promises jobs, economic growth, and a level of strategic importance that the country has rarely experienced, its current importance to the economy is often overrated. Government income from mining is low, hovering at around 3 percent to 5 percent of the export value, compared to a typical target of 7 percent to 10 percent. The field is dominated by predatory and poorly regulated junior companies with track records of overpromising and underdelivering.

In part this is a result of the government signing deals that may be excessively generous. Several companies have negotiated arrangements that allow them to avoid royalty payments and that provide wide-ranging tax exemptions. By late 2010 there was enough concern about the terms for President Koroma to announce a complete review of all major mining contracts (Melik 2010). By mid-2011 this process had resulted in the successful renegotiation of two of the large mining contracts and improved terms for the government.

The country does not have a solid track record when it comes to managing the conduct of large extractive companies. Several parts of the country, particularly around Kono in the east, are struggling with the environmental legacy of past mining operations, both artisanal and industrial. The financial benefits are divided nationally, but negative environmental impacts are mostly localized in rural areas with vulnerable communities. Small-scale and artisanal mining, mostly for gold and diamonds, and quarrying for construction stone are important sources of employment but also a major cause of land degradation in some areas.

The agricultural sector

Sierra Leone's agricultural potential is less well known than its mineral resources, but a wave of new agricultural investment is beginning. In 2010 a Switzerland-based bio-energy company, Addax, received a 57,000-hectare concession near the center of the country to grow sugarcane to supply Europe's growing market for ethanol. Nedoil, a private entity attached to the Lion Heart Foundation (a not-for-profit health-focused charity), has plans for a 50,000-hectare oil palm plantation. Others are likely to follow. In mid-2011 the California-based Oakland Institute estimated that roughly 500,000 hectares of arable land (about 10 percent of the country's total) were under negotiation or had already been leased to agribusiness in Sierra Leone (Baxter 2011). The investments have caused concern in a country where roughly 70 percent of the population is engaged in subsistence agriculture, land ownership is a highly sensitive and politicized subject, and food security is an ongoing worry (Green Scenery 2010).

Because tenure security is lacking, many farmers become agricultural workers on large-scale plantations, where they are often paid low wages and provided with little social or legal protection. For the government to maximize the benefits from agricultural resources, it must facilitate and manage large-scale investment to attract responsible investors who ensure a fair and equitable financial return to the nation, and promote and protect the well-being of the natural and social environment.

Environmental governance

The civil war had a dramatic impact on Sierra Leone's people and infrastructure. But the period of governmental mismanagement that led up to the conflict arguably had a more pernicious impact on environmental management, which almost entirely collapsed. With numerous priorities requiring attention in the immediate aftermath of the conflict, it is perhaps little surprise that natural resource management and environmental protection have been largely overlooked.

Sierra Leone placed last in Yale University's 2010 Environmental Protection Index, a ranking of 163 countries' environmental management that noted some serious regressions in Sierra Leone since the end of the civil war. The country scored particularly low in the area of environmental health; this underlines the effects of environmental degradation on the personal health of the Sierra Leonean people (Yale Center for Environmental Law and Policy 2010).

Several institutions are part of the framework for environmental governance, with ministerial functions of the national government centered in the capital city, Freetown, and local-level administration split between the traditional paramount chiefs and the modern district councils. Though this is now changing with the creation of the EPA-SL, historically the capacity of institutional authorities was inadequate, with little environmental planning taking place in most places and sectors. The planning that has been done since the end of the civil war has tended to involve a limited range of stakeholders and little in the way of consultation (UNEP 2010).

The national institutions for environmental management have gone through a few incarnations. The Environmental Protection Act of 2000 was passed before the peace agreement and the disarmament, demobilization, and reintegration process had put an end to major hostilities. The legislation established a Division of the Environment that came to rest within the Ministry of Lands, Country Planning, and the Environment (UNEP 2010).

In 2005, the National Commission for Environment and Forestry was created under the auspices of the Office of the President to coordinate and facilitate environmental governance. However, its legal status was never resolved, and in 2008 a new Environment Protection Act replaced the National Commission with the Sierra Leone Environment Protection Agency (originally called SLEPA but now known by the acronym EPA-SL).

The 2008 Act (which was amended in 2010) devolved most responsibility for environmental management to the self-standing EPA-SL, which reports directly to the Office of the President. The EPA-SL is the focal point of all environment matters; it formulates policy advice and coordinates overall guidance for environmental management in the country.

ENVIRONMENTAL ASSESSMENT

One of the EPA-SL's central responsibilities is to monitor the environmental impacts of major development projects and to enforce the projects' compliance with their own environmental management plans and with nationally determined environmental standards. This involves reviewing EIAs submitted by project proponents, issuing environmental licenses, and monitoring the environmental performance of mining and agribusiness companies. The 2009 Mines and Minerals Act also requires that mining companies submit EIAs and receive environmental licenses before they are eligible to apply for a mining license.

In early 2011, over the objections of several of the large mining companies, parliament passed a fee schedule that sets out a point system to quantify the environmental footprint of a project, determines what sort of EIA is needed, and allows the agency to recoup its costs from the license award process and subsequent monitoring.[2] At a higher level, the EPA-SL uses SEAs to formulate overall guidance for environmental management.

Throughout much of 2011, the Extractive Industries Project, funded by the World Bank and the United Kingdom's Department for International Development, developed a series of environmental and social regulations. These clarified the need for project proponents to conduct EIAs of varying detail, depending on the scope and scale of their projects. The regulations lay out clear expectations with regard to the EIAs, establish timetables for submission of the EIAs and for their review by the EPA-SL, and prompt the EPA-SL to conduct SEAs of districts where artisanal and industrial mining has been most prevalent.

UNEP's 2010 assessment confirmed that environmental degradation is widespread in both rural and urban areas of the country. In the future it is particularly important that the longstanding environmental and natural resource issues that contributed to the initial conflict are managed, that any growing tensions over the use of natural resources are defused, and that Sierra Leone's considerable natural resource assets are used in a way that supports stability and long-term development. Many of the impacts experienced in the past may be prevented in the future if environmental planning and management tools, including EIAs and SEAs, are applied consistently at both the policy and project levels. There can be no durable peace if the natural resources that sustain people's livelihoods are damaged, degraded, or destroyed (UNEP 2009, 2010).

Environmental assessment is an important tool for at least five reasons. First, universally applied and rigorously enforced environmental planning and assessment helps to weed out the most poorly performing companies: those that are unable or unwilling to submit EIAs should, according to legislation and the evolving regulations, cease operations. This should help to ensure that the country is not left dealing with damaging social and environmental impacts that can take decades to play out, cost millions to clean up, and be highly destabilizing.

Second, environmental assessment helps to raise the floor of environmental expectations in a way that spreads best practices and helps better-performing companies to operate profitably in the country. Thus it helps to create a better investment climate for companies that are prepared to devote more time, energy, and resources to minimizing their environmental impacts, ideally triggering a race to the top rather than a slump to the bottom.

Third, exercises like SEAs can help to forge a common vision for how the country should exploit its natural resources. Better planning leads to better practices. A participatory, inclusive approach can also help to predict and prevent potential conflicts over the management of natural resources and over the division of revenues derived from them.

---

[2] Environmental Impact Assessment License, Environment Protection Agency Regulations, 2010.

Fourth, environmental planning that is fact based and science led may have spillover benefits for other dimensions of governance, helping to depoliticize sensitive disputes over natural resources, increasing transparency, increasing confidence in politics and the legitimacy of government, and professionalizing decision making.

Finally, stakeholder engagement in environmental assessment processes can provide a platform for bringing divided communities together or create new channels for different segments of society to communicate and cooperate over a common issue.

Although issuing environmental permits and developing environmental planning tools might seem to be dull bureaucratic processes, they are key entry points for ensuring that negative impacts can be predicted and that appropriate social and environmental safeguards are put in place. This is perhaps the only time in the lifespan of an investment when the government has significant leverage over the type and nature of a mine or plantation. Getting the process right is one of the principal ways that any government can influence the design, technology, and financial models used in large-scale developments to ensure that long-term social and economic benefits accrue to the country with minimal environmental and social damage. Therefore, environmental assessment is a key opportunity to identify and mitigate potential sources of conflict caused by an investment.

Capacity building for environmental assessment

Historically, environmental assessment tools have rarely been applied, monitored, or enforced in Sierra Leone. Prior to 2008, although EIAs were required by law, they were often not done as part of development planning. If they were done, they were often of poor quality, and their results, including their environmental management plans, were often ignored by proponents of projects and decision makers alike. Compounding the problem, developers in large-, medium-, and small-scale enterprises often used outdated and inappropriate technology.

After the 2008 Environmental Protection Act was passed, EIAs were undertaken more commonly. However, limited capacity to review them at the EPA-SL led to a large backlog. This, in turn, slowed down the process for developers hoping to obtain mining and plantation licenses. It also encouraged developers to ignore or subvert what environmental standards and processes did exist.

SEA is not required by law, and it has rarely been applied at the policy, plan, or program level, either in government or by the private sector. A National Environmental Action Plan (the sort of product that can be created by SEA) was developed in the early 1990s with support from the World Bank; however, it was published in 1995 in the middle of the conflict, so any policy directions it recommended seem to have been quickly overcome by the chaos caused by the civil war. In 2010 it took several months to even uncover a copy of the plan, and there is little evidence that it ever informed policy in a substantial way.

A root-cause analysis was conducted in Sierra Leone in late 2010 to determine the underlying reasons for problems with environmental assessment (SAIEA 2010). Researchers learned that institutions tasked with regulating environmental assessment at various government and sectoral levels were weak and poorly resourced and that implementation tended to proceed on an ad hoc basis. In development planning, high-level government and private decision makers often assigned low priority to environmental protection. Quality control over environmental assessment was inadequate, and external reviews of EIAs and SEAs were conducted only rarely.

Training and research institutions were found to have insufficient capacity related to environmental assessment, and the media rarely reported on stories involving environmental assessments. For the most part, therefore, policy makers and the general public had a very limited understanding of assessment processes (SAIEA 2010).

The UNEP project

Building the EPA-SL's capacity to serve as a platform for managing Sierra Leone's natural resources was one objective of a country program initiated by UNEP in July 2010 and partly conducted in cooperation with SAIEA. UNEP and SAIEA's work with the EPA-SL took several forms. First, they conducted a capacity needs assessment to locate the gaps in capacity and determine what support the EPA-SL might need. Second, for several weeks SAIEA experts helped staff from the EPA-SL to work through the backlog of EIAs waiting for review. SAIEA experts from a variety of countries across southern Africa who are familiar with both mining issues and the particular challenges of operating in African developing countries worked alongside EPA-SL staff to review EIAs and compare their conclusions—an approach to technical assistance that was neither condescending nor displacing. Third, SAIEA staff provided training in EIA techniques and best practices for government and civil society representatives. Finally, SAIEA and UNEP personnel accompanied EPA-SL staff as they carried out monitoring inspections of mining and agribusiness sites.

LESSONS LEARNED

The experiences of the EPA-SL, UNEP, SAIEA, and other entities that are active in capacity building for environmental management in Sierra Leone may provide valuable lessons to other countries in a similar position. At least six elements are important components of an overall strategy: awareness raising, capacity building, streamlining of systems, training and regulation of practitioners, stakeholder participation, and regular monitoring.

Awareness raising

Raising awareness about the benefits of environmental assessment as a tool of development is a prerequisite for the creation of a functional environmental assessment system in any country. In the case of Sierra Leone, there is a powerful argument to be made that it is also an investment in long-term peacebuilding.

Unfortunately, environmental assessment is often perceived to be a green hand brake that is designed to protect the natural environment against the threat of human development. But when implemented properly, it enhances the benefits of development projects and policies while it minimizes negative impacts. This needs to be understood by decision makers at all levels. Support from high-level political leaders can be an important way of giving these issues greater priority.

Awareness-raising workshops for high-level decision makers demonstrate the value of environmental assessment and clarify these links. EPA-SL, SAIEA, and UNEP organized one such awareness raising event in December 2010, at which President Koroma himself issued a statement underlining the importance of environmental assessment (Kalokoh 2010).

Objective and regular public reporting on environmental issues and environmental assessment processes improves people's awareness about the importance of environmental safeguards and promotes transparency in decision making. Nurturing journalists' understanding of the environment and environmental assessment can promote better reporting, which results in greater awareness and understanding of environmental assessment and its benefits. Given that transparency contributes to the building of the population's confidence and trust in government, reporting on the environment can also be an important peacebuilding tool.

Capacity building

Building staff, skills, and capacity is another prerequisite for more effective environmental assessment. Training on best practices and quality control of environmental assessment can be offered to key staff, line ministry environmental authorities, regional and local authorities, and parastatal environmental officers.

In Sierra Leone this training took the form of short-term courses and experienced practitioners' accompaniment of EPA-SL staff into the field to deliver hands-on training, especially in post-implementation monitoring and auditing.

Networking opportunities can help government and private environmental assessment practitioners. For example, practitioners can join international bodies, such as the International Association for Impact Assessment, and attend their annual conferences. This exposure to global thinking and well-established and supportive international networks can complement other capacity-building efforts.

Streamlining of systems

Streamlining of systems is necessary to ensure that environmental authorities do not become log-jammed with hundreds of reports waiting for review. Consultants can be brought in to assist in tackling a backlog, but a longer-term, less expensive solution is to improve the officials' capacity to conduct professional reviews.

Publishing best practice guidelines for EIAs and environmental management plans and making them widely available can help environmental practitioners and proponents of new projects to know what the law requires.

Training and regulation of practitioners

Training and regulation of practitioners builds up a professional cadre of environmental planners and assessors. A certification scheme for environmental practitioners improves the credibility of this growing sector and prevents unqualified people from conducting EIAs and SEAs. However, certification alone is not adequate; there needs to be a parallel process of quality control and a system of deregistering practitioners who are demonstrably incompetent or unethical.

Stakeholder participation

Stakeholder participation helps to build a coalition for transparent and effective environmental assessment. Public participation improves transparency, ensures consideration of community issues, and increases the likelihood that win-win solutions will be found in project planning and implementation. Actions that can improve public participation include the drafting of legislation to require it; training in public participation for governmental staff, environmental practitioners, and academic personnel; and project proponents' preparation and wide public circulation of well-illustrated, simply written, and succinct background information documents. Dissemination of background information at the onset of a project helps the public to understand the project components at an early stage and improves their ability to participate in discussions. All relevant documentation should be publicly available, ideally in a central location but also in the vicinity of the project area itself.

Regular monitoring

Regular monitoring of mining and agribusiness companies is critical to ensuring that proper environmental standards are enforced, but it is much easier said than done. Effective monitoring requires technical expertise across a wide range of areas, a great deal of expensive sampling equipment, and extensive experience in the various technical challenges presented by mining and agribusiness operations. It also requires careful management to ensure that the staff carrying out the monitoring resist any offers of bribes. Finally, it requires an architecture of law enforcement to ensure that any transgressions are properly redressed.

CONCLUSIONS

Post-conflict countries with weak environmental management and plans for growth that are fueled by access to natural resources face daunting challenges. The imperative to kick-start economic growth using those natural resources can override the imperative to manage and mitigate the full social and environmental costs of extractive projects. Ensuring that economic growth does not come at the expense of the country's natural resource base and people's human rights requires considerable skill, equipment, and judgment. Getting it wrong can increase the risk that conflict will resume.

In any post-conflict situation, improved governance of natural resources and the environment is a litmus test of government stability and effectiveness (UNEP 2010). The challenge is to select the best possible investments and then monitor those investments long after the ink dries on the contract.

Environmental assessment at a macro level, through SEA, and at a project level, through EIA, has proven to be an important part of natural resource management and should be seen as a critical catalytic activity that warrants its own investment by government, civil society, and the international community in post-conflict states. These processes offer at least four concrete benefits for peacebuilding.

First, they act as a platform for citizen participation in decision making and provide an arena where divided groups can work together toward a common goal.

Second, if managed effectively, they can help build confidence in the government, demonstrate the government's legitimacy, and lead to a range of additional benefits, including greater transparency and more fact-based decision making.

Third, fact-based environmental assessment that is the subject of extensive consultation can help to strip the politics away from the power dynamics that often surround natural resources, and thus help to articulate a common vision for the role that natural resources should play as the country moves forward.

Finally, environmental assessment helps policy makers choose among companies, and it forces companies to be responsible environmental stewards, especially when assessments are followed by sustained monitoring and enforcement. It limits the negative environmental impacts of mining and agribusiness projects, thereby protecting health and livelihoods, reducing the likelihood that costly environmental remediation will be necessary, and preventing conflict.

REFERENCES

Adam Smith Institute. 2007. *The economic and fiscal potential of mining sector reform in Sierra Leone*. London.

AP (Associated Press). 2010. Oil producer Anadarko announces light sweet crude discovery off Sierra Leone's coastline. November 15.

Baxter, J. 2011. *Understanding land investment deals in Africa: Country report, Sierra Leone*. Oakland, CA: Oakland Institute

Economy Watch. 2011. Sierra Leone economic statistics and indicators. www.economywatch.com/economic-statistics/country/Sierra-Leone.

FAO (Food and Agriculture Organization of the United Nations). n.d. National aquaculture sector overview: Sierra Leone. www.fao.org/fishery/countrysector/naso_sierraleone/en.

Green Scenery. 2011. *The Socfin land deal missing out on best practices: Fact-finding mission to Malen Chiefcom, Pujehun District, Sierra Leone.* Freetown.

Kalokoh, I. 2010. We must conserve Salone's natural resources says President Ernest Bai Koroma. *For di People*, December 17.

Melik, J. 2010. Selling Sierra Leone to investors. BBC News, November 26. www.bbc.co.uk/news/business-11774744.

Ministry of Mineral Resources. 2010. An overview of the Sierra Leone minerals sector. www.slminerals.org/content/index.php?option=com_content&view=article&id=4&Itemid=7.

National Advocacy Coalition on Extractives. 2009. Sierra Leone at the crossroads: Seizing the chance to benefit from mining. Freetown.

OECD (Organisation for Economic Co-operation and Development). 2006. *Applying strategic environmental assessment: Good practice guidance for development cooperation.* DAC Guidelines and Reference Series. Paris.

SAIEA (Southern African Institute for Environmental Assessment). 2010. A root cause analysis. Unpublished report. Windhoek, Namibia.

Statistics Sierra Leone. 2006. *Annual statistical digest 2005/2006.* www.statistics.sl/final_digest_2006.pdf.

UN (United Nations). 1997. Glossary of environment statistics. Studies in Methods. ST/ESA/STAT/SER.F/67. New York.

UNDP (United Nations Development Programme). 2010. *The real wealth of nations: Pathways to human development.* New York.

UNEP (United Nations Environment Programme). 2009. *From conflict to peacebuilding: The role of natural resources and the environment.* Nairobi, Kenya. http://postconflict.unep.ch/publications/pcdmb_policy_01.pdf.

———. 2010. *Sierra Leone: Environment, conflict and peacebuilding assessment; Technical report.* Geneva, Switzerland. http://postconflict.unep.ch/publications/Sierra_Leone.pdf.

UNIPO (United Nations Integrated Peacebuilding Office). 2008. *Joint vision for Sierra Leone of the United Nations family.* Freetown.

UNSC (United Nations Security Council). 2000. Report of the UN Panel of Experts on Sierra Leone diamonds and arms. S/2000/1195. New York.

von der Schulenburg, M. 2010. Sierra Leone: Statement to the Security Council. September 28. New York: United Nations. http://unipsil.unmissions.org/portals/unipsil/media/documents/statement_SC_280910.pdf.

Yale Center for Environmental Law and Policy. 2010. *Environmental performance index 2010.* New Haven, CT: Yale University. www.ciesin.columbia.edu/documents/EPI_2010_report.pdf.

Natural resources, post-conflict reconstruction, and regional integration: Lessons from the Marshall Plan and other reconstruction efforts

Carl Bruch, Ross Wolfarth, and Vladislav Michalcik

On April 17, 2002, George W. Bush invoked the Marshall Plan as a model for building a peaceful and prosperous Afghanistan (Bush 2002). According to President Bush, U.S. support for rebuilding Europe after World War II was a "beacon to light the path" toward effective post-conflict peacebuilding processes in the twenty-first century. In 2005, the Wallonia Regional Government in Belgium announced what they dubbed a Marshall plan for economic revitalization (Chaidron 2005). To the Walloons, the plan would lead to renewed local prosperity.[1] Proposals for other Marshall plans are found in the political rhetoric on Iraq (Kemp 2007), Haiti (Novacek, Mederly, and Armand 2007), the Third World (Korb and Cohen 2005), the environment (Ohlsson 2004), and even the streets of Los Angeles (Newsmax.com 2007).

It would be easy to dismiss the original Marshall Plan as nothing more than a rhetorical tool. Yet the post–World War II reconstruction of Europe—in which the Marshall Plan was instrumental—was peacebuilding worthy of emulation. A region whose rivalries spawned two of the most destructive conflicts in human history has been more or less at peace for the last sixty years. Indeed, George Marshall received the Nobel Peace Prize in 1953, in large part, for the effect of the eponymous plan on building long-term peace. The Marshall Plan enabled Europe's recovery by providing external support for regional cooperation and integration. The plan helped form the basis for international institutions that persist, including the predecessors of the Organisation for Economic Co-operation and Development (OECD) and the European Union (EU). The management of

---

Carl Bruch is a senior attorney and codirector of international programs at the Environmental Law Institute. He also cochairs the Specialist Group on Armed Conflict and the Environment of the Commission on Environmental Law of the International Union for Conservation of Nature. Ross Wolfarth is a law student at Columbia University, and Vladislav Michalcik is a research scholar-in-residence at the Washington College of Law, American University. This chapter was developed with support from the Center for Global Partnership of the Japan Foundation.

[1] While there has been no civil war recently in Belgium, the country has been in political crisis since 2007, raising the possibility of partition.

natural resources, particularly coal, contributed significantly to the development and implementation of regional reconstruction and integration plans, as well as the creation of accompanying institutions. The Marshall Plan casts a long shadow. A survey by the Brookings Institution of 450 professors of history and political science regarding the greatest achievements of the U.S. government in the past half-century rated the rebuilding of Europe after World War II as the greatest achievement (Light 2000).

In the last two decades, Central America and the Western Balkans have taken concerted and moderately effective approaches to regional peacebuilding based in part on natural resource management. Experiences elsewhere, however, demonstrate the potential pitfalls of a regional approach to post-conflict reconstruction. Tracing the history of achievement and disappointment illustrates how, under the right circumstances, regional cooperation in managing natural resources can support the transition to a durable peace.

By comparing seven post-conflict approaches to regional integration involving natural resources—some successful, some problematic—this chapter identifies several common aspects of successful attempts by donors to promote post-conflict regional integration. Effective management of natural resources to support post-conflict regional integration requires an appropriate resource; a well-defined region; political will; significant commitments of financial and technical resources by donors; a coordinated, time-bound plan of action; and a high degree of adaptability. This chapter also discusses the key role of natural resources in post-conflict regional reconstruction and explores how lessons learned may be applied to Afghanistan and other post-conflict situations.

EXPERIENCES IN REGIONAL POST-CONFLICT INTEGRATION AND NATURAL RESOURCE MANAGEMENT

This section describes three well-developed efforts at post-conflict regional integration that have utilized natural resource management. It then briefly reviews four other experiences that illuminate potential difficulties in applying this peacebuilding strategy.

The Marshall Plan displayed a high degree of donor and recipient commitment to reconstruction and regional integration, and was an adaptable approach to distributing aid that incorporated natural resources. The Marshall Plan's role in the emergence of the European Coal and Steel Community (ECSC) and its successor, the EU, showed that post-conflict cooperation on natural resources could lay the foundation for and support the development of more advanced forms of political and economic integration. In the 1990s, peacebuilding and regional integration in Central America grew out of cooperation on environmental issues, which were perceived as peripheral and therefore "safe," in contrast to more sensitive economic and political issues. Western Balkan reconstruction following the post–Cold War breakup of Yugoslavia illustrates how the European integration process continues and how the neglect of natural resources

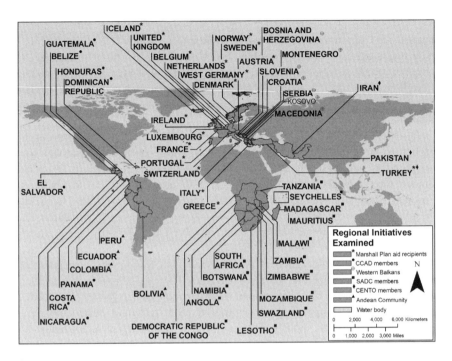

Notes:
At the time of writing, Kosovo is not a UN member state.
CCAD: Central American Commission on Environment and Development; SADC: Southern African Development Community; CENTO: Central Treaty Organization.

can retard progress toward post-conflict regional integration. Experiences in Southern Africa, West Asia, South America, and Japan reveal some of the pitfalls and constraints of donor-supported regional natural resource management as a peacebuilding tool.

The Marshall Plan

When George Marshall announced the United States' startlingly ambitious foreign aid program in 1947, he called it "the business of the Europeans" (Marshall 1947). Throughout its relatively brief existence (1948–1952), the Marshall Plan engaged Europe as a unit while devolving substantial authority to individual European governments. The willingness of the Economic Cooperation Administration (ECA), which was formed by the U.S. government to distribute Marshall Plan aid, to grant significant control to European authorities and national governments was remarkable given the scale of the program. At its peak in 1948, the Marshall Plan consumed 1.98 percent of the U.S. gross national product (Machado 2007), whereas in 2007 U.S. foreign aid totaled only 0.16 percent of the gross national product (Shah 2009).

Before the plan's approval by the U.S. Congress, sixteen nations met in Paris as the Committee on European Economic Cooperation (CEEC) to calculate how much aid each country needed. The United States refused to accept any proposal for aid distribution that did not result from a regional agreement. Leading European diplomats felt that the Marshall Plan negotiations at the CEEC defined Europe (Geremek 2008). In fact, the organizational ties created by the Marshall Plan would last far longer than direct ECA funding: the CEEC would outlive the reconstruction effort and evolve into the OECD. The Soviets would prevent the participation of Eastern Europe, and the plan would solidify the post-war split between East and West. The Marshall Plan supported Austria, Belgium, Denmark, France, Greece, Iceland, Ireland, Italy, Luxembourg, the Netherlands, Norway, Portugal, Sweden, Switzerland, Turkey, the United Kingdom, and West Germany. Despite the wide dispersal of decision-making authority to national leaders and the sheer quantity of money and personnel involved, the Marshall Plan produced only a single public scandal (Machado 2007).

The day-to-day operation of the Marshall Plan was far less dependent on regional cooperation than its founding had been. The only genuinely international project funded by the ECA was a joint Austrian and German power plant (Arkes 1973). The ECA shipped large quantities of food, fuel, and other supplies to European governments, which sold the goods to their citizens in exchange for local currency, or "counterpart funds" that the governments then reinvested for the general good. The governments had extensive leeway in spending counterpart funds, although there was oversight by the ECA. Great Britain used virtually all of its funds on debt relief. Italy invested 46 percent of its lira in improving agriculture, including swamp drainage and other land reclamation projects, and in infrastructure for transporting agricultural goods to market (Machado 2007). Italy failed through its investments to close the regional prosperity gap between the South and the North but improved the quality of life in southern Italian villages (Machado 2007). France was exceedingly successful in reviving its economy by rebuilding its infrastructure (Machado 2008). Counterpart funds also supported less comprehensive natural resource successes across Europe. The funds supported efforts to fight tuberculosis in cows (Mills 2008), develop large-scale rice cultivation in Greece (Machado 2007), and construct a series of hydroelectric dams along the Rhone River that dwarfed those erected in the 1930s by the Tennessee Valley Authority in the United States (Behrman 2007).

Technical-assistance programs, which in many cases focused on agriculture, were not formalized until later but became so popular and successful that they outlasted the Marshall Plan. Through 1957, five years after the official end of the plan, more than 19,000 Europeans learned U.S. production methods, and more than 15,000 Americans traveled to Europe to share their expertise, often on agriculture (Wasser 2005).

The Marshall Plan also helped support the creation of the European Coal and Steel Community (ECSC). The brainchild of French diplomat Jean Monnet, the ECSC sought to achieve lasting European peace by internationalizing control of the coal- and steel-producing regions of the Rhineland, Ruhr, and Saar, which had long driven conflict between France and Germany (Fransen 2001). However, in the immediate aftermath of war, integration with Germany was decidedly unpopular among the French people. American officials administering occupied Germany in 1948 were admonished not to allow the Germans' standard of living to exceed that of the French. American and French leaders believed that the existence of well-fed Germans would ignite French anger, even communism (Machado 2007).

By 1950, French sentiment had drastically changed. When proposing the creation of the ECSC, French foreign minister Robert Schuman recommended that France and Germany form "an embrace so close that neither could draw back far enough to hit the other" (Behrman 2007, 288). Considering the history of conflict between France and Germany, it was remarkable that Schuman could recommend integration with Germany without destroying his political career. The transformation of the French people's burning desire for revenge into a willingness to work with Germany would have been unlikely without the support of the Marshall Plan for improving the material conditions and forming functional European organizations such as the CEEC.

Shared natural resource management drew together France and Germany—and Italy, Belgium, Luxembourg, and the Netherlands—as they joined the ECSC negotiations. Coal was essential not only to reconstruction and macroeconomic recovery but also to war. Thus placing the coal reserves of traditional antagonists into the hands of a supranational authority was a long-term strategy to prevent another war. Although the actual functioning of the ECSC was at times rocky, its administrators benefited from access to the successor aid mechanisms of the Marshall Plan for financial and informal support (MacDonald 2009). The ECSC would eventually serve as one of the first building blocks of the EU, demonstrating how post-conflict cooperation through natural resource management can feed into deeper political and economic cooperation.

The Central American Commission on Environment and Development (CCAD)

The 1980s was a period of turmoil in Central America. Guerrilla warfare with Cold War overtones consumed El Salvador, Guatemala, Honduras, and Nicaragua. The U.S. military ousted a Panamanian strongman installed by the United States. Only Costa Rica (and Belize, a state more culturally and economically oriented toward the Caribbean) avoided serious internal instability and violent government repression. Although none of the Central American conflicts were formal international wars and there were no pitched battles between national armies, porous borders and chaotic legal environments allowed establishment of training camps in neighboring countries and helped to generate regional instability and economic stagnation (Robinson 1991).

The convoluted international structure of the Central American conflicts called for a regional resolution to the conflicts. The first attempt, thwarted by the United States, was the Contadora peace process led by Colombia, Mexico, Panama, and Venezuela. The United States, even though it lacked credibility among certain parties to the conflict, was unwilling to relinquish its position as the preeminent foreign power in Central America.

Peace, therefore, had to be negotiated by the countries of Central America, led by Costa Rican president Óscar Arias Sánchez. In 1987, five Central American presidents signed the Esquipulas II Accords. The treaty opened the doors for substantial international economic assistance, mainly from the United States, and gradually moved Central America from a conflict to a post-conflict region. By 1992, all the civil wars had ended, except for the Guatemalan conflict, which persisted until 1996.

During the same period, regional and international concern about environmental degradation grew. The overexploitation of natural resources for immediate economic benefit had depleted forests, soils, and fisheries and threatened biodiversity (USAID 1989). Combating environmental exploitation and degradation allowed Central American nations to work together on a politically neutral issue. The Central American Commission on Environment and Development (Comisión Centroamericana de Ambiente y Desarrollo, or CCAD) was established in 1989 by Costa Rica, El Salvador, Guatemala, Honduras, and Nicaragua "to cooperate on environmental issues in an effort to facilitate peace in the strife-torn region" (Page and Schwarz 1996, 3).

The United States quickly recognized the importance of CCAD as a tool for building Central American cooperation and for more effectively managing Central American resources. Beginning in 1989, the USAID Regional Environmental and Natural Resources Management Project provided financial support to the CCAD Executive Secretariat and later funded CCAD policy formulation (USAID 1994).

Progress was swift. The commission's first unified effort was the Central American Tropical Forest Action Plan of 1991. By the 1992 United Nations Conference on Environment and Development, CCAD had derived the consensus-based Central American Agenda on Environment and Development. In 1993, CCAD founded the Central American Council on Forests, which brought together forest-service directors, farmers' unions, industry organizations, and nongovernmental organizations throughout the region (Page and Schwarz 1996). CCAD was instrumental in launching the Inter-Parliamentary Commission on the Environment, which assembled legislative representatives throughout the region to push for ratification of international conventions and policy reform in their national congresses (UNEP 1997). Perhaps most notably, CCAD has repeatedly coordinated a unified environmental approach for Central American nations, including the development of shared positions for negotiating the 1997 Kyoto Protocol and other multilateral environmental agreements, and has led efforts to develop, harmonize, and adapt national environmental legislation in the region.

Just as shared management of European coal fed into the EU, the international ties established through CCAD contributed to the creation of the Central American Integration System (Sistema de la Integración Centroamericana, or

SICA) in 1991. In both cases, environmental cooperation laid the foundation for continuing regional integration. CCAD became the environmental branch of the larger system for integration and remains one of the most successful branches of SICA (SICA n.d.). CCAD's operations have also expanded. Since 1994, CCAD has overseen the Alliance for Sustainable Development (Alianza para el Desarrollo Sostenible de Centroamérica, or ALIDES), which expanded CCAD's work to include political, cultural, economic, and social spheres while focusing on the environment.

With the December 10, 1994, signing of the Central America–United States of America Joint Accord (Conjunto Centroamericano–USA, or CONCAUSA), the United States became an extra-regional member of ALIDES. The agreement identified four areas that required action: biodiversity conservation, energy use, legal and institutional frameworks, and the harmonization of environmental protection standards across the region.[2]

Early partnerships developed around Central American cooperation on environmental issues have expanded into region-wide systems promoting environmental, political, economic, and social integration. By initially addressing environmental concerns popular in the international community, Central America gained support from major international donors, and early success in relatively noncontroversial areas allowed CCAD to bring in more international partners and expand the number of regional program areas. The process helped to transform Central America from a region torn by civil war to a (somewhat) unified bloc working cooperatively to promote development, governance, and peace.

EU post-conflict recovery programs in the Balkans

The breakup of Yugoslavia in the 1990s ignited war in Europe for the first time since the Greek civil war ended with the assistance of the Marshall Plan. The disintegration of the multiethnic state created seven new countries: Slovenia, Croatia, Bosnia and Herzegovina, Macedonia, Montenegro, Serbia, and (perhaps) Kosovo.[3] The processes that led to the new states ranged from the peaceful secession of Montenegro, to the swift pseudo-war that resulted in Slovenia, to the bloody and protracted ethnic strife in Kosovo. These processes left some of the new states economically and politically devastated and others relatively strong (Bennet 1997). The varied, comprehensive, and generally popular destruction of

---

[2] For the complete text of the accord, see "CONCAUSA Declaration and Action Plan: Text of Declaration Signed Following a Meeting between the U.S. and Central American Governments, Miami, Florida, December 10, 1994," *Dispatch* 6 (May 1995), suppl. no. 2. http://dosfan.lib.uic.edu/ERC/briefing/dispatch/1995/html/Dispatchv6Sup2.html.

[3] The international status of Kosovo is still in dispute, with some countries recognizing it as a state. The 2010 Advisory Opinion of the International Court of Justice regarding the unilateral declaration of independence of Kosovo addressed the matter to some extent (see www.icj-cij.org/docket/files/141/15987.pdf), but as of April 2012, ninety UN member states (less than half of the membership of the UN) had formally recognized Kosovo as a state.

a multiethnic state might be expected to yield a region unsuited to and uninterested in a regional approach to post-conflict reconstruction. Yet the shared goal of EU membership convinced the Western Balkan states to act in concert.

When the foreign minister of Luxembourg helped negotiate the Slovenian treaty that ended the first Balkan war, he stated, "this is the hour of Europe" (Bennet 1997, 159). The nations of the Western Balkans were promised participation not only in the rhetorical heir to the Marshall Plan but also in the actual institutional successor to post–World War II recovery and cooperation—the European Union. The Western Balkan states were placed on a post-conflict path designed to end in EU membership, a path smoothed by the EU accession process.

The European Council has affirmed and reaffirmed over the last twenty years that "the future of the Western Balkans lies within the European Union" (European Commission 2008b, 2). Conflict has both expanded the role of the EU in the region and retarded the progress of those Balkan states toward European integration. Only Slovenia, which experienced a relatively nondestructive secession process, was able to enter the EU during the 2004 enlargement that incorporated most of post-communist Eastern Europe. The other six states are in varying stages of accession to the EU, with Croatia the most advanced and Kosovo the least (European Commission 2008a).

In general, the new states of the Western Balkans see membership in the EU as a means to long-term prosperity and stability. The long-term promise has been complemented with the concrete and immediate benefits of EU accession. Billions of euros of EU assistance to the countries of the region have been explicitly tied to their efforts to gain EU membership. The Community Assistance for Reconstruction, Development, and Stabilisation program (CARDS) was the primary tool for distributing EU funds in the region from 2000 to 2006; it distributed 5.16 billion euros over its lifetime (European Commission n.d.b). In 2006, the Instrument for Pre-Accession Assistance (IPA) replaced CARDS.

The level of EU support provided through IPA, which is divided into five categories, is contingent on progress toward EU membership. All participating countries are eligible to receive funds for two of the categories: transition assistance and institution building, and cross-border cooperation. Only countries that have become formal candidates for accession can receive funding for the other three categories: regional development (for regions within countries), human resource development, and rural development (European Commission n.d.a). By structuring IPA to reward success in a series of steps toward EU membership, the EU has created a context in which each Balkan nation is concerned about the economic consequences of falling behind its peers in EU accession (Pond 2006).

From a natural resource management perspective, it is unfortunate that regional and rural development moneys are only available late in the EU accession process. Indeed, natural resources have received a small percentage of CARDS and IPA assistance in the Western Balkans. Less than 4.5 percent of CARDS funds in 2005 and 2006 were targeted toward environment and natural resources (European Commission n.d.b). IPA similarly builds capacity for natural resource management only when the accession process (and presumably post-conflict reconstruction) has significantly progressed.

The lack of focus on natural resource issues has created challenges for the EU accession process. One of the key components of the transition from candidate to member is the incorporation into national legislation of 80,000 pages of standardized EU rules, the *acquis communitaire*, which are divided into thirty-five chapters. According to one Croatian leader, the three most problematic chapters for Croatia (the only Balkan state currently in negotiations) were Agriculture and Rural Development, Fisheries, and Environment (Grdesic 2009). By delaying funding for natural resource management until Croatia achieves candidate status, the EU may prolong the nation's journey toward EU membership and European integration.

More progress has been made in encouraging regional coordination in natural resource management. In addition to its adherence to the strict requirements of the acquis, the EU requires the Western Balkan states seeking EU membership to cooperate with each other and their Southeastern European neighbors (Pond 2006). The allure of EU membership has been somewhat successful in fostering the development of a functional Southeastern European grouping. Natural resources have played a significant role in the cooperation. The first joint treaty signed by the new Western Balkan nations focused on joint management of the Sava River (Čolakhodžić et al. 2013).

In 2004, the European Commission, in conjunction with the Balkan states and neighboring allies, established the Energy Community of South East Europe (ECSEE). The ECSEE sought to streamline Western Balkan progress toward EU membership and to promote the development of local energy reserves.[4] The new energy community was explicitly modeled on the post–World War II ECSC (Liebscher et al. 2005). Through the ECSEE, the EU sought to replicate the model of post-conflict regional integration through natural resource management that had contributed to the origins of the EU.

The success of post–World War II European reconstruction has fostered a continental belief in regional approaches to peacebuilding. The regional approach has been central to post-conflict recovery of the Western Balkan states; and natural resources played a substantial role in fostering regional cooperation and integration, as well as possibly slowing EU accession where not addressed early in the process.

Other examples

Although the Western European, Central American, and Balkan experiences offer appealing stories of post-conflict regional integration using natural resources, experiences from other regions highlight various challenges to and caveats for

---

[4] For the text of the Treaty Establishing the Energy Community, 2004, see www.eihp.hr/hrvatski/pdf/zakoni/ect2005.pdf.

regional approaches to using natural resources in post-conflict reconstruction. Four examples are useful in considering the limitations of regional approaches: the first three examine situations in which regional integration involving natural resources has not lived up to expectations. The fourth is a success story that happened in parallel with the Marshall Plan but was undertaken at the national rather than regional level. The experience (in Japan) reveals that while natural resources can be crucial to post-conflict recovery at the national and regional levels, a regional approach is not necessary for successful recovery.

Southern African Development Community (SADC)

The Southern African regional institutions created in the 1970s and 1980s were anticolonial, antiapartheid, and anti–South African. With the fall of apartheid in South Africa in the early 1990s, Southern African countries reorganized these organizations to establish the Southern African Development Community to encourage regional cooperation and economic integration alongside, rather than in opposition to, the regionally dominant nation, South Africa. For the smaller nations battered in the 1980s by South Africa's destabilizing "Total Strategy," SADC held the promise of a regional Marshall plan whereby South Africa could make amends for its past colonialist wrongs by helping its poorer neighbors (Omari and Macaringue 2007).

South Africa, despite regional preeminence, lacked the economic power to support a massive program for regional development and integration. SADC's 2003 development plan presented a laudable list of goals and methods for regional action (SADC 2003), yet funding for projects has been inconsistent and piecemeal. Bilateral aid from Finland covers forestry education; aid from Italy funds research in plant biodiversity; and an aquaculture program deemed necessary by SADC was discontinued in 2004 because of lack of funds. In the absence of a strong, consistent, and independent financial base, SADC's ability to conduct integrated development projects is constrained both in the natural resource sector and more broadly.

SADC coordinating initiatives have been more successful than those involving money. For instance, a 2000 protocol to standardize mining regulations in all member states, except the Democratic Republic of the Congo, and regional protocols for environmental and transboundary water management have been developed. SADC has become a platform for encouraging natural resource cooperation and development of environmental standards in the region, although it has yet to harness the full development potential of the resources of Southern Africa. The potential of natural resource cooperation to contribute to economic and political integration as peacebuilding tools has, therefore, been limited. It is difficult to see the situation changing without outside donors either dramatically increasing aid budgets in the region or making the unlikely choice of prioritizing regional integration over issues of poverty, public health, and environmental degradation at the national and subnational levels (GON 2008).

Central Treaty Organization (CENTO)

The Central Treaty Organization (CENTO) sought to integrate Turkey, Iran, and Pakistan and was the least successful of the U.S.-led Cold War alliances. The lack of common security orientations prevented development of a lasting union. Turkey feared Soviet expansion; Pakistan was more concerned with the threat of India; and Iran was fearful of enemies within the Arab world. CENTO is remembered as an icon of Cold War U.S. hubris and exemplifies the U.S. fantasy of a bipolar world.

Yet beginning in 1959, CENTO housed the first regional authority for the dispersal of U.S. aid since the Marshall Plan. CENTO was coordinated by John McDonald, a former staff member of the secretariat of the Organisation for European Economic Co-operation. He had direct experience with the mechanisms of regional supervision and authority that began with the Marshall Plan. Regional International Cooperation Administration (ICA) coordination was central to a number of infrastructure projects, including the construction of a still-functioning railroad connecting Tehran and Ankara (McDonald and Zanolli 2008). The ICA built capacity and fostered cooperation between professionals in the three countries through a symposium on mining. It also brought together agricultural economists from the region and the West to change the agricultural credit system by providing low-interest loans (McDonald and Zanolli 2008).

CENTO utterly failed to reproduce the anti-Soviet successes of Europe's North Atlantic Treaty Organization. But individuals focused on replicating Marshall Plan–type development in Central Asia achieved modest success. They were able to foster cross-border cooperation with positive results for agricultural production and other forms of natural resource management. Although the efforts did not lead to deeper cooperation in a region artificially defined by proximity to the Soviet Union, they nevertheless made some positive contributions to the well-being of local populations.

The Alliance for Progress and Andean integration

In 1961, John F. Kennedy proposed U.S. foreign aid for Latin America on a grand scale. Aid plans with regional scope or substantial budgets are often compared with the Marshall Plan, but the Alliance for Progress was the rare successor that rivaled the original in ambition, if not execution. Kennedy's speech pledged U.S. support for economic integration in Latin America (Kennedy 1961), but the results of the Alliance for Progress were less than stellar. The lack of financial, popular, and institutional support within the United States and the fundamental differences between a war-ravaged Europe and a chronically underdeveloped Latin America led to its demise (Rabe 1999).

The Alliance for Progress nevertheless contributed to the creation of a number of Latin American regional organizations, including the Andean Common Market. Created in 1969, the Andean Common Market included the two primary countries of the alliance, Colombia and Chile (Collier and Slater 1996). Though greatly encouraged by the United States, the organization's formation was a response to tensions within Latin America. In its early years, the Andean Common Market developed plans for joint control of a wide range of products, including the area's ample natural resources. In the Andean Petrochemical Agreement, production of thirty-nine petrochemical products was divided among the five member nations. Each product could be produced by no more than two of the countries (Kearns 1972). Similar agreements were contemplated for other natural resources, but protectionist and nationalist trends, including the takeover of Chile by Augusto Pinochet in 1973, prevented the plans and agreements from evolving into functional integrationist institutions.

While the cause of Andean integration was delayed, it was not destroyed, and the Andean Common Market reemerged in the 1990s as the Andean Community. The modern community is oriented toward a political integration unseen in the plans of the 1960s and facilitates cooperation on many issues, including the environment and natural resources. U.S. funds helped underwrite the formation of an Andean integration system of the 1960s, but political and economic development realities prevented significant progress until the more favorable political environment of the 1990s and 2000s. Funds and plans are insufficient to create action for regional integration in the absence of political will among the participating countries.

Japan

Not all post-conflict countries can be easily and productively fit into a regional model, nor should they be. At the same time the United States crafted the Marshall Plan for Europe, it administered the reconstruction of Japan in an entirely non-integrationist fashion, partially because of the internal peculiarities of the U.S. government. The army, particularly General Douglas MacArthur, was bureaucratically and materially unchallenged during most of the occupation of Japan. In contrast to the United States' long tradition of civilian diplomatic action in Europe, during the occupation of Japan, only a single high-level State Department official visited the country (Finn 1992). MacArthur himself was not inclined to pursue integrationist goals, in part because the logical partners, China and Korea, were focused on resisting the military advance of communism (Finn 1992).

The absence of an integrationist agenda did not prevent a focus on natural resources. The occupation authority swiftly conducted "surveys in the fields of mining and geology, agriculture, fisheries, and forestry reveal[ing] the extent to which utilization of Japan's meager natural resources had been dislocated by the war" (Mueller 1949). The surveys led to constructive action, beginning with the emergency support of Japanese food production through the supply of seed, fertilizer, and fuel. In addition to short-term emergency measures to address food and fuel, longer-term measures sought to increase Japanese production of coal, oil, and timber, as well as for replanting over-forested areas and restoring fishery fleets (Scheiber and Jones 2013).[5] The isolation of Japan may have been inspired by geography, historical coincidence, and even racism, but it did not preclude a substantial role for natural resources in post-conflict recovery, nor did it prevent an economic revitalization that rivaled and sometimes exceeded that of states participating in the Marshall Plan.

LESSONS

The general successes of Western Europe, Central America, and the Western Balkans are the products of particular post-conflict situations. Caution needs to be exercised before seeking to replicate the Marshall Plan, CCAD, or CARDS and IPA elsewhere. The historical record suggests a number of factors that affect the success of post-conflict peacebuilding efforts to use natural resources in regional integration. These factors include an appropriate resource, a well-defined and logical region, political will, significant commitments of resources by outside donors, a coordinated and potentially time-bound plan of action, and a willingness to adapt to local conditions.

Regional peacebuilding cannot succeed without a clearly and logically defined region. Furthermore, shared natural resources can often help to identify the region and provide a context for regional cooperation and peacebuilding. When George Marshall testified before the U.S. Senate in 1947 in defense of the Marshall Plan, he was immediately asked why the plan should include Germany. Marshall's response was emphatic: "The inclusion, or integration, of western Germany into the program is essential. Coal alone provides one of the great essentials to the recovery program, and Germany is a major source of coal" (Gimbel 1976, 266). For Marshall, natural resources helped to define the acceptable limits of the regional recovery program: the integration of Germany into the ECA was necessary because the integration of Germany's resources was indispensable to recovery. The apolitical reality of coal distribution mandated that the Marshall Plan treat Axis and Allied countries alike. A plan that had failed to treat Europe as a region would not have had the same impact on recovery or peacebuilding. Conversely, CENTO was a political disaster because the "central" region of Iran, Pakistan, and Turkey was a geopolitical fantasy developed in Washington, and the target countries did not sufficiently share national goals, interests, or identities. Accordingly, attempts at unified natural resource management and regional integration were short-lived.

Regions cannot be defined by outside donors; they must reflect the interests of post-conflict countries. Although successful post-conflict regional integration has occurred in readily understood areas, such as Western Europe, Central America, and the Western Balkans, regional integration processes inherently politicize

---

[5] For more information on Japanese post–World War II reconstruction efforts, see Mikiyasu Nakayama, "Making Best Use of Domestic Energy Sources: The Priority Production System for Coal Mining and Steel Production in Post-World War II," in this book.

geographic identity. The cooperative and integrative efforts of CCAD and its successors have helped to make the people of Central America somewhat more "Central American" than before. Their common identity can act as a deterrent against conflict recurrence, albeit an imperfect one.

Proximity and similar historical experience do not ensure integration. The Andean Common Market failed in the 1960s because the ambitious plans for the regional management of various natural resources were never executed for political reasons. Shared natural resource interests—from the interconnected natural environments of small nations in Central America to distribution of European coal—can be key to convincing international actors that geographical proximity and common interests are a sufficient basis for substantive cooperation. Long before sharing political authority is politically or socially acceptable, co-ordinated natural resource management can allow technical and administrative cooperation. Joint natural resource management can lay the foundation not only for medium-term cooperation but also for long-term regional integration.

A conflict with interstate dimensions can be a strong incentive for taking a regional tack after hostilities. World War II was an interstate war; the Western Balkan conflicts were internationalized civil wars; and Central America's civil wars featured combatants who frequently crossed international borders. The conflicts showed how strife generated by one country in a region could have devastating consequences on the entire area. At the same time, the shared experience of conflict helped build a common interest in and perspective on reconstruction. With outside donor support, the perspective formed the basis for justifying integration as a guarantor of regional peace.

For integration to make its full contribution to post-conflict reconstruction, belief in the positive benefits of a regional approach must extend to external donors. The Marshall Plan was so integrative in its original conception in part because key U.S. decision makers felt that a United States of Europe would be the best ally and companion for the United States of America. To U.S. senator William Fulbright, European integration "was an objective so dramatic and so full of hope that the enthusiasm of a tired and disillusioned people could be aroused" by it in the United States and Europe (Fulbright 1948, 152). Although donors of the past thirty years may have lacked Fulbright's enthusiasm—there is frequent reference to "donor fatigue"—EU belief in a regional approach to reconstruction in the Western Balkans and U.S. faith in a regional approach in Central America have been crucial to fostering a regional approach to post-conflict reconstruction in the two regions. In contrast, there was no serious interest in a United States of Asia in the 1940s, and there has been only modest donor rhetoric or support for the development of integrative institutions in Southern Africa.

A lack of commitment and political will from participating countries or donors has the power to destroy any possibility of regional integration for peace. Regional integration is not painless, and it often requires participating countries to make real sacrifices of sovereignty. Great Britain dropped out of the Marshall Plan at the end of 1950, so it could retain its special links to Commonwealth countries rather than integrate more fully with Europe (Behrman 2007). It eventually joined the EU in 1973.

As Japan's post-war reconstruction illustrates, a regional approach is not necessary for effective peacebuilding. Substantial investments of assistance at the national level can yield dramatic results. There are few (if any) successful post-conflict recoveries that do not rely at least partially on natural resources, and Japan's recovery depended in no small part on managing their coal, steel, fisheries, agriculture, and other natural resources.

Post-conflict regional integration depends on substantial commitments of funds and other support from outside donors for management of shared natural resources. The generous monetary contributions made by the EU to the Western Balkans through CARDS and IPA have been essential in moving the region toward European and Southeastern European integration. Successful regional integration and peacebuilding efforts frequently entail a combination of financial, technical, and other commitments from donors. Funding is essential but insufficient, as seen in the politically driven collapses of CENTO and the Alliance for Progress. The efficient allocation of funds is critical for maximizing the impact of financial commitments. In the natural resource sector, successful efforts have historically emphasized technical assistance, cooperation, and harmonizing legislation across international borders. Furthermore, integrationist reconstruction cannot occur without a solid base of security and peace. Thus peacekeeping assistance can be an essential donor contribution. CARDS was facilitated by a UN peacekeeping force that made continued interstate war in the Western Balkans impossible, and the presence of the U.S. Army was instrumental in enabling Western Europe to focus its resources on civilian reconstruction during the Marshall Plan.

The goodwill generated by the Marshall Plan far exceeds any realistic assessment of its economic impacts (Behrman 2007). The Marshall Plan's reputation was burnished by the ECA's extensive propaganda efforts, which produced numerous documentary films for European consumption and even sent troubadours through the Sicilian countryside to sing of the wonders of Marshall Plan penicillin (Ellwood 1998). The psychological boost of a well-funded and well-publicized integrationist dream for a better future should not be underestimated. Senator Fulbright's belief that a united Europe would contribute to a prosperous and peaceful Europe has been borne out by the last sixty years.

Donor commitments need to be coordinated but should not be unlimited. The Marshall Plan had a strict five-year cutoff date and was actually canceled early due to an unexpectedly vibrant European recovery. Although some of the most successful elements of the plan continued for decades (for example, the technical assistance program, cooperation through the OECD, etc.), the massive allocation of funds at the core of the Marshall Plan was a relatively short-lived phenomenon (Arkes 1973). Similarly, although there seems little chance of IPA no longer funding the Western Balkan states, full admittance to the EU and eligibility for all EU benefits are limited to Western Balkan countries that manage to incorporate the entirety of the acquis, including the natural resource requirements.

These limitations force post-conflict states to assume ownership and responsibility for their own recovery and future prosperity. Donor support for regional integration must be a tool to help national governments set their investment priorities, including proper consideration of natural resources. For Croatia, insufficient attention to natural resources appears to have prolonged its accession to the EU, potentially affecting the momentum of regional integration.

Every region requires a different approach to post-conflict integration, and every regional approach must adapt to the specific context of the countries involved. No two post-war regional integration efforts utilizing natural resource management are identical. In the case of the Marshall Plan, and to some extent the Western Balkans, reconstruction targeted a population and a region dissimilar from most modern post-conflict situations. Before World War II, Western Europe was one of the most prosperous and industrially advanced areas of the world and possessed ample natural resources to harness for economic progress. The task of the Marshall Plan was to rebuild capacity that had been destroyed by war and to restore the coal mines and the shipping infrastructure, not to design a modern economy from scratch. Although U.S. technical assistance substantially improved European production and cultivation techniques, Europeans already possessed many economically valuable skills and had education levels far higher than those of Central Americans in the 1990s or of most citizens of other modern post-conflict states. It has been argued that the Marshall Plan's early focus on regional integration and its incredible success were only possible because Western European countries were already developed—although the experience of Central America calls that argument into question.

The claims also ignore the nature of the Marshall Plan. Although Europe's post–World War II advantages are undeniable, the Marshall Plan confronted wide disparities in economic conditions among participating countries and responded by structuring its activities on a country-by-country basis. The Marshall Plan in Greece was not the Marshall Plan in France, just as a Marshall plan for Croatia would not be a Marshall plan for Kosovo. Countries that needed massive investment in agricultural capacity used counterpart funds, while nations better positioned to invest in heavy infrastructure could make different choices. Similarly, EU accession in the Western Balkans, while valuing Southeastern European cooperation, has been structured so that each post-conflict country can proceed at its own pace. In the Western Balkans, the donor makes most of the decisions, whereas countries participating in the Marshall Plan played a central role in allocating funds. In both the Marshall Plan and the Western Balkans, collaboratively developed programs attuned to local conditions were essential.

Especially following interstate conflicts, post-conflict countries may be unusually aware of the role of their neighbors in national prosperity and security. The awareness can foster cooperation and regional integration that can contribute to long-term peacebuilding and fulfill immediate reconstruction needs. In the past, natural resources have inspired efforts at regional cooperation, which in turn have expanded into regional integration.

APPLYING THE LESSONS OF POST-CONFLICT REGIONAL INTEGRATION: A MARSHALL PLAN FOR AFGHANISTAN?

According to at least one Afghan official, the 2008 Afghanistan National Development Strategy is a Marshall plan for Afghanistan (Haidari 2008). Yet the document does not reflect a regional approach beyond a few scattered projects for regional hydropower and irrigation (IRA 2006). A real Marshall plan for Afghanistan would need to be far more regionally oriented and ambitious.

The geographic scope of a would-be Afghanistan Marshall plan is not obvious. Lack of stability along the Afghanistan-Pakistan border could inspire Pakistan to participate in a regional attempt to rebuild Afghanistan, but two highly unequal countries do not a region make. There is less incentive for Afghanistan's other neighbors—particularly the Central Asian republics of Turkmenistan, Kyrgyzstan, and Kazakhstan—to surrender sovereignty in support of cooperation or integration. Shared water management could be a promising context for cooperation between Afghanistan and its Central Asian neighbors, but Afghanistan is in a poor position to negotiate effectively given its lack of institutional capacity, data, and geopolitical power—at least without strong donor assistance (Ahmad 2004). More positively, donor support of post-conflict Afghanistan will presumably remain substantial in the near future, and many donors will likely be open to regional approaches to peacebuilding. Of course, a Marshall plan would need to be adapted to Afghanistan's history and level of development, as well as to ethnic differences within the country.

The central lesson of past post-conflict regional integration efforts is not that enormous sums of money can produce economic miracles under perfect conditions. It is that a carefully structured foreign commitment can foster both post-war recovery and long-term regional peace and stability. The cooperative management of natural resources was essential to post-conflict regional integration in post-conflict Europe and Central America. Regional integration of natural resource management in Afghanistan and other post-conflict areas could similarly become a key tool in advancing economic development and peace—and create an embrace between countries so close that no country would have the desire or capacity to pull back its fist to pummel another. But the right conditions are necessary, and the approach must be tailored.

With the right conditions, leadership, and approaches, post-conflict reconstruction can lead to long-term peace and prosperity. Regional approaches, such as the Marshall Plan and its conceptual progeny in Central America and the Western Balkans, can be particularly effective. However, as the less successful regional approaches illustrate, regional integration by no means guarantees peace. If a regional approach is adopted, natural resources can and should be part of the strategy to build confidence (e.g., cooperating on environmental issues in Central America before extending cooperation to political and economic spheres), facilitate cooperation (e.g., in managing shared waters in the Western Balkans), foster shared identity (e.g., through harmonized environmental laws and joint international environmental negotiating positions in Central America), and link economies (e.g., through coal and steel management in Europe).

A regional approach can be valuable but not necessarily indispensable to post-conflict peacebuilding. As this book shows, however, natural resources appear to be indispensable to most peacebuilding processes. Rather than calls for new Marshall plans, international assistance may be more effectively and efficiently deployed to manage natural resources for livelihoods, economic recovery, basic services, restoring governance capacity, and other objectives of peacebuilding.

REFERENCES

Ahmad, M. 2004. *Water resource development in Northern Afghanistan and its implications for Amu Darya Basin.* Washington, D.C.: World Bank.

Arkes, H. 1973. *Bureaucracy, the Marshall Plan, and the national interest.* Princeton, NJ: Princeton University Press.

Behrman, G. 2007. *The most noble adventure: The Marshall Plan and how America helped rebuild Europe.* New York: Free Press.

Bennet, C. 1997. *Yugoslavia's bloody collapse.* New York: NYU Press.

Bush, G. W. 2002. Remarks by the president to the George C. Marshall ROTC Award Seminar on National Security, Lexington, VA, April 17. http://usa.usembassy.de/gemeinsam/bush041702.htm.

Chaidron, A. 2005. Walloon government launches plan for economic recovery. *European Industrial Relations Observatory On-line,* October 25. www.eurofound.europa.eu/eiro/2005/10/feature/be0510304f.htm.

Čolakhodžić, A., M. Filipović, J. Kovandžić, and S. Stec. 2013. The Sava River: Transitioning to peace in the former Yugoslavia. In *Water and post-conflict peacebuilding,* ed. E. Weinthal, J. Troell, and M. Nakayama. London: Earthscan.

Collier, S., and W. F. Slater. 1996. *A history of Chile: 1808–1994.* New York: Cambridge University Press.

Ellwood, D. 1998. You too can be like us: Selling the Marshall Plan. *History Today,* October. http://ics.leeds.ac.uk/papers/vp01.cfm?outfit=pmt&folder=715&paper=1131.

European Commission. 2008a. Western Balkans: Enhancing the European perspective. Communication from the Commission to the European Parliament and the Council, SEC 288. http://ec.europa.eu/enlargement/pdf/balkans_communication/western_balkans_communication_050308_en.pdf.

———. 2008b. Enlargement strategy and main challenges 2008–2009. Communication from the Commission to the Council and the European Parliament, 674 (2008). http://ec.europa.eu/enlargement/pdf/press_corner/key-documents/reports_nov_2008/strategy_paper_incl_country_conclu_en.pdf.

———. n.d.a. Enlargement statistics 2000–2006. http://ec.europa.eu/enlargement/how-does-it-work/financial-assistance/cards/statistics2000-2006_en.htm.

———. n.d.b. Enlargement: Instrument for pre-accession assistance (IPA). http://ec.europa.eu/enlargement/how-does-it-work/financial-assistance/instrument-pre-accession_en.htm.

Finn, R. 1992. *Winners in peace: MacArthur, Yoshida, and postwar Japan.* Berkeley: University of California Press.

Fransen, F. 2001. *The supranational politics of Jean Monnet: Ideas and origins of the European Community.* Westport, CT: Greenwood Press.

Fulbright, J. W. 1948. A United States of Europe? In *Peace settlements of World War II (May)*. Vol. 257 of *Annals of the American Academy of Political and Social Science*. Philadelphia, PA: Sage Publications.

Geremek, B. 2008. The Marshall Plan and European integration. In *The Marshall Plan: Lessons learned for the 21st century*, ed. E. Sorel and P. C. Padoan. Paris: Organisation for Economic Co-operation and Development.

Gimbel, J. 1976. *The origins of the Marshall Plan*. Stanford, CA: Stanford University Press.

GON (Government of Norway). 2008. Speech at the SADC Summit Mauritius, April 20. www.tmcnet.com/usubmit/2008/04/21/3398987.htm.

Grdesic, I. 2009. Presentation at Federal Conference: Innovative Strategies for European Integration of the Western Balkans, Woodrow Wilson International Center for Scholars, Washington, D.C., May 6. www.wilsoncenter.org/event/federal-conference-innovative-strategies-for-european-integration-the-western-balkans.

Haidari, M. A. 2008. NATO needs Marshall Plan to secure Afghanistan. *Quqnoos*, March 31. http://e-ariana.com/ariana/eariana.nsf/allPrintDocs/952e9576703dd6138725741d005cd9c4!OpenDocument&Click=.

IRA (Islamic Republic of Afghanistan). 2006. *Afghanistan national development strategy summary report: An interim strategy for security, governance, economic growth and poverty reduction*. June 30. http://reliefweb.int/sites/reliefweb.int/files/resources/AFA4970B33A0505E49257107000811C6-unama-afg-30jan2.pdf.

Kearns, K. 1972. The Andean Common Market: A new thrust at economic integration in South America. *Journal of Interamerican Studies and World Affairs* 14 (2): 225–249.

Kemp, J. 2007. The president's plan is our one last hope. Townhall.com, January 8. http://townhall.com/columnists/JackKemp/2007/01/08/the_presidents_plan_is_our_one_last_hope.

Kennedy, J. F. 1961. On the Alliance for Progress. In *Modern history sourcebook*. www.fordham.edu/halsall/mod/1961kennedy-afp1.html.

Korb, L., and A. Cohen. 2005. A Marshall plan for the third world. *Boston Globe*, November 15.

Liebscher, K., J. Christl, P. Mooslechner, and D. Ritzberger-Grünwald, eds. 2005. *European economic integration and South-East Europe: Challenges and prospects*. Cheltenham, UK: Edward Elgar.

Light, P. C. 2000. Government's greatest achievements. Reform Watch Paper No. 2. Washington, D.C.: Brookings Institution.

Machado, B. 2007. *In search of a usable past: The Marshall Plan and postwar reconstruction today*. George C. Marshall Foundation. www.marshallfoundation.org/library/doc_in_search.html.

———. 2008. A usable Marshall plan. In *The Marshall Plan: Lessons learned for the 21st century*, ed. E. Sorel and P. C. Padoan. Paris: Organisation for Economic Co-operation and Development.

Marshall, G. 1947. The Marshall Plan speech, Harvard University, Cambridge, Massachusetts, June 5. www.oecd.org/document/10/0,3343,en_2649_201185_1876938_1_1_1_1,00.html.

McDonald, J. W. 2009. Interview by authors of former U.S. Department of State official, former U.S. economic coordinator for the Central Treaty Organization, and current chairman of the Institute for Multi-Track Diplomacy. March 4. Arlington, VA.

McDonald, J. W., and N. Zanolli. 2008. *The shifting ground of conflict and peacebuilding: Stories and lessons.* Lanham, MD: Lexington Books.

Mills, N. 2008. *Winning the peace: The Marshall Plan and America's coming of age as a superpower.* Hoboken, NJ: John Wiley and Sons.

Mueller, P. J. 1949. *Occupied Japan: A progress report.* www.army.mil/article/4613/.

Newsmax.com. 2007. LA needs Marshall plan to stop gangs. January 13. http://archive.newsmax.com/archives/ic/2007/1/13/184315.shtml.

Nováček, P., P. Mederly, P. C. Armand, and I. Skácelová. 2007. Marshall plan for Haiti: Initial project of the Global Partnership for Development. *Foresight* 9:59–66.

Ohlsson, L. 2004. Arguing the case for an environmental Marshall plan. Background paper for The Hague Conference on Environment, Security and Sustainable Development, May 9–12. www.envirosecurity.org/conference/working/EnvironmentalMarshallPlan.html.

Omari, A., and P. Macaringue. 2007. Southern African security in a historical perspective. In *Security and democracy in Southern Africa,* ed. G. Cawthra, A. du Pisani, and A. Omari. Johannesburg, South Africa: Wits University Press; Ottawa, Canada: International Development Research Center.

Page, K. D., and M. Schwarz. 1996. USAID capacity building in the environment: A case study of the Central American Commission for Environment and Development. July 31. http://pdf.usaid.gov/pdf_docs/PNABZ225.pdf.

Pond, E. 2006. *Endgame in the Balkans.* Washington, D.C.: Brookings Institution.

Rabe, S. 1999. *The most dangerous area in the world: John F. Kennedy confronts communist revolution in Latin America.* Chapel Hill: University of North Carolina.

Robinson, L. 1991. *Intervention or neglect: The United States and Central America beyond the 1980s.* New York: Council on Foreign Relations Press.

SADC (Southern African Development Community). 2003. Regional indicative strategic development plan. Gaborone, Botswana. www.sadc.int/attachment/download/file/74.

Scheiber, H., and B. Jones. 2013. Fisheries policies and the problem of instituting sustainable management: The case of occupied Japan. In *Livelihoods, natural resources, and post-conflict peacebuilding,* ed. H. Young and L. Goldman. London: Earthscan.

Shah, A. 2009. U.S. and foreign aid assistance. www.globalissues.org/article/35/us-and-foreign-aid-assistance.

SICA (Central American Integration System). n.d. Purposes of SICA. www.sica.int/sica/propositos_en.aspx?IdEnt=401&IdmStyle=2&Idm=2.

UNEP (United Nations Environment Programme). 1997. Policy responses and directions. In *Global environment outlook-1.* www.unep.org/geo/geo1/ch/ch3_21.htm.

USAID (United States Agency for International Development). 1989. *Environmental and natural resource management in Central America: A strategy for AID assistance.* Washington, D.C.

———. 1994. *Regional environmental and natural resources management project midterm evaluation.* Washington, D.C.

Wasser, S. F. 2005. BLS and the Marshall Plan: The forgotten story. *Monthly Labor Review* 128 (6): 44–52.

Making best use of domestic energy sources: The Priority Production System for coal mining and steel production in post–World War II Japan

Mikiyasu Nakayama

For Japan, World War II ended with its surrender in August 1945 and a cease-fire agreement with the Allied Forces in September. Japan was thereafter occupied by the United States until the San Francisco Peace Treaty in September 1951. The six years between August 1945 and September 1951 are generally considered the post-conflict period in Japan.

One of the main reasons Japan entered World War II was to secure sources of energy in Asia and the Pacific region, particularly oil wells such as the Minas oil field on Sumatra in the Dutch colony of Indonesia. Although oil filled only 10 percent of energy needs in post–World War II Japan, it was indispensable to transportation and the military, so the country had to rely on imported oil, as it had before the war.[1] Although there were oil wells on mainland Japan, production of crude oil could meet only a tiny fraction of the country's energy demands.

In the post–World War II period, Japan suffered from an energy shortage. The means for producing domestic coal—Japan's only resort—were destroyed toward the end of the war. Moreover, many immigrant coal miners from former colonies (particularly Korea) went home shortly after the war.

Because coal fueled civilian activities and industry, including production of fertilizer and synthetic fiber, the Japanese government introduced the Priority Production System in December 1946 to support the revitalization of domestic coal mining. The system's major aim, after strengthening coal production, was to restore steel manufacturing to drive Japanese industry as a whole. Steel was, in turn, given to coal mines, to help accelerate the extraction of more coal, and to other industrial and export businesses (see figure 1).

The Priority Production System relied on funds from the Reconstruction Finance Bank, which raised money by selling reconstruction finance bonds to the Bank of Japan. The Bank of Japan thus continued to print bank notes,

---

Mikiyasu Nakayama is a professor in the Department of International Studies, Graduate School of Frontier Sciences, University of Tokyo.

[1] Before the war in 1937, coal and hydropower provided 62 percent and 18 percent of Japan's energy needs, respectively (Oba 2009).

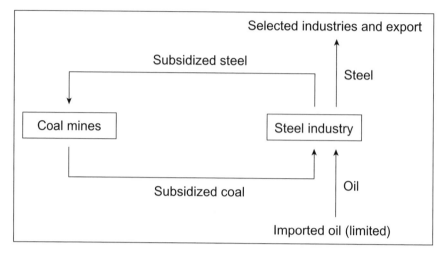

Figure 1. Concept of the Priority Production System in post–World War II Japan
Source: Data from Agency of Natural Resources and Energy (2002).

which led to inflation. Then, in the mid-1950s to 1960s, with increasing imports of oil and coal, many coal mines closed, and workers lost their jobs.

This chapter describes how the Priority Production System was developed, why it was accepted so readily by the Japanese, why it was successfully implemented, what it cost, and how other post-conflict societies can learn from Japan's experience.

THE PRIORITY PRODUCTION SYSTEM IN POST–WORLD WAR II JAPAN

The major objectives of the Priority Production System for economic reconstruction were to stimulate industry and restrain hyperinflation. The government believed that increasing the production of coal, electric power, and steel would improve the economy. With more coal, electric power and marine transportation increased significantly. Industrial production of chemical fertilizer reached 70 percent of its pre-war level by December 1948 (Saito 2000).

Before World War II, some 60 percent of coal was used by industry and 40 percent by other sectors, such as transportation and thermal power. After the war, demand for energy became immense; therefore, increasing domestic coal production for industry became critical (Johnson 1983). In 1947, the coal and steel industries were prioritized. Beginning in 1946, approximately 20 to 30 percent of the general account budget was devoted to priority production in the form of price subsidies and indemnities for losses (see table 1). Because many workers from former colonies went home after the war, Japan had a serious shortage of labor. The few remaining miners received food and housing benefits in exchange for working extended hours in a three-shift, twenty-four-hour schedule (Johnson 1983).

Table 1. Price subsidies and indemnities: Government payments and percent of general account budget, Japan, 1940–1952

Year	Total general account budget expenditures		Price subsidies (kakaku chōsei hi)		Indemnities for losses (sonshitsu hoshō hi)	
	(Million yen)					
1940	5,856	(100%)	17	(0.3%)	60	(1.0%)
1941	7,929	(100)	95	(1.2)	55	(0.7)
1942	8,271	(100)	305	(3.7)	240	(2.9)
1943	12,491	(100)	510	(4.1)	265	(2.1)
1944	19,872	(100)	1,266	(6.4)	567	(2.8)
1946	115,207	(100)	3,731	(3.2)	22,661	(20.0)
1947	205,841	(100)	28,178	(13.7)	8,566	(4.2)
1948	461,974	(100)	93,118	(20.2)	16,632	(3.6)
1949	699,448	(100)	179,284	(25.6)	31,838	(4.6)
1950	633,259	(100)	60,162	(9.5)	7,830	(1.2)
1951	749,836	(100)	26,975	(3.6)	9,560	(1.3)
1952	873,942	(100)	40,308	(4.6)	8,183	(0.9)

Source: Johnson (1983).

Priority production proved successful by 1948. Coal production recovered in 1948 to about 60 percent of its highest level during the war (Johnson 1983). The Economic Stabilization Board stated in its first economic white paper, published on July 22, 1947, that a two-fold increase in coal production would lead to a four-fold increase in general manufacturing (Johnson 1983). Economic recovery was accelerated as more industries were included in the Priority Production System. Electricity was prioritized in November 1947, the railway in January 1948, and chemical fertilizers (especially ammonium sulfate) in March 1948 (Nakamura and Odaka 2004). In the 1948 fiscal year, production nearly met or (in many instances) exceeded targets, with 97 percent for coal, 94 percent for steel, 102 percent for ironware, 101 percent for ammonium sulfate, 115 percent for electric power, 110 percent for caustic soda, 113 percent for cement, and 67 percent for cotton thread. Coal, steel, and ammonium sulfate recovered to prewar levels in 1948, 1950, and 1947, respectively (Nakamura and Odaka 2004).

Inflation: The cost of the Priority Production System

Immediately after World War II, the production base in Japan was disorganized, and the government lost control of commodity prices. Inflation accelerated toward the end of the war; the highest price increases occurred in 1946, the year after the war ended (see table 2) (Saito 2000).

The Priority Production System made prevailing inflation worse, and countermeasures were necessitated. Accordingly, in 1949, Joseph Dodge, finance advisor to General Douglas MacArthur who led General Headquarters (GHQ, the occupation forces of the United States), advised the Japanese government to balance the budget. Through implementation of what became commonly known as the

Table 2. Inflation rate, Japan, 1944–1955

	Inflation rate by year					
	1944	1945	1946	1947	1948	1949
Wholesale price	13.3	51.0	364.5	195.9	165.6	63.3
Consumer price	n.a.	n.a.	n.a.	125.3	75.9	25.6
	1950	1951	1952	1953	1954	1955
Wholesale price	18.2	38.8	19.6	0.7	−0.7	−1.8
Consumer price	−4.0	15.2	4.8	7.0	5.9	0.1

Source: Saito (2000).

Dodge Line, the Reconstruction Finance Bank suspended lending to firms. Postal rates and the fares on the national railway also increased substantially (Saito 2000). The Japanese government enforced tax collection, cut expenditures to balance the budget, decreased the volume of the Bank of Japan notes, progressed remarkably in abolishing commodity and price controls, and increased productivity.

Unequal distribution of wealth

Some criticize the Priority Production System on the grounds that it maintained or led to unequal distribution of wealth. Socialist Kihachiro Kimura insisted that the Priority Production System only served the interests of the "capitalist class." He argued that inflation was due to floating capital during the war and unfair profits made during priority production. He maintained that the Japanese government was obliged to eliminate inflation at the expense of business interests, and that concentration on steel and other industrial production provided capitalists a way to earn money with ease (Kimura 1947).

Hiromi Arisawa, an economist and later a professor at the University of Tokyo, developed the Priority Production System and advocated it to Prime Minister Shigeru Yoshida. Arisawa specialized in Marxist economics while serving as an economist in the Japanese army during World War II. He was thus knowledgeable about the Japanese economy during the war, when Japan was under a military government. Prime Minister Yoshida relied upon Arisawa and decided to implement priority production, even though the Japanese viewed Arisawa as a "red economist." Arisawa, who was not expected to back the capital class, maintained that the system would revitalize the Japanese economy. He was against a tight monetary policy and believed that industrial production should be given the highest priority (Gao 1997).

Criticisms of the Priority Production System reflected the rapidly changing ideological environment of Japan just after the war. Ideas of social equity and balanced distribution of wealth had been suppressed from the early 1930s to the end of the war. After the war, criticisms were not strong enough to change the wartime ideology of Japanese industrial policy (Gao 1997). But ideological imbalance in a post-conflict society may be inevitable.

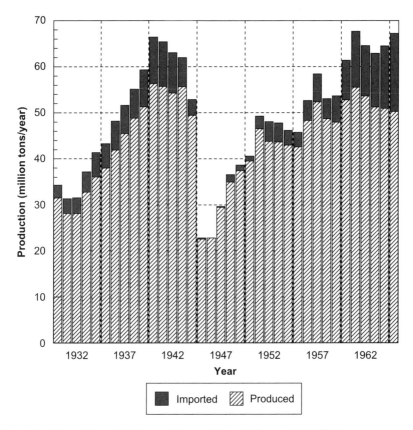

Figure 2. Domestic production and imported coal, Japan, 1930–1965
Source: Data from Agency of Natural Resources and Energy (2002).

Massive unemployment of coal miners

Once the balance of payments improved in the late 1950s, Japan began to import cheaper and higher-quality coal (see figure 2). Because there was less demand for domestic coal, Japanese coal mines were adversely affected. As coal mines closed from the 1950s to the 1970s (see figure 3), unemployment increased, leading to social unrest and many strikes.

Most former coal miners were absorbed by other sectors while Japan enjoyed rapid economic growth in the 1960s and 1970s. The Temporary Law to Deal with Redundant Coal Miners was adopted in December 1959 to adjust the labor-market structure by encouraging worker turnover. The policy prompted many laborers to move to manufacturing, lowering and stabilizing unemployment. Thereafter, no substantial employment policies were implemented (Ohtake 2004).

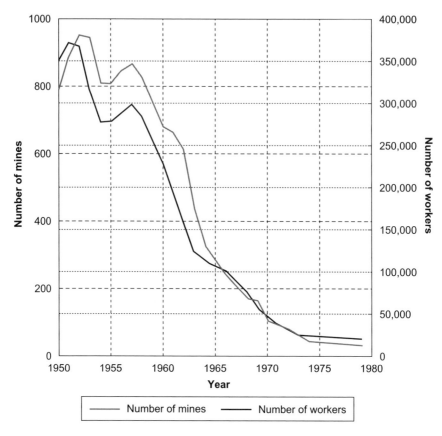

Figure 3. Number of coal mines and workers, Japan, 1950–1970s
Source: Data from Agency of Natural Resources and Energy (2002).

FACTORS THAT AFFECTED THE SUCCESS OF THE PRIORITY PRODUCTION SYSTEM

One of the main prerequisites for successful implementation of the Priority Production System was strong governmental control of the national economy. In other words, the Priority Production System was essentially a socialist planned economy, not a free economy. It was also based on the recovery of heavy industry, with steel production constituting the major component. Such an industry-based, socialistic system was made possible by several factors.

First, Japanese citizens were accustomed to a planned economy before and during the war. Thus the Japanese expressed no strong objection to the Priority Production System. Civilian use of oil had been strictly controlled since 1938, when the Japanese government enacted the Revised Materials Mobilization Plan to control many strategic materials. For example, free commercial transactions of gasoline, coal, and rice were prohibited; people had to use government vouchers to purchase them. Later, during the war, civilians were not allowed to purchase gasoline.

Second, before the war, Japan constructed military vessels and met other military and civilian needs through heavy industry. After the war and as a means to accelerate economic recovery, Japan's reliance on heavy industry continued. Provision of coal and steel were thus essential to revitalizing heavy industry. Technically knowledgeable and highly skilled engineers, who had survived the war, promoted the recovery of Japanese heavy industry. Shortly after the war, there were few miners and industrial workers because men had been drafted. The labor shortage was resolved by employing up to 6 million ex-soldiers and Japanese workers who had returned from former colonies to mainland Japan.

Finally, although the Priority Production System relied on coal, industry and civilians still needed oil. To meet the demand, the GHQ organized the Petroleum Advisory Group (PAG) shortly after the war in October 1945. American oil companies, such as Cal-Tex and Shell, participated in PAG. The GHQ provided the Japanese with petroleum products as part of its emergency aid program as early as November 1945 and light oil in December 1945 to cope with the first winter. Assistance given by the United States, the occupier, was therefore instrumental.

LESSONS LEARNED

The success of the Priority Production System was due to several factors:

- The use of coal—a domestic energy source—fueled the steel industry and other sectors before and during World War II.
- Although production of coal was severely hampered during the war (see figure 4), the technical resources for coal mining survived the conflict.
- The lack of labor shortly after the war was resolved by employing ex-soldiers and Japanese workers who had returned from former colonies.
- The Japanese population was accustomed to a planned economy before and during the war, so the Priority Production System was not disconcerting.

Post-conflict societies may benefit from making good use of domestic energy sources when imported ones are lacking. Unlike in Japan after World War II, a heavy industry–driven economy may not be feasible in all countries emerging from conflict. Still, domestic energy sources have advantages over imported ones. Intensive use of domestic energy sources might also conserve hard currency, which is often lacking in post-conflict countries.

Developing, and especially post-conflict, countries usually lack technical resources to make the best use of domestic energy. Donor countries and organizations should thus give full support to expanding technical resources in the energy sector and help train the short supply of workers.

Absorbing excombatants and returning refugees into society is difficult for most post-conflict countries. The Japanese Priority Production System led to

Figure 4. Monthly coal production and number of miners, Japan, 1944–1946
Source: Data from Agency of Natural Resources and Energy (2002).

employment for 6 million ex-soldiers and civilians. Similar measures could be taken in other post-conflict countries to prioritize labor-intensive domestic energy production (taking into account new technologies to reduce carbon emissions).

Some researchers assume that the Priority Production System was based on the Japanese Revised Materials Mobilization Plan, which was put into effect in 1938 in anticipation of the war (Johnson 1983). For several years thereafter, the Japanese population endured scarcity and strict control of indispensable commodities such as oil. Consequently, they could cope with yet another planned-economy scheme.

Other analysts argue that the Priority Production System was not that effective. Critics point out that the proliferation of underground markets in post-conflict Japan indicated that the Japanese government had failed to control the material flows on which the Priority Production System was based. Still, critics generally assume that the Japanese economy would not have recovered as rapidly as it did after the war without the Priority Production System. Perhaps the key lesson is that post-conflict societies should consider stronger control of some aspects of their economies in the early recovery period rather than relying solely on the free market.

CONCLUSION

The Priority Production System was successful in post–World War II Japan. Countries that implement their own priority production systems should be familiar with government-controlled economies.

Defeated countries might rationally take advantage of domestic resources and give priority to certain industries or sectors, especially when they cannot obtain imports. Priority production tends to require money and human resources, so countries should adopt policies to absorb surplus manpower, such as former soldiers and refugees. Governments also need to consider how to employ the same populations in other sectors when priority production systems end.

The massive unemployment and hyperinflation observed in post-conflict Japan revealed the risk of short-term solutions like the Priority Production System. Societies should understand that priority production systems are emergency government measures, and governments may need outside advice, as Japan received. Because the Priority Production System was a large-scale experiment carried out in a defeated country, it might serve as an interesting and stimulating example for other post-conflict societies.

REFERENCES

Agency of Natural Resources and Energy. 2002. *Coal note* [*Koru noto*]. Tokyo: Shigen Sangyo Shimbun Sha.
Gao, B. 1997. *Economic ideology and Japanese industrial policy*. Cambridge, UK: Cambridge University Press.
Johnson, C. A. 1983. *MITI and the Japanese miracle: The growth of industrial policy, 1925–1975*. Palo Alto, CA: Stanford University Press.
Kimura, K. 1947. The precondition of economic recovery [Keizai saiken no zentei]. *Asahi Review* [*Asahi hyoron*] November: 12–20.
Nakamura, T., and K. Odaka. 2004. *Economic history of Japan 1914–1955*. Oxford, UK: Oxford University Press.
Oba, Y. 2009. Study of the energy revolution [Enerugie kakumeino keiei kenkyu]. *Proceedings of Hokkai-Gakuen University* [*Hokkai-Gakuen Daigaku Ronshu*] 141: 41–89.
Ohtake, F. 2004. Structural unemployment measures in Japan. *Japan Labor Review* 1 (2): 26–53.
Saito, M. 2000. *The Japanese economy*. Vol. 1 of *Economic ideas leading to the 21st century*, ed. L. R. Klein and V. Su. River Edge, NJ: World Scientific Publishing.

Road infrastructure reconstruction as a peacebuilding priority in Afghanistan: Negative implications for land rights

Jon Unruh and Mourad Shalaby

The international community's understanding of war-affected societies and the processes leading to peace have improved significantly in recent years, particularly with the need for effective approaches to deal with unstable, failed, recovering, volatile, and poorly governed states and their restive populations. As knowledge grows of how and why civil wars occur, end, and often recur, efforts must progress beyond the pursuit of peacebuilding priorities as separate endeavors toward their integration. The need comes with the realization that conflict-related and stable settings are profoundly different. Peacebuilding projects and policies, although derived and implemented separately and on their own merits, interact on the ground in a largely unplanned and unexamined manner. Success in one area of peacebuilding can cause problems in another, and there can be unexpected and often volatile repercussions from interactions between priorities. As lessons learned in peacebuilding become more widely known, the opportunity emerges to examine harmful interactions between priorities to mitigate acutely negative outcomes at a minimum and, more ideally, enhance prospects for interactions to contribute to durable peace.

Although peacebuilding priorities vary according to country and conflict, two that are widely recognized as critically important are road-infrastructure (re)construction[1] and reconstitution of land and property rights systems. Based on a literature review of Afghanistan's land tenure and conflict and the experience of the authors in war-torn settings, this chapter examines the interaction between the two priorities in Afghanistan. It focuses specifically on how the road-infrastructure (re)construction effort by international donors affects land rights, which the Afghan

---

Jon Unruh is a professor in the Department of Geography at McGill University and an expert in post-conflict land tenure in the developing world. Mourad Shalaby, who has wide international experience in land use issues, is a graduate student in geography at McGill University. This chapter is an adapted version of Jon Unruh and Mourad Shalaby, "A Volatile Interaction between Peacebuilding Priorities: Road Infrastructure (Re)Construction and Land Rights in Afghanistan," *Progress in Development Studies* 12 (2012): 47–61. It was developed with support from the Center for Global Partnership of the Japan Foundation.

[1] Parentheses are used to indicate that infrastructure was either reconstructed (it previously existed) or constructed for the first time (it had not previously existed).

government, with assistance from the international community, is attempting to recognize formally. The chapter presents some of the destructive interactions between road (re)construction and land tenure in Afghanistan to illustrate the need for better integration of peacebuilding priorities, raise awareness of the potential negative repercussions of well-intentioned investments, and contribute to understanding of how outcomes differ between war-torn and stable scenarios.

Donors who plan, fund, and implement projects believe that the (re)construction of road infrastructure in war-torn countries contributes substantially and independently to peacebuilding and post-war recovery. Road (re)construction is intended to ease trade and economic linkages; facilitate access to schools, health clinics, courts, and other services; boost agricultural yields; connect rural areas to the marketplace; provide security to rural communities; and lead to development in other sectors (JICA 2003, 2004, 2006; JSCE 2002; USAID 2006). Realizing the benefits is important for economic and livelihood recovery and development and thus to winning hearts and minds of people living in unstable and volatile sociopolitical settings (JICA 2004; Meilahn 2007; Mockaitis 2003).

The reconstitution of land and property rights systems in conflict-affected settings is crucial for the return of dislocated populations; restitution; agricultural recovery and food security; broad economic recovery; dispute resolution; and addressing ethnic, tribal, and religious claims and attachments to land (Bruch et al. 2009; Unruh 2009). Reconstitution of functional land and property rights systems also leads to resolution of political problems associated with areas claimed, gained, or lost in battle (Andre 2003; Banks 2007; Unruh 2003, 2004). Land rights issues can also lead to armed conflict.[2] Ethnic cleansing, evictions, retribution, inequality in land and property, legal pluralism that favors some sectors of society over others, legal systems that are noninclusive or exploitive, and land-related grievances and animosities exacerbate conflict.[3]

Although road (re)construction and land rights do not interact at the levels of analysis, policy, planning, programming, implementation, and evaluation—and the Afghanistan case is particularly illustrative—they often interact quite negatively on the ground in an unplanned and to-date unexamined way (ANDS 2008; JICA 2003, 2004, 2006; USAID 2006). Some interactions work against peace and can be particularly problematic when a military response is perceived as the only answer.

The primary reason for not examining the interaction between peacebuilding priorities is the assumption that projects and activities will produce outcomes similar to those expected in stable settings (JICA 2006; MRRD and MPW 2007; U.S. DOD 2009). But one of the main lessons learned is that conflict settings differ profoundly from peaceful ones.[4] Much additional work is needed on how the differences affect the interaction of peacebuilding priorities. After describing

---

[2] See Bailliet (2003); Barquero (2004); Bruch et al. (2009); Cohen (1993); Unruh (2009).
[3] See Bruch et al. (2009); Cohen (1993); DW (2005); Unruh (2009); Alden Wily (2003).
[4] See Bruch et al. (2009); Goovaerts, Gasser, and Inbal (2005); Junne and Verkoren (2005); UNEP (2009).

Road reconstruction and land rights in Afghanistan

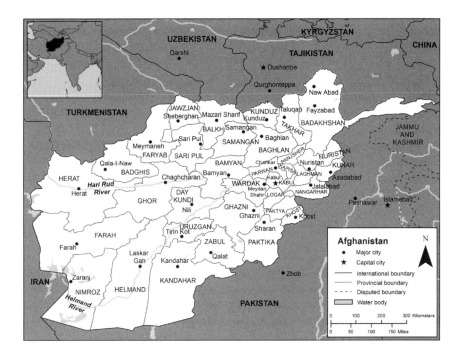

road (re)construction and land rights in Afghanistan and showing how they differ from those in stable contexts, the chapter provides an analysis of the volatile interaction between them.

ROAD INFRASTRUCTURE

Decades of war and neglect have made Afghanistan's limited roads and bridges nearly impassable (Glasser 2002). International donors presume that road (re)construction will help win over local populations and lead to peace (JICA 2003, 2004, 2006; JSCE 2002; USAID 2006). After security expenditures, road (re)construction absorbs the most aid and is the largest component of Afghanistan's economic recovery and development (Delesgues 2007; Olesen and Strand 2005). The United States and Japan have undertaken most of the road projects at a cost of several billion U.S. dollars to help grow the economy, improve security, and integrate isolated parts of the country (Delesgues 2007).[5] For the Afghan government, road (re)construction is "key to raising rural livelihoods and reducing poverty and vulnerability in rural areas. Better rural roads will improve market access and opportunities for rural households" (ANDS 2008, 9). Road (re)construction is also thought to improve the following (U.S. DOD 2009):

---

[5] See also JICA (2003, 2004, 2006); JSCE (2002); Schell (2009); USAID (2006).

- Access to schools, health clinics, courthouses, and other government and social services.
- Trade and economic links within Afghanistan.
- Trade with other Central Asian countries.
- Access to mineral resources.
- Peace, local-level security, and stability.
- National security.
- National integration of ethnic groups, clans, and religions.
- Administrative, trade, and economic contacts between district headquarters and provincial capitals.
- Bringing the hinterland into commercial contact with the market place.
- Transportation costs for agricultural produce to and from markets.
- Capacity and efficiency of all sectors.
- Access to markets for farming communities.
- Response time of military agencies to security concerns.
- Creation of businesses.

Of particular importance is the three-thousand-kilometer Ring Road connecting Kabul, Herat, and Kandahar (see figure 1). When completed, 60 percent of Afghans (approximately 17 million people) will live within fifty kilometers of the road (U.S. DOD 2009). Donors in different parts of the country are constructing provincial and feeder roads and bridges that will connect many areas of rural Afghanistan (MRRD and MPW 2007). The United States built 715 kilometers of the northern Ring Road and rebuilt six provincial roads and 0.4 kilometers of bridges to benefit some 5.3 million people. Current measures of success of road (re)construction are highly selective, easily calculated, and almost entirely based on logistics: reduced vehicle and transport costs, lower travel times and passenger fares, new businesses, increased traffic, and movement of more freight (U.S. DOD 2009). The measures of success fail to assess impacts on land rights, land grabbing, or conflict.[6]

LAND RIGHTS

Long periods of armed conflict, beginning with the Soviet occupation, have profoundly altered the statutory and customary land tenure systems of Afghanistan. Land tenure is based on confusing and highly divisive statutory, customary, ad hoc, Islamic, and warlord laws and regulations; is rife with problems; and is lacking in nationally legitimate, workable approaches (IWPR 2008; Alden Wily 2003).

---

[6] Land grabbing is the illegal or coerced seizure of land in the absence or against the will of the owner or legitimate landholder, whether or not the land is held under statutory law.

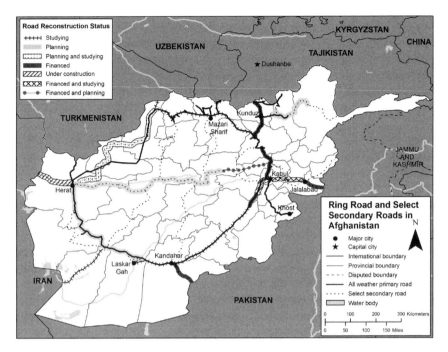

Figure 1. Ring Road and select secondary roads in Afghanistan
Source: AIMS (2003).

With the capture of the state by the mujahideen in 1992, the land tenure system began to disintegrate rapidly. Tenure security has since plummeted, and extortion, asset stripping, and land grabbing thrive as warlords, militias, and other powerful interests have emerged to acquire land (Alden Wily 2003). Customary agreements and land documents have become meaningless, and the poor are unable to pay the necessary bribes to keep the militias away from their land. As a result, land is among the most difficult issues confronting the Afghan government (IWPR 2008).

Disarmament, demobilization, and reintegration in Afghanistan depend on agriculture (Sato 2010), and the long-term stability of the country hinges on recovery and resilience at the local level (Rogers 2010). Rural and peri-urban lands are often invaded and degraded, and there are waves of land grabbing when individuals and groups gain or lose power (Alden Wily 2003). Land values have increased dramatically.[7] And although the 2007 National Land Policy (IRA 2007) acknowledges problems, it assumes that the government has control over the whole country, that corrupt officials will not use the law to seize lands, and that local warlords and other leaders will cooperate.

---

[7] See Batson (2008); InfoSud (2009); IRA (2007); Irvine (2007); IWPR (2008); Maletta (2007); Sherin (2009); Synovitz (2003).

THE PROBLEM OF CONTEXT

Although many concerned with post-war recovery in the international community appreciate that the sociopolitical context of a war-torn nation differs from that of a stable country, they have not examined how context affects peacebuilding in a way relevant to policy and programming.

The road (re)construction context

Even though road (re)construction always seems promising, some analysts have expressed concern about its impact on livelihoods, security, and society in Afghanistan. Lorenzo Delesgues comments on the cost of (re)construction and the increased insecurity and benefits to warlords and other well-positioned elites that result (Delesgues 2007). The consulting firm Mott MacDonald—commissioned by the United Kingdom's Department for International Development—examined problems with post-conflict infrastructure redevelopment: corruption, problems with disenfranchised and marginalized groups, access to essential services, coordination, security, and the aggravation or reemergence of grievances and tensions (Mott MacDonald 2005). The resulting report finds that "in most situations, the triggers for conflict can be related to power and/or resources and, while the reconstruction phase provides opportunities to mitigate underlying tensions, it is also possible to exacerbate them inadvertently" (Mott MacDonald 2005, 10). Bastiaan Philip Reydon also notes that a primary reason for land grabbing in conflict scenarios is power (Reydon 2006).

Absent from Japanese and U.S. road (re)construction programs was understanding of the potentially detrimental land rights and sociopolitical outcomes of peacebuilding. The U.S. infrastructure (re)construction effort took into account twenty-three Afghan laws relevant to road (re)construction (U.S. DOD 2009) but failed to consider national laws on land and environment or customary land law and tenure through which most people in the country access and claim land.

A broader concern in post-conflict road (re)construction is the disconnect between international donors, who see projects' economic and societal advantages, and local inhabitants affected by changing sociopolitical patterns. The former generalize based on understandings of the market economy, access to services, mobility, and security in largely stable settings. The latter worry about land grabbing; control of agricultural production; speculation; rent seeking; recruitment of indentured labor; and increased access to villages for exploitation by corrupt government officials, the Taliban, or foreign troops.

From the foreign military viewpoint, access is the explicit purpose of road (re)construction (Rogers 2010; U.S. DOD 2009). Taliban insurgents heavily target roads (Catarious 2010). In 2010, violence in the more peaceful north "escalated as the Taliban converge[d] on roads that bring supplies from Central Asia to military bases in Afghanistan" (Rahim 2010). Roads used for military operations and for extending the government's reach are attractive locations for placement of improvised explosive devices (IEDs). In the first six months of 2010, there were 94 percent more incidents involving IEDs than there had been in the same period in 2009 (UNSC 2010). Civilians are dislocated as a result of IED-related violence, and land tenure is thus severely affected. As a local resident of Dara-e-Pachaye in Kabul's Paghman District noted, "foreign forces came to our village and said they want[ed] to asphalt the road but we said no. We know the road is good but we also know that an asphalted road brings ISAF [International Security Assistance Force] patrols and with them come suicide and roadside attacks" (IRIN 2010b). At times, villages call international forces to destroy bridges, including those used by the Taliban (Hauslohner 2010). National and international private security forces also abuse the citizenry, particularly on the country's roads (Ahmad 2010). The problem is so severe that President Hamid Karzai called in August 2010 for all private security groups in the country to disband. He cited the need "to better provide security for the lives and property of citizens, fight corruption, prevent irregularities and the misuse of arms, military uniforms and equipment by private security companies that have caused heartbreaking and tragic incidents" (Ahmad 2010).

Particularly problematic are donor assumptions that road infrastructure will benefit all or most of society equally and that economic development and access to services will result. But societies in or emerging from conflict are highly fractured, lawless, desperate, and grievance based. They evidence a culture of impunity, power struggles, subjugation, and exploitation. Road redevelopment thus takes place where seeking advantage and protecting oneself (or one's group) by any means is the norm. In a stable setting, by contrast, rule of law facilitates more equitable realization of benefits from road construction.

Donors assume that the state, local government, nongovernmental organizations, and internationally funded programs will provide social services and that access to the services will contribute to increased well-being and durable peace. In stable countries, institutions intervene in land conflicts and land grabbing. They also handle surveying, titling, land registration, and use of land as collateral. But in a war-related context, such as Afghanistan, institutions are often nonexistent, weak, or highly corrupt. Insurgents capitalize on their absence or dysfunction by providing missing social services (Berman 2009; Stern 2010). Insurgents even destroy development and reconstruction projects and target aid workers and state institutions, so they can create need for their hospitals, schools, courts, and other institutions (Oppel 2010; Stern 2010). At the same time, they intimidate, attack, or kill those who cooperate with the government (Hammond 2010).[8] Where insurgents provide justice, security, employment, education, and welfare, they are much more able to recruit and assert control of the economy, for example (Stern 2010). Thus the greater the insurgents' monopoly on government functions, the greater their

---

[8] The UN reported that civilian casualties increased 31 percent and assassinations and executions over 90 percent in the first half of 2010 (Hammond 2010).

control of their constituencies is (Berman 2009). Insurgent groups go to great lengths to establish and maintain their ability to provide social services (Berman 2009). To the extent that road (re)construction increases access to services provided or imposed by insurgents, it detracts from durable peace and, in Afghanistan, allows the Taliban to move more easily.[9] General Stanley McChrystal, former commander of all foreign forces in Afghanistan, observed that "in places, [the Taliban] control roads, collect revenues and mete out swift justice" (IRIN 2010a).

The land rights context

In Afghanistan, population dislocation and return, widespread corruption, landmines, and landmine clearance create an exceedingly difficult land rights context for road-infrastructure (re)construction.

Although over 5 million refugees have returned to the country since 2002, in the largest-ever repatriation (U.S. DOS 2010), as of 2009 there were still approximately 2.7 million Afghan refugees in Pakistan and Iran (Rehmani 2009; UNHCR 2009) and approximately 235,000 internally displaced persons (IDPs) in Afghanistan (IRIN 2009). Dislocations continue to occur due to ongoing insecurity and conflict between the Taliban and the Afghan population (Hammond 2010) and between the Taliban and national and international forces. The massive population displacement results in large-scale abandonment of land and property, to which the owners intend to return.

Pervasive corruption in Afghanistan hinders the country's recovery and is a primary point of contention between the government and the international community (Gebauer and Volkery 2010; UNODC 2010). War-torn countries are generally the most corrupt (BBC News 2009); only Somalia ranks higher than Afghanistan in this regard (TI 2010). According to Integrity Watch Afghanistan, corruption in the country has doubled since 2007, and by UN accounts, 59 percent of Afghans believe that corruption is a greater threat to the country than the lack of security (IWA 2010). Afghans find services impossible to obtain without paying bribes. With corruption higher in rural areas, land tenure is in considerable jeopardy (UNODC 2010).

Among its eight recommendations, Integrity Watch Afghanistan included combating land sector corruption (IWA 2010). Land seizures and evictions are increasing, and the corruption money leaving Afghanistan is more often coming from landgrabs (Bowman 2010). Threats of land seizure are frequently used for extortion (World Bank et al. 2007). Because the justice system is the most corrupt sector of the government (IWA 2010), Afghans are driven to the Taliban

---

[9] T. Hayashi, Japan International Cooperation Agency (JICA), personal communication with the authors at the Second International Symposium on Strengthening Post-conflict Security and Diplomacy: Policy Recommendations to Integrate Natural Resources, Infrastructure, and Peacebuilding, Tokyo, Japan, June 25, 2010.

for recourse in land conflicts (Carlstrom 2010; Giampaoli and Aggarwal 2010). The "popular perception is that property rights are for sale by the government to insiders with influence" (USAID 2008, 24).

Landmine clearance plays a significant part in Afghanistan's recovery. The country is the most mined in the world,[10] and it has the largest and longest mine action program (Landmine and Cluster Munition Monitor n.d.).[11] A Mine Clearance Planning Agency report found that agricultural and grazing land accounted for 95 percent of mined areas (ICBL n.d.). IEDs are concentrated along roads, hindering farmers' access to their land and putting communities, particularly along the Ring Road, at risk (Villano 2009).

Mine-related dislocation and post-clearance land reoccupation greatly affect land rights (AusCare 2008; Unruh, Heynen, and Hossler 2003). In Cambodia, post-clearance land tenure was so contentious that authorities considered not clearing properties if ownership could not be ascertained (AusCare 2008).[12] When demined land is near reconstructed or new roads, it rises in value. Thus the likelihood increases that the rich and powerful will grab it and that the magnitude and severity of subsequent land disputes will prevent further clearance and development (AusCare 2008). In Afghanistan, the resulting tenure insecurity may lead to less advantaged households' abandoning cleared land and further marginalize the poor, impede development (AusCare 2008), and ease recruitment by insurgents.

LAND GRABBING: A VOLATILE OUTCOME OF THE ROAD-LAND INTERACTION

When road (re)construction and land tenure issues collide, there is often a surge in land grabbing, which is driven by large increases in land values after road (re)construction, weak customary and statutory tenure systems, increased access to land, flourishing corruption, and the absence of landowners, tenants, and their relatives or heirs. The nine provinces with the most seized land (Reydon 2006) are along the Ring Road. In six of them, 80 percent or more of the agricultural area has been grabbed. Land can be grabbed once, even twice: all of the land in three provinces has been grabbed, and much of the land in Logor Province has been grabbed a second time (Reydon 2006). A "land mafia" seizes, subdivides, and sells land in a number of areas (Irvine 2007; IWPR 2008).

The recent discovery of large mineral deposits (Risen 2010; Rubin and Mashal 2010) will require more road (re)construction to facilitate exploitation and may result in seizure of land above mineral deposits and along new access roads. The road

---

[10] R. Okumura, Osaka School of International Public Policy, Osaka University, Japan, personal communication with the authors, June 23, 2010.
[11] Some put the number of landmines as high as 10 million (George 2002).
[12] For further information on demining strategies and operations in Cambodia, see Nao Shimoyachi-Yuzawa, "Linking Demining to Post-Conflict Peacebuilding: A Case Study of Cambodia," in this book.

construction will likely raise suspicions that foreign builders want to control land that contains minerals[13]—fears the Taliban, among others, will likely encourage.

In Afghanistan, land grabbing by powerful interests, including government officials, militia commanders (Sherin 2009; Synovitz 2003), former military commanders, and members of parliament, is pervasive and firmly related to the corruption and dislocation of people (Irvine 2007). Land grabbing is lucrative, widely known, and historically volatile (Batson 2008; Irvine 2007; Sherin 2009). It may push the country into renewed civil unrest (Batson 2008; IWPR 2008), even decades of conflict (*PakTribune* 2003).

Land grabbing creates economic, social, and political instability (Reydon 2006; Sherin 2009). The economic development thought to follow road (re)construction is made more difficult by illegal seizure of land, including government-owned property for which development projects are planned (Irvine 2007). According to the National Land Policy, "land grabbing has been one of the most problematic aspects of land management throughout the country" (IRA 2007, 6). There is little law enforcement, and Afghans are not convinced that the statutory courts can resolve land disputes. Although the legal code outlaws land grabbing, legal redress is nearly impossible (InfoSud 2009).[14] Refugees and returning IDPs trying to regain land do not trust the authorities and courts (Olesen and Strand 2005).[15] Through the state land tenure system, government officials often know about the location, size, potential value of lands and properties, and from whom land can be most easily seized. Greater access to state services associated with road infrastructure (re)construction increases access to lands by corrupt officials and works against peace and economic development. Consequently, local inhabitants search for alternatives to state institutions for land security.

The Taliban are only too eager to provide an alternative, especially when it leads to violent action against state actors and non-Taliban warlords. The Taliban supply disgruntled and disenfranchised villagers with weapons to use against land-grabbing government officials (Sato 2010) and recruit those who want retribution because of land grabbing. As sympathy and support for the Taliban grow among the general population (Sato 2010), elites and warlords remain unwilling to relinquish land they have forcibly grabbed from the peasantry

---

[13] M. Nishimura, Japan Institute of International Affairs, personal communication with the authors at the Second International Symposium on Strengthening Post-Conflict Security and Diplomacy: Policy Recommendations to Integrate Natural Resources, Infrastructure, and Peacebuilding, Tokyo, Japan, June 25, 2010.

[14] Complaints to the Human Rights Commission regarding landgrabs have doubled between 2007 and 2009 (Bowman 2010).

[15] Chandet (2010) and J. Ironside (University of Otago, New Zealand, personal correspondence with the authors at the International Research Workshop on Collective Action, Property Rights, and Conflict in Natural Resources Management in Siem Reap, Cambodia, June 28–July 1, 2010) note a similar relationship between new roads and land grabbing in Cambodia, where courts are also corrupt, distrusted, and difficult to access.

(McAuslan 2009). In neighboring Pakistan's Swat Valley, the Taliban were able to gain control by taking advantage of landlessness, unresolved land disputes, land-related corruption, and the local population's desire for an alternative to the corrupt, ineffective state (Perlez and Zubair 2009).

CONCLUSION AND RECOMMENDATIONS

Donors assume that road (re)construction will lead to economic development, peace, and security. But the interaction between road (re)construction and land tenure in a stable political environment is different from that in a war-torn country such as Afghanistan. As far as most Afghans are concerned, road (re)construction has undermined the land tenure system.

Given the interaction's often-negative outcomes in conflict-affected areas, there should be consideration of whether or not to (re)construct roads—despite their positive effects on some localities—until peace reigns in Afghanistan. Those tasked with security and development should at least change their approach to construction of road infrastructure so that well-placed Afghans do not benefit at the expense of the majority who cannot legally or nonviolently defend their rights. There must be a realistic examination and understanding of how (re)construction contributes to or undermines peacebuilding in Afghanistan and other war-torn parts of the world.

REFERENCES

Ahmad, S. 2010. Karzai formally orders security firms to disband. DefenseNews.com, August 17. www.defensenews.com/story.php?i=4749128.

AIMS (Afghanistan Information Management Service). 2003. Program for development of the road network (2004–2015). www.ecoi.net/index.php?countrychooser_country=188769::afghanistan&command=showcountryhome&doctype=5&next=421.

Alden Wily, L. 2003. *Land rights in crisis: Restoring tenure security in Afghanistan*. Kabul: Afghanistan Research and Evaluation Unit. http://unpan1.un.org/intradoc/groups/public/documents/APCITY/UNPAN016656.pdf.

Andre, C. 2003. Custom, contracts and cadastres in north-west Rwanda. In *Securing land rights in Africa*, ed. T. A. Benjaminsen and C. Lund. London: CASS Publishing.

ANDS (Afghanistan National Development Strategy). 2008. *Afghanistan national development strategy 2008–2013: A strategy for security, governance, economic growth and poverty reduction*. Kabul: Islamic Republic of Afghanistan.

AusCare. 2008. *Tackling poverty in conflict-affected countries: Linking development, security and the remnants of conflict*. www.gichd.org/fileadmin/pdf/ma_development/practitioners-network/wk-nov2008/LMAD-Wk-SUMMARY-REPORT-Nov2008.pdf.

Bailliet, C. 2003. Property restitution in Guatemala: A transnational dilemma. In *Returning home: Housing and property restitution rights of refugees and displaced persons*, ed. S. Leckie. Ardsley, NY: Transnational Publishers.

Banks, P. 2007. *Issues paper on reforming Liberia's legal and judicial system towards enhancing the rule of law*. Monrovia, Liberia: Governance Reform Commission.

Barquero, R. 2004. *Access to land in post-conflict situations: A case study in Nicaragua*. Rome: Food and Agriculture Organization of the United Nations.

Batson, D. 2008. *Registering the human terrain: A valuation of cadastre*. Washington, D.C.: Center for Strategic Intelligence Research / National Drug Intelligence Center.

BBC News. 2009. War-torn nations "most corrupt." November 17. http://news.bbc.co.uk/2/hi/8363599.stm.

Berman, E. 2009. *Radical, religious and violent: The new economics of terrorism*. Cambridge, MA: MIT Press.

Bowman, T. 2010. Karzai's brother tied to corrupt Afghan land deals. NPR.org, February 1. www.npr.org/templates/story/story.php?storyId=123223248.

Bruch, C., D. Jensen, M. Nakayama, J. Unruh, R. Gruby, and R. Wolfarth. 2009. Post-conflict peacebuilding and natural resources. *Yearbook of International Environmental Law* 19: 58–96.

Carlstrom, G. 2010. Study says Afghan graft worsening. Aljazeera, July 13.

Catarious, D. 2010. The impacts of Afghan and U.S. counternarcotics efforts on the Afghan poppy farmers. Paper presented at the Second International Symposium on Strengthening Post-Conflict Security and Diplomacy: Policy Recommendations to Integrate Natural Resources, Infrastructure and Peacebuilding, University of Tokyo, Japan, June 24.

Chandet, H. 2010. Whose land is this anyway? The role of collective action in maintaining community rights to the land in Kratie, Cambodia. Paper presented at the International Research Workshop on Collective Action, Property Rights, and Conflict in Natural Resources Management, Siem Reap, Cambodia.

Cohen, S. 1993. *The politics of planting: Israeli-Palestinian competition for control of land in the Jerusalem periphery*. Chicago, IL: University of Chicago Press.

Delesgues, L. 2007. *Afghan roads reconstruction: Deconstruction of a lucrative assistance*. Kabul: Integrity Watch Afghanistan. www.iwaweb.org/reports/DeconstructionofaLucrativeAssistance2006.html.

DW (Development Workshop). 2005. *Terra: Urban land reform in postwar Angola; Research, advocacy and policy development*. Luanda, Angola.

Gebauer, M., and C. Volkery. 2010. Corruption in Afghanistan. *Spiegel Online International*, January 19.

George, M. 2002. Afghanistan's landmine legacy. BBC News Online, July 28.

Giampaoli, P., and S. Aggarwal. 2010. *Land tenure and property rights in Afghanistan: Do LTPR conflicts and grievances foster support for the Taliban*. USAID Issue Brief, January. http://usaidlandtenure.net/usaidltprproducts/issue-briefs/issue-brief-afghanistan/view.

Glasser, S. 2002. Project to build Afghanistan's roads going nowhere, despite promises. *Washington Post*, August 7.

Goovaerts, P., M. Gasser, and A. Inbal. 2005. Demand driven approaches to livelihood support in post-war contexts: A joint ILO-World Bank study. Social Development Paper No. 29. Washington, D.C.: World Bank. http://siteresources.worldbank.org/INTCDD/214574-1107382173398/20877452/WP29_Web.pdf.

Hammond, A. 2010. Civilian casualties up 31%: UN. Reuters, August 10. www.reuters.com/article/2010/08/10/us-afghanistan-civilians-idUSTRE6790UI20100810.

Hauslohner, A. 2010. Battling IEDs in Afghanistan. *Time*, June 15. www.time.com/time/world/article/0,8599,1996636,00.html.

ICBL (International Campaign to Ban Landmines). n.d. Afghanistan: Landmine fact sheet. www.afghan-network.net/Landmines.

InfoSud. 2009. Land and home grab in Afghanistan. *InfoSud Human Rights Tribune*, August 20. www.infosud.org/spip.php?article4863.
IRA (Islamic Republic of Afghanistan). 2007. *Draft land policy of the Afghan Ministry of Agriculture and the Ministry of Urban Development*. Kabul.
IRIN (Integrated Regional Information Networks). 2009. Afghanistan: Insecurity, lack of aid prompt IDPs to leave camp. IRIN Humanitarian News and Analysis, June 21. www.irinnews.org/Report.aspx?ReportId=84926.
———. 2010a. Afghanistan: Driven into the arms of the Taliban. IRIN Humanitarian News and Analysis, March 10. www.irinnews.org/Report.aspx?ReportId=88372.
———. 2010b. Afghanistan: Military convoys put civilians "at risk." IRIN Humanitarian News and Analysis, June 16. http://irinnews.org/Report.aspx?ReportID=89507.
Irvine, S. 2007. Powerful grab Afghanistan land. BBC News, September 6. http://news.bbc.co.uk/go/pr/fr/-/2/hi/south_asia/6981035.stm.
IWA (Integrity Watch Afghanistan). 2010. *Afghan perceptions and experiences of corruption: A national survey 2010*. www.iwaweb.org/Reports/PDF/IWA%20corruption%20survey%202010.pdf.
IWPR (Institute for War and Peace Reporting). 2008. Afghan environmental health problems legacy of land-grab. Environmental News Service, November 21. www.ens-newswire.com/ens/nov2008/2008-11-21-01.html.
JICA (Japan International Cooperation Agency). 2003. *The urgent rehabilitation support program in Afghanistan: Rehabilitation planning of the south western area and public transportation study of Kabul*. Tokyo.
———. 2004. *Afghanistan assistance: From reconstruction to development*. Tokyo. www.jica.go.jp/english/publications/jica_archive/brochures/2006/pdf/afghanistan.pdf.
———. 2006. *The project formulation study on road maintenance and management sector in Afghanistan*. Tokyo.
JSCE (Japan Society of Civil Engineers). 2002. *Afghanistan reconstruction vision*. www.jsce.or.jp/strategy/files/Afgan-vision.pdf.
Junne, G., and W. Verkoren. 2005. *Postconflict development: Meeting new challenges*. Boulder, CO: Lynne Rienner.
Landmine and Cluster Munition Monitor. n.d. Afghanistan. www.the-monitor.org/index.php/publications/display?url=lm/2007/afghanistan.html.
Maletta, H. E. 2007. Arable land tenure in Afghanistan in the post-Taliban era. *African and Asian Studies* 6 (1–2): 13–52.
McAuslan, P. 2009. Emergency lex—and other improbable tales from the law zone. www.dpu-associates.net/node/180.
Meilahn, K. 2007. Cultural understanding within context as a tool for countering irregular threats and as a force for peace. *Strategic Insights* 6 (2).
Mockaitis, T. 2003. Winning hearts and minds in the "war on terrorism." *Small Wars and Insurgencies* 14:21–38.
Mott MacDonald 2005. *Provision of infrastructure in post conflict situations*. London: Department for International Development. http://ti-up.dfid.gov.uk/uploads/public/documents/Key%20Documents/Infrastructure%20in%20Post%20Conflict.pdf.
MRRD (Ministry of Rural Rehabilitation and Development) and MPW (Ministry of Public Works). 2007. National Rural Access Program (NRAP). Kabul: Islamic Republic of Afghanistan.
Olesen, G., and A. Strand. 2005. *Evaluating post war interventions: The case of Afghanistan*. Copenhagen, Denmark: Danish International Development Agency.

Oppel, R. 2010. Bombers hit U.S. aid compound in Afghanistan. *New York Times*, July 3.
PakTribune. 2003. UN accuses top Afghan ministers of land grab. September 12. www.rawa.org/land.htm.
Perlez, J., and P. Zubair. 2009. Taliban exploit class rifts in Pakistan. *New York Times*, April 16.
Rahim, G. 2010. Three foreigners among dead in Afghan Taliban attack. *Sydney Morning Herald*, July 2. http://news.smh.com.au/breaking-news-world/three-foreigners-among-dead-in-afghan-taliban-attack-20100702-ztoy.html.
Rehmani, F. 2009. 100,000 refugees return home. *Pajhwok Afghan News*, September 29.
Reydon, B. P. 2006. Social embeddedness, institutions for rural land management and land grabbing: The cases of Afghanistan and Brazil. Land Tenure Centre / Terra Institute. www.terrainstitute.org/pdf/Social%20Embeddedness.pdf.
Risen, J. 2010. U.S. identifies vast mineral riches in Afghanistan. *New York Times*, June 13. www.nytimes.com/2010/06/14/world/asia/14minerals.html.
Rogers, W. 2010. Military to military engagement on environment and natural disasters: Lessons learned for post conflict peacebuilding. Paper presented at the "Second International Symposium on Strengthening Post-Conflict Security and Diplomacy: Policy Recommendations to Integrate Natural Resources, Infrastructure and Peacebuilding," University of Tokyo, Japan, June 24.
Rubin, A., and M. Mashal. 2010. Afghanistan moves quickly to tap newfound mineral reserves. *New York Times*, June 17. www.nytimes.com/2010/06/18/world/asia/18afghan.html.
Sato, M. 2010. Demobilization, reintegration and natural resources in Afghanistan: Afghanistan's New Beginnings Programme (ANBP). Paper presented at the "Second International Symposium on Strengthening Post-Conflict Security and Diplomacy: Policy Recommendations to Integrate Natural Resources, Infrastructure and Peacebuilding," University of Tokyo, Japan, June 24.
Schell, B. 2009. Afghanistan: A white elephant called the Ring Road. IDN-InDepthNews Service, www.indepthnews.net/news/news.php?key1=2009-10-05%2003:29:19&key2=1.
Sherin, L. A. 2009. Land and home grab in Afghanistan. *InfoSud Human Rights Tribune*, August 20. www.infosud.org/spip.php?article4863.
Stern, L. 2010. Do-gooder terrorism. Canwest News Services, June 1. www2.canada.com/ottawacitizen/columnists/story.html?id=406deb39-279c-495e-814e-e188f2373ced&p=2.
Synovitz, R. 2003. Afghanistan: Land-grab scandal in Kabul rocks the government. Radio Free Europe and Radio Liberty, September 16. www.rferl.org/content/article/1104367.html.
TI (Transparency International). 2010. *Transparency International annual report 2009*. Berlin, Germany. www.transparency.org/publications/annual_report.
UNEP (United Nations Environment Programme). 2009. *From conflict to peacebuilding: The role of natural resources and the environment*. Nairobi, Kenya. www.unep.org/pdf/pcdmb_policy_01.pdf.
UNHCR (United Nations High Commissioner for Refugees). 2009. UNHCR and Pakistan sign new agreement on stay of Afghan refugees. March 13. www.unhcr.org/49ba5db92.html.
UNODC (United Nations Office on Drugs and Crime). 2010. *Corruption in Afghanistan: Bribery as reported by the victims*. www.unodc.org/documents/data-and-analysis/Afghanistan/Afghanistan-corruption-survey2010-Eng.pdf.
Unruh, J. D. 2003. Land tenure and legal pluralism in the peace process. *Peace and Change* 28:352–376.

———. 2004. Rural property rights in a peace process: Lessons from Mozambique. In *WorldMinds: 100 Geographical Perspectives on 100 Problems*, ed. B. Warf, D. Janelle, and K. Hanson. Dordrecht, Netherlands: Kluwer Academic Publishers.

———. 2009. Land rights in postwar Liberia: The volatile part of the peace process. *Land Use Policy* 26:425–433.

Unruh, J. D., N. C. Heynen, and P. Hossler. 2003. The political ecology of recovery from armed conflict: The case of landmines in Mozambique. *Political Geography* 22: 841–861.

UNSC (United Nations Security Council). 2010. *Report of the Secretary-General pursuant to paragraph 40 of resolution 1917 (2010).* http://unama.unmissions.org/Portals/UNAMA/SG%20Reports/June182010_SG_Report.pdf.

USAID (United States Agency for International Development). 2006. Data sheet: Afghanistan. www.usaid.gov/policy/budget/cbj2006/ane/pdf/af306-004.pdf.

———. 2008. *Case study of the poultry and grape/raisin subsectors in Afghanistan.* Washington D.C. http://pdf.usaid.gov/pdf_docs/PNADN388.pdf.

U.S. DOD (United States Department of Defense). 2009. *Progress toward security and stability in Afghanistan.* www.defense.gov/pubs/November_1230_Report_FINAL.pdf.

U.S. DOS (United States Department of State). 2010. Background note: Afghanistan. www.state.gov/r/pa/ei/bgn/5380.htm.

Villano, P. 2009. Afghanistan: Landmine clearance safeguards communities one square kilometer at a time. Dipnote Blog, September 16. www.state.gov/t/pm/rls/othr/c32882.htm.

World Bank, Asian Development Bank, DFID (Department for International Development, United Kingdom), UNDP (United Nations Development Programme), and UNODC (United Nations Office on Drugs and Crime). 2007. Fighting corruption in Afghanistan: A roadmap for strategy and action. Informal discussion paper. www.unodc.org/pdf/afg/anti_corruption_roadmap.pdf.

Evaluating post-conflict assistance

Suppiramaniam Nanthikesan and Juha I. Uitto

In post-conflict and post-crisis settings in which people's livelihoods are at stake and situations remain fluid, there is an urgency to ensure not only that emergency responses and development interventions are on track but that they do not further exacerbate the problems. There is a real risk that external interventions in post-crisis situations could worsen inequalities that may have been the original cause of the crisis, or weaken the unifying ties among conflicting communities. Certain interventions may not be appropriate for the social, cultural, or economic situation prevailing in the area. Evaluation is a tool to ensure that an intervention is cognizant of such factors. At the same time, the evaluation must be timely.

Many evaluations are driven by the interests of the agencies and donors who wish to assess the effectiveness and efficiency of their interventions. In those cases, accountability is directed upward to the agency and its funders, frequently the taxpayers in the donor country. But what about the people the interventions are intended to benefit? Downward accountability to beneficiaries is equally if not more important. In the evaluation of post-conflict assistance, the focus on downward accountability has been weak.

This chapter explores some of the evaluation challenges particular to post-conflict situations, the importance of natural resource management to recovering from conflict, and the key role that evaluation can play in shaping effective interventions in these areas. It begins by defining evaluation and describing its role in accountability, learning, and program improvement. It examines conceptual and practical challenges to evaluating post-conflict interventions, and proceeds by discussing the limitations of the quantitative approach to evaluation, an approach currently emphasized by donors. The chapter continues with an examination of alternative approaches to effective evaluation in post-conflict situations. It discusses how evaluation can promote downward accountability and help identify unintended consequences of interventions. The chapter argues for taking a comprehensive approach to evaluation, going beyond individual interventions. To make this case, lessons for evaluating the role of natural resource management in moving from recovery to sustainable development are highlighted based on evaluations conducted.

Suppiramaniam Nanthikesan is monitoring and evaluation advisor for the Regional Bureau for Africa of the United Nations Development Programme (UNDP). Juha I. Uitto is deputy director of UNDP's Evaluation Office.

THE ROLE OF EVALUATION

Evaluation is a powerful instrument for strengthening development effectiveness. Its role ranges from summative assessments of what was achieved and measuring the program's achievements against its objectives, to formative assessments, in which the lessons learned are used to improve current and future programs. But there is no real dichotomy between accountability and learning, for both approaches require credible and verifiable evidence of the performance of the evaluand (subject of the evaluation), whether it is a project, program, strategy, policy, or organization.

There are several definitions of evaluation, but their gist is usually the same. The United Nations Development Programme (UNDP), for example, defines *evaluation* as "a rigorous and independent assessment of either completed or ongoing activities to determine the extent to which they are achieving stated objectives and contributing to decision making" (UNDP 2009, 8).

Monitoring and evaluation are often mentioned interchangeably as oversight functions. They share the aim of providing information to managers, stakeholders, and claim holders that can help inform decisions, improve performance, achieve planned results, and hold duty bearers to account.[1] However, monitoring and evaluation have important differences. Monitoring is essentially a management function, carried out by those who create and run a program, while evaluations are done independently to provide an objective assessment of whether a development initiative is on track. Such independence can be achieved either by engaging an external entity to design and carry out the evaluation or through internal mechanisms, such as an independent evaluation unit within an agency.[2] Evaluations are also more rigorous than monitoring in their procedures, design, and methodology, and go beyond mere description of what was achieved to an analysis of what worked and why. Most importantly, evaluations are able to bring out not only the intended results but also the unintended consequences of a development initiative—an issue that is especially important when determining whether the claim holders, or beneficiaries of a program, actually receive the benefits of an intervention.

The standards adopted by the United Nations Evaluation Group, a professional network of heads of evaluation in the United Nations system, contain principles such as the intention to use the evaluation findings; impartiality, including methodological rigor and absence of bias in the evaluation process;

---

[1] In this chapter, *claim holders* refers to the beneficiaries of an intervention; *duty bearers* refers to donors or authorities who have the responsibility to ensure the rights of claim holders; and *stakeholders* refers to all those who have a stake in the development intervention—primarily claim holders and duty bearers.

[2] The degree of such independence varies among agencies. In UNDP and the World Bank, for example, the evaluation units report directly to the respective governing bodies, which also approve their program of work and budget for evaluation. The program office whose project is being evaluated has no control or influence over how the evaluation is carried out or its results.

independence from management, to avoid undue influence and conflict of interest; and transparency and consultation with major stakeholders (UNEG 2005).

The practice of evaluation contains a wide variety of approaches. While the focus is frequently on programs or projects, it is often important to take a thematic or sector-wide approach to evaluation. This is particularly the case in post-conflict situations, where focusing on a single intervention may not be adequate. In virtually all cases there are a number of interventions consisting of a set of projects that interact and are intended to contribute to the larger outcome of conflict resolution and peacebuilding. These interventions may be nationally initiated or external, involving domestic and foreign actors, both bilateral and multilateral organizations, civil society, and others. For programmatic evaluations to be fully meaningful, they should be conducted in a manner that captures the whole picture. This is especially the case with natural resources, given their interconnected and crosscutting nature.

Timely feedback to management is critical in post-conflict settings, in which situations often evolve rapidly. Approaches have been developed for evaluating interventions in real time in order to support adaptive management. In such approaches it is important to maintain adequate distance from the program implementers, lest these evaluations slip into routine monitoring of activities and outputs.

THE CHALLENGES TO EVALUATING POST-CONFLICT INTERVENTIONS

Post-conflict evaluations face all of the challenges of routine development evaluations (that is, those not conducted in a post-conflict situation) as well as their own particular challenges. The challenges in post-conflict evaluations are both conceptual and practical.

One conceptual challenge is related to the ideal of national ownership of evaluations and the issues surrounding the legitimacy of the state. Development programming and evaluations enshrine the principle of national ownership as embodied in the Paris Declaration on Aid Effectiveness, endorsed in 2005 by over one hundred countries and agencies.[3] That means that a national government assumes responsibility for an intervention and exerts effective leadership toward

---

[3] The Paris Declaration on Aid Effectiveness defines *ownership* this way:

Partner countries commit to:
- Exercise leadership in developing and implementing their national development strategies through broad consultative processes.
- Translate these national development strategies into prioritised results-oriented operational programmes as expressed in medium-term expenditure frameworks and annual budgets (Indicator 1).
- Take the lead in co-ordinating aid at all levels in conjunction with other development resources in dialogue with donors and encouraging the participation of civil society and the private sector (OECD 2005, 3).

its success. However, because the state is itself almost always a party to the conflict, there is a concern as to whether the state can and should "own" a post-conflict evaluation. A post-conflict government may, in fact, have an interest in undermining programs that might benefit its former enemies and may therefore attempt to influence the findings of the evaluation.

Second, multiple factors affect the capacity of parties to a conflict to reconcile or to amplify their differences. The interconnected and dynamic nature of these factors poses significant challenges to fully understanding the root causes of conflict and assessing changes.

A third conceptual challenge arises from the deep fragmentation of society associated with the conflict. Peacebuilding efforts recognize this fragmentation and work to address it. But what may appear to one group as a successful or effective intervention may be seen as counterproductive by another. In this context, claims of achievements and statements about what works and why are likely to be contested. Thus the design of evaluations, particularly methods of data validation, faces significant challenges.

There are practical challenges as well. Conflicts weaken or destroy existing institutional capacity to gather data. Countries facing an urgent need to rebuild and a scarcity of resources may not be able to devote the manpower or money to create a framework for gathering evidence for evaluations. Even when data exist, their credibility and objectivity cannot be taken for granted. Thus there are significant challenges to obtaining baseline information or monitoring progress toward intended results.

Limitations of quantitative approaches

The current donor emphasis on quantitative approaches,[4] such as results frameworks with indicators and logical frameworks,[5] may well be premature and may crowd out efforts to achieve in-depth understanding of the assumptions and explanations surrounding conflicts (OECD/DAC 2007). Rigorous alternative evaluation approaches exist and should be used.

Many donors, facing pressure to report to their constituencies on the performance of their investments, are seeking to demonstrate tangible results and

---

[4] Strictly speaking, qualitative and quantitative approaches refer to the types of data collected and not the categories of design (Weiss 1998). However, this chapter adopts the common usage whereby quantitative and qualitative approaches refer to type of designs. Quantitative approaches involve data that can be subject to statistical analysis and reporting, and these approaches focus on the size of effects and the significance of statistical relationships. Qualitative approaches rely primarily on data collected through nonstandardized methods (for instance, through semistructured or unstructured interviews) and do not have to be amenable to statistical analysis.

[5] A results framework outlines the development hypothesis of how the program objectives are to be achieved. It presents the causal linkages between the goal, strategic objectives, and specific program outcomes, as well as the underlying assumptions.

are thus increasingly favoring quantitative approaches, in particular impact evaluations, which attempt to attribute changes in conditions to specific interventions, rather than just assessing what happened.[6] Donor agencies frequently want to be able to identify the effects produced by their projects—often in order to be able to report such results to their funders or the taxpayers in the donor country. However, it is often impossible to isolate the effects of one particular intervention. This is especially true in complex post-conflict situations where conditions change rapidly and are influenced by multiple actors. The same can also be said for natural resource management interventions.

Impact evaluations also attempt to identify the counterfactual—what would have happened in the absence of a given intervention. They tend to emphasize experimental designs using quantitative methods derived from experimental sciences, such as randomized control trials—for example, comparing a village that received the intervention with one that did not.

Impact evaluations have shortcomings that limit their use in evaluating post-crisis responses. First, they can only be credibly used for fairly simple individual interventions that have clear and measurable objectives (Picciotto 2007). For example, in evaluating a program to vaccinate children against a specific disease, the occurrence of that disease among vaccinated and unvaccinated children could be measured, and the difference attributed to the campaign. Even in such a case, the impact evaluation would focus only on the dimension of immediate effects of the vaccination and might not look at possible unintended consequences in the community if, for instance, the campaign promoted forced vaccinations. Although in this case, the primary objective of vaccinating children would be achieved, the approach might undermine community buy-in and the long-term sustainability of the effort.

Second, real development is about not only the end result but also the means by which it is achieved. A key question for evaluations guided by human development principles is: Do the means enhance human agency and freedom? In other words, they evaluate not only the results but also the processes by which the results are achieved. Experimental (and quasi-experimental) methods, such as randomized trials, are ill-suited to handle this aspect. Furthermore, establishing the counterfactual (what would have occurred in the absence of the intervention) is rarely feasible in real-life post-crisis situations and would involve ethical challenges—if there was evidence that an intervention was indeed working, would it be ethical to deprive a control group of its benefits?

A more significant challenge comes from the issue of unintended consequences, which is an essential element of downward accountability. That is, were the intended benefits of an intervention associated with an unforeseen negative effect? However, tracking unintended consequences is by definition outside

---

[6] Groups such as the Washington-based Center for Global Development and the relatively new International Initiative for Impact Evaluation (known as 3ie), based in Cairo, have been established with donor support to promote impact evaluation.

the results framework, and hence cannot be captured by experimental or quasi-experimental methods.

For these reasons, impact evaluation methods do not fit well into post-conflict and post-crisis situations, which are often messy and require complex interventions and management that can adapt to the unexpected.

In this context, rigorously assessing and identifying which programs are making a difference and which are merely feel-good exercises without real results has become a challenge. Finding a middle ground between quantitative approaches (which use experimental and quasi-experimental methods) and qualitative approaches (which rely on ethnographic research) is a familiar challenge to those who have been following the debates on development evaluations (Chen 1990).

Extending this analysis to monitoring and evaluation of peacebuilding and conflict-resolution efforts, Reina Neufeldt has presented the debate in terms of two strands of thinking among practitioners (Neufeldt 2007). *Frameworkers*, Nuefeldt writes, believe that peacebuilding efforts can be interpreted through linear causal chains laid out in logical frameworks and thus can be monitored and evaluated quantitatively, using indicators that measure the achievement of predetermined activities and outputs and their contribution to higher-order objectives and goals. *Circlers*, on the other hand, take a more flexible and responsive approach, emphasizing the importance of context and the uniqueness of interventions and the communities in which they take place. They argue that events in conflict environments are unpredictable, depend on organic community processes in which causality is not clear, and thus require a qualitative approach. These two approaches reflect significant differences in understanding "how the world operates, how we interact within that world, how we can determine the impact of our programming interventions upon that world, the role of different worldviews and the purpose of determining impact" (Neufeldt 2007, 16).

EFFECTIVE POST-CONFLICT EVALUATION APPROACHES

In a post-conflict situation, the most effective evaluation approach is shaped by the nature of the conflict, the objectives and scale of the evaluation, and the resources available to carry it out. Clearly, the end of a long-standing, low-intensity conflict (for instance, Peru in the 2000s) and of a relatively brief but devastating conflict (Rwanda in the mid-1990s) present different constraints on the nature and breadth of the evaluation. Depending on the circumstances, it may be necessary to evaluate (1) specific projects or programs, (2) the performance of a particular sector (for example, health), or (3) all efforts related to a theme (for example, livelihoods). Occasionally it is necessary to take stock of the entire external assistance effort in response to a crisis (such as the Rwandan genocide).

These three types of evaluation—project, sector-wide, and thematic—share some fundamental features, such as rigorous methods, but involve different instruments and different techniques for collecting and validating data. Sector-wide assessments often require joint evaluations involving multiple actors and often have considerable resources at their disposal. This in turn permits an elaborate and rigorous design that could include time- and resource-consuming instruments such as broad-based claim holder surveys. An evaluation of a small project, on the other hand, usually involves a much smaller budget and effort. But the smaller scale rules out certain instruments—for instance, without a substantial budget it would not be possible to conduct a survey of all claim holders. When timely evidence is needed on whether to reorient the program, real-time evaluations are necessary.

Rigorous evaluations: A theory-based approach

In the face of the challenges outlined previously, qualitative approaches to post-conflict evaluation are often more feasible than quantitative approaches. It is now well established that qualitative approaches can be rigorous. Since the 1980s the theory-based approach has been advanced as a way to conduct rigorous performance assessments that avoid the pitfalls of qualitative approaches (Birckmayer and Weiss 2000). This approach is based on a program theory—"a plausible and sensible model of how a program is supposed to work" (Bickman 1987, 5). The theory explains how the planned intervention will lead to the desired social and developmental changes and points out the risks and assumptions involved in every step. It also provides the basis for evaluations to assess progress toward results. When quantitative measures are not readily available, as is the case in many post-conflict situations, theory-driven approaches are the most viable option to ensure rigor.

Programs and projects are often initiated without a clear picture of how specific interventions will lead to the desired end result. Many post-conflict projects and programs substitute experience and intuition for theory. Even when interventions start with a theory, the dynamics of a post-conflict situation may leave the theory outdated by the time the intervention is evaluated. The role of evaluation is to scrutinize whether the theory holds and whether the activities, which are promoted in good faith, actually improve the lot of those affected by the crisis. If there have been unintended consequences, the theory needs to be revised to account for these consequences. Consequently, evaluations may need to reconstruct a theory, based on an understanding of the intervention and on consultations with the designers and implementers of the intervention.

Because relapse into conflict is a risk in most post-conflict situations, a viable theory must recognize the opportunities to bring conflicting communities together as well as the threats that could exacerbate their divisions. Constructing such a theory requires a full understanding of the root and proximate causes of the conflict, local history, traditions, institutions, power relations, and the economies of the conflicting parties. A well-constructed theory needs inputs from a range of specialists, including anthropologists, historians, economists, political theorists, and civil-society activists.

Conflict signifies a fundamental difference in the way actors interpret the world. Even in peacetime, there have been situations that required development evaluations to devise an alternative theory (Carvalho and White 2004). It may be the case that no single theory would ever be agreeable to all stakeholders. Techniques such as multi-criteria decision aid can help to gauge claim holders' values and to assess alternative strategies for program intervention (Vaessen 2006).[7]

In a theory-based approach, the program theory allows the construction of a results chain—a description of how inputs and activities lead to desired outputs and outcomes. It is then possible to construct context-appropriate indicators for the outputs and outcomes on a case-by-case basis.

Despite the advantages of a theory-based approach, there is still considerable pressure to develop and use universal indicators when planning and evaluating peacebuilding efforts. In this regard, it is worth quoting at length from an important 2007 paper on this subject by the Development Assistance Committee (DAC) of the Organisation for Economic Co-operation and Development:

> There is no single proved methodology for preventing violence and building peace. This reality led many . . . to be concerned by recent donor emphasis on establishing standard (or universal) conflict prevention and peacebuilding indicators, specifying detailed logframe analyses of intended activities, and linking evaluations to funding decisions. Many note that they now see evaluations as existing "only" or "primarily" to meet a donor requirement.
>
> Given the reality of what we do not know, conflict prevention and peacebuilding evaluations in the coming years should be directed toward gathering evidence and learning from it, and on testing and challenging commonly held theories and assumptions about peace and conflict, rather than on establishing fixed universal indicators of peace/conflict. Clarity on indicators (and whether or not they can be generalised in a useful way) may emerge in the process, but the focus and approach at this time should avoid over-specification of anticipated indicators as benchmarks for evaluation. Upcoming conflict prevention and peacebuilding evaluations should focus on gathering experience and analysing it cumulatively and comparatively across contexts, to improve our collective learning (OECD/DAC 2007, 14).

The progress toward the intended results thus identified can be evaluated using the DAC evaluation criteria modified and amended as necessary. Possible criteria for peacebuilding efforts include relevance and appropriateness, effectiveness, efficiency, impact, sustainability, linkages, coverage, and consistency with conflict-prevention and peacebuilding values. Achieving rigor is not feasible without

---

[7] *Multi-criteria decision making* generally refers to techniques that explicitly consider multiple criteria in evaluating possible courses of action or decisions. Such decisions may have to be taken in situations that involve conflicting criteria, multiple stakeholder groups, or a lack of information (Mendoza and Martins 2006).

meaningful involvement of local experts in developing the theory of change and designing the evaluation. Involvement of local experts is equally necessary in implementing the evaluations—stakeholder mapping as well as collecting, interpreting, and validating data. The evaluation team must have the expertise in the conflict prevention and peacebuilding field, as well as the ability to interpret local customs and traditions and to fully understand the local interlocutors.

Joint evaluations

Post-conflict program support often involves multiple themes and sectors. For instance, a needs assessment has to be conducted; resources mobilized; efforts of diverse actors coordinated; relevant capacities strengthened; and links between relief, recovery, and development established. Relevant capacities of duty bearers include the ability to govern and implement law enforcement, public administration, and service delivery, while relevant capacities for claim holders include the ability to access and utilize services and to hold duty bearers accountable.

Joint evaluations are the best method to get a full picture of the peacebuilding dynamics—not only of the effects of individual efforts but also of the interactions among the multiple efforts. Joint evaluations tend to have greater objectivity and legitimacy and make it easier to capture attribution. They also are capable of strengthening downward accountability. Joint evaluations are also more effective advocacy tools to convince policy makers or program managers to address the findings and recommendations. Joint evaluations addressing the broader set of interventions are not perceived to advance any single actor's perspective. These advantages often outweigh the disadvantages associated with joint evaluations, which include higher transaction costs and complexity.

One possible method for a joint evaluation is to conduct parallel evaluations on different themes and then synthesize all evaluations to produce a single report. This approach has been followed in many thematic evaluations by UNDP and was used by the Tsunami Evaluation Coalition discussed later in this chapter (Telford, Cosgrave, and Houghton 2006). The latter evaluation was organized in five parallel thematic areas: needs assessment, coordination, impact on local and national capacities, resource mobilization, and links between relief and development. Each thematic evaluation was conducted jointly but led by one agency. A dedicated team member was assigned from the beginning to ensure that a synthesis of all thematic studies would be feasible at the end. To do so, it was necessary to ensure that evaluation questions reflected this need and used uniform standards for data collection, analysis, and reporting. A synthesis report was in fact successfully prepared.

Real-time evaluations

A real-time evaluation is conducted at the early stages of a program and focuses on the effectiveness and efficiency of implementation, rather than the ultimate results. It provides timely evidence to address ongoing programming needs in response to the dynamic context. Procedurally, real-time evaluations can be conducted also as joint evaluations. The evaluation is conducted while a program is still being implemented, and the results are fed back to the program for immediate use. Approaches to real-time evaluation have been developed by entities that operate in crisis situations, such as the Active Learning Network for Accountability and Performance in Humanitarian Action. Agencies interviewed for a United Nations Children's Fund desk review of real-time evaluations generally found the rapid feedback valuable (Sandison 2003). Another review of real-time evaluation practice also emphasized its timeliness and usefulness to program staff (Herson and Mitchell 2005).

The risk with a real-time evaluation, however, is that it can blur the distinction between monitoring and evaluation. In such a case, a real-time evaluation (like monitoring) only focuses on program performance and delivery, rather than constantly evaluating whether the program strategy continues to make sense. Therefore, it is important to ensure the independence of the evaluation function to enable it to constantly question the assumptions behind the intervention's logic and to verify the results with the claim holders.

Real-time evaluation is just one type of rapid evaluation and assessment.[8] A common challenge for all such methods is finding a balance between speed and trustworthiness (McNall and Foster-Fishman 2007). In order to be truly useful, real-time evaluation must be removed from program management and retain its independence, credibility, and rigor.

DOWNWARD ACCOUNTABILITY AND UNINTENDED CONSEQUENCES

In an ideal world, the accountability to the duty bearers and funders of an intervention (upward accountability) would mean the same thing as accountability to the claim holders (downward accountability), and the methodologies of evaluations commissioned by the duty bearers would be no different from those commissioned by or on behalf of claim holders. In that world, both types of evaluation would assess the full range of consequences (positive and negative, intended and unintended) that interventions had for claim holders. These would be goal-free evaluations (Scriven and Patton 1972).

However, reality is often different, by omission if not by design. Evaluations are designed to assess progress toward intended results, or goals. Results, and reporting practices based on them, guide evaluations in this direction. Evaluations commissioned by donors focus mainly on the results that are of interest to them.

---

[8] Other techniques include participatory rural appraisal, which is often used to assess claim holders' perceptions of their conditions and the programs intended to benefit them; rapid evaluation methods, developed by the World Health Organization to assess the quality of health-care services; and rapid (ethnographic) assessments, associated with action research, which aim to assess local conditions and improve the design of interventions.

Claim holders, on the other hand, are concerned with any consequences, intended or unintended, that affect their lives.

Thus the key difference between upward accountability and downward accountability in the real world is how they treat unintended results. Downward accountability does not distinguish unintended results from intended results, while upward accountability generally ignores them. This might not be an issue if unintended results were minimal. However, in complex post-conflict humanitarian and recovery interventions, the unintended consequences of aid can dwarf the intended consequences (Anderson 1999; Rieff 2002; Kennedy 2004; IFRC 2005). Although evidence clearly points to the need for evaluations to go beyond assessing intended results, actual evaluation practice consistently fails to take unintended consequences seriously (Harvey et al. 2010). It seems clear that the methodologies available now are not fully equipped to capture and assess unintended consequences. Moreover, the pursuit of methodological rigor inhibits the assessment of the extent to which unintended consequences affect the claim holders.

Evaluations recognize the need to distinguish between unintended consequences that are avoidable (occur because of errors in programming) and those that are a consequence of the complex and unpredictable nature of the post-conflict situation (Anderson 1999). It is feasible for evaluations to address unintended results (Vaux 2001; Telford, Cosgrave, and Houghton 2006).

One example is the recent joint evaluation conducted by the Tsunami Evaluation Coalition, consisting of forty-two international agencies, to assess the impact of international assistance to countries affected by the 2004 Indian Ocean tsunami (Telford, Cosgrave, and Houghton 2006). In that evaluation, two of the four case studies involved regions also affected by conflict at the time of the tsunami (Sri Lanka and the Aceh region in Indonesia). The Tsunami Evaluation Coalition addressed downward accountability through four steps.

1. To assess the performance of disaster response, the evaluation set the benchmarks using international agreements and standards—the *Code of Conduct for the International Red Cross and Red Crescent Movement and Non-Governmental Organisations (NGOs) in Disaster Relief* (IFRC 1994); the Sphere Project's *Humanitarian Charter and Minimum Standards in Disaster Response* (Sphere Project 2004); *Principles and Good Practice of Humanitarian Donorship* (Good Humanitarian Donorship 2003); and the UN's Guiding Principles on International Displacement (UN 1998)—rather than those of the individual agencies conducting the evaluation.
2. In delineating the evaluand, which was the effect of assistance on local and national capacities, it explicitly included the ability to hold duty bearers to account as a dimension of these capacities.[9]

---

[9] The evaluation defined *capacity* as the "interconnected set of skills and abilities to access services and programmes, to influence and set policies and longer term recovery/reconstruction agendas, and . . . to hold duty-bearers at all levels accountable" (Scheper et al. 2006, 17).

3. The methodology identified the vulnerable and marginalized populations (taking into consideration gender, age, social status, physical disability, and geographic region) in every case study to facilitate the assessment of changes in the capacities of these groups.
4. Since downward accountability requires participatory approaches to evaluation that gauge the perceptions of claim holders, the evaluation included broad-based claim holder surveys and exit stakeholder consultations with affected communities (represented by community-based organizations) to validate its findings.

Qualitative methods were the only possible source of evidence for this evaluation. Lessons from evaluative experience also point to the need to design evaluations that clearly recognize the power relations between the duty bearers and the claim holders, as well as among all stakeholders.

Evaluations conducted by individual agencies are ill equipped to fully address downward accountability issues. To fully understand and assess the consequences of international support, sector-wide joint evaluations are seen as necessary. Evaluations conducted jointly by all key actors in a given sector will help pin down the overall contribution of international support. This became apparent in the Tsunami Evaluation Coalition study, in which claim holders could not differentiate among the different United Nations agencies and tended to regard them all as simply the United Nations (Telford, Cosgrave, and Houghton 2006). Similarly, from their perspective, very often the differences between other donor agencies and international organizations were blurred.

The tsunami, and the international assistance that followed, strengthened the efforts underway for the resolution of the conflict in Aceh.[10] In Sri Lanka, the results were the opposite. Though the initial response of the population was overwhelmingly to ignore ethnic boundaries and reach out to the affected, subsequent events led to the breakdown of the fragile peace agreement. Even though aid was not the major factor leading to this breakdown, the way the national government chose to disburse international assistance became a contentious issue. This result was a consequence of a complex web of interactions between the demography of the relief and recovery needs and the political upheavals in the country.

To ensure recovery and the ability to "build back better," it is critical that assistance programs recognize the different social groups, the social position of each, and the relationships among them. Evaluation must address whether the response is contributing to building bridges among divided social groups or merely responding to pressure to disburse funds as quickly as possible. Three of the four case studies undertaken by the Tsunami Evaluation Coalition found that aid was disbursed disproportionately to areas that were easily served by transportation, rather than based on need, and that the old and the disabled were often

---

[10] For another perspective on post-tsunami Aceh, see Renner (2013).

excluded from benefits because they were poorly informed about them. A recovery support that clearly recognizes groups at risk and an evaluation designed to assess the differentiated progress of these different groups are vital to speedy recovery.

A number of broad-based claim holder surveys were conducted as part of the tsunami aid evaluation. For instance, in Sri Lanka and Indonesia, surveys involving over 1,000 affected people were conducted for one of the thematic components of the evaluations. These surveys provided an important channel for feedback from a number of claim holders who could not have been reached otherwise. For two reasons, the surveys would not have been possible if this had not been a joint evaluation. First, resources from all participating agencies were needed to make the survey viable. Second, the time and capacity requirements for the design and conduct of the surveys were only met because it was a joint exercise. Joint evaluations provide a necessary but not sufficient condition for experimenting to broaden the reach of the evaluation.

EVALUATING NATURAL RESOURCE MANAGEMENT IN POST-CONFLICT SITUATIONS: ASSESSMENTS OF DEVELOPMENT RESULTS

A comprehensive understanding of the context and situations affecting people's lives and well-being in post-conflict situations is essential. In order for any intervention to reach the intended beneficiaries and to improve the lives of claim holders, it is important to grasp the full picture of the political, economic, and social forces that impinge on them. Consequently, narrowly evaluating a particular project or intervention without giving consideration to the wider context may generate an irrelevant assessment at best and, at worst, miss significant unintended and unforeseen consequences of the intervention. This section discusses lessons from country-level evaluations in a range of conflict-affected countries conducted by the UNDP Evaluation Office. These evaluations—called assessments of development results (ADRs)—are better able to capture the full situation and analyze how specific interventions influence outputs because ADRs take a comprehensive look and apply an endogenous perspective. What may have to be sacrificed in this approach is attributing change to limited external interventions. Such attribution, especially in a complex post-conflict situation, would in any case be futile.

Many post-conflict societies and communities depend on natural resources for their livelihoods, yet as other chapters in this book have demonstrated, agriculture, forestry, and fisheries are often disrupted during conflict and in some cases intentionally destroyed. Thus natural resource management issues must be a key focus for evaluation as the post-conflict transition moves from emergency relief to long-term development. In that transition, evaluation must move beyond considering immediate outputs such as reduction in fighting, increased safety, and access to shelter and food. Evaluation can enhance understanding of people's needs and preferences around natural resources, and of the social dynamics—such as power relations between different groups or between genders—that is essential for any intervention to succeed.

Natural resources can be both a cause of conflict and a factor enabling post-conflict recovery and development. Their role in conflicts is well documented (UNEP 2009). Post-conflict strategies and interventions must address any conflict over natural resources in a fair, balanced, and realistic manner. Otherwise, they risk perpetuating the root causes of the conflict and jeopardizing the peace. Evaluations can play a key role in ensuring that this issue is addressed. Even when natural resource issues are not a source of conflict, peoples' long-term ability to support themselves often depends on their access to natural resources such as water and land. In post-conflict and post-disaster situations, displaced people may actually increase the pressure on resources in a way that reduces sustainability. Therefore, evaluation must focus on how the program manages access to natural resources and resolves related disputes. Management of the environment and natural resources should not be an afterthought during evaluation.

As independent evaluations, ADRs assess UNDP's contributions to development results at the country level and provide lessons for strategies in the future. The evaluations take a longer perspective than is usual for evaluations of individual interventions, normally analyzing UNDP's work in the country over a period of seven to ten years. In post-conflict countries, the perspective may be somewhat shorter, depending on whether UNDP remained present in the country during the conflict or whether it returned only after hostilities ended. In either case, the evaluations look at the full range of projects and nonproject activities (such as policy dialogue and advocacy) that UNDP has been involved in. The purpose of these evaluations is to contribute to UNDP's accountability toward the organization's executive board, as well as national stakeholders and partners, to serve as a means of quality assurance for UNDP's interventions at the country level, and to contribute to learning at the country, regional, and corporate levels. While the evaluations focus on UNDP's performance and results, these are presented against the in-country situation and development trends in the country. It is not satisfactory for the projects to reach their objectives, operating effectively and efficiently, if there is no real improvement in the development situation in the country and in the lives of the people. The country's development context and status thus become important benchmarks against which UNDP's strategic positioning and results are mapped.

On the other hand, what ultimately happens in the country depends primarily on the national actors and a wide range of other partners. It is most often difficult, if not impossible, to attribute the final development results to UNDP or any other single actor. Apart from other actors and organizations, the results depend on a number of external factors, notably the overall political, economic, and security trends. Similarly, the ways that UNDP's interventions affect change may be indirect and complex, triggering actions by various actors in the country that, combined with other actions, may lead to the desired outcomes. For instance, if UNDP supports the organization of elections in a post-conflict situation, assessing whether the elections resulted in democratization and sustainable development at the societal level in the long term would go far beyond evaluating UNDP's performance. If UNDP's thrust is to advocate and provide policy advice to national authorities for inclusive development that reflects the needs of vulnerable populations, it is again impossible to attribute the eventual reduction in vulnerability of, for instance, female farmers to the policy dialogue UNDP had with the government. However, it is possible to identify the contributions of UNDP to processes and whether these processes led to desired results or whether there were unforeseen factors or consequences that reduced or even reversed the benefits.

The ADRs use mixed methods to collect and analyze much data and information on the national development situation and trends, as well as on UNDP's strategies and interventions. Data collection and analysis include: review of project and program documents, monitoring and review reports, and project-level evaluations; identification and interviews with a wide range of stakeholder groups; and field visits to observe the situation on the ground and to interview claim holders. It is important to spend adequate time scoping the evaluation and mapping the stakeholders before embarking on the evaluation. When identifying the stakeholders and persons to be interviewed, it is important to include different categories, such as government officials, political parties (or opposing sides in a conflict), civil society representatives, academics, journalists, international development partners, and key groups that have a stake in the process. It is also important to reach out to groups that are not involved in the interventions to gauge whether the interventions have had noticeable effects—either positive or negative—beyond the direct stakeholders. A key analytical tool used to enhance the validity of the findings is triangulation, referring to a deliberate effort to confirm information from multiple data sources, using multiple methods and repeated observations over time, and analyzing findings against multiple hypotheses (UNDP EO 2011).

Taking a long-term and comprehensive perspective to analyzing UNDP's support to two conflict-affected countries in the African Great Lakes region (Rwanda and Uganda), ADRs were able to assess the relevance, effectiveness, efficiency, and sustainability of the organization's strategies and interventions. Although the individual projects were mostly found to be operating as expected, the evaluations pointed out certain shortcomings that reduced the overall results in both countries.

Almost two decades later, Rwanda is still feeling the aftermath of the 1994 genocide. Particularly vulnerable groups include widows and orphans (in 2006, almost a quarter of Rwandan households were headed by women and 0.7 percent by children), recently returned refugees, and resettled internally displaced persons (UNDP EO 2008). Similarly, families of those detained as suspects of crimes related to the genocide are vulnerable. In a country where agriculture employs some 80 percent of the population, management of land and water is critical (UNEP 2011). In the Land of a Thousand Hills, as Rwanda is often called, it is estimated that half of the country's farmland suffers from moderate to severe erosion (UNEP 2011). Due to its high rural population density (with 350 people per square kilometer, Rwanda is the most densely populated country in Africa) and continued population growth of 2.5 percent per year, agriculture has been pushed to steep slopes and to seasonally flooded valley bottoms that are ecologically fragile (UNEP 2011; UNDP EO 2008). During the genocide, erosion-control structures were abandoned, and they remain neglected.

Environmental management has received little attention from the government, despite the key role sustainable agriculture could play in recovery from the conflict. Looking beyond the immediate aftermath of the conflict, an ADR—covering the period from 2000 to 2006—highlighted the need for addressing issues related to sustainable management of natural resources, including neglected land management works. The evaluation found that UNDP did not adequately prioritize its assistance to the government to address this development gap and ensure the effective incorporation of environment and sustainable development into the economic development and poverty reduction strategy (UNDP EO 2008). The longer time window and comprehensive view taken in the evaluation allowed for the identification of such gaps, like the critical linkages between poverty and environment and the pressure on arable land that remains a potential source of conflict (Diamond 2005; Boudreaux 2009).

In neighboring Uganda, economic development has been one of the fastest in sub-Saharan Africa, with sustained growth rates averaging 7.8 percent since 2000. In the north, however, two decades of conflict between the government and the Lord's Resistance Army and other rebel groups took a toll on economic and social development; about 1.8 million people were internally displaced, and thousands were killed. Although the hostilities officially ended in 2006, the region still lags severely behind the rest of the country in social and economic development. Reducing this disparity is a major challenge for the government (UNDP EO 2009b).

With up to 80 percent of the population engaged in agriculture and a rapidly growing population (3.3 percent per year), sustainable use and management of the environment is key to human and economic development. As part of its early recovery and human security interventions in the northern parts of the country, UNDP has promoted livelihood projects for internally displaced persons. However, an ADR discovered that while these projects, some of which were directly related to agriculture and food security, were seen as positive, the results were mixed because of their short-term nature, implementation delays, and lack of community consultation in their design (UNDP EO 2009b).

Both evaluations reinforce the conclusion that paying attention to natural resource management and livelihoods is essential in a post-conflict situation in which most people depend on agriculture for their sustenance. They also showed the importance of integrating such considerations in policies and long-term strategies, beyond individual projects, in order to achieve sustainable benefits for the conflict-affected populations. This empirical analysis provides further evidence to the potential role of natural resources, not only as sources of conflict, but as an area around which cooperation can be built in the Great Lakes region, provided that they are properly factored into post-conflict development visions (Kameri-Mbote 2007; UNEP 2009).

An ADR conducted in Afghanistan provided different, albeit equally critical, lessons for working on local development in a conflict situation. International attention in Afghanistan has focused understandably on insecurity and the continued conflict with the Taliban. But the evaluation showed that exclusive focus on ending conflict in insecure areas can undermine the transition to development.

The United Nations is present in Afghanistan under a Security Council mandate and operates as an integrated mission. Assistance to Afghanistan by the United Nations and the international community more broadly has focused on dealing with the immediate issues pertaining to the conflict and post-conflict recovery. Like most donors, UNDP has concentrated its efforts in Afghanistan on the provinces with the most security problems. An ADR conducted in 2009 suggested that this approach may have failed to create incentives to reduce armed conflict—as peace and security, where they have been established, have not brought significant social and economic benefits. Despite its expertise in and experience with promoting community-based development programs and concepts in many countries, UNDP as part of the integrated mission also focused on post-conflict recovery and only later became active in promoting economic development and livelihoods. Such activities are crucial, however, as the lack of jobs and income opportunities make people more likely to join insurgent activities (UNDP EO 2009a).

This echoes the conclusion from a more general evaluation of UNDP support to conflict-affected countries (UNDP EO 2006). These evaluations recommended that UNDP advocate strongly for the international community to drop the incremental, phased approach to post-conflict assistance in favor of one that immediately begins to build the capacity of the institutions necessary for lasting peace and development. This should give priority early on to issues such as reintegration of refugees and internally displaced persons and support for sustainable livelihoods. In countries that are highly dependent on agriculture, support for natural resource management is crucial.

CONCLUSIONS

Evaluation can determine whether post-conflict peacebuilding objectives are being met, and can also provide lessons for how to improve performance. In order for evaluations to provide reliable feedback, they need to incorporate a number of considerations.

Evaluators must understand the dynamics that either help or hamper people's efforts to improve their lives after conflict ends. To this end, they need to have a full grasp of the nuances of the local context—including a comprehensive understanding of the social, political, and economic causes that fueled the crisis, and of existing local capacities with which recovery efforts need to engage. They must particularly keep in mind inequalities, power relations, gender dimensions, social exclusion, and vulnerabilities that exist in the communities. The various links to natural resource ownership, control, access, and management should also be considered.

Experience shows that the international community tends to repeat its own mistakes in responding to post-conflict and post-crisis situations because situations that in fact are quite variant are seen as interchangeable and amenable to standardized solutions. But national, political, social, economic, and ethnic issues, among others, as well as the sources of conflict, vary significantly from one situation to the next. Interventions do not take place in a vacuum; there are always other factors taking place. This variability creates challenges to the meaningful utilization of preexisting frameworks of analysis in post-conflict countries.

In post-conflict evaluations there are no easy solutions involving tick boxes or simple indicators. The evaluations should provide both upward accountability, to the funders of the program interventions, and downward accountability, to those the program is intended to benefit. Surveys, focus groups, and interviews with key informants all play a role, but they must be carefully crafted so as not to bias the findings in favor of particular groups or interests. Another important element is triangulation, or validating the findings from interviews through other means, such as document review, statistical data on actual trends, and direct observation.

Evaluations should go beyond intended results and dig deeper to look at the full spectrum of consequences, both intended and unintended, of development initiatives. Any changes in the well-being of claim holders are affected not only by the intended effects but also by the unintended consequences. In post-conflict situations, unintended consequences could be significant compared to the intended ones. The failure of most post-conflict evaluations to assess intended and unintended results on an equal footing has resulted in these evaluations not reflecting downward accountability and raises questions about their rigor and reliability.

To capture the full spectrum of consequences, evaluation approaches to recovery efforts must be based on a thorough understanding of the experiences of the local populations as collected through interviews and surveys. In addition, assessment of sector-wide efforts should be preferred over individual interventions. Effort must be made to document evidence accumulating from post-conflict evaluations to build a body of knowledge that will help test and refine assumptions and hypotheses about providing post-conflict support. At the same time, evaluation can also help improve our collective understanding regarding the role of natural resource management in both conflict and effective peacebuilding.

REFERENCES

Anderson, M. B. 1999. *Do no harm: How aid can support peace—or war.* London: Lynne Rienner.

Bickman, L. 1987. The functions of a programme theory. In *Using programme theory in evaluation,* ed. L. Bickman. San Francisco, CA: Jossey-Bass.

Birckmayer, J. D., and C. H. Weiss. 2000. Theory-based evaluation in practice: What do we learn? *Evaluation Review* 24 (4): 407–431.

Boudreaux, K. 2009. Land conflict and genocide in Rwanda. *Electronic Journal of Sustainable Development* 1 (3): 85–95.
Carvalho, S., and H. White. 2004. Theory-based evaluation: The case of social funds. *American Journal of Evaluation* 25 (2): 141–160.
Chen, H.-T. 1990. *Theory-driven evaluations.* Thousand Oaks, CA: Sage Publications.
Diamond, J. 2005. *Collapse: How societies choose to fail or succeed.* New York: Viking.
Good Humanitarian Donorship. 2003. *Principles and good practice of humanitarian donorship.* Stockholm, Sweden. www.goodhumanitariandonorship.org/Libraries/Ireland_Doc _Manager/EN-23-Principles-and-Good-Practice-of-Humanitarian-Donorship.sflb.ashx.
Harvey, P., A. Stoddard, A. Harmer, and G. Taylor. 2010. *The state of the humanitarian system: Assessing performance and progress; A pilot study.* With V. DiDomenico and L. Brander. London: Active Learning Network for Accountability and Performance in Humanitarian Action. www.alnap.org/pool/files/alnap-sohs-final.pdf.
Herson, M., and J. Mitchell. 2005. Real-time evaluation: Where does its value lie? *Humanitarian Exchange Magazine* 32:43–45.
IFRC (International Federation of Red Cross and Red Crescent Societies). 1994. *Code of conduct for the International Red Cross and Red Crescent movement and non-governmental organisations (NGOs) in disaster relief.* Geneva, Switzerland.
———. 2005. *World disasters report 2005: Focus on information in disasters.* Bloomfield, CT: Kumarian Press.
Kameri-Mbote, P. 2007. *Conflict and cooperation: Making the case for environmental pathways to peacebuilding in the Great Lakes region.* Environmental Change and Security Program Report 12. Washington, D.C.: Woodrow Wilson Center / United States Agency for International Development. www.wilsoncenter.org/sites/default/files/ECSP _report_12.pdf.
Kennedy, D. 2004. *The dark side of virtue: Reassessing international humanitarianism.* Princeton, NJ: Princeton University Press.
McNall, M., and P. G. Foster-Fishman. 2007. Methods of rapid evaluation, assessment, and appraisal. *American Journal of Evaluation* 28 (2): 151–168.
Mendoza, G. A., and H. Martins. 2006. Multi-criteria decision analysis in natural resource management: A critical review of methods and new modelling paradigms. *Forest Ecology and Management* 230 (1–3): 1–22.
Neufeldt, R. C. 2007. *"Frameworkers" and "circlers"—Exploring assumptions in peace and conflict impact assessment.* Berlin, Germany: Berghof Research Center.
OECD (Organisation for Economic Co-operation and Development). 2005. Paris declaration on aid effectiveness. Paris. www.unrol.org/files/34428351.pdf.
OECD/DAC (Organisation for Economic Co-operation and Development, Development Assistance Committee). 2007. Encouraging effective evaluation of conflict prevention and peacebuilding activities: Towards DAC guidance. *OECD Journal on Development* 8 (3): 7–106.
Picciotto, R. 2007. The new environment for development evaluation. *American Journal of Evaluation* 28 (4): 509–521.
Renner, M. 2013. Post-tsunami Aceh: Successful peacemaking, uncertain peacebuilding. In *Livelihoods, natural resources, and post-conflict peacebuilding,* ed. H. Young and L. Goldman. London: Earthscan.
Rieff, D. 2002. *A Bed for the night: Humanitarianism in crisis.* New York: Simon and Schuster.

Sandison, P. 2003. Desk review of real-time evaluation experience. Evaluation working paper. New York: United Nations Children's Fund.

Scheper, E., A. Parakrama, S. Patel, and T. Vaux. 2006. *Impact of the tsunami response on local and national capacities.* London: Tsunami Evaluation Coalition.

Scriven, M., and M. Q. Patton. 1972. Pros and cons about goal-free evaluation. *Evaluation Comment: The Journal of Educational Evaluation* 3 (4): 1–7.

Sphere Project. 2004. *Humanitarian charter and minimum standards in disaster response.* Geneva, Switzerland. http://ocw.jhsph.edu/courses/refugeehealthcare/PDFs/SphereProject Handbook.pdf.

Telford, J., J. Cosgrave, and R. Houghton. 2006. *Joint evaluation of the international response to the Indian Ocean tsunami: Synthesis report.* London: Tsunami Evaluation Coalition.

UN (United Nations). 1998. Guiding principles on internal displacement. E/CN.4/1998/53/Add.2. www.unhcr.org/refworld/docid/3d4f95e11.html.

UNDP (United Nations Development Programme). 2009. *Handbook on planning, monitoring and evaluating for development results.* New York: web.undp.org/evaluation/handbook/documents/english/pme-handbook.pdf.

UNDP EO (United Nations Development Programme, Evaluation Office). 2006. *Evaluation of UNDP assistance to conflict-affected countries.* New York. http://web.undp.org/evaluation/documents/thematic/conflict/ConflictEvaluation2006.pdf.

———. 2008. *Assessment of development results: Rwanda; Evaluation of UNDP contribution.* New York. www.oecd.org/dataoecd/61/0/41105593.pdf.

———. 2009a. *Assessment of development results: Islamic Republic of Afghanistan; Evaluation of UNDP contribution.* New York. www.undp.org.af/publications/KeyDocuments/ADR_Afghanistan.pdf.

———. 2009b. *Assessment of development results: Uganda; Evaluation of UNDP contribution.* New York. http://web.undp.org/evaluation/documents/ADR/ADR_Reports/Uganda/Uganda_ADR_2009.pdf.

———. 2011. *ADR method manual.* New York.

UNEG (United Nations Evaluation Group). 2005. *Norms for evaluation in the UN system.* New York. www.uneval.org/papersandpubs/documentdetail.jsp?doc_id=21.

UNEP (United Nations Environment Programme). 2009. *From conflict to peacebuilding: The role of natural resources and the environment.* Nairobi, Kenya. www.unep.org/pdf/pcdmb_policy_01.pdf.

———. 2011. *Rwanda: From post-conflict to environmentally sustainable development.* Nairobi, Kenya. http://postconflict.unep.ch/publications/UNEP_Rwanda.pdf.

Vaessen, J. 2006. Programme theory evaluation, multicriteria decision aid and stakeholder values: A methodological framework. *Evaluation* 12 (4): 397–417.

Vaux, T. 2001. *Independent evaluation: The DEC response to the earthquake in Gujarat.* London: Disasters Emergency Committee.

Weiss, C. 1998. *Evaluation.* 2nd ed. Upper Saddle River, NJ: Prentice-Hall.

PART 5

Lessons learned

Natural resources and post-conflict assessment, remediation, restoration, and reconstruction: Lessons and emerging issues

David Jensen and Steve Lonergan

Post-conflict situations are often characterized by multiple transition processes, including not only the transition from conflict to peace, but also democratization, decentralization, and market liberalization. The transformation of conflict-affected countries into peaceful, stable, and more prosperous ones is an immensely complex task, often susceptible to contradictory pressures and to the risk of relapsing into violence (UNDP and World Bank 2007).

Among the immediate challenges in post-conflict situations are (1) defining needs and assigning priorities to them, (2) coordinating response and reconstruction, and (3) implementing a coherent plan to consolidate peace and prevent the relapse of violence. Simultaneous activities are also undertaken to lay the future foundations for good governance and sustainable development. All of these efforts must respond and adapt to a complex and fluid political environment, pressure for rapid recovery and growth, and expressions of investment interest from the private sector.

Assigning priority to the management of natural resources and the environment is often difficult, given competing priorities that include security sector reform; disarmament, demobilization, and reintegration; the return of displaced persons; and the organization of national elections. In many cases, the drive for rapid reconstruction comes at the expense of transparency, equitable sharing of resource wealth, and the sustainable management of natural resources. In the worst circumstances, natural resources are captured by elites, provide an avenue for corruption, and are used to sustain short-term political interests.

Although countries emerging from conflict often delay decisions on natural resource management until stability is restored, this approach can prove disastrous for long-term sustainability. As the cases in this book demonstrate, natural resources are essential assets in the peacebuilding process, and decisions about

---

David Jensen is the head of the Environmental Cooperation for Peacebuilding program of the United Nations Environment Programme (UNEP). Steve Lonergan is a professor emeritus of geography at the University of Victoria and the former director of the UNEP Division of Early Warning and Assessment.

how they will be managed, owned, allocated, and accessed cannot be put off. Poor choices made early on (including the choice to defer action) may establish trajectories that will undermine the fragile foundations of peace. Moreover, in the absence of clear policies and laws, some choices are inevitably made by the most powerful stakeholders; when such choices become institutionalized, it may take decades to undo then. The key challenges are (1) to identify those natural resources that have the greatest potential to contribute to conflict and peace, and (2) to determine how they should be managed and which stakeholders should be engaged in the process. Early decisions about resource governance can be critical, in the long run, in determining whether social relations follow a peaceful or a violent path (Conca and Wallace 2012*).[1]

Furthermore, failure to respond to the environmental needs of war-torn societies can greatly complicate the difficult tasks of peacebuilding. For example, the degradation or contamination of renewable resources, such as water and arable land, can deepen human suffering and increase vulnerability to natural disasters. At worst, tensions triggered by environmental damage or contested access to natural resources may lead to renewed violent conflict. Ultimately, poor governance of natural resources can threaten the effective functioning of the governmental, economic, and social institutions necessary for sustained peace (Conca and Wallace 2012*).

Too often, environmental governance and the sustainable management of natural resources are perceived as being distinct from—and sometimes even in conflict with—peacebuilding and development. Both this book and the other books in the series clearly demonstrate that this view is mistaken. In fact, natural resources and the environment hold tremendous peacebuilding potential and underpin many peacebuilding priorities. For example, opportunities to kick-start economic growth often depend on oil, minerals, and other high-value natural resources, and the creation of new jobs and sustainable livelihoods typically relies on a range of natural assets, including land, water, forest resources, and minerals (Brown et al. 2012*). Post-conflict governments also rely on revenues derived from the extraction, sale, and trade of natural resources. And shared natural resources or common environmental threats can create platforms for dialogue, confidence building, and cooperation between divided groups (Conca and Wallace 2012*). In short, natural resources can be a fundamental engine of economic growth and stability in post-conflict countries, provided that they are managed transparently, equitably, and sustainably. In some cases, they can also be used as the basis for regional cooperation and economic integration (Bruch, Wolfarth, and Michalcik 2012*).

To unlock this potential, it is essential to determine, at the outset of the reconstruction process, how natural resource management and environmental governance can concretely support conflict prevention, peacebuilding, and broader

---

[1] Citations marked with an asterisk refer to chapters within this book.

development goals. The next steps involve the development of action plans, capacity-building programs, environmental remediation and restoration projects, and investments in key infrastructure. Throughout the reconstruction process, it is essential to minimize the environmental impacts of reconstruction itself; practitioners must also be on the alert for potential negative interactions between different peacebuilding priorities (Unruh and Shalaby 2012*). Particularly in the case of natural resources that are being used to support multiple peacebuilding goals and that are therefore subject to multiple competitive pressures, success in one area of peacebuilding may have unintended consequences in another (Nanthikesan and Uitto 2012*).

This book is designed to help domestic and international actors understand how to achieve these multiple objectives more effectively. The twenty-one chapters in the book were written by thirty-five specialists representing a cross section of practitioners from United Nations agencies, government ministries, nongovernmental organizations, academia, and the military. Taken together, the case studies demonstrate that environmental and natural resource governance can support more effective peacebuilding and can be better integrated into peacebuilding programs, policies, and practices.

This chapter consists of seven major sections that cover the following topics: (1) post-conflict environmental assessment; (2) remediation of environmental hot spots; (3) restoration of natural resources and ecosystems; (4) environmental dimensions of infrastructure and reconstruction; (5) crosscutting lessons; (6) coordinating and sequencing interventions; and (7) future outlook.

POST-CONFLICT ENVIRONMENTAL ASSESSMENT

In the immediate aftermath of conflict, among the first steps taken by domestic and international actors are to identify needs, define priorities, and determine the amount of financing that will be required for relief, recovery, and peacebuilding. Priorities and funding needs are often identified through needs assessments conducted jointly by domestic stakeholders and international organizations such as the UN, the World Bank, and the European Union.

For the first two to four years after conflict, needs assessments provide the basis for donor financing and influence the direction of reconstruction. It is thus imperative to ensure, from the outset, that needs assessments pay particular attention to natural resource management and environmental governance issues, in order to help prevent conflict relapse and support stabilization and peacebuilding. The inclusion of such issues provides a critically important basis for financing and reconstruction. If environmental and natural resource issues are neglected or marginalized in the needs assessment process, it may be years before they are addressed—and the country in question will miss a critical window of opportunity for reform.

At the outset of the reconstruction process, a rapid environmental assessment should be undertaken to identify the key impacts, risks, and opportunities that must be integrated into the peacebuilding process and addressed within the first two years. Rapid assessments can then be followed by comprehensive assessments or by sector- or region-specific assessments designed to collect information that is more quantitative. Because post-conflict situations are fluid and politically complex—and involve winners and losers who have competing interests, needs, and agendas—one of the main challenges is to ensure that assessments are impartial and backed by sound scientific data.

In fragmented countries—where natural resource ownership, access, and allocation may be highly politicized, divided along ethnic lines, or both, and where certain stakeholders may be attempting to protect vested interests in such resources—international organizations typically lead environmental and natural resource assessments. Even where adequate institutions exist and rule of law applies, domestic authorities may lack the necessary scientific expertise and operational capacity to carry out assessments, and may call on the international community for assistance. International support may also be requested when a conflict causes transboundary environmental damage. Since 1999, international organizations such as the United Nations Environment Programme (UNEP), the United Nations Development Programme (UNDP), and the World Bank have been asked to oversee the design and implementation of more than thirty post-conflict assessments, which have been conducted in cooperation with domestic partners.

The cases in this book that address environmental assessment reveal eight key lessons—highlighted in the following sections—about (1) the scope and approach of effective post-conflict environmental assessments, and (2) the importance of integrating environmental governance and natural resource management into reconstruction plans and peacebuilding strategies.

Direct and indirect pathways of environmental damage

Post-conflict environmental assessments conducted since 1999 have revealed that conflict can damage or affect natural resources and the environment through many pathways, both direct and indirect (UNEP 2009a; Jensen 2012*; Conca and Wallace 2012*; Briggs and Weissbecker 2012*). The six principal pathways for direct environmental damage that have been identified are as follows:

- Toxic hazards from the bombardment of industrial sites and urban infrastructure.
- A legacy of weapons, landmines, unexploded ordnance, and depleted uranium munitions.
- Human displacement.
- The use of extractive industries to fund conflict.
- The loss of water supply, sanitation, and waste disposal infrastructure.
- Direct targeting of natural resources, particularly as part of scorched-earth military tactics.

For the safety of local populations and international workers in post-conflict situations, assessments must evaluate the short- and long-term risks to human health and recommend mitigation measures (Burger 2012*; Briggs and Weissbecker 2012*).

It is also essential to understand indirect pathways to environmental damage, two of which are particularly relevant. First, violent conflict and the loss of economic opportunity may compel affected populations to engage in unsustainable coping mechanisms or survival strategies, such as overharvesting or the liquidation of natural resources. In some regions of Afghanistan, for example, residents removed as much as 99 percent of the forest cover to sell as charcoal, or so that the land could be used for agriculture and grazing (Jensen 2012*). In many cases, economic activity shifts from a formal to an informal basis, operating outside government regulation. And conflict economies often emerge that consist of several distinct but intertwined segments: the remains of the formal economy, the international aid economy, the informal economy, and the criminal economy (Conca and Wallace 2012*). Second, violent conflict disrupts state and local institutions and initiatives, undermining the enforcement of laws and the protection of resource rights. Conflict thus leads to poor resource governance; loss of capacity; abundant space for illegality, corruption, and land grabbing;[2] and the collapse of positive resource management practices (Conca and Wallace 2012*). The impacts of conflict on land tenure have significant implications not only for future land and resource use but also for livelihoods and commercial investments (Unruh and Shalaby 2012*). Though there is little question that violent conflict often causes tremendous direct damage to the environment, in many cases, indirect impacts cast a darker shadow because of their capacity to undermine institutions, disrupt livelihoods, affect land and resource tenure, alter social practices, and change economic systems (Carius and Maas 2012*; Conca and Wallace 2012*; Jensen 2012*; Unruh and Shalaby 2012*; Lonergan 2012*).

Assessing natural resource risks and opportunities—and building governance capacity to address them

In addition to evaluating the direct and indirect environmental damage caused by conflict, assessments should take into account the specific role natural resources played in the conflict itself and in the national political economy. In particular, assessments should attempt (1) to understand how the mismanagement of natural resources triggered, sustained, fueled, or financed conflict, and (2) to identify the key actors that shape resource governance (Liljedahl et al. 2012*; Jensen 2012*). Such efforts should also include an analysis of the risk of potential conflict relapse from new sources of conflict, such as those that might emerge from tensions over extractive industries, renewable resources, or land.

---

[2] Land grabbing is the illegal or coerced seizure of land in the absence or against the will of the owner or legitimate landholder, whether or not the land is held under statutory law.

An analysis of relapse risk typically focuses on specific conflict drivers and risk factors, including the following (Nanthikesan and Uitto 2012*; UNDG 2012):

- The sharing of resource wealth and its attendant benefits.
- Transparency with regard to resource contracts, payments, and the potential social and environmental impacts of the extraction process.
- Increasing competition over scarce resources.
- Environmental degradation.
- Tensions over land tenure and resource rights.
- Stakeholder and civil society participation in decision making.
- Transboundary dynamics.
- National and local capacity for resolving disputes and grievances.

Where extractive resources provide a substantial part of a country's revenues, or where large portions of the population depend on land and renewable resources, there is particular vulnerability to conflict relapse in the absence of improved governance.

Once the risks of conflict relapse have been identified, an assessment must be undertaken to determine how the environment and natural resources can support peacebuilding and national development priorities—such as reconciliation and political inclusion, good governance, revenue generation, the restoration of basic services, economic recovery, and the creation of jobs and livelihoods for all, including returnees and excombatants. Demonstrating, through such an assessment, how natural resources underpin peacebuilding priorities can help build a stronger case for strengthening national resource management and environmental governance capacity at the outset of reconstruction. Assessments conducted by UNEP in the Central African Republic, the Democratic Republic of the Congo, and Sierra Leone, for example, demonstrated how natural resources could support national peacebuilding priorities associated with human development, livelihoods, and governance, thereby paving the way for the integration of natural resource management into peacebuilding and reconstruction (UNEP 2010, 2011a; Jensen, Halle, and Lehtonen 2009; Brown et al. 2012*).

The final step, once conflict relapse risks and resource-related peacebuilding opportunities have been identified, is to assess national and local capacities to address them. Such an assessment must reach beyond formal state institutions to engage the social and local context in which most resource governance actually occurs. Among the specific factors that must be assessed are the quality of institutions, the legal and policy framework, coordination mechanisms, financial and operational resources, technical expertise, and the capacity of civil society to participate in decision making and monitor compliance with relevant laws. Finally, the assessment should identify ongoing international support to the environmental and natural resource sectors and inventory all international environmental agreements the country has ratified (Conca and Wallace 2012*).

Emerging areas for post-conflict environmental assessment

Post-conflict assessments conducted by international organizations or agencies have given insufficient attention to four emerging areas. First, the assessments have failed to reflect the complexity of post-conflict economies, which typically include several distinct but intertwined segments: the remains of the formal economy, the international aid economy, the informal economy, and the criminal economy. Each of these segments has a different relationship to natural resources, and it is essential to understand not only how they are embedded in transnational commodity chains, but also how private sector interests exploit weak governance to accelerate extraction and minimize payments for resource concessions (Conca and Wallace 2012*). The linkages between post-conflict economies and national, regional, and global criminal networks, and the ways in which these networks drive insecurity, corruption, and violence, must also be carefully considered. By failing to address the different segments, peacebuilding strategies risk overemphasizing one while ignoring others; there is also a danger of implementing initiatives that work at cross-purposes to each other or to peacebuilding goals.

Second, post-conflict environmental assessments have generally failed to address the differential effects of conflict on men and women, particularly with respect to (1) gender-specific risks from and impacts of conflict-related environmental degradation; (2) gender-specific impacts with respect to resource access, benefits sharing, rights, and ownership; (3) opportunities for women's participation and empowerment in decision making regarding natural resources; and (4) the risk of gender-based violence that is linked to resource use. Conflict often precipitates the breakdown of cultural norms and structures: communities are displaced, combatants violate the social compact, and traditional power structures are thrown into upheaval. But such changes affect men and women in quite different ways; to improve the design and implementation of recovery programs, it is essential to take such differences into account (Benard et al. 2008).

Third, assessments must consider the potential for (1) negative interactions between different peacebuilding priorities, and (2) unintended harm to natural resources caused by peacebuilding interventions (Nanthikesan and Uitto 2012*; Unruh and Shalaby 2012*; Carius and Maas 2012*), both of which can lead to serious repercussions. Conflict-affected settings differ profoundly from peaceful ones, but little is known about the ways in which peacebuilding priorities interact, particularly when they rely on or compete for the same natural resources. To date, efforts to address such interactions have been largely unplanned and inadequately thought through. For example, efforts to expand and improve roads in Afghanistan, which has a weak system for protecting land rights, failed to consider the potential effects on land and livelihoods; one result was extensive land grabbing, as land values increased near the new roads (Unruh and Shalaby 2012*). Assessments should begin to systematically identify where potential interactions between priorities or unintended environmental harm could occur.

Finally, assessments should address the vulnerability of the environment and natural resources to natural hazards and climate change. In particular, it is critical to determine how changing precipitation patterns, rising sea levels, and increases in the frequency and intensity of extreme weather might undermine livelihoods, reduce the productivity of key economic sectors, disrupt human health, and alter settlement and migration patterns (Matthew and Hammill 2012*). Assessments should also identify specific measures that can enable fragile societies to (1) better cope with the additional stress of climate impacts, and (2) build national and local capacity to better manage climate and disaster risk.

Dealing with complexity, uncertainty, and the future

Many forces can affect the resource base during post-conflict recovery: the resurgence of economic development; the return of refugees and internally displaced persons; population growth; the award of major resource concessions; increasing resource scarcity; and resource consumption resulting from reconstruction work. Climate change, which is likely to drastically alter regional and local environments and to redraw political, economic, and social maps, will further complicate the analysis of post-conflict situations (Matthew and Hammill 2012*). Finally, other influences, such as changes in global markets and regional politics, can also transform the post-conflict context (Carius and Maas 2012*).

Although standard post-conflict environmental assessments are useful for understanding impacts, risks, and opportunities, they provide only a snapshot of conditions at a given moment. In other words, they attempt, with limited information, to rationalize and simplify a high degree of complexity. To account for the dynamic nature of natural resources and the rapid change that characterizes post-conflict situations, however, practitioners' analytical tools must be increasingly forward looking (Carius and Maas 2012*).

After a major conflict, it takes at least a generation for the social contract to be renewed and for reconciliation to occur (Lederach 2005). Thus, it is imperative to outline, discuss, and attempt to understand the likely shape of the world in which reconstruction will occur. To address the challenges posed by a dynamic environment requires scenario-based approaches that incorporate realistic projections of likely changes and their effects. Actively integrating stakeholders into such a process is crucial and can improve both their awareness of environmental concerns and their sense of ownership. Discussions of the future also require great sensitivity: stakeholders who anticipate that they will be adversely affected by coming changes may take immediate steps to attempt to interfere with the changes (Carius and Maas 2012*).

Once a few distinct scenarios have been established, a process known as "backcasting" comes into play, in which pathways that can potentially link the current situation to a desirable future are identified; the next step is to determine what specific events must occur in order to realize a desirable scenario, what the potential obstacles might be, and how to overcome those obstacles (Carius and

Maas 2012*). In the case of the Iraqi marshlands, for example, one of the authors, working in consultation with Iraqi experts, developed three scenarios to identify the factors that needed to be addressed to reach each outcome. The exercise revealed that one of the scenarios was impossible because of ongoing development efforts and political issues in the wider region. The analysis not only helped stakeholders to understand what was possible but also enabled them to rally around a common vision (Lonergan 2012*).

The limits of predominantly technical approaches to environmental assessment

Post-conflict assessments, such as those undertaken by UNEP, are generally based on the assumption that those who are conducting the assessments are impartial and functioning in a depoliticized environment. Thus, international organizations act as honest brokers, conducting scientific assessments on the basis of field sampling, laboratory analyses, satellite images, secondary data, and stakeholder interviews. If the UN or the European Union is to work effectively with governments and other stakeholders in war-torn societies subject to competing agendas, there may be little alternative to this approach. Indeed, impartiality has been the core source of added value in UNEP's approach since the outset, and a principal factor in the broad level of support its assessment reports have received.

Nevertheless, it is important to recognize the trade-offs involved in a predominantly technical approach to assessment. In societies that have been affected by violent conflict, different actors will bring different realities and "ways of knowing" to the table. Large segments of the population may find the discourse of modern science inaccessible—and may regard "facts" as political matters. Under such circumstances, efforts to depoliticize knowledge may make it more feasible to work under complex and difficult circumstances; nevertheless, technical approaches risk reducing the extent to which the intended beneficiaries of peacebuilding interventions understand and take ownership of assessment results. Moreover, focusing almost exclusively on what can be quantified may prevent questions of resource governance and equity from being addressed (Conca and Wallace 2012*; Nanthikesan and Uitto 2012*).

As the UN embarks on the use of new models of post-conflict environmental assessment—which call for partnerships that extend beyond a country's environmental ministry, and a focus on cooperation grounded in shared environmental knowledge—the potential value of broadening the approach to assessment will likely come to the foreground. If environmental assessments are to serve not only as resource management guides but also as confidence-building tools, the task of widening the audience for the assessments becomes central (Conca and Wallace 2012*). It may not be a coincidence that UNEP's most successful post-conflict assessment, which was conducted in Sudan, included more than six months of consultation with stakeholders (Jensen 2012*).

Using a tailored approach to stakeholder consultation and national ownership

In the typical post-conflict situation, historical data are lacking, environmental monitoring is sporadic, and interagency coordination (assuming that agencies exist and are functioning) is poor to nonexistent. And even where monitoring capacity exists, large-scale environmental assessments require access to information, data exchange, and institutional transparency in settings often dominated by suspicion and exclusion (Conca and Wallace 2012*; Anand 2012*).

To overcome such challenges, international agencies or organizations are often asked to lead impartial assessments. But maintaining an impartial and scientific approach to the assessment process, while simultaneously securing stakeholder buy-in and creating a sense of national ownership, creates difficulties of its own. The cases featured in this book suggest a number of ways to overcome this problem.

First, to build credibility, create a sense of national ownership, and enhance transparency, assessments should employ both international specialists and representatives of government and civil society (Jensen 2012*). When this model is used, however, it is essential to clarify—from the outset, and in writing—both the scope of the work and the participants' roles and responsibilities; it is also necessary to define the role of the assessment in relation to national priorities and follow-up plans. In the post-conflict environmental assessments in Afghanistan and Sudan, for example, experts from across the UN system and from domestic and international nongovernmental organizations took part in the assessment process and continued to play key roles in implementing the recommendations (UNEP 2003, 2007a).

Second, to maximize the transparency of the assessment process and help all parties agree on a common set of analytical techniques, it is useful to divide field samples among the principal parties in the conflict and have them conduct independent analyses (UNEP 2009b). Environmental science, including field sampling, has proved to be a powerful means of putting facts on the table and preventing politicization. UNEP assessments conducted in both Gaza and Lebanon used this approach (Jensen 2012*).

Third, one of the best means of securing stakeholder buy-in is to conduct extensive consultations at each step of the assessment process: from determining the initial scope of the assessment, to implementing the assessment plan, to creating the final assessment report. Engaging stakeholders in highly participatory processes such as workshops and public meetings demonstrates that their voices are being heard, strengthens their sense of ownership in the process, and increases their acceptance of analytical findings and recommendations (Carius and Maas 2012*). UNEP's assessment in Sudan, for example, included six months of consultation that was crucial to the project's success: it validated the fieldwork, ensured that the study was attuned to local issues and needs, and paved the way for national endorsement of assessment outcomes. As part of the process, UNEP also worked closely with the Government of National Unity and the government of Southern Sudan to align UNEP's assessment activities with the National Plan for Environmental Management (Jensen 2012*).

Fourth, for consultation to succeed, it is critical to identify the needs of target audiences and determine how best to engage them and present findings. Engaging audiences by means of stakeholder workshops, discussing findings with the participants, and developing comprehensive reports that reflect results and priorities in terms that are accessible to the target audience not only helps to ensure that an analysis is perceived as legitimate but can also support the development of a sense of ownership (Carius and Maas 2012*).

Finally, although international agencies, donors, and nongovernmental organizations may take a lead technical role in identifying needs, national actors should ideally be responsible for assigning priorities to those needs. The assignment of priorities should occur at the national level, through approaches that are designed to secure inputs from a wide range of stakeholders. International actors can support such efforts by convening workshops on priorities, sharing experiences and best practices from other post-conflict countries, and ensuring the participation of key stakeholders; they should also help to ensure that the process is run in a fair, open, and transparent way, and that wide national buy-in is achieved. Once priorities have been identified, the utility of post-conflict environmental assessments is significantly increased if the national government and its international partners develop a detailed action plan. Dedicated efforts must then be made to communicate the action plan to key donors and to fully integrate it into the relevant post-conflict policy frameworks.

Attuning assessments to context and policy processes

The cases featured in this book demonstrate that post-conflict environmental assessments can be an effective tool for identifying critical environmental needs and integrating them into relief, recovery, and peacebuilding policies and processes. A key lesson derived from such efforts is that the most successful assessments are tailored to the particular post-conflict context and to the political and policy processes they are meant to inform. In particular, assessments that are (1) designed to directly inform an ongoing policy process, and (2) written in terms that the target audience can understand have a greater impact than stand-alone assessments (Jensen 2012*). The structure and language of the environmental, conflict, and peacebuilding assessments conducted by UNEP in the Central African Republic and Sierra Leone, for example, were tailored to inform a larger peacebuilding strategy (UNEP 2010; Jensen, Halle, and Lehtonen 2009). In Iraq, in contrast, the environmental needs assessments were not properly aligned to the policy process; as a result, the final needs assessment document did not fully reflect the needs of the policy process (UN and World Bank 2003).

With respect to policy change, mobilization of financial resources, and media coverage, four principal factors have determined the overall impact of UNEP's post-conflict environmental assessments (Jensen 2012*):

- The amount of funding and time available for the assessment.
- The overall level of national ownership and stakeholder buy-in.
- Clearly identifying priority needs and developing a detailed budget to meet those needs.
- The ability to secure early and sustained financial and political support from donors.

In all cases, trade-offs must be made between the assessment budget, the timing of the assessment, and the scope of the assessment. Trade-offs must also be made between speed and comprehensiveness, qualitative and quantitative approaches, and degree of national ownership. The cases in this book suggest that a rapid but broad assessment that will render information available as soon as possible is essential to early post-conflict policy formation and priority setting. Ideally, however, such rapid assessments should be followed by more comprehensive ones that can inform on-the-ground programming (Jensen 2012*; Conca and Wallace 2012*).

All assessments must be designed to take context into account, including the duration, intensity, geographic distribution, and root causes of the conflict; the weapons technology and military tactics used; and the nature of both the conflict economy and the current political economy. As post-conflict environmental assessments continue to mature, it will become increasingly important to tailor the format and findings to the needs of specific post-conflict policy processes and frameworks, such as humanitarian appeals, early recovery plans, national development plans, peacebuilding strategies, poverty reduction strategies, UN common country assessments, and UN development assistance frameworks (Jensen 2012*; Carius and Maas 2012*).

Evaluating the cost of addressing environmental damage and assigning priorities to needs and economic opportunities are becoming standard elements in post-conflict assessments. In particular, it is essential to conduct a detailed economic analysis of the financing required for a two- to three-year period and to identify the principal actors who are responsible for follow-up. Costing was one of the core features of the assessments that UNEP and the World Bank conducted in Somalia in 2005, and of those conducted in Lebanon after the 2006 conflict with Israel (UN and World Bank 2007; UNDP 2007; World Bank 2007; UNEP 2007b; Jensen 2012*); it was also a major component of the environmental assessments undertaken for the Democratic Republic of the Congo and Sudan (UNEP 2007a, 2011a).

Improving coordination and the use of outside capacity

Many different agencies within the UN system are potential sources of expertise and information on the environment and natural resources. For example, UNEP typically focuses on renewable resources, biodiversity, environmental quality, and transboundary dynamics; UN-HABITAT (the United Nations Human Settlements Programme) on land and urban settlements; the Food and Agriculture

Organization of the United Nations on agriculture, forests, and fisheries; the World Health Organization (WHO) on health and chemicals; the United Nations Industrial Development Organization on industry; UNICEF (the United Nations Children's Fund) on water and sanitation; and the United Nations Development Programme (UNDP), in partnership with the World Bank, on governance and extractive industries. Yet in many cases, agencies have conducted full or sector-specific environmental assessments without fully coordinating such efforts with other agencies or sharing findings. UNEP, UNDP, and the World Bank, for example, all conducted independent environmental assessments in Lebanon, sharing only limited amounts of field data (Jensen 2012*).

UNEP has conducted the majority of post-conflict environmental assessments, but there are few mechanisms in place to obtain assistance from thematic or regional experts from other UN agencies or to request access to country-specific information held by resident agencies. Similarly, mechanisms that would enable UNEP to draw on civilian capacity and expertise from outside the UN system need strengthening.

To take advantage of the potential both within and outside the UN system, a more strategic approach is required that would both coordinate more fully with an expanded set of international peacebuilding actors and engage a wider set of domestic stakeholders (Conca and Wallace 2012*).

REMEDIATION OF ENVIRONMENTAL HOT SPOTS

In addition to causing loss of life and destroying homes, industries, and public infrastructure, many conflicts create a legacy of chemical contamination, hazardous waste, landmines, and unexploded ordnance, all of which can pose significant risks to human health and disrupt recovery efforts. While the cost of remediating such hot spots may be high, it is outweighed by the benefits of protecting human health and restoring the quality of critical resources such as land and water (Briggs and Weissbecker 2012*).

A number of post-conflict countries or regions, including Cambodia, Iraq, Lebanon, Serbia, and Sierra Leone, have had to remediate environmental hot spots created by conflict. In many cases, the countries or regions lacked sufficient technical capacity to safely identify and dispose of hazardous materials; as a result, international actors have played an essential role, not only in identifying hot spots but also in designing and implementing remediation plans.

It is critically important for the designers of remediation programs to identify all the ways in which a site may have been (or could be) contaminated. Thus, in setting the scope of a remediation program, project leaders must address three major questions (Thummarukudy, Brown, and Moosa 2012*):

- What causes of contamination, both preexisting and conflict-related, should be addressed during remediation? (Some level of environmental contamination often predates the conflict.)

- What level of remediation and restoration should the project achieve? (For example, should the goal be to return to natural conditions, to pre-conflict conditions, or to some other condition?)
- What new or existing sources of pollution may recontaminate the site?

The following six subsections highlight lessons from the case studies that address post-conflict remediation of environmental hot spots—severely polluted areas that pose a threat to human health, the environment, or both.

Addressing environmental hot spots: An immediate need

Addressing the risks associated with environmental hot spots should be a humanitarian priority—both to protect human health and to prevent the further degradation of crucial resources such as drinking water and fertile land (Briggs and Weissbecker 2012*; Thummarukudy, Brown, and Moosa 2012*). Left unattended, the risks associated with contamination can undermine public confidence in government. At the same time, the rapid remediation of environmental hot spots can serve as an early and visible peace dividend, and should therefore be considered as a possible quick-impact peacebuilding project (Tamer-Chammas 2012*; Thummarukudy, Brown, and Moosa 2012*).

When it comes to chemical contamination, the main lesson is that cleanup costs tend to increase with time, as contaminants migrate through the soil and spread to groundwater, as occurred in Serbia. Chemicals that remain on the surface, in contrast, can be remediated more easily and at a lower cost. Thus, rapid assessments should be used to identify hot spots as soon as possible—and, once they are identified, domestic agencies and organizations and the international community should assign priority to their remediation (Thummarukudy, Brown, and Moosa 2012*).

When environmental assessments identify acute environmental risks from contaminated sites, public-awareness campaigns are also needed to alert residents to risks; to inform them of safe practices; and to prevent the spread of misinformation and panic. After the escalation of hostilities in Gaza in late 2008 and early 2009, for example, the public was alerted to the risk of drinking contaminated water and consuming contaminated vegetables (UNEP 2009b). Finally, where public health is at risk, changes in environmental quality and public health should be monitored, both during and after remediation (Briggs and Weissbecker 2012*; Burger 2012*; Thummarukudy, Brown, and Moosa 2012*).

It is important to note that in post-conflict situations, remediation is often only one small step in a much longer and larger process that encompasses both environmental restoration and improved governance of natural resources. In many cases, the cleanup of environmental hot spots can be a starting point for increasing environmental awareness, building public support for environmental protection and management, and catalyzing greater political interest in the broader environmental challenges facing the country (Thummarukudy, Brown, and Moosa 2012*).

Using a full-life-cycle approach to hazardous waste

Regardless of whether hazardous waste is generated by military or peacekeeping operations, there is no quick fix. From the outset of a remediation project, the complete hazardous waste life cycle must be taken into account: from collection to storage, transport, treatment, and final disposal. Because many post-conflict countries lack sufficient expertise and capacity to treat and dispose of hazardous waste, storage is often used as a temporary solution. Experience suggests, however, that this approach can create more problems in the long run:

- Poor storage of hazardous waste creates secondary contamination sites, thus compounding health risks. Examples of improperly stored hazardous waste include oil waste in Lebanon and asbestos in Gaza (UNEP 2006, 2007b).
- Storage sites are seldom secure, and storage methods are rarely in accordance with international best practices (Thummarukudy, Brown, and Moosa 2012*).
- Local waste management contractors in some countries, including Afghanistan, have illegally dumped hazardous waste instead of storing it (UNEP 2012).
- The temporary storage of hazardous waste often triggers an "out of sight, out of mind" reaction; as a result, donor support wanes when immediate risks are mitigated. Instead of continuing to address the full cost of treatment and disposal, donors may leave the problem to national authorities, who generally lack the necessary resources and expertise.

The case studies featured in this book also show, however, that it is seldom feasible to build a hazardous waste treatment and disposal facility in a post-conflict setting. First, as many as ten years may be required to create adequate capacity for regulation, operation, monitoring, and enforcement; second, competing priorities are likely to render management and maintenance costs unaffordable. The best solution is a regional one: to the extent possible, neighboring countries with internationally accredited treatment and disposal facilities should be used. Where there are no regional facilities, international ones should be sought.

Hazardous waste that crosses international borders must comply with the Basel Convention on the Control of Transboundary Movements of Hazardous Wastes and Their Disposal and related regional agreements (such as the Bamako Convention, which bans the import of hazardous waste into Africa and controls the transboundary movement and management of hazardous waste within Africa).[3]

---

[3] For the text of the Basel Convention and additional information, see www.basel.int. The text of the Bamako Convention is available at www.africa-union.org/root/au/documents/treaties/Text/hazardouswastes.pdf.

And where local contractors are used to transport hazardous waste to treatment or disposal sites, chain-of-custody systems (including monitoring and enforcement) should be implemented to prevent illegal dumping.

In addition to generating hazardous waste, many conflicts—in particular, short-duration, high-intensity conflicts—generate significant amounts of rubble and debris. For example, during the escalation of hostilities between Israel and Hamas in late 2008 and early 2009, the destruction of buildings and infrastructure in Gaza generated an estimated 600,000 tons of rubble and demolition waste (UNEP 2009b). After the 2008 conflict in Lebanon, waste estimates initially ranged from 2.5 to 3 million cubic meters, but the actual volume of waste removed was 5.75 million cubic meters (Tamer-Chammas 2012*).

In many cases, debris and rubble can be recycled and used to construct buildings or roads. To avoid creating new contamination and health risks, however, care must be taken to screen for and remove any hazardous materials, such as asbestos. In Lebanon, 65,000 tons of rubble were screened and safely recycled for reconstruction—an example of good practice; unfortunately, most of the rubble was disposed of illegally, without environmental safeguards, or both (Tamer-Chammas 2012*).

Assigning priority to cleanup sites

Because post-conflict cleanup may exceed available financing (Jensen 2012*), it is often necessary to assign priority to particular sites (Thummarukudy, Brown, and Moosa 2012*). To support this process, a transparent decision-making framework should be developed that will allow stakeholders to rank sites on the basis of priority. The rankings should be informed, however, by technical findings based on the source-pathway-receptor approach, which identifies and determines the significance of the risks posed to possible receptors through specific pathways (air, soil, food, and water).

The source-pathway-receptor approach should be adapted to post-conflict situations in three ways. First, sites containing highly toxic chemicals may be assigned priority, regardless of the presence or absence of a pathway, because they could be targeted by those who oppose the peace process. In Iraq, for example, Qadissiya was an abandoned industrial site that contained 150 drums of highly toxic sodium cyanide; Suwaira, another abandoned industrial site, contained twenty-seven drums of chlorophenyl mercury, another highly toxic compound (Thummarukudy, Brown, and Moosa 2012*). To ensure that the chemicals were not used by insurgents, these sites were assigned priority for cleanup. Second, because security conditions may prevent access to certain sites, such conditions should be included in the ranking criteria. Third, if the remediation of particular sites could directly contribute to peacebuilding outcomes, that information should be factored into the ranking criteria. Examples of such sites include those where government authority and credibility need to be restored, or where divided communities could collaborate on cleanup.

Remediation design: Flexibility, capacity building, and improved practices

Where practicable and affordable, remediation should comply with domestic or international standards. In exceptional cases, where the costs of full cleanup may be prohibitive, a risk analysis may indicate that a lower standard can safely be used. Although assessment and remediation efforts should draw on existing approaches, implementation must be sufficiently flexible to adapt to the particular situation, including evolving security conditions. A one-size-fits-all approach and strict adherence to a specific and inflexible framework should be avoided (Thummarukudy, Brown, and Moosa 2012*).

In addition, priority should be given to solutions that use locally appropriate technology and maximize employment opportunities. For example, in the cleanup program for environmental hot spots in Serbia, 75 percent of all contracts were awarded to local companies or institutions that employed local experts and used local technologies (Thummarukudy, Brown, and Moosa 2012*), thereby contributing to capacity building and supporting the generation of local income, employment, expertise, and technological innovation.

Ideally, cleanup should not focus solely on reversing environmental harm but should jump-start long-term environmental restoration and lay the foundation for environmentally sound site management. To achieve these goals, cleanup operations at industrial sites may need to be accompanied by technology upgrades and training in cleaner production methods (Thummarukudy, Brown, and Moosa 2012*).

Where trade-offs need to be made between the costs and benefits of various levels of risk reduction, key stakeholders should participate in decision making. In addition to increasing community ownership of the remediation effort, stakeholder involvement can build trust between communities, local and national government agencies, and international actors.

Depleted uranium: A precautionary approach

Like other heavy metals, depleted uranium (DU) is toxic when inhaled or ingested (Burger 2012*). If certain uranium compounds accumulate in the kidneys, severe poisoning can result within hours or days. Although DU's chemical toxicity is usually considered a greater danger than its radioactivity, the long-term health risks of low-level radiation are still uncertain; thus, DU-contaminated sites require a precautionary approach. In practical terms, this means that DU munitions (including penetrators), fragments, and dust should be treated as hazardous and radioactive waste, and should be managed according to the standards set by the WHO and the International Atomic Energy Agency. At attack sites, visible DU penetrators should be collected, removed, and properly disposed of; DU dust that has contaminated buildings or vehicles should be removed and properly disposed of; and groundwater should be systematically monitored. In addition, public information campaigns should be undertaken to raise community awareness of

(1) the health hazards associated with the remnants of DU weapons, and (2) procedures for the safe handling, storage, and disposal of DU by local authorities; community members should also be provided with contact information for relevant authorities. More broadly, financial responsibility for cleanup costs associated with the use of DU should be the subject of international dialogue.

The potential environmental impacts of new generations of weapons, such as dense inert metallic explosives, have yet to be studied in the post-conflict context. Additional research is needed on potential risks and remediation options.

Land tenure and the remediation of contaminated or mined land

A number of specific challenges to land tenure need to be taken into account during the remediation of contaminated or mined land (Shimoyachi-Yuzawa 2012*; Tamer-Chammas 2012*). First, under customary tenure regimes, tenure rights or access rights may be lost when land is not used productively for a few years. Second, in many post-conflict situations, both ownership records and traditional land use practices may have been lost or destroyed. As a result, when land becomes available after remediation or demining, questions may arise about ownership, access, and use. In particular, it is common for elites to engage in land grabbing, leading to new tensions and conflicts within communities.

To prevent land grabbing and ensure that land is returned to those who previously held rights to it, land tenure should be addressed at the outset of the remediation process, and remediation projects should be linked to overall land management programs, including registration and titling. In Cambodia, for example, land titling was addressed from the beginning of the demining program; moreover, a community-based, bottom-up process was used for the annual selection of the areas that would be demined (Shimoyachi-Yuzawa 2012*).

RESTORATION OF NATURAL RESOURCES AND ECOSYSTEMS

In combination, violent conflict and the coping strategies of local populations can cause extensive damage and degradation to natural resources and the environment. Moreover, such harm is often in addition to long-term environmental degradation from pre-conflict unsustainable practices. Because resources such as arable land, water, wetlands, and forests are essential to livelihoods, basic services (including water, sanitation, and energy), and economic development, restoration of the natural resource base can support a range of peacebuilding priorities. Moreover, restoration can build confidence both in the government and in the value of peace. Examples of successful restorations that have supported peacebuilding include the Mesopotamian marshlands in Iraq; pastures and woodlands in Afghanistan; forests in Haiti; and orchards and other agricultural areas in Lebanon (Lonergan 2012*; Shovic 2005; Gingembre 2012*; Tamer-Chammas 2012*).

Communities in severely degraded environments are usually aware of the need for restoration, but they often lack the necessary capital, technology, and expertise to identify and implement viable alternatives. In post-conflict situations, where the need for restoration is even more acute, external actors must play a key role in restoration efforts.

Successful restoration programs typically require five to ten years of technical and financial support, which must be provided in a way that builds local capacity, provides incentives for local ownership, demonstrates improved quality of life, and facilitates eventual independence and sustainability. Learning by doing, innovating, and adapting projects in response to real-time evaluations and lessons learned are also essential to success. Although the tangible benefits of restoration may not materialize for several years, it is nonetheless important to incorporate metrics from the outset that will make it possible to assess progress toward restoration goals. Evaluation is particularly important to justify renewed support from donors who must make funding decisions within time frames that are shorter than those associated with the completion of a restoration project. The three subsections that follow highlight lessons from the case studies that focus on restoration in post-conflict situations.

Facing the challenges of large-scale restoration projects

Restoration programs in post-conflict countries can be overwhelmingly complex. In addition to meeting formidable technical challenges, such efforts face a number of other difficulties, including insecurity, political change, corruption, lack of institutional capacity, competing forms of land use, transboundary management issues, and the necessity of ensuring community ownership of the project (Gingembre 2012*; Tamer-Chammas 2012*; Lonergan 2012*).

The case studies suggest that post-conflict resource restoration is gradually evolving from a purely technical and isolated endeavor to a more comprehensive and integrated effort. For example, in recognition of the importance of community ownership, many restoration projects are specifically designed to empower local communities, to build institutional capacity for long-term management, and to link natural resource restoration to income generation. Despite evolving in a positive direction, however, restoration still faces several implementation challenges, including the lack of long-term funding and follow-up; the absence of mechanisms to ensure that key lessons are shared; and a lack of coordination among different projects located in the same area.

While the restoration of the Iraqi marshlands may be unique in terms of scale, it offers an excellent example of how scenarios can be used as a means of guiding natural resource restoration. First, possible future scenarios for the marshlands were defined, and then backcasting was used to determine the political and technical pathways that would be needed to achieve each scenario. Ultimately, ten socioeconomic, political, and technical issues were identified that would need to be addressed as part of the restoration process (Lonergan

2012*). Thus, scenarios were used to identify the key challenges of ecosystem restoration.

In Haiti, restoration projects needed to tackle a number of issues simultaneously, including governance, economic and social development, disaster risk reduction, land tenure, agricultural productivity and food security, energy and water access and management, and conflict resolution. One encouraging development is that many large donors in Haiti—such as the Inter-American Development Bank, the U.S. Agency for International Development (USAID), the Canadian International Development Agency, UNDP, and UNEP—are rehabilitating larger, more vulnerable geographic areas on a ridge-to-reef basis, throughout entire water catchment areas. Nevertheless, a review of the restoration projects in Haiti also found that only six of the forty-three projects included a cross-border element with the Dominican Republic, despite the interdependence of the two countries' ecosystems, their shared vulnerability to natural disasters, and the need to improve relations. A likely explanation is that transboundary projects typically require more coordination and negotiation than domestic projects, as well as strong commitment from the two governments, from their implementing agencies, and from communities in both countries. Likewise, climate change adaptation strategies were found to have been systematically ignored (Gingembre 2012*). This is a critical concern: implementing restoration projects without considering climate risks fosters maladaptation, increasing vulnerability to climate-related hazards, especially over the long term, and undermining or reversing development gains and the benefits of restoration (Matthew and Hammill 2012*).

All the restoration case studies point to land tenure as a crucial piece in the restoration puzzle. Land tenure disputes are among the most common problems facing restoration projects; in fact, tenure insecurity—where landholders constantly face dispossession—often prevents long-term investment in restoration and sustainable management. In Haiti, for example, informal land tenure arrangements are more important than formal titles, which are more expensive and less flexible. Thus, investment decisions are based on the duration of access to a plot, regardless of formal tenure; duration of access depends, in turn, on social capital and position. Uncertainty about the duration of access to land acts as a disincentive to restoration investments and sustainable management (Smucker et al. 2005).

Determining the degree of restoration

Although restoring an ecosystem or natural resource to its "natural" or pre-conflict condition may be technically possible, numerous political, social, and economic barriers often constrain restoration options. These include lack of institutional capacity, time, resources, or political will; established land use patterns and practices; and the absence of viable livelihood alternatives. All these elements were in play, for example, with the Iraqi marshlands (Lonergan 2012*).

If the long-term goal of a specific restoration project is to fully restore the proper functioning of the ecosystem, the feasibility of this intention should be evaluated in detail. At the time of writing, such evaluations were being conducted for severely degraded watersheds in Haiti, where watersheds were being grouped into at least three categories: functional, functional but at risk, and nonfunctional. Once a watershed is nonfunctional, the effort, cost, and time required for recovery increase dramatically. Therefore, Haiti's nonfunctional watersheds were being restored only when such efforts were not at the expense of at-risk watersheds, or when restoration was needed as an investment in disaster risk reduction.

In some cases, the investment required to achieve full restoration may be too high, and limited funds could be better spent on more immediate needs. Stakeholders—including community members, technical experts, and funding agencies—must then discuss what level of restoration is possible and conduct a scenario-based analysis of alternative conditions and land use options. In many cases, communities assign priority to restoration projects that contribute directly and immediately to livelihoods recovery, job creation, and reconciliation, rather than to broader goals of ecosystem recovery.

Careful consideration should also be given to potential threats from climate change and to the "climate-proofing" of restoration projects (Matthew and Hammill 2012*). At a minimum, such efforts would include systematic use of climate data to inform early peacebuilding decisions (regarding land use planning, resource prospecting, and investment, for example) that commit post-conflict countries to long-term development pathways. Efforts to address the risks of climate change also require greater emphasis on early warning, and on tools and strategies to reduce disaster risks and resolve disputes over increasingly scarce resources.

Keys to success: Community ownership and an overarching national framework

The case studies demonstrate that successful restoration of damaged or degraded natural resources can be critical to revitalizing livelihoods and providing visible peace dividends. Such results can be achieved, however, only when restoration programs are led and owned by the affected communities, with the support of local authorities. In practical terms, communities must help identify the challenges they face, find solutions, choose methodologies, and organize project activities. Moreover, affected communities must be involved at every stage of the project, from needs assessment to project design, implementation, monitoring, and evaluation.

Participation is most effective when stakeholders (1) have sufficient opportunity to contribute, (2) can openly express their aspirations and concerns throughout the decision-making process, and (3) can participate without being discriminated against on the basis of racial or ethnic background, religion, socioeconomic group, or gender. Successful participation requires clearly defined roles and responsibilities for community members. It also requires an accountable process, under which (1) affected populations can register complaints if participation is inadequate, and (2) the decision-making process will be suspended until adequate participation is achieved. Financial and material contributions from communities need to be agreed upon beforehand—through partnership agreements, for example. Generally, strengthening existing local structures—instead of creating new, ad hoc structures—results in greater community acceptance; it also increases the long-term sustainability of restoration projects (Gingembre 2012*).

Given the timescale of restoration efforts (often between ten and twenty years), local processes should have national-level political backing and should be clearly linked to a national restoration framework. At the national level, policies and the legislative framework need to support community-based natural resource management (CBNRM) and to render CBNRM attractive to local communities.

In most post-conflict countries, there are thousands of rural development projects that contain elements of environmental restoration, but there is little coordination between them, or between local actors and the national government. If such projects are linked to an overarching national-level program, restoration is more likely to be well coordinated, coherent, and successful at the national scale. For instance, Afghanistan's National Solidarity Programme (ANSP), which supports small-scale rural development projects in 22,000 villages in Afghanistan, offers a good example of community-level restoration and rural development projects that were brought under a single framework. The ANSP also established a social and environmental management framework, which was designed to strengthen the positive environmental and social outcomes of rural development projects, while preventing environmental degradation resulting from either individual subprojects or their cumulative effects (ANSP 2010).

International agencies and organizations use three main criteria for selecting communities for restoration projects (Gingembre 2012*; Lonergan 2012*):

- The community must demonstrate a commitment to and ownership of a specific restoration vision.
- The community must have the capacity to handle project finances and administration and to ensure that community members meet project commitments.
- The community must match external financing with in-kind resources, such as labor and management time.

Restoration projects are complex, long-term endeavors that typically require flexibility, innovation, and adaptive management. In post-conflict countries, insecurity, community division, ethnic or religious strife, the erosion of rule of law, and weak governance institutions impose significant complications. Because of the complexity of the projects and the significant challenges they face, it is essential at the outset of a national environmental restoration program to assign priority to secure areas, within which approaches can be pilot tested and key lessons identified before decisions are made about whether and how to extend restoration efforts. Projects may take three or four years to yield tangible benefits—but once success can be demonstrated in more secure regions, projects in insecure areas can be considered.

ENVIRONMENTAL DIMENSIONS OF INFRASTRUCTURE AND RECONSTRUCTION

Armed conflict often damages public infrastructure and interferes with basic services (including waste collection and disposal, and the provision of water and energy) for years. In addition to being a visible and painful reminder of conflict, a lack of basic services can also foster feelings of marginalization and resentment and undermine livelihoods, worker productivity (and thus economic development), and well-being (Anand 2012*). Finally, in combination with other factors, lack of services may strengthen grievances, which can then be taken advantage of by groups seeking to undermine the peace process.

As a result of the conflict in Lebanon, extensive damage was inflicted on the country's water and sanitation infrastructure: rivers were polluted by industrial facilities and demolition waste; and water tanks, transmission lines, pumping stations, artesian wells, and water treatment systems were heavily damaged or destroyed. Because the conflict had effectively brought water and sanitation services to a halt, restoration of those services was assigned priority during the post-conflict period. Direct expenditures for early recovery and reconstruction were estimated to be US$2.8 billion, of which the government of Lebanon was to cover US$1.75 billion (Tamer-Chammas 2012*).

In many post-conflict countries, investing in water, waste, and energy infrastructure and restoring basic services may be one of the principal means of providing visible peace dividends, rebuilding public confidence in government, creating jobs, and encouraging the return of displaced persons. In fact, "the condition of infrastructure is often a barometer of whether a society will slip further into violence or make a peaceful transition out of the conflict cycle" (Mashatt, Long, and Crum 2008, 1). Meeting reconstruction needs typically involves a flurry of rebuilding and a massive injection of foreign capital: according to estimates, post-conflict countries receive between six and twenty times more aid per capita for reconstruction than is awarded in course of regular development assistance (IMF 2002; Jensen 2009). Although post-conflict aid may be high on a per capita basis and in relation to the size of the recipient economy, it often declines rapidly once the initial emergency phase is over (IMF 2002; Jensen 2009).

A World Bank analysis of post-conflict investment patterns revealed that telecommunications investments, particularly in mobile networks, materialize soon after the end of conflict (Schwartz, Hahn, and Bannon 2004). Electricity generation and distribution projects are often completed approximately three years after conflict and increase in frequency after year five. Private investment in water and transportation tends to come much later than investments in other basic services. Within the transport sector, seaports receive the majority of private investment.

The pressures to meet humanitarian needs and rapidly rebuild can place high demands on essential natural resources such as water, wood, sand, gravel, iron, and petroleum. Indeed, depending on the rate of reconstruction, a single year of post-conflict redevelopment can consume the same amount of resources that, under normal circumstances, would be used over a much longer period (Bouma 2012*). To ensure that reconstruction (including infrastructure projects) does not create environmental impacts that could compound poverty or become a new source of tension, reconstruction plans, programs, and projects should be subjected to environmental impact assessment.

Infrastructure repair and reconstruction involve trade-offs in relation to natural resources (Anand 2012*). The dilemma is whether to focus on infrastructure that will aid in the rapid extraction and exportation of natural resources, so that the country can earn much-needed foreign exchange to pay for recovery—or, alternatively, to focus on services that have a more significant impact on the dimensions of human development that are not directly related to immediate income generation, such as education. When state institutions are controlled by nonstate entities whose goal is to extract income from natural resources, however, infrastructure investments may be designed to facilitate resource extraction and sale, rather than to serve the broader needs of the populace (Verstegen 2001; Bardhan 2004; Addison and Bruck 2009).

The rebuilding of Japan's infrastructure and economy after World War II highlights many resource-related pressures and opportunities. Faced with energy shortages that threatened its post-war recovery, Japan developed the Priority Production System, which focused on managing domestic coal and steel production (Nakayama 2012*). The endeavor was inherently unsustainable, but it was sufficient to rebuild the country's infrastructure, jump-start its economy, and provide thousands of jobs for excombatants and returning Japanese civilians. After the system had been in place for ten years, however, the number of coal mines and miners fell rapidly—leading to unemployment and social unrest, and necessitating adjustments to Japan's economic strategies. Although the use of domestic coal was unsustainable, it allowed Japan to exploit its domestic coal reserves until it could secure other energy resources and shift its economy to other sectors.

The following five sections highlight the lessons learned since the early 1990s regarding (1) the planning and implementation of reconstruction programs, and (2) the delivery of energy, water, sanitation, and waste infrastructure in ways that are conflict sensitive and avoid creating new sources of environmental damage.

Delivering conflict-sensitive and sustainable infrastructure reconstruction

The repair and reconstruction of the infrastructure needed for energy, water, sanitation, and waste is a key element in peacebuilding and in the restoration of governmental legitimacy (Mott MacDonald 2005). Such projects also contribute to the sense that normal life has returned, and can serve as important platforms for reconciliation (Tamer-Chammas 2012*). Finally, infrastructure projects provide both direct benefits (restoration of services) and significant opportunities for employment. These two outcomes can be a source of conflict, however, if they are not equally distributed. Thus, international agencies and organizations must bear in mind that unless infrastructure investments are informed by an understanding of the original conflict as well as current tensions (that is, they are conflict sensitive), they have the capacity to do harm as well as good.

Thus, the principal challenge in selecting infrastructure projects is to meet immediate needs while ensuring longer-term sustainability, conflict prevention, and peace consolidation. In practical terms, this means that infrastructure provision must be (1) conflict sensitive, and (2) based on an analysis of local management capacities, the needs of key stakeholders and user groups, and options for the sustainable management of natural resources (Anand 2012*; Carius and Maas 2012*). In the absence of deliberate precautions, interventions risk intensifying the inequalities that may have been among the original causes of the conflict, or weakening developing ties among conflicting communities (Nanthikesan and Uitto 2012*). In short, infrastructure reconstruction should not be intended to simply rebuild what was destroyed, without consideration of equity or sustainability. The primary considerations that must be addressed are how the infrastructure will be governed and maintained, how the benefits will be shared, how natural resources will be managed, and how reconstruction can contribute to peacebuilding.

The assumption on the part of donors that infrastructure will benefit all or most of society equally—and that nationwide economic development and access to services will result—is particularly problematic. Societies affected by or emerging from conflict are highly fragmented, lawless, desperate, and rife with grievances, and their history is one of impunity, power struggles, subjugation, and exploitation. Infrastructure reconstruction thus occurs in an environment where seeking advantage and protecting oneself (or one's group) by any means has become the norm (Unruh and Shalaby 2012*).

Approaches that focus on simply rebuilding the services that existed before the conflict, or that target areas where there is a significant willingness to pay, tend to neglect the poorest and most vulnerable segments of the population and reinforce existing inequalities (Anand 2012*; Pinera and Reed 2013). Following the 2008 conflict in Lebanon, UNDP implemented a US$2 million project in 143 communities in southern Lebanon, funding initiatives that targeted quick repair of water and wastewater networks, cleanup and rehabilitation of sewage systems, and the reinstallation of streetlights. To foster equity and prevent conflict, UNDP chose not to simply restore and improve preexisting infrastructure; instead, it included nearly all municipalities in the project, including those that had not previously had such services (Tamer-Chammas 2012*).

The role of infrastructure investment in peacebuilding is an emerging area of study; nevertheless, anecdotal evidence from Iraq suggests that infrastructure investment supports stability and prevents conflict at the local level (Barwari 2012). Such investment should not be undertaken exclusively in hotbeds of insurgency, however, as doing so fosters the view that only violence attracts donor attention and investment and creates a perverse incentive to engage in violence. Investments should be strategic—that is, balanced across different types of communities and among urban and rural environments throughout the country (Anand 2012*).

Addressing the unintended consequences of infrastructure projects

Practitioners and donors alike must reexamine the commonly held assumption that reconstruction projects in conflict-affected countries will produce outcomes similar to those produced in stable settings (Unruh and Shalaby 2012*). Conflict-affected settings differ profoundly from peaceful ones, and one area that merits further study concerns the ways in which infrastructure reconstruction interacts with other peacebuilding priorities and with conflict dynamics.

One of the most critical issues raised by the case studies in this book is access to and ownership of land and natural resources that may be needed for, or may be negatively affected by, major infrastructure projects. Resolution of land use disputes and compensation for damage or lost access are often essential prerequisites to infrastructure development (Brookings Institution and University of Bern 2007; Solomon et al. 2009). In Lebanon, for example, land tenure is among the principal factors undermining reconstruction and peacebuilding efforts. In rural areas, land tenure is affected by monopolistic landowning patterns; corrupt land administration practices; unclear or overlapping land rights (caused by legal ambiguity and customary practices); land encroachment and illegal settlers; and zoning difficulties (resulting from the failure to survey land) (UN-HABITAT 2008). Reconstruction cannot proceed on a sustainable basis until these issues are addressed.

In Afghanistan, road reconstruction and land rights are both priorities in peacebuilding plans, but they are being addressed in isolation; moreover, interactions between the two categories of activity are having undesirable consequences. Land tenure in Afghanistan is rife with problems: the country lacks any nationally legitimate, workable approaches to tenure; instead, tenure is based on confusing and highly divisive statutory, customary, ad hoc, Islamic, and warlord-derived laws or regulations (IWPR 2008; Alden Wily 2003). Tenure security is virtually nonexistent—and warlords, militias, and other powerful interests engage in extortion, asset stripping, and land grabbing with impunity (Alden Wily 2003).

Nevertheless, a number of major road reconstruction programs failed to attend to the complexity of land tenure. For example, U.S. reconstruction efforts took into account twenty-three Afghan laws relevant to road reconstruction but ignored customary land law and tenure, national land laws, and national environmental laws (U.S. DOD 2009).

A number of factors—including corruption; increases in land values after road reconstruction; the weakness of customary and statutory tenure systems; increasing access to land; and the absence of landowners, tenants, and their relatives or heirs—can lead to a surge in land grabbing near infrastructure projects. In Afghanistan, for example, the nine provinces most subject to land grabbing all border the reconstructed Ring Road (Unruh and Shalaby 2012*). The discovery of large mineral deposits in Afghanistan will likely lead to more road construction, to facilitate exploitation; one result will be a serious risk of speculative land seizure, both above mineral deposits and along new access roads (Risen 2010).

The interaction between different peacebuilding priorities in Afghanistan also highlights another concern: namely, the disconnect between international donors, which are focused on projects' economic and social benefits, and local communities, which are subject to changes in sociopolitical patterns as a consequence of new infrastructure. As noted earlier, donors' expectations of the effects of infrastructure construction are based largely on their effects in stable settings. But conflict-affected communities worry about speculation; land grabbing; control of agricultural production; rent seeking; the recruitment of indentured labor; and increased access to villages susceptible to exploitation by corrupt government officials, foreign troops, or the Taliban (Unruh and Shalaby 2012*). Thus, there is a critical need to examine both the intended and unintended consequences of infrastructure, and to increase the extent to which project proponents are accountable to the beneficiaries of infrastructure projects (Nanthikesan and Uitto 2012*).

Reconstruction and environmental assessment

Although environmental impact assessments (EIAs) can identify and help to mitigate the potential impacts of reconstruction, they also face a number of challenges in post-conflict environments, including a lack of baseline environmental data, poor community-level participation, inconsistent monitoring, and noncompliance with mitigation plans (Anand 2012*). The principal obstacle that EIAs face, however, is the commonly held perception that environmental reviews slow recovery and hinder the timely delivery of peace dividends to conflict victims. When this misperception is combined with political interests and the demand for quick recovery, environmental reviews may be ignored or simply not conducted, which not only results in further environmental damage and greater hardship for conflict-affected populations, but also potentially sows the seeds for future conflict (Kelly 2012*).

The work of donors such as USAID offers a number of lessons on the conduct of EIAs in post-conflict countries. USAID-supported projects demonstrate that EIAs can, in fact, be streamlined and effectively applied in post-conflict countries without causing significant approval delays (Kelly 2012*). The four strengths of the USAID environmental-review process are as follows:

- A clearly defined process, well-trained staff, and internal compliance mechanisms.
- Flexibility regarding the amount of information needed for a review.
- Continuous monitoring and review of environmental issues during project implementation.
- The use of standard references and forms to guide the review process and help implement project activities in an environmentally sound manner.

The USAID review process also focuses more on the type of activity, such as school repair, rather than on specific activities, such as repairing particular schools on the basis of damage reports. This lack of precision is common during transitions from conflict to recovery (Kelly 2012*).

The USAID approach to expedited environmental reviews has two principal limitations. The first is a primary focus on the effects of activities on the environment, and a failure to address the potential social, economic, security, and political consequences of those effects. Ideally, such broader impacts should be assessed during an environmental review, particularly for the purpose of evaluating indirect and cumulative impacts and cost-benefit trade-offs. The EIA for road building in Afghanistan, for example, did not cover the impact of road repair on land tenure or illicit activities, such as timber harvesting (Unruh and Shalaby 2012*). Expanding the USAID process to consider such linkages would reduce the unanticipated and unintended negative outcomes of international assistance and could help build a stronger case for mitigation of harmful side effects (Kelly 2012*).

The second limitation is that the agencies undertaking EIAs for reconstruction projects have not systematically collaborated with local organizations, nor have they necessarily observed local regulatory requirements. As a result, opportunities were lost to strengthen conflict-affected governments through capacity building and knowledge sharing in the environmental reviews presented in this book. Moreover, it was unclear to what extent target populations were consulted during the development of the environmental reviews or about the environmental trade-offs incorporated into the final versions of the reviews. Consultation with intended beneficiaries is a core principle of development assistance and should be part of the environmental-review process even in conflict-affected countries (Kelly 2012*).

Despite these concerns, the expedited environmental-review processes developed by USAID could serve as a good model for other donors and aid agencies working in post-conflict countries. A uniform process, based on the USAID approach, would give all providers of assistance a consistent approach to identifying and addressing the potential adverse environmental impacts of projects. A common process could also lead to the more effective use of staff (who could, for example, serve several projects and organizations at the same time), and to more opportunities to involve national- and local-level government, as well as civil society, in the review and monitoring of peacebuilding assistance.

Strategic environmental assessments: An alternative to EIAs

Despite the potential benefits of EIAs, a number of factors—including weak governance, inadequate legal frameworks, insufficient technical skills, and limited baseline data—may prevent national authorities in post-conflict countries from undertaking them. In Afghanistan between 2004 and 2006, for example, only six environmental impact statements were provided to the National Environmental Protection Agency, and these were submitted only for information and comment, rather than for approval—despite the fact that approval was required by law (Bouma 2012*). In Ethiopia, the EIA system has developed more as a result of donors' demands than in response to the desires of decision makers. As a result, EIAs are conducted through a top-down process that often lacks national ownership and consistent application.

Between coordinating aid and learning to understand their institutional responsibilities, post-conflict governments are often overwhelmed, and an EIA process is rarely a priority. Furthermore, it can take ten years or longer to develop a functional, project-based EIA system that is fully integrated into the fabric of governance and applied as a decision-making tool. Given these constraints, alternative approaches are needed in post-conflict countries (Bouma 2012*).

One alternative to conducting a project-level EIA is to conduct strategic environmental assessments (SEAs) at the sector or program level. The primary reason to undertake SEAs is to identify the programs or sectors that have the potential to cause the greatest environmental impact, so that practitioners can focus on a broad set of preventive and mitigation measures. At the very least, the key programs or sectors, the key actors, and the proportion of projects that may have an environmental impact can be identified. Transforming this information into changes in plans, policies, and programs has been more challenging, however (Bouma 2012*).

Two characteristics of the SEA process are worth noting. First, SEAs use a variety of approaches and methods; second, a good SEA is tailored to the context in which it is applied. In practical terms, this means that the design of an SEA process can take into account the existing post-conflict institutional capacity and legal framework; it can also incorporate the option for adjustments as capacities increase or laws change (Bouma 2012*). As the principal form of reconstruction capital for the first three to five years after conflict, official development assistance (ODA) could benefit significantly from a process that helps to identify potential cumulative environmental impacts within and across the main ODA sectors; a tailor-made SEA is just such a process.

One of the key lessons from the case studies is the importance of finding suitable entry points for the application of an SEA process (or a streamlined SEA-like process) to an ODA framework. In Afghanistan, Iraq, and Sudan, the entry points were a donor-assistance database, a UN multi-donor trust fund, and UN work plans, respectively (Bouma 2012*). Experiences with SEA in these three countries suggest that there are six main sectors in which significant environmental impacts can be expected: extractive industries, energy, water and sanitation, transportation, agriculture and livestock, and livelihoods recovery. The main impacts are related to waste disposal; the quality and quantity of surface water; and the sustainable use of natural resources such as forests, fisheries, and soil. Efforts to use the entry points referred to earlier to develop broad environmental safeguards in each sector have had mixed success, however. In both Afghanistan and Iraq, the governments adopted no general safeguards, and none of the projects with potential impacts were amended. In short, the political will to apply safeguards could not be sustained.

In Sudan, however, the 2008 SEA of the UN work plan had three major impacts (Bouma 2012*):

- The UN country team and its partners began to understand the potential environmental impacts of each sector and to more systematically incorporate environmental issues into project design from the outset.
- Groundwater monitoring finally became common practice for all water and sanitation projects across Darfur—an important sectoral safeguard.
- New approaches to mitigating the environmental impact of humanitarian response were initiated through a specific budget line (US$1 million from the Common Humanitarian Fund, known as the Green Pot).

The UN country team's heightened environmental awareness had a major influence on the approach taken during the drafting of the UN Development Assistance Framework (UNDAF) for 2009–2012 (Bouma 2012*). Development priorities were organized according to four main pillars: peacebuilding; governance, rule of law, and capacity building; livelihoods and productive sectors; and basic services. Detailed environmental outcomes were included for each pillar, together with budgets and lists of responsible organizations and their partners. The total budget for natural resource management projects was US$419 million, approximately 18 percent of the total UNDAF budget of US$2.3 billion.

If donor-assistance databases, UN multi-donor trust funds, UN work plans, and similar instruments are to be used as the entry points for conducting post-conflict SEAs in the future, several conditions need to be met:

- A consistent way to categorize environmental impacts needs to be established at the outset, along with a clear allocation of responsibility. Ideally, project proponents should be required to undertake the classification and to consider environmental issues at the earliest possible phase of project design. Only

when an insufficient number of proponents have the capacity to conduct the classification should third parties take responsibility.
- All projects—humanitarian as well as recovery and development—should undergo environmental screening. Systematic screening of all projects will help to identify the sectors that are most in need of environmental mitigation.
- Additional information should be incorporated into project information sheets—in particular, the geographic location. This would allow a more fine-scaled review of the geographic areas where projects are to be concentrated and a better analysis of potential impacts and cumulative effects.
- Domestic stakeholders need support to identify and mitigate the environmental risks inherent in particular sectors and to develop capacity for compliance monitoring. An SEA can be a starting point for mitigating sector-level environmental impacts, but a policy that includes project-specific EIAs should eventually be adopted. Capacity-building programs should keep longer-term EIA needs in mind as post-conflict SEA approaches are further developed (Kelly 2012*; Bouma 2012*).

Addressing the environmental implications of extractive industries and agribusiness

Post-conflict countries that are rich in land and nonrenewable natural resources often plan to use these assets to finance the recovery process; however, this approach can create unique challenges for both governance and peace consolidation. Pressure to kick-start economic growth through the use of natural resources can override the imperative to manage and mitigate the full social and environmental costs of such use. Ensuring that economic growth does not come at the expense of human rights and the natural resource base requires considerable skill and judgment, and the stakes are high: a misstep can increase the risk that conflict will resume. The challenge is to select the best possible investments, then monitor them to ensure that they are delivering the expected benefits while minimizing social and environmental costs.

In any post-conflict situation, improved governance of natural resources and the environment is a test of governmental stability and effectiveness (UNEP 2009a, 2010). It is thus essential to use natural resource management both to build confidence in the wider political process of peace consolidation and as an entry point for public participation in decision making. It is also critical to establish and maintain transparency and accountability with respect to contracts, payments, and the social and environmental impacts of agribusiness and the extractive sector (Brown et al. 2012*). EIA processes tailored to the industry in question can be indispensable tools for achieving these goals, particularly when combined with other instruments such as the Extractive Industries Transparency Initiative.[4]

---

[4] For more information on the Extractive Industries Transparency Initiative, see http://eiti.org; see also Rich and Warner (2012) and Rustad, Lujala, and Le Billon (2012).

EIAs, environmental permits, and the use of environmental planning tools create valuable opportunities to identify potential harmful impacts from agribusiness and the extractive sector and to put social and environmental safeguards in place. The planning and approval phases are perhaps the only time in the life span of a multibillion-dollar investment when the government has significant leverage over the nature of a mine or plantation. Getting the process right is one of the principal ways that a government can influence the design, technology, scope, and financial models of large-scale developments, to ensure that the country receives long-term social and economic benefits and suffers minimal environmental or social damage.

In Sierra Leone, the application of EIA to the extractive sector yielded four major benefits (Brown et al. 2012*):

- Universally applied EIA processes help weed out poorly performing companies. Those that are either unable or unwilling to submit EIAs are excluded from bidding on concessions—and, according to legislation and evolving regulations, should cease operations. Ideally, if only those companies that are willing to invest time, energy, and resources in minimizing their environmental impacts are permitted to bid, there will be a race to the top—rather than a slump to the bottom.
- Environmental planning that is led by science and based on facts may have spillover benefits for other dimensions of governance: in particular, it can increase transparency with respect to contracts, payments, and impacts; strengthen confidence in political processes and in the legitimacy of government; and help to professionalize decision making. A fact-based environmental assessment that is subject to extensive review and consultation can also help to depoliticize disputes over natural resources; by stripping away the power dynamics that often characterize such disputes, a deliberative and science-based environmental assessment can help stakeholders identify and articulate a common vision for the role of natural resources in the future of the country.
- Stakeholder engagement in environmental assessment can help unify divided communities and create opportunities for different segments of society to communicate and cooperate. A participatory, inclusive approach can also help to predict and prevent potential conflicts over the management of natural resources and the distribution of the resulting revenues. Finally, stakeholder engagement can help to forge a common vision for how the country should exploit its natural resources and share the benefits of extraction.
- The successful application of EIA limits the negative environmental impacts of mining and agribusiness projects, thereby preventing conflict, protecting health and livelihoods, and reducing the likelihood that costly environmental remediation will be necessary.

Some companies and governmental decision makers still perceive EIAs as "green hand brakes" that are designed to protect the natural environment against the perceived perils of economic development (Brown et al. 2012*). When implemented properly, however, EIAs can actually increase the benefits of extractive industries and commercial agriculture, while minimizing negative social and environmental impacts. Investing in environmental assessment is cost-effective in post-conflict states because EIAs are catalytic interventions that have long-lived implications for governance and sustainable natural resource use. The timing and sequencing will depend on the specific case, but such interventions should be in step with increased investment activity in post-conflict countries.

The full benefits of EIAs can only be achieved, however, when capacity is sufficient to support sustained monitoring and enforcement by both national authorities and civil society. In Sierra Leone, for example, government support for EIAs throughout the extractive sectors hinged on political backing from the president. Without top-level support, the advances made toward the development of EIA law and policy in Sierra Leone would not have been possible.

CROSSCUTTING LESSONS

In addition to the specific lessons learned about assessment, remediation, restoration, and reconstruction, the case studies in this book also revealed a number of crosscutting lessons, which are described in the next five sections.

Using the environment as a platform for cooperation and reconciliation

Reconciliation between divided groups, communities, or countries is often a central peacebuilding priority. Identifying opportunities to rebuild severed relationships and strengthen the bonds of trust between conflict-affected parties is thus an immediate post-conflict task.

Environmental assessment, remediation, restoration, and reconstruction projects offer important platforms for promoting dialogue, cooperation, and confidence building between divided groups as well as different levels of government. In particular, peacebuilding programs should carefully consider the deliberate use of environmental projects as bridges to peace and arenas for political inclusion, relationship building, and reconciliation (Mott MacDonald 2005; Nanthikesan and Uitto 2012*; Conca and Wallace 2012*).

Potential risks from climate change or other transboundary environmental threats can also be used as the basis for dialogue between divided groups. Because these threats are to some extent abstract, external, and neutral, they can form the basis for discussions that are less politicized than those that address the post-conflict situation (Carius and Maas 2012*).

Building national capacity through assessment, remediation, restoration, and reconstruction

Despite the fact that the environment and natural resources underpin human health and livelihoods, environmental ministries in both developed and developing countries often lack effective governance and institutional capacity and are starved of financial resources, authority, and staff. Such problems are even more acute in post-conflict countries, where warfare may have destroyed records, led staff to flee, diverted resources, undermined the rule of law, and weakened governance institutions. Thus, ministries of the environment (and line ministries with environmental and natural resource management functions) often benefit from international support until they can develop sufficient capacity to function independently. Such support might include lending staff; providing equipment, technical and financial assistance; training; and mentoring. International partners may also assist environmental and natural resource management institutions to negotiate realistic and sustainable operational budgets—an often-overlooked task that, left unattended, can undermine the sustainability of capacity-building efforts. Finally, because capacity building is a long-term process, often requiring ten years or more if new institutions must be built from scratch, it is critical for international partners to provide support without replacing or undermining the authority of the national entity.

Although many initial capacity-building efforts focus on policy and legal reform, it is imperative to also use environmental assessment, remediation, restoration, and reconstruction as opportunities for capacity building. One way to do so is to include government staff in every step of each project, from design to financing, implementation, monitoring, and evaluation. Community-led restoration projects can also be good complements to national capacity-building programs, because they demonstrate the tangible benefits of resource management policies and sustainable land use practices. Such projects also help national policy makers and technical staff understand community-level needs for legal reforms that address ownership, access, management, and dispute resolution regarding natural resources.

Using natural resources as a basis for regional cooperation and economic integration

In some instances, the coordinated or shared management of natural resources has created a foundation for regional reconstruction and economic integration. For example, after World War II, shared natural resource management was the means of drawing together France and Germany—and, eventually, Belgium, Italy, Luxembourg, and the Netherlands as well (Bruch, Wolfarth, and Michalcik 2012*). In this case, coal and steel production was placed into the hands of a supranational authority, the European Coal and Steel Community—which evolved, over decades, into the European Union. In this example, shared management of natural resources at the regional level led not only to economic cooperation but, ultimately, to deeper political cooperation.

Similarly, after the turmoil that gripped Central America in the 1980s, efforts to coordinate natural resource management and combat environmental degradation offered a politically neutral platform that enabled the various nations to work together (Bruch, Wolfarth, and Michalcik 2012*; King et al. 2013). Eventually, cooperation on environmental issues laid the foundation for regional reconstruction and integration efforts that continue to this day.[5]

If natural resources are to be successfully used as a basis for regional cooperation and reintegration, however, such efforts must be adapted to the context of the countries involved; in particular, the region in question must be defined logically from a political, cultural, and historical perspective (Bruch, Wolfarth, and Michalcik 2012*). Coordinated and time-bound donor support is another essential element.

Evaluation and monitoring: Emerging trends

Many evaluations are driven by the interests of agencies that wish to assess the effectiveness and efficiency of their interventions. In those cases, accountability is directed upward, to the agency and its funders—often the taxpayers in the donor country. But downward accountability—that is, to the people the interventions are intended to benefit—is equally if not more important (Nanthikesan and Uitto 2012*).

Many donors, facing pressure to report to their constituencies on the performance of their investments, want to be able to demonstrate tangible results, and are thus increasingly favoring quantitative approaches—in particular, impact evaluations, which attempt to attribute changes in conditions to specific interventions. But it is often impossible to isolate the effects of a specific intervention—particularly in post-conflict situations, where conditions change rapidly and are influenced by multiple actors and dynamics. With respect to natural resource management interventions, the post-conflict environment is unpredictable, and the effects of interventions will depend on organic community processes in which causality is not clear. Thus, a qualitative approach is essential to effectively evaluate natural resource–related interventions in post-conflict situations (Nanthikesan and Uitto 2012*).

The current donor emphasis on quantitative evaluation may be premature, and may crowd out efforts to achieve an in-depth understanding of conflict (OECD/DAC 2007). Rigorous alternative evaluation approaches exist and should be used. Because so much is still unknown about conflict, conflict prevention and peacebuilding evaluations in the coming years should focus on gathering evidence and learning from it, and on testing commonly held theories and

---

[5] For an analysis of the cooperation among post-conflict Balkan states in the Sava River area, see Čolakhodžić et al. (2013).

assumptions about peace and conflict, rather than on establishing fixed, universal indicators of peace or conflict. Clarity regarding indicators (and whether they can be generalized in a useful way) may emerge in the process—but at this point, evaluations should steer clear of excessively specific indicators. Instead, the emphasis should be on improving collective understanding through the cumulative and comparative analysis of experience across contexts (Nanthikesan and Uitto 2012*).

Although joint evaluations have several disadvantages, including greater complexity and higher transaction costs, they are the best means of getting a full picture of peacebuilding dynamics. Among the advantages of joint evaluations are the following:

- They reveal not only the effects of individual efforts, but also of interactions among multiple efforts.
- They tend to be more objective, because the participation of multiple parties tends to reduce conflicts of interest and agency bias.
- Because they are not perceived to advance the perspective of any one actor, they have greater legitimacy.
- They make it easier to capture attribution, because multiple factors and projects can be considered as potential contributions to particular outcomes.
- They can strengthen downward accountability.
- When it comes to persuading policy makers or program managers to address findings and recommendations, joint evaluations are more effective advocacy tools.

Evaluation processes can be useful in highlighting critical programmatic gaps related to natural resources. For example, evaluations of UNDP programs in two post-conflict countries (Rwanda and Uganda) demonstrated that the programs failed to adequately incorporate the environment or sustainable development into economic development and poverty reduction strategies (Nanthikesan and Uitto 2012*). The evaluations also confirmed that in post-conflict situations in which most people depend on agriculture for sustenance, it is essential to address natural resource management and livelihoods. Moreover, in order to achieve sustainable benefits for conflict-affected populations, such considerations must not only be integrated into individual projects, but also into policies and long-term strategies. Finally, the evaluations provide further evidence that in addition to being a source of conflict, natural resources can be the focus of cooperation, provided that they are properly factored into post-conflict development visions.

Further developments in monitoring and evaluation can improve future project design and implementation. In Lebanon, interventions proposed for green recovery (such as promotion of sustainable cropping patterns) and for mitigating the environmental impacts of the conflict (such as sustainable management of demolition waste) were ignored. Since this pattern is all too common, evaluations should more systematically monitor the implementation of recommendations

(Tamer-Chammas 2012*). A related challenge is that organizations and funders generally categorize projects by sector; for example, governance or conflict mitigation projects have governance- and conflict-related indicators, and natural resource management projects have resource-related indicators. Depending on how a project is categorized, sector-based monitoring and evaluation may not capture its full impact (Brady et al. 2013). Since many post-conflict environmental and natural resource projects have various peacebuilding dimensions, such projects should be monitored and evaluated on the basis of broader, cross-sectoral indicators.

The importance of conflict sensitivity

In post-conflict countries, a number of factors combine to create significant complications for natural resource management and environmental governance; these include insecurity, community division, ethnic or religious strife, erosion of the rule of law, weak governance institutions, environmental variability, climate change, and the risk of natural hazards. Given the complexity of post-conflict situations, even the most benign interventions can disrupt access to natural resources; affect traditional land use practices; stir up latent conflicts; and contribute to political, social, and economic tensions (Matthew and Hammill 2012*). It is thus essential for all actors to adopt conflict-sensitive approaches to project design, implementation, and evaluation.

Conflict sensitivity requires an understanding not only of the context in which an intervention will be undertaken but also of the potential interactions between the intervention and that context; it is also necessary to act upon that understanding, in order to maximize positive impacts and avoid negative impacts (Ruckstuhl 2009). In particular, a systematic conflict analysis and monitoring process should consider how a policy, program, or project may affect resource availability and access; the governance of natural resources and the environment with respect benefit sharing, public participation, transparency, and access to information; and transboundary dynamics and pressures.

COORDINATING AND SEQUENCING INTERVENTIONS

In most post-conflict situations, the number of national and international organizations working on humanitarian relief, peacekeeping, and peacebuilding is staggering. In some of the more complex cases (such as post-conflict Sierra Leone), there may be well over 400 different governmental, international, and nongovernmental organizations on the ground. Although it is nearly impossible to ensure that all activities are well coordinated, lack of coordination can lead to a number of unintended consequences, including duplication of efforts and competition for scarce resources.

Various international assessment and programming tools can serve as platforms for setting priorities and coordinating assistance; examples include the UN's consolidated appeal process, post-conflict needs assessment process, integrated mission planning process, and development assistance framework. Improved coordination is needed, however, across the UN system; between the UN system, donors, and domestic authorities; and between the national and subnational levels. Many actors complain about the high investment required to ensure full coordination, and the resulting diversion of resources from needs on the ground. At the very least, however, it is essential for all actors to share information regarding who is doing what and where, and to have a common vision of overall priorities and approach.

In addition to coordinating the activities of various actors, it is also necessary to properly time, prioritize, and sequence activities so that they support and build on each other. Given that the issues identified in needs assessments cannot all be addressed at once, the selection of priorities for post-conflict reconstruction is inherently complex. As noted earlier, peacebuilding priorities should be determined by national actors, with support and cooperation from international agencies and organizations.

One effort to improve programming for fragile states, including post-conflict countries, is the Busan New Deal.[6] Under the Busan New Deal, nineteen fragile and conflict-affected countries, their development partners, and international organizations agreed on a set of peacebuilding and state-building goals, as well as on new processes for periodically assessing fragility, monitoring progress, involving stakeholders, and building mutual trust. These goals and processes will be reflected in a country-specific compact, which is to be (1) developed in accordance with the views of a wide variety and a significant number of stakeholders, and (2) reviewed annually, through an inclusive process. The principal purpose of the compact is to ensure donor coordination and harmonization and to reduce duplication, fragmentation, and proliferation among programs. In recognition of differences in national context and level of fragility, and of the possibility that the compacts may need adjustment during the transition out of fragility, each compact will be tailored to the needs of the country in question (International Dialogue on Peacebuilding and Statebuilding 2011).

Although the UN's existing assessment and programming approaches do not fully account for the links between the environment, natural resources, conflict, and peacebuilding, the UN's approach is starting to shift. Specifically, the UN is developing a new understanding of security threats and sources of conflict that encompasses economic and social issues, including natural resources, the environment, and climate change. This new understanding has led to a number of high-level reports, policies, and resolutions that reflect the UN's growing commitment to addressing natural resource issues in post-conflict countries. For example, the 2010 *Progress Report of the Secretary-General on Peacebuilding in the Immediate Aftermath of Conflict* highlights natural resources as an area

---

[6] For more information on the Busan New Deal, see www.aideffectiveness.org/busanhlf4/about/new-deal-for-engagement-in-fragile-states.html.

of "increasing concern where greater efforts will be needed to deliver a more effective United Nations response" and calls on "Member States and the United Nations system to make questions of natural resource allocation, ownership and access an integral part of peacebuilding strategies" (UNSG 2010, 11–12). In mid-2012, in response to this call, the United Nations Development Group, through a process chaired by UNEP, adopted UN-wide guidelines on addressing natural resources in post-conflict transitional settings (UNDG 2012). The United Nations–European Union Partnership for Preventing and Managing Land and Natural Resource Conflicts also adopted a series of guidance notes on natural resources and conflict prevention. Finally, the Busan New Deal offers important new entry points for assessing and addressing the linkages between fragility, environmental degradation, and poor resource governance.

In post-conflict countries and fragile states, assigning the appropriate priority to natural resources and the environment, given competing needs, can be a challenge. Historically, human health and safety have been given the highest priority. In the absence of major health risks, however, natural resources have been given priority in peacebuilding if poor natural resource governance creates a significant risk of conflict relapse, or if natural resources played a substantial role in the onset, conduct, or financing of conflict. For example, natural resource management features prominently in the peacebuilding efforts of Sierra Leone and Sudan, where natural resources were significant drivers of conflict (Brown et al. 2012*; Jensen 2012*). Finally, natural resources and the environment may be assigned priority in peacebuilding contexts if they can be shown to directly support peacebuilding and state-building objectives such as economic recovery, restoration of governance and revenues, job creation, sustainable livelihoods, basic services, and reconciliation.

Table 1 highlights potential actions related to assessment, remediation, restoration, and reconstruction in the two principal stages of the peace process (immediate aftermath and peace consolidation). As noted earlier, there is no one recipe for resource management in post-conflict countries: approaches must be selected and timed to meet the needs of the specific context. Depending on context, some approaches may not be appropriate at all, or may be used in peacebuilding phases other than those suggested in the table.

FUTURE OUTLOOK

In post-conflict situations, which are often characterized by serious humanitarian and security concerns, national priorities are driven mainly by immediate peacebuilding needs, and by human welfare in particular. Given competing needs, assigning priority to natural resource management is often a difficult prospect, and environmental sustainability is rarely on the agenda. Nevertheless, natural resource management and environmental governance can become a national priority under three cases: when assessments clearly identify environmental impacts from conflict that threaten human health, livelihoods, and security; when assessments demonstrate

Table 1. Approaches to post-conflict assessment, remediation, restoration, and reconstruction

	Immediate aftermath	Peace consolidation

Assessment	Assess direct impacts of conflict on natural resources from
	  Toxic hazards.
	  Legacy of weapons, landmines, and unexploded ordnance.
	  Human displacement.
	  Use of extractive industries to finance conflict.
	  Loss of water supply, sanitation, and waste infrastructure.
	  Direct targeting of natural resources, particularly as part of scorched-earth military tactics.
	Assess indirect impacts of conflict on natural resources from
	  Livelihood-coping mechanisms and survival strategies.
	  Conflict economy (formal, international aid, informal, criminal).
	  Resource tenure.
	  Resource management institutions and capacity.
	  Dispute resolution capacity.
	Assess conflict relapse risks related to natural resources, including
	  Natural resources as conflict drivers.
	  Mechanisms for wealth and benefit sharing.
	  Level of resource scarcity and competition.
	  Transparency of contracts, payments, and impacts.
	  Public participation in decision making.
	  Dispute resolution capacity.
	  Transboundary dynamics.
	Assess peacebuilding opportunities related to natural resources, including
	  Safety and security.
	  Provision of basic services.
	  Restoration of government functions and revenues.
	  Reconciliation and political inclusion.
	  Economic recovery and livelihoods.
		Conduct thematic assessments of
		  Risks from natural hazards and climate change.
		  Long-term population and resource consumption trends.
		  Priorities and feasibility of resource and ecosystem restoration.
		  Sustainable livelihoods.
		  Opportunities to maximize employment from resource value chains.

Lessons and emerging issues 451

Assess capacity to govern natural resources, including
  Laws, regulations, and policies.
  Institutional capacity for planning, spending, and implementation.
  Enforcement and coordination mechanisms.
  Financial and operational resources.
  Technical expertise.
  Capacity of civil society to monitor compliance with laws.
  Public participation in decision making.
Additional considerations to take into account:
  Differential impacts and resource access for men and women.
  Differential impacts and resource access stemming from age or ethnicity.
  Negative interactions between peacebuilding priorities.
  Mainstreaming conflict sensitivity in programming.
  Major vulnerabilities to climate change and natural hazards.
Tools to be employed:
  Field sampling.
  Geographic information systems and remote sensing.
  Household surveys.
  Civilian capacity and expertise (international and national rosters).
  Gender-sensitive assessment approaches.
  Rapid or comprehensive versus thematic assessments.

Remediation Focus on hot spots whose remediation
  Will address direct and acute risks to human health and livelihoods.
  Offers visible peace dividends.
  Can strengthen public confidence in government.
  Can generate short-term employment.
Additional considerations to take into account:
  New grievances over natural resources.
  Ongoing interactions between peacebuilding priorities (positive and negative).
  New resource pressures stemming from population growth and the return of displaced populations.
  Level of illegal resource exploitation and trade.
Tools to be employed:
  Civilian capacity and expertise (local networks).
  Public consultation.
  Scenario analysis.
  Benchmarks and indicators.
  Cost-benefit analysis.
Expand scope to address hot spots that
  Pose chronic risks to drinking water, arable land, and air quality.
  Were not directly caused by the conflict.
  Can help catalyze investments in cleaner production.
  Can form part of a broader cleanup, restoration, and job-creation program.

Table 1. *(cont'd)*

	Immediate aftermath	Peace consolidation
Remediation *(cont'd)*	In the design of hot spot remediation programs, take account of Priorities determined by the source-pathway-receptor model. The complete life cycle of the waste, from cleanup to final disposal. Land tenure and ownership issues. The need for parallel public-awareness campaigns. Other forms of ongoing site contamination. Opportunities to maximize the use of locally available labor and technologies. Hazardous wastes should be Treated with extreme caution, in accordance with international health and safety standards. Screened, sorted, and removed from rubble- and waste-recycling streams. Kept out of municipal landfills that lack specific capacity. Temporarily stored in secure sites until transport and final disposal can be conducted. During hot spot cleanup operations Provide operators with training and personal protective equipment. Design projects to provide maximum emergency employment. Secure the site and prevent valuable or hazardous materials from being looted. Monitor risks to staff and local populations. Regularly update residents on risk reduction measures and cleanup progress. Conduct site-specific monitoring of acute environmental risks until remediation targets are achieved. Implement measures to prevent land grabbing.	In the design of hot spot remediation programs, take account of Opportunities to use remediation projects to build mutual trust and cooperation between divided groups. Opportunities to involve local communities in decisions about hot spot remediation priorities. Parallel investments in restoring or establishing landfills that incorporate environmental safeguards. Hazardous wastes should be Handled with consideration for the full life cycle. Disposed of according to international best practice. Transported across international borders in accordance with the Basel Convention on the Control of Transboundary Movements of Hazardous Wastes and Their Disposal. During hot spot cleanup operations Provide more detailed training to operators, to create a technical basis and skill set for longer-term employment. Use remediation projects to increase political and public interest in resource governance. Use remediation projects to build environmental awareness and public support for projects that safeguard the environment. Establish environmental-quality monitoring programs in and around high-risk areas. Ensure that new investments at cleanup sites do not create new sources of pollution and contamination.

Restoration	Focus restoration programs on areas where Direct, short-term benefits to livelihoods or disaster risk reduction can be achieved (for example, food, water, and energy security) within a single growing season. Restoration projects will show rapid and visible peace dividends and strengthen public confidence in government. The maximum amount of short-term employment can be generated. Short-term investments can lay the foundation for longer-term recovery of sustainable livelihoods. Local communities have a direct stake in restoration and have identified the restoration project as a priority. In the design of restoration programs, take into account Land tenure and ownership issues. Incentives and measures to control site access. Varying implementation capacities among communities. Future livelihood needs. Conflict sensitivity. Impacts that can be achieved within a single growing season.	Expand the scope of restoration programs to include areas where restoration yields both livelihood and ecosystem benefits (for example, reforestation, wetlands recovery, protected areas). In the design of restoration programs, take additional opportunities into account, including Using restoration programs to build trust, cooperation, and reconciliation between divided groups. Using restoration projects to reconnect and rebuild trust between communities, local authorities, and the national government. Establishing transboundary cooperation around resource restoration. Expanding the scope of restoration programs to larger geographic areas (including on a ridge-to-reef basis). Developing short-term indicators to track progress against long-term goals. Using scenario analysis to develop restoration options that reflect political, technical, and social constraints. Incorporating disaster and climate risks.

Lessons and emerging issues 453

Table 1. *(cont'd)*

	Immediate aftermath	*Peace consolidation*
Restoration *(cont'd)*	Design restoration programs to Provide maximum emergency employment. Be led and owned by communities (including through the provision of labor). Receive financing on an incremental basis, in accordance with the achievement of agreed-upon milestones.	Design restoration programs to Provide operators with more detailed training, to create a technical basis and skill set for longer-term employment. Address the need for corresponding legislation. Increase political and public interest in resource governance. Provide the legislative framework for decentralized, community-based natural resource management. Monitor the direct livelihood impact of successful restoration and disseminate lessons learned.
Reconstruction	Consider the following when conducting environmental assessments: Environmental impact assessments (EIAs) should be undertaken for all relief and reconstruction projects by international agencies or organizations acting in accordance with their internal policies and procedures, but with respect for domestic legislation. Where domestic EIA legislation or capacity does not exist, broad environmental and social safeguards can be adopted at the sector level to prevent reconstruction projects from causing major harmful impacts. Strategic environmental assessments of the main reconstruction sectors can also be conducted using entry points in official development assistance. Full-scale, ad hoc EIAs should be conducted for major infrastructure projects and major resource and agricultural concessions.	Consider the following when building national capacity to conduct environmental assessments: Moving toward requirements that all international assistance projects respect domestic EIA legislation. Gradually increasing EIA capacity in step with increasing government capacity, rule of law, and private sector investment. Building domestic authorities' capacity to monitor compliance with EIA plans and operating permits. Using EIAs for medium- to large-scale investments, as a means of building public confidence in the wider political processes of peace consolidation. Using EIAs as initial entry points for public participation in decision making.

Lessons and emerging issues

	Conduct immediate repair of infrastructure	Construct new infrastructure with
	In a conflict-sensitive way.	Conflict sensitivity.
	With consideration for how benefits will be apportioned between (or perceived by) divided groups.	Attention to the sustainable use of natural resources.
	So as to create immediate peace dividends.	Consideration for competition for scarce resources among different users and economic sectors.
	In response to local needs and priorities.	Attention to how the infrastructure will be governed.
	With attention to land tenure and ownership issues.	Attention to how the infrastructure will be maintained and financed by domestic authorities.
	So as to link infrastructure repair to livelihoods recovery, through an integrated and stepwise approach.	

Crosscutting issues	Design and implement all assessment, remediation, restoration, and reconstruction projects in a conflict-sensitive way, and ensure that they are based on a theory of change that is grounded in how the projects are expected to contribute to peace and security.
	Integrate gender considerations across all assessment, remediation, restoration, and reconstruction work, taking account of the following:
	    Gender-specific risks of and impacts from conflict-related environmental degradation.
	    Gender-specific impacts with respect to resource access, benefit sharing, rights, and ownership.
	    Opportunities for women's participation and empowerment in decision making regarding natural resources.
	    The risk of gender-based violence that is linked to resource use.
	Where possible, use environmental assessment, remediation, restoration, and reconstruction as platforms for
	    Cooperation and reconciliation between divided groups.
	    Political inclusion.
	    The restoration of relationships between levels of government and across ministries.
	    Building confidence in government.
	    Transboundary cooperation.
	    Strengthening public confidence in government.
	Where possible, design environmental assessment, remediation, restoration, and reconstruction projects to contribute to capacity building of
	    National and local governmental authorities.
	    Host communities.
	    Civil society.	

that conflict drivers or relapse risks are related to natural resource governance; or when assessments demonstrate tangible peacebuilding benefits from natural resources, such as economic and livelihood recovery, government revenues, job creation, and opportunities for reconciliation and political inclusion.

Immediately after the end of a conflict, a window of opportunity opens for rebuilding, establishing security, and consolidating peace. The parties to the conflict are often willing to reexamine conflict causes and development challenges and to collaborate in the design of new strategies to address them. And there may be unprecedented opportunities to transform or build institutions anew and to develop capacity on the basis of new principles and practices. In particular, this period offers opportunities to transform and rebuild institutions that are related to the management of natural resources in ways that would otherwise be politically difficult to achieve. Capitalizing on such early opportunities is particularly critical if the economy depends on natural resources, if resources contributed to the onset or financing of conflict, or if resources are undermining state-building efforts. Despite domestic and international efforts, however, a risk of conflict relapse may remain, particularly if conflict drivers are not sufficiently addressed and capacities for peace reinforced (UNDG 2012).

Natural resource governance is likely to contribute to peace consolidation if the power to make decisions about vital resources can be contested by different stakeholders without violence. Achieving this goal, in turn, requires (1) a government that is capable, accountable, transparent, and responsive to the wishes and needs of its population, and (2) a civil society that trusts the governing structures and processes, and is ready and able to engage with government to manage natural resources in a sustainable, profitable, equitable, and nonviolent manner. External actors can help build the capacity of conflict-affected and fragile societies to understand, manage, mediate, and respond to natural resource conflicts without violence, but the process must be led from within. A key challenge for the UN is to promote positive social transformation through the effective management of natural assets, while simultaneously mitigating the risks and potential impacts of violent conflict (UNDG 2012).

Despite the fact that natural resources are essential to most peacebuilding activities, the design and implementation of peacebuilding policies and programs have often failed to effectively analyze or address natural resources. This book draws attention to the important role that assessment, remediation, restoration, and reconstruction play, both individually and collectively, in the peacebuilding context. It highlights the importance of integrating natural resource management and environmental sustainability into peacebuilding processes and activities, and offers lessons on how to undertake that integration. Finally, it addresses some of the unique challenges of implementing assessment, remediation, restoration, and reconstruction projects in conflict-affected countries.

The most important peacebuilding work may take place before conflict even occurs—in the form of proactive, preventive measures. Investment in effective, equitable, and conflict-sensitive strategies for natural resource management may lessen incentives for conflict, reduce the impact of conflict on people and the environment when conflict does occur, and strengthen the chances for durable peace (Conca and Wallace 2012*). At the time of writing, the Organisation for Economic Co-operation and Development list of fragile states included forty-five countries (OECD 2011). Approximately 95 percent of those countries contain transboundary waters at risk, biodiversity hot spots of global significance, or both (Wolf, Yoffe, and Giordano 2003; CI 2005); 67 percent contain World Heritage sites (UNESCO 2011); and 80 percent contain extractive resources of strategic significance to the global economy (USGS 2010; IEA 2011). Fragile states can be viewed as the final frontier in the global scramble to secure rights to remaining resource supplies in a world of increasing resource scarcity (Klare 2012). Understanding how to prevent natural resources from contributing to instability and conflict in fragile regions is a critical need, as is the provision of immediate technical and political support in the event of violence. Preventing the pillage and plunder of natural resources in fragile states and ensuring their sustainable, transparent, and equitable management will be one of the key challenges of the next decade.

REFERENCES

Addison, T., and T. Bruck, eds. 2009. *Making peace work: The challenge of social and economic reconstruction.* London: Palgrave Macmillan.

Alden Wily, L. 2003. *Land rights in crisis: Restoring tenure security in Afghanistan.* Kabul: Afghanistan Research and Evaluation Unit. http://unpan1.un.org/intradoc/groups/public/documents/APCITY/UNPAN016656.pdf.

Anand, P. B. 2012. Addressing infrastructure needs in post-conflict reconstruction: An introduction to alternative planning approaches. In *Assessing and restoring natural resources in post-conflict peacebuilding*, ed. D. Jensen and S. Lonergan. London: Earthscan.

ANSP (Afghanistan National Solidarity Programme). 2010. Environmental and social management framework. Kabul.

Bardhan, P. 2004. *Scarcity, conflicts, and cooperation: Essays in the political and institutional economics of development.* Cambridge, MA: MIT Press.

Barwari, N. 2012. Rebuilding peace: Land and water management in the Kurdistan Region of northern Iraq. In *Land and post-conflict peacebuilding*, ed. J. Unruh and R. C. Williams. London: Earthscan.

Benard, C., S. G. Jones, O. Oliker, C. Q. Thurston, B. K. Stearns, and K. Cordell. 2008. *Women and nation-building.* Santa Monica, CA: RAND Corporation. www.rand.org/pubs/monographs/2008/RAND_MG579.pdf.

Bouma, G. 2012. Challenges and opportunities for mainstreaming environmental assessment tools in post-conflict settings. In *Assessing and restoring natural resources in post-conflict peacebuilding*, ed. D. Jensen and S. Lonergan. London: Earthscan.

Brady, C., O. Agoncillo, M. Z. Butardo-Toribio, B. Dolom, and C. V. Olvida. 2013. Improving natural resource governance and building peace and stability in Mindanao, Philippines. In *Livelihoods, natural resources, and post-conflict peacebuilding*, ed. H. Young and L. Goldman. London: Earthscan.

Briggs, C., and I. Weissbecker. 2012. Salting the Earth: Environmental health challenges in post-conflict reconstruction. In *Assessing and restoring natural resources in post-conflict peacebuilding*, ed. D. Jensen and S. Lonergan. London: Earthscan.

Brookings Institution and University of Bern. 2007. *Addressing internal displacement in peace processes, peace agreements and peace-building*. Washington, D.C.: Brookings–Bern Project on Internal Displacement.

Brown, O., M. Hauptfleisch, H. Jallow, and P. Tarr. 2012. Environmental assessment as a tool for peacebuilding and development: Initial lessons from capacity building in Sierra Leone. In *Assessing and restoring natural resources in post-conflict peacebuilding*, ed. D. Jensen and S. Lonergan. London: Earthscan.

Bruch, C., R. Wolfarth, and V. Michalcik. 2012. Natural resources, post-conflict reconstruction, and regional integration: Lessons from the Marshall Plan and other reconstruction efforts. In *Assessing and restoring natural resources in post-conflict peacebuilding*, ed. D. Jensen and S. Lonergan. London: Earthscan.

Burger, M. 2012. The risks of depleted uranium contamination in post-conflict countries: Findings and lessons learned from UNEP field assessments. In *Assessing and restoring natural resources in post-conflict peacebuilding*, ed. D. Jensen and S. Lonergan. London: Earthscan.

Carius, A., and A. Maas. 2012. Thinking back-end: Improving post-conflict analysis through consulting, adapting to change, and scenario building. In *Assessing and restoring natural resources in post-conflict peacebuilding*, ed. D. Jensen and S. Lonergan. London: Earthscan.

CI (Conservation International). 2005. *Biodiversity hotspots*. Arlington, VA.

Čolakhodžić, A., M. Filipović, J. Kovandžić, and S. Stec. 2013. The Sava River: Transitioning to peace in the former Yugoslavia. In *Water and post-conflict peacebuilding*, ed. E. Weinthal, J. Troell, and M. Nakayama. London: Earthscan.

Conca, K., and J. Wallace. 2012. Environment and peacebuilding in war-torn societies: Lessons from the UN Environment Programme's experience with post-conflict assessment. In *Assessing and restoring natural resources in post-conflict peacebuilding*, ed. D. Jensen and S. Lonergan. London: Earthscan.

Gingembre, L. 2012. Haiti: Lessons learned and way forward in natural resource management projects. In *Assessing and restoring natural resources in post-conflict peacebuilding*, ed. D. Jensen and S. Lonergan. London: Earthscan.

IEA (International Energy Agency). 2011. *Key world energy statistics*. Paris.

IMF (International Monetary Fund). 2002. Economics of post-conflict aid. IMF Working Paper. Washington, D.C.

International Dialogue on Peacebuilding and Statebuilding. 2011. A new deal for engagement in fragile states. www.oecd.org/international%20dialogue/49151944.pdf.

IWPR (Institute for War and Peace Reporting). 2008. Afghan environmental health problems legacy of land-grab. Environment News Service, November 21. www.ens-newswire.com/ens/nov2008/2008-11-21-01.html.

Jensen, D. 2009. From conflict to peacebuilding: UNEP's role in environmental assessment and recovery. *Environmental Change and Security Program Report*, no. 13. Washington, D.C.: Woodrow Wilson International Center for Scholars.

———. 2012. Evaluating the impact of UNEP's post-conflict environmental assessments. In *Assessing and restoring natural resources in post-conflict peacebuilding*, ed. D. Jensen and S. Lonergan. London: Earthscan.

Jensen, D., M. Halle, and M. Lehtonen. 2009. UNEP mission report: Risks and opportunities from natural resources and the environment for peacebuilding in the Central

African Republic. Draft. United Nations Environment Programme. www.unep.org/dnc/Portals/155/dnc/docs/UNEP_car_mission_Report_August_2009_draft_rev_1.pdf.

Kelly, C. 2012. Mitigating the environmental impacts of post-conflict assistance: Assessing USAID's approach. In *Assessing and restoring natural resources in post-conflict peacebuilding*, ed. D. Jensen and S. Lonergan. London: Earthscan.

King, M. W., M. A. González Pastora, M. Castro Salazar, C. M. Rodriguez. 2013. Environmental governance and peacebuilding in post-conflict Central America: Lessons from the Central American Commission for Environment and Development. In *Governance, natural resources, and post-conflict peacebuilding*, ed. C. Bruch, C. Muffett, and S. S. Nichols. London: Earthscan.

Klare, M. T. 2012: *The race for what's left: the global scramble for the world's last resources*. New York: Metropolitan Books.

Lederach, J. P. 2005. *The moral imagination: The art and soul of building peace*. New York: Oxford University Press.

Liljedahl, B., A. Waleij, B. Sandström, and L. Simonsson. 2012. Medical and environmental intelligence in peace and crisis-management operations. In *Assessing and restoring natural resources in post-conflict peacebuilding*, ed. D. Jensen and S. Lonergan. London: Earthscan.

Lonergan, S. 2012. Ecological restoration and peacebuilding: The case of the Iraqi marshes. In *Assessing and restoring natural resources in post-conflict peacebuilding*, ed. D. Jensen and S. Lonergan. London: Earthscan.

Mashatt, M., D. Long, and J. Crum. 2008. Conflict-sensitive approach to infrastructure development. Special Report. Washington, D.C.: United States Institute of Peace. www.usip.org/files/resources/sr197.pdf.

Matthew, R., and A. Hammill. 2012. Peacebuilding and adaptation to climate change. In *Assessing and restoring natural resources in post-conflict peacebuilding*, ed. D. Jensen and S. Lonergan. London: Earthscan.

Mott MacDonald. 2005. *Provision of infrastructure in post conflict situations*. London: Department for International Development. http://ti-up.dfid.gov.uk/uploads/public/documents/Key%20Documents/Infrastructure%20in%20Post%20Conflict.pdf.

Nakayama, M. 2012. Making best use of domestic energy sources: The Priority Production System for coal mining and steel production in post-World War II Japan. In *Assessing and restoring natural resources in post-conflict peacebuilding*, ed. D. Jensen and S. Lonergan. London: Earthscan.

Nanthikesan, S., and J. Uitto. 2012. Evaluating post-conflict assistance. In *Assessing and restoring natural resources in post-conflict peacebuilding*, ed. D. Jensen and S. Lonergan. London: Earthscan.

OECD (Organisation for Economic Co-operation and Development). 2011. *Ensuring fragile states are not left behind*. Paris.

OECD/DAC (Organisation for Economic Co-operation and Development, Development Assistance Committee). 2007. Encouraging effective evaluation of conflict prevention and peacebuilding activities: Towards DAC guidance. *OECD Journal on Development* 8 (3): 7–106.

Pinera, J.-F., and R. A. Reed. 2013. A tale of two cities: Restoring water services in Kabul and Monrovia. In *Water and post-conflict peacebuilding*, ed. E. Weinthal, J. Troell, and M. Nakayama. London: Earthscan.

Rich, E., and T. N. Warner. 2012. Addressing the roots of Liberia's conflict through the Extractive Industries Transparency Initiative. In *High-value natural resources and post-conflict peacebuilding*, ed. P. Lujala and S. A. Rustad. London: Earthscan.

Risen, J. 2010. U.S. identifies vast mineral riches in Afghanistan. *New York Times*, June 13. www.nytimes.com/2010/06/14/world/asia/14minerals.html.

Ruckstuhl, S. 2009. *Renewable natural resources: Practical lessons for conflict-sensitive development*. Washington, D.C.: World Bank.

Rustad, S. A., P. Lujala, and P. Le Billon. 2012. Building or spoiling peace? Lessons from the management of high-value natural resources. In *High-value natural resources and post-conflict peacebuilding*, ed. P. Lujala and S. A. Rustad. London: Earthscan.

Schwartz, J., S. Hahn, and I. Bannon. 2004. The private sector's role in the provision of infrastructure in post-conflict countries: Patterns and policy options. Social Development Paper No. 16. Washington, D.C.: World Bank.

Shimoyachi-Yuzawa, N. 2012. Linking demining to post-conflict peacebuilding: A case study of Cambodia. In *Assessing and restoring natural resources in post-conflict peacebuilding*, ed. D. Jensen and S. Lonergan. London: Earthscan.

Shovic, H. 2005. Continuing pistachio woodland rehabilitation in Afghanistan. Pistachio Woodlands TDY-2: Report. www.shovic.com/henryshovic/AssetsGeography/Documents/PistachioTDY2ReportShovic12022005.pdf.

Smucker, G. R., G. Fleurantin, M. McGahuey, and B. Swartley. 2005. *Agriculture in a fragile environment: Market incentives for natural resource management in Haiti*. Port-au-Prince: United States Agency for International Development. http://pdf.usaid.gov/pdf_docs/PDACN884.pdf.

Solomon, A., Y. Bouka, J. O'Neil, G. Pouliot, and S. Al-Sarraf. 2009. Forced displacement and housing, land, and property ownership challenges in post-conflict and reconstruction. INPROL Consolidated Response (09-003). Washington, D.C.: International Network to Promote the Rule of Law.

Tamer-Chammas, A. 2012. Restoration of damaged land in societies recovering from conflict: The case of Lebanon. In *Assessing and restoring natural resources in post-conflict peacebuilding*, ed. D. Jensen and S. Lonergan. London: Earthscan.

Thummarukudy, M., O. Brown, and H. Moosa. 2012. Remediation of polluted sites in the Balkans, Iraq, and Sierra Leone. In *Assessing and restoring natural resources in post-conflict peacebuilding*, ed. D. Jensen and S. Lonergan. London: Earthscan.

UN (United Nations) and World Bank. 2003. *Joint Iraq needs assessment report*. Baghdad. http://siteresources.worldbank.org/IRFFI/Resources/Joint+Needs+Assessment.pdf.

———. 2007. *Somali joint needs assessment: Productive sectors and the environment cluster report*. www.somali-jna.org/downloads/vol5_V.pdf.

UNDG (United Nations Development Group). 2012. Guidance note: Natural resource management in transition settings. New York.

UNDP (United Nations Development Programme). 2007. *Lebanon rapid environmental assessment for greening recovery, reconstruction and reform—2006*. Beirut. www.undp.org.lb/events/docs/DraftReport.pdf.

UNDP and World Bank. 2007. Joint guidance note on integrated recovery planning using post conflict needs assessments and transitional results frameworks. New York. http://ochanet.unocha.org/p/Documents/Joint%20Guidance%20Note%20on%20Integrated%20Recovery%20Planning.pdf.

UNEP (United Nations Environment Programme). 2003. *Afghanistan: Post-conflict environmental assessment*. Geneva, Switzerland. http://postconflict.unep.ch/publications/afghanistanpcajanuary2003.pdf.

———. 2006. *Environmental assessment of the areas disengaged by Israel in the Gaza Strip*. Nairobi, Kenya. http://postconflict.unep.ch/publications/UNEP_Gaza_web.pdf.

―――. 2007a. *Sudan: Post-conflict environmental assessment.* Nairobi, Kenya. http://postconflict.unep.ch/publications/UNEP_Sudan.pdf.

―――. 2007b. *Lebanon: Post-conflict environmental assessment.* Nairobi, Kenya. http://postconflict.unep.ch/publications/UNEP_Lebanon.pdf.

―――. 2009a. *From conflict to peacebuilding: The role of natural resources and the environment.* Nairobi, Kenya. http://postconflict.unep.ch/publications/pcdmb_policy_01.pdf.

―――. 2009b. *Environmental assessment of the Gaza Strip following the escalation of hostilities in December 2008–January 2009.* Nairobi, Kenya. www.unep.org/PDF/dmb/UNEP_Gaza_EA.pdf.

―――. 2010. *Sierra Leone: Environment, conflict and peacebuilding assessment; Technical report.* Geneva, Switzerland. http://postconflict.unep.ch/publications/Sierra_Leone.pdf.

―――. 2011a. *The Democratic Republic of the Congo: Post-conflict environmental assessment synthesis for policy makers.* Nairobi, Kenya. http://postconflict.unep.ch/publications/UNEP_DRC_PCEA_EN.pdf.

―――. 2011b. *Rwanda: From post-conflict to environmentally sustainable development.* Nairobi, Kenya. http://postconflict.unep.ch/publications/UNEP_Rwanda.pdf.

―――. 2012. *Greening the blue helmets: Environment, natural resources and UN peacekeeping operations.* Nairobi, Kenya. http://postconflict.unep.ch/publications/UNEP_greening_blue_helmets.pdf.

UNESCO (United Nations Educational, Scientific and Cultural Organization). 2011. *World Heritage List.* Paris.

UNSG (United Nations Secretary-General). 2010. *Progress report of the Secretary-General on peacebuilding in the immediate aftermath of conflict.* A/64/866–S/2010/386. July 16 (reissued on August 19 for technical reasons). New York. www.un.org/ga/search/view_doc.asp?symbol=A/64/866.

UN-HABITAT (United Nations Human Settlements Programme). 2008. *Country programme document 2008–2009: Lebanon.* Nairobi, Kenya. www.unhabitat.org/pmss/listItemDetails.aspx?publicationID=2706.

Unruh, J., and M. Shalaby. 2012. Road infrastructure reconstruction as a peacebuilding priority in Afghanistan: Negative implications for land rights. In *Assessing and restoring natural resources in post-conflict peacebuilding,* ed. D. Jensen and S. Lonergan. London: Earthscan.

U.S. DOD (United States Department of Defense). 2009. *Progress toward security and stability in Afghanistan.* Kabul.

USGS (United States Geological Survey). 2010. *Minerals yearbook.* Reston, VA.

Verstegen, S. 2001. Poverty and conflict: An entitlement perspective. CPN Briefing Paper. Brussels, Belgium: Conflict Prevention Network.

Wolf, A. T., S. B. Yoffe, and M. Giordano. 2003. *International waters: Indicators for identifying basins at risk.* Paris: United Nations Educational, Scientific and Cultural Organization.

World Bank. 2007. *Republic of Lebanon: Economic assessment of environmental degradation due to the July 2006 hostilities; Sector note.* Report No. 39787-LB. http://siteresources.worldbank.org/LEBANONEXTN/Resources/LB_env_Oct2007.pdf?resourceurlname=LB_env_Oct2007.pdf.

APPENDIX 1
List of abbreviations

ADR: assessment of development results
AECID: Ministry of Foreign Affairs and Cooperation (Ministerio de Asuntos Exteriores y de Cooperación) (Spain)
ALI: annual limit on intake
ALIDES: Alliance for Sustainable Development (Alianza para el Desarrollo Sostenible de Centroamérica)
AME: Asia and Middle East
ANDS: Afghanistan National Development Strategy
ATSDR: U.S. Agency for Toxic Substances and Disease Registry
BAPPENAS: National Development Planning Agency (Badan Perencanaan dan Pembangunan Nasional) (Indonesia)
BEO: bureau environmental officer
CAP: consolidated appeal process
CARDS: Community Assistance for Reconstruction, Development, and Stabilization
CBD: community-based demining
CBNRM: community-based natural resource management
CBRN: chemical, biological, radiological, and nuclear
CCA: common country assessment
CCAD: Central American Commission on Environment and Development
CEDRO: Community Energy Efficiency and Renewable Energy Demonstration Project for the Recovery of Lebanon
CEEC: Committee on European Economic Cooperation
CENTO: Central Treaty Organization
CIDA: Canadian International Development Agency
CMAA: Cambodian Mine Action and Victim Assistance Authority
CMAC: Cambodian Mine Action Center
CONCAUSA: Central America-United States of America Joint Accord (Conjunto Centroamericano–USA)
CPA: Coalition Provisional Authority (Iraq)
CPA: Comprehensive Peace Agreement

DAC: Development Assistance Committee
DACs: derived-air concentrations
DAD: donor assistance database
DALYs: disability-adjusted life years
DCHA: Democracy, Conflict, and Humanitarian Assistance
DEED: Economic Development for a Sustainable Environment
DU: depleted uranium
DWG: District Working Group
EC: European Commission
ECA: Economic Cooperation Administration
ECHO: European Commission for Humanitarian Aid
ECSC: European Coal and Steel Community
ECSEE: Energy Community of South East Europe
EDC: ethylene dichloride
EIA: environmental impact assessment
EIHH: environmental and industrial health hazards
EPA: Environmental Protection Agency
EPA-SL: Environment Protection Agency-Sierra Leone
ESA: environmental site assessment
EU: European Union
EVA: environmental vulnerability assessment
FAES: Economic and Social Assistance Fund (Fonds d'Assistance Economique et Sociale) (Haiti)
FAO: Food and Agriculture Organization of the United Nations
FDA: Forest Development Authority
FRY: Federal Republic of Yugoslavia
GDP: Gross domestic product
GICHD: Geneva International Centre for Humanitarian Demining
GIRoA: Government of the Islamic Republic of Afghanistan
GIS: geographic information system
GNU: Government of National Unity
GOI: government of Indonesia
GOL: government of Lebanon
GOSS: Government of Southern Sudan (prior to July 9, 2011); Government of South Sudan (as of July 9, 2011)
GTZ: German Society for International Cooperation
HIP Azotara: Pancevo fertilizer factory
HIP Petrohemija: Pancevo petrochemical plant
HPSC: Healthy Practices, Strong Communities Program
IAEA: International Atomic Energy Agency
ICA: International Cooperation Administration
ICBL: International Campaign to Ban Landmines
ICRP: International Commission on Radiological Protection
IDB: Inter-American Development Bank

IED: improvised explosive device
IEE: initial environmental examination
IMF: International Monetary Fund
INARA: Haitian Institute of Agrarian Reform
IDPs: Internally displaced persons
IPA: Instrument for Pre-Accession Assistance
IUCN: International Union for the Conservation of Nature
JMAS: Japan Mine Action Service
LAMAA: Land Administration in Mine Affected Areas
LER: Lebanon's Early Recovery
LMAC: Lebanese Mine Action Centre
LUPU: land use planning unit
MAPU: Mine Action Planning Unit
MEO: mission environmental officer
MRL: minimal risk level
MTDP: Medium Term Development Plan
NATO: North Atlantic Treaty Organization
NDS: National Development Strategy
NECOLIB: National Environmental Commission of Liberia
NEPA: National Environmental Protection Agency
NGO: nongovernmental organizations
NIS-RNP: Pancevo oil refinery
NIS-RNS: Novi Sad oil refinery
NSP: National Strategic Plan
ODA: official development assistance
OECD: Organisation for Economic Co-operation and Development
oPt: occupied Palestinian territories
ORE: Organization for the Rehabilitation of the Environment (L'Organisation pour la Réhabilitation de l'Environnement) (Haiti)
OTI: Office of Transition Initiatives
PADELAN: Oxfam Quebec Support for Local Development and Agroforestry project in Nippes
PAG: Petroleum Advisory Group
PCBs: polychlorinated biphenyls
PCDMB: Post-Conflict and Disaster Management Branch
PCNA: post-conflict needs assessment
PERSUAP: pesticide evaluation report and safe-user plan
PLO: Palestine Liberation Organization
PMAC: Provincial Mine Action Committee
PRSP: poverty reduction strategy paper
REA: regional environmental advisor
RPC: Radiation Protection Center (Iraq)
RUF: Revolutionary United Front (Sierra Leone)
SADC: Southern African Development Community

SAF: Securing Afghanistan's Future
SAIEA: Southern African Institute for Environmental Assessment
SCA: Sudan Country Analysis
SEA: strategic environmental assessment
SICA: Central American Integration System (Sistema de la Integración Centroamericana)
SPLM: Sudan People's Liberation Movement
STL: Special Tribunal for Lebanon
TDI: tolerable daily intake
TEL: tetraethyl lead
UN: United Nations
UNAMSIL: United Nations Mission in Sierra Leone
UNAS: United Nations Assistance Strategy for Iraq
UNCHS: United Nations Centre for Human Settlements
UNDAF: United Nations Development Assistance Framework
UNDP: United Nations Development Programme
UNEP: United Nations Environment Programme
UNICEF: United Nations Children's Fund
UNIFIL: United Nations Interim Force in Lebanon
UNIPSIL: United Nations Integrated Peacebuilding Office in Sierra Leone
UNMAS: United Nations Mine Acton Service
UNTAC: United Nations Transitional Authority in Cambodia
USAID: U.S. Agency for International Development
UXO: unexploded ordnance
VCM: vinyl chloride monomer
WHO: World Health Organization
WINNER: Watershed Initiative for National Natural Environmental Resources

APPENDIX 2
Author biographies

P. B. Anand is a reader in environmental economics and public policy at the University of Bradford. His research focuses on sustainable human development in resource-rich societies, human rights and capabilities in the context of water governance, and the role of participatory and citizen-centered mechanisms in promoting accountability. Anand has written on the resolution of river water conflicts, Millennium Development Goals, and transboundary mechanisms for cooperative infrastructure planning. He holds degrees in engineering and urban planning from institutions in India, and a Ph.D. in economics from the University of Strathclyde, Glasgow.

George Bouma is a policy advisor for the Environment and Energy Group in the Bureau for Development Policy of the United Nations Development Programme (UNDP). He began working in international development in 2000, as a civil affairs officer with the UN mission in Timor-Leste. From 2004 to 2006, he served as an environmental impact assessment expert in Afghanistan, working with the Environmental Governance and Capacity Building Programme of the United Nations Environment Programme (UNEP). In 2007, he worked for UNEP as a consultant on UNEP-sponsored post-conflict and post-disaster projects. In 2009, Bouma returned to peacekeeping operations as a natural resources advisor to the United Nations Mission in Liberia. He holds a B.Sc. and an M.Sc. in environmental science from Murdoch University and an M.A. in international development from the University of Melbourne.

Chad Briggs holds the Minerva Chair of Energy and Environmental Security at the Air University of the U.S. Air Force; is a principal at Global Interconnections LLC, in Ottawa; and is a fellow at the Institute for Environmental Security in The Hague. Briggs was previously senior advisor for international security affairs at the Environmental Security Directorate of the U.S. Department of Energy. His work focuses on scenario planning for environmental change and international security, environmental health risks in post-conflict and post-disaster regions, and the security risks of climate and environmental change. Briggs has published on vulnerability assessments for environmentally fragile regions and systems, water resource management, and the security implications of tropical disease, and was the project leader on security assessments under conditions of abrupt climate change for GlobalEESE (Global Energy and Environment Strategic Ecosystem). He holds a Ph.D. in political science from Carleton University, has been a visiting scholar in geography at University College London, and was a Fulbright professor in Budapest and Berlin.

Oli Brown is the environmental affairs officer for the United Nations in Sierra Leone, where he coordinates a program, sponsored by the United Nations Environment Programme (UNEP), to develop capacity for natural resource management. He was previously a senior researcher with the Environment and Security Program of the International Institute for Sustainable Development, where he coordinated an expert advisory group that worked with UNEP to develop ways to integrate environmental and natural resource concerns into the UN's conflict prevention and peacebuilding work. Brown holds degrees in anthropology, history, and international relations, and is a coauthor (with Richard Matthew and David Jensen) of the 2009 UNEP publication *From Conflict to Peacebuilding: The Role of Natural Resources and the Environment*.

Carl Bruch is a senior attorney and codirector of international programs at the Environmental Law Institute; he also cochairs the Specialist Group on Armed Conflict and the Environment of the Commission on Environmental Law of the International Union for Conservation of Nature. Bruch's research focuses on making environmental law work. He has helped countries in Africa, Asia, Eastern Europe, and Latin America develop and implement laws, policies, and institutional frameworks to effectively manage water resources, biodiversity, forests, and other natural resources. Much of his work has focused on the means of preventing, reducing, mitigating, and compensating for environmental damage resulting from armed conflict. He is a series editor of the six-book series on Post-Conflict Peacebuilding and Natural Resource Management (Earthscan, 2012–2013). He has edited or coedited six other books, including *The Environmental Consequences of War: Legal, Economic, and Scientific Perspectives* (with Jay Austin) (Cambridge University Press, 2000); coauthored *Post-Conflict Peacebuilding and Natural Resources: The Promise and the Peril* (with David Jensen, Mikiyasu Nakayama, and Jon Unruh) (Cambridge University Press, forthcoming); and authored dozens of scholarly articles. He holds a B.S. in physics from Michigan State University, an M.A. in physics from the University of Texas at Austin, and a J.D. from Northwestern School of Law of Lewis & Clark College.

Mario Burger is the head of the physics department at Spiez Laboratory, an institute of the Swiss Ministry of Defense, Civil Protection and Sports. He also consults regularly for the United Nations Environment Programme, where he serves as a senior scientific advisor to the Post-Conflict and Disaster Management Branch. Burger first joined the UN in the 1990s, when he was nominated to serve as the chief inspector of the UNSCOM (United Nations Special Commission) Chemical Group in Iraq. Burger holds a Ph.D. in chemistry from the University of Bern.

Alexander Carius, the cofounder and codirector of Adelphi, specializes in international relations and development cooperation. The main fields of his research and consulting are resources and governance, climate and energy, and development and security. He is a senior advisor to federal ministries, aid agencies, the European Commission, and various international and regional organizations. Carius is an experienced facilitator of national and international stakeholder dialogues and consultation processes, and designs and leads complex international programs and projects for donor agencies and international organizations. Since 1995, he has served as a team leader for more than one hundred projects in the areas of environment, development, and foreign policy, and has published over 200 research reports, articles, and books. Carius has studied political science, law, and journalism, and holds an M.A. in political science from the Free University of Berlin.

Ken Conca is a professor of international relations at the School of International Service at American University, where he also directs the Global Environmental Politics Program. His research and teaching focus on global environmental politics, environmental policy, social movements in world politics, and peace and conflict studies. He is the author or editor of seven books, including *The Crisis of Global Environmental Governance* (Routledge, 2008), *Governing Water* (MIT Press, 2006), and *Confronting Consumption* (MIT Press, 2002). Conca received the Chadwick Alger Prize, awarded by the International Studies Association (ISA), for the best book on international organization, and is a two-time recipient of the ISA's Harold and Margaret Sprout Award for the best book on international environmental affairs. Conca is an associate editor of *Global Environmental Politics* and a member of the Expert Advisory Group on Environment, Conflict and Peacebuilding of the United Nations Environment Programme.

Lucile Gingembre is an associate program officer for the Post-Conflict and Disaster Management Branch of the United Nations Environment Programme (UNEP); in that role, she participated in the design, planning, and implementation of the UNEP Haiti country program, which focuses on reducing poverty, disaster vulnerability, and environmental degradation in the country. Before joining UNEP, Gingembre worked in a province of northern Uruguay, serving as area manager for the ART International Initiative, a local development program sponsored by the United Nations Development Programme. Her field experience also includes several years of volunteering for a nongovernmental organization in Morocco that focused on improving education for children and creating income-generating activities for women. She has studied in China, France, and Spain, and holds a master's degree in international relations and development from Sciences Po, Paris, and a master's degree in international law from Pantheon-Assas Paris II University.

Anne Hammill is a senior researcher for the International Institute for Sustainable Development, where she works on two programs: Climate Change and Energy, and Environment and Security. Much of her work focuses on understanding how environmental management can contribute to human security by supporting conflict prevention, peacebuilding, and resilience in the face of climate stress. Her most recent work has involved field research, training, and policy analysis on climate change adaptation and conflict-sensitive conservation in Eastern and Central Africa. She holds a B.A. in geography and environmental studies from McMaster University and an M.A. in geography from the University of Victoria.

Morgan Hauptfleisch is the principal scientist for the Southern African Institute for Environmental Assessment (SAIEA), in Namibia; in that capacity, he co-ordinated SAIEA's role in the multi-donor Capacity Development and Linkages for Environmental Assessment in Africa Program. At SAIEA, Hauptfleisch's work focuses on conservation and environmental management planning, environmental assessment training, and quality control. A lecturer at the Polytechnic of Namibia and an accomplished trainer, facilitator, and planner, Hauptfleisch is currently completing a Ph.D. in environmental management at the University of the Free State, in South Africa.

Haddijatou Jallow is the executive chairperson of the Sierra Leone Environment Protection Agency, a semiautonomous regulatory institution that coordinates all environmental matters and drafts environmental policy for the government of Sierra Leone. Jallow is also a member of Sierra Leone's negotiating team for United Nations–sponsored climate change negotiations. Previously, she served on several environmental boards and was a legal advisor to the Gambia National Environment Management Agency. Jallow has a master's degree in environmental law from George Washington University and a master's degree in international law from the University of Lagos.

David Jensen heads the Environmental Cooperation for Peacebuilding Program of the United Nations Environment Programme (UNEP). Since 2000, he has worked on fifteen operations that assessed post-conflict environmental damage and natural resource degradation, and their implications for human health, livelihoods, and security. His current work focuses on the links between natural resources and conflict, and on approaches to natural resource management that create jobs, sustain livelihoods, and contribute to economic recovery and peacebuilding without creating new grievances or significant environmental degradation. In addition to conducting fieldwork, Jensen focuses on integrating natural resource risks and opportunities into UN policies on conflict prevention, mediation, peacekeeping, and peacebuilding. He is a series editor of the six-book series on Post-Conflict Peacebuilding and Natural Resource Management (Earthscan, 2012–2013), co-author of *Post-Conflict Peacebuilding and Natural Resources: The Promise and the Peril* (with Carl Bruch, Mikiyasu Nakayama, and Jon Unruh) (Cambridge University Press, forthcoming), and the managing coeditor of a UNEP policy series on environment, conflict, and peacebuilding. He holds a bachelor's degree in geography from the University of Victoria and a master's degree in biology from the University of Oxford.

Author biographies

Charles Kelly has more than thirty years of field experience in humanitarian assistance programs addressing droughts, food insecurity, hurricanes, epidemics, floods, war, and other emergencies in developing countries. He has performed field and senior management tasks in more than twenty disaster response operations. Kelly's recent professional work includes risk assessment, disaster risk reduction, management capacity building, and the assessment of environmental impacts during disasters. He has worked in more than sixty countries and published more than forty-five articles on disaster management, including impact assessment, disaster-environment linkages, and disaster management systems. Kelly is an affiliate of the Aon Benfield Hazard Research Centre, University College London, and a member of the International Research Committee on Disasters, the Society of Risk Analysis, the International Emergency Management Society, and ProAct Network.

Birgitta Liljedahl is a senior analyst at the Swedish Defence Research Agency (FOI), with a specialty in environmental impact assessments and health hazard assessments in conflict and disaster areas. Since 2001, she has been the project manager for FOI support for the Swedish Armed Forces in the area of environmental and medical intelligence; in that role, she has conducted environmental vulnerability assessments in Afghanistan, Chad, Darfur, the Democratic Republic of the Congo, Lebanon, Libya, Somalia, and other countries. Since 2006, Liljedahl has been the project coordinator for Environment and Health in Peacekeeping, a program financed by the Swedish Ministry for Foreign Affairs that has developed pilot projects in cooperation with the United Nations Department of Peacekeeping Operations, the United Nations Department of Field Support, and the United Nations Mission in South Sudan. Liljedahl's background is in environmental geology, and she holds an M.Sc. from Uppsala University.

Steve Lonergan is an emeritus professor in the Department of Geography at the University of Victoria. Lonergan began his academic career at McMaster University, in Hamilton, Ontario, and has held visiting posts at the University of Auckland, in New Zealand; the University of Malaysia; and Monash University, in Australia. From 2003 to 2005, he was the director of the Division of Early Warning and Assessment at the United Nations Environment Programme in Nairobi, Kenya. Lonergan's research focuses on water resources in the Middle East, environmental change and population movement, and the impacts of climate change. He is the author of two books and more than sixty journal articles and reports. His most recent book, *Riding in a Matatu* (Tiny Tembo Publishing, 2012), is a humorous account of the time he spent living in Kenya and working for the United Nations. Lonergan holds a B.Sc. from Duke University and an M.A. and Ph.D. from the University of Pennsylvania.

Achim Maas is a senior project manager at Adelphi. His main areas of work are the interlinkages between natural resources, violent conflict, and peace at all levels of society. Within these areas, he focuses primarily on the security implications of climate change and on the development of analytical frameworks and methodologies. Maas is a member of the editorial staff of the *Environment, Conflict and Cooperation* newsletter. He studied political science, sociology, history, and economics at Johann Wolfgang Goethe University, Frankfurt am Main, Germany, and holds a master's degree in international politics and security studies from the University of Bradford, United Kingdom.

Richard Matthew is a professor of international and environmental politics in the Schools of Social Ecology and Social Science at the University of California, Irvine, and the founding director of the Center for Unconventional Security Affairs. He is also the Senior Fellow for Security at the International Institute for Sustainable Development; a member of the Expert Advisory Group on Environment, Conflict and Peacebuilding of the United Nations Environment Programme; and a member of the Commission on Environmental, Economic and Social Policy of the International Union for the Conservation of Nature. His field-based research focuses on international relations in the developing world, especially South Asia and East Africa. He has published widely on transnational security threats, including climate change, infectious disease, terrorism, and landmines. Matthew has worked closely with major U.S. corporations, the United Nations, numerous international nonprofit organizations, and a variety of U.S. government departments and agencies, and has received certificates of recognition from the U.S. Congress, the California State Legislature, and the City of Los Angeles. He holds a B.A. from McGill University and a Ph.D. from Princeton University.

Vladislav Michalcik was a research scholar in residence from 2009 to 2011 at American University Washington College of Law (AU WCL), where he focused on the human rights of older people and on the connections between those rights, access to justice, and rule of law. Under the auspices of the United Nations Development Fund, Michalcik also coordinated a project, implemented by AU, that led to the development of a handbook on regional, national, and global standards for the rights of older people. Previously, Michalcik was a Dean's Fellow at the Center for Human Rights and Humanitarian Law at AU WCL, and a visiting scholar at the Environmental Law Institute. He has also worked at the European Center for Minority Issues, Human Rights Watch, the Institute for Multi-Track Diplomacy, and International Campaign for Tibet. Michalcik holds an LL.M. in international legal studies from AU WCL and a degree in law and legal science from the Masaryk University, Czech Republic.

Hannah Moosa is a Ph.D. student at the Munk School of Global Affairs and the Department of Political Science at the University of Toronto. Her doctoral research focuses on water resource management, conflict, and peacebuilding in the Nile and Jordan river basins. From June 2009 to June 2011, Moosa worked as a research assistant for the Post-Conflict and Disaster Management Branch of the United Nations Environment Programme. From July to December 2010, she conducted research for the Forum of Federations on federalist options for Sudan and constitutional design in post-conflict societies. Moosa has been active in Model UN debating since 2001, and from March 2009 to March 2010 served as the Secretary-General of the first Global Model United Nations Conference, which was organized by the United Nations Department of Public Information. Moosa holds a B.A. in international affairs and economics from the University of Toronto Mississauga, and an M.A. in international relations from the Munk School of Global Affairs.

Mikiyasu Nakayama is a professor in the Department of International Studies, Graduate School of Frontier Sciences, University of Tokyo. Nakayama's research subjects include the application of satellite remote-sensing data for the environmental monitoring of lake basins, the use of geographic information systems for the environmental management of river and lake basins, environmental impact assessment methodologies applicable to involuntary resettlement caused by the construction of dams, and the involvement of international organizations in the management of international water bodies. He is a series editor of the six-book series on Post-Conflict Peacebuilding and Natural Resource Management (Earthscan, 2012–2013) and coauthor of *Post-Conflict Peacebuilding and Natural Resources: The Promise and the Peril* (with Carl Bruch, David Jensen, and Jon Unruh) (Cambridge University Press, forthcoming). He holds a B.A., M.Sc., and Ph.D., all in agricultural engineering, from the University of Tokyo.

Suppiramaniam Nanthikesan is an evaluation advisor at the Regional Bureau for Africa of the United Nations Development Programme (UNDP). Previously, he spent several years as an evaluation advisor at the UNDP Evaluation Office, where he was responsible for a number of thematic evaluations, including the evaluation of UNDP assistance to conflict-affected countries; in addition, as part of the Tsunami Evaluation Coalition, he participated in the joint evaluation of the impact of the tsunami response on local and national capacities. Before joining UNDP, Nanthikesan spent fifteen years teaching in Sri Lanka and working in both academia and the private sector in the United States. A native of Sri Lanka, Nanthikesan holds an M.P.A. from Harvard University and a Ph.D. in civil engineering from the Massachusetts Institute of Technology.

Björn Sandström is a deputy research director at the Swedish Defence Research Agency, where his work focuses primarily on radiation safety and radiation security issues, and includes information gathering in support of Swedish Armed Forces intelligence and crisis-management operations in various countries and regions, including Afghanistan, Africa, and the Balkans. Sandström is also an assistant professor of experimental clinical chemistry at Umeå University, Sweden. Since the early 1990s, he has represented Sweden in various North Atlantic Treaty Organization research working groups dealing with chemical, biological, radiological, and nuclear weapons issues. Sandström holds a Ph.D. in physical biology from Uppsala University.

Mourad Shalaby is pursuing a master's degree in geography at McGill University, where he is investigating the relationship between climate change, development, and adaptation in the Congo forest region. His previous work has focused on the analysis of air pollution in Cairo, the history of planning and transport policy in Montreal, and the evaluation of quality of life in Montreal. Shalaby has a bachelor's degree in human environmental geography from the University of Montreal, where he conducted studies on urban issues in developing countries, geographic information systems and cartography, field assessments of land management, environmental impact assessments, and natural resources management. He also has a certificate in trade, development, and the environment from the London School of Economics, where he conducted research on the role of the United States in climate change.

Nao Shimoyachi-Yuzawa is a research fellow with the Japan Institute of International Affairs (JIIA). Before joining JIIA, in 2006, she was a program officer at the Foundation for International Development/Relief, where she coordinated a medical project in Cambodia. She is also a former staff writer for *The Japan Times*, where she covered national security, politics, and social issues. Shimoyachi-Yuzawa holds an M.A. in peace studies from the University of Bradford, United Kingdom, and an LL.B. from the University of Tokyo.

Louise Simonsson is a researcher at the Swedish Defence Research Agency, where her work focuses on natural resources, environmental and climate change, risks and hazards, vulnerability and adaptation, and associated methodologies. Previously, Simonsson worked at the Swedish Emergency Management Authority, the Stockholm Environment Institute, and the Centre for Climate Science and Policy Research. Her fieldwork and research have been carried out in several least developed countries, as well as in the Nordic countries. Simonsson has published in the fields of risk perception, vulnerability to environmental and climate change, and participatory and interdisciplinary methodologies. Simonsson holds an M.Sc. in physical geography, a licentiate's degree in earth sciences, and a Ph.D. in environmental analysis, all from Uppsala University.

Aïda Tamer-Chammas is a Ph.D. candidate at the School of Oriental and African Studies (SOAS), University of London, where her thesis focuses on accountability under international law for environmental damage arising from armed conflict. Her research interests include humanitarian law and international environmental law. After graduating, in 1986, from Pantheon-Assas Paris II University, Tamer-Chammas studied international law and economics at the Fletcher School of Law and Diplomacy, Tufts University. From 1988 to 1995, she practiced as a corporate and finance lawyer in Paris; during that time, she participated in a one-year project funded by the World Bank, in which she served as part of a team that advised the government of Lebanon on the restructuring of its telecommunications sector. In 1999, she obtained an LL.M. in international environmental law from SOAS.

Peter Tarr is the executive director of the Southern African Institute for Environmental Assessment. He has more than twenty years of experience, first as a conservationist and later as an environmentalist focused on environmental assessment. He previously served as a senior official in the Namibian government, where he oversaw the development of environmental assessment legislation and a national environmental assessment policy. He has conducted, guided, and reviewed more than eighty environmental impact assessments, strategic environmental assessments, and environmental management plans for development initiatives in various sectors throughout sub-Saharan Africa. He is involved in a number of capacity-building initiatives, conducts training-needs assessments, and develops and delivers a variety of training courses throughout the region. Tarr has a Ph.D. in environmental management and planning from the University of Aberdeen.

Muralee Thummarukudy is chief of disaster risk reduction at the United Nations Environment Programme (UNEP). Before joining UNEP, he was a corporate environmental advisor at Petroleum Development Oman and head of environmental studies at Brunei Shell Petroleum Company. Thummarukudy has more than twenty years' experience in environmental assessment and cleanup, emergency response, and contaminated site management. He has led international multidisciplinary project teams undertaking assessments in the wake of many major conflicts and disasters of the twenty-first century, including those in Iraq and in the occupied Palestinian territories. He holds a Ph.D. in engineering from the Indian Institute of Technology.

Juha I. Uitto is deputy director of the Evaluation Office of the United Nations Development Programme (UNDP), where he has managed several programmatic and thematic evaluations at the country and regional levels, as well as global evaluations focused on UNDP's contributions in the areas of environmental management, energy, and poverty-environment linkages. Before joining UNDP, Uitto worked at the Global Environment Facility and as a researcher and consultant in international development; he was also on the faculty of the United Nations University for nine years. A geographer by training, Uitto holds an M.Sc. from the University of Helsinki, and a Ph.D. in social and economic geography from the University of Lund, in Sweden.

Jon Unruh is an associate professor in the Department of Geography at McGill University. Since the early 1990s, his research and policy work have focused on post-conflict land tenure in the developing world. His work focuses on conflict resolution, land law and policy, legal pluralism, approaches to reconciling customary and formal land tenure systems, and agriculture in post-war and peacebuilding contexts. Unruh's research and policy experience includes work in Cameroon, Central America, Ethiopia, Liberia, Madagascar, Mozambique, Peru, Sierra Leone, Somalia, Timor-Leste, Uganda, Zambia, and Zanzibar. He is a series editor of the six-book series on Post-Conflict Peacebuilding and Natural Resource Management (Earthscan, 2012–2013) and coauthor of *Post-Conflict Peacebuilding and Natural Resources: The Promise and the Peril* (with Carl Bruch, David Jensen, and Mikiyasu Nakayama) (Cambridge University Press, forthcoming).

Unruh holds a bachelors degree in environmental studies from the University of Kansas–Lawrence, a masters degree in environmental studies from the University of Wisconsin–Madison, and a doctorate in geography and rural development from the University of Arizona.

Annica Waleij is a senior analyst and project manager at the Swedish Defence Research Agency. Her work includes the provision of environmental intelligence support to the Swedish Armed Forces and environmental expertise to Swedish peace and crisis-management operations in a number of locations, including Afghanistan, Africa, and the Balkans. Waleij also participates in the design and implementation of environmental awareness training for military and civilian deploying organizations; provides expert support to the United Nations Department of Field Support; and represents Sweden on the Science for Peace and Security Programme of the North Atlantic Treaty Organization. Waleij holds a B.Sc. in environmental health and a M.Sc. in environmental chemistry, both from Umeå University, in Sweden.

Jennifer Wallace is a Ph.D. candidate in the Department of Government and Politics at the University of Maryland and an affiliate of the Harrison Program on the Future Global Agenda. Her research interests focus primarily on environmental linkages to conflict, with particular attention to natural resource management and environmental degradation. Wallace previously worked in Switzerland as a training course coordinator at the Geneva Centre for Security Policy, part of Switzerland's contribution to the Partnership for Peace, a program of bilateral cooperation between individual partner countries and the North Atlantic Treaty Organization. She holds a B.A. from Sarah Lawrence College, a Certificate of Advanced Studies in Environmental Diplomacy from the University of Geneva, and an M.A. in political science from the Graduate Institute of International and Development Studies, in Geneva.

Inka Weissbecker works for the International Medical Corps as a global mental health and psychosocial advisor. She has represented the International Union of Psychological Science at the United Nations Economic and Social Council and the United Nations Department of Public Information, and has served on the NGO Committee on Mental Health in New York. Weissbecker has published several peer-reviewed manuscripts and has been involved in research and mental health projects in Afghanistan, Belize, Gaza, Libya, Sierra Leone, and Tanzania. She holds an M.P.H. from the Harvard School of Public Health, with an emphasis on global health and humanitarian studies, and a Ph.D. in clinical psychology from the University of Louisville. She completed her clinical psychology internship, with a focus on public policy, at the University of South Florida.

Ross Wolfarth is a law student at Columbia University. In 2008, he served as a research intern at the Environmental Law Institute, where he focused on post-conflict natural resource management. He holds a B.A. in history from Amherst College.

APPENDIX 3
Table of contents for *Post-Conflict Peacebuilding and Natural Resource Management*

This book is one of a set of six edited books on post-conflict peacebuilding and natural resource management, all published by Earthscan. Following is the table of contents for the full set. Titles and authors are subject to change.

HIGH-VALUE NATURAL RESOURCES AND POST-CONFLICT PEACEBUILDING
Edited by Päivi Lujala and Siri Aas Rustad

Foreword
Ellen Johnson Sirleaf

High-value natural resources: A blessing or a curse for peace?
Päivi Lujala and Siri Aas Rustad

Part 1: Extraction and extractive industries

Introduction

Bankrupting peace spoilers: Can peacekeepers curtail belligerents' access to resource revenues?
Philippe Le Billon

Mitigating risks and realizing opportunities: Environmental and social standards for foreign direct investment in high-value natural resources
Jill Shankleman

Contract renegotiation and asset recovery in post-conflict settings
Philippe Le Billon

Reopening and developing mines in post-conflict settings: The challenge of company-community relations
Volker Boege and Daniel M. Franks

Diamonds in war, diamonds for peace: Diamond sector management and kimberlite mining in Sierra Leone
Kazumi Kawamoto

Assigned corporate social responsibility in a rentier state: The case of Angola
Arne Wiig and Ivar Kolstad

Part 2: Commodity and revenue tracking

Introduction

The Kimberley Process at ten: Reflections on a decade of efforts to end the trade in conflict diamonds
J. Andrew Grant

The Kimberley Process Certification Scheme: A model negotiation?
Clive Wright

The Kimberley Process Certification Scheme: The primary safeguard for the diamond industry
Andrew Bone

A more formal engagement: A constructive critique of certification as a means of preventing conflict and building peace
Harrison Mitchell

Addressing the roots of Liberia's conflict through the Extractive Industries Transparency Initiative
Eddie Rich and T. Negbalee Warner

Excluding illegal timber and improving forest governance: The European Union's Forest Law Enforcement, Governance and Trade Initiative
Duncan Brack

Part 3: Revenue distribution

Introduction

Sharing natural resource wealth during war-to-peace transitions
Achim Wennmann

Horizontal inequality, decentralizing the distribution of natural resource revenues, and peace
Michael L. Ross, Päivi Lujala, and Siri Aas Rustad

The Diamond Area Community Development Fund: Micropolitics and community-led development in post-war Sierra Leone
Roy Maconachie

Direct distribution of natural resource revenues as a policy for peacebuilding
Martin E. Sandbu

Part 4: Allocation and institution building

Introduction

High-value natural resources, development, and conflict: Channels of causation
Paul Collier and Anke Hoeffler

Petroleum blues: The political economy of resources and conflict in Chad
John A. Gould and Matthew S. Winters

Leveraging high-value natural resources to restore the rule of law: The role of the Liberia Forest Initiative in Liberia's transition to stability
Stephanie L. Altman, Sandra S. Nichols, and John T. Woods

Forest resources and peacebuilding: Preliminary lessons from Liberia and Sierra Leone
Michael D. Beevers

An inescapable curse? Resource management, violent conflict, and peacebuilding in the Niger Delta
Annegret Mähler

The legal framework for managing oil in post-conflict Iraq: A pattern of abuse and violence over natural resources
Mishkat Al Moumin

The capitalist civil peace: Some theory and empirical evidence
Indra de Soysa

Part 5: Livelihoods

Introduction

Counternarcotics efforts and Afghan poppy farmers: Finding the right approach
David M. Catarious Jr. and Alison Russell

The Janus nature of opium poppy: A view from the field
Adam Pain

Peace through sustainable forest management in Asia: The USAID Forest Conflict Initiative
Jennifer Wallace and Ken Conca

Women in the artisanal and small-scale mining sector of the Democratic Republic of the Congo
Karen Hayes and Rachel Perks

Forest user groups and peacebuilding in Nepal
Tina Sanio and Binod Chapagain

Lurking beneath the surface: Oil, environmental degradation, and armed conflict in Sudan
Luke A. Patey

Part 6: Lessons learned

Building or spoiling peace? Lessons from the management of high-value natural resources
Siri Aas Rustad, Päivi Lujala, and Philippe Le Billon

LAND AND POST-CONFLICT PEACEBUILDING
Edited by Jon Unruh and Rhodri C. Williams

Foreword
Jeffrey D. Sachs

Land: A foundation for peacebuilding
Jon Unruh and Rhodri C. Williams

Part 1: Peace negotiations

Introduction

The Abyei territorial dispute between North and South Sudan: Why has its resolution proven difficult?
Salman M. A. Salman

Land tenure and peace negotiations in Mindanao, Philippines
Yuri Oki

Part 2: Response to displacement and dispossession

Introduction

The role of restitution in post-conflict situations
Barbara McCallin

Land issues in post-conflict return and recovery
Samir Elhawary and Sara Pantuliano

Return of land in post-conflict Rwanda: International standards, improvisation, and the role of international humanitarian organizations
John W. Bruce

Post-conflict land tenure issues in Bosnia: Privatization and the politics of reintegrating the displaced
Rhodri C. Williams

Angola: Land resources and conflict
Allan Cain

Refugees and legal reform in Iraq: The Iraqi Civil Code, international standards for the treatment of displaced persons, and the art of attainable solutions
Dan E. Stigall

Part 3: Land management

Introduction

Snow leopards and cadastres: Rare sightings in post-conflict Afghanistan
Douglas E. Batson

Community documentation of land tenure and its contribution to state building in Afghanistan
J. D. Stanfield, Jennifer Brick Murtazashvili, M. Y. Safar, and Akram Salam

Title wave: Land tenure and peacebuilding in Aceh
Arthur Green

Beyond land redistribution: Lessons learned from El Salvador's unfulfilled agrarian revolution
Alexandre Corriveau-Bourque

Institutional aspects of resolving land disputes in post-conflict societies
Peter Van der Auweraert

Rebuilding peace: Land and water management in the Kurdistan Region of northern Iraq
Nesreen Barwari

Transboundary resource management strategies in the Pamir mountain region of Tajikistan
Ian D. Hannam

Part 4: Laws and policies

Introduction

Title through possession or position? Respect for housing, land, and property rights in Cambodia
Rhodri C. Williams

Land conflicts and land registration in Cambodia
Manami Sekiguchi and Naomi Hatsukano

Legal frameworks and land issues in Muslim Mindanao
Paula Defensor Knack

Unexplored dimensions: Islamic land systems in Afghanistan, Indonesia, Iraq, and Somalia
Siraj Sait

Customary law and community-based natural resource management in post-conflict Timor-Leste
Naori Miyazawa

Part 5: Lessons learned

Lesson learned in land tenure and natural resource management in post-conflict societies
Jon Unruh and Rhodri C. Williams

WATER AND POST-CONFLICT PEACEBUILDING
Edited by Erika Weinthal, Jessica Troell, and Mikiyasu Nakayama

Foreword
Mikhail Gorbachev

Shoring up peace: Water and post-conflict peacebuilding
Jessica Troell and Erika Weinthal

Part 1: Basic services and human security

Introduction

The role of informal service providers in post-conflict reconstruction and state building
Jeremy Allouche

A tale of two cities: Restoring water services in Kabul and Monrovia
Jean-François Pinera and Robert Reed

Conflict and collaboration for water resources in Angola's post-war cities
Allan Cain and Martin Mulenga

Thirsty for peace: The water sector in South Sudan
Sam Huston

Community water management: Experiences from the Democratic Republic of the Congo, Afghanistan, and Liberia
Murray Burt and Bilha Joy Keiru

Environmental management of the Iraqi marshlands in the post-conflict period
Chizuru Aoki, Sivapragasam Kugaprasatham, and Ali Al-Lami

Part 2: Livelihoods

Introduction

Lessons of water resource management from perspectives of irrigation water-use management and flood control: A case study of Japan after World War II
Mikiko Sugiura, Yuka Toguchi, and Mona Funiciello

Refugee rehabilitation and transboundary cooperation: India, Pakistan, and the Indus River system
Neda A. Zawahri

Despite the best intentions? The political ecology of water resource management in northern Afghanistan
Jennifer McCarthy and Daanish Mustafa

Water's role in security and stabilization in Helmand Province, Afghanistan
Laura Jean Palmer-Moloney

Part 3: Peace processes, cooperation, and confidence building

Introduction

The Jordan River Basin: A conflict like no other
Munther J. Haddadin

Transboundary cooperation in the Lower Jordan River Basin
Munqeth Mehyar, Nader Khateeb, Gidon Bromberg, and Elizabeth Ya'ari

The Sava River: Transitioning to peace in the former Yugoslavia
Amar Čolakhodžić, Marija Filipović, Jana Kovandžić, and Stephen Stec

Transnational cooperation over shared water resources in the South Caucasus: Reflections on USAID interventions
Marina Vardanyan and Richard Volk

Water security and scarcity: Potential destabilization in western Afghanistan and Iranian Sistan and Baluchestan due to transboundary water conflicts
Alex Dehgan, Laura Jean Palmer-Moloney, and Mehdi Mirzaee

484   Assessing and restoring natural resources in post-conflict peacebuilding

Water resources in the Sudan North-South peace process and the ramifications of the secession of South Sudan
Salman M. A. Salman

Part 4: Legal frameworks

Introduction

Management of waters in post-Dayton Bosnia and Herzegovina: Policy, legal, and institutional aspects
Slavko Bogdanovic

The right to water and sanitation in post-conflict legal mechanisms: An emerging regime?
Mara Tignino

Part 5: Lessons learned

Harnessing water management for more effective peacebuilding: Lessons learned
Jessica Troell and Erika Weinthal

LIVELIHOODS, NATURAL RESOURCES, AND POST-CONFLICT PEACEBUILDING
Edited by Helen Young and Lisa Goldman

Foreword
Jan Egeland

Managing natural resources for livelihoods: Helping post-conflict communities survive and thrive
Helen Young and Lisa Goldman

Part 1: Natural resource conflicts, livelihoods, and peacebuilding approaches

Introduction

Social identity, natural resources, and peacebuilding
Arthur Green

Swords into ploughshares? Access to natural resources and securing agricultural livelihoods in rural Afghanistan
Alan Roe

Forest resources in Cambodia's transition to peace: Lessons for peacebuilding
Srey Chanthy and Jim Schweithelm

Post-tsunami Aceh: Successful peacemaking, uncertain peacebuilding
Michael Renner

Manufacturing peace in "no man's land": Livestock and access to resources in the Karimojong Cluster of Kenya and Uganda
Jeremy Lind

Resolving natural resource conflicts to help prevent war: A case from Afghanistan
Liz Alden Wily

Part 2: Innovative livelihoods approaches in post-conflict settings

Introduction

The opportunities and challenges of protected areas for post-conflict peacebuilding
Carol Westrik

A peace park in the Balkans: Cross-border cooperation and livelihood creation through coordinated environmental conservation
J. Todd Walters

Mountain gorilla ecotourism: Supporting macroeconomic growth and providing local livelihoods
Miko Maekawa, Annette Lanjouw, Eugène Rutagarama, and Doug Sharp

The interface between natural resources and disarmament, demobilization, and reintegration: Enhancing human security in post-conflict settings
Glaucia Boyer and Adrienne Stork

Demobilized combatants as park rangers: Post-conflict natural resource management in Gorongosa National Park
Matthew Pritchard

Utilizing alternative livelihood schemes to solve conflict problems in Sierra Leone's artisanal diamond mining industry
Andrew Keili and Bocar Thiam

Linking to peace: Using BioTrade for biodiversity conservation and peacebuilding in Colombia
Lorena Jaramillo Castro and Adrienne Stork

Part 3: The institutional and policy context

Introduction

Fisheries policies and the problem of instituting sustainable management: The case of occupied Japan
Harry N. Scheiber and Benjamin Jones

Developing capacity for natural resource management in Afghanistan: Process, challenges, and lessons learned by UNEP
Belinda Bowling and Asif Zaidi

Building resilience in rural livelihood systems as an investment in conflict prevention
Blake Ratner

Improving natural resource governance and building peace and stability in Mindanao, Philippines
Cynthia Brady, Oliver Agoncillo, Maria Zita Butardo-Toribio, Buenaventura Dolom, and Casimiro V. Olvida

Commerce in the chaos: Charcoal, bananas, fisheries, and conflict in Somalia
Christian Webersik and Alec Crawford

Part 4: Lessons learned

Managing natural resources for livelihoods in post-conflict societies: Lessons learned
Lisa Goldman and Helen Young

ASSESSING AND RESTORING NATURAL RESOURCES IN POST-CONFLICT PEACEBUILDING
Edited by David Jensen and Steve Lonergan

Foreword
Klaus Töpfer

Placing environment and natural resource risks, impacts, and opportunities on the post-conflict peacebuilding agenda
David Jensen and Steve Lonergan

Part 1: Post-conflict environmental assessments

Introduction

Evaluating the impact of UNEP's post-conflict environmental assessments
David Jensen

Environment and peacebuilding in war-torn societies: Lessons from the UN Environment Programme's experience with post-conflict assessment
Ken Conca and Jennifer Wallace

Medical and environmental intelligence in peace and crisis-management operations
Birgitta Liljedahl, Annica Waleij, Björn Sandström, and Louise Simonsson

Thinking back-end: Improving post-conflict analysis through consulting, adapting to change, and scenario building
Alexander Carius and Achim Maas

Part 2: Remediation of environmental hot spots

Introduction

Salting the Earth: Environmental health challenges in post-conflict reconstruction
Chad Briggs and Inka Weissbecker

Remediation of polluted sites in the Balkans, Iraq, and Sierra Leone
Muralee Thummarukudy, Oli Brown, and Hannah Moosa

The risks of depleted uranium contamination in post-conflict countries: Findings and lessons learned from UNEP field assessments
Mario Burger

Linking demining to post-conflict peacebuilding: A case study of Cambodia
Nao Shimoyachi-Yuzawa

Part 3: Restoration of natural resources and ecosystems

Introduction

Restoration of damaged land in societies recovering from conflict: The case of Lebanon
Aïda Tamer-Chammas

Ecological restoration and peacebuilding: The case of the Iraqi marshes
Steve Lonergan

Haiti: Lessons learned and way forward in natural resource management projects
Lucile Gingembre

Peacebuilding and adaptation to climate change
Richard Matthew and Anne Hammill

Part 4: Environmental dimensions of infrastructure and reconstruction

Introduction

Addressing infrastructure needs in post-conflict reconstruction: An introduction to alternative planning approaches
P. B. Anand

Mitigating the environmental impacts of post-conflict assistance: Assessing USAID's approach
Charles Kelly

Challenges and opportunities for mainstreaming environmental assessment tools in post-conflict settings
George Bouma

Environmental assessment as a tool for peacebuilding and development: Initial lessons from capacity building in Sierra Leone
Oli Brown, Morgan Hauptfleisch, Haddijatou Jallow, and Peter Tarr

Natural resources, post-conflict reconstruction, and regional integration: Lessons from the Marshall Plan and other reconstruction efforts
Carl Bruch, Ross Wolfarth, and Vladislav Michalcik

Making best use of domestic energy sources: The Priority Production System for coal mining and steel production in post–World War II Japan
Mikiyasu Nakayama

Road infrastructure reconstruction as a peacebuilding priority in Afghanistan: Negative implications for land rights
Jon Unruh and Mourad Shalaby

Evaluating post-conflict assistance
Suppiramaniam Nanthikesan and Juha I. Uitto

Part 5: Lessons learned

Natural resources and post-conflict assessment, remediation, restoration, and reconstruction: Lessons and emerging issues
David Jensen and Steve Lonergan

GOVERNANCE, NATURAL RESOURCES, AND POST-CONFLICT PEACEBUILDING
Edited by Carl Bruch, Carroll Muffett, and Sandra S. Nichols

Foreword
Óscar Arias Sánchez

Natural resources and post-conflict governance: Building a sustainable peace
Carl Bruch, Carroll Muffett, and Sandra S. Nichols

Part 1: Frameworks for peace

Introduction

Reducing the risk of conflict recurrence: The relevance of natural resource management
Christian Webersik and Marc Levy

Stepping stones to peace? Natural resource provisions in peace agreements
Simon J. A. Mason, Damiano A. Sguaitamatti, and Pilar Ramirez Gröbli

Considerations for determining when to include natural resources in peace agreements ending internal armed conflicts
Marcia A. Dawes

Peacebuilding through natural resource management: The UN Peacebuilding Commission's first five years
Matti Lehtonen

Preparing for peace: A case study of Darfur, Sudan
Margie Buchanan-Smith and Brendan Bromwich

Part 2: Peacekeepers, the military, and natural resources

Introduction

Environmental experiences and developments in United Nations peacekeeping operations
Sophie Ravier, Anne-Cécile Vialle, Russ Doran, and John Stokes

Crime, credibility, and effective peacekeeping: Lessons from the field
Annica Waleij

Environmental stewardship in peace operations: The role of the military
Annica Waleij, Timothy Bosetti, Russ Doran, and Birgitta Liljedahl

Taking the gun out of extraction: UN responses to the role of natural resources in conflicts
Mark B. Taylor and Mike Davis

Military-to-military cooperation on the environment and natural disasters: Engagement for peacebuilding
Geoffrey D. Dabelko and Will Rogers

Civil-military coordination and cooperation in peacebuilding and natural resource management: An enabling framework, challenges, and incremental progress
Melanne A. Civic

Part 3: Good governance

Introduction

Burma's ceasefire regime: Two decades of unaccountable natural resource exploitation
Kirk Talbott, Yuki Akimoto, and Katrina Cuskelly

Taming predatory elites in the Democratic Republic of the Congo: Regulation of property rights to adjust incentives and improve economic performance in the mining sector
Nicholas Garrett

Process and substance: Environmental law in post-conflict peacebuilding
Sandra S. Nichols and Mishkat Al Moumin

Post-conflict environmental governance: Lessons from Rwanda
Roy Brooke and Richard Matthew

Corruption and natural resources in post-conflict transition
Christine Cheng and Dominik Zaum

Stopping the plunder of natural resources to provide for a sustainable peace in Côte d'Ivoire
Michel Yoboue

Sartor resartus: Liberian concession reviews and the prospects for effective internationalized solutions
K. W. James Rochow

Social benefits in the Liberian forestry sector: An experiment in post-conflict institution building for resilience
John Waugh and James Murombedzi

Preventing violent conflict over natural resources: Lessons from an early action fund
Juan Dumas

Part 4: Local institutions and marginalized populations

Introduction

Legal pluralism in post-conflict environments: Problem or opportunity for natural resource management?
Ruth Meinzen-Dick and Rajendra Pradhan

The role of conservation in promoting sustainability and security in at-risk communities
Peter Zahler, David Wilkie, Michael Painter, and J. Carter Ingram

Integrating gender into post-conflict natural resource management
Njeri Karuru and Louise H. Yeung

Indigenous peoples, natural resources, and peacebuilding in Colombia
Juan Mayr Maldonado and Luisz Olmedo Martínez

Part 5: Transitional justice and accountability

Introduction

Building momentum and constituencies for peace: The role of natural resources in transitional justice and peacebuilding
Emily E. Harwell

Peace through justice: International tribunals and accountability for wartime environmental wrongs
Anne-Cécile Vialle, Carl Bruch, Reinhold Gallmetzer, and Akiva Fishman

Legal liability for environmental damage: The United Nations Compensation Commission and the 1990–1991 Gulf War
Cymie Payne

Reflections on the United Nations Compensation Commission experience
Lalanath de Silva

Part 6: Confidence building

Introduction

Environmental governance and peacebuilding in post-conflict Central America: Lessons from the Central American Commission for Environment and Development
Matthew Wilburn King, Marco Antonio González Pastora, Mauricio Castro Salazar, and Carlos Manuel Rodriguez

Promoting transboundary environmental cooperation in Central Asia: The Environment and Security Initiative in Kazakhstan and Kyrgyzstan
Saba Nordström

The Perú and Ecuador peace park: One decade after the peace settlement
Yolanda Kakabadse, Jorge Caillaux, and Juan Dumas

Transboundary collaboration in the Greater Virunga Landscape: From gorilla conservation to conflict-sensitive transboundary landscape management
Johannes Refisch and Johann Jenson

Part 7: Integration of natural resources into other post-conflict priorities

Introduction

Consolidating peace through the "Aceh Green" strategy
Sadaf Lakhani

Natural resource management and post-conflict settings: Programmatic evolution in a humanitarian and development agency
Jim Jarvie

Mainstreaming natural resources into post-conflict humanitarian and development action
Judy Oglethorpe, Anita Van Breda, Leah Kintner, Shubash Lohani, and Owen Williams

Using economic evaluation to integrate natural resource management into Rwanda's post-conflict poverty reduction strategy paper
Louise Wrist Sorensen

Mitigating natural resource conflicts through development projects: Lessons from World Bank experience in Nigeria
Sandra Ruckstuhl

Natural resources and peacebuilding: What role for the private sector?
Diana Klein and Ulrike Joras

Part 8: Lessons learned

Fueling conflict or facilitating peace: Lessons in post-conflict governance and natural resource management
Sandra S. Nichols, Carroll Muffett, and Carl Bruch

Index

abundance, 68
Abyei, Sudan, 4–5, 126–127
Aceh
  Free Aceh Movement, 301, 400
  Indian Ocean tsunami of 2004, 292, 397, 399–401
adaptation to change, 16, 101, 274–276
  anticipatory approaches to, 274
  continuum of, 275–276
  hybrid approaches to, 274–275
Additional Protocol I of the Geneva Conventions, 3–4
Afghanistan
  access to environmental information, 72–73
  Afghanistan National Development Strategy (ANDS), 29, 30, 58, 359–360
  Afghanistan National Solidarity Programme (ANSP), 432
  Afghanistan Stabilization Initiative, 299
  agriculture, 377, 381
  Bonn Agreement, 28
  capacity building, 30–31
  corruption, 380–381
  deforestation, 415
  donor-assistance database, 316–317, 440
  economic development, 75–76
  electricity, 291–292
  environmental governance, 77–79, 425
  environmental impact assessment (EIA), 299–301, 314, 316–317, 439, 440
  environmental impacts of conflict, 69
  environmental vulnerability assessment (EVA), 89
  health-peace initiatives, 128
  humanitarian projects, 322–323
  infrastructure repair programs, 287, 290–292, 314, 316–317, 373–383, 436–437
  land disputes, 287, 373–383, 417, 436–437
  land grabbing, 381–383, 417, 436–437
  landmines and IEDs, 378–381
  map, 6, 19, 65, 375, 377
  mineral resources, 381–382, 417
  official development assistance, 313n
  peacebuilding activities, 57
  pistachio wood harvesting, 72
  refugees and internally displaced persons, 380
  regional management approaches, 359–360
  road reconstruction, 373–383, 417, 436–437
  rural development projects, 432
  Taliban activity, 378–380, 382–383
  UNDP assessment of development result (ADR), 405
  UNEP post-conflict assessment, 15, 18, 20, 21*t*, 22, 28–32, 56, 64, 66*t*, 69, 72–73, 75–79, 420
  USAID involvement, 299–301, 306, 307
  water and sanitation, 72
An Agenda for Peace, 269
Agent Orange, 3, 109, 114–116

494 Index

Agent Orange Act of 1991, 115
agriculture, 401, 424
   Afghanistan, 377, 381
   climate change, 268
   environmental impact assessment, 441–443
   ethanol production, 334
   Haiti, 242
   Iraq, 238
   land. *See* land rights
   Lebanon, 122, 212–213
   Sierra Leone, 268, 328, 330, 334
   Uganda, 302–303
aid economy, 76
Albania, 7n
   access to environmental information, 73
   map, 65
   NGOs in, 73n
   UNEP post-conflict assessment, 64, 66*t*
Alliance for Progress, 353, 357
ammonia, 140–141
Anan, Kofi, xv
Anand, P. B., 285
Andean Common Market, 353–354, 356
annual radiation-exposure limit (ALI), 165
annual work plans, 312, 315, 320–321
anticipatory adaptation, 274–275
antipersonnel mines. *See* landmines
antitank mines, 192
Aoun, Michel, 204n
Arab-Israeli War of 1948, 204–205
Arafat, Yasser, 36, 205n
Arias Sánchez, Óscar, 348
Arisawa, Hiromi, 366
Aristide, Jean-Bertrand, 261
assessment of development results (ADR), 401–405
   Afghanistan, 405
   methods, 403
   Rwanda, 403–404
   triangulation, 403
   Uganda, 404–405
assessment of the post-conflict environment, 6–7, 15–16, 56–59, 219, 413–423, 450–451*t*
   actors and participation, 7, 20, 55, 57, 100–101
   adapting to change, 16, 101, 104–105

   baseline data, 209
   capacity building, 30–31, 58, 77–79, 147
   climate change, 418
   confidence building, 72–75
   consultation approaches, 16, 100–101, 105
   on environmental governance, 77–79, 413, 415–416
   on environmental impacts of conflict, 69–72
   environmental vulnerability assessment (EVA), 16, 85–96
   field sampling, 420
   financial resources, 54–55, 56, 413, 422
   gender-specific risks and impacts, 417
   impact analysis, 18, 22–24
   information exchange, 93–96
   infrastructure repair. *See* environmental impact assessment (EIA)
   institutional neutrality, 55
   limitations, 419
   national ownership, 55
   partnership approach, 419–421
   peacebuilding agendas, 57, 63–64
   on peacebuilding linkages, 79–81
   policy context of, 20–22, 421–422
   post-conflict economies in, 75–77, 411–412, 417
   priority setting, 411–412, 422
   relapse risk, 415–416
   role of uncertainty in, 418–419
   scenario-building approaches, 16, 101–105
   scope, 59
   success factors, 53–56
   timing, 7, 55–56
   types of assessment, 18–20, 21*t*, 54*t*
   UNEP assessment. *See* UNEP post-conflict assessment
   unintended consequences, 417
   use of outside capacity, 422–423
   See also evaluation of post-conflict interventions

backcasting, 103, 418–419, 429–430
Balkan region

Index   495

Joint UN-HABITAT Balkans Task Force, xv, xvi
regional management approaches, 344, 349–351, 356, 358
See also Albania; Bosnia and Herzegovina; Former Yugoslav Republic of Macedonia; Kosovo; Serbia and Montenegro/Federal Republic of Yugoslavia (FYR)
Ban Ki-Moon, xii, xvi, 64
Bannon, Ian, 290
Basel Convention on the Control of Transboundary Movements and Hazardous Waste and Their Disposal, 145, 156, 159, 425
basic services/restoration of, 2
Belgium, 343
Bijlsma, Martijn, 69
Bint Jbeil (Lebanon), 203
Biodiversity Support Program, 69
biological hazards, 87*t*
Bor (Serbia), 146–147
Bosnia and Herzegovina, 349
 access to environmental information, 73
 depleted uranium (DU), 69, 70, 73, 163
 map, 6, 65
 NATO bombings, 171
 UNEP post-conflict assessment, 64, 66*t*, 166, 170–171
Bouma, George, 286
Boustani, Emile, 205n
Boutros-Ghali, Boutros, 269
Briggs, Chad, 109
Brown, Oli, 109, 286
Bruch, Carl, 286–287
Burger, Mario, 109
Busan New Deal, 448, 449
Bush, George W., 343

calcium cyanide, 152
Cambodia
 Cambodia Mine/UXO Victim Information System, 184
 Cambodian Mine Action and Victim Assistance Authority (CMAA), 186, 187*f*, 189–191
 Cambodian Mine Action Center (CMAC), 186, 187*f*, 189–192
 community-based demining (CBD) programs, 192–194, 195
 demining and poverty reduction program, 185–190
 environmental governance, 77
 international assistance, 191–194
 Khmer Rouge, 182–183, 186
 landmines, 110, 181–195, 423, 428
 land rights, 186–188, 381, 382n, 428
 land use planning process, 189–190, 195
 map, 6
 peacekeeping missions, 4–5, 191
 unexploded ordnance (UXO) casualties, 184
 UN Transitional Authority, 186
Canadian International Development Agency, 430
capacity building, 444, 455*t*
 assessment of the post-conflict environment, 30–31, 58, 77–79, 147
 environmental governance, 30–31, 58, 77–79, 147, 160–161, 327–341, 415–416
 reconstruction of infrastructure, 327–341
 remediation of environmental hot spots, 160–161, 427
Carius, Alexander, 16
Central African Republic
 access to environmental information, 73
 map, 65
 UNEP post-conflict assessment, 64, 66*t*, 416, 421
Central American Commission on Environment and Development (CCAD), 344, 347–349, 356
Central American Integration System (SICA), 348–349
Central Marshes (Iraq), 223, 228
Central Treaty Organization (CENTO), 353, 355, 357
Chad, 89, 93
chain-of-custody systems, 426
chemical hazards, 87*t*, 424, 426
 defoliants, 3, 109, 114–116
 petrochemicals, 138–140, 150–151

Chile, 353–354
chlorophenyl mercury, 152
circlers, 394
Civilian Capacity in the Aftermath of Conflict, xii
claim holders, 390n
cleanup. *See* remediation of environmental hot spots
climate change, 272–274, 443
  adaptations, 101, 104, 274–280
  assessment of the post-conflict environment, 418
  drought, 229, 231
  Haiti, 430
  health care, 278
  infrastructure projects, 278
  Mesopotamian marshlands, 229, 231
  peacebuilding considerations of, 201, 202, 267–280
  population displacement, 268
  restoration of natural resources, 8, 101, 104, 201, 202, 229, 267–280, 430, 431
  Sierra Leone, 202, 268
  transition to sustainable development, 268, 269
cluster bombs
  Iraq, 119
  Lebanon, 122, 201, 211–212
  UN Convention on Cluster Munitions, 123
Colombia
  Andean Common Market, 353–354
  Contadora peace process, 348
  map, 6
common country assessment (CCA), 22, 58
Common Humanitarian Fund, 50, 321, 440
Community Assistance for Reconstruction, Development, and Stabilisation (CARDS), 350–351, 357
community-based demining (CBD), 193–194, 195
community-based natural resources management (CBNRM), 78–79, 432
compensation for environmental damage, 4

comprehensive assessment, 18, 20, 48–50, 53, 54*t*, 55, 59
Conca, Ken, 15, 68
confidence-building potential, 72–75
  access to environmental information, 72–73
  neutral knowledge brokers, 74–75
conflict diamonds, 4n, 5, 49, 76–77, 329
  definition, 271n
  Extractive Industries Transparency Initiative (EITI), 5, 441–442
conflict economies, 1, 76–77, 415
conflict resources, 4–5, 76–77, 402, 414–415
  Liberia, 40, 41–42
  Sierra Leone, 271–272, 329–330
conflict sensitivity, 447, 455*t*, 456–457
consolidated appeal process (CAP), 21, 448
consultation, 16, 100–101, 105
Contadora peace process, 348
Convention on Biological Diversity, 236
Convention on Cluster Munitions, 123
Convention on the Law of Non-Navigational Uses of International Watercourses, 236
Convention on the Prohibition of Military or Any Other Hostile Use of Environmental Modification Techniques (ENMOD), 3, 112
Convention on the Prohibition of the Use, Stockpiling, Production and Transfer of Anti-Personnel Mines and on Their Destruction, 119, 181–185, 191
Convention on Wetlands of International Importance (Ramsar Convention), 229n, 236, 237
coordination of intervention, 447–449
Costa Rica, 347–349
Côte d'Ivoire, 4n
criminal economies, 415, 417
crisis-management operations. *See* peacekeeping missions
Croatia, 349, 350–351
Crum, James, 289–290

Dabelko, Geoffrey D., 68
damage to natural resources. *See* environmental impacts of conflict

Darfur, 48, 125
  civil war, 125, 126
  environmental governance, 78
  environmental impact assessment, 320–321, 440
  environmental vulnerability assessment (EVA), 89, 93
  human displacement, 69, 126, 323
  UN and Partners Work Plan, 320–321, 323
  water and sanitation, 320–321, 440
defoliants, 3, 109, 114–116
deforestation, 70
degradation. *See* environmental impacts of conflict
Delesgues, Lorenzo, 378
demand-driven planning, 293
demining machines, 192
Democratic Republic of the Congo
  climate change, 202, 280
  economic development, 75
  health-peace initiatives, 128
  map, 65
  natural resource governance, 4–5
  UNEP post-conflict assessment, 64, 66*t*, 67n, 416
  Virunga National Park resettlement, 279
depleted uranium (DU), 73, 109, 118–119, 163–178, 414, 427–428
  Bosnia and Herzegovina, 69, 70, 73, 163, 170–171
  contamination rates, 175–177
  degradation, 171
  drinking water supplies, 171, 176, 178
  health impacts, 164–166
  Iraq, 163, 172–175
  Kosovo, 69, 70, 73, 163, 167–168
  Lebanon, 70
  radioactivity level, 163
  recommendations, 177–178
  safety precautions, 174–176
  sampling procedures, 167n, 171n, 172–173
  Serbia and Montenegro, 70, 73, 163, 168–170
  uses, 163–164, 171n
Desert Storm. *See* Gulf War
desk studies, 18–19, 53, 54, 59, 147

destruction of natural resources. *See* environmental impacts of conflict
diamonds, 68
  as conflict resources, 4n, 5, 49, 76–77, 271n, 329
  Extractive Industries Transparency Initiative (EITI), 5, 441–442
  Kimberley Process, 5
  Liberia, 42
  Sierra Leone, 271–272, 328, 333–334
dioxin, 115, 116
  See also Agent Orange
dirty war index, 128
disability-adjusted life years (DALYs), 113
displaced persons camps, 323
Dodge, Joseph, 365
donor-assistance databases, 312, 315–317, 322–325
donors. *See* evaluation of post-conflict interventions
downward accountability, 398–399, 400, 406
duty bearers, 390n

East Timor. *See* Timor-Leste
Economic Cooperation Administration (ECA). *See* Marshall Plan
economic infrastructure (definition), 289
economic restoration, 2, 75–77
  aid economy, 76
  climate change, 267–280
  evaluation and monitoring phase, 389
  neoliberal (free-market) reforms, 75, 120n
  post-conflict assessment, 411–412, 417
  regional economic integration, 444–445
  sustainable development, 75n
ecosystem services, 273n
Effects of Environmental Conditions on Soldiers project, 94–95
EIA. *See* environmental impact assessment (EIA)
electricity infrastructure, 289, 290, 434
El Salvador
  health-peace initiatives, 128
  regional integration, 347–349

498 Index

Energy Community of south East Europe (ECSEE), 351
energy infrastructure reconstruction, 214–215, 289, 290, 434
ENMOD (Convention on the Prohibition of Military or Any Other Hostile Use of Environmental Modification Techniques), 3, 112
environmental assessment. *See* assessment of the post-conflict environment; environmental impact assessment (EIA)
Environmental Foundation of Africa, 73
environmental governance, 1–9, 401–402, 411–413, 449, 456–457
   capacity building, 30–31, 58, 77–79, 147, 160–161, 327–341, 415–416
   community-based natural resource management, 78–79
   environmental impact assessment, 340, 441–443
   infrastructure repair. *See* reconstruction of infrastructure
   link with economic development, 75–77
   peacebuilding, 1–9, 129, 331–341
   peacekeeping missions, 4–5
   post-conflict environmental assessment. *See* assessment of the post-conflict environment
   regional management approaches, 343–360
   restoration of natural resources. *See* restoration of natural resources and ecosystems
   sanctions, 5
   shared challenges and social capital, 64, 68–69
environmental health hazards. *See* health hazards
environmental impact assessment (EIA), 8, 285–286, 297–308, 328n, 339, 437–439
   Afghanistan, 299–301, 314, 316–317, 322, 439
   compliance with local law, 306–307, 308
   Darfur/Sudan, 320–321, 323
   displaced persons camps, 323
   exclusions and exemptions, 298–299, 307
   extractive industries, 441–443
   governance and capacity building, 327–341
   Indonesia, 301–302
   Iraq, 317–320, 322
   linkage, 307–308
   local collaboration, 308
   monitoring and enforcement, 340, 441–443
   occupied Palestinian territories, 303–304
   official development assistance (ODA), 311–313, 324–325, 439–440
   project-specific assessment, 323–324
   raising awareness, 338–339
   Sierra Leone, 327–341, 442–443
   staffing challenges, 307
   stakeholder participation, 340, 442
   systematic screening approaches, 313–325
   timing, 306, 314
   training programs, 340
   Uganda, 302–303
   USAID review process, 285–286, 297–308, 437–439
   See also strategic environmental assessment (SEA)
environmental impacts of conflict, 1, 67–72, 111–112, 414–415, 416
   duration, 70
   impacts, 69–70
   indirect linkages, 70–72
   institutional effects, 71–72
   pre-conflict environment, 71
   as risk factor, 64
   unsustainable actions, 72
environmental peacemaking, 208
Environmental Protection Index, 335
environmental scarcity, 67–68
environmental vulnerability assessment (EVA), 16, 85–96
   content and format, 89–90, 91–92*t*
   implementation, 93
   purpose, 89
   quality of data scale, 89

sharing of information, 93–95
vulnerability estimates, 88, 93
Esquipulas II Accords, 348
ethanol, 334
Ethiopia
  environmental impact assessment, 314, 439
  official development assistance, 313n
ethnographic assessment, 398n
ethylene dichloride (EDC), 137–138, 140
Euphrates River, 223, 226, 228, 230, 236
European Coal and Steel Community (ECSC), 344, 346–347, 444
European Commission, 64
European Union (EU), xvi, 343, 344, 444–445
  Balkan regional integration, 349–351, 356
  membership, 357
  post-conflict needs assessment (PCNA), 21
  pre-membership programs, 350–351, 357–358
EVA. *See* environmental vulnerability assessment (EVA)
evaluation of post-conflict interventions, 287, 389–406, 445–447
  accountability, 398–399, 400, 406
  circler approaches, 394
  definition, 390
  framework approaches, 394
  impact evaluation, 393–394
  joint evaluation, 397, 401, 446
  national ownership and responsibility, 391–392
  project evaluation, 394–395
  quantitative *vs.* qualitative approaches, 392–394, 445–446
  real-time evaluation, 397–398
  role, 390
  sector-wide evaluation, 394–395, 447
  standards, 390–391
  sustainable development goals, 389
  thematic evaluation, 394–395, 401
  theory-based approaches, 395–397
  triangulation, 403, 406
  UNDP assessment of development results (ADR), 401–405, 446
  unintended consequences, 398–401, 406
  universal indicators, 396–397
explosive devises. *See* unexploded ordnance (UXO)
extractive industries. *See* Extractive Industries Transparency Initiative (EITI); oil, gas, and mining
Extractive Industries Project, 336
Extractive Industries Transparency Initiative (EITI), 5, 441–442

Fauna and Flora International, 40
Federal Republic of Yugoslavia (FYR). *See* Serbia and Montenegro/Federal Republic of Yugoslavia (FYR)
field sampling, 420
financial impact indicators, 18, 23, 53–54t, 55, 56
  Afghanistan, 31, 32t
  Federal Republic of Yugoslavia, 26, 27t
  Iraq, 38, 39t
  Lebanon, 46, 47f
  Liberia, 43, 44f
  occupied Palestinian territories, 34, 35t
  Sudan, 52t, 53
financing of conflict. *See* conflict resources
fisheries, 268, 328
flash appeal process, 21
Food and Agriculture Organization of the UN (FAO), 422–423
food insecurity, 112–113, 126
  Haiti, 256–257
  Iraq, 120
forestry, 70, 401
Former Yugoslav Republic of Macedonia, 7n, 349
  human displacement, 69–70
  map, 65
  pre-conflict environment, 71
  UNEP post-conflict assessment, 64, 66t
fragile states, 9, 313n, 448, 449, 457
frameworkers, 394
Free Aceh Movement (GAM), 301, 400
free-phase oil, 141–142
Fulbright, William, 356, 357
future-oriented assessment. *See* scenario building

future risk, 9
FYR. *See* Serbia and Montenegro/Federal Republic of Yugoslavia (FYR)

Gaza
 conflict of 2008–2009, 70, 72
 remediation of environmental hot spots, 425
 rubble removal, 426
 water and sanitation, 70, 424
 See also occupied Palestinian territories (oPt)
gender considerations, 417, 455*t*
Geneva International Centre for Humanitarian Demining (GICHD), 185
Georgia
 map, 65
 UNEP post-conflict assessment, 64, 66*t*
German Advisory Council on Global Climate Change, 273
Ghajar (Lebanon), 206
Gingembre, Lucile, 202
global warming. *See* climate change
Global Witness, 40
Gomes-Mugumya, Albert, 293–294
governance and institutions, 71, 415
 institutional infrastructure (definition), 289
 rebuilding, 2, 411
 reestablishment of, 2, 109
 See also environmental governance
Green Pot, 50, 321, 440
Guatemala
 map, 6
 regional integration, 347–349
Gulf War, 36, 116
 depleted uranium (DU), 118–119, 172
 draining of the Mesopotamian marshlands, 3–4, 201, 226
 oil spills and fires, 3, 117–118

Haavisto, Pekka, 25, 28, 36
 on knowledge controversies, 74
 on pre-conflict environment, 71
Hahn, Shelly, 290
Haiti
 agriculture, 242
 deforestation and erosion, 242–243
 earthquake of January 2010, 242, 244, 257, 259
 environmental vulnerability assessment (EVA), 89
 fisheries, 242–243
 food- and cash-for-work programs, 256–257
 food insecurity, 256–257
 forestry projects, 254–255
 fruit tree value chains, 255–256
 Haiti Regeneration Initiative, 202, 241, 246–264
 income generation programs, 254–258
 integrated large-scale rehabilitation projects, 249–250
 international funding, 261–262, 430
 landscape engineering rehabilitation projects, 247
 land tenure challenges, 253, 430
 local participation and empowerment, 250–254
 long-term approaches, 261–264
 map, 6, 65
 national-level capacity building, 258–260
 natural disasters, 242–244
 poverty and instability, 244–246, 259–260
 restoration of natural resources, 201–202, 241–264, 428, 430–431
 soil conservation projects, 255
 transboundary projects, 430
 UNEP post-conflict assessment, 64, 66*t*
 watershed-based rehabilitation projects, 248–249, 430–431
Hammar Marsh (Iraq), 223, 228, 238
Hammill, Anne, 202
Hariri, Rafik, 206
Hauptfleisch, Morgan, 286
Hawizeh Marsh (Iraq and Iran), 223, 228–229, 230, 238
hazardous waste, 7
 Basel Convention on, 145, 156, 159, 425
 life-cycle of, 158–159, 425–426
 transportation of, 145–146, 156, 159, 425–426
 See also hot spots

health hazards, 414–415, 449
　ammonia, 140–141
　calcium cyanide, 152
　chemical defoliants, 3, 109, 114–116
　chlorophenyl mercury, 152
　civilian morbidity and mortality rates, 109, 112–113, 126
　climate change, 278
　data collection, 128
　depleted uranium (DU), 69, 70, 73, 109, 118–119, 163–178, 427–428
　developmental abnormalities, 115, 118
　dirty war index, 128
　disability-adjusted life years (DALYs), 113
　environmental and industrial health hazards network, 94–95
　environmental hot spots. *See* hot spots
　ethylene dichloride, 137–138, 140
　fertilizers, 140–141
　food insecurity and malnutrition, 112–113, 120, 126
　heavy metals, 149
　hexavalent chromium salt, 152–153
　industrial waste, 136–147
　infectious disease, 126
　maternal health, 126
　oil spills and fire, 117–118, 139–143, 204, 209
　peacekeeping/unrelated to combat, 86, 87*t*
　pesticides, 150, 152
　petrochemicals, 138–140, 150–151
　polychlorinated biphenyls (PCBs), 143–145, 146
　polyvinylchloride, 140–141
　respiratory illness, 117–118
　scrapping activities, 151
　sewage, 143
　sodium cyanide, 149–150, 152
　sodium hydroxide, 152–153
　sulfur fires, 151
　tetraethyl lead (TEL), 153–156
　transportation of hazardous waste, 145–146, 156, 159
　unexploded ordnance (UXO), 110, 112, 115–117, 122, 125–126
　water and sanitation infrastructure, 70–72, 119–120, 125–126, 138–143, 424

heavy metals, 149
hexavalent chromium salt, 152–153
Hezbollah, 121–122, 203, 204–208, 216–217
　See also Lebanon
Hicks, Madelyn H., 128
high-value natural resources. *See* conflict resources; oil, gas, and mining
Honduras, 347–349
hot spots, 7, 105, 109–110, 414, 423
　definition, 109
　Iraq and Kuwait, 116–121, 147–153, 423, 426
　Lebanon, 69, 121–123
　occupied Palestinian territories, 71, 74
　remediation. *See* remediation of environmental hot spots
　Serbia, 135–147
　Sierra Leone, 153–156, 423
　Sudan, 123–127
　Viet Nam, 113–116
human displacement, 69–70, 414
　See also refugees and internally displaced persons
humanitarian assistance, 2
　environmental assessment, 21, 25, 37
　environmental impact assessment (EIA), 441
humanitarian law, xvi
　Additional Protocol I of the Geneva Conventions, 3–4
　Convention on the Prohibition of Military or Any Other Hostile Use of Environmental Modification Techniques (ENMOD), 3–4, 112
Hurricane Jeanne, 244
Hussein, Saddam, 201
　draining of the Mesopotamian marshes, 224–226, 228, 234
　regime fall of 2003, 235
　See also Iraq

immediate aftermath of conflict. *See* post-conflict period
impact evaluation, 393–394
　See also evaluation of post-conflict interventions
imposed strategic planning, 292

incremental infrastructure repair, 291–292
Indian Ocean tsunami of 2004, 292, 397, 399–401
Indonesia
  environmental impact assessment (EIA), 301–302
  Free Aceh Movement (GAM), 301, 400
  Indian Ocean tsunami of 2004, 292
  map, 6
  Tsunami Evaluation Coalition, 397, 399–401
  USAID involvement, 301–302, 306
infectious disease, 126
informal economies, 415, 417
information exchange, 1, 93–96
infrastructure
  definition, 289
  economic infrastructure (definition), 289
  electricity infrastructure, 289, 290, 434
  energy infrastructure, 214–215, 289, 290, 434
  institutional infrastructure (definition), 289
  repair. *See* reconstruction of infrastructure
  social infrastructure (definition), 289
  transportation infrastructure, 290, 373–383, 434
  water and sanitation infrastructure, 70–72, 119–120, 125–126, 138–143, 424
institutional infrastructure (definition), 289
institutions. *See* governance and institutions
Instrument for Pre-Accession Assistance (IPA), 350–351, 357
integrated mission planning, 448
intelligence assessment. *See* assessment of the post-conflict environment
Inter-American Development Bank, 430
International Atomic Energy Agency (IAEA), 166–167, 172, 175, 427
International Campaign to Ban Landmines (ICBL), 181
International Day for Preventing the Exploitation of the Environment in War and Armed Conflict, 4

international law
  Additional Protocol I of the Geneva Conventions, 3–4
  compensation for environmental damage, 4
  Convention on the Prohibition of Military or Any Other Hostile Use of Environmental Modification Techniques (ENMOD), 3–4, 112
International Monetary Fund, 22
International Union for the Conservation of Nature (IUCN), 40
investment. *See* economic restoration
ionizing radiation, 163
  See also depleted uranium (DU)
Iran
  Afghan refugees, 380
  Central Treaty Organization (CENTO), 353
  Hezbollah connections, 217
  Mesopotamian marshlands, 228–229, 230, 235–236, 238
  water use policies, 228
Iran-Iraq War, 36, 116, 224, 226
Iraq, 116–121
  access to environmental information, 73
  actors and participants, 36, 38–40
  Coalition Provisional Authority (CPA), 120
  depleted uranium (DU), 109, 118–119, 163
  donor-assistance database, 440
  environmental governance, 77, 147
  environmental health risks, 111
  environmental impact assessment (EIA), 317–320, 440
  environmental impacts of conflict, 69
  environmental relief, 37
  food insecurity, 120
  humanitarian projects, 21, 322–323
  infrastructure repair, 292, 436
  invasion of Kuwait, 4
  map, 6, 19, 65, 224–227, 232–234
  Mesopotamian marshlands, 3–4, 147, 201, 223–238, 419, 428–430
  official development assistance, 313n
  oil industry, 238

oil spills and fires, 3, 117–118
peacebuilding activities, 57
post-conflict assessment, 15, 19, 21–22, 36–40, 55, 56, 64, 66*t*, 147–149, 172–175, 292
pre-conflict environment, 71
Ramsar Convention, 229n, 236
remediation of environmental hot spots, 109, 118–121, 423, 426
restoration of natural resources and ecosystems, 223–238, 428–430
UNEP post-conflict assessment, 421
UNEP remediation projects, 147–153, 158–161, 426
unexploded ordnance (UXO), 117
UN multi-donor trust fund, 317–320, 322
wars and occupation, 3–4, 36, 116, 147, 172, 224–225
water and sanitation, 119–120, 226, 231, 235–236
Iraq Trust Fund, 317–320, 322
ISO/IEC 17025, 172n
Israel
  conflict with Lebanon. *See* Lebanon
  Gaza conflict of 2008–2009, 70, 72
  institutions and governance, 71
  knowledge controversies, 74
  settlements, 71
  See also occupied Palestinian territories (oPt)

Jallow, Haddijatou, 286
Janjaweed militias, 125
Japan
  coal and steel production, 363–371, 434
  economic inequality, 366
  employment policies, 367
  energy needs, 363, 364, 369
  heavy industry economy, 369
  inflation, 365–366
  infrastructure repair plan, 287, 354–355, 434
  map, 6
  Priority Production System, 287, 363–371, 434
  regional management approaches, 357

jatropha, 255
Jensen, David, 15
joint evaluation, 397, 398, 401, 446
Joint UNEP/UN-HABITAT Balkans Task Force, xv, xvi

Karzai, Hamid, 379
Kelly, Charles, 285–286
Kennedy, John F., 353
Khan Dhari petrochemical warehouses (Iraq), 150–151
Khmer Rouge, 182, 186
  See also Cambodia
Kimberley Process (KP), 5, 42
Kimura, Kihachiro, 366
Kissy Refinery (Sierra Leone), 153–156, 158
Klein, Naomi, 120n
Koroma, Ernest, 334, 339
Kosovo, 24–28, 135–136, 349n, 350
  depleted uranium (DU), 69, 70, 73, 163, 167–168
  map, 6, 65
  NATO bombing, 167
  UNEP post-conflict assessment, 65n, 66*t*, 136, 166–168
The Kosovo Conflict: Consequences for the Environment and Human Settlements, xv
Kragujevac industrial complex (Serbia), 143–146
Kreilkamp, Jacob, 269
Kuwait, 116–121
  depleted uranium (DU), 118–119
  environmental health risks, 111
  map, 6
  oil spills and fires, 117–118
  unexploded ordnance (UXO), 117
Kyoto Protocol, 348

land grabbing, 415, 428
  Afghanistan, 381–383, 417, 436–437
  definition, 415n
landmines, 70, 414
  Afghanistan, 380–381
  antitank mines, 192
  Cambodia, 110, 181–195, 381, 423, 428

community-based demining (CBD)
  programs, 192–194, 195
 death toll, 182n
 demining and poverty reduction
  programs, 185–190
 demining guidelines, 185
 demining machines, 192
 Information Management System for
  Mine Action, 185
 international assistance, 191–194
 Iraq, 117
 Lebanon, 122–123, 203–204, 211–212
 mine action programs, 182n
 Mine Ban Treaty, 119, 181–185, 191
 Sudan, 125
 Viet Nam, 115
land rights, 415
 Afghanistan's road repair program, 287,
  373–383, 417, 436–437
 Cambodia, 381, 382n, 428
 Haiti, 253, 430
 Lebanon, 436
 remediation of environmental hot spots,
  110, 428
 restoration of natural resources, 430
 Sierra Leone, 334
Laos, 185
Lebanon, 121–123
 access to environmental information,
  73
 agriculture, 122, 212–213
 civil society, 216–217
 civil war, 204n, 206, 211n
 conflicts with Israel, 43, 45, 70, 121–
  122, 201, 203–208, 210n
 demining programs, 203–204, 211–212
 depleted uranium (DU), 70
 environmental health risks, 111
 environmental vulnerability assessment
  (EVA), 89, 93
 green recovery plan, 214–215,
  446–447
 Hezbollah, 121–122, 203–208,
  216–217
 infrastructure rehabilitation, 209–210,
  213–215, 433
 international actors, 206, 217
 Jiyeh oil spill, 70, 74, 204, 209
 land tenure, 436
 Lebanon Mine Action Center (LMAC),
  211–212, 218
 map, 6, 19, 65, 205
 National Mine Action Policy, 122–123
 Palestinian refugees, 204n, 211n
 peacebuilding activities, 57, 207–208,
  215–217
 politics and governance, 215–216,
  217n, 218–219
 post-conflict assessment, 15, 18, 20,
  21t, 22, 43–46, 47f, 64, 66t, 208–
  209, 219
 remediation of environmental hot spots,
  122–123, 425
 restoration of natural resources and
  ecosystems, 201, 203–219, 428
 rubble removal, 210–211, 426
 toxic spills, 69
 unexploded ordnance (UXO), 70, 72,
  122, 201, 211–212, 218
 UN Interim Force in Lebanon
  (UNIFIL), 207, 212n
 water and sanitation, 70, 213–214, 215,
  433
Liberia
 access to environmental information,
  73
 cattle industry, 77
 civil wars, 40
 conflict resources, 40, 41–42
 environmental governance, 78
 Forestry Development Authority, 71
 institutions and governance, 71
 Kimberley Process, 42
 Lift Liberia plan, 42
 mangrove harvesting, 72
 map, 6, 19, 65
 natural resource governance, 4–5
 peacebuilding activities, 81
 pre-conflict environment, 71
 rubber industry, 77
 sustainable economic development,
  75–77
 UNEP post-conflict assessment, 15,
  18–22, 40–43, 55, 56, 58, 64, 66t
light-footprint approaches, 87–88
Liljedahl, Birgitta, 16

livelihood recovery, 8
logging industry, 70, 72, 401
Lomé Peace Accord, 330
Lonergan, Steve, 201
Long, Daniel, 289–290
Lopez, Alan D., 113
Lord's Resistance Army, 404
  See also Uganda

Maas, Achim, 16, 273
MacArthur, Douglas, 354, 365
Macedonia. *See* Former Yugoslav Republic of Macedonia
malnutrition, 112–113, 120
mangrove forests
  Haiti, 242–243
  Liberia, 72, 81
  Saudi Arabia, 117
  Viet Nam, 3, 115
market liberalization, 75, 120n
Marshall, George, 345, 355
Marshall Plan, 286–287, 343–347, 355–358
Mashatt, Merriam, 289–290
maternal health, 126
Matthew, Richard, 68, 202
McChrystal, Stanley, 380
McDonald, John, 353
McGray, Heather, 275–276
media campaigns, 159, 177, 424
media impact indicators, 18, 23, 53–54*t*, 59
  Afghanistan, 31, 32*t*
  Federal Republic of Yugoslavia, 26, 27*t*
  Iraq, 38, 39*t*
  Lebanon, 46, 47*f*
  Liberia, 43, 44*f*
  occupied Palestinian territories, 34, 35*t*
  Sudan, 52*t*, 53
medical intelligence. *See* environmental vulnerability assessment (EVA)
Mesopotamian marshlands, 3–4, 147, 201, 223–238, 419
  draining, 225, 226
  drought, 229, 231
  fragmentation, 228–229
  international and regional efforts, 225, 230–231, 235–236, 237

land and water use strategies, 231–232
map, 224–227, 232–234
population, 223, 226, 228
recommendations and future scenarios, 230–234
restoration, 227–230, 234–237, 428
salinity levels, 231
wildlife, 223
Michalcik, Vladislav, 286–287
Millennium Development Goals (MDGs), 185, 313, 318, 324
mine action programs, 182n
Mine Ban Treaty, 119, 181–185, 191
mines. *See* landmines
mining. *See* oil, gas, and mining
Mishraq sulfur mining complex (Iraq), 151
monitoring of post-conflict interventions, 290, 445–447
  See also evaluation of post-conflict interventions
Monnet, Jean, 346–347
Montenegro, 6, 24n, 349
  See also Serbia and Montenegro/ Federal Republic of Yugoslavia (FYR)
Moosa, Hannah, 109
morbidity and mortality rates, 109, 112–113, 126
multi-donor trust funds, 312, 315, 317–320, 322–325
Murray, Christopher J. L., 113

Nabatiye (Lebanon), 203, 212
Nakayama, Mikiyasu, 287
Nanthikesan, Suppiramaniam, 287
National Congress Party (Sudan), 123–124
National Development Strategy (NDS), 21–22, 37–38
National Security and the Threat of Climate Change, 273
NATO, 94–95
natural hazards. *See* climate change
natural resources, 8
  abundance *vs.* scarcity, 67–68
  conflict resources, 5, 40–42, 76–77, 271–272, 329–330, 402, 415

506 Index

definition, 2
financing of conflict, 4–5, 414
management. *See* environmental governance
relapse risk, 415–416
resource wealth, 68, 411–412
restoration. *See* restoration of natural resources and ecosystems
needs assessment. *See* desk studies; post-conflict needs assessment (PCNA); UNEP post-conflict assessment
Neufeldt, Reina, 394
Nicaragua, 347–349
nongovernmental organizations (NGOs), 64, 73n
Novi Sad oil refinery (Serbia), 141–143
nuclear hazards, 87*t*

occupied Palestinian territories (oPt)
   access to environmental information, 73
   environmental impact assessment, 303–304
   environmental impacts of conflict, 69
   infrastructure, 71
   institutions and governance, 71
   Israeli settlements, 71
   knowledge controversies, 74
   map, 6, 19, 65
   official development assistance (ODA), 313n
   peacebuilding activities, 57, 81
   pre-conflict environment, 71
   refugees, 204n
   toxic waste, 71, 74
   UNEP post-conflict assessment, 15, 18, 19, 21*t*, 22, 33–36, 56, 65, 66*t*
   USAID involvement, 303–304, 306
   See also Gaza
official development assistance (ODA), 311–313, 324–325, 439–440
oil, gas, and mining, 68–69, 457
   Afghanistan, 381–382
   artisanal mining, 334
   environmental impact assessment, 335–338, 441–443
   Extractive Industries Project, 336
   Extractive Industries Transparency Initiative, 5, 441–442

free-phase oil, 141–142
Gulf War oil well destruction, 3, 117–118
health hazards, 117–118, 139–143, 204, 209
Japan's coal and steel production, 363–371
Jiyeh oil spill (Lebanon), 70, 74, 204, 209
SADC's regional management approach, 352
Serbian oil refinery bombings, 139–143
Sierra Leone, 271–272, 286, 327–328, 331–334
Sudan and South Sudan, 124–125
sulfur fires, 151
operations security, 94n
Organisation for Economic Cooperation and Development (OECD), 343, 346
   on countries at risk, 9, 457
   SEA guidelines, 315
Oslo II agreements, 74

Pakistan
   Afghan refugees, 380
   regional integration programs, 353, 359
   Taliban land grabs, 383
Palestine Liberation Organization (PLO), 204–205
Palestinian Authority, 71
Palestinian territories. *See* Gaza; occupied Palestinian territories (oPt)
Pancevo industrial center (Serbia), 137–141, 157
parallel evaluation, 397
Paris, Roland, 67, 75
Paris Declaration on Aid Effectiveness, 314, 324, 391–392
participatory rural appraisal, 398n
peacebuilding, 57, 63–64, 79–81, 269–272, 374, 416, 443
   actors, 2
   adapting to change, 16, 101, 104–110
   capacity building, 30–31, 58, 77–79, 147, 160–161, 267, 288, 327–341
   climate change, 101, 104, 201, 202, 267–269, 272–280

Index 507

coordination of interventions, 447–449
environmental governance, 1–9, 129, 412–413
future outlook, 449, 456–457
infrastructure repair. *See* reconstruction of infrastructure
Lebanon, 207–208, 215–217
Marshall Plan models, 343–360
political governance, 218–219, 270, 277, 413
prioritization and sequencing, 271–272, 447–449, 450–455*t*
regional focus, 219
remediation of environmental hot spots. *See* remediation of environmental hot spots
restoration of natural resources. *See* restoration of natural resources and ecosystems
security concerns, 270–271, 277
shared challenges, 64, 68–69
Sierra Leone, 271–272, 330–331
social, economic, and environmental dimension, 218–219, 270, 278
sustainable development, 64, 75–77, 267, 389
terminology, 2, 64
truth and reconciliation, 101, 271, 277, 392, 418, 443, 455*t*
unintended consequences, 417
Peacebuilding Commission, xi–xii, xv, 64
peace consolidation period, 2, 411–413, 450–455*t*, 456
peace (definition), 64
peace-health initiatives, 128–129
peacekeeping missions
community impact, 86–87
definition, 269–270
environmental vulnerability assessment (EVA), 85–96
health risks unrelated to combat, 86, 87*t*
information exchange, 93–96
life-cycle of operations, 88*f*
light-footprint approaches, 87–88
natural resource governance, 4–5
peacemaking, 2, 208, 269
pesticides, 150, 152

petrochemicals, 138–140, 150–151
Pinochet, Augusto, 354
policy impact indicators, 18, 22–23, 53–54*t*, 56, 59
Afghanistan, 31, 32*t*
Federal Republic of Yugoslavia, 26, 27*t*
Iraq, 38, 39*t*
Lebanon, 46, 47*f*
Liberia, 43, 44*f*
occupied Palestinian territories, 34, 35*t*, 36
Sudan, 52*t*, 53
political processes. *See* governance and institutions
Pol Pot, 183, 193
polychlorinated biphenyls (PCBs), 143–145, 146
polyvinylchloride, 140–141
Post-Conflict and Disaster Management Branch (PCDMB), xv–xvi, 5, 64, 74–75
post-conflict environmental assessment. *See* assessment of the post-conflict environment; UNEP post-conflict assessment
post-conflict needs assessment (PCNA), 21, 36, 37, 54, 58, 414, 448
post-conflict period, 2
definition, 207
environmental assessment. *See* assessment of the post-conflict environment
environmental management. *See* environmental governance
immediate aftermath of conflict period, 2
infrastructure repair. *See* reconstruction of infrastructure
peace consolidation period, 2, 411–413, 450–455*t*, 456
See also peacebuilding
poverty reduction strategy paper (PRSP), 22
Priority Production System, 363–371, 434
program theory, 395–397
Progress Report of the Secretary General on Peacebuilding in the Immediate Aftermath of Conflict, 448–449

project evaluation, 394–395
public health. *See* health hazards

Qadissiya metal-plating facility (Iraq), 148–152, 426
qualitative evaluation, 392n, 394
  joint evaluation, 397, 398
  theory-based evaluation, 395–397
quantitative evaluation, 392n, 394
quantitative risk assessment, 18, 19–20, 53–56, 59
  Serbia and Montenegro, 25–28
Quireej military scrapyard (Iraq), 151–152

Rabin, Yitzak, 206n
radiological hazards, 87*t*
Ramsar Convention, 229n, 236, 237
rapid (ethnographic) assessment, 398n
rapid (health-care) evaluation, 398n
real-time evaluation, 397–398
reconciliation, 101, 271, 277, 392, 418, 443, 455*t*
reconstruction of infrastructure, 8–9, 285–288, 411–413, 433–443, 454–455*t*
  Afghanistan, 287, 290–292, 299–301, 314, 316–317, 373–383, 436–437
  bottom-up planning, 292–293
  capacity building, 327–341
  challenges, 290–291, 322–325, 435–436
  climate change, 278
  Darfur/Sudan, 320–321
  demand-based planning, 293
  energy infrastructure, 214–215, 289, 290, 434
  environmental impact assessment. *See* environmental impact assessment (EIA)
  European Union programs, 350–351
  evaluation methods, 287, 389–406
  financing and investment, 433–436
  health hazards. *See* health hazards
  incremental approaches, 291–292
  Indonesia, 301–302
  insurgent responses, 378–380
  Iraq, 292, 317–320
  Japan's coal and steel industry, 363–371, 434
  land- and property-rights systems, 287, 373–383, 436–437
  Lebanon, 209–210, 213–215, 433, 435–436
  occupied Palestinian territories, 303–304
  peacebuilding links, 287, 327–341
  planning approaches, 285, 289–295
  project selection, 435–436
  regional integration approaches, 286–287, 343–360
  regional management approaches, 343–360
  rights and security-based approaches, 293–294
  sanitation. *See* water and sanitation
  Sierra Leone, 286, 327–341
  strategic environmental assessment (SEA), 286, 313–325
  telecommunications systems, 290, 433–434
  tension triggers, 378
  top-down needs-based planning, 292, 314
  transportation infrastructure, 290, 373–383, 434
  Uganda, 301, 302–303
  unintended consequences, 436–437
  USAID's approach, 285–286, 297–308
  water. *See* water and sanitation
  Work Plan Projects Database, 320–321
refugees and internally displaced persons, 69–70, 414
  Afghanistan, 380
  camps, 323
  Darfur, 69, 126, 323
  environmental impact assessment, 323
  Former Yugoslav Republic of Macedonia, 69–70
  Palestinian refugees, 204n, 211n
  Rwanda, 274–275, 278, 279
  Sierra Leone, 69–70
  Viet Nam, 116
regional cooperation, 444–445
Regional Environmental and Natural Resources Management Project, 348

regional management approaches, 286–287, 343–360
  Afghanistan, 359–360
  Alliance for Progress, 353
  Andean Common Market, 353–354, 356
  Balkan region, 349–351, 356
  Central America, 347–349, 356
  Central Treaty Organization (CENTO), 353, 355
  donor commitment, 356–358
  identification of logical regions, 355–356
  Japan, 354–355, 357
  Marshall Plan, 343–347, 355–358
  political will, 356–357
  Southern Africa, 352
Regulation 216 (USAID), 298–299
rehabilitation of natural resources. *See* restoration of natural resources and ecosystems
relapse risk, 415–416
relief. *See* humanitarian assistance
remediation of environmental hot spots, 7, 109–110, 127–129, 413, 423–428, 451–452*t*
  Cambodia, 110, 181–195, 423
  capacity building, 160–161, 427
  data collection, 127–128
  Federal Republic of Yugoslavia, 135–147, 423, 424
  flexibility and contingency plans, 157–158, 427
  Gaza, 70, 72, 424, 425
  Iraq and Kuwait, 116–121, 147–153, 423, 426
  landmines and unexploded ordnance, 110, 115, 119, 181–195, 423
  land rights and use, 110, 428
  Lebanon, 122–123, 425
  life-cycle of hazardous waste, 158–159, 425–426
  local employment, 161, 427
  media campaigns, 159, 177, 424
  peacebuilding benefits, 109, 127–129
  prioritization, 158, 426–427
  scope of cleanup, 157
  secondary contamination sites, 425
  source-pathway-receptor approach, 426–427
  stakeholders and partners, 159–160, 427
  subsurface dump sites, 157–158
  Sudan, 126–127
  timing considerations, 156–157, 424
  UNEP projects. *See* UNEP remediation of environmental hot spots
  Viet Nam, 116
Report of the Secretary-General on Peacebuilding in the Immediate Aftermath of Conflict, xii, xvi, 64
Republic of Macedonia. *See* Former Yugoslav Republic of Macedonia
restoration of natural resources and ecosystems, 8, 201–202, 413, 427–433, 453–454*t*
  best practices, 246–247
  capacity building, 444
  climate change, 8, 101, 104, 201, 202, 229, 267–280, 430, 431
  feasibility, 430–431
  Haiti, 201–202, 241–264, 428, 430–431
  land tenure, 430
  Lebanon, 201, 203–219, 428
  local involvement, 202, 431–433
  Mesopotamian marshlands, 201, 223–238, 428–430
  metrics and evaluation, 429
  national frameworks, 432
  resilience of ecosystems, 201, 237
  Sierra Leone, 331–341
  timeframes, 429, 432, 433, 456
  transboundary management, 201, 430
results frameworks, 392n
Revolutionary United Front (RUF), 153–154, 329–330
Reydon, Bastiaan Philip, 378
Richmond, Oliver, 75
Ricigliano, Robert, 218
Rio Declaration on Environment and Development, 4
road reconstruction, 287, 373–383, 417, 436–437
Ross, Michael L., 68
rubble recycling, 210–211, 426

rural development projects, 432
Rwanda
  climate change, 202, 274–275, 278, 279, 280
  map, 6
  refugee resettlement, 274–275, 278, 279
  UNDP assessment of development results (ADR), 403–405, 446
  UNEP post-conflict assessment, 65, 66t, 67n

sanctions, 5
Sanderson, John, 186
San Francisco Peace Treaty of 1951, 363
sanitation. *See* water and sanitation
Sandström, Björn, 16
Sava River, 351
Save the Environment Afghanistan, 73
scarcity, 67–68
scenario building, 16, 101–105
  backcasting and pathway development, 103, 418–419, 429–430
  creative-narrative approach, 102
  definition, 102
  goals, 103–104
Schuman, Robert, 347
Schwartz, Jordan, 290
scrapping, 151
scratch sampling, 171n
SEA. *See* strategic environmental assessment (SEA)
secondary contamination sites, 425
sector-wide evaluation, 394–395, 447
security/establishment of, 2, 64
Serbia and Montenegro/Federal Republic of Yugoslavia (FYR), 6, 24n, 65
  access to environmental information, 73
  depleted uranium (DU), 70, 73, 163, 168–170
  environmental governance, 78
  humanitarian priorities, 21, 25, 26, 28
  map, 6, 19, 65
  NATO bombings, 24, 70, 137, 143, 146, 168
  peacebuilding activities, 57
  release of industrial chemicals, 72
  remediation of environmental hot spots, 78, 109, 136–147, 423, 424, 427
  UNEP post-conflict assessment, 15, 18, 20, 21, 24–28, 55, 65, 66t, 135–136, 166, 168–170
  UNEP remediation projects, 137–147, 161
  water and sanitation infrastructure, 138–143, 424
Shalaby, Mourad, 287
Sharon, Ariel, 36
Shatt al-Arab River, 223, 232
Shebaa Farms (Lebanon), 206
Shimoyachi-Yuzawa, Nao, 110
Sierra Leone
  access to environmental information, 73
  agriculture, 268, 328, 330, 334
  artisanal mining, 334
  civil war, 329–330
  climate change, 202, 268, 277, 280
  economic investment, 278, 332
  environmental impact assessment (EIA), 286, 327–341, 442–443
  environmental impacts of conflict, 70
  Extractive Industries Project, 336
  fisheries, 268, 328
  hot spot remediation, 109, 423
  human displacement, 69–70
  Lomé Peace Accord, 330
  map, 6, 65, 329
  minerals and mining sector, 271–272, 286, 327, 328, 331–334, 442–443
  natural resource governance, 4–5, 78, 331–341, 442–443
  peacebuilding, 271–272, 330–331
  peacekeeping missions, 4–5
  UNEP post-conflict assessment, 65, 66t, 330–331, 416, 421
  UNEP remediation projects, 153–160, 423
  water and sanitation, 330
Simonsson, Louise, 16
Sirleaf, Ellen Johnson, 42
Slovenia, 349, 350
smear sampling, 167n
Smith, Dan, 273–274, 279–380
social infrastructure (definition), 289

social relations
  access to environmental information, 72–73
  impact of environmental hot spots on, 109
  media campaigns, 159, 177, 424
  reconciliation, 101, 418, 443, 455*t*
  shared challenges of resource management, 64, 68–69
sodium cyanide, 149–150, 152
sodium hydroxide, 152–153
Somalia
  corruption, 380
  institutions and governance, 71
  map, 6, 65
  sustainable economic development, 76
  UNEP post-conflict assessment, 65, 66*t*
source-pathway-receptor approach, 426–427
Southern Africa Development Community (SADC), 352
South Lebanon. *See* Lebanon
South Sudan, 19, 65, 123–125
  border agreement, 127
  civilian morbidity and mortality rates, 126
  Comprehensive Peace Agreement, 48, 123–124, 126
  environmental governance, 78, 421
  independence, 127
  map, 6
  oil production, 124–125, 126
Spagat, Michael, 128
Sri Lanka, 400–401
stakeholders, 390n
strategic environmental assessment (SEA), 286, 311–325, 439–441
  accuracy and consistency challenges, 322
  donor-assistance databases, 316–317, 322–325
  entry points, 315
  OECD guidelines, 315
  Sierra Leone, 327–328, 336–337
  streamlined approach, 315
  UN and Partners Work Plans, 320–325
  UN multi-donor trust funds, 317–320, 322–325

strategic post-conflict assessment, 18, 20, 29, 53, 54*t*, 59
Sudan, 123–127
  civil wars, 48, 123–126
  Comprehensive Peace Agreement, 48, 123–124, 126
  Darfur region. *See* Darfur
  donor-assistance database, 440
  environmental governance, 79, 421
  environmental health risks, 111
  environmental impact assessment, 320–321, 322, 440
  Government of National Unity, 420–421
  map, 6, 19, 65
  natural resources, 123–126
  official development assistance, 313n
  oil production, 124–125, 126
  peacebuilding activities, 57, 81
  pre-conflict environment, 71
  remediation of environmental hot spots, 126
  southern Sudan. *See* South Sudan
  sustainable economic development, 76
  UN and Partners Work Plan, 320–321, 323
  UNDAF, 51–52, 58–59, 440
  UNEP post-conflict assessment, 15, 18–22, 46–56, 65, 66*t*, 419, 420–421
  unexploded ordnance (UXO), 125–126
  water controversies, 74, 125–126
Sudan People's Liberation Movement (SPLM), 48, 123–124, 126–127
  See also South Sudan
sulfur fires, 151
sustainable development, 75–77, 411–412
  climate change, 267–280
  definition, 75n
  evaluation and monitoring, 389
Suwaira pesticides warehouse complex, 150, 152, 426
Swedish Armed Forces and Defence Research Agency, 16, 85–96
Swedish Medical Intelligence Network, 88
Syria, 204n, 206, 209n, 226, 230, 235–236

Taliban. *See* Afghanistan
Tamer-Chammas, Aïda, 201
Tänzler, Dennis, 273
Tarr, Peter, 286
telecommunications systems, 290, 433–434
teratogens, 114
tetraethyl lead (TEL), 153–156
thematic evaluation, 394–395, 401
theory-based evaluation, 395–397
Thummarukudy, Muralee, 109
Tigris River, 223, 226, 228, 230, 236
timber industry, 70, 72, 401
Timor-Leste, 6, 75
tolerable daily intake (TDI), 165
Töpfer, Klaus, 36, 74
toxic waste. *See* hazardous waste; hot spots
transboundary management, 455*t*, 457
transparency, 411–412
transportation infrastructure, 290, 373–383, 434
truth and reconciliation practices, 101, 271, 277, 392, 418, 443, 455*t*
Tsunami Evaluation Coalition, 397, 399–401
Turkey
  Central Treaty Organization (CENTO), 353
  water use policies, 226, 228, 230, 235–236
Tyre (Lebanon), 203

Uganda
  agriculture, 302–303
  environmental impact assessment, 302–303
  health care delivery, 302
  map, 6
  official development assistance, 313n
  UNDP assessment of development results (ADR), 403–405, 446
  USAID involvement, 302–303, 306
  water and sanitation, 302–303
Uitto, Juha I., 287
UN, 448–449
  International Day for Preventing the Exploitation of the Environment in War and Armed Conflict, 4
  member states, 6
  Peacebuilding Commission, 64
  UN and Partners Work Plans, 312, 315, 320–325
  UN Assistance Strategy for Iraq (UNAS), 38, 40
  UN Centre for Human Settlements (UNCHS), 65n, 135–136
  UN Children's Fund (UNICEF), 40, 423
  UN Compensation Commission, 4
  UN Consolidated Inter-Agency Appeal for Southeastern Europe Humanitarian Operations, 25–26
  UN Development Assistance Framework (UNDAF), 22, 29–30, 50–51, 58–59, 321n, 440, 448
  UN Development Group
    natural resources guidelines, 449
    post-conflict needs assessment (PCNA), 21
  UN Development Programme (UNDP), 414, 423
    assessment of development results (ADR), 401–405
    Haiti, 430
    joint evaluation approach, 390, 397, 446
    Lebanon, 45–47, 209–214, 215n, 217, 435–436
    Liberia, 40
    Mesopotamian marshlands, 227
  UN Environment Programme (UNEP), 112
    Afghanistan's donor-assistance database, 316–317
    Green Pot, 50, 321, 440
    Haiti Regeneration Initiative, 202, 241, 246–264, 430
    Mesopotamian marshlands, 234–236
    neutrality of, 74–75, 419, 420
    Post-Conflict and Disaster Management Branch, xv–xvi, 5, 64, 74–75
    Sierra Leone infrastructure projects, 327–328, 338
    strategic priorities, 64, 80–81
    Sudan's Work Plan, 320–321
  UNEP post-conflict assessment, 15–59, 64–67, 69, 414, 422

Index 513

Afghanistan, 15, 18, 20, 21*t*, 22, 28–32, 56, 64, 66*t*, 69, 72–73, 75–79, 420
Albania, 73
Bosnia and Herzegovina, 69, 70, 73, 166, 170–171
Central African Republic, 73, 416, 421
common country assessment (CCA), 22, 58
comprehensive assessment, 18, 20, 48–50, 53, 54*t*, 55, 59
confidence building, 72–75
consolidated appeal process, 21, 448
Darfur, 69
Democratic Republic of the Congo, 67n, 75, 416
desk studies, 18–19, 53, 54, 59, 147
 on economic development links, 75–77
 on environmental governance, 77–79
 on environmental impacts of conflict, 69–72
flash appeal process, 21
Former Yugoslav Republic of Macedonia, 69, 71
Gaza, 70, 72
impact analysis, 18, 22–24, 43, 53–54*t*, 55, 59
impartiality, 419, 420
Iraq, 36–40, 55, 56, 69, 73, 77, 147–149, 172–175, 421
Kosovo, 69, 70, 74, 166–168
Lebanon, 43–46, 47*f*, 70, 73, 208–209
lessons learned, 56–59
Liberia, 15, 18–22, 40–43, 55, 56, 58, 71, 72, 73, 75–77, 81
National Development Strategy, 21–22, 37–38
national ownership, 55
occupied Palestinian territories, 33–36, 56, 69, 71, 74, 81
partnership approach, 419–421
peacebuilding linkages, 79–81
policy frameworks, 20–22, 47*f*
post-conflict needs assessment (PCNA), 21, 36, 37, 58, 414, 448
poverty reduction strategy papers, 22
quantitative risk assessment, 18, 19–20, 53, 54*t*, 55–56, 59

Rwanda, 67n
Serbia and Montenegro, 24–28, 55, 70, 73, 78, 135–136, 166, 168–170
Sierra Leone, 69–70, 73, 78, 154–155, 330–331, 416, 421
Somalia, 71, 76
strategic assessment, 18, 20, 29, 53, 54*t*, 59
success factors, 53–56
Sudan, 46–56, 69–71, 74, 79, 419–421
Timor-Leste, 75
types of assessment, 18–20, 21*t*, 54*t*, 65, 67
UN Assistance Strategy for Iraq (UNAS), 38, 40
UN Development Assistance Framework (UNDAF), 22, 29–30, 50–51
UNEP remediation of environmental hot spots, 109, 135–161
 capacity building, 160–161
 flexibility and contingency plans, 157–158
 Iraq, 147–153, 158–161, 426
 life-cycle of hazardous waste, 158–159, 425–426
 local employment, 161
 media campaigns, 159
 prioritization decisions, 158
 scope of cleanup, 157
 Serbia, 136–147, 161
 Sierra Leone, 153–160, 423
 stakeholders and partners, 159–160
 timing considerations, 156–157
UN–EU Partnership for Preventing and Managing Land and Natural Resources Conflicts, 449
UN Evaluation Group, 390–391
unexploded ordnance (UXO), 70, 112, 414
 Afghanistan, 380–381
 Cambodia, 110, 181–195
 Iraq, 119
 Lebanon, 122–123, 201, 211–212, 218
 Sudan, 125
 Viet Nam, 115–116
UN Food and Agriculture Organization (FAO), 422–423

514 Index

UN Human Settlements Programme (UN-HABITAT), 65n, 422
  Balkans Task Force, xv, xvi
  Lebanon, 214
UN Industrial Development Organization (UNIDO), 423
UN Integrated Peacebuilding Office in Sierra Leone (UNIPSIL), 330, 331
unintended consequences, 398–401, 406, 417, 436–437
UN Interim Force in Lebanon (UNIFIL), 207, 212n
UN Mine Action Service, 182n, 185
UN Mission in Sierra Leone (UNAMSIL), 330
UN multi-donor trust funds, 312, 315, 317–320, 322–325
UN Peacebuilding Commission, xi–xii, xv, 330
Unruh, Jon, 287
UN Transitional Authority in Cambodia (UNTAC), 186
upward accountability, 398–399, 406
uranium, 164–166
  See also depleted uranium (DU)
uranium oxide dust, 164
U.S. Agency for International Development (USAID)
  Afghanistan, 299–301, 306, 307
  Biodiversity Support Program, 69
  compliance with local law, 306–307, 308
  environmental impact assessment (EIA), 285–286, 297–308, 437–439
  exclusions and exemptions, 298–299, 307
  Haiti, 430
  Indonesia, 301–302, 306
  linkage, 307–308
  local collaboration, 308
  monitoring and evaluation procedures, 306
  occupied Palestinian territories, 303–304, 306
  Regional Environmental and Natural Resources Management Project, 348
  Regulation 216, 298–299
  staffing challenges, 307
  standardization of procedures, 305
  SWIFT funding mechanism, 303n
  Uganda, 302–303, 306
Utstein Group, 270n

value chains, 255–256
Verheem, R., 315
Vieira de Mello, Sergio, 25
Viet Nam, 113–116
  Agent Orange Central Payments Programme, 115
  Agent Orange use, 3, 109, 114–115, 116
  cleanup operations, 116
  economic sanctions, 116
  environmental health risks, 111
  map, 6
  refugees and population shifts, 116
  unexploded ordnance (UXO), 115–116
Vivekananda, Janani, 273–274, 279–280
von der Schulenberg, Michael, 331

Waleij, Annica, 16
Wallace, Jennifer, 15
water and sanitation, 70–72, 112–113, 424
  Darfur, 320–21, 440
  depleted uranium (DU), 171, 176, 178
  groundwater monitoring, 142–143
  infrastructure repair, 290
  Iraq, 119–120
  Lebanon, 213–214, 215, 433, 435–436
  oil contamination and cleanup, 141–142
  Serbia, 138–143
  sewage treatment facilities, 143
  Sierra Leone, 330
  Sudan, 125
  Uganda, 302–303
Weissbecker, Inka, 109
West Bank/Gaza. *See* Gaza; occupied Palestinian territories (oPt)
Western Balkans. *See* Balkan region
wetlands
  Ramsar Convention, 229n, 236, 237
  See also Mesopotamian marshlands

Wolfarth, Ross, 286–287
women, 126, 417, 455t
Work Plan Projects Database, 320–321
World Bank, xii, 423
    post-conflict needs assessment (PCNA), 21, 40, 45–47, 414
    poverty reduction strategy papers, 22
World Health Organization (WHO), 40, 423
    radioactive waste management standards, 427
    rapid evaluation methods, 398n
World Heritage sites, 457

World in Transition: Climate Change as a Security Risk, 273
World Wildlife Fund, 64

Yale Environmental Protection Index, 335
Yoshida, Shigeru, 366
Yugoslavia. *See* Bosnia and Herzegovina; Former Yugoslav Republic of Macedonia; Kosovo; Serbia and Montenegro/Federal Republic of Yugoslavia (FYR)

zero-footprint approaches, 87–88